The Cambridge Handbook of Human Dignity

This introduction to human dignity explores the history of the notion from antiquity to the nineteenth century, and the way in which dignity is conceptualized in non-Western contexts. Building on this, it addresses a range of systematic conceptualizations, considers the theoretical and legal conditions for human dignity as a useful notion and analyzes a number of philosophical and conceptual approaches to dignity. Finally, the book introduces current debates, paying particular attention to legal implementation, human rights, justice and conflicts, medicine and bioethics, and provides an explicit systematic framework for discussing human dignity. Adopting a wide range of perspectives and taking into account numerous cultures and contexts, this handbook is a valuable resource for students, scholars and professionals working in philosophy, law, history and theology.

Marcus Düwell is Professor for Philosophical Ethics and Director at the Ethics Institute at Utrecht University, The Netherlands.

Jens Braarvig is Professor of Religious Studies at the University of Oslo, Norway.

Roger Brownsword is Professor of Law at King's College London. He is also an Honorary Professor in Law at the University of Sheffield and a Visiting Professor at Singapore Management University.

Dietmar Mieth is Professor (Emeritus) of Theological Ethics and Social Ethics at the University of Tübingen, Germany and Longtime Fellow at the Max Weber Center for Advanced Cultural and Social Studies at the University of Erfurt, Germany.

The Cambridge Handbook of Human Dignity

Interdisciplinary Perspectives

Edited by

MARCUS DÜWELL

JENS BRAARVIG

ROGER BROWNSWORD

and

DIETMAR MIETH

Assisted by

NAOMI VAN STEENBERGEN

and

DASCHA DÜRING

CAMBRIDGE
UNIVERSITY PRESS

CAMBRIDGE
UNIVERSITY PRESS

University Printing House, Cambridge CB2 8BS, United Kingdom

Cambridge University Press is part of the University of Cambridge.

It furthers the University's mission by disseminating knowledge in the pursuit of education, learning and research at the highest international levels of excellence.

www.cambridge.org
Information on this title: www.cambridge.org/9780521195782

First published 2014

A catalogue record for this publication is available from the British Library

Library of Congress Cataloguing in Publication data
The Cambridge handbook of human dignity : interdisciplinary perspectives / edited by Marcus Düwell, Jens Braarvig, Roger Brownsword and Dietmar Mieth ; assisted by Naomi van Steenbergen and Dascha Düring.
pages cm
Includes bibliographical references and index.
ISBN 978-0-521-19578-2 (hardback)
1. Respect for persons – Law and legislation. I. Düwell, Marcus, 1962– editor of compilation. II. Braarvig, Jens, editor of compilation. III. Brownsword, Roger, editor of compilation. IV. Mieth, Dietmar, editor of compilation.
K3249.C36 2014
341.4'8 – dc23 2013030652

ISBN 978-0-521-19578-2 Hardback

Contents

Contributors

ANDERSON, ELIZABETH John Rawls Collegiate Professor of Philosophy and Women's Studies at the University of Michigan, Ann Arbor (USA)

ATTERTON, PETER Professor of Philosophy at San Diego State University (USA)

BAXI, UPRENDA Emeritus Professor of Law at the Universities of Warwick (UK) and Delhi (India)

BAYER, OSWALD Emeritus Professor of Systematic Theology at the University of Tübingen (Germany)

BEYLEVELD, DERYCK Professor of Law and Bioethics at Durham University (UK) and Professor of Moral Philosophy and Applied Ethics at the Department of Philosophy at Utrecht University (the Netherlands)

BRAARVIG, JENS Professor of Religious Studies at the University of Oslo and Member of the Norwegian Academy of Science and Letters (Norway)

BROWNSWORD, ROGER Professor of Law at King's College London, he is also an Honorary Professor in Law at the University of Sheffield and a Visiting Professor at Singapore Management University.

BYK, CHRISTIAN Judge at the Court of Appeal in Paris and Secretary general at the International Association of Law, Ethics and Science (France)

CAMPAGNA, NORBERT Associate Professor of Philosophy at the Université du Luxembourg and philosophy teacher at the Lycée de Garçons Esch (Luxembourg)

CAMPBELL, ALASTAIR V. Chen Su Lan Centennial Chair in Medical Ethics and Director of the Centre for Biomedical Ethics, National University of Singapore (Singapore)

CLAASSEN, RUTGER Associate Professor for Ethics and Political Philosophy at the Department of Philosophy at Utrecht University (the Netherlands)

COLLSTE, GÖRAN Professor of Applied Ethics at Linköping University (Sweden) and Chief International Academic Advisor, Harbin Institute of Technology (China)

DAVIS, ZACHARY Assistant Professor at St John's University, New York (USA)

DE GAAY FORTMAN, BAS Honorary Professor of Political Economy of Human Rights at Utrecht University and Emeritus Chair in Political Economy of the International Institute of Social Studies of Erasmus University Rotterdam (the Netherlands)

DEN HARTOGH, GOVERT Emeritus Professor of Moral Philosophy at the University of Amsterdam (the Netherlands)

DREIER, HORST Professor of Legal Philosophy, Constitutional and Administrative Law at the University of Würzburg (Germany)

DÜWELL, MARCUS Professor for Philosophical Ethics, Director at the Research Institute for Philosophy and Religious Studies and the director of the Ethics Institute at Utrecht University (the Netherlands)

FAGAN, ANTON W. P. Schreiner Chair in Law at the University of Cape Town (South Africa)

GRAUMANN, SIGRID Professor of Ethics at the Protestant University of Applied Sciences Rhineland-Westphalia-Lippe in Bochum (Germany)

HASENCLEVER, ANDREAS Professor of Peace Studies and International Politics at the University of Tübingen (Germany)

HEEGER, ROBERT Emeritus Professor of Ethics at the Ethics Institute of Utrecht University (the Netherlands)

HENNETTE-VAUCHEZ, STÉPHANIE Professor of Public Law, Université Paris Ouest Nanterre La Défense (France)

HILL, THOMAS E., JR Kenan Professor of Philosophy at the University of North Carolina at Chapel Hill (USA)

HOLLENBACH, DAVID Professor of Theology, University Chair in Human Rights and International Justice and Director of the Center for Human Rights and International Justice at Boston College (USA)

HÜBENTHAL, CHRISTOPH Professor of Systematic Theology at Radbond University Nijmegen (the Netherlands)

ILLIES, CHRISTIAN Professor of Practical Philosophy at the University of Bamberg (Germany)

IMBACH, RUEDI Professor of Medieval Philosophy at the University of Paris-Sorbonne (Paris IV) (France)

JUNKER-KENNY, MAUREEN Professor in Theology and Head of the Department of Religions and Theology, Trinity College Dublin (Ireland)

KELLER, PERRY Senior Lecturer in Law at King's College London (UK)

KERSTEIN, SAMUEL Professor of Philosophy at the University of Maryland (USA)

KLANG, MATHIAS Senior Lecturer in Applied Information Technology at the University of Gothenburg (Sweden)

LIMA MARQUES, CLAUDIA Chair of Private International Law at the Federal University of Rio Grande do Sul (Brazil)

LINDEMANN, GESA Professor of Sociology at the University of Oldenburg (Germany)

LIXINSKI, LUCAS Lecturer at the University of New South Wales (Australia)

LOHMANN, GEORG Emeritus Professor of Practical Philosophy at the University of Magdeburg (Germany)

LORBERBAUM, YAIR Professor of Law and Philosophy at Bar-Ilan University (Israel)

LUBAN, DAVID University Professor and Professor of Law and Philosophy at Georgetown University (USA)

LUO, AN'XIAN Professor for Classical Chinese Philosophy at Renmin University of China

MARÓTH, MIKLÓS Emeritus Chair of the Faculty of Humanities at the Pázmány Péter Catholic University, Vice-President (Social Sciences) of the Hungarian Academy of Sciences (MTA) and President of the Union Académique Internationale 2007–10 (Hungary)

MATSUI, SHIGENORI Professor of Law and Director of Japanese Legal Studies at the University of British Columbia (Canada)

MAYER, ANN E. Associate Professor of Legal Studies and Business Ethics at the Wharton School, University of Pennsylvania (USA)

MENKE, CHRISTOPH Professor of Practical Philosophy at the University of Frankfurt (Germany)

METZ, THADDEUS Humanities Research Professor of Philosophy at the University of Johannesburg (South Africa)

MIETH, DIETMAR Emeritus Professor of Theological Ethics at the Eberhard Karls University Tübingen, President of the Meister-Eckhart-Gesellschaft and Longtime Fellow at the Max Weber Center for Advanced Cultural and Social Studies at the University of Erfurt (Germany)

NEUHÄUSER, CHRISTIAN Lecturer in Philosophy at the Philosophy Department of the University of Lucerne (Switzerland)

OBER, JOSIAH Mitsotakis Professor of Political Science and Classics, and Professor, by courtesy, of Philosophy at Stanford University (USA)

PHARO, LARS KIRKHUSMO Research Associate, Moses Mesoamerican Archive, Harvard University, Research Associate, Institute for Signifying Scriptures (ISS), Claremont Graduate University (USA), Affiliated Scholar, The Centre for Development and the Environment (SUM), University of Oslo (Norway)

POGGE, THOMAS Leitner Professor of Philosophy and International Affairs and Director of the Global Justice Program at Yale University (USA) and Professor of Human Rights and Global Justice at the University of Sydney (Australia)

QIAO, QING-JU Professor of Philosophy and Director of the Research Institute for Chinese Philosophy at Nankai University (China)

SCHABER, PETER Professor of Applied Ethics and Director of the Centre for Ethics at the University of Zürich (Switzerland)

SNEAD, CARTER William P. and Hazel B. White Director of the Center for Ethics and Culture and Professor of Law at the University of Notre Dame (USA)

STEENBAKKERS, PIET Senior Lecturer in the History of Modern Philosophy at Utrecht University, and holder of the endowed chair of Spinoza Studies at Erasmus University Rotterdam (the Netherlands)

STEIGLEDER, KLAUS Professor of Applied Ethics at Ruhr University Bochum (Germany)

STOECKER, RALF Professor of Practical Philosophy at Bielefeld University (Germany)

THIEM, ANNIKA Professor of Philosophy at Villanova University (USA)

VALADIER, PAUL Emeritus Professor at the Centre Sèvres, Facultés jésuites de Paris (France)

VERBEEK, THEO Emeritus Professor for the History of Modern Philosophy at Utrecht University (the Netherlands)

WEISS, MARTIN G. Assistant Professor in Philosophy at the Alpen-Adria-Universität Klagenfurt (Austria)

WERNER, MICHA Professor of Philosophy with the Focus on Practical Philosophy at the University of Greifswald (Germany)

WESTERMAN, PAULINE Professor for Philosophy of Law at the University of Groningen and member of staff at the Academy for Legislation in The Hague (the Netherlands)

Foreword

Professor Alain Plantey, the well-known French jurist, who represented the French Academy of Moral and Political Sciences in the International Union of Academies (IUA), proposed a project for joint research by the member-academies on the subject of human rights. After long discussion, the Bureau of the IUA modified the subject-matter of the investigation by converting it to a project to investigate human dignity, so as to give the opportunity to non-European academies to participate. The General Assembly of the IUA accepted the project in this form.

The project is unique amongst the projects patronized by the IUA for several reasons. The investigation is not being carried out by two or more interested academies according to a previously fixed timetable, but rather is open to all member academies. At the start of the project, with the financial aid of the European Science Foundation (ESF), three meetings of experts were organized by the Bureau of the IUA in cooperation with three member academies, as follows:

- 'Human Dignity: Religious and Historical Aspects', Jerusalem, 17–18 December 2006, organized by G. Stroumsa
- 'Human Dignity: Sociological, Ethical and Bioethical Perspectives', Rabat, 26–27 June 2007, organized by M. Düwell, G. Stroumsa and I. Khalil
- 'Human Dignity: Juridical and Philosophical Perspectives', Barcelona, 16–17 July 2007, organized by S. Giner, G. Stroumsa and M. Düwell.

A closing session was held on 1–4 October 2007 in Vadstena (Sweden), where, based on the experience gained during the previous sessions, the necessary conclusions were drawn by the participants. The organizers were M. Düwell and G. Stroumsa.

As a result of these preparatory meetings, the General Assembly of the IUA approved guidelines for further research, according to which the most important first step was to collect a volume of studies which would sum up the outcome of the conferences held so far, on the one hand, and, by delineating the problem in general, could serve as starting-point for future work, on the other.

The General Assembly entrusted the Norwegian Academy of Sciences with the organization and supervision of future activities in this field, and with the composition of the present volume.

The IUA hopes that this volume will prompt further research in order to enrich the outcome of these investigations, and will also prompt politicians to implement the results achieved by scholars.

MIKLÓS MARÓTH
President of the International Union of Academies, 2007–10

Why a handbook on human dignity?

Why human dignity?

Human Dignity was established in 1948 as the foundational concept of the Universal Declaration of Human Rights (UDHR, reproduced in Appendix 2 to this volume). The Preamble to the Declaration opens with the following statement: 'Whereas recognition of the inherent dignity and of the equal and inalienable rights of all members of the human family is the foundation of freedom, justice and peace in the world . . . '. In Article 1, we read: 'All human beings are born free and equal in dignity and rights. They are endowed with reason and conscience and should act towards one another in a spirit of brotherhood.' And, in 1966, the United Nations declared: 'These [human] rights derive from the inherent dignity of the human person.'[1] During preparation of the Declaration (1946–8),[2] there were discussions about whether there was a need for such a foundational concept and, if so, which notion that should be. Choosing human dignity immediately after the Second World War was a statement against the Shoah, against totalitarianism, and against the atrocities of the war. However, by choosing human dignity, a concept was selected that has an impressive history in various traditions. The Stoic philosopher Cicero saw it as a central requirement of a virtuous life that one should behave in a way that is appropriate to the dignity of a human being; and, famously, for Immanuel Kant, the dignity of the human person is at the centre of his moral philosophy. During the drafting process of the UDHR, the philosopher Peng Chuan Chang claimed that the Confucian notion of humanity (*ren*) would have the same meaning as human dignity in the Western tradition; the South African President, Jan Smuts, could make sense of this notion within the Calvinist-reformed tradition; and the philosopher Jacques Maritain, who acted as the representative of the Vatican, held a similar view in relation to the Thomist tradition.

This apparent consensus raises the question whether, upon further reflection, all those traditions would really coincide in a common understanding of human

[1] United Nations, International Covenant on Economic, Social and Cultural Rights, 1966; International Covenant on Civil and Political Rights, 1966.

[2] For the history of the Declaration, see Morsink 1999, for a discussion about the role in particular of human dignity, see Tiedemann 2012, 20–8.

dignity. Nevertheless, one could reasonably assume that this concept represents a basic concept of the modern world: at least since the eighteenth century, we have seen the human being as the central point of justification of basic political and social institutions. For Hugo Grotius, the distinctive features of the human being served as the justification for a particular structure of the international order; and the American and French Revolutions referred explicitly to the idea of the rights of man. However, the extent to which a commitment to human rights implies a concept of human dignity is moot; and, what is more, it is contested how this modern idea of human dignity relates to earlier understandings in the Middle Ages and the Renaissance as well as the relationship of these debates to traditions outside the cultural contexts of Europe and North America. These are all significant topics for discussion.

After 1948, in the course of the further establishment of the UDHR, human dignity became a widely accepted concept, but its reception remained ambivalent. On the one hand, it has often been perceived as vague and open, hardly explained and conceptually unclear, perhaps even completely empty; the suspicion was that everybody could 'sign up' to human dignity because, with this agreement, one would not commit oneself to any specific conviction or position. Some scholars even assumed that this was precisely the reason for the success of this notion. Moreover, some feared that, insofar as human dignity is assumed in various legal contexts to override the interests of an individual human, its adoption could endanger the commitment to human rights. If human dignity is a concept with an under-determined content but which could trump human rights, it could be a kind of Trojan horse in relation to the human rights regime.

On the other hand, human dignity was seen by scholars from various traditions as the foundational and basic concept of the entire human rights regime from which the whole set of human rights should be derived. Indeed, in the legal context, human dignity was implemented in various constitutions and became a key part of the national legal order in, for example Germany and Israel. From this perspective, the relevance of the concept would be to offer more than a conceptual understanding of why human beings are so important that we should ascribe to them inalienable rights. Such a legal foundation would be seen as a practical necessity because concrete human rights are constantly undergoing changes in the process of political and legal interpretation.

Beside the importance of human dignity as a foundational concept, in the first decades after the war, there were many debates about the implementation and content of the human rights regime but human dignity was not a focal point. Rather, human dignity was a notion in the background of the UDHR. However, in recent years, there has been a remarkable change in this position. The most significant debates about human dignity have been in bioethics. For example, there have been discussions about which beings – human embryos, comatose patients, and perhaps (at least some) animals – have dignity (and what this entails); appeals to 'dying with dignity' have been prominent in debates about the permissibility of assisted suicide and euthanasia; and the value of human dignity is a central focus for debates about reproductive cloning, genetic modification, and human enhancement (for example, Beyleveld and Brownsword 2001; Kass 2002; President's Council on Bioethics 2008). At the same time, we can see a growing *philosophical* interest in human rights in general, focusing on the appropriate interpretation of human rights (for example, Gewirth 1996; Griffin 2008; Beitz 2009) as well as on the question of whether or not human rights are the appropriate normative framework for matters of international politics in a globalized and multicultural world (for example, Mutua 2002). In short, discussions around human dignity have been galvanized in the last few years, these debates being found in legal (McCrudden 2008; Capps 2009) as well as in philosophical contexts (Gaita 2000; Benhabib 2011; Kateb 2011; Waldron 2012). Sometimes, we even find quite a polemical dimension in the debate when human dignity is suggested to be the intellectual property of a specific conservative heritage or when sceptics find harsh words about the vagueness of the concept.

The concept of dignity may, all in all, seem paradoxical, in the way that value or dignity is something that has to do with *differences* between people. But, as with the UDHR, and in a broader sense with humanism in its various formulations in different traditions, and in particular after the French Revolution, one has tried to create an idea of a shared and equal dignity for all humans, as an *inherent* quality. This militates against many historical views where human dignity is for the few, and, indeed, an egalitarian ideal is not present in many historical traditions, European, or others. Dignity is something to be earned, or maybe, more often, something that certain persons are born with, as in the upper classes of a society. Clearly, human dignity in the modern and UDHR sense, as *inherent*, is rather a concept that does not, and probably cannot, exist in a society without laws to protect the *rights* that flow from it rather than the principle itself. Thus, we may find lofty ideas of an egalitarian view of dignity in ideologies, in places and situations where still human rights are not protected. The idea of inherent dignity is very closely connected with the *individual*; however, the implementation of laws on the rights, traditions and moral rules, may well also be connected with *collective* entities, and *group dignity* may well be detrimental to the dignity of the *individual*. In this way, the discussion on human rights is closely linked to the principle of dignity, and one may argue that the equal rights of all is the *practical outcome* of the dignity concept. In the UDHR, inherent dignity is indeed the presupposition on which the rights are built, and the reason why the rights should be legally protected.

A handbook on human dignity?

It is not only timely to have an intense debate about human dignity, it is surely a matter of intellectual honesty to try to attain a more comprehensive understanding of this concept. Given that human dignity forms the basis of many legal frameworks (international, regional and national), that it is deeply interwoven with various moral and religious traditions, and that it functions as a reference point for a number of contemporary social and political debates, it should be carefully investigated before we judge whether it is a useful, meaningful, vague or problematic concept. Whether one wants to embrace human dignity enthusiastically or criticize its political and legal dominance, in any case one should understand the concept, its normative status, its history and the principles of its applicability. That requires, however, intense interdisciplinary studies from various points of view, particularly legal, philosophical and historical.

We have chosen a structure that combines a *pragmatic attitude* with an attempt to cover a broad range of perspectives. Our attitude is pragmatic insofar as the handbook has no encyclopaedic ambition; since discussions about human dignity are related to the cosmological, moral, legal and religious position of the human being in general, a comprehensive discussion of human dignity would cover more or less the intellectual, moral and legal history of humankind. Accordingly, instead of making a futile attempt at completeness, we have tried to highlight a variety of perspectives that we think are central for an understanding of the history and the contemporary understanding of the concept. For the whole handbook, we have chosen to take the understanding of human dignity in the UDHR as a *point of departure.* That does not mean that we want to claim that in all approaches to human dignity this human-rights-related understanding is presupposed, which would be obviously wrong. However, we asked our authors to relate all discussions to the concept of human dignity as it was developed within the contexts of human rights. This seemed to us to be the natural focal point since it is precisely the foundational role of human dignity within the human rights framework that is the reason for its presence in contemporary debates.

In the introductory part of the handbook, there are two chapters: the first focuses on the *legal* discussions, starting with the history of the UDHR and the many references to human dignity in international and regional instruments; it then discusses the place of human dignity in a comparative legal perspective; and, finally, it considers the arguments for and against a legal role for human dignity. The second chapter introduces the *conceptual* aspects of human dignity (as we find it in various historical and contemporary approaches) and the various *philosophical* attempts to reconstruct and justify its meanings. This conceptual and philosophical analysis is intended to provide the reader with some important background to relate the various historical perspectives and contemporary debates to each other. We believe that this quite open approach is preferable to an attempt at synthesizing the whole book, which would be necessarily an arbitrary and one-sided endeavour.

Part I offers an attempt to reconstruct the *history* and the *Begriffsgeschichte* of human dignity with regard to some especially prominent parts of its history. A first subsection focuses on European history, from antiquity to the socialistic tradition of the nineteenth century. A particular chapter is dedicated to the role of human dignity in the Jewish tradition. This selection, which is not guided by the ambition of completeness, is not arbitrary – the traditions that are selected are those that need to be considered in order fully to understand the contemporary discourse. We discuss the Kantian and phenomenological tradition in the second Part and not in this historical Part. The second subsection presents concepts of human dignity beyond the scope of the European tradition. We discuss the Islamic tradition in this context, even though we are aware that Islam is also a part of European history. The selection focuses on those traditions that have some kind of systematic and written elaboration. We are aware that this attempt to engage in a debate in the global richness of historical and cultural perspectives is just a first step to broaden the scope of the debate in a direction that would do justice to the universal ambition of the human dignity concept. It will be a task of future research to bring other perspectives into the debate (for example, some oral traditions) and to investigate in greater detail the differences and similarities between the various perspectives.

Part II offers an overview of the most important *philosophical* approaches to the reconstruction and justification of the meaning of human dignity. To focus so strongly on the philosophical discussion is based on the assumption that human dignity has a central role in the moral and philosophical self-interpretation of human beings, and that the central place of the concept in legal regulations is derived from this fact. This overview includes various philosophical approaches that draw on more analytical and continental traditions than are currently present in the debate. It also includes some debates that are not clearly related to one traditional philosophical school (such as discussions about 'collective dignity' or 'posthumanism') as well as a discussion about sociological approaches to human dignity.

Part III discusses the role of human dignity in various legal traditions, and then introduces a variety of contemporary societal, moral and political debates in which human dignity is contested, ranging from issues in bioethics, to questions of just war and gender equality. We selected some discussions where the concept of human dignity already plays some role, but of course there would be further relevant contexts. The ambition of this Part is, in the first place, to show the range of contexts in which human dignity plays a role and to discuss what that role is or could be. The ambition of this Part will be fulfilled if the reader develops an understanding of the conceptual possibilities of human dignity to gain a sense of its normative orientation.

The future of human dignity

We see this handbook as an opening, rather than a concluding, publication for an understanding of the history, the meaning and the normative function of human dignity. Much remains to be debated: it will be the task of future research to write a comprehensive history of human dignity, and it will need more philosophical and legal scholarship to understand in which ways human dignity can fulfil its foundational role within the context of human rights. It will, in particular, be important to engage more strongly in a dialogue between the existing philosophical approaches and philological and historical research about various intellectual traditions from the whole globe. From our point of view, an international debate about human dignity, its historical and cultural roots, and its philosophical justification, has only just begun. All attempts to conclude these debates would be inappropriate given the lively discussions that have been a feature of recent years. We hope that this handbook can provide the necessary tools for future debate and discussion so that a more comprehensive understanding of human dignity is possible.

MARCUS DÜWELL
JENS BRAARVIG
ROGER BROWNSWORD
DIETMAR MIETH

References

Beitz, C. 2009. *The Idea of Human Rights.* Oxford University Press

Benhabib, S. 2011. *Dignity in Adversity: Human Rights in Troubled Times.* Cambridge: Polity Press

Beyleveld, D., and Brownsword, R. 2001. *Human Dignity in Bioethics and Biolaw.* Oxford University Press

Capps, P. 2009. *Human Dignity and the Foundations of International Law.* Oxford, Portland, OR: Hart Publishing

Gaita, R. 2000. *A Common Humanity: Thinking about Love and Truth and Justice.* London, New York: Routledge

Gewirth, A. 1992. 'Human Dignity as the Basis of Rights'. in M. J. Meyer and W. A. Parent (eds.). *The Constitution of Rights: Human Dignity and American Values.* Ithaca, NY: Cornell University Press, 10–28

1996. *Community of Rights.* Chicago University Press

Griffin, J. 2008. *On Human Rights.* Oxford University Press

Kass, L. R. 2002. *Life, Liberty and the Defense of Dignity: The Challenge for Bioethics.* San Francisco: Encounter Books

Kateb, G. 2011. *Human Dignity.* Cambridge, MA, London: Belknap Press of Harvard University Press

McCrudden, C. 2008. 'Human Dignity and Judicial Interpretation of Human Rights', *European Journal of International Law* 19(4): 655–724

Morsink, J. 1999. *The Universal Declaration of Human Rights: Origins, Drafting and Intent.* University of Philadelphia Press

Mutua, M. 2002. *Human Rights: A Political and Cultural Critique.* Philadelphia, PA: University of Pennsylvania Press

President's Council on Bioethics. 2008. *Human Dignity and Bioethics: Essays Commissioned by the President's Council on Bioethics.* Washington, DC, http://bioethics.georgetown.edu/pcbe/reports/human_dignity/chapter14.html

President's Council on Bioethics. 2008. *Human Dignity and Bioethics.* Washington, DC

Tiedemann, P. 2012. *Menschenwürde als Rechtsbegriff: Eine philosophische Klärung.* Berlin: Berliner Wissenschaftsverlag

Waldron, J. 2012. *Dignity, Rank and Rights*, ed. Meir Dan-Cohen. Oxford University Press

Acknowledgments

The Cambridge Handbook of Human Dignity is the result of a long-running project. In the first instance, in 2006–7, the International Union of Academies (IUA) and the European Science Foundation (ESF) initiated a series of workshops and a conference at which scholars from around the world, and from different disciplines, met to discuss various aspects of the topic of human dignity. Following those discussions, the editors developed the idea of a multidisciplinary handbook on human dignity and, happily, they found an enthusiastic reaction when inviting various scholars to participate in this enterprise.

We have received much help, encouragement and support in producing this handbook. First, we are particularly grateful to the former Presidents, Agostino Paravicini Bagliani and Miklós Maróth, and the Secretary General of the IUA, Jean-Luc de Pape, for their support for this project. In the same way, we are very grateful for the support of the ESF, and in particular that of Rüdiger Klein. Second, we wish to acknowledge the support shown by Cambridge University Press, as the development process of the book took much longer than expected. Our special thanks go to Finola O'Sullivan and Richard Woodham, who managed the process with great professionalism and patience and to Jonathan Ratcliffe for his careful editing of the manuscript. Third, we wish to record our appreciation of the enormous editorial contributions made by Naomi van Steenbergen and Dascha Düring. Naomi and Dascha did a great job, showing exceptional commitment and care. We want to thank both of them for their excellent work.

1

Human dignity from a legal perspective

ROGER BROWNSWORD

Introduction

As the contributions to this handbook make clear, human dignity is a fundamental value in many legal systems. In both the northern and the southern hemispheres, in common law and civilian legal systems, we find that human dignity plays a prominent role. It is also a cornerstone concept of many regional and international conventions and declarations. However, the jurisprudence of human dignity betrays a familiar tension. Whereas, in some cases, human dignity is articulated and applied in a 'liberal' spirit (underpinned by an 'empowerment' conception), in others the guiding spirit is 'conservative' (underpinned by a conception of 'human dignity as constraint') (Beyleveld and Brownsword 2001). Broadly speaking, while liberals appeal to human dignity in order to protect and to extend the sphere of individual choice, conservatives appeal to human dignity in order to impose limits on what they see as the legitimate sphere of individual choice.

Introducing the legal section of the handbook, three general issues are addressed. First, there is the question of how we should view the burgeoning references to human dignity (often in conjunction with human rights) in international and regional instruments. Second, there is the question of how we should understand the role of human dignity in national legal systems. Finally, there is the question of whether positive law is enhanced by references to human dignity or whether it would be an improvement to eliminate all such legal allusions.

Human dignity and human rights as universal values: from one declaration to another

The notion of human dignity is intimately connected to the cornerstones of modern human rights thinking – that is, to the United Nations' Universal Declaration of Human Rights (UDHR) of 1948, together with its two partner Covenants, the International Covenant on Economic, Social and Cultural Rights and the International Covenant on Civil and Political Rights, both of 1966. In the Preamble to each of these instruments, we read that 'recognition of the inherent dignity and of the equal and inalienable rights of all members of the human family is the foundation of freedom, justice and peace in the world'; and Article 1 of the UDHR famously proclaims that 'All human beings are born free and equal in dignity and rights.'

In the early years of the present century, in the particular context of 'medicine, [the] life sciences and associated technologies', UNESCO has made a comparable attempt to underline the centrality of respect for human rights and human dignity. Notably, the Universal Declaration on Bioethics and Human Rights, 2005, is peppered with references to human dignity. For example, Article 2(d) states that one of the aims of the Declaration is to recognize 'the importance of freedom of scientific research and the benefits derived from scientific and technological developments, while stressing the need for such research and development to . . . respect human dignity, human rights and fundamental freedoms'.

We find a similar story in Europe, where the Council of Europe copied across the spirit, if not quite the letter, of the UDHR in the European Convention on Human Rights, 1950 (ECHR). Even the European Community, with its constitutive *economic* objectives, has recognized the binding nature of the Convention rights. Indeed, after the Treaty of Lisbon, Article 2 of the (amended) Treaty on the European Union provides that the EU 'is founded on the values of respect for human dignity, freedom, democracy, equality, the rule of law and respect for human rights'. Moreover, Article 6(1) of the Treaty now accords to the Charter of Fundamental Rights of the European Union – a Charter that is founded on the indivisible and universal values of human dignity, freedom, equality and solidarity – the same legally binding status as the Treaties.

On the face of it, these affirmations and reaffirmations of respect for human rights and human dignity testify to a consolidation of the project started by the United Nations – in particular, they testify to human rights and human dignity being universally supported as fundamental values for the conduct of public life as well as for the governance of science, medicine and technological development. However, although the rhetoric of human rights and human dignity commands widespread support, the liberal thinking that underlies the UDHR and the ECHR is rather different to the conservative ethic that underlies both the UNESCO Declaration and the Council of Europe's Convention on Human Rights and Biomedicine, 1996.

The Universal Declaration of Human Rights

According to the distinguished judge and jurist, Michael Kirby, the purpose of the UN Charter (1945) in conjunction with the UDHR was 'to design a new world order for the safety of humanity, the more equitable sharing of its wealth and the defence of fundamental rights' (Kirby 2010: 789). Specifically, the UDHR reflected the efforts that had been made in some countries to 'express universal values that attach to being a member of the community' (Kirby *ibid.*).

In other words, the principal purpose of the UDHR was to put down a non-negotiable marker against the denial of human dignity. From the Declaration onwards, governments should not be permitted to say to any human being, 'you do not count, you have no value as an individual'. This did not require a deep philosophical justification; and it was a cosmopolitan principle that applied to all humans in their dealings with governments. Quite simply, humans have a dignity – a dignity that governments should always respect.

Having placed their preambular markers in support of 'the inherent dignity . . . of all members of the human family', it was not necessary for the Declaration or its partner Covenants to make repeated references to human dignity. Indeed, in the UDHR, after the proclamation in Article 1, there are only two further explicit references to human dignity – first, in Article 22 (concerning the right to social security and the economic, social and cultural rights indispensable for dignity and the free development of personality), and then in Article 23(3) (concerning the right to just and favourable remuneration such as to ensure an existence worthy of human dignity). Similarly, in the Covenants, the only further references to human dignity are in Article 13 of the International Covenant on Economic, Social and Cultural Rights (where it is agreed that 'education shall be directed to the full development of the human personality and the sense of its dignity'), and in Article 10 of the International Covenant on Civil and Political Rights (to the effect that 'All persons deprived of their liberty shall be treated with humanity and with respect for the inherent dignity of the human person').

These provisions are firmly tied to an important cluster of ideas: namely, that each and every human being has inherent *dignity*; that it is this *inherent* dignity that grounds (or accounts for) the possession of human rights; that these are *inalienable* rights; and that, because all humans have dignity, they hold these rights *equally*. So understood, human dignity is the foundation on which the superstructure of human rights is built. Given this relationship between human dignity and human rights, the primary *practical* and *political* discourse becomes that of human rights; and, while those who seek a deeper justification for human rights might need to revisit the idea of human dignity, the practical business of pressing one's interests against others (particularly against powerful states) will be conducted in terms of claimed human rights (see, for example, Kolnai 1976: 257–9; and Goodin 1981).

Accepting the preambular axioms – human dignity signifying that each human has inherent value and is worthy of respect – which particular rights are presupposed by human dignity? According to Joseph Raz (1979: 221), '[r]especting human dignity entails treating humans as persons capable of planning and plotting their future. Thus, respecting people's dignity includes respecting their autonomy, their right to control their future.' It follows that, if the capacity to control one's actions by reference to the choices one has made is the distinctive source of human worth, then to deny a human the opportunity to choose and control, whether by insult, enslavement or manipulation, is to offend against his or her dignity – it is, in fact, a double offence, a denial of rights as well as a denial of responsibility.

However, the International Bill of Rights is not limited to such offences against dignity. Rather, it is designed to specify a constellation of particular negative and positive rights that create the right kind of environment for humans to flourish. In this light, Andrew Clapham (1993: 148–9) maintains that the protection of human dignity involves (1) respect for everyone's humanity, and (2) the creation and protection of 'the conditions for everyone's self-fulfilment (or autonomy or self-realization)'. While the former is said to relate to *direct* attacks on dignity (such as killing, torture, slavery, trafficking in persons, coercion, verbal abuse, discrimination and maltreatment), the latter can be understood as relating to *indirect* attacks (such as a denial of the right to associate, to make love, to take part in social life, to express one's intellectual, artistic or cultural ideas, or to enjoy a decent standard of living and healthcare). This latter approach, Clapham points out, is picked up in Article 22 of the UDHR – and the same point could be made in respect of Article 23(3).

The UNESCO Universal Declaration on Bioethics and Human Rights

UNESCO has been in the vanguard of attempts to forge a worldwide bioethical consensus, publishing three major instruments, namely, the Universal Declaration on the Human Genome and Human Rights in 1997, the International Declaration on Human Genetic Data in 2003, and most significantly – or, at any rate, certainly most ambitiously – the Universal Declaration on Bioethics and Human Rights in 2005 (see, ten Have and Jean 2009). This five-part Declaration opens by speaking to its scope (namely, medicine and the life sciences) and then to its aims (particularly to ensure that developments in science and technology are compatible with respect for human dignity, human rights and fundamental freedoms).

Starting in Article 3(1) with the principle that '[h]uman dignity, human rights and fundamental freedoms are to be fully respected', the second and longest part of the Declaration articulates familiar principles relating to the maximization of benefit and the minimization of harm (Article 4), the importance of individual autonomy (Article 5) and consent (Article 6), and requiring respect for privacy and confidentiality (Article 9). However, not all persons are robust individualists able to look after their own interests, and the Declaration emphasizes the importance of respecting human vulnerability and integrity (Article 8), as well as setting out principles of equality (Article 10) and non-discrimination or stigmatization (qua 'violation of human dignity, human rights and fundamental freedoms') (Article 11). The Declaration, too, conveys the sense of our essential connectedness (and, concomitantly, our mutual responsibilities) in a series of articles that relate to solidarity and cooperation (Article 13), social responsibility and health (Article 14), benefit-sharing (Article 15) and the protection of future generations (Article 16) and the environment (Article 17). Last but not least, in the middle of this list, we find Article 12, which underlines the 'importance of cultural diversity and pluralism' but only so long as difference is not 'invoked to infringe upon human dignity, human rights and fundamental freedoms' (compare Appiah 2006).

For present purposes, we can skip over the remaining three parts of the Declaration because, to the extent that it is an ethical milestone, it is in its first two parts that its significance lies. On one reading, the different facets of human dignity are brought together in a complementary way: hence, despite its general nature, 'the idea of human dignity provides the necessary conceptual background for responding to the new concerns about respect for persons in clinical and research settings, and for humanity as a whole' (Andorno 2009: 96). However, the counter-reading is that the insistent demand that human dignity must not be compromised not only sets limits on pushing ahead with the science, it is also in tension with respect for human rights (Brownsword 2008).

Europe

Although the ECHR does not explicitly refer to or rely on the notion of human dignity, there is no doubt that, by implication, the European Convention on Human Rights asserts the value of respect for human dignity. Moreover, in the Strasbourg jurisprudence, it is clear that human dignity is implicated in the Convention's protective regime. For example, in the *Pretty* case, the Grand Chamber of the European Court of Human Rights affirmed that 'the very essence of the [Convention] is respect for human dignity and human freedom'.[1] By and large, the terms of the Convention together with the jurisprudence of the Court stick closely to the idea of human dignity as the supportive underpinning for (autonomy-driven) human rights. Yet, in the Convention on Human Rights and Biomedicine, Article 1 of which declares that the parties 'shall protect the dignity and identity of all human beings', the Council switches to a more conservative European bioethics.

The contrast in the thinking that underlies the two Conventions is not immediately obvious. So, in the Explanatory Report accompanying the later Convention, we read that 'human dignity . . . constitutes the essential value to be upheld [. . . and] is at the basis of most of the values emphasized in the Convention' (paragraph 9); that all articles must be interpreted in light of the aim of the Convention – 'which is to protect human rights and dignity' (paragraph 22); and that the principle of respect for human dignity is central to Articles 15 (the general rule with regard to scientific research) (paragraph 96), 17 (protection of persons not able to consent to research) (paragraphs 106 and 111) and 21 (which provides that '[t]he human body and its parts shall not, as such, give rise to financial gain' (paragraph 131)). Additionally, the Preamble to the Protocol to the Convention dealing with the cloning of human beings tells us

[1] *Pretty* v. *United Kingdom* 2002-III; 35 EHRR 1, para. 65. See also *SW* v. *United Kingdom* and *CR* v. *United Kingdom* (1996) 21 EHRR 363, 402, para. 44/42.

that the Protocol is guided by the consideration that 'the instrumentalization of human beings through the deliberate creation of genetically identical human beings is contrary to human dignity and thus constitutes a misuse of biology and medicine'.

While these explanatory comments suggest a greater readiness to identify human dignity with a number of specific offences (particularly relating to the commercialization and commodification of the human body, the sanctity of human life, and so on) (see Caulfield and Brownsword 2006), this kind of tagging does not of itself indicate that a rival conception is incorporated in the Convention. Nevertheless, there are grounds for thinking that the Convention reflects more than a new fashion for drafting. In particular, human dignity is deployed not only to give protection to human life from the point of conception (including human embryos) but also to constrain actions which, although *prima facie* merely self-regarding, are judged to compromise human dignity (whether located in the actor's own person or humanity or, so to speak, in the community's collective conscience).

The UN declaration on human cloning

All 191 members of the United Nations agree that human reproductive cloning is incompatible with respect for human dignity; and, accordingly, they support its prohibition. However, members disagree about the ethics of so-called therapeutic cloning. In 2005, the General Assembly accepted a recommendation that members should be called on 'to prohibit all forms of human cloning inasmuch as they are incompatible with human dignity and the protection of human life'.[2] This non-binding Declaration purports to cover all forms of human cloning, but its drafting allows members to persist with their different views about whether therapeutic cloning is compatible with human dignity. First, the use of the phrase 'inasmuch as' allows for both a narrow ('to the extent that') and a broad ('for the reason that') interpretation of the prohibition on human cloning. Second, and for present purposes more significantly, this ambiguity reaches through to invite reading the prohibition in line with one's favoured conception of human dignity. And, third, as pointed out by several of the members who voted against adopting the Declaration, the reference to the protection of human life begs all the difficult questions about the status of the human embryo (see, further, Brownsword 2007).

Taking stock

In one Declaration after another, the importance of human dignity has been affirmed. In the political arena, human dignity founds a regime of human

[2] Eighty-four members voted in favour of the (non-binding) UN Declaration on Human Cloning, with thirty-four against and thirty-seven abstentions (UN press release GA/10333, www.un.org/News/Press/docs/2005/ga10333.doc.htm).

rights that acknowledges that each human has a view, a voice and a value. In the modern biomedical Declarations, human dignity again underpins the idea that each human counts and should not be used merely as a research resource. However, in the more recent Declarations, human dignity also signals some limits to individual autonomy as well as the responsibilities that we have to human life in its developmental stages.

As foreshadowed in our introductory remarks, there is a fault line in the international jurisprudence of human dignity. Whereas, on the one side, we find a liberal ethic that treats human dignity as the underpinning of human rights, on the other, we have a conservative ethic holding that the fundamental duty is not to compromise human dignity (Brownsword 2003). Until this tension is resolved, we can expect international legal instruments to engage with human dignity in more than one way and to be articulated in one of three forms: first, they might follow the UDHR in adopting a particular conception of human dignity (and, concomitantly, a particular underlying ethic); or, second, they might try to conceal the tension by drafting either at a very high level of generality or in suitably vague terms; or, third, they might follow the UNESCO Universal Declaration by taking a more pluralist approach which invites different interpretations depending upon one's ethical approach.

Human dignity in modern legal systems

Turning from the international to the national scene, we find that human dignity is a key concept in many legal systems. However, the contributions to this handbook paint a picture that suggests some unevenness and unpredictability in the various appeals that are made to it and in its application. Not surprisingly, we find that the tensions already detected at the international level are replicated nationally.

There are many different ways of classifying the elements of legal systems. For present purposes, a three-level model of the ordering (or governance) of human societies will be employed. For convenience, we can term these levels: the 'constitutive', the 'public' and the 'private'. Following some clarifying remarks about this organizing scheme, we can consider how human dignity shapes features of both the public and the private order, before broaching the important question of why it is that, in some cases, human dignity underlines the importance of consent and yet, in others, repudiates it (Fletcher 1996; Beyleveld and Brownsword 2007).

The organizing scheme

Assuming a three-level legal ordering, the first task for a society is to declare its constitutive values. These values indicate the mission of that society, its direction and the values that set the limits to what it regards as acceptable conduct. All legal operations within a society need to be compatible with this constitutive order. When we say that human dignity is treated as a fundamental legal value, this ordinarily means that it is either itself one of the explicit constitutive values or that it is an implicit value that is the basis of, or ground for, the expressed values. Second, there is public order, giving the public life of each society its distinctive features. Broadly conceived, the public order includes the criminal justice system but also the regulation of health, education, the economy, transport, the information society and a myriad other matters. Third, there is private ordering, at which level individuals have the opportunity for self-governance. In the case of contract law, for example, it is not simply that parties may make their own trades; more significantly, it is that they may (within public policy limits which, of course, will be sensitive to the order's constitutive and public values) set their own terms of trade (Brownsword 2006).

Against this backcloth, the law operates in ways that reflect the influence of a host of credos and beliefs, or so to speak 'ideologies' (Adams and Brownsword 2006). As political institutions take greater responsibility for making the law, leaving courts to settle particular disputes and to hold government to the constitutive values of the legal order, it is surely unsurprising that particular legislative enactments reflect the political ideologies of their promoters. Nevertheless, we might expect that the constitutive values themselves are above politics and, for this reason, immune to the influence of political ideology – and, indeed, to some extent, this might be so. The fact is, however, that, in one instance after another, we see that human dignity cannot escape the influence of ideology (McCrudden 2008).

In a seminal paper, David Feldman cautioned that we should not 'assume that the idea of dignity is inextricably linked to a liberal-individualist view of human beings as people whose life-choices deserve respect' (Feldman 1999: 685). To the contrary, 'human dignity may subvert rather than enhance choice . . . Once it becomes a tool in the hands of lawmakers and judges, the concept of human dignity is a two-edged sword' (*ibid.*). Applying this insight, we can chart the application of human dignity relative to both liberal and conservative readings, the former pushing (other things being equal) for the protection and extension of the sphere of individual choice, the latter emphasizing the limits to this sphere of legitimate choice. Of course, this is a very broad-brush contrast. On the liberal side, there are important differences between, for example, consequentialist (usually utilitarian) and rights-based approaches, and between approaches that recognize only negative rights and those that recognize also positive rights; similarly, on the conservative side, there are important differences between communitarian and other duty-based approaches (Brownsword 2003); and we should not forget that there are approaches that treat human dignity as the ground not only for permitting individuals to make their own choices but also for setting limits to the sphere of free choice. However, for present purposes, the double-edged sword (albeit a relatively blunt instrument) suffices.

Public order

Where a legal system orients itself towards a liberal reading of human dignity, this will impact on matters of institutional design and process as well as on the substantive law. According to Green:

> Principles . . . which directly or indirectly recognize and protect human dignity include: like cases must be treated alike; any curtailment of the freedom of an individual is prima facie unlawful unless justified by a positive law; a private person may do anything which is not prohibited or which does not infringe the rights of others; when it is making a decision affecting the interests of individuals a public authority is required to observe procedural fairness or natural justice and various presumptions of statutory interpretation designed to protect individual rights and freedoms. (Green 2007: 153)

Arguably, then, many of the features of the due process model of criminal justice (Packer 1969) – for example, the presumption of innocence, the right to know the reason for one's arrest, the right to legal representation, the right to remain silent, the requirement that guilt be established beyond any reasonable doubt, and so on – flow from (or, at the very least, are in line with) the liberal conception of human dignity. Similarly, for example, section 35 of the Constitution of the Republic of South Africa provides that the conditions of detention (of arrested, detained and accused persons) must be consistent with human dignity, including at least exercise and the provision, at state expense, of adequate accommodation, nutrition, reading material and medical treatment. In the German *Life Imprisonment* case,[3] too, the Federal Constitutional Court emphasized that, even where offenders are deprived of their liberty following the commission of a crime, they do not lose their inherent dignity and, by implication, their membership of a community of rights. Elaborating on this, the Court held that cruel, inhuman and degrading punishments are strictly prohibited by the 'commandment of human dignity';[4] and, in the *Honecker* decision,[5] the Court suggested that human dignity is violated where an individual is 'degraded to a mere object of state action' by being kept in custody when he is seriously ill and close to death.[6] Although this latter suggestion was controversial, the idea that human dignity is violated where persons are subjected to conditions that are demeaning or degrading is commonly relied on – not merely in the context of deprivation of liberty, but also in relation to housing and employment conditions.

While much of the liberal-inspired design of criminal justice is opposed to the ideology of 'crime control' (Packer 1969), rather than to the conservative reading of human dignity, the latter famously opposes liberal thinking in relation to the limits to be set on individual choice. For liberals, the way in which human dignity is respected is by recognizing that individuals should be free to make their own

[3] BVerfGE 45 (1977) 187. [4] *Ibid.*: 228.

[5] BerlVerfGH NJW 1993, 515. [6] *Ibid.*: 517.

choices, and act on them, unless such actions trench on the rights or freedoms of others. Against this, conservative communitarians see human dignity as a value that binds the group together by setting community-defining limits to individual freedom. So, for example, in the US case of *State* v. *Braxton*,[7] the appellate court withdrew the option of surgical castration that the trial court had offered to the convicted defendant (this being instead of a thirty-year custodial sentence). Why limit the defendant's options, and, if surgical castration is permissible in a medical context, why not in a juridical context? According to Meir Dan-Cohen (2002), the answer is that, in the latter case but not in the former, the procedure is seen as expressing an affront to human dignity. As Dan-Cohen puts it, the 'negative connotations with regard to human dignity of physical mutilation extend to even such unusual punitive circumstances as those presented by *Braxton*, but they do not extend to the very different practices of medical treatment' (Dan-Cohen 2002: 163).

The conservative dignitarian manifesto pushes for the criminalization of conduct that it regards as off limits – for example, acts that involve the commercialization or the commodification of the human body (compare the earlier analysis of the Convention on Human Rights and Biomedicine). However, its opposition to the liberal pro-choice view is nowhere sharper than in relation to end-of-life decisions. Here, as many have remarked, we witness an initially puzzling exchange between those would-be reformers who appeal to 'death with dignity' to argue for a permissive legal position and those who insist that the prohibitions against assisted suicide and euthanasia must be retained lest human dignity should be compromised.

Where activities need to be licensed, and where appeals to human dignity are made, it is easy to find further examples of conflict – for example, the conservative ideology failed to prevail in recent English cases concerning the licensing of research using human embryos and the tissue typing of an embryo for 'saviour sibling' purposes;[8] but it was successful in the well-known (German) *Peep-Show* decision,[9] where the Federal Administrative Tribunal denied a licence for a mechanical peep-show on the ground that the performance would violate human dignity. Anticipating a later point in this discussion, the Tribunal said:

> The consent of the women concerned can only exclude a violation of human dignity if such a violation is based only on the lack of consent to the relevant actions or omissions of the women concerned. However, this is not the situation here because in the case at issue . . . the human dignity of the women concerned

[7] 326 SE 2d 410 (SC 1985).

[8] *R (Quintavalle on behalf of Comment on Reproductive Ethics)* v. *Human Fertilization and Embryology Authority* [2002] EWHC 2785 (Admin); [2003] EWCA 667; [2005] UKHL 28; and *R* v. *Secretary of State for Health ex parte Quintavalle (on behalf of Pro-Life Alliance)* [2001] EWHC 918 (Admin) (Crane J); [2002] EWCA Civ 29; [2003] UKHL 13.

[9] BVerwGE 64 (1981) 274.

> is violated by the exposition typical of these performances. Here, human dignity, because its significance reaches beyond the individual, must be protected even against the wishes of the woman concerned whose own subjective ideas deviate from the objective value of human dignity.[10]

No doubt, many further illustrations of the tension could be given. However, there is already more than enough to indicate that, where the public ordering of a society is orientated towards a constitutive value of human dignity, the way in which that ordering is articulated will depend on the competing influences of the liberal (empowering) and conservative (constraining) views.

Private order

In the sphere of private ordering, it will sometimes be agreed that there should be a particular limit on transactional freedom – for example, that there should be limits on the validity and enforceability of contracts concerning slavery, the procurement of human organs, surrogacy, various kinds of sexual services, gaming and so on. The reasons for recognizing these limits might be quite distinct and different – whereas liberals will be concerned about the extent to which such transactions are truly 'free', conservatives will find the purposes of the transactions offensive. Nevertheless, at the points of convergence, it is at least agreed that cases of this kind are where support for, and encouragement of, contracts should reach their end.

Such overlapping agreement notwithstanding, liberals and conservatives have very different approaches to transactional freedom. Whilst the pressure of liberalism is towards deregulation, in order to make room for private governance, it is characteristic of conservative thinking that human dignity needs to be conserved, that transactions should respect community values (Brownsword 2001). The tension can be detected in *'Jerusalem Community' Funeral Society* v. *Lionel Aryeh Kestenbaum*,[11] a decision of the Supreme Court of Israel. The contract at issue concerned the funeral arrangements for the respondent's wife. According to the respondent, it was his deceased wife's wish that her tombstone should show her name and her Gregorian date of birth and date of death in Latin characters. However, the funeral society refused to accede to this wish, relying on its standard form provisions which allowed only for the engraving of letters in the Hebrew alphabet. The question for the Court was whether this restrictive and non-negotiable standard-form provision was valid. For the minority, this was a legitimate attempt by the funeral society to preserve its traditions. However, for the majority, this was an unacceptable restriction on the respondent's freedom and, ultimately, it was a violation of his dignity. The term was invalid.

In an era of rapid developments in human genetics (Brownsword, Cornish and Llewelyn 1998), there might be broad support for a precautionary view

[10] *Ibid.*: 277–9. [11] CA 294/91, 46 (2) PD 464 (Hebrew).

of some emerging transactional practices – for instance, the circulation of personal genetic information in the context of employment and insurance contracts (which might lead to unacceptable forms of discrimination), the supply of direct-to-consumer genetic services, and various kinds of enhancement contracts. However, in the longer run, it is the conservative ideology that will resist such transactions in the name of respect for human dignity (see, for example, Sandel 2007).

Consent

The remarks of the Federal Administrative Tribunal in the *Peep-Show* decision (above) prefigure an enormously important point. Whereas liberals picture humans expressing their dignity through the choices that they make, including the choices that they make in giving or withholding their consent where this is an issue, conservative dignitarians treat consent as irrelevant. Quite distinctively, as the Tribunal emphasizes, where an act is judged to compromise human dignity, the fact that the offending act is a consensual one makes absolutely no difference to its impermissibility. According to this view, where an act involving two or more persons is categorically prohibited (because it compromises human dignity), that prohibition is not susceptible to being lifted by the persons involved giving their consent to the act.

In case after case, we see this lesson repeated. In the UK, we see it in *R* v. *Brown*,[12] where the majority of the House of Lords ruled that consent was no defence to the assaults and woundings inflicted during sado-masochistic sexual practices; we see it in another *Brown* case,[13] this time in the US, where the court rejected the defendant's defence that his alcoholic wife consented to the beatings that he administered when she drank; in France, we see it in the famous dwarf-throwing case;[14] and, in Germany, in addition to the *Peep-Show* decision, there is, of course, the more recent *Omega* case,[15] in which the fact that the participants were freely consenting adults failed to salvage the Laserdrome's licence.

By contrast, where liberal thinking prevails, the fact that the parties are consenting is a central (although not sufficient) consideration that pushes towards permission. Thus, in a famous chapter of US constitutional jurisprudence, the Supreme Court, having been divided about the criminalization of consensual

12 [1993] 2 All ER 75.

13 *State* v. *Brown*, 364 A 2d 27 (NJ Super. Ct Law Div, 1976), affirmed 381 A 2d 1231 (NJ Super. Ct App. Div. 1977).

14 Conseil d'Etat (27 October 1995) req. nos. 136-727 (Commune de Morsang-sur-Orge) and 143-578 (Ville d'Aix-en-Provence).

15 *Omega Spielhallen- und Automatenaufstellungs-GmbH* v. *Oberbürgermeisterin der Bundesstadt Bonn* (Case C-36/02) (14 October 2004); OJ C 300, 04.12.2004 p. 3.

adult homosexual acts, eventually decided in *Lawrence* v. *Texas*[16] that restrictions on sexual freedom violate human dignity. For the majority, the earlier jurisprudence failed to grasp the breadth and depth of the liberty interest at stake and to appreciate that 'adults may choose to enter upon [such a sexual] relationship in the confines of their homes and their own private lives and still retain their dignity as free persons'.[17] Summing up, the majority opinion concludes:

> The case [involves] two adults who, with full and mutual consent from each other, engaged in sexual practices common to a homosexual lifestyle. The petitioners are entitled to respect for their private lives. The State cannot demean their existence or control their destiny by making their private sexual conduct a crime.[18]

While consent does not do all the work here, on the liberal view of human dignity, it is material; and, other things being equal, it is decisive.

Taking stock

Where a legal system is constitutively committed to respect for human rights, much of its business will be conducted with reference to particular rights. Sometimes, the underlying (constitutive) value of human dignity will make an appearance, particularly it seems where privacy is the right at issue or where the right against cruel and unusual punishment is central; but, for much of the time, it is a silent partner. Such liberal regimes can and do encounter cultural and legal resistance, particularly where there is a reluctance to move away from tradition or where there is a fear of dramatic and disruptive change. Here, we find recourse to a conservative notion of human dignity, designed to hold the line in both public and private ordering. In short, we might say that in those legal systems that have embraced the modern, the liberal view rules; but, in those systems that either hanker after the past or that fear the future, human dignity serves as a rallying point for conservative views (compare Matsui, in Chapter 45 below).

The legal embedding of human dignity: positives and negatives

While legal references to human dignity abound, there would be little support for the proposition that there should be a law providing, quite simply, that it is a criminal offence to act in a way that fails to respect, or that compromises, human dignity. Many would argue that this would violate the canons of the Rule of Law – or, at any rate, this would be so unless the context was one in which it was perfectly well understood in which circumstances the offence would be committed. In the same way, imagine that a legal system recognized claims for compensation where the tort (or delict) of violating human dignity

[16] 123 SCt 2472. [17] *Ibid.*: 2478. [18] *Ibid.*: 2484.

was proved. Even though this branch of the law exposes defendants to claims for compensation rather than to punishment and stigma, it might be objected that such a vaguely formulated claim should not be recognized. What should we make of this? Are there good arguments in favour of expressly recognizing human dignity as a positive legal value? Or, is the better view that the positive law should exclude such references to human dignity?

Addressing these questions, we can start by sketching three arguments against the explicit referencing of human dignity in the positive law. The first two arguments – one based on fairness (particularly in relation to the criminal law) and the other based on utility (particularly in the area of commercial law) – treat the vague and contestable nature of the concept of human dignity as a problem. The third argument, based on liberal values of respect for human rights and fundamental freedoms, is not so much concerned that there should be clarity and calculability in the law as that references to human dignity might prove to be a hostage to fortune, inviting illiberal interpretations and applications.

In response to these arguments, three counter-considerations are outlined. First, for those who subscribe to a conservative dignitarian ethic, it is important that this constraint on free choice is reflected in the law. Second, even if one rejects such an ethic, one might see some utility in there being express reference to human dignity in certain legal contexts – for example, in those areas of law that are trying to regulate technological and cultural change (where the function of such references to human dignity is not action-guiding as such but rather to provide an opportunity for debate and reflection together with some flexibility), and, similarly, where attempts are being made to develop a degree of consensus in the context of value pluralism (the vagueness of the concept of human dignity being a virtue in such a context). Third, there is a rights-based argument in favour of transparency in legal decision-making. It follows that, if human dignity is the implicit ground for a decision, the parties to the dispute are entitled to have it made explicit.

The upshot of this discussion is that the question does not seem to have an all-or-nothing answer. For, unless the range of law is specified in extremely narrow terms, there seem to be some aspects of the legal enterprise in which the express referencing of human dignity might be functional and appropriate. However, there is a further complication: namely, that the judgments that we make about functionality and appropriateness will be driven by competing ethics that go right back to the contested nature of human dignity itself. In other words, it is not just a matter of which particular part of the legal enterprise is in the spotlight, but also of which particular ethic is energizing the light.

Three negative arguments

In this part of the discussion, three arguments against the explicit referencing of human dignity in the positive law are sketched. These are: (1) the argument from fairness; (2) the argument from utility and commercial need; and (3) the argument from respect for human rights and fundamental freedoms.

The argument from fairness

Let us start with the hypothetical criminal law that provides that it is an offence to act in a way that fails to respect, or that compromises, human dignity. Without some context, it is difficult to assess such a provision. If this is the one and only offence in the criminal code, and if the setting is anything like a modern society, it would be difficult to know where one stood, to know whether one's acts were or were not criminal offences. In such circumstances, this would seem to be a serious departure from the guiding principles represented by the Rule of Law (Fuller 1969).

If our hypothetical criminal law is to do any better, the circumstances need to be modified in one or other of two ways. One way is to change the setting, so that we are supposing a small homogeneous community with well-understood social norms (Roberts 1979). In such a community, the one-provision criminal code might capture the spirit of the group's more particularized normative order. In such a context, the provision would be of no more than symbolic significance; it would not be intended to have any action-guiding function and so it would have some immunity against the Rule of Law objection.

The other way in which the hypothetical might be modified is by retaining the setting of a modern pluralistic society but with a developed and particularized criminal code. So long as the human dignity provision appears as one offence amongst many others, and so long as those many other offences are action-guiding, the legal order is less clearly pathological. Nevertheless, the question arises: what is the role and function of the human dignity offence? As with the simpler society, the answer might be that the function of the provision is symbolic – it has no utility but it does no harm. On the other hand, the answer might be that the offence can be brought into play where prosecutors can find no other offence that fits the 'crime'. If this is the answer, then once again the provision is likely to fall foul of Rule of Law values (see Lima Marques and Lixinski, in Chapter 41 below).

The demand made by the Rule of Law that legal provisions should be clear is at its strongest where non-compliance attracts penal sanctions. Here, it is commonly said that defendants must be given 'fair warning' that they are breaking the law;[19] and that, in the event of an ambiguity, any benefit of the doubt must be given to the accused. Accordingly, to resort to the human dignity offence where all else fails is unfair; and no encouragement should be given to such provisions of last resort.[20]

[19] For a well-known example, see *McBoyle* v. *US*, 283 US 25 (1931).

[20] Compare Lord Diplock in *DPP* v. *Withers* [1974] 3 WLR 751, 761, criticizing the prosecution's reliance on a conspiracy charge.

The argument from utility and commercial need

Common lawyers believe that commercial people, especially commercial contractors, need to have calculable trading rules. For this reason, there is a degree of suspicion, probably at its highest amongst English contract lawyers, of general clauses (for example, clauses that require good faith and fair dealing in transactions) of the kind that are commonplace in both civilian contract codes and some common law jurisdictions as well as in harmonizing (regional and international) instruments (Brownsword 2006). Some take the view that the concern is overstated, claiming that the incorporation of explicit general clauses of this kind makes little practical difference (neither for better nor for worse). Nevertheless, the fact that English contract law, with its emphasis on calculability and its eschewal of good faith and the like, is the law of choice for many international traders suggests that there might be some substance in the concern for certainty. Taking such a view, even at the margins of contract law, appeals to human dignity should not be encouraged.

Turning from contracts to patents, those who invest in research and development (like contractors) need to know where they stand – in particular, they need to know that, if they develop innovative products or processes, they will be in a position to claim patent protection. Broadly speaking, patent regimes are geared for granting patents provided that the applicant shows that the work is inventive and has some utility. However, in Europe, the regional patent regime – which is rooted in the European Patent Convention 1973 and Directive 98/44/EC on the Legal Protection of Biotechnological Inventions – has an explicit moral exclusion in relation to patentability. In a string of controversial cases, the European Patent Office (EPO) has attempted to apply this exclusion to claims made in relation to genetically engineered animals and plants, as well as to coding sections of the human genome and the products of human embryonic stem cell research. While the moral arguments have not always centred on human dignity, appeals to human dignity are strongly encouraged by recital 38 of the Directive which underlines that, in addition to the specific exclusions that are identified in Article 6(2) of the Directive, any invention that compromises human dignity is to be excluded from patentability.

Although the moral exclusion has greatly agitated patent lawyers, and not just the English, the EPO managed for some years to reduce its practical impact by insisting that moral objections would not have exclusionary effect unless they were backed by an overwhelming consensus – which meant that contested concepts such as human dignity were marginalized (Brownsword and Goodwin 2012). However, in the *Wisconsin Alumni Research Foundation* (WARF) case,[21] the Enlarged Board of Appeal (EBA) at the EPO was asked by the Technical Board of Appeal[22] to rule, *inter alia*, on whether Article 6(2)(c) of the Directive – which provides that uses of human embryos for industrial or commercial purposes

[21] Case G 0002/06, 25 November 2008.

[22] T 1374/04 (OJ EPO 2007, 313).

shall be treated as unpatentable – forbids the patenting of a human embryonic stem cell culture. Holding that the patent was excluded, the EBA said:

> On its face, the provision . . . is straightforward and prohibits the patenting if a human embryo is used for industrial or commercial purposes. Such a reading is also in line with the concern of the legislator to prevent a misuse in the sense of a commodification of human embryos . . . and with one of the essential objectives of the whole Directive to protect human dignity.[23]

With this turn in the jurisprudence – and, *a fortiori*, after the parallel confirming decision of the European Court of Justice in *Oliver Brüstle* v. *Greenpeace eV*[24] – critics can say, with some justification, that the patentability (in Europe) of leading-edge biotechnological work has been thrown into doubt; that this is bad for biotechnology and innovation in Europe; and, more generally, that the uncertainty surrounding the moral exclusion (and, concomitantly, its protection of human dignity) creates an unhelpful regulatory environment for innovators (Plomer and Torremans 2009).

The argument from respect for human rights and fundamental freedoms

There is a third and rather different argument against the use of explicit legal references to human dignity. So far, the two arguments have been more concerned with the law having clear and calculable applications than with the substance of legal provisions. However, the third argument is precisely that references to human dignity can permit interpretations and applications that are incompatible with respect for human rights and fundamental freedoms.

On the face of it, this is a strange objection; for the modern demand that human rights and fundamental freedoms should be respected is predicated on respect for human dignity. Nevertheless, proponents of human rights may well feel that positive law can be articulated and applied in ways that are compatible with human rights without the need for any reference to human dignity. After all, the European Convention on Human Rights seems to work perfectly well without such an explicit reference – and, indeed, liberals have a real cause for concern if the Strasbourg court, relying on implicit references to human dignity, allows in conservative views as good reasons for restricting the Convention's rights.[25]

Taking this approach, there might be some concern that, with human dignity in the mix, there is too much constitutional noise and that this leads to a risk that there might be a loss of clarity as to the scope and function of particular human rights (Fagan 1998). However, the greater concern is that explicit references to human dignity will support legal applications that evince a lack of respect

[23] Case G 0002/06, para. 18. [24] Case C-34/10, OJ C 362, 10.12.2011.

[25] Compare the case of *SH* v. *Austria* (Application No. 57813/00 (1 April 2010). The judgment of the Grand Chamber was given on 3 November 2011).

for autonomy and self-determination. Famously, for example, in the dwarf-throwing ('*lancer de nain*') case,[26] the Conseil d'Etat held that, where police powers had been exercised to ban dwarf-throwing in clubs, such steps were lawfully taken in order to secure respect for human dignity and *ordre public*. However, the legality of the bans was challenged by, among others, one of the dwarfs, who argued that he freely participated in the activity, that the work brought him a monthly wage, and that, if dwarf-throwing was banned, he would find himself unemployed again. To this, the Conseil d'Etat responded that the dwarf compromised his own dignity by allowing himself to be used as a projectile, as a mere thing, and that no such concession could be allowed.

While cases of this kind are not commonplace, it is not just dwarf-throwing that has been banned in the name of human dignity.[27] More generally, as we have already remarked, whenever the human body or body parts are commodified or commercialized, or whenever there seems to be a lack of respect for the sanctity of human life, dignitarian values will tend to push for legal prohibition – and, where the law expressly references human dignity (even if the founding intentions were quite different), there is an available legal peg on which to hang the argument for restriction (Kadidal 1996).

Three positive arguments

Against the three negative arguments, we can suggest three counter-arguments. Whereas the first of these counter-arguments is unashamedly dignitarian, maintaining that the culture of respect for individual 'autonomy', 'choice' and 'consumerism' has gone too far, the second and third counter-arguments do not presuppose such values. Rather, these latter arguments return to the principles of utility, fairness and rights upon which the negative arguments rely.

The conservative dignitarian argument

Many national constitutions take it as axiomatic that human dignity should be respected. Where, as in Article 1 of the German Basic Law, the constitutive importance of human dignity is declared and embedded, the interpretive work remains to be done. Over time, the jurisprudence might develop in a way that is more or less consistent with the founding intentions, more or less consistent with liberal or conservative takes on human dignity, and so on. For conservative dignitarians, anything other than a jurisprudence that sticks to the script that captures the essence of humanity will not do. In other words, the dignitarian

[26] Conseil d'Etat (27 October 1995) req. nos. 136-727 (Commune de Morsang-sur-Orge) and 143-578 (Ville d'Aix-en-Provence).

[27] Compare, for example, *Omega Spielhallen-und Automatenaufstellungs-GmbH* v. *Oberbürgermeisterin der Bundesstadt Bonn* (Case C-36/02) (14 October 2004); OJ C 300, 04.12.2004 p. 3.

argument in favour of the explicit legal referencing of human dignity is not sufficient; it matters that the right kind of dignitarianism is fixed in the law.

Clearly, this kind of position will be opposed by liberals. However, there is a more subtle argument in favour of the referencing of human dignity that appeals to some common ground between the protagonists. The idea is that liberals and conservatives alike hold that individuals should try to do the right thing (to act ethically) for the right reason (Brownsword 2010). Insofar as modern regulatory technologies amplify prudential reasons for compliance with the law (as in the case of CCTV, or DNA profiling, or various kinds of biometrics), the moral signal is weakened (Larsen 2011); and, where the technologies render non-compliance impracticable or impossible, the moral signal is weakened even further. If humans are to express their dignity by doing the right thing for the right reason, they need a context in which they can develop moral virtue and then act on it. One of the key roles that the express legal referencing of human dignity might play in an increasingly technological setting, is to compel regulators to be very careful about employing strategies that might corrode the essential context for moral virtue (Brownsword 2008; Brownsword 2011).

The argument from utility

Where law is intended to be action-guiding, there are good arguments that favour its guidance being clear and its responses calculable. However, these arguments lose some traction as we move away from 'hard' law to 'softer' forms of law, to codes, informal guidance, voluntary standards, and the like. Soft law of this kind might be nested within hard law frameworks (for example, as with codes of practice that are anticipated by legislative frameworks) or it might be the kind of early stage governance that is relied on before a hard law intervention is viable. In the context of the various uncertainties associated with emerging technologies, such a strategy seems to have considerable utility (Dorbeck-Jung and van Amerom 2008; Mandel 2009). To the extent that these uncertainties concern the nature or extent of the risks to human health, safety, or the environment, it is not obvious that a softer law strategy needs to be built specifically around respect for human dignity. For human dignity to serve as a focal point for deliberation, consultation and debate, there needs to be a cultural concern – indeed, just the kind of concern elicited by human genetics, new reproductive technologies, synthetic biologies, technologies for human enhancement, nanomedicine, sophisticated brain imaging machines, and the like. In such cases, the technology is culturally disruptive and, by putting down a marker for human dignity, the law facilitates a serious debate about the direction of society.

Flowing from the previous point, in a world of value pluralism, it can be difficult to articulate agreements in terms that command all-round support. In this context, those who draft international soft law instruments will often make use of concepts such as human dignity as a means of establishing a working level of consensus. Arguably, the UNESCO Universal Declaration on the Human

Genome and Human Rights in 1997 and, even more so, the Universal Declaration on Bioethics and Human Rights in 2005, are examples of this approach to consensus-formation (see Byk, Chapter 37 below).

The argument from fairness and rights

One of the arguments that figures in the debates about general clauses in contract law is that, in the absence of such clauses, judges resort to indirect strategies to achieve results that could have been achieved directly had such clauses been in play. It is said, in other words, that such clauses promote honesty, transparency and integrity in adjudication. Similarly, in those patent law regimes that do not have explicit moral exclusions, it is said that moral considerations can covertly shape the reasoning of patent examiners and courts. What these arguments add up to is the claim that litigants and the public have a right to transparent and accurate reasons for legal decisions – and so, where (rightly or wrongly) decision-makers are going to reason from human dignity, this needs to be expressly represented in the law. Quite simply, fairness so dictates.

Taking stock

The question of the explicit legal referencing of human dignity is more complex than we might first suppose. However, should we also conclude that the arguments for and against are evenly balanced? If we are able to privilege liberal human rights over conservative dignitarian values, or *vice versa*, we will not so conclude. Rather, we will seek to embed a particular conception of human dignity in the law. Short of being able to specify a particular conception of human dignity, much will depend upon whether we are able to privilege a particular ethical approach – for example, rights over utility, or *vice versa*. However, even if we can do this, the 'take-home message' is not simple: if utility is the test, we might find the express referencing of human dignity a useful addition to some parts of the law but less useful in others; and, if fairness and rights is the test, we will almost certainly reject an ostensibly action-guiding reference to human dignity in the heartland of the criminal law, but, elsewhere in the law, such a reference might be supportive of rights.

Concluding remarks

Legal debates that revolve around human rights and human dignity are full of twists, turns, and unresolved difficulties. Liberals and conservatives seem to be destined to disagree. However, the fact that such debates are a feature of legal discourse underlines that, as humans, we share a concern, individually and collectively, to try to do the right thing. In an era of rapid technological development, operating in conjunction with the globalization of markets and trade, this is especially important. In such a context, it is imperative that communities with moral aspirations challenge the dominance of regulators who operate with a narrow risk-management (instrumental) mentality. It is also important to keep an eye on the complexion of the regulatory environment, particularly the replacement of normative legal and moral signals with technological management (various forms of coding, design, architecture, and the like) (Brownsword 2011). In our life and times, there is a danger that we lose sight of the simple virtue of doing the right thing. If our current preoccupation with human dignity leads us to ponder and to persist with such questions, then (*pace* the sceptics) we need to keep it and its questions firmly in the regulatory foreground (Brownsword 2013).

References

Adams, J. N., and Brownsword, R. 2006. *Understanding Law.* London: Sweet & Maxwell

Andorno, R. 2009. 'Article 3: Human Dignity and Human Rights', in H. A. M. J. ten Have and M. S. Jean (eds.), *The UNESCO Universal Declaration on Bioethics and Human Rights.* Paris: UNESCO, 91–8

Appiah, K. A. 2006. *Cosmopolitanism.* London: Penguin, Allen Lane

Beyleveld, D., and Brownsword, R. 2001. *Human Dignity in Bioethics and Biolaw.* Oxford University Press

2007. *Consent in the Law.* Oxford: Hart Publishing

Brownsword, R. 2001. 'Freedom of Contract, Human Rights and Human Dignity', in D. Friedmann and D. Barak-Erez (eds.), *Human Rights in Private Law.* Oxford: Hart Publishing, 181–99

2003. 'Bioethics Today, Bioethics Tomorrow: Stem Cell Research and the "Dignitarian Alliance"', *University of Notre Dame Journal of Law, Ethics and Public Policy* 17: 15–51

2006. *Contract Law: Themes for the Twenty-First Century.* Oxford University Press

2007. 'Ethical Pluralism and the Regulation of Modern Biotechnology', in F. Francioni (ed.), *Biotechnologies and International Human Rights.* Oxford: Hart Publishing, 45–70

2008. *Rights, Regulation, and the Technological Revolution.* Oxford University Press

2010. 'Regulating the Life Sciences, Pluralism, and the Limits of Deliberative Democracy', *Singapore Academy of Law Journal* 22: 801–32

2011. 'Lost in Translation: Legality, Regulatory Margins, and Technological Management', *Berkeley Technology Law Journal* 26: 1321–65

2013. 'Human Dignity, Human Rights, and Simply Trying To Do the Right Thing', in C. McCrudden (ed.), *Understanding Human Dignity.* Proceedings of the British Academy. Oxford University Press, 470–90

Brownsword, R., Cornish, W. R., and Llewelyn, M. (eds.). 1998. *Law and Human Genetics: Regulating a Revolution.* Oxford: Hart Publishing

Brownsword, R., and Goodwin, M. 2012. *Law and the Technologies of the Twenty-First Century.* Cambridge University Press

Caulfield, T., and Brownsword, R. 2006. 'Human Dignity: A Guide to Policy Making in the Biotechnology Era', *Nature Reviews Genetics* 7: 72–6

Clapham, A. 1993. *Human Rights in the Private Sphere.* Oxford: Clarendon Press

Dan-Cohen, M. 2002. *Harmful Thoughts: Essays on Law, Self, and Morality.* Princeton University Press

Dorbeck-Jung, B., and van Amerom, M. 2008. 'The Hardness of Soft Law in the United Kingdom: State and Non-State Regulatory Activities Related to Nanotechnological Development', in H. van Schooten and J. Verschuuren (eds.), *International Governance and Law*. Cheltenham: Edward Elgar, 129–50

Fagan, A. 1998. 'Dignity and Unfair Discrimination: A Value Misplaced and a Right Misunderstood', *South African Journal on Human Rights* 14: 220–47

Feldman, D. 1999. 'Human Dignity as a Legal Value: Part I', *Public Law* 682–702

Fletcher, G. P. 1996. *Basic Concepts of Legal Thought*. Oxford University Press

Fuller, Lon L. 1969. *The Morality of Law*. New Haven, CT: Yale University Press

Goodin, R. E. 1981. 'The Political Theories of Choice and Dignity', *American Philosophical Quarterly* 18: 91–100

Green, Sir G. 2007. 'Human Dignity and the Law', in J. Malpas and N. Lickiss (eds.), *Perspectives on Human Dignity: A Conversation*. Dordrecht: Springer, 151–6

Kadidal, S. 1996. 'Obscenity in the Age of Mechanical Reproduction', *American Journal of Comparative Law* 44: 353–85

Kirby, M. 2010. 'Health Care and Global Justice', *Singapore Academy of Law Journal* 22: 785–800

Kolnai, A. 1976. 'Dignity', *Philosophy* 51: 251–71

Larsen, B. von S. T. 2011. *Setting the Watch: Privacy and the Ethics of CCTV Surveillance*. Oxford: Hart Publishing

Mandel, G. N. 2009. 'Regulating Emerging Technologies', *Law, Innovation, and Technology* 1: 75–92

McCrudden, C. 2008. 'Human Dignity and Judicial Interpretation of Human Rights', *European Journal of International Law* 19: 655–724

Packer, H. L. 1969. *The Limits of the Criminal Sanction*. Stanford University Press

Plomer, A., and Torremans, P. (eds.). 2009. *Embryonic Stem Cell Patents–European Law and Ethics*. Oxford University Press

Raz, J. 1979. *The Authority of Law*. Oxford: Clarendon Press

Roberts, S. 1979. *Order and Dispute*. London: Penguin

Sandel, M. 2007. *The Case Against Perfection: Ethics in the Age of Genetic Engineering*. Cambridge, MA: Harvard University Press

Ten Have, H. A. M. J., and Jean, M. S. (eds.). 2009. *The UNESCO Universal Declaration on Bioethics and Human Rights*. Paris: UNESCO

2

Human dignity: concepts, discussions, philosophical perspectives

MARCUS DÜWELL

The following introduction aims at an overview of relevant conceptual and philosophical distinctions and questions that discussions about human dignity are confronted with. I will mainly focus on questions about 'human dignity' that are relevant within the context of the human rights framework. First, I will explain why we are in need of a philosophical account of human dignity at all. Second, I will distinguish different ideal typical models of (human) dignity. Third, I will distinguish different conceptual questions related to different approaches to human dignity and their philosophical articulations. Fourth, I will investigate some relevant questions on the way towards an ethics of human dignity. Finally, I will propose some topics that I consider to be important questions for future philosophical debates about this concept.

Why develop a philosophical account of human dignity?

When in 1948 the Universal Declaration of Human Rights (UDHR) was signed, human dignity was introduced as a kind of moral reference point for an agreement that could provide normative guidance for the interpretation of the human rights framework in general. Most people believed that they knew what human dignity was about: a consensus within the humanistic tradition, a secularized version of the Judeo-Christian concept of Imago Dei, an overlap between the ethical doctrines of important thinkers like Kant and Confucius, the normative core of the natural law tradition, a moral–political statement against the atrocities of the Nazi regime etc. Although obviously not everyone endorsed the notion, it was generally assumed that its meaning and status were clear – and thus it appeared superfluous to strive for a theoretical explanation and justification of the concept.

The number of publications in recent years demonstrates that this attitude has changed. It seems that the concept has lost its innocence: in discussions about cloning, embryo protection and euthanasia, the concept of 'human dignity' has been embraced by various societal groups with very different intentions. This emphatic use of the concept to articulate highly controversial issues made others hesitant to use this notion. For instance, one could consider debates in the United States, where the publications of the President's Council of Bioethics in the last decade created the impression that a conservative programme would be promoted under the title 'human dignity' (for example, President's Council on Bioethics 2008). An example on the European level was the attempt by Peter Kemp *et al.* (2000) to formulate four core bioethical principles – dignity, integrity, vulnerability and autonomy – that should function as the European alternative to more liberal bioethical principles as autonomy, non-maleficence, beneficence and justice (Beauchamp and Childress 2013). Other examples were verdicts of the highest courts in France and Germany to forbid participation in activities such as peep shows or dwarf-throwing: these were judged as being incompatible with the dignity of the person and thus illegitimate – even though those participating claimed to do so on the basis of their own free decision. Such developments create the impression that human dignity formulates an alternative to the traditional liberal ethos for which a concept of autonomy would be fundamental; Brownsword (2003) speaks in this context of a 'dignitarian alliance' in bioethics that uses the concept of human dignity to undermine important starting-points of the human rights concept.

Ambivalences about the concept of 'human dignity' are so important because of the central position the concept adopts within the human rights framework. The United Nations ascribed a foundational role to this concept by declaring: 'These [human] rights derive from the inherent dignity of the human person.'[1] Similarly we find in Article 1 of the German Constitution: 'Human dignity shall be inviolable. To respect and protect it shall be the duty of all state authority.' And in Article 2 we read: 'The German people therefore acknowledges inviolable and inalienable human rights as the basis of every community, of peace and of justice in the world.' The 'therefore' in Article 2 suggests that human rights follow from human dignity, an idea we also find in the Declarations.[2]

In this light, it is clear that the way we understand human dignity influences our understanding of the human rights framework as such. But what is the normative content of human dignity? Often, human dignity is understood as a condemnation of the 'instrumentalization' of human beings, to treat them as mere objects.[3] But how would that relate to the foundational role of human dignity? It is quite possible to avoid a reduction of human beings to mere objects, as in the Shoah, without being committed to the whole set of human

[1] United Nations, International Covenant on Economic, Social and Cultural Rights, 1966; International Covenant on Civil and Political Rights, 1966.

[2] See Chapter 39 by Dreier in this volume for a detailed explanation.

[3] Dürig's view is that respect for human dignity prevents one from treating human beings only as objects (Dürig 1956). He refers at least implicitly to Kant's 'formula of humanity', which prescribes that human beings may not be treated 'merely as a means' (Kant 1996: 429). But this is not unproblematic: in Kant the understanding is much broader in the sense that Kant proscribes treating humanity always 'as an end' which goes beyond the negative formulation that forbids instrumentalization. If I don't help a person in need, I don't treat him merely as a means to my end; I just don't treat him at all. But a different question is whether I respect him as an end in himself.

rights. To emphasize that human beings have a right not to be a victim of such extreme forms of dehumanization would entail identifying violations of human dignity with a subset of human rights violations, and subsequently to declare these forms of violations illegitimate. This interpretation of a *distinct* normative content of human dignity is different from an understanding of human dignity as the *basic principle* of the legal order. And if we would understand human dignity as a fundamental principle, how should we determine its normative content? How can the human rights be derived from human dignity? What would be the rule of interpretation?

These considerations are particularly important because human dignity is assumed to be of overriding importance. While the diverse rights have to be weighed against each other, this is not the case with human dignity. Human dignity will always trump other considerations. But this means that it may easily be a Trojan horse if we do not understand what it means and how to use it: if we have a concept that can trump the human rights while there is no principled understanding of how it is used, this could ultimately undermine the legal status and the moral authority of the entire human rights framework. As such, the conceptual clarification of human dignity is a very important philosophical task. In the following, I will therefore try to set out an overview of the questions necessary to develop an understanding of the concept. These questions are also relevant for those scholars who are sceptical whether human dignity is a meaningful, worthwhile or useful concept at all. Such a negative judgment should be the result of a careful examination of all questions mentioned below.

The concept of human dignity

I will in the following distinguish some ideal typical models of human dignity. Two preliminary remarks are necessary. First, I will refer to different historical models, but it is not my aim to reconstruct an evolution of the concept. Second, It is difficult to identify different models of human dignity by reference to terminology alone. The decisive question would be whether we can find the *concept* in other traditions – in for example Hebrew or Confucian texts – and that is a question of interpretation. Let me now distinguish five ideal typical ways of conceptualizing human dignity.

(1) *Rank*. Some have reconstructed dignity as primarily linked to a kind of *nobility* or *rank*.[4] In that sense, it is to some extent a concept that marks a distinction: the one who has rank and honour is distinct from those who do not. It is unclear whether this exclusionary aspect is decisive: it is relevant that the honourable person has a dignity which is a reason to treat him or her with respect, and which at the same time forms a reason for him to

[4] See Chapter 3 by Ober and Chapter 31 by Neuhäuser and Stoecker in this volume; and Waldron (2012).

behave according to this status. However, dignity related to rank does not imply universalizability and is not inalienable – rank may be lost.

(2) *Virtue and duty.* As early as in ancient times, dignity was seen as a concept of universal nobility, for example in Cicero (1913: I.30: 105–6).[5] The universal status of a human, rational being was seen as a reason to behave in accordance with this status. Specific roles are connected to specific duties: similarly to the duties a person has in his quality of father or judge, a human being has duties that are implications of his status as a human being – a being endowed with rational capacities. The content of these obligations is simply to exercise one's rational capacities: a being with dignity should behave in a way that is appropriate to her rational capacities, it should exercise rational control in action, it should master the emotions, it has to stay sober in order to stay in control of himself, in short, it has to behave like a rational being should behave. In that sense, human dignity formulates duties to ourselves, but it is not concerned with the protection of the dignity of the other. There are some obligations towards other human beings involved, but the core of this concept are the duties of the agent to behave according to his status – not the respect for the dignity of the other. This concept is universal but not inalienable: a human being can lose his or her dignity by not living according to his or her duties and it can hardly be reconstructed as the foundation of rights.

(3) *Dignity and religious status.* Dignity in accordance with the duties of a human being can be translated into various religious contexts. In that case the duties are seen not as a result of our rational nature, but as a result of divine commands; of course, our rational nature is necessary for us to understand those commands and to behave accordingly. In some religious traditions, these divine commands would be the result of divine revelation, which according to some approaches would coincide with our rational insight. The model of human dignity would be comparable to the previous one, differing only in that the duties of the virtuous man are determined on the basis of divine commands. This concept may be universal when religious law is thought to be the valid law for all human beings. And, as with the previous model, dignity may be lost if one does not live up to one's duties. It is impossible here to reconstruct to what extent the religious tradition is related to the development of the human rights concept; however, it is important to point out that there is no conceptually necessary relationship between religious status and respect for human rights.

(4) *The cosmological status of the human being.* Human dignity can be a concept that refers to the specificity of human beings. Pico della Mirandola would in this sense describe the human being as specifically different from animals (humans are free), from the angels (humans are free and vulnerable) and from God (humans are not perfect). This anthropological self-reflection is

[5] See Chapter 17 by Luo in this volume.

a kind of interpretation of the role from human beings in the cosmos, which of course would have implications for the political order.[6] This cosmological and anthropological speculation can perhaps explain why the human being is an admirable creature, and this insight could be a reason to see him as a creative and curious being, whose nature is linked to the discovery of the world and the creation of new possibilities. But this whole concept has only indirect links to the moral and political dimension. The concept is universal but it does not specifically justify that the human being has rights.

(5) *Respect for the dignity of the individual human being.* From general considerations about the cosmological or religious status of the human being, the specific idea can be distinguished that each single human individual would have dignity. In this line, human dignity should be seen as an expression that signifies a status which other human beings and political institutions have to respect. This respect can be interpreted primarily in a sense of moral obligations or – as happened in the twentieth century – in the sense of individual rights that can be legally enforced. And since this respect is of immanent importance from a moral point of view, it can be seen as a reason to understand the entire legal and political state and international order as based on the respect for the dignity and rights of each individual human being. This concept of 'human dignity', as opposed to those named above, is *universal*: it signifies a status that cannot be lost, and thus may provide a foundation of rights.

Questions regarding human dignity in the context of the human rights regime

A first inventory of models shows that there exists a variety of ways in which human dignity may be conceptualized, some close to one specific ideal type and others more mixed. By way of exclusion, one can identify aspects of how human dignity is *not* understood in contemporary discourse: human dignity is not understood in terms of *honour*, it is not about the particular honour of specific beings with dignity (even so, some would think that human dignity would be a kind of universalization of the honour-idea). It is also not a *perfectionist* concept – references to human dignity do not tell us how to live a good, virtuous or excellent life; perhaps it is about securing the necessary precondition of a good life but it is not about the goals of the good life itself. Rather, the scope of ascription of human dignity is *universal* in the sense that it applies to all human beings, it is *egalitarian* insofar as each human being is equal with regard to his dignity and references to human dignity are justifying *duties towards others* that have the form of *categorical* obligations. Under categorical obligations we understand: duties that are overriding with regard to other action-guiding considerations. That does not mean that those duties cannot be weighted against

[6] See Chapter 6 by Steenbakkers in this volume; and Trinkaus (1970).

other considerations, but that the duties that follow from human dignity can only be weighted against other duties that follow from the respect for human dignity. By emphasizing that human dignity justifies duties to others, I do not exclude the possibility that respect for human dignity may imply duties towards myself as well (as in Kant) but it forms *at least* a ground for strict duties towards others.

But, even thus identified, there exists a broad variety of ways in which the modern concept of dignity may be conceived. In order to understand the differences between various approaches, I would propose to distinguish five questions with regard to which each account should be able to explain its position.

(1) What is the relationship between human dignity and human rights?
(2) What is the relationship between a moral and a legal interpretation of human dignity?
(3) Who has dignity?
(4) What is the normative content of human dignity?
(5) What are the necessary presuppositions for a commitment to human dignity?

What is the relationship between human dignity and human rights?

If we focus on human dignity approaches within the human rights context, we can distinguish various forms of conceptual relationships between human dignity and human rights.[7] The way this relationship is conceptualized determines fundamentally the role of human dignity within the human rights framework. Therefore, I will now present some possibilities of conceptualizing the relation between human dignity and human rights; these considerations would thus be applicable also to a moral and a legal interpretation of human dignity. We can broadly distinguish the interpretation of human dignity as a *right*, as a *norm* and as a *principle*.

If we see human dignity as a *right*, it would be an individual right with a special status. We could think of a right that is to some extent less specific than other rights, a kind of container concept to protect those forms of disrespect for human beings that are not covered by other human rights – a last resort that compensates imperfections in the human rights system. A second option would be to understand it as a right that condemns systematic and structural forms of rights violations so immense that they are not just denials of specific rights, but forms of disrespect for the human being as such. That seems to be the idea behind the critic of instrumentalization or critic of forms of dehumanization (cf. Dürig 1956). But this understanding would just see violations of human dignity

[7] See for this part Düwell (2010); and, as an antithesis, Chapter 20 by Den Hartogh in this volume.

as violations of a *subcategory* of the most fundamental rights, the normative core of the human rights, for which a stronger form of protection would be required. The question would then be how other rights can be derived from the respect for these fundamental rights: one can, for example, see genocide, slavery and systematic degradations of human beings as deeply immoral without deriving further normative consequences from this insight, like political or social and cultural rights. The idea that rights are derived from human dignity would require that human dignity is different from the human rights in a much more fundamental sense. A third option would be to understand human dignity – in line with Hannah Arendt – as a 'right to have rights'.[8] Human dignity would, in this line of thought, be a legitimate claim that each human being has to be a member of a political order that gives her rights as a citizen, a right to inclusion in a legal order. The rights that are granted within the legal order would not be human rights, but legal rights resulting from political struggles. Human dignity would not determine which rights that should be; it would refer to the prior entitlement to have this status of a right-holder at all.

We could also think that human dignity is not a right but a kind of fundamental *norm* that requires respect for humanity in general without an internal link to human rights. This norm would condemn some actions as objective violations of 'humanity'. It would allow for restrictions of rights and liberties for other reasons than direct rights violations. In some contexts, such an understanding is related to the rules of conduct and customs of a specific society. Such a concept could of course be used by all kinds of societal groups to support their particular ideals of human behaviour: dwarf-throwing or peep shows could then be seen as violations of human dignity; likewise it could be a violation of human dignity if unmarried couples live together, if homosexuals have sexual intercourse or if women appear in public without a head-covering. If human dignity as a norm were as under-determined yet nonetheless had overriding power *vis-à-vis* human rights, it could potentially rule out human rights altogether. This would really be the Trojan horse of the human rights regime.

A third possibility would be to understand human dignity as a *principle* – and I will distinguish two interpretations of such a principle. The generally used concept of 'principle' stems from a bioethical debate and was developed by Beauchamp and Childress (2013). These authors argue that we have to start normative evaluations by referring to several mid-level principles that are generally accepted points of departure in normative discourse. These principles have to be specified in concrete situations and have to be balanced against each other. In some bioethical discussions, human dignity is used in this line: as one principle amongst others. Such an understanding would ignore a conceptual relationship to the human rights and it would not give human dignity the

[8] See Chapter 34 by Menke in this volume. In this direction, see also the considerations about 'a right to justification' in Forst (2012).

status of a concept that overrides other practical considerations and from which rights can be derived. Such a principle would certainly not be the concept of human dignity within the human rights framework. A completely different understanding would conceive 'principle' as *overarching*: such a concept would ascribe worth to human beings that forms the basis for the respect we owe to them. This principle overrides other practical considerations and is categorically binding for all actions. Different from the understanding of mid-level principles, this principle cannot be balanced against other principles and would have a unique status as the primary source of moral and legal obligations. This principle would explain the central position of the human person in the legal order, is guiding for the interpretation of the entire set of human rights, and would see human rights as 'derived' from human dignity – Kant's categorical imperative would be a model for the explanation of such a principle (see also Gewirth 1992).

But would human dignity as a principle in this latter sense only prescribe respect for the rights of individuals? Often it is claimed that human dignity would also protect more general conditions for a human life or that it is related to respect for humanity in general. Would such an interpretation of human dignity be in line with its role as a basis for the human rights? An interpretation could proceed as follows: human beings have human rights because they have human dignity. Human dignity would be the principle to respect human beings in their possibility to live a life appropriate to a being with autonomous capacities. The duties with respect to human dignity are duties to protect the necessary conditions to live a life of an autonomous being. This consideration justifies rights of individuals but it justifies also duties to protect the general conditions that are required for an autonomous life. Those general conditions would have to do with a safe environment and institutions that secure the conditions of a life with dignity. These rights are also of course the rights of each individual but they are to some extent unspecific. Gewirth would speak in this context of 'generic rights' (Gewirth 1978: 64) which would be rights that are necessary for all kind of actions, human beings would need them in general, independently of the concrete goals they may want to achieve. These would not necessarily be the most basic rights in a minimalistic sense (as rights to just the goods that are necessary for survival). It would be rights to conditions of life that make the enjoyment of our goals possible in the first place. If we see human dignity as a commitment to the general conditions that make it meaningful to claim and make use of human rights, we would give human dignity a very fundamental role in the understanding of human rights. The most important consequence is that this understanding would not generate all kinds of collective goods that bypass the individual human being's liberty. It would rather be an emphasis on a commitment to those conditions that make the rights of all individuals possible in the first place.

This short overview of different conceptualizations shows that it is by no means evident what the role of human dignity in the human rights context is: approaches to human dignity need therefore to explicate the conceptual relationship.

What is the relationship between a moral and legal interpretation of human dignity?

So far, I have discussed human dignity independently of the distinction between a legal and a moral perspective. Not all traditions of human dignity would see this concept in a legal perspective. The virtue-ethical tradition knows only obligations for the virtuous life. But the modern human rights tradition clearly has a legal dimension. But the legal chapters in this volume demonstrate that legal provisions about 'human dignity' fulfil very different functions in the various legal systems.[9] It can be a concept that grants a kind of exceptional protection against the most fundamental rights violations, it can prohibit forms of significant disrespect for human beings, and is seen as the foundational concept of the entire concept of human or civil rights. This exceptional position implies that references to human dignity in normal legal praxis are a kind of last resort. With regard to human dignity as a foundational concept, the default would be not to refer to human dignity so easily. It would, however, be more likely to decide concrete legal questions by reference to specific rights. Human dignity would then particularly be discussed if the interpretation of specific rights, their relative weight, and their interrelationship is at stake on a more fundamental level. We would have to distinguish between this foundational role for the entire corpus of human rights on the one hand and, on the other, for more specific functions, such as an explicit condemnation of various extreme forms of disrespect of human beings (for example, genocide and torture). These specific functions presuppose, however, the foundational understanding of human dignity, because only if respect for the human being is categorically required in general do we have reasons to see these particular forms of denial of respect also as categorically wrong.

This categorical condemnation of disrespect for the human being is not an invention of the UDHR. It is therefore plausible to assume that human dignity has not only a legal origin, but also a moral one. It is important to note that scholars use different understandings of morality in this context: some would see morality as the articulation of a prior specific 'moral position', in the sense that the 'moral point of view' is characterized by independent considerations of the interests of all; by for example the specific morality of the golden rule, or those convictions that are traditionally seen as natural law. These would be attempts to define morality by references to a specific normative content. One can also understand the distinctive feature of morality in a more formal sense. Under that perspective, moral convictions would be distinct from other convictions in that they confront us with requirements for action that we may

[9] See Chapter 1 by Brownsword in this volume, and McCrudden (2008).

reasonably see as categorically binding. Such a formal definition could deal with the fact that different moral doctrines would present distinct normative content to be obligatory. A chauvinist moral doctrine could be seen as *a* moral doctrine; that does not mean that such a doctrine is a good one, but it belongs to the category of moral doctrines. So, in discussing the relationship between morality and (international) law, it would be important to be aware of the different interpretations of morality.

Many are reluctant to refer to morality in legal discourse, because they hold the view that the legal order must be morally neutral and open to various moral convictions and worldviews. There is, furthermore, a hesitancy to interpret human rights directly as a continuation of the natural rights tradition of the eighteenth century. Some scholars even try to interpret the entire human rights approach only or primarily as a system that has a function via the various human rights instruments in international law, and, resulting from this function, some roles also in political discourses (Beitz 2009).

There are, however, several arguments why human dignity can only be adequately understood – even in the legal context – if one sees the relationship to the moral understanding of the concept. It is difficult to ignore the historical context of implementation: for the UDHR, and also for the many (in particular the German) constitutions, human dignity was introduced after the Second World War, and the moral dimension is hard to dismiss – 'human dignity' is obviously at least partly a moral–political answer to the atrocities of the Shoah and the war (Morsink 1999, Chapter 2). A similar explanation would be relevant for the South African Constitution. In other words, it would be difficult to understand the choice of such a concept and its prominent role in international law, if its legal function were completely independent from the role this concept played in the history of moral philosophy and plays in broadly shared moral intuitions and convictions.

If there is indeed a connection, this could mean that the political–legal would not be neutral but rather based on some moral assumptions. Human dignity would as such articulate the basic moral claim that we should see ourselves as obliged to order the legal and political institutions in such a way that a respect for the dignity of all human beings is secured. That means that the reason why human dignity has such a central place in the legal order is understood as a response to a moral demand. That makes it both plausible and necessary to assess the validity of this demand by moral arguments.

Such a 'moral grounding' of the human rights framework would not imply that one would have to understand the human rights framework as an institutionalization of a set of moral rights, as if the UDHR were a kind of written version of the natural law. One should rather understand the human rights as a legal institution. To see human rights as based on or derived from respect for human dignity would here be the recognition that it is morally required to respect human dignity, to ensure the legal provisions of the human rights would be an institutionalized answer to this moral requirement. In that sense, it would be plausible that different historical and cultural situations ask for different institutionalizations because of the different challenges human dignity is confronted with. On this view, a critic of human rights in general or specific human rights provisions could either question the moral authority of human dignity, could disagree with the perception of challenges human dignity is confronted with, or could question whether the human rights provisions are appropriate institutional means to protect human dignity against these challenges. In any case, one can expect that accounts of human dignity are explicit about the assumed relationship between law and morality.

Who has dignity?

So far, we have discussed the conceptual status of human dignity in its relationship to the human rights and in the tensions between the legal and moral dimensions. There are also various questions concerning the subject and the content of human dignity. It may be thought surprising how many debates concern the question of the subject of human dignity.[10] The adjective 'human' seems to suggest an answer to the question to whom we should attribute human dignity, and that answer is: to *all* human beings and *only* to human beings. This answer, however, gave rise to a variety of other questions: what does 'all human beings' precisely mean? When does a human being start to have dignity (with conception, at birth etc.)? And when does it cease to be a being with dignity? Should we see human beings who will never develop rational capacities as beings with dignity? And why should we ascribe this status only to humans? Are not at least some animals worthy of the same respect we owe to human beings?

It would be necessary to explain the criteria we use to determine who has human dignity and how these criteria can be justified. It would further be necessary to determine what that means for the scope of duties corresponding to the respect for human dignity. A first candidate would be: membership in the biological species, *homo sapiens.* This criterion is, however, dubious because it is unclear why membership of a biological species by itself should be a sufficient ground to ascribe the dignity status from which the human rights are derived. Under pragmatic criteria to determine the legal scope of human dignity, the membership in the biological species can play a specific role (since the law would have to work with empirically robust criteria) but this cannot be the justificatory ground for the ascription of the dignity status. Some would just refer to the will of God, but either that is an arbitrary selection simply grounded on a divine decision, or a decision by God that is further elaborated in terms of reasons. Thus, there must be something in the human being that may justify his special status. And, even if we would have reasons to broaden the scope of dignity-holders beyond the species, this extension would have to be justified by

[10] See for example Chapter 53 by Graumann and Chapter 58 by Düwell in this volume.

the fact that some animals would share these features with us, or that we at least are uncertain to what extent they do.

Thus, what is it in the human being that makes it plausible that it has the status of a being with dignity? If we refer to features that are distinctly human, we could think about man's curiosity, creativity, or power to use instruments, as features that are preconditions for an understanding of and domination over the world. In line with an honour concept of dignity, these features may indeed be reasons for admiration (or sometimes for fear and anger), but they are not reasons for moral respect. One could also refer to the fact that human beings have interests and needs, are vulnerable, have the capacity to act at all and are able to act morally. All those elements can be constitutive for the possibility of having, granting, respecting or refraining from exercising the rights. Only if human beings have needs and interests, if they care about something, is it reasonable to assume that there may be rights that protect and support them. And at the same time the capacity of agents to respect or disrespect rights is necessary for an understanding of the status of a rights-holder. I do not want to go into all the relevant distinctions of the various rights theories, but it seems evident that those features that are necessary to ascribe the status of a rights-holder are also necessary for the ascription of human dignity. If human rights are derived from human dignity, then the status of human dignity must contain those features that are necessary for the ascription of rights. The possibilities to justify the moral relevance of these features will be discussed in the next chapter.

If we determine the status of a being with dignity as a ground for rights by such features, the question would be how this status would relate to the obligations to other beings, particularly our duties towards animals. The problem may be posed as follows: (a) if dignity is the status ascribed to (living) human beings, (b) if the respect for dignity of human beings implies that they have liberties that can only be limited by the rights of others, and (c) if the obligations we have towards beings with this status are overriding with regard to other action-guiding considerations, then (d) it is not possible to limit the rights of human beings in order to protect animals, nature or something else. The only legitimate form to restrict the rights of human beings in the exercise of their liberties is within this framework the reference to rights of other human beings. We can of course often show that specific goods are necessary for human beings to effectuate their rights; this holds for example for various ecological considerations. We can furthermore show that collective goods demand protection because they have value for human beings. This can perhaps go much beyond the instrumental value that some natural goods have for us: it can for example also include aesthetic values of specific cultural and natural goods or the importance of specific values for the identity of human beings. But it would be problematic to limit the respect for human dignity in favour of other beings that are assumed to have a status of their own.[11]

[11] See Chapter 60 by Heeger and Chapter 61 by Schaber in this volume.

In that case, we would have four conceptual options: (1) we could deny that animals or non-living nature have a status independent from the relevance they have for human beings. In these discussions, the basis on which we ascribe a feature of human dignity would of course be relevant. If we ascribe it on the basis of rational capacities that human beings typically develop, we would of course have to investigate to what extent animals have them. It could be the case that with regard to some animals (for example, some apes or dolphins) we are quite uncertain about their capacities. This could be a reason to treat them with the same respect as human beings for precautionary reasons. (2) We could ascribe the dignity status independently of rational capacities and include (at least some) animals. We would have to discuss the basis of the grounds on which beings would have dignity, and which animals would fall inside the scope of the protection afforded by human dignity. This ascription would result in severe changes in the application of the human rights. Their status would then be the same as that of human beings. (3) We could ascribe a different moral status to animals than we do to human beings, which would force us to assume that the exercise of rights by human beings can be restricted by considerations that fall outside the regime of human rights. This would imply that human rights and human dignity are not overriding, which again would change the very nature of the human rights approach. We would have to discuss under what circumstances it would be permissible to restrict human rights due to other considerations. That would imply that respect for human dignity from which the rights are derived would sometimes not be categorically required. (4) We could introduce a kind of graduated concept: moral status may come in degrees. That would mean that we would assume that (living) human beings would have the full status of human dignity with all the rights following from that, while we would ascribe another (lower) moral status to animals (and perhaps also to human embryos: see below). For developing such an approach, two questions need to be answered. First, on the basis of what capacities do we ascribe animals a specific moral status? Animals purportedly lack rationality or for example the capacity to envisage future existence, but on the basis of which capacities ought we to grant them respect? Second, we would have to formulate rules that explicate in which cases the status of an animal may overrule respect for beings with human dignity: when must respect for human dignity be limited to protect that of an animal?

Such questions do not arise only with regard to animals. Most of the discussions in the literature deal with the questions of when the required status of a being with dignity begins, when it ends and what is the status of human beings who have lost or will never develop rational capacities. We can either assume that the ascription of human dignity is independent of those capacities that we typically find within human beings (then the question would be on basis of which features we would ascribe dignity at all and why a human being deserves another form of respect than a stone or a bicycle), or we can assume that there are reasons to include human beings before birth or those with severe mental disabilities within the protection we owe to human persons. There are various arguments brought forward for justifying such an inclusion. Some of the arguments are more pragmatic in nature, such as lack of knowledge about human capacities and the need for precautionary ways of dealing with this problem. Other arguments are more fundamental, such as arguments that claim that potential persons should be treated with the same respect we owe to human persons. I discuss these arguments in more detail in Chapter 58 below.

A further question would be to what extent the *human species would have dignity as such*, whether there is something like collective dignity. Human dignity within the human rights framework ascribes this specific status to each human being. But, in doing so, it is assumed that it is morally fundamentally important to have those features that are characteristic of beings with dignity. In that sense, the ascription involves a general evaluative judgment about the importance of being human. There are furthermore some goods relevant for all agents. For example, some ecological conditions have to be fulfilled in order to enable human beings to live an autonomous life. Therefore, the right to have those goods preserved may be a very important part of the human rights regime that would even affect the possibility of living human life on Earth in general. Here, the rights of all individuals are at stake and not just those of specific individuals. In any case, we cannot interpret a concept of the 'dignity of the species' or of 'collective dignity' independently of the dignity of individual human beings.

The question as to who has dignity plays a fundamental role in all kinds of debates – from abortion and euthanasia, animal ethics, to sustainability and future generations. The variety of discussions in which the question adopts a prominent role makes it difficult to develop an encompassing concept of human dignity in an uncontroversial manner – but also all the more urgent.

What is the normative content of human dignity?

While the previous section discussed who has dignity, the current section will deal with the question what kind of obligations would follow from the required respect for human dignity. In the current debate it is often assumed that human dignity is an empty concept: various groups can give very diverse meanings to it, verdicts that see participation in dwarf-throwing or peep shows as violations of human dignity seem to support this view. Others assume that talking about human dignity is redundant because it would not have any meaning that goes beyond what 'respect for autonomy' would require (Macklin 2003). However, those critics normally only demonstrate that the concept is used in different and often arbitrary ways – and what better reason is there for a *more* philosophical investigation. To say that the concept is empty or useless would require an argument that makes it plausible that there are no conceptual *possibilities* to enlighten the content of this concept in a non-arbitrary way.

What would be required to determine the normative content of human dignity in terms of criteria that allow for determining those obligations that follow from respect for human dignity? In light of the above discussion, we could say: if we were to understand human dignity as an 'open norm', the normative content of human dignity would depend on the image of appropriate behaviour (the cultural customs or habits) that is upheld in a specific society. If human dignity is understood as the right to the status of a citizen (the right to have rights), the normative content of human dignity would simply entail granting this status. If human dignity were understood as a normative prohibition against completely reducing a human being to an object, this would probably imply merely obligations to ensure that very extreme forms of humiliation and degradation cannot happen; the scope of the corresponding obligations would be quite limited (see above).

But what if we understand human dignity as a principle that determines the entire content of the human rights? This obviously touches upon our whole understanding of human rights, and it is therefore impossible to discuss this comprehensively, but I will mention some aspects.

First, we would have to ask what kind of concept of rights we presuppose. With regard to the traditional distinctions of Hohfeld (1964), it seems quite obvious that those kinds of rights that human dignity would justify are *claim rights* (in opposition to privileges, powers or immunities), that is, rights that are strictly correlated to duties on the side of others. But what is the content of these rights? We can distinguish an *interest concept of rights* from a *will concept of rights* (Hart 1955). An interest theory would see rights as protecting a (basic) interest of all human beings. Interest theories may be further distinguished with regard to the scope of the interest they would see as justifications for rights. A will theory would protect the control of the agent over himself. With regard to those theories, we could further distinguish between concepts that would only give a right to the agent not to be infringed upon by others in the exercise of his will, from others that would also protect those conditions that are necessary for him to do so. With regard to human dignity, one could for example wonder whether rape or genocide are dignity violations because some basic interests of the dignity-holder are denied, or rather because she is treated with disrespect as a person with the capacity to decide about herself. It is contested to what extent approaches of human dignity are compatible with all kinds of rights accounts.

A *second* question would be whether respect for dignity would only require respect for the *negative rights* of the dignity-holder or for *positive rights* as well.[12] Whatever it is a right-holder has a right to, negative rights would impose a duty on others to refrain from interfering with these rights, while positive rights would impose a duty on them also to support the right-holder. If I had a right to develop my basic intellectual capacities, a negative right would oblige others not to interfere with this development, while a positive right would also create an obligation to give me assistance, for example by education. Both kinds of rights have corresponding obligations, but there may be asymmetries: with regard to

[12] For this distinction, see in particular Gewirth (1996; 31–70). See also Shue (1996).

negative rights, each agent has obligations, while from the viewpoint of positive rights, this may be a topic of discussion. And with regard to positive rights, there may also be debate on the degrees of required support. Some usages of the concept of human dignity see respect for human dignity simply as requiring protection of a minimal threshold of basic interests or the most fundamental capacity as an agent. The idea that human dignity is the basis of human rights would, however, entail that the whole range of rights provisions would be a consequence of the protection of human dignity; if we relate that to the existing human rights regime this would include a variety of positive rights.

If human rights are derived from the respect for human dignity, one could wonder whether all rights-provisions have the same importance for the protection of human dignity. It does not seem plausible to assume that the right to education has here the same relevance as the provisions against torture. While torture will probably affect the core of the personality of the dignity-holder in a central and irreversible way, lack of access to education reduces the opportunities of the agent in a severe way but is not comparably irreversible and devastating. There may thus be a hierarchy of rights (some rights are more urgent and important than others) and it may be that we are entitled to weigh some rights against each other while other rights should not be weighed at all or weighed only to a very limited degree. Gewirth has made a proposal for such a hierarchy (1978 and 1992). He proposed viewing human dignity as a ground for the rights to the necessary conditions to live a life of one's own. This approach presupposes a will theory of rights, so the agent should be seen as capable of controlling his own life. He should be seen as having the right to exercise his own will as well as to develop his own capacities in a way that he has the ability to choose and realize important goals for himself. Rights are in that sense the protection of the necessary conditions for the possibility to live and flourish as an agent. This would imply negative and positive rights, it would include rights to empowerment to live a life of one's own. But, within the rights, Gewirth would see a specific hierarchy that is justified by the *different degrees of necessity* of the respective rights for the maintenance and development of this basic ability. One is a level of *most basic rights*: I must be alive, must have access to food and sometimes healthcare and must have some basic control over myself in order to live a life of my own. If others influence these basic conditions of my life, the respect for my dignity requires that they refrain from intervening negatively and help me if they are able to do so. There are other, less basic levels of rights. Gewirth would distinguish next-to-basic rights, those rights that are important to *maintain* the capacities I have in order to reach the goals of my life, and rights that are important to *develop my capacities further*. Between these different levels of rights, he would assume a *hierarchy* in the sense that some rights are more fundamental to protect the dignity of a human being due to the necessity of the goods in question to live a life of my own. Gewirth would not assume that such a hierarchy is fixed, but that these distinctions would help to determine in a context-specific sense the relative weight of the concrete rights. This would provide an understanding of human dignity that allows for a structure of the human rights in terms of importance and urgency. The systematic question for other approaches to human dignity would be whether they would assume that all rights deriving from human dignity have the same level of importance, or whether they would propose an alternative hierarchy – which then obviously is in need of justification.

The normative content of human dignity would be concretized by human rights, and those rights would be grounds for obligations on the side of the duty-bearer. To determine who the duty-bearer is, is not a simple question. There are some obvious cases: for example if I have a right to life, nobody has the right to kill me (except in the case of self-defence etc.). But there are various cases wherein it is not so clear who the carrier of the corresponding obligations is. It seems at least plausible that the ability to grant protection plays a crucial role in the determination of possible duty-bearers.

In the case of the human rights, the general understanding of the human rights regime presupposes that the corresponding obligations lie with the state, that is required to realize the obligations following from the rights of human beings. This follows from the very nature of the human rights law as based on contracts between states. If, however, we assume that human rights are based on moral assumptions, and if we assume that this moral ground of the human rights is the reason why the human rights law has been installed in the first place, then the human rights are based on a set of moral convictions which involve obligations to individuals as well as other collective actors than states alone.

A further remark is necessary with regard to the idea that the human rights are 'derived' from human dignity. It could evoke the idea of a deduction or specification: it might be thought that the human rights could be best determined by a philosopher who would just think hard enough to derive a comprehensive set of human rights from the concept of human dignity. Such an understanding would, however, neglect that the rights are responses to possible or probable context-embedded threats. In this sense, human rights can, will and must change over time.

There are at least five factors that are important for the determination of new rights:

(1) Respect for and protection of *human dignity forms the normative basis* of the entire human rights regime.
(2) *Changes in the needs, desires and vulnerabilities* of human beings are factors that may affect the perspective under which their dignity can be violated. My possibility of seeing myself as an agent that is able to control myself will depend on various cultural-dependent factors.
(3) There may be new threats to living a life in dignity. Examples are climate change or the possibilities in the digital world that may change the living conditions so severely that a life in dignity is threatened in new ways.

Climate change may endanger the possibility to live an autonomous life in whole parts of the Earth.

(4) There are also new forms of *possible protections* of human dignity. The possibilities of the Internet can create new opportunities for rights-fulfilments (for example, by enabling people to be a more competent actor).

(5) The possible duty-bearers can change by for example the evolution of new (international or global) institutions that have new abilities to protect human beings.

The list of human rights (in a moral as well as in a legal sense) will never be complete, and it would never have been expected that we would be able in 1948 to outline a list of rights that would be valid until the end of the world. If there are new threats to human beings, for example by changes in the financial system or by changes in the natural environment, it would be immoral not to respond to these threats by establishing new forms of protection. But, to hold the moral authority of the human rights, it would be necessary for us to be able to interpret these changes not just as a reflection of changes in power relationships but as new forms of protection of human dignity. In that sense, human dignity would function as the normative basis of the human rights that is necessary for the moral integrity of the human rights process as such.

What are the necessary presuppositions for a commitment to human dignity?

A last set of considerations is related to the question to what extent a commitment to human dignity depends on specific conceptions of nature, individuality, rationality, religion and time that are culturally contingent. And would not such dependencies be a challenge for the universality of human dignity? The development of the concept of human dignity in Western history could be an indicator for this. It is therefore relevant in a systematic, philosophical discussion to reflect on the necessary presuppositions of the concept.

One candidate for a culturally contingent but perhaps necessary presupposition would be the assumption that we need a religious horizon in order to understand why the human person is sacrosanct. Such a religious genealogy could, however, only explain that there are some elements seen as sacrosanct in a religious worldview at all, but we would need additional explanations for the ascriptions of rights to the human person. One could try to reconstruct ideas of natural rights in developments in the late middle age by criticism of religious authorities.[13] But those reconstructions would not affect a possible universality in the ascription of human rights because it is quite possible to develop insights into the worth of human beings in other contexts as well. It could be that

[13] See Tuck (1979); and Chapter 4 by Imbach and Chapter 5 by Mieth in this volume.

there are some elements in the Christian tradition that are also necessary for an understanding of the rights-approach of human dignity. Candidates could be a linear conception of history and time (as opposed to a circular understanding) that would be needed to understand the importance that is given to the singular individual that is understood in such a way that it cannot be substituted by another individual. Another genealogy[14] would connect the concept of human dignity inherently to ideas central to modernity. Human dignity would ascribe a status to human beings as persons with equal individual rights, the opportunity to develop economically, governed by a state that is acknowledged by all citizens and ensures those rights by an effective legal system.

I would propose three kinds of methodological considerations that would be helpful to relate those genealogical approaches to the systematic discussion about the moral and legal role of human dignity:

(1) To assess the plausibility of these genealogies, it would be decisive to what extent they can explain the concept of human dignity in all its dimensions. A reconstruction of the central role of the individual in eighteenth-century culture, as Hunt (2007) presented it, can for example not explain how the development of this idea is related to the justification of government as the human rights regime aims to do. And a functionalistic reconstruction of the role of the individual within the modern differentiated society can as such not explain that all human beings and not only all citizens are declared to have dignity. As such, the plausibility of those reconstructions should be measured by the degree to which they can explain the dependency of the core conceptual elements of human dignity in a sociological and historical perspective. The further question would be whether those reconstructed evolutions in the development of a concept of human dignity would exclude that in other cultural contexts other evolutions are possible. It is quite plausible to assume that we 'discovered' the unconditional worth of the human being after the atrocities of the Shoah, but why should that be the only way of gaining this insight?

(2) It is obviously plausible that a commitment to human dignity is not neutral with regard to the institutions that are accompanied by it. Human dignity may indeed be necessarily linked to a state that is characterized by a distinction between the private and public sphere, equality before the law, formalized contractual relationships, the rule of law, and that each individual has rights to decide about fundamental aspects of his life etc. If those elements are necessary features of a society based on human dignity, this may be interpreted in two ways: either it can be seen to indicate that only societies with those features will develop a concept of human dignity, or it can be a reason to assume that a commitment to human dignity implies

[14] See for this context Chapter 19 by Lindemann in this volume, Jellinek 1901 and Hunt 2007.

the moral obligation to organize the society according to these features. Whether the universal obligation in the latter sense is valid would precisely depend on the question whether we are able to justify that human beings have a right to live in such societies.

(3) If we interpret the societal and legal consequences that would follow from a commitment to human dignity, it is not self-evident that these consequences are necessarily coherent or even compatible with the way in which modern societies are designed. If the commitment to human dignity implies a moral commitment to secure the conditions necessary for living an autonomous life, we may raise many questions with regard to contemporary societies. Would this commitment to human dignity not imply a requirement to make all reasonable efforts to realize at least decent standards of living on a global scale and to secure the conditions for future generations to live their own life? One could even be suspicious that in Western society human rights are just functionalized to secure the welfare prospects of the richer part of the world. It seems quite obvious that the traditional nation-state would not be the institutional setting that can secure the moral requirements a commitment to human dignity would ask from us. The question what institutions and what kind of a society and culture would fulfil those requirements, is still open.

So accounts of human dignity would have to investigate to what extent their plausibility depends on culturally specific presuppositions. If we can justify the universality of the claim to live in societies that are able to protect the possibility of each human being to live an autonomous life or to live under conditions in which he or she can flourish, the question would arise what kind of political, civil and legal institutions would be required to ensure this possibility.

Towards an ethics of human dignity

Against the background of the conceptual aspects I discussed above, I want to outline some of the questions in moral philosophy an ethics of human dignity would have to deal with. I assume here, as discussed above, that the legal concept of human dignity is grounded in a moral concept and that such a moral concept is in need of conceptual explanation and justification. I will now outline some of the philosophical challenges of this concept.

The ontological status of human dignity

It was often said that there is a tension between the idea that we cannot lose human dignity but that it can be violated. Why should we protect human dignity if it cannot be lost? Is human dignity a property we have that may be endangered and in need of protection, or is it a claim we have against others? In the latter case, we should interpret the proposition 'human beings have human dignity' as 'we are categorically obliged to treat human beings with respect'. If human beings have dignity in this sense, their claim to be treated with respect can be violated, but the normative claim to be treated with respect will still be valid; as long as someone is a human being, he ought to be treated with respect. There are two kinds of reservations against such a reading. The first would be the concern that we endanger the unconditional respect we owe to human beings by seeing it as an *ascription*. If human dignity is something we ascribe, it may be thought to lose some of its normative force because it is a matter of choice – and thus to an extent arbitrary – whether we ascribe dignity to someone or not. This is, however, not necessary. One could reply to this consideration that it is of course possible that an ascription must not be an arbitrary ascription. It is also possible that there is a moment of decision involved (human beings have to decide to grant each other the status as a being with dignity) but that this ascription is rationally necessary (we cannot understand ourselves consistently as agents if we do not make this ascription).

A second reservation against the idea of an ascription concerns the phenomenological plausibility: we experience the other as confronting us with a claim to respect him, we experience in ourselves a disposition to treat other people with respect. Reflecting on the question 'ought I to treat another with respect?' might be an example of the notorious 'one thought too many'. In line with Ricœur or Lévinas, one could say: the phenomenology of moral experiences confronts us with the worth of the other,[15] the other has some authority over us that is the origin of the respect we owe to him. One can accept that there is such a phenomenological experience, so that human beings see themselves on a pre-reflexive level confronted with the claim of respect. But it is disputable whether the phenomenological experience makes it superfluous to reflect on the reasons we have to ascribe this status to human beings. The pre-reflexive experience may confront us with a strong experiential force to embrace the conviction that human beings have to be treated with respect, but it is not clear why the pre-reflexive experience urges us to affirm the unconditional worth of human beings as an ultimate commitment. As rational beings, we can reflect on this status of human dignity, and, moreover: phenomenological experience alone cannot account for the insight that it would be right, obligatory and important to ascribe this status to each other.

A normative theory of human dignity

Since respect for human dignity cannot be overridden by other practical considerations, a normative theory of human dignity must be able to account

[15] See in this context Chapter 29 by Atterton and Chapter 30 by Junker-Kenny in this volume.

for categorical obligations. This makes it dubious whether we can think of it in terms of (long-term) self-interest: seeing moral norms as based in shared self-interest would make respect for the other conditional in the sense that we should respect the interest of the other as long as it coincides with our own interest (at least in the long run). As far as it is employed in terms of social contract theory, human dignity would be a form of social contract that would not justify the social contract in terms of self-interest, but would see the social contract as grounded in obligations to respect each individual. Typically, one would think that a deontological theory would be appropriate for the conceptualization of such a form of respect; unconditional worth or human dignity would even be the standard examples for deontological concepts. But there is a problem if we conceptualize deontological normative theories as opposed to consequentialist theories (for example, Pettit 1977). The distinctive feature of these theories is that consequentialist theories would define the moral right (that which is morally obligatory) in terms of the consequences of our actions alone, while deontological theories would define the moral right not solely, or not at all, in terms of consequences (for example, good motives, good intentions or God's will). A consequentialist theory would therefore claim that those actions that bring about the best consequences are morally obligatory, while deontological theories would determine the obligatory actions not solely, or not at all, on the basis of their consequences. If human dignity were a deontological concept in that sense, it would be difficult to spell it out in terms of human rights; to see those actions as morally obligatory which consequences (probably) respect the requirements of human rights. This would thus imply that the right actions are determined in terms of the consequences of our actions: we should always choose those actions whose consequences respect the rights of others.

But there is another option to conceptualize a deontological ethics, which we find in Frankena (1973). Frankena introduces the opposition between deontological and teleological forms of ethics. Frankena defined teleological ethics by seeing the moral right (our moral obligations) as a function of a non-morally good (Frankena 1973: 14). Standard cases for such a theory would be classical hedonistic utilitarianism or welfarism that would claim that we are morally obliged to act such that the overall happiness would be maximized. In such a theory, the moral right would be defined in terms of a non-moral good (happiness). 'Non-moral' does not mean that it is immoral (morally wrong) to be happy, but rather that happiness is a good independently of whether we see ourselves as obliged to strive for it; it is simply a good that we naturally want to achieve. While – in Frankena's terms – a teleological ethics sees the moral obligation as a function of the non-moral good, a deontological ethics does not. In that sense, it is possible to see ourselves as morally obliged to do our duty even if the fulfilment of the duty does not maximize happiness. In the latter sense we should understand human dignity as a deontological concept since the respect for the other is seen as a highest principle. This respect cannot be conceptualized in terms of maximalization and naturally not in terms of maximalization of happiness. If we have to respect the will of the people and if we ensure that they can act as free agents, then it is not evident that this action supports overall happiness in the world; at least happiness is not the ultimate measure for the rightness of our action.

If we see human dignity within the field of normative theories, we could say that it is a deontological concept insofar as it forms the ground for categorical obligations that trump other practical considerations, and human dignity is not functional to the maximalization of a non-moral good. But at the same time the concept is not necessarily non-consequentialist in the sense that the moral right is determined by the consequences of our actions alone: only the consequences of our actions for the rights of others are decisive if respect for the other agent is of overriding importance for the human dignity approach. This does not exclude the possibility that human dignity will imply more obligations than just to respect the rights of the other, for example obligations towards ourselves or the obligations to develop or cultivate specific virtues, obligations that would go beyond the scope of consequentialist considerations. In light of the role of human dignity within the human rights framework, it would be controversial to assume that human dignity would not take the consequences of our action into account. But the main problem of this whole debate is connected to conceptual ambiguities in the use of the concepts 'deontological', 'consequentialist' or 'teleological' ethics.

Justification of human dignity

Respect for human dignity imposes categorical obligations upon us. This claim is so important that it overrides other practical considerations and forms the basis of the legitimation of the political order. But how can we justify this claim? If we understand human dignity as a concept that legitimizes a distinct moral order, an order that ascribes equal moral status to all human beings and that claims to be universally valid, then we must admit that this claim is factually contested: that it is not intuitively plausible to everybody. A justification thus seems to be necessary. If human dignity is understood as a moral principle from which other moral insights can be derived (as rights and more concrete principles or rules), it seems difficult to see a justification along the lines of a particularistic approach that rejects the role of principles altogether (Dancy 2004). Approaches that have room only for mid-level principles face similar difficulties (Beauchamp and Childress 2013), as well as pluralistic approaches that have a non-reducible plurality of moral principles that forbid for example killing or lying. Those approaches have a plurality of moral principles that have to be weighed against each other in moral judgments, and thus they cannot account for the *overriding* authority of human dignity. Of course, such a plurality of principles can be understood as the specification of human dignity in particular contexts, but we cannot understand human dignity in line with those principles. I will now shortly discuss three candidates for an ethical account of human dignity.

If we have in mind that human dignity was introduced in the UDHR as a concept on which different worldviews could agree, one might think that the overlapping consensus of Rawls' *Political Liberalism* (1995) could form a helpful model. Human dignity would then have to be interpreted in line with a consensus between different worldviews. As a consequence, we should not try to elaborate a philosophical account of this concept, but should try to understand it from the political practices where the dignity of human beings is contested. Such an account would have the advantage that it would give room for a diversity of ways to access the concept, and that it would account for the genuinely political nature of struggles about human dignity. But one might wonder whether we can develop it as a critical concept that can account for the specific idea of human dignity as a foundation of human rights.

Another possibility that seems to offer a justification for the overriding authority and universality of the concept would be a justification in terms of a *moral realism*, that would see the authority of moral concept as based in a subject-independent concept of a moral truth. A strong concept of moral truth could indeed guarantee the universality of the concept. Such a realist concept, however, most probably has a disadvantage: it is quite likely that the moral truths could only be justified in an intuitive manner, that is, by referring to some form of insight we have without further rational justification. Such an intuitive approach would, however, be quite implausible with regard to human dignity. We may perhaps have a kind of generally shared intuition that it is wrong to kill people or that it is good to tell the truth. But it is very implausible to assume that human beings generally share intuitions with regard to the concept of human dignity as it is presupposed within the human rights framework.

A third possibility would elaborate the universality of human dignity by a *transcendental or reflexive justification*. Such a justification would understand the specific status of human dignity by reference to our status as beings that have the capacity to set goals, and are the sources of moral responsibility. A transcendental or self-reflective justification would show that the agent cannot deny himself the status of a right-holder without contradicting himself. This strategy has been defended by Kant, Gewirth (1978) and Korsgaard (1996).[16] Such a strategy would make plausible that we ascribe human dignity to ourselves simply in our quality of being a (moral) agent, and, because what we morally evaluate are the *capacities* necessary for action at all, we are obliged to ascribe the dignity status to every being in possession of these capacities. Such an approach claims universal validity for the concept of human dignity without claiming a subject-independent moral truth.

[16] See Chapter 22 by Hill, Chapter 23 by Kerstein and Chapter 24 by Beyleveld in this volume.

Tasks for further research

This short introduction aimed at an overview of the scope of questions one is confronted with if one focuses on human dignity as the foundational concept of the human rights regime. The different chapters of this handbook will focus on various aspects of the problem. I want to conclude this introduction by focusing on some research questions which I submit require further investigation. The list is of course not complete:

(1) A *history of human dignity* in the sense of an *Ideengeschichte* needs to be written. Such a history faces at least a double task: it needs to reconstruct the development of the ideas of human rights in the West, and combine it with an understanding and legitimation of modern political institutions. This would have to be related to the main ideas in the conceptual developments of human dignity. It would be important to understand how the perfectionistic, virtue-ethical tradition relates to the modern rights-oriented concept.

(2) It would be important to *reconstruct the underlying assumptions* that are necessary for an ethics of human dignity. Is the potential commitment to the principle of human dignity dependent on specific concepts of individuality, on the relationship between the individual and the state, on specific forms of states, on specific views on religion, time and history etc.? If human dignity articulates the basis for protection of the rights of the individual, is this protection only possible in specific forms of a liberal society? Do we need specific social systems or specific institutions in order to protect human dignity effectively? Is protection of human dignity dependent on the specific modern idea of a nation-state with his institutions? Or can we think about a diversity of institutions as an articulation of the commitment to human dignity?

(3) The latter questions are necessary for a conceptual and philosophical guided discussion about the *relationship between the rights-centred concept of human dignity to non-European or non-Western traditions.* Such investigations are only possible on the basis of a conceptual understanding of the necessary underlying assumptions of the concept.

(4) A comprehensive investigation into the possibilities of a *philosophical conceptualization and justification* of human dignity would be necessary. That would also include an understanding of the guiding principles for the use of the concept within the application of the human rights framework. For reaching this goal, a discussion of the underlying assumptions as described under (2) and (3) would be particularly important.

References

Beauchamp, T. L., and Childress, J. F. 2013. *Principles of Biomedical Ethics.* 7th edn, Oxford University Press

Beitz, C. 2009. *The Idea of Human Rights.* Oxford University Press

Brownsword, R. 2003. 'Bioethics Today, Bioethics Tomorrow: Stem Cell Research and the "Dignitarian Alliance"', *Notre Dame Journal of Law, Ethics and Public Policy* 17: 15–51

Cicero, M. Tullius. 1913. *De officiis*, ed. and trans. W. Miller. Cambridge, MA: Harvard University Press

Dancy, J. 2004. *Ethics Without Principles.* Oxford University Press

Dürig, G. 1956. 'Der Grundrechtssatz von der Menschenwürde', *Archiv des öffentlichen Rechts* 81: 117–56

Düwell, M. 2010. 'Human Dignity and Human Rights', in P. Kaufmann, H. Kuch, C. Neuhäuser and E. Webster (eds.). *Humiliation, Degradation, Dehumanization – Human Dignity Violated.* Dordrecht: Springer, 215–30

Forst, R. 2012. *The Right to Justification.* New York: Columbia University Press

Frankena, W. K. 1973. *Ethics.* Englewood Cliffs, NJ: Prentice-Hall

Gewirth, A. 1978. *Reason and Morality.* Chicago University Press

1992. 'Human Dignity as the Basis of Rights', in M. J. Meyer and W. A. Parent (eds.). *The Constitution of Rights: Human Dignity and American Values.* Ithaca, NY: Cornell University Press, 10–28

1996. *Community of Rights.* Chicago University Press

Hart, H. L. A. 1955. 'Are There Any Natural Rights?', *Philosophical Review* 64(2): 175–91

Hohfeld, W. N. 1964. *Fundamental Legal Conceptions as Applied in Judicial Reasoning.* 3rd edn, New Haven, CT: Yale University Press

Hunt, L. 2007. *Inventing Human Rights: A History.* New York, London: Norton

Jellinek, G. 1901. *The Declaration of the Rights of Men and Citizens: A Contribution to Modern Constitutional History*, trans. M. Farrand. New York: Holt (online edition, http://oll.libertyfund.org/index)

Kant, I. 1996. *Groundwork of the Metaphysics of Morals*, trans. M. Gregor, in *Immanuel Kant: Practical Philosophy.* Cambridge University Press

Kemp, P., Rendtorff, J., and Johansen, N. M. (eds.). 2000. *Bioethics and Biolaw*, vol. II, *Four Ethical Principles.* Copenhagen: Rhodos International Science and Art Publishers and Centre for Ethics and Law

Korsgaard, C. M. 1996. *Creating the Kingdom of Ends.* Cambridge University Press

Macklin, R. 2003. 'Dignity as a Useless Concept', *British Medical Journal* 327: 1419–20

McCrudden, C. 2008. 'Human Dignity and Judicial Interpretation of Human Rights', *European Journal of International Law* 19(4): 655–724

Morsink, J. 1999. *The Universal Declaration of Human Rights: Origins, Drafting and Intent.* University of Philadelphia Press

Pettit, P. 1977. 'The Consequentialist Perspective', in M. W. Baron, P. Pettit and M. Slote (eds.), *Three Methods of Ethics: A Debate.* Oxford: Blackwell, 92–174

President's Council on Bioethics. 2008. *Human Dignity and Bioethics: Essays Commissioned by the President's Council on Bioethics.* Washington, DC, http://bioethics.georgetown.edu/pcbe/reports/human_dignity/chapter14.html

Rawls, J. 1993. *Political Liberalism.* New York: Columbia University Press

Shue, H. 1996. *Basic Rights: Subsistence, Affluence, and US Foreign Policy.* Princeton University Press

Trinkaus, C. 1970. *In Our Image and Likeness: Humanity and Divinity in Italian Humanist Thought.* Chicago University Press

Tuck, R. 1979. *Natural Rights Theories: Their Origin and Development.* Cambridge University Press

Waldron, J. 2012. *Dignity, Rank and Rights*, ed. M. Dan-Cohen. Oxford University Press

Part I
Origins of the concept in European history

3

Meritocratic and civic dignity in Greco-Roman antiquity

JOSIAH OBER

Jeremy Waldron (2012) has pointed out conceptual similarities between the Kantian conception of universal human dignity as intrinsic and rights-generating, and an older conception of dignity as high standing. Waldron suggests that human dignity generalizes to all humanity the high standing formerly reserved for a privileged few. This chapter suggests that our understanding of dignity would benefit from attention to an intermediate stage: civic dignity, equal high standing among citizens, as it was practiced in classical Athens. Attending to how civic dignity was protected by coordinated citizen action in Athens reminds us that individuals are secure in their dignity only when others are willing and able to defend it. This chapter distinguishes rights-based human dignity from two predecessor forms in the ancient Greco-Roman world: meritocratic and civic dignity. Ancient conceptions of dignity must be understood in light of three assumptions, common to Greek and Roman ethical thought. First, the fundamental question of ethics is what it is for a life to go well. Second, because humans are social beings, as a practical matter ethics is inseparable from politics. Third, we understand politics better when we attend to history.[1]

Dignity as non-humiliation and non-infantilization

For the Greeks and Romans, living with dignity meant, figuratively and literally, holding one's head up in the company of others and being properly acknowledged by them. This entails having one's claims recognized by others, having their respect, having some measure of control over one's life, having a say in decisions and having responsibility for one's choices. Like liberty, which has been variously defined by contemporary theorists as 'non-interference' (Berlin 1969) or 'non-domination' (Skinner 1998; Pettit 1997), Greco-Roman conceptions of dignity may best be expressed by what they stand against: dignity can be defined as *non-humiliation* and *non-infantilization*. We suffer indignity – humiliation and/or infantilization – when our public presence goes unacknowledged, when we cringe before the powerful, when we are unduly subject to the paternalistic

[1] For a fuller discussion of the arguments presented here, see Ober 2012.

will of others and when we are denied the opportunity to employ our reason and voice in making choices that affect us.

Greco-Roman dignity, meritocratic and civic alike, was a social value and could not be reduced to an internal state of the individual. Dignity is, on this view, a matter of the respect we accord to one another. It is because we live in communities, structured by rules, that the ethical question about lives going well became a question for political theory. From this perspective, the best political regime is the one that provides the best conditions for lives to go well – including the preservation of dignity. Dignity that is held in common by an extensive yet bounded body of citizens stands between the personality and exclusivity of meritocratic dignity and the impersonality and universality of human dignity. Moreover, once it is established among citizens, civic dignity may provide a bridge from meritocratic to human dignity, by facilitating the recognition that everyone has an interest in living with dignity.

Meritocratic dignity

Meritocratic *dignity* was not a formal theory but a basic set of social practices that was partially canonized in custom and law. Meritocratic dignity is best construed as respect and recognition accorded to persons of high standing, with that high standing arising from the exclusive possession of characteristics regarded by relevant observers as meritorious. High standing is sustained by personalized relations: family, friendship, patronage and enmity determine where one stands and how one is treated. Meritocratic dignity is most clearly manifest in archaic societies. The society depicted in Homeric epic provides a model case in that the distinguishing features of meritocratic dignity – its grounding in personal relations and the fragility of equality at the top – are starkly to the fore.

In a system of meritocratic dignity, my dignity or lack thereof is determined by the place I hold in a hierarchy of merit, and on others' acknowledgment that I am worthy of that place. Meritocratic dignity admits of equality among those of equally high rank. Yet true equality is acknowledged *only* among those who are equal in every relevant particular. In Homeric society, this included ancestry, military prowess, number of retainers and wealth. Equality among elites is precarious because there is limited room at the top and because the ultimate goal is to excel, to be 'best'. The fraught question, 'who is the best of the Achaeans?' (Agamemnon because he commands most men? Achilles because he is the greatest warrior?) drives the action of the *Iliad* (Nagy 1979). The question of pre-eminence can only be answered contingently, based on changing contexts and ongoing competitions. In the inherently agonistic system of meritocratic dignity, recognition arises from vertical relationships, from structured inequality and patronage. Those beneath me in the hierarchy offer me their deference: they recognize my superiority, as I offer deference to and recognize the superiority of those above me. Cooperative relations among persons of similarly high rank (for example, Agamemnon and Achilles) are always threatened by ongoing contests seeking to establish who is best.

Meritocratic dignity is a scarce social resource and it is distributed by high-stakes contests. Establishing and preserving my dignity is ultimately my own responsibility. I must be able to demonstrate that I deserve my place and only those with whom I have a strong personal relationship (for example, my kinsmen and my clients: Agamemnon's brother or Achilles' Myrmidons) will help me to defend it. Because my dignity is fragile, I must remain vigilantly on guard against slights and affronts, as others seek to increase their social standing at my expense. I must be ready to protect my dignity against any hint of presumed superiority from those I regard as my peers. As a result, social interaction among elites in Homeric society was marked by incessant feuding, dueling and flyting (Martin 1989).

Threats also arise from below and so I must enforce deference from those beneath me on the social scale. Society is therefore characterized by systematic expressions of disrespect (sometimes ritualized and sometimes violent) towards inferiors, who must be 'kept in their place' if they are not to threaten the standing of those above them (cf. Odysseus' beating of Thersites in Book II of the *Iliad*). Well-known ancient examples of how meritocratic dignity leads to political crisis include Achilles' catastrophic anger (motivated by Agamemnon's appropriation of his war-prize) in the *Iliad* and Julius Caesar's choice in 49 BC to overthrow the Roman Republic rather than to accept a slight to his dignity (Latin: *dignitas*).[2]

Civic dignity

Civic dignity, like meritocratic dignity, was not a formal theory, but a set of historic practices that was regularized as custom and law at certain times and places in history. Meritocratic dignity, as we have seen, is predicated on intensely personalized relationships. Human dignity, as an inherent attribute of the individual, rests neither on personal nor on political relationships among people. Civic dignity stands in between these poles: it is predicated on a shared status of political equality among a body of citizens – a defined set of people who are jointly committed to the preservation of a public domain (Greek: *politeia*; Latin: *res publica*), but who are not social peers and who may have no personal ties with one another. Civic dignity is available to and protected by free citizens who have an equal opportunity to participate in a public domain of decision and action. Because civic dignity is grounded in *political* and not in personal relations, it cannot be reduced, conceptually, to meritocratic or to universal human dignity.

[2] Achilles, *Iliad*, Book 1; Caesar, Suetonius, *Divus Julius*, 33.

The ambit of civic dignity appears very broad when compared to highly exclusive meritocratic dignity, yet very parsimonious when compared to universal human dignity. Historically, civic dignity generalizes and stabilizes the high standing associated with archaic meritocratic dignity among an extensive body of citizens. Citizen dignity is robust insofar as it is sustained by rational self-interest, well-known and well-respected rules, and by the habitual behaviour developed as a result of living according to those rules. Dignity is transformed in the civic realm, from a scarce resource distributed by competitive zero-sum games, to a common pool resource sustained by a coordination game. By building common knowledge among citizens, and providing incentives for individuals to act in the public good, the common pool resource of dignity resists devolution into a commons tragedy.

In common with other forms of dignity, an individual's civic dignity is sustained by having the recognition and respect of others. Civic dignity differs from meritocratic dignity in that its defence is the collective responsibility of a clearly defined set of people, the citizens, who do not share personal ties. Recognition that their lives do indeed go better under a regime of civic dignity, on the part of the majority of citizens who would be denied high standing under a meritocratic regime, provides a rational motive for defence of the civic regime. Mobilization is facilitated by rules specifying sanctions and remedies: the institutions established by the community must provide both well-understood mechanisms and adequate incentives for specific individuals (public officials or otherwise) to come to the defence of those suffering dignitary harms. When the rules are properly structured, any member, or group of members, of a civic community suffering indignity can expect aid from their fellow citizens – most obviously in the guise of their peers sitting as a jury in a court of law, but potentially in the form of direct and collective action by the citizenry.

Virtues of civic dignity

Calling to account individuals, groups or corporate entities that seek to humiliate others requires a certain level of courage, and thus the defence of civic dignity requires the virtue of courage (cf. Balot 2004). Yet civic dignity does not place an extraordinary burden of courage on citizens: no one need be super-courageous so long as other citizens can and will coordinate their actions, by establishing and supporting rules that enable a ready response to dignitary threats. As a citizen of a community with well-structured rules, I can reasonably expect members of my community to act (and to have acted, pre-emptively, by establishing the right institutions) in defence of my dignity. I can expect that because they recognize that to do so is ultimately in their own interest, as well as in mine. It is in their interest as persons who may in turn be threatened by the arrogance of the strong, as persons concerned with the defence of their own dignity, and as persons who recognize that defence of dignity requires the aid of fellow citizens. Civic dignity is thus at once virtuous, reciprocal and rational.

In civic dignity, the responsibility of a group of civic peers to maintain the dignity of each and all is specified in law and in political culture. The law serves as a focal point enabling the actions of officials and citizens to be effectively coordinated (Weingast 1997). Because the mutuality of responsibility for responding to dignitary threats is common knowledge, when I choose to act in another's defence I can assume that my choice accords with the preferences and interests of my fellow citizens, and my actions will be coordinated with theirs. By coming to another's defence I am not, therefore, naively subjecting myself to a 'sucker's payoff'. And so, once again, our collective dignity, as a citizen body, is guaranteed by the rational commitment of each individual to the system that guarantees his and her own welfare.

Sustaining a regime of respect and recognition among an extensive population of diverse individuals entails a second virtue: self-restraint (Greek: *sôphrosunê*). As citizens, we ought voluntarily to restrain ourselves from self-aggrandizing actions that compromise another's dignity. Yet once again, rationality limits the demands placed on individual virtue. As citizens, we rationally restrain ourselves from arrogant behaviour for three overlapping reasons. First, because we know the rules and expect that we will be sanctioned for infractions. Next, because we have come to believe that it is in our real, long-term interest to deny ourselves short-term gratification at the expense of the dignity of others. And, third, having internalized dignity as a value, acting arrogantly is no longer a source of pleasure.[3]

Defending dignity by coordinated citizen action

The key to sustaining a regime of civic dignity is a joint commitment to, and an agreement on the definition of, right action in respect to dignity and threats to it. That commitment and agreement are strengthened by seeing dignity as a matter of coordination rather than (as in the meritocratic regime) competition: mutual recognition of our common interest in sustaining the system of dignity leads us to assume mutual responsibility for doing so. Each of us acknowledges that we have some duties to one another and to the community, and we each grasp that doing our duty is also a rational choice. If each of us does the right thing, acts rationally, and thus fulfils those duties, then our own dignity is sustained in common. If we coordinate our behaviour by using legal rules as focal points for aligning choices and actions, then no one is left unprotected – no matter how individually weak he or she may be.

The system is reinforced by reputation effects when the citizen body joins in blaming and sanctioning those who fail to do their part in sustaining the regime

[3] Self-restraint/moderation (*sôphosunê*) is a virtue that was manifest, in democratic Athenian evaluative vocabulary, by the middling/moderate/dignified (*metrios*) citizen. I am drawing here on Aristotle's (*Nicomachean Ethics*) theory of moral training by habituation and practice (*askêsis*).

of dignity, while praising and rewarding those whose service in its defence is outstanding. Civic dignity retains space for recognizing and for according special respect and honour for extraordinary merit. Civic dignity need not be opposed to the desire to excel or the expectation that one will be appropriately recognized for achievement. An appropriately restrained version of competitive meritocracy may flourish within a regime of civic dignity, so long as the drive to excellence remains oriented towards pro-social ends. Likewise, the concern for defence of dignity among a body of citizens need not dull the concern felt by citizens for the dignity of those outside the citizen body. Although a complacent localism may emerge within a body of citizens, by the same token a sensitivity to the dangers posed by threats to civic dignity may sharpen the recognition of the value of human dignity.

Dignity and democracy in classical Athens

The practice of civic dignity developed in classical Athens in close association with democracy. In the immediate aftermath of the Athenian Revolution of 508 BC, all males then resident in Athenian territory became citizens – that is, full members of the community with substantial immunities and participation rights. In effect, the male community collectively took for itself, jointly and severally, the high standing once reserved for a few members of an elite of birth and wealth. Civic dignity was promoted and defended by an expansive (in historical terms) conception of citizenship. Athenian concern for civic dignity was manifest in new democratic rules and political culture. Moreover, because in Athens there was no property qualification for active citizenship, some citizens were richer and better educated – and thus had greater access to social power – than others. In light of the survival of meritocratic ideals among the elite, there always remained the danger that the stronger members of the citizen body would seek to humiliate or infantilize their weaker fellows. If it were to be sustained, civic dignity thus had to be actively defended by laws backed up by habits of behaviour. The development of democratic Athenian law and public discourse can be understood, at least in part, as a successful move on the part of the ordinary citizens of Athens to build an institutional and political-cultural system that effectively protected the dignity of all citizens.[4]

Democracy did not drive out meritocratic dignity, but it changed the way in which honour was gained and how claims to merit special consideration could legitimately be expressed in public. With the consolidation of Athenian democracy, traditional meritocratic values (for example, *eugeneia*: high birth-status; *kalokagathia*: inherent excellence manifest in physical beauty; *andreia*: manly courage) were appropriated by democratic discourse (in assembly and law

[4] Athenian revolution: Ober 2007 (with literature review); Democratic institutions: Ober 2008; political culture: Ober 1989.

courts) and generalized as values appropriately possessed by all citizens. Democratic rules and ideology emphasized the conjoined values of liberty (*eleutheria*) of the citizen and equality among citizens (key terms were *isonomia*: equality before the law; *isopsêphia*: equality of vote; *isêgoria*: equality in respect to public speech). The laws of the democracy (notably the law against *hubris*, considered below) criminalized the expression of social superiority (humiliation by word and deed) that was a behavioural foundation of archaic meritocratic society. Wealthy Athenians were now expected to exercise self-restraint in speech and action. If they sought special recognition, they were expected to demonstrate their meritorious love of honour (*philotimia*) by providing resources to the community in excess of their legal obligations. The community in turn expressed its appreciation with public expressions of approval: most notably, inscriptions recording public decrees recognizing the generosity and public-spiritedness of elite public benefactors.[5]

A speech of prosecution, written by the orator-politician Demosthenes for a criminal trial in 346 BC, provides a window into the mature democratic understanding of civic dignity and the role of the law and political culture in sustaining it. The defendant, a prominent Athenian politician named Meidias, was accused of violating the norms of dignity – Demosthenes repeatedly describes Meidias' public behaviour as *hubris*: wilful and harmful infliction of humiliation upon another. At the conclusion to his speech, Demosthenes reminded the citizen-jurors of the security (*bebaiotês*) in which each Athenian 'goes on his way':

> Consider: in a moment, when the court rises, each of you will go away home, not wondering whether it will be someone friendly or someone unfriendly who will meet you on the way, or if he will be big or small, or if he will be strong or weak, or anything of that sort. Why so? Because in his heart [each citizen] knows, and is sure, and has put his trust in the constitution, that no one will take hold of him, or be insolent to him, or hit him. (Demosthenes 1990: 21.221)[6]

Demosthenes' point is that the individual citizen can walk down the streets of Athens with his head up because he trusts in the formal rules governing the behaviour of others. He can go about his public and private business without worrying about threats to his dignity – without fear of humiliation. And this was, according to Demosthenes, because of Athens' democratic constitution. Yet law was not enough, in and of itself. Rules and the habit of acting in support of them must be mutually reinforcing. In his peroration, Demosthenes offers a theory of how legal institutions enable the mobilization of citizens in collective action

[5] Appropriation of meritocratic values and terms: Ober 1989; Whitehead 1993; law against *hubris*: Fisher 1992; *philotimia* in the democratic state: Whitehead 1983; public benefactors: Domingo Gygax (forthcoming).

[6] References to Demosthenes provide speech number and specify the section.

to support the public domain; this description neatly captures the mechanism underlying the defence of civic dignity.

> For in fact, if you cared to consider and investigate the question of what it is that gives power and control over everything in the polis to those of you who are jurors at any given time . . . you would find that the reason is not that you alone of the citizens are armed and mobilized in ranks, nor that you are physically the best and strongest, nor that you are youngest in age, nor anything of the sort, but rather you'd find that you are powerful through the laws. And what is the power of the laws? Is it that, if any of you is attacked and gives a shout, they'll come running to your aid? No, they are just inscribed letters and have no ability to do that. What then is their motive power? You are, if you secure them and make them authoritative whenever anyone asks for aid. So the laws are powerful through you and you through the laws. You must therefore stand up for them in just the same way as any individual would stand up for himself if attacked; you must take the view that offenses against the law are common concerns. (Demosthenes 1990: 21.223–5)

Demosthenes' description of a world in which relatively poor and weak citizens went about their daily business with their heads held high, unafraid of dignitary threats, contrasts sharply with the conditions of pre-democratic Athens. The archaic Athenian poet-lawgiver Solon described evil conditions (which he sought to correct by his laws) in which wealthy and powerful Athenians enslaved their poorer and weaker fellows, and weak Athenians, for their part, 'trembled at the whims of their masters' (quoted in [Aristotle] *Constitution of Athens* 12.4). Solon's sharply framed poetic image conjoins humiliation (trembling) with infantilization (subjection to the master's whim). By seeking an end to those conditions of systematic humiliation and infantilization, Solon's law code set Athens on the road to civic dignity. Three generations later, in 508 BC, the ordinary people of Athens rose up in arms, defying elite leaders and risking vengeance by the powerful Spartans, to establish a regime of greater collective dignity. They rose up against the threat of return to conditions in which free men would tremble at the whims of masters and in anticipation of a community in which the dignity of citizens would be secure.

The result was a new democratic political order that, over the next 180 years, systematically promoted mutual respect and recognition among citizens, while enhancing opportunities for public participation and private risk-taking across the citizen population. The democracy enforced laws criminalizing wilful disrespect (*hubris*). It promoted mutual recognition by bringing together citizens from different walks of life in new institutions (artificial tribes, an agenda-setting council, people's courts). By instituting new forms of social insurance (for example, support for orphans and the disabled), the democracy enabled citizens to take more calculated risks, individually and collectively.

One indication that Athens' democratic regime effectively defended civic dignity is the absence of evidence for personal patronage at Athens. Other well-documented societies of classical antiquity, including citizen-centred yet non-democratic societies such as Sparta and Rome, were grounded in personal patronage. In both Sparta and Rome, the dignity associated with citizenship remained limited; Sparta and Rome remained essentially meritocratic. By contrast, historians have searched in vain for evidence of patron–client relationships in democratic Athens, where a strong form of civic dignity was the norm.[7]

Dignity of non-citizens

The Athenian regime of democratic law and culture was focused, in the first instance, on civic dignity for citizens and defended by citizens. Yet dignity was, at least in principle, defended well *beyond* the ranks of citizens. In the same speech (Demosthenes 1990: 21.48–50) in which he reminded jurors of the meaning of their secure possession of civic dignity, Demosthenes noted that Athenian law protected '*any person*, either child or woman or man, free or slave', against intentional disrespect (*hubris*) and other unlawful (*paranomon*) treatment. Demosthenes notes that the Athenians 'do not think it right to treat with disrespect even the slaves whom they acquire by paying a price for them, but have publicly made this law to prevent it'.[8]

The law to which Demosthenes refers presumably dates back at least to the fifth century BC, since 'the Old Oligarch' – an anonymous anti-democratic writer of the later fifth century – points out to his intended elite readers that in Athens 'you' are not permitted (*oute... exestin*) to hit slaves and foreigners at will. Nor, he adds, will an Athenian slave stand aside for you in the road. The Old Oligarch explains the Athenians' motive for this law against hitting at will as concern for providing a sort of public risk insurance. He points out that lower-class Athenian citizens could not be readily distinguished, by dress or appearance, from slaves and resident foreigners. Hence, he says, if powerful men were allowed to please themselves by striking slaves or foreigners at will, they might mistakenly strike an Athenian citizen (1.10). And so, claims the Old Oligarch, it was in order to ensure their own security that the Athenian citizenry forbade mistreatment of slaves and foreigners.

We cannot hope to recover the actual motives and intentions of the legislator who wrote the Athenian law against *hubris* to include non-citizens, or of the Athenian citizens who affirmed it. Regardless of the Athenians' actual legislative intent, their extension of some legal protection to non-citizens points to

[7] Patronage in classical antiquity: Wallace-Hadrill 1989; no patronage at Athens: Millett 1989.

[8] In contrast to Kant, Demosthenes imagines that putting a price on humans and dignity (as non-humiliation) are compatible. Demosthenes' comment underlines both the recognition of something like human dignity (even slaves ought not to be unnecessarily humiliated) but also the limited range of actions that recognition motivated.

how the recognition of dignity as a general attribute of humans might arise from active defence of civic dignity as a common pool resource. The Greeks and Romans never developed the conception of intrinsic human dignity as the foundational premise of human rights, either in morality or in law. There is no ancient equivalent of the United Nations Universal Declaration of Human Rights, or of Article 1 of the German Constitution. Yet the idea that each human being naturally possesses an inherent dignity was developed and widely disseminated by the ancient Stoics. Stoicism began with Zeno of Citium, who lived as a resident foreigner in Athens beginning in about 300 BC This was an era in which perhaps half of the Greek city-states had democratic governments. If we had more than mere fragments of Zeno's *Republic*, we might be able to say more about how the historical experience of civic dignity affected the earliest philosophical development of the concept of inherent human dignity.

References

Balot, R. K. 2004. 'Courage in the Democratic Polis', *Classical Quarterly* 54: 406–23

Berlin, I. 1969. *Four Essays on Liberty*. Oxford University Press

Demosthenes. 1990. *Demosthenes, Against Meidias: Oration 21*, ed. and trans. D. M. MacDowell. Oxford, New York: Clarendon Press

Domingo Gygax, M. Forthcoming. *Benefaction and Rewards in the Ancient Greek City: The Origins of Euergetism*. Cambridge University Press

Fisher, N. R. E. 1992. *Hybris: A Study in the Values of Honour and Shame in Ancient Greece*. Warminster: Aris & Phillips

Martin, R. P. 1989. *The Language of Heroes: Speech and Performance in the Iliad*. Ithaca, NY: Cornell University Press

Millett, P. C. 1989. 'Patronage and Its Avoidance in Classical Athens', in A. Wallace-Hadrill (ed.), *Patronage in Ancient Society*. London: Routledge, 15–48

Nagy, G. 1979. *The Best of the Achaeans: Concepts of the Hero in Archaic Greek poetry*. Baltimore, MD: Johns Hopkins University Press

Ober, J. 1989. *Mass and Elite in Democratic Athens: Rhetoric, Ideology, and the Power of the People*. Princeton University Press

2007. '"I Besieged That Man": Democracy's Revolutionary Start', in K. Raaflaub, J. Ober and R. W. Wallace (eds.), *The Origins of Democracy in Ancient Greece*. Berkeley, CA: University of California Press, 83–104

2008. *Democracy and Knowledge: Innovation and Learning in Classical Athens*. Princeton University Press

2012. 'Democracy's Dignity', *American Political Science Review* 106(4): 827–46

Pettit, P. 1997. *Republicanism: A Theory of Freedom and Government*. Oxford, New York: Clarendon Press

Skinner, Q. 1998. *Liberty Before Liberalism*. Cambridge University Press

Waldron, J. 2012. *Dignity, Rank, and Rights*. Oxford University Press

Wallace-Hadrill, A. (ed.). 1989. *Patronage in Ancient Society*. London: Routledge

Weingast, B. R. 1997. 'The Political Foundations of Democracy and the Rule of Law', *American Political Science Review* 91: 245–63

Whitehead, D. 1983. 'Competitive Outlay and Community Profit: Philotimia in Democratic Athens', *Classica et Mediaevalia* 34: 55–74

1993. 'Cardinal Virtues: The Language of Public Approbation in Democratic Athens', *Classica et Mediaevalia* 44: 37–75

4

Human dignity in the Middle Ages (twelfth to fourteenth century)

RUEDI IMBACH

Any discourse on human dignity presupposes a specific anthropology. This is equally true for reflection on human dignity in the Middle Ages. The medieval efforts to interpret the human being occur in dialogue with two kinds of sources: on the one hand with biblical statements regarding the human being, and on the other hand with works from antiquity along with the Arabic and Jewish texts that discuss these works. Of interest in the first tradition is primarily the interpretation of the human being as the image of God, expressed most notably in Genesis 1:26 and Wisdom 2:23. At the core of the influence of ancient philosophy, in contrast, is the interpretation of the human being as *animal rationale* and as *animal sociale* and *politicum*. While the decisive texts of Aristotle in which this twofold designation of human beings is developed (the *Nicomachean Ethics* and *Politics*) only became fully accessible to the Latin world in the course of the thirteenth century, the notion of humans as rational beings had never sunk into oblivion.[1] From ancient philosophy, Christian speculation had taken the problem of immortality, while the theme of beatitude and the final destination of humans in relation to eternal bliss and the sight of God was taken up and strongly enriched by theological reflection. This also holds for the development of the notion of a person, which was deepened in the light of the Trinitarian debate.[2] What may not be overlooked is the propagation and redevelopment of ethics through the interaction not only with biblical guidelines, but especially through the questions of sin, grace, and the proper way to live one's life.

Human dignity and the idea of humans as the image or likeness of God

In the Middle Ages, the biblical doctrine of human beings as the image (*imago*) and likeness (*similitudo*) of God was, on the basis of patristic models, interpreted and developed in a number of very distinct ways. An important group of authors considers human beings' likeness to God to be grounded first and foremost in

[1] On the rediscovery of Aristotle in the Middle Ages, see Brams 2003.

[2] On the history of the notion of personhood, see Kobusch 1997; Wéber 1991; Boureau 2008.

their rational nature. Hugo of Saint Victor (c.1096–1141), for instance, argues that the human being is 'image according to reason (*ratio*), likeness in accordance with love' (*De sacramentis* I, 6, 2). In Anselm of Canterbury (1033–1109), this interpretation is closely connected to the idea of a proportionality between knowledge of oneself and knowledge of God: the better humans know themselves, the better they know God (*Monologion* c. 66). Even Augustine (354–430) had already repeatedly emphasized this relation, which manifests the dignity of human beings in a special sense – in a famous passage in the *Soliloquia*, he writes that if a person were to recognize himself, he would recognize God: 'noverim me, noverim te' (*Soliloquia* II, 1, 1). Bernard of Clairvaux (1090–1153), in contrast, is of the opinion that it is freedom that designates humans as the image of God (*De gratia et libero arbitrio* IX, 28). Human dignity exists in freedom: 'For the human being, I consider dignity (*dignitas*) free will, through which it is given to him not only to be superior to other creatures, but also to rule them.'[3] Bonaventura (1217–74), finally, interprets the three activities of the human mind – remembering, cognizing and willing – in light of its being an image of God (*Itinerarium mentis in deum* III, 1). In Thomas Aquinas' (c.1224–74) anthropology, the human likeness to God is the very goal of the creation of rational creatures; the rational nature of human beings allows them to imitate God through self-knowledge and self-love (*Summa theologiae* I, q. 93, Art. 4).[4] Reason accounts for human dignity.[5] The theologoumenon of humans as a likeness or image of God also explains the anthropocentrism of many medieval thinkers. When Hildegard of Bingen (1098–1179) writes that the human being stands in the middle of the structure of the world, she summarizes this special conception of the world order and emphasizes the dignity of the human person, 'because he is more powerful than any other creature'.[6] As geocentrism and anthropocentrism expand, these are expressed in the theological–philosophical thesis that the world was created for the sake of human beings: 'In a certain way, the entirety of corporeal nature exists for the sake of the human being, insofar as he is a rational creature. Therefore, the consummation of the entire corporeal world to an extent depends on the consummation of the human being.'[7] In light of Psalm 8 (verse 6), where it is said that God has placed everything under the humans' feet, it can be concluded that humans may use 'all kinds of things

[3] *De diligendo Deo* II, 2, *Opera*, 3, p. 121: 'dignitatem in homine liberum dico arbitrium, in quo ei nimirum datum est ceteris non solum praeeminere, sed et praesidere animantibus.'

[4] See *Summa theologiae* I, q. 93, Art. 4.

[5] Note the remarkable formulation: 'Recessus autem a ratione, in qua tota dignitas humana consistit', in *De veritate*, q. 25, Art. 6 ad 2.

[6] Liber divinorum operum, I, visio I, PL 197, 761B.

[7] Thomas Aquinas, 'Compendium theologiae', I, c. 148, Leonina, 138: 'quodam modo propter hominem, in quantum est rationale animal, tota natura corporalis esse videtur. Ex consummatione igitur hominis consummatio totius creature corporalis quodam modo dependet.'

to his advantage', even the 'end of celestial motion' is arranged around him.[8] This arrangement of the entire creation around the human being attests to [is evidence of] the dignity of humans.[9]

The priority of self-knowledge

The Socratic tradition, which sees the essence of philosophical activity in the Delphic imperative of self-knowledge, is alive throughout the Middle Ages in a number of different ways (Courcelle 1974–5). Its presence is, again, particularly powerful in Bernard of Clairvaux, for instance when he tersely summarizes his intentions in a sermon: 'I wish, therefore, that the soul, before anything else, know itself.'[10] From an epistemological perspective, the soul is the first object of knowledge in two different ways: it is that which is closest to us, and at the same time it is the most significant object of questioning. The primacy of self-knowledge must therefore be understood both chronologically and hierarchically. In a deservedly famous passage of *De consideratione* (a treatise addressed to the Pope), Bernard summarizes the decisive elements. As a question regarding what I am myself, self-knowledge includes the demarcation from what I am not, whether it rises above or lies below me. *Te, circa te, sub te* and *supra te* are the four stages of introspection that Bernard here indicates. Of particular importance in this context is the fact that the self is said to be the beginning and the end of reflection: 'For you, begin with reflecting on yourself, so that you will not uselessly concern yourself with others while neglecting yourself. What use it is for you to gain the entire world while losing yourself?'[11]

Other thinkers describe the process of self-examination in very similar ways. Richard of Saint Victor (*c.*1110–73), in contrast, calls on philosophers to concentrate on themselves in order to contemplate the nature and possibilities of human existence. However, he who dares to look inside himself will almost be infatuated with the depth and beauty of what shows itself to him, for he will discover a new world, and much that invokes admiration.[12]

[8] *Summa contra gentiles* III, c. 22, n. 2032: 'Si igitur motio ipsius caeli ordinatur ad generationem; generatio autem tota ordinatur ad hominem sicut in ultimum finem huius generis: manifestum est quod finis motionis caeli ordinatur ad hominem sicut in ultimum finem in genere generabilium et mobiliium.'

[9] *In symbolum apostolorum*, Art. 1, n. 886: 'Quinto ducimur ex hoc in cognitionem dignitatis humanae. Deus enim omnia facit propter hominem, sicut dicitur in Psal. VIII, 8: Omnia subiectisti sub pedibus eius.'

[10] *Super cantica canticorum* 36, *Opera omnia*, vol. 1, p. 568.

[11] *De consideratione* II, iii, 6, *Opera*, vol. 3, p. 414.

[12] *Benjamin maior* III, c. 8, ed. Aris/Andres, 65: 'In hoc sane profundo invenies multa stupenda et admiratione digna, ibi invenire licet alium quendam orbem, latum quidem et amplum, et aliam quandam plenitudinem orbis terrarum. Ibi sua quaedam terra, suum habet caelum.'

It is entirely clear that the self-knowledge demanded by these authors is not conceived as an isolated or self-contained end, but embedded in a conception of the spiritual itinerary of human beings. In these texts, self-knowledge is one stage of a mystagogy. Even as many authors, most notably those of the twelfth century, agree on the priority of self-knowledge, there are nevertheless significant differences with respect to the fruits such self-knowledge is taken to bear for people themselves. While some authors, such as William of St Thierry (1080/85–1148)[13] and Hugo of Saint Victor consider capturing beauty and human dignity as an achievement, others, for instance Bernard or Helinand of Froidmont (*c.*1160–after 1226),[14] emphasize that the person who studies himself becomes aware of his nullity and his misery. As Bernard summarized it incisively: 'We realise, that we are nothing.'[15] In the context of their appropriation of the *cognosce te ipsum*, these twelfth-century authors plead – through their critique of a mode of philosophizing that was common at the time – for a way of philosophical questioning that would blossom again in the early Renaissance of the fourteenth century in Francesco Petrarca (1304–74). Petrarca is exemplary of the view that, a philosophy which, as a human practice, does not primarily realize contemplation of human life, does not fulfil its true task. This is impressively shown in the invective *De sui ipsius multorum ignorantia*, in which Petrarca argues for a mode of philosophy that gains a view of the ultimate possibility of human beings in thinking about itself (Imbach 2004a).

The dignity of the person

As indicated above, Trinitarian speculation in particular – which was concerned with capturing and describing the unity of the divine being and the trinity of the persons as clearly and precisely as possible – promoted reflection on the human being. Decisive for the development of the notion was first of all the definition proposed by Boethius (*c.*480–524), which connects the concept of nature with substantiality and individuality, and reserves the notion of 'person' for God, angels and humans: 'When therefore personhood is only in substances, in fact in rational ones, when every substance is nature and exists not in the universal, but in the individual, the definition of the person has been found: an individual substance of rational nature' (*naturae rationalis individua substantia*; *Contra Eutychen et Nestorium* III). However, two further definitions were of great importance. Richard of Saint Victor emphasizes the unique and

[13] On St Thierry's interpretation of human dignity, see first and foremost his commentary on the Song of Songs: Saint-Thierry 1962.

[14] The eighth book of his world chronicle is titled *De cognitione sui*. The work was published in PL 212, pp. 771–1082.

[15] On this important topic of *miseria hominis*, see Courcelle's key study 'Le thème antique de la misère humaine', in Courcelle 1974–5, pp. 295–324.

incommunicable nature of persons[16] in describing them as 'incommunicable existence' of an intellectual nature (*incommunicabilis existentia*), and stressing the particular phenomenon of existing-for-oneself (*existens per se*). This is a quality that only ever applies to individuals – it does not describe a universal (*quid*), but is the answer to the question 'who?' (*quis*).[17] Finally, Alexander of Hales (*c.*1185–1245) describes the person as a 'hypostasis distinguished by a property pertinent to dignity' (*hypostasis distincta proprietate ad dignitatem pertinente*).[18] Alexander connects the notion of dignity with the concept of persons, who 'are moral beings, since they signify the quality of dignity'.[19] According to Bonaventura, persons are not only characterized by singularity and incommunicability, but especially by the *supereminens dignitas* that is also discussed by Albertus Magnus (*c.*1200–80) when he describes persons as rational supposita that are 'characterized by natural and moral dignity'.[20] Thomas Aquinas emphasizes the special mode of being of persons, which is identified as existing-through-itself and comprises individuality. This mode of being of rational substances, which is said to be the most dignified of all (*dignissimus*),[21] implies self-governance (*dominium sui*), that is, independence in acting (*Summa theologiae* I, q. 29, Art. 1), thinking and willing. Thomas does not hesitate to claim that the independent existence of rational substances – that is, personhood – is the most perfect being in the whole of nature.[22] The dignity of human beings thus coincides with the dignity of personhood.

In praise of freedom

For a number of authors, freedom is the constitutive moment of human existence. Thomas Aquinas, for instance, opens the central ethical section of his *Summa* by discussing the free human being as the origin (principle) of his own deeds. According to Dante Alighieri (1265–1321), human freedom is the greatest gift of the divine goodness (*Paradiso* V, 19–24). Since human freedom

16 For what follows, see Ebneter 2005, who discusses particular aspects of Richard of Saint Victor's concept in detail, as well as the 1985 edition of *De trinitate*.

17 See Ebneter 2005: 68–9.

18 With regard to what follows, see the valuable article 'Person, Mittelalter', in *Historisches Wörterbuch der Philosophie*, vol. 7 (Basel, 1989), 283–300.

19 *Glossa in quatuor libros sententiarum Petri Lombardi* 3, 5, 20: 'persona res moris est, quia dicit proprietatem dignitatis'.

20 *De incarnatione*, 3, Art. 4, in *Opera omnia* (Borgnet), vol. 26, p. 200: 'distinctum proprietate pertinente ad dignitatem vel naturalem vel moralem.'

21 *De potentia* q. 9, Art. 3: 'Natura autem, quam persona in sua significatione includit, est omnium naturarum dignissima, scilicet natura intellectualis secundum genus suum.'

22 *Summa theologiae* I, q. 29, Art. 3: 'Persona significat id quod est perfectissimum in tota natura.'

is the basis for responsibility and morality (see *Purgatorio* XVIII, 64–66), it functions more or less as the cornerstone of the entire *Divine Comedy*. The Church has often denounced determinist approaches, and theologians have defended freedom.[23] In William of Ockham (*c.*1285 to *c.*1349), human freedom is significantly radicalized;[24] a move that is initiated by John Duns Scotus (*c.*1265–1308).[25] According to Ockham, freedom should not be understood in the first place as an absence of coercion, but as the capacity to act or refrain from acting. While, for Ockham, the specific human form of freedom cannot be proven, the freedom particular to human beings cannot be proven, it solely presents itself through experience.[26] The radicalization of the notion of freedom in Ockham becomes clear when he claims that human beings have the capacity not to desire eternal bliss.[27] This is an hypothesis that would be unthinkable for a Thomist, who would take the human desire for blessedness to be ontologically grounded. According to Ockham, the human will can reject any object, and thus even God. This doctrine of human and divine freedom yields important consequences not merely for ethics, but also for politics, since the primacy of freedom means that both acting morally and political authority presuppose the recognition of the freedom of others. On this basis, legitimate political authority can only be founded on mutual agreement.[28]

Political dimensions

The rediscovery of Aristotle's texts on practical philosophy fundamentally changed the basis for the consideration of human beings as social creatures. It introduced the possibility of conceiving the social order without recourse to theological theses. The human being as *animal politicum* constituted the central object of this line of research, whose foundations – in contrast to 'political Augustinianism' – no longer rest in the supernatural.[29] In this way, dignity (re)emerges as a concept grounded in man's social nature. As such a political creature, human beings are after inner-worldly happiness, of the kind that appears exemplarily in Dante's *Monarchia* as a goal that is philosophically recognizable and that can be reached in a natural manner.[30] In this horizon, being part of the *civitas* becomes a fundamental component of *humanitas*. Dante's contemporary, the Florentine Dominican Remigio dei Girolami, expressed this insight in an exceedingly pointed way by stating that whoever is not a citizen

[23] At this point, the Paris condemnation of 1277 should be particularly noted: *La condamnation parisienne de 1277*, trans. and ed. D. Piché. Paris: Vrin, 1999.

[24] On Ockham's approach, see McCord Adams 1987.

[25] Introduction by Ingham 2004.

[26] *Quodlibetum* I, q. 16, *Opera theologica* IX, pp. 87–9.

[27] I *Sent.*, d. 1, q. 6, *Opera theologica* I, pp. 503–6.

[28] See McGrade 2002. [29] Arquillière 1934. [30] See Dante 1998.

is not a human being (*si non est civis, non est homo*, Dei Girolami 1985). But Thomas too highly valued the Aristotelian conception of the human as political creature. The linguistic ability clearly shows that humans are the most expressive animal.[31] As the doctrine of natural law confirms, sociability is anchored in human nature. According to Thomas, the first ground rules of natural law can be identified by way of the inclinations (*inclinationes*) that move human beings. Humans share with all other living creatures their striving for self-preservation, and with animals reproduction and the rearing of offspring. Specifically human, in contrast, is the desire for knowledge and for life in a community.[32] From these inclinations, we can not only determine the first ground rules of the unchangeable law of nature, this understanding of the dynamic human nature, on which the entirety of Thomist ethics and politics is grounded, also proves to be a further interpretation of Aristotle's double determination of human beings as rational and social animals. Thomas stresses the social nature of humans in a particularly memorable manner when, following Aristotle, he points out that every human is every other's friend: 'Every man is naturally every man's friend by a certain general love.'[33]

The limits of the medieval conception of human dignity

While it cannot be denied that medieval philosophers and theologians made essential contributions to our thinking about human dignity, and that much of what they have formulated on the matter has not lost any of its relevance and meaning, from a contemporary view there exist many problems with these conceptions of human dignity. First, their anthropological reflections had a strongly androcentric character. That is, their theories on human beings were almost exclusively developed from a male perspective. Certainly, the reasons for this can largely be found in the social structures of the time, but they are also closely connected with the relevant philosophical and theological sources. Misogyny was encouraged and theoretically supported not only by the thirteenth-century reactualization of the Aristotelian notion of the woman as a failed man, that is, as a creature that went awry due to reproductive infelicities (*mas occasionatus*; *De generatione animalium* II, 3; 737a27), but also by leading patristic theologoumena. But also two further features render these accounts of human dignity problematic from a contemporary view – that demands they are

[31] See the comments on this matter in the first chapter of the treatise *De regno* (Leonina XLII, p. 450a): 'magis igitur homo est communicatiuus alteri quam quodcumque aliud animal quod gregale uidetur.'

[32] *Summa theologiae*, I-II, q. 94, Art. 2; see Imbach 2004b.

[33] *Summa theologiae* II-II, q. 114 a. 1 ad 2: 'Dicendum quod omnis homo naturaliter omni homini est *amicus* quodam generali amore.' Also see *Summa contra gentiles* IV, c. 54, n. 6.

comprehensive and without reservation: the attempts to justify the death penalty and the legitimation of slavery. With regard to these two points, it should be kept in mind that the reception of Aristotle in the thirteenth century supported the idea of natural inequality amongst human beings. Given a hierarchical conception of reality, the questionability of slavery remains obscured: 'For those who lack in reason, yet are physically powerful, appear to be determined by nature to serve; this is how Aristotle puts it in his Politics.'[34] While Thomas does not claim that slavery is grounded in natural law, he does believe that it can be deduced from natural law, and that it belongs to the law of peoples (*Summa theologiae* II-II, q. 57, Art. 3 ad 2).

With regard to the death penalty, I shall here only point out the influential position of Thomas Aquinas, who, on the basis of the thesis that the part is subordinate to the whole, argued as follows: 'If therefore a man, on account of a transgression, becomes a danger and corruptive influence to society, it is rational and beneficial to kill him in order to save the common good' (*Summa theologiae* II-II, q. 64, Art. 2). Someone who sins, the Dominicans moreover believe, falls from human dignity (*Summa theologiae* II-II, q. 64, Art. 2 ad 3). Still, this claim cannot be taken literally, but can only mean that this person does not act in accordance with the dignity of his nature.

References

Alexander von Hales. 1951–7. *Glossa in quatuor libros sententiarum Petri Lombardi*, 4 vols. Florence: Quaracchi

Anicius Manlius Severinus Boethius. 1973. *The Theological Tractates; the Consolation of Philosophy*, ed. H. F. Stewart, E. K. Rand and S. J. Tester. Cambridge, MA: Harvard University Press

Anselm of Canterbury. 1998. *The Major Works*, ed. B. Davies and G. R. Evans. Oxford University Press

Arquillière, H.-X. 1934. *L'augustinisme politique: Essai sur la formation des théories politiques du Moyen Âge.* Paris: Vrin

Augustinus. 2000. *Soliloquia, PL 32, 869–904 – Soliloquies: Augustine's Interior Dialogue*, trans. K. Pfaffenroth and J. E. Rotelle. Hyde Park, NY: New City Press

Bernard of Clairvaux. 1957. *Super cantica canticorum*, vols. 1–2. Rome: Editiones cistercienses

1963a. 'De consideratione', in *Opera omnia*, ed. J. Leclercq and H. Rochais, vol. 3. Rome: Editiones cistercienses, 393–439

1963b. 'De gratia et libero arbitrio', in *Opera omnia*, ed. J. Leclercq and H. Rochais, vol. 3. Rome: Editiones cistercienses, 165–203

Bonaventura. 1891. 'Itinerarium mentis in Deum', in *Opera omnia*, vol. V, *Quaracchi*, 285–316

[34] Summa contra gentiles III, c. 81.

1978. *The Soul's Journey into God, The Tree of Life, The Life of St Francis*, trans. E. Cousins. Mahwah, NJ: Paulist Press

Boureau, A. 2008. *De vagues individus: La condition humaine dans la pensée scolastique.* Paris: Les Belles Lettres

Brams, J. 2003. *La riscoperta di Aristotele in occidente.* Milan: Jaca Books

Courcelle, P. 1974–5. *Connais-toi toi-même de Socrate à Saint Bernard*, 3 vols. Paris: Etudes augustiniennes

Dante. 1998. *Monarchia*, trans. R. Kay. Toronto: Pontifical Institute of Mediaeval Studies

De Saint-Thierry, G. 1962. *Exposé sur le cantique des cantiques*, ed. J. M. Déchanet and M. Dumontier. Paris: Cerf

Dei Girolami, R. 1985. 'De bono communi', in *Memorie Domenicane* 16, ed. E. Panella, 123–68

Ebneter, Th. 2005. *Existere: Zur Persondefinition der Trinitätslehre de Richard von Sankt Viktor.* Fribourg: Academic Press

Hildegard of Bingen. 1996. *Liber divinorum operum*, PL 197, ed. A. Derolz and P. Dronke. Turnhout: Brepols (CCCM 92)

Hugo de Sancto Victore, *De sacramentis*, PL 176, 173–618

Imbach, R. 2004a. 'Virtus illiterata: Zur philosophischen Bedeutung des Scholastikkritik in Petrarcas Schrift "De sui ipsius et multorum ignorantia"', in *Miscellanea mediaevalia* 31, 84–104

2004b. 'Thomas von Aquino: Das Gesetz', in *Klassiker der Philosophie heute*, ed. A. Beckermann and D. Perler. Stuttgart: Reclam, 143–65

Ingham, M. E. 2004. *The Philosophical Vision of John Duns Scotus: An Introduction.* Washington, DC: Catholic University of America Press

Kobusch, Th. 1997. *Die Entdeckung der Person: Metaphysik der Freiheit und modernes Menschenbild.* Darmstadt: Herder

La condamnation parisienne de 1277. 1999. trans. and ed. D. Piché. Paris: Vrin

McCord Adams, M. 1987. *William of Ockham.* Notre Dame, IN: University of Notre Dame Press

McGrade, A. S. 2002. *The Political Thought of William Ockham.* Cambridge University Press

Richard de Saint-Victor. 1958. *De trinitate*, ed. J. Ribaillier. Paris: Vrin

1996. 'Benjamin maior', in M. A. Aris, *Contemplatio, Philosophische Studien zum Traktat Benjamin Maior des Richard von St Viktor.* Frankfurt am Main: Josef Knecht

Thomas Aquinas, 'Compendium theologiae', in *Opera omnia*, Editio Leonina, vol. XLII, 83–205

1949. 'Quaestiones disputatae de potentia', in *Quaestiones disputatae* II, ed. P. Biazzi and M. Calcaterra *et al.* Turin: Marietti

1961. *Liber de veritate catholicae fidei contra errores infidelium seu summa contra gentiles*, ed. C. Pera, P. Marc and D. P. Caramello. Turin: Marietti

1979. 'De regno', in *Opera omnia*, Editio Leonina, vol. XLII, Rome: San Tommaso, 449–71

1972. 'In symbolum apostolorum', in *Opuscula theologica*, vol. II, ed. R. M. Spiazzi. Turin: Marietti, 193–217

1975. *Quaestiones disputatae de veritate*, Editio Leonina, vol. XXII. Rome: San Tommaso

1988. *Summa theologiae*, Editio Paulina, Rome: San Tommaso

Wéber, E. H. 1991. *La personne humaine au XIIIe siècle*. Paris: Vrin
William of Ockham. 1967. *Scriptum in librum primum Sententiarum*. Ordinatio, vol. I (*Opera theologica* IX), ed. G. Gál, New York: St Bonaventure
1980. *Quodlibeta septem* (*Opera theologica* IX), ed. J. C. Wey. New York: St Bonaventure

5

Human dignity in late-medieval spiritual and political conflicts

DIETMAR MIETH*

Human dignity in the late Middle Ages: mysticism and the law of nations

Recently, medievalists have started to address the question of individuality in the Middle Ages. They broadly agree that Leopold von Ranke, Jakob Burkhardt and others were misguided in understanding the Renaissance as a break with the dark medieval collectivism.[1] The same holds – to an extent that is yet to be determined – for the understanding and justification of human dignity. In the Middle Ages, a number of perspectives arise that break ground for the idea of dignity and equality between humans. At the same time, though, there are numerous medieval approaches that vigorously challenge such ideas.

The Church Fathers connected the ancient idea that human beings have a special place in the world because of their rational capacities and their ability for self-formation (the Stoics, Cicero), with the Christian doctrine of the human being as created in the image of God (*imago Dei*) or the redeemed (baptized) human as similar to God (*similitudo*). That is, by participating in God in being His image, human beings at the same time participate in God's reason. Humans have the capacity to reflect on themselves, and to exercise free will (*liberum arbitrium*). The particular theory of human dignity as springing from freedom – especially the individual's freedom of the will and his capacity for self-determination and self-knowledge – does not (as is often assumed) originate from Pico della Mirandola's work, *De hominis dignitate*, but can already be found in Alcuin of York's *De dignitate conditionis humanae* (cf. Marenbon 1981), as well as in several twelfth-century texts. Peter Abelard develops an account of the will as a reflexive structure and the unity of human beings as rational creatures. The 'I' in this theory – the conscious and reflexive relation of people to their own will – is determined by rationality, which humans employ to evaluate possible actions and to decide to act in a particular way. Yet such a *secundum*

* Translated by Naomi van Steenbergen in collaboration with the author.

[1] Cf. Aertsen and Speer 1996, particularly the introduction by Jan A. Aertsen, Ibid.: ix ff. In the same vein, Richard Tuck (1979) and Brian Tierney (1997; 2008) demonstrate that the idea of (individual) human rights is based in medieval scholastic thought.

rationem agere was already identified by Pseudo-Dionysus as the ethical capacity of the human being; one that is not only a form of freedom, but also a responsibility.[2]

Yet from the Christian perspective, humans are confronted with contingency, sin and the need for salvation. This raises the question whether dignity can be lost or revoked. Must dignity first be re-established by baptism? In other words, is dignity possible at all outside of the Church as an institution of salvation, which through its sacraments brings salvation by Christ within reach? In the medieval literature, the notion of a *dignitas* that applies universally to all persons has a theological basis. It corresponds to the assumption that human beings were created for their own sake, and that therefore they have inherent worth. Besides the place of humans in the world, what forms the basis for human dignity in the Middle Ages is their rational, deliberate self-determination. In the late-twelfth-century work, *De miseria humanae conditionis*, Lotario dei Conti di Segni, later Pope Innocent III, contrasts the *dignitas humanae naturae* with the *vilitas humanae conditionis*. On the basis of their divine nature, human beings can be considered to have worth in themselves, yet their actual condition is wretched (cf. Innocent III; Sturlese 2007: 35–45). In the thirteenth century, two concepts stood in opposition: the emphasis on the dignity of creation, which could never be lost, and the dignity of salvation that humans could lose through sin. Insofar as in this context the emphasis was put on original sin, which could be redeemed by baptism, the unbaptized did not partake in the dignity of salvation. This could be understood to mean either that these persons were not given the dignity of creation either, or that they were deprived of it.

The following selection of late-medieval tendencies proceeds, as it were, from the inside outwards. Essential to late-medieval mysticism is the *homo divinus*, who at the same time, figuratively, is the *homo nobilis* (the noble human). The doctrine of *homo divinus* dominates mysticism as well as the movement of the Free Spirit from the end of the thirteenth and throughout the fourteenth century. The similarity between the doctrines of *homo divinus* and *homo nobilis* in so-called German mysticism consists in the fact that 'humanity', against a theological–philosophical backdrop, is drawn upon in order to legitimize a special kind of dignity and special rights. In this way, reflection on what is human is deeply embedded in the Middle Ages, well before Humanism. Around the same time, the canonistic schools of Bologna and Padua develop the *ius gentium*, the law of nations, in a way that, while referring to the doctrines of *homo divinus* and *homo nobilis*, is distinct from it. The *ius gentium* too can serve to show how the right of the unbaptized (persons as well as nations) could advance under new political constellations in the first three decades of the fifteenth century – even in the political environment of the Council of Constance.

[2] This formula frequently occurs in Thomas Aquinas; see for instance Q *Quaestiones disputatae de veritate*. 16,1,9; STh 1–2, 18,5.

Homo divinus et nobilis: the motive of human dignity in Meister Eckhart

Late-medieval mysticism prepares the way of self-withdrawal and the nobility of the soul that leads towards the universal equality of human beings especially through Meister Eckhart and Marguerite Porete. Alongside the hierarchies of the Church and the state, the internal hierarchy of the soul appeared. The motif of inwardness as relational motif – for Eckhart in the shape of an intellectual relation, for Marguerite Porete as a relation of the will – expands in the social domain to the equality of all human beings. For the nobility of the soul has to do with humanity, no more and no less. For Meister Eckhart (*c.*1260–1328), Christ's act of redemption is not present in its original form; often, it is eclipsed by God's general devotion to men in the event of incarnation. At the centre is always 'humanity'.

As Kurt Flasch emphasizes, what is at stake is a theory of recognition. God is self-evidently given, but can his recognition be accounted for? (Flasch 2010: 52–5, 268f) God's divine–human nature must be recognizable in humanity as reason and free will, that is to say, in ethics. Whatever human criteria humans can acutely perceive and recognize can be used as criteria for our image of God: if God did not mean righteousness, then he would not mean anything to the righteous person. This means that the ethical recognition of righteousness becomes relevant as a theological criterion too. Theology is not separated from rationality; indeed, it is entrusted to it all the more clearly, since faith is to be explained through the 'natural grounds of rationality'. This is why Eckhart's commentary on John describes ethics more precisely as the relation between faith and reason:

> In the beginning was the word. With respect to morality, we teach that the principle of all our intentions and actions must be God... Yet we also teach that our work ought to be rational, and that it ought to be a work that is controlled by the direction and order of reason. For 'In the beginning was the word' also means: in the beginning was reason... What is done in accordance with reason... emanates from God's countenance. (Psalm 16:2, John, Meister Eckhart 1936: vol. III, n. 51: 42)

Eckhart is revolutionary in his influence, even if he did not exactly intend to be so. He lays the groundwork for freedom in the self-abnegation of any human being. In his defence during his trial, he refers to his 'efforts for justice (or righteousness)' that earned him hostility and prosecution (cf. Meister Eckhart 1936: vol. V, n. 77: 275). Eckhart's revaluation of human beings from the inside out did not result in new institutions or external reforms, but his revaluation created a new self-awareness that was accessible to everyone, one that kept cropping up after him and that did not exclusively involve Christians. After Eckhart, this kind of self-awareness can be found in the theological schools of Cracow and Salamanca, respectively one and two centuries later.

The *homo divinus*, as Loris Sturlese characterizes the subject of 'the philosophical projects in the thirteenth and fourteenth centuries', is aware of his divine constitution.[3] This awareness does not deny the role of Church and politics as institutions, but views them as accompanying, not constitutive, instances. The subject's sense of self advances. For Eckhart, Christology becomes a reference point for the nobility of the soul. This also deeply relativizes the distinction between Christians, Jews and Muslims. This development was wholly in line with the openness to debate at the time.

We may conclude: the *homo divinus* of Eckhart and his spiritual contemporaries heightens the significance of the individual, yet does not carry this significance over into the domain of human rights. Certainly, the rise of the individual in mysticism is a source from which Humanism and the Reformation can draw. On the one hand, this stems from a philosophical intellectualism, which puts considerable emphasis on rationality; on the other hand, it stems from the right to personally assure oneself of one's faith.

The ius gentium and the recognition of equal humanity in the context of the dispute between Poland and the Teutonic Order at the time of the Council of Constance

In Eckhart's younger contemporary, Marsilius of Padua (1280–1342/3), a state philosopher had stood up who 'questioned the grounds and legitimacy of state authority' (Imbach 1989: 162). On the basis of the Roman-canonical principle according to which everything that pertains to all must be decided by all, he 'provided the beginnings of a theory of a sovereignty of the people' (*ibid.*: 162). Admittedly, what this doctrine refers to is a *universitas civium*, which leaves the question who can *be* a civilian unanswered, especially since whenever this issue occurs Marsilius falls back on Aristotle, for whom only the rights of full citizens are taken into account. And what is at stake here are not civil rights, but universal human rights, on which civil rights rest. This is what Marsilius seems to allude to when he writes that 'the design of political authority ought to be based on the consensus of all those affected' (*ibid.*: 163). Imbach shows that this 'truly fundamental idea in the Middle Ages was first formulated by Duns Scotus in connection with the debate on property'. For Marsilius, power over people and material goods is prescribed neither in laws of nature nor by divine command. This means that it rests on a consensus, 'on the voluntary agreement of free persons' (*ibid.*: 163, 164, n. 85). The sentence from Dante's *De monarchia* that Imbach cites (I, xii, 10) allows us to transfer to the considerations that will follow: 'Upright governments have liberty as their aim, that men may live for themselves' (Imbach 1989: 164). For what is at stake in what is to follow is the *propter se* (for themselves) of human beings as the source of political

[3] *Homo divinus* is the title of Sturlese's essay collection that came out in 2007. Relevant here are mostly pp. 34–45.

institutions. At the beginning of the fourteenth century, however, philosophers considered this question fundamentally in relation to the emancipation of all laity from the demands of the Church. The canonists on the other hand had fewer problems with papalism – for instance as an authority that embodied the law of peoples but was bound by natural law. Insofar as they did not only consider the established *civitates*, but also the coexistence of 'Christian' and 'pagan' nations, they did not argue on the basis of a consensus theory, but, as we shall see, with natural law, which at the same time curtailed the rights of the Pope as an institution for the law of nations.

The relation between the justification of wars, human dignity and human rights shows itself in the medieval example of a highly theorized legal-moral debate that took place at and around the Council of Constance (1414–18). In the present context, the arguments relating to natural law or the law of reason are from particular interest. These were used by the Cracow Academy[4] to argue – in a debate with the legal scholars of the universities of Pisa, Padua and Bologna who were well-grounded in the theory of the state, and with the Dominican Falkenberg as the chief ideologist of the Teutonic Order – that it is not permitted to wage war on pagan nations, since they too are God's creatures. While such motives – that even pagans are God's 'handiwork' – can already be found in Wolfram von Eschenbach's *Willehalm* or in Raimundus Lullus (*c.*1300), wars against infidels were considered the work of God: God wills it (*Dieu lo vult*) had been the motto of the crusades since the eleventh century.

With respect to pre-modern engagement with human dignity, one might think of Pico della Mirandola, whose argument still lies entirely within the framework of creation and the idea of human beings as the *imago Dei*, or of the Schools of Salamanca, Vittoria and Las Casas. The latter are of particular significance since their ideas – propagated in the sixteenth-century debate at the Council of Valladolid against Sepúlveda, who was an adherent of the Aristotelian theory of slavery – were of great importance for the New World. A similar debate on the dignity and rights of heathens had taken place more than a hundred years earlier between Johannes von Falkenberg, the Dominican theologian of the Teutonic Order, and Paulus Wladimiri. On a canonist basis, following natural law, the latter contested (along with Stanislaus Skarbimierz, who was to become one of his successors as a rector) the right of the Pope to assign pagan territories to the Teutonic Order. He advocated requiring justification for all wars, regardless against which peoples, and he emphasized the right to coexistence of Christian and non-Christian nations. Wladimiri's arguments, which were grounded in the interpretation of canon law by the School of Padua, were not uncommon. They found favour with many at the Council of Constance.

[4] The Cracow Academy was formed by the theological and canonist faculties of the Polish University of Cracow (founded in 1364; the theological faculty in 1397) that were led by Paulus Wladimiri.

The secondary literature is ambivalent about the treaties and corresponding rights that were negotiated in the thirteenth century between several rulers and the Teutonic Order. The Teutonic Order had understood its powers and entitlement to territories extensively, and enslaved or oppressed the pagan Prussians without mustering a whole lot of interest for their peaceful conversion, which after all would have relativized the reason for the conquests. Instead, the Order installed itself majestically in the centre of Marienburg, and took charge of important trading towns such as Thorn and Danzig. The initial good relations with Poland gradually disintegrated in the course of the fourteenth century, and came to a definitive end when Ladislaus Jagiełło, a pagan Lithuanian monarch, converted to Christianity in order to become King of Poland. In 1410, the dispute led to a war, which, due to considerable propaganda from both parties, involved western European knights and mercenaries as well. In the first instance, the military dispute ended in the battle of Tannenberg (or, in Polish, Grunwald) where the Order suffered a dramatic loss against the Polish–Lithuanian coalition, resulting in the Peace of Thorn (1411). The conflict kept flaring up though, and was brought to the Council of Constance. An arbitral verdict by Emperor Sigismund in favour of the Order did not end the dispute. The conflict continued to preoccupy the curia of Pope Martin V, who was elected at Constance. The next step was to draw upon advisors from the universities of Pisa, Padua and Florence. Paulus Wladimiri, who had been educated at the Italian universities as well as at the University of Prague, was a prominent member of the Polish delegation, both in Constance with Emperor Sigismund and at the papal curia. Of interest for the current chapter is not the way the conflict evolved, but the arguments on human rights and the rights of nations (especially of pagan peoples) that were used in it. The arguments can be easily reconstructed from the documentation. In order to do so, I shall consider first the expert testimony from the legal experts from Padua, Florence and Pisa (cf. Wos 1971: 99–123), followed by Paulus Wladimiri's *magnum opus*,[5] and finally a text by Ladislaus Skarbimierz from the same early 'Cracow Academy' (Skarbimierza 1979).

The Padua advice was mostly concerned with the validity of the fourteenth-century agreements between the Order and Kasimir III of Poland. The formal objection that the Order was not able to produce and provide the complete set of relevant documents was complemented by the argument that, even if the documents had been ratified by the king, he would not have been authorized to do so, since as a king he represented and was responsible for the people and the territory. His task, according to the objection, was to protect the rights of the people, whether heathen or Christian, as well as the integrity of his country. This was a standpoint that later came to be adopted by his successor, Jagiełło. In this line of argument, the position deriving from natural law and the law of

[5] Cf. the most important works of Wladimir: *Saevientibus* (1415), *Opini ostiensis* (1415) and *Ad aperiendam* (1416), edited by Ehrlich (1969).

reason that presupposes all human beings to have rationality and freedom – that is to say, human dignity and human rights – is already taken as a given. In contrast, the protection of Christian faith, on which this advice does insist, is permitted only in the case of prosecution by pagans and only in order to secure pre-established rights. In this context, the Teutonic Order had not only referred to attacks of the Samaiten, which it considered itself justified in fending off (mostly through pre-emptive defence), but also to the deeds of the Tatars in the army of the Lithuanian leader Vytautas (Withold) in the 1410 war, who had pillaged and burnt down a town, driving citizens into a church and burning them alive. War crimes on the side of the Order have been reported as well. In Paulus Wladimiri's biography, they form a central reason for his concern with the rights of the heathens (cf. Wos 1971: 77).

From where does Wladimiri derive his theses? He mostly follows three leads. First, the *lex divina*, which he understands as the authoritative interpretation of the *lex naturalis* – that is to say, he introduces this law as a rational authority. The natural or rational law is embodied in the Ten Commandments as well as in the commandment to love one's neighbour as oneself. Historically, it is continued in the collected legal texts of the Church (the papal decretals), which transcend regional legal provisions and therefore, according to numerous commentaries, are the only normative standards that can be drawn upon with respect to legal matters that apply to entire peoples. The second lead – not explicitly declared as in the *lex divina* – is the *lex naturae*, a law that is comprehensible through rational knowledge by non-believers as well, and which, one might say, forms a 'reflexive equilibrium' of rational insights with the standards expressed by the Church. The third lead is a theoretical debate with Cardinal 'Ostiensis', Henricus de Segusio (*c.*1194–1271), a famous interpreter of the collection of decretals whose conception of right is adopted by representatives of the Teutonic Order, amongst whom Johannes von Falkenberg (cf. Sénko 1986; Ehrlich 1966–9: 113–43). Against him, Wladimiri refers to the interpretation of the decretals by Innocent IV (*c.*1195–1254) as well as to Thomas Aquinas.

In his contribution to the mission of conversion, Innocent IV had appointed bishops in the regions around the Baltic Sea, and granted heathens the right to their own state. Ostiensis, in contrast, put a much stronger emphasis on the papal-political supremacy, and took the Pope, as an authority higher than the emperor and as an absolutely comprehensive institution, to be able to overrule regional authorities. According to Ostiensis, rights were primarily Christian rights, and concerned both the propagation and the defence of faith. This perspective curtailed the moral and legal restrictions of the *ius ad bellum* against heathens. Heathens did not possess originary rights. In light of the right of creation and the *ius naturale*, heathendom equalled self-deprivation of rights. For this reason, a heathen can be enslaved, and when converted he can be forced to work. Ostiensis interpreted Christ as *caput universalis* from a monistic perspective that made the Pope into a central authority, without regard for the self-reliance of creation. Interestingly, those who followed this interpretation were the Renaissance Popes such as Nicholas V (a humanist!) in reference to Portugal's African conquests, and Alexander VI with his infamous bull *Inter cetera*, which allowed the Spanish Crown to disenfranchise the Indians and their states. It is important to realize, though, that these theological texts were employed as convenient – they did not justify the exploitation, but were used to silence its opponents. Ultimately, power determined more than the legal position of those concerned.

In contrast to Ostiensis, the teachings of Paulus Wladimiri, close in content to the doctrine of Pope Innocent IV, can be summarized in the following ten points:

(1) The original equality of all human beings is grounded in the fact that humans are the image of God; a fact that is established in creation and that applies to every human being. Even though the original sin casts a shadow on the dignity that is thus given, sin does not annul this dignity. Wladimiri is therefore opposed to a theory according to which one can be deprived of this dignity, which is supposed to be true for those who are unbaptized and remain in sin. It seems likely that such a theory underlies Ostiensis' interpretations.

(2) In light of the message of Christianity, violence calls for particularly strong justification. The doctrine of a 'just' war should therefore be understood exactly as a doctrine of reasons or justification, even though war remains an evil that is to be avoided. The conditions *auctoritas legitima, iusta causa* (in the case of defence), *ultima ratio* and *iustis mediis* may not be annulled or modified on the grounds of lesser or derivative rights of the heathens.

(3) Pagan states or areas under pagan control are not necessarily unjust communities that can be eradicated by Christian occupation. They are to be considered equal partners, and their territorial integrity ought to be respected.

(4) No government – monarch, emperor, pope – may terminate or compromise the territorial integrity of its own state. This holds in particular for the agreements between Poland and the Teutonic Order. Property rights in the sense of sovereign rights cannot be granted in this manner.

(5) The authority of the Pope, understood as the primary authority (for instance, *vis-à-vis* emperors and kings; the priority of the spiritual over the worldly sword, such as in the case of Innocent IV) does not entail absolute rule-making authority (the Pope is not a world monarch, as the theological 'legalists' Ostiensis and Falkenberg envisage). This is a rejection of the idea that the Pope can take command of countries and intervene in their integrity without heeding their governmental autonomy. What remains are only subsidiary possibilities, that is – with respect to pagan territories – defence and the protection of Christian Believers against prosecution. If the violence of the Pope is thus restricted, this holds *a fortiori* for the Christian emperors, kings, etc.

(6) A particular outgrowth of the delegitimization of pagan human rights is the manner of warfare of the Order, which animated the western knighthood to – almost as a kind of sport – join it in campaigns into pagan land in order to go looting or asserting themselves against poorly armed resistance. It is perfectly possible that Paulus Wladimiri, whose family and homeland were damaged by such looting campaigns, would have found such behaviour particularly abhorrent.

(7) The service of faith is determined by the condition that conversion should not be attained violently. In the thirteenth century, dioceses in which both Christians and heathens lived had been established in Prussia for this very purpose. Instead of peaceful coexistence, the Order had caused unrest in these places. Indeed, doubts were raised as to whether the Order was at all interested in establishing states of Christians endowed with rights.

(8) Important was the question whether it was permissible to wage war in the name of rights (human rights and territorial rights) in military alliances with heathens and heretics (which referred to orthodox Christians!). As mentioned above, in the battle of Tannenberg, Tatars (also Muslims) and orthodox Christians from Lithuania had fought on the side of Poland. (The Christian outrage also related to war atrocities. Therefore, the question was: what was positively permissible, and what should be put up with? At the same time, this was a question of *iustis mediis*. From the perspective of natural law, the participation of heathens in a just battle was less of a problem than putting up with war atrocities, which one should obviously not want as such. In my opinion, Skarbimierz' reasoning in particular is rather one-sided.)

(9) Until the nineteenth century, the Council of Constance was the largest convention of the Church and of those nations who self-identified as western-Christian. In addition, Conciliarism sparked the hope of international understanding, and constituted a comprehensive institution for transnational cooperation. For this reason, the Cracovians are close to the Conciliarists, even if they do not wish to take up an anti-hierocratic standpoint explicitly.

(10) The possibility of international settlement of conflicts is theoretically grounded in the priority of non-violence, and in the idea of the recognition of sovereignties regardless of their relation to Christian faith. The ethical attitude that is demanded by faith and confirmed by natural law in this case takes priority over the Christian-monistic attitude that drove the legalists to grant rights only to those baptized, indeed to deny neophytes the same rights as Christian conquerors. Nicholas V's bull *Romanus Pontifex* (1455), in contrast, granted the Portuguese conquerors in Africa the right to take possession of all goods, and to subject the original inhabitants to 'everlasting slavery'. It is evident that the will to spread Christianity was just a feeble guise.

In strong contrast to Wladimiri's arguments, the bulls of later Popes such as Nicholas V and Alexander VI allowed slavery, without even referring to the School of Padua or its continuation in the Cracow Academy.[6] They were an enormous step backwards. History developed differently in Prussia than in Latin America. The implementation of these earlier progressive ideas in the *leyes nuevas* of King Charles V could not be sustained in the Latin American colonies. The movement of recognition of equality in the sense of the law of nations was more successful in eastern Europe, since it could be connected with power-political motives; something that failed in Latin America. In the late Middle Ages, the political circumstances worked in favour of human rights and of sovereignty rights independent of faith.

References

Aegidius Romanus. 1929. *De ecclesiastica potestate*, ed. R. Scholz, Weimar; Hermann Boehlau Nachfolger (English edition: Aegius Romanus. *De ecclesiastica potestate*, ed. R. W. Dyson. New York: Columbia University Press, 2004)

Aertsen, J. A., and Speer, A. (eds.). 1996. *Individuum und Individualität im Mittelalter.* Berlin, New York: Walter de Gruyter

Alexandrowicz, Ch. H. 1963. 'Paulus Vladimiri and the Development of the Doctrine of Coexistence of Christian and Non-Christian Countries', *British Yearbook of International Law* 39: 441–8

Belch, S. F. (ed.). 1965. *Paulus Vladimiri and His Doctrine Concerning International Law and Politics*, vols. 1–2. The Hague, Paris: Mouton and Co.

Böckenförde, E. W. 2006. *Geschichte der Rechts- und Staatsphilosophie: Antike und Mittelalter*, 2nd edn, Tübingen: Mohr Siebeck – Uni-Taschenbuch

Ehrlich, L. 1966–9. *Works of Paul Wladimiri, a Selection (Latin, English)*, vols. I–III. Warsaw: Instytut Wydawnicy PAX

Flasch, K. 2010. *Meister Eckhart: Philosoph des Christentums.* Munich: C. H. Beck

Grewe, W. G. (ed.). 1988–95. *Fontes historiae jus gentium.* 3 vols. Berlin: Walter de Gruyter

Grewe, W. G., and Evers, M. 2000. *The Epoches of International Law.* Berlin, New York: Walter de Gruyter

Imbach, R. 1989. *Laien in der Philosophie des Mittelalters Hinweise und Anregungen zu einem vernachlässigten Thema.* Bochum: B. R. Grüner

Marenbon, J. 1981. *From the Circle of Alcuin to the School of Auxerre: Logic, Theology and Philosophy in the Early Middle Ages.* Cambridge University Press

Meister Eckhart. 1936. *Die Lateinischen Werke*, vols. 1–5, ed. Loris Sturlese, Stuttgart: Kohlhammer

Sénko, W. 1973. 'Les tendances préhumnaistes dans la philosophie polonaise au XVe siècle', in Academia Polaca della Scienza, Biblioteca e Centro di Studi di Roma, fasc.62, Wroclaw *et al.*

[6] The papal documents (Bulls) that were important for the question concerning the Indians are: Nicholas V, *Romanus pontifex* (to King Alphons V of Portugal); Alexander VI, *Inter cetera* of 1493 (to Isabella and Ferdinand of Spain), and Paul III, *Sublimus Dei* of 9 June 1537; the latter can be understood as an 'abrogation' of the earlier ones.

1986. *Johannis Falkenberga 'De Monarchia Mundi'* (Texts and Studia, Historа Theologica in Polonia Ex Cultu Spectantia, vol. XX). Warsaw: Academia Teologii Katholikiej

Skarbimierza, Stanislaw Ze. 1979. *Sermones Sapientiales*, ed. B. Chmielowska, Textus et Studia, vol. IV, fasc. 1. Warsaw: Academia Teologii Katholikiej

Sturlese, L. 2007. *Homo divinus: philosophische Projekte in Deutschland zwischen Meister Eckhart und Heinrich Seuse.* Stuttgart: Kohlhammer

Tierney, B. 1997. *The Idea of Natural Rights: Studies on Natural Rights, Natural Law and Church Law 1150–1625*. Atlanta, GA: Scholar Press

2008. *Religions, Law and the Growth of Constitutional Thought 1150–1650*. Cambridge University Press

Thomas Aquinas. 1953. *Quaestiones disputatae de veritate – Truth, Questions 10–20*, trans. J. V. McGlynn SJ. Chicago: Henry Regnery Company, http://dhspriory.org/thomas/QDdeVer.htm

Thomas Aquinas, 'New English Translation of St Thomas Aquinas's Summa Theologiae', trans. A. J. Freddoso, University of Notre Dame. Parts 1 and 2, www3.nd.edu/~afreddos/summa-translation/TOC-part1-2.htm

Tuck, R. 1979. *Natural Rights Theories: Their Origin and Development.* Cambridge University Press

Wos, Jan Wladislaw. 1971. 'Appunti per la biografia di Paulus Wladimiri Canonista Polacco del seculo XV', in *Studi Senesi*, vol. LXXXIII, 57–124, Appendix II, 'A Latin Edition of the Expert Opinion of Canonists from Padova, Fiorentina and Siena to the Juridical Questions Between the Teutonic Order and Poland'

6

Human dignity in Renaissance humanism

PIET STEENBAKKERS

Renaissance humanism

As a topic worthy of sustained and systematic scrutiny, human dignity first appeared on the philosophical agenda in the Renaissance. An indication of this is the appearance, from the middle of the fifteenth century onwards, of several tracts about the dignity and excellence of man. Yet, in spite of this apparently straightforward state of affairs, the Renaissance treatment of human dignity has also given rise to confusion. The reason for this is that we tend to read our own conceptions of human dignity into Renaissance discussions of it. Moreover, the new interest in human dignity in the fifteenth century is related to the revival of classical culture known as 'Renaissance humanism'. The tendency to conflate this movement with later systems that have been labelled 'humanism', too, has been pervasive since the middle of the nineteenth century. In order to clear the ground, I must first disentangle the different meanings of the elastic notion of humanism.

The word 'Humanismus' was coined in 1808 by the German theologian and pedagogue, Friedrich Niethammer, to denote the educational current that laid much store by the study of the classical languages and literature (Niethammer 1808). In the course of the nineteenth century, however, the word came to be applied to a variety of currents, positions and worldviews. Particularly influential was Georg Voigt's use of the term to label the Renaissance programme of restoring ancient learning (Voigt 1859). Though the Renaissance scholars and thinkers who brought this movement about did not call themselves 'humanists',[1] the label caught on. Since that time, 'Renaissance humanism' refers to the educational and cultural project to re-establish the liberal arts or *studia humanitatis* of antiquity,[2] the pursuit of which was considered to be the privilege of free

[1] The word '(h)umanista' did exist, but it had a very limited application: in Italian university terminology, the *umanista* was the teacher of the liberal arts, as the *jurista* was the professor of law. For the links between *umanista* and *humanism*, see Kristeller 1979: Chapter 1. On the occurrence and use of 'humanist' in the sixteenth and seventeenth centuries, see Ramminger 2007.

[2] In the fifteenth century, these arts comprised grammar, rhetoric, history, poetry and moral philosophy (Kristeller 1979: 22). They constitute the 'middle ground between

persons (as distinct from slaves). But, apart from this well-defined acceptation, 'humanism' acquired a wide range of other (sometimes conflicting) meanings.[3] Here is a suitably loose description that attempts to cover some of their common features: 'Humanism is also [i.e. in addition to being the designation for the cultural movement of the Renaissance] any philosophy which recognizes the value or dignity of man and makes him the measure of all things or somehow takes human nature, its limits, or its interests as its theme.' Since such features have also been perceived in the culture of the Renaissance,[4] the different meanings have blurred. Even though scholars will insist on the historical specificity of Renaissance humanism,[5] there is an indelible popular image of the Renaissance. In this view, humanism carries the connotation of a turn towards humanity, implying that the Renaissance drew away from the divine and eternal which formed the focus of the medieval world picture, and began to discover the human and secular instead. Thus, the Renaissance is conceived as the first stage of a progress towards modernity, a process characterized by secularization and the rise of a humanist worldview. It is this confusion that makes it difficult for us to gauge what Renaissance authors are up to when they sing the praises of man's dignity and excellence.

This is not to say that it is mistaken to regard the Renaissance as an early stage of the process that shaped the modern world as we know it. I do, however, reject the tacit assumptions underlying the popular image. The most important of these is that Renaissance humanism is somehow continued by present-day humanism, which is characterized by a secular, liberal and individualist outlook. An implication of this is that the Renaissance veered away from religion. As we shall see in this chapter, these assumptions are erroneous. I will briefly return to this in the conclusion to this chapter.

Excellence, superiority and dignity

In employing 'dignity', 'excellence' and 'superiority' as equivalent terms, Renaissance authors take their cue from Cicero's *De officiis*:

purely practical studies such as law, medicine, or the mechanical arts on the one hand, and purely theoretical studies such as natural philosophy, advanced logical theory, metaphysics, and theology on the other' (Hankins 2007: 32).

3 For the historical development, see Menze 1974; for an attempt to classify its usage in later philosophy, see, for example, Luik 1998.

4 Here, Jacob Burckhardt's classic study, *Die Cultur der Renaissance in Italien* (1860), was a major influence. Among the defining characteristics of the period, Burckhardt stresses the development of the individual ('*Zweiter Abschnitt: Entwicklung des Individuums*') and the discovery of the world and of man ('*Vierter Abschnitt: Die Entdeckung der Welt und des Menschen*').

5 See, for example, Trinkaus 1983: 3–31; and Hankins 2007; for further suggestions see the helpful bibliographical references in Copenhaver and Schmitt 1992: 24, n. 20.

> But it is essential to every inquiry about duty that we keep before our eyes how far superior man is by nature to cattle and other beasts: they have no thought except for sensual pleasure and this they are impelled by every instinct to seek; but man's mind is nurtured by study and meditation; he is always either investigating or doing, and he is captivated by the pleasure of seeing and hearing . . . From this we see that sensual pleasure is quite unworthy of the dignity [*praestantia*] of man and that we ought to despise it and cast it from us; but if someone should be found who sets some value upon sensual gratification, he must keep strictly within the limits of moderate indulgence. One's physical comforts and wants, therefore, should be ordered according to the demands of health and strength, not according to the calls of pleasure. And if we will only bear in mind the superiority and dignity [*excellentia et dignitas*] of our nature, we shall realize how wrong it is to abandon ourselves to excess and to live in luxury and voluptuousness, and how right it is to live in thrift, self-denial, simplicity, and sobriety. (Cicero 1913: I.30: 105–6)

Cicero identifies *excellentia* and *praestantia* ('pre-eminence, superiority') and links these notions to *dignitas*: 'to us Nature herself has assigned a character of surpassing excellence, far superior to that of all other living creatures [*magna cum excellentia praestantiaque animantium reliquarum*]' (*ibid.*: 97: I.28). This idea of human dignity, which is Stoic in origin,[6] was the guiding inspiration for humanist authors from Petrarch onwards: it is a summons to rise above animal existence by using the distinctively human gift of reason. The Renaissance view of human dignity was the result of an absorption of classical sources, in an attempt to understand the human condition as more complex and less wretched than it had commonly been pictured in the Christian tradition the humanist authors inherited from and shared with their medieval predecessors.

At the end of the eleventh century, Lothar of Segni, who was to become Pope Innocent III, wrote an immensely popular tract on the misery of the human condition. His intention was to complement this with another text on the dignity of human nature, but that was never realized. Around 1357, a friend of Francesco Petrarca, Giovanni Birel Limosino (Prior General of the Carthusians) implored him to supply this missing treatise, but Petrarch politely declined. Instead, he inserted a dialogue on 'Sadness and Misery' in his *De remediis utriusque fortunae* ('Remedies for Both Faces of Fortune'), in which he set forth his thoughts on the issue (Petrarch 1869–70: 513–22).[7] There Petrarch – or rather his spokesperson, Reason personified – observed that authors find it a good deal easier to write about human misery than about happiness (Petrarch 1975: 220: I.93). Fortune has two faces, but moral philosophy tends to over-emphasize the negative side: original sin and the ensuing human wretchedness. Petrarch and Renaissance thinkers generally regretted the one-sidedness of this picture, which did not do justice to real life, nor to the biblical view of man as made in God's image

[6] More particularly Cleanthes and Chrysippus (Horstmann 1980: 1124).

[7] See also R. Schottlaender's note to his edition of Petrarch's *De remediis*: Petrarch 1975: 220.

(Genesis 1:26) and as ruler of the Earth (Genesis 1:28) (Trinkaus 1983: 136–7; Kraye 1988: 306–11). Apart from extolling human dignity as the distinguishing feature of human nature, Cicero had also given a narrower interpretation, namely, that of political dignity or notability. Petrarch had elaborated that theme (as well as that of moral dignity) in his *De viris illustribus.* In the dialogue on sadness and misery, he acknowledges that the miserable aspects of the human condition are indeed huge and manifold. That should not, however, make us blind to the many things that make life happy and agreeable, though that is something nobody has ever written about (or so Petrarch alleges). And yet, the likeness of the Creator's image is inscribed in the human soul; we have talents, eloquence, memory and foresight; inventions and discoveries, arts and sciences. Petrarch then enumerates the beautiful things in the world that give us joy, and mentions the admirable features of the human body. Moreover, man's dignity even surpasses that of the angels: for God became a man, not another creature. Petrarch's moderate optimism evinces the energetic and inquisitive attitude of the beginnings of Renaissance humanism. It blends with a profoundly Christian outlook on the ambiguity of the human condition, with God's likeness and the Incarnation of Christ as the ultimate foundations of the excellence and dignity of man.

Bartolomeo Facio (or Faccio) opens his short treatise 'On the Excellence and Preeminence of Man' of 1448 with an explicit reference to Innocent III: it aims at supplying the complementary volume that Innocent III never wrote.[8] This was not a spontaneous idea: the work was commissioned by Alfonso of Aragon, King of Naples. Facio connects the Christian idea of man's central position in creation with the partly classical and partly theological celebration of a contemplative life. Man was made in God's image, and it is human reason and in particular the immortality of the mind that confers something of a divine nature to man. Accordingly, the greatest part of Facio's argument is taken up by a discussion of the immortality of the soul and of a future life, based on religious and philosophical authorities. Human happiness consists in contemplating God: Facio's treatise shows no interest in the active life.

Apparently, Alfonso was not yet satisfied with this rather perfunctory interpretation, for he then asked Giannozzo Manetti for a work on the same topic.[9] Manetti wrote his *De dignitate et excellentia hominis* around 1450.[10] It differs

[8] *De excellentia ac praestantia hominis liber* was written in 1447–8, but first published in 1611 as an appendix to Marquard Freher's edition of Felino Sandeo's *De regibus Siciliae et Apuleia.* The reference to Innocent III is on p. 149 of that edition.

[9] Both Facio and Manetti had been asked to write on human dignity not only by Alfonso, but also by the Benedictine monk Antonius Bargensis (Antonio da Barga), who had sent them a manuscript of his own on this very subject. Barga's treatment was preponderantly theological, and Facio appears to have followed his example fairly closely. See Kristeller 1965: 68; Trinkaus 1973: 143.

[10] For the genesis of the text, see A. Buck, 'Einleitung', and Manetti's dedication to Alfonso, in Manetti 1990.

considerably from Facio's treatise in size and scope. He insists on the active life as one of the features that define human dignity and excellence. It is precisely the combination of acting and understanding that makes human beings superior. Manetti develops his argument systematically, and in a continuous dialogue with authors who had dwelt upon human misery (among them Innocent III): Book I deals with the excellent properties of the human body, Book II with those of the soul; Book III elaborates the creative power that the combination of body and soul is capable of. The world of civilization, the arts and sciences was created by human beings, out of the raw material of the natural world in which they found themselves. The fourth book then concludes with a detailed repudiation of the arguments for human wretchedness.

The core of Manetti's argument is the exposition of human superiority in the third book. It is founded on the idea that God created and arranged the world for the sake of human beings alone (Manetti 1990: 68: Book III, para. 5). He created them last of all, in his own likeness, endowed with senses and intellect (*ibid.*: 69: para. 7).[11] Men's talents (*ingenium*) enabled them to create buildings, cities, pictures, sculptures, arts, sciences, wisdom and infinitely many other achievements (*ibid.*: 77: para. 20). Our wisdom is ultimately rooted in knowledge and worship of God (*ibid.*: 78–9: paras. 21–2). The sage, who (unlike animals) is capable of controlling anger and desire, is presented as the highest form of human existence (*ibid.*: 79–80: para. 24). Men are exceedingly rich and powerful, the lords of all creation, and they may use all creatures for their own benefit (*ibid.*: 80–1, 83: paras. 25–7, 30). Manetti endorses his argument with many references to the Bible and to classical authors. Quoting with approval Cicero (who in turn refers to Aristotle), he describes man as a mortal god, born for two things: understanding and acting (*ibid.*: 91: para. 47).[12] When God created man, he wanted him to strive for faith and wisdom (*ibid.*: 91–2, 95: paras. 48, 55). The third book concludes with a short paragraph in which the Incarnation is offered as the final proof of human superiority (*ibid.*: 97, para. 59).

Giovanni Pico della Mirandola

In spite of the wide variety of sources Manetti adduces, the general drift of his argument is still basically the early humanist mixture of Stoic and Christian positions that is already to be found in Petrarch. In the final decade of the fifteenth century, a crucial development in Renaissance philosophy will lead to new perspectives on human dignity. Owing to the work of Marsilio Ficino, an abundance of Platonic sources rapidly becomes available in Latin: Plato's works,

[11] Cf. *De excellentia ac praestantia hominis liber* (note 8 above), p. 117, para. 45, which runs thus in the Latin text: 'tum fecit [Deus] ipse sibi simulacrum sensibile atque intelligens, hoc est ad imaginis suijpsius formam, qua nihil poterat esse perfectius.'

[12] See also Cicero, *De finibus* II, 13, 40, referring to Aristotle, *Eth. Nic.* I 6, 1097b28–33.

Plotinus and the so-called *Corpus hermeticum*.[13] In addition, Ficino produced a series of highly influential commentaries, and developed a Platonic philosophy (or theology, as he himself styled it) of his own (cf. Copenhaver and Schmitt 1992: Chapter 3; Celenza 2007). His revival of Platonism profoundly influenced the course of Western philosophy in the centuries to come. One immediate effect was a revision of the relationship between action and contemplation:

> Ficino presented the contemplative life as the final step in a hierarchy of human action that led people to surpass the active life without utterly denying it: lived well, the active life becomes a step on the way to escaping matter and uniting with God. (Copenhaver and Schmitt 1992: 144)

As Ficino argues in his *Theologia Platonica*, what this union with God comes down to is that we become godlike when our intellect understands God through contemplation (Kraye 1988: 349). The impact of this hefty treatise 'on the immortality of the soul', written in 1474, was greatly reinforced by a revolutionary new invention: it appeared in print in 1482.

Giovanni Pico della Mirandola was a pupil and friend of Ficino, and he incorporated the latter's brand of Platonism into his own original, albeit eclectic, system. Although he was only thirty-one years old when he died in 1494, he left a considerable *œuvre*. His fame, however, rests on a single short work, published posthumously: an oration that he never delivered, and that received its title 'Oration on the Dignity of Man' only in an edition of 1557.[14] In 1486, Pico drew up 900 theses (*Conclusiones*) about all things knowable, on which he wanted to organize a huge public dispute in Rome.[15] The (untitled) *Oration* was written as an inaugural address to open this debate. Pope Innocent VIII condemned the project and prevented the dispute. Only the first part of the *Oration* deals with the topic of human dignity; the rest discusses Pico's selection of theses and authorities. On principle, Pico refuses to limit himself to particular schools or currents:

> I have wished to bring into view the things taught not merely according to one doctrine (as some would desire), but things taught according to every sort of doctrine, that by this comparison of very many sects and by the discussion of manifold philosophy, that radiance of truth which Plato mentions in his *Letters* might shine more clearly upon our minds, like the sun rising from the deep. (Pico della Mirandola 1998: 23)

Pico begins by expressing his dissatisfaction with the arguments traditionally adduced for the superiority (*praestantia*) of human nature and asserting that

13 On the *Corpus Hermeticum*, allegedly a collection of very ancient writings but in 1614 shown by Isaac Casaubon to be an early Christian fabrication from the first or second century CE, see (for example) Walker 1972; Yates 1964.

14 Buck, 'Einleitung', XVII, in Pico della Mirandola 1990.

15 Farmer 1998; on the turbulent events surrounding the dispute that eventually did not take place: *Ibid.*: 1–18.

he has finally discovered why man is the happiest living being, 'what the state is that is allotted to man in the succession of things, and that is capable of arousing envy not only in the brutes but also in the stars and even in the minds beyond the world' (*ibid.*: 3). When God had created the rest of the world, he wanted there to be someone who would understand and appreciate it and love its beauty, and so he created man. But all properties had already been dispensed, and all seats were occupied. God then decided

> that that to which nothing of its very own could be given should be, in composite fashion, whatsoever had belonged individually to each and every thing. Therefore He took up man, a work of indeterminate form; and, placing him at the midpoint of the world, He spoke to him as follows: '. . . In conformity with thy free judgment, in whose hands I have placed thee, thou art confined by no bounds; and thou wilt fix limits of nature for thyself. I have placed thee at the center of the world . . . Neither heavenly nor earthly, neither mortal nor immortal have We made thee . . . Thou canst grow downward into the lower natures which are brutes. Thou canst again grow upward from thy soul's reason into the higher natures which are divine.' (Pico della Mirandola 1998: 4–5)

Taking up the traditional Aristotelian and scholastic division of functions of the soul into nutrition, sensation and cognition, Pico asserts that each person's development will depend on the aspect they cultivate: those who cultivate the nutritive and reproductive part will become plants, those who cultivate the senses will be brutes, but if reason and understanding are pursued, they will be angels, sons of God (*ibid.*: 5). Nor does it stop there: he who retreats into the centre of his own unity is 'made one spirit with God' (*ibid.*):

> If you come upon a pure contemplator, ignorant of the body, banished to the innermost places of the mind, he is not an earthly, not a heavenly animal; he more superbly is a divinity clothed with human flesh. (Pico della Mirandola 1998: 6)

Here we see Ficino's Platonic programme of uniting with God through contemplation integrated into a dynamic conception of human superiority as an unlimited capacity for growth and development. Though Pico does not depart from the ascetic perspective inherited from the Stoic idea of human dignity, the focus is now on the creative power of man.

The originality of Pico's *Oration* is its bold preference for the power to choose between different routes of development as the distinctive feature of human dignity. There is no external pressure to opt for one rather than the other: 'thou art confined by no bounds'. Yet it would be a mistake to conclude that the choice is genuinely open: throughout the *Oration*, Pico vividly depicts the hierarchical organization of creation. Human beings may take the intellectual way to contemplation, or the animal or even vegetable way to physical satisfaction, but God's intention is clear. Those who develop the intellect will be rewarded by peace of mind, those who degenerate into a sensual or vegetative existence will be punished by transforming themselves into lower beings.

Conclusion

Renaissance humanism developed a sophisticated notion of human dignity. A survey of the three most important treatises on the topic, by Facio, Manetti and Pico, shows that – in spite of the many traditional influences they assimilated, pagan and Christian, philosophical and theological – their contributions have been original and innovative, too. The most important effect was probably the sustained attention for human assets, achievements and successes. If there is a link between the Renaissance philosophy of man and modernity, it will have to be situated here. Their positive approach to human potential responded to the needs of a dynamic society on the threshold of an era of incomparable development. Yet their ideas on human dignity did not evolve to present-day views, let alone in a linear fashion. For all Renaissance thinkers, human excellence, superiority and dignity are a gift from God, a result of the plan of his creation. They conceived of dignity as a feature shared by all human beings, but for them this did not imply that all were entitled to inalienable human rights – rights that can be claimed merely by dint of being human. In fact, they saw dignity as an assignment; those who failed to realize it thereby proved that they were unworthy of the honorary name of man:

> if you see a man given over to his belly and crawling upon the ground, it is a bush not a man that you see. If you see anyone blinded by the illusions of his empty and Calypso-like imagination . . . delivered over to the senses, it is a brute not a man that you see. (Pico della Mirandola 1998: 6)

Thus, dignity will apply to some people but not to others, even to the point of excluding them from humanity – 'Wen solche Lehren nicht erfreun, verdienet nicht ein Mensch zu sein.'[16] In this respect, Renaissance humanism has nothing in common with a humanist worldview as it is now generally understood.

References

Burckhardt, J. 1860. *Die Cultur der Renaissance in Italien: Ein Versuch*. Basel: Schweighauser

Celenza, C. 2007. 'The Revival of Platonic Philosophy', in J. Hankins (ed.), *The Cambridge Companion to Renaissance Philosophy*. Cambridge University Press, 72–96

[16] Emanuel Schikaneder, libretto to Mozart's *Die Zauberflöte* (1791, KV 620), Act 2, Scene 3, No. 15: Sarastro's aria 'In diesen heil'gen Hallen'. In English: 'Whoever is not delighted by these doctrines does not deserve to be a human being.'

Cicero, M. Tullius. 1913. *De officiis*, with an English translation, ed. and trans. W. Miller. Cambridge, MA: Harvard University Press, Loeb edition (retrieved 10 June 2013 from urn:cts:latinLit:phi0474.phi055.perseus-lat1 (Latin text) and urn:cts:latinLit:phi0474.phi055.perseus-eng1 (English translation))

Copenhaver, B. P., and Schmitt, C. B. 1992. *Renaissance Philosophy*. Oxford University Press

Facio, B. 1611. 'De excellentia ac praestantia hominis', in F. Sandeo, *De regibus Siciliae et Apuleiae*, ed. M. Freher. Hanau: Aubry's Heirs, 149–68

Farmer, S. A. 1998. *Syncretism in the West: Pico's 900 Theses (1486): The Evolution of Traditional Religious and Philosophical Systems*, with Text, Translation and Commentary. Tempe, AZ: Medieval and Renaissance Texts and Studies

Hankins, J. 2007. 'Humanism, Scholasticism, and Renaissance Philosophy', in J. Hankins (ed.), *The Cambridge Companion to Renaissance Philosophy*. Cambridge University Press, 30–48

Horstmann, R. P. 1980. 'Menschenwürde', in J. Ritter and K. Gründer (eds.), *Historisches Wörterbuch der Philosophie*, vol. 5. Basel: Schwabe, 1124–7

Kraye, J. 1988. 'Moral Philosophy', in C. B. Schmitt, Q. Skinner, E. Kessler and J. Kraye (eds.), *The Cambridge History of Renaissance Philosophy*. Cambridge University Press, 301–86

Kristeller, P. O. 1965. 'The Humanist Bartolomeo Facio and His Unknown Correspondence', in Ch. Carter (ed.), *From the Renaissance to the Counter-Reformation: Essays in Honor of Garrett Mattingly*. New York: Random House, 56–74

1979. *Renaissance Thought and Its Sources*, ed. M. Mooney. New York: Columbia University Press

1998. 'Humanism', in C. B. Schmitt, Q. Skinner, E. Kessler and J. Kraye (eds.), *The Cambridge History of Renaissance Philosophy*. Cambridge University Press: 1113–17

Luik, J. C. 1998. 'Humanism', in E. Craig (ed.), *Routledge Encyclopedia of Philosophy*. London: Routledge (online edition, www.rep.routledge.com/article/N025SECT4 (accessed 7 June 2013))

Manetti, G. 1532. *De dignitate et excellentia hominis libri IV*. Basel: Andreas Cratander, http://dx.doi.org/10.3931/e-rara-1740

1990. *Über die Würde und Erhabenheit des Menschen*, trans. H. Leppin, introd. A. Buck. Hamburg: Meiner

Menze, C. 1974. 'Humanismus, Humanität I', in J. Ritter (ed.), *Historisches Wörterbuch der Philosophie*, vol. 3. Basel: Schwabe, 1217–20

Niethammer, F. I. 1808. *Der Streit des Philanthropinismus und Humanismus in der Theorie des Erziehungs-Unterrichts unsrer Zeit*. Jena: Frommann

Petrarca, F. 1869–70. *Lettere senili*, trans. G. Fracassetti, 2 vols. Florence: Successori Le Monnier

1975. *De remediis utriusque fortunae*, zweisprachige Ausgabe in Auswahl, trans. and ed. R. Schottlaender, bibliogr. E. Keßler. Munich: Fink

Pico della Mirandola, G. 1990. *De hominis dignitate/Über die Würde des Menschen*, trans. N. Baumgarten, introd. A. Buck. Hamburg: Meiner

1998. 'On the Dignity of Man', trans. C. Wallis (revised by P. Miller), in G. Pico della Mirandola, *On the Dignity of Man: On Being and the One: Heptaplus*, trans. C.

Wallis, P. Miller and D. Carmichael, introd. P. Miller. Indianapolis, IN: Hackett, 1–34

Ramminger, J. 2007. '"Nur ein Humanist . . . ": Einige neue Beispiele für *humanista* im 16. und 17. Jahrhundert', in M. Pade (ed.), *Album amicorum: Festskrift til Karsten Friis-Jensen i anledning af hans 60 års fødselsdag/Studies in Honour of Karsten Friis-Jensen on the Occasion of his Sixtieth Birthday* (*Renæssanceforum*, vol. 3), www.renaessanceforum.dk/rf_3_2007.htm (accessed 7 June 2013)

Trinkaus, C. 1973. 'Renaissance Idea of the Dignity of Man', in P. Wiener (ed.), *Dictionary of the History of Ideas: Studies of Selected Pivotal Ideas*, vol. 4. New York: Scribner, 136–47

1983. *The Scope of Renaissance Humanism*. Ann Arbor, MI: University of Michigan Press

Voigt, G. 1859. *Die Wiederbelebung des classischen Alterthums oder das erste Jahrhundert des Humanismus*. Berlin: Reimer

Walker, D. P. 1972. *The Ancient Theology: Studies in Christian Platonism from the Fifteenth to the Eighteenth Century*. London: Duckworth

Yates, F. A. 1964. *Giordano Bruno and the Hermetic Tradition*. London: Routledge & Kegan Paul

7

The Council of Valladolid (1550–1551): a European disputation about the human dignity of indigenous peoples of the Americas

LARS KIRKHUSMO PHARO

Historical background to the Council of Valladolid

From the late-fifteenth century, the 'discovery' of continents and different cultures had a profound philosophical and theological impact upon the European conception of non-European and non-Christian peoples. Spain's war, conquest and ensuing colonization of the continent later denominated as 'America' from the beginning of the sixteenth century constitutes the political, economic and religious background to a principle moral debate on the human dignity and rights of non-European and non-Christian people. About fifty years after the 'discovery' of 'America', a disputation was organized by King Charles I of Spain (1500–58)[1] at the Colegio de San Gregorio in the Spanish city of Valladolid during the period of 1550 to 1551. He assembled a *junta* (council) of fourteen distinguished theologians who were specialists in Catholic canon law – the Consejo Real de las Indias (also known as the 'Council of the Fourteen') – with the purpose of issuing a ruling whether the methods of war and conquest of America were just. Another important subject was the manner in which the indigenous American peoples were to be converted to Catholicism as had been demanded by various papal bulls. The current situation in colonial 'Spanish America' was enforced conversion to Christianity, compulsory labour, tribute and violent treatment of indigenous people within the *encomienda* system. King Charles I suspended the war and conquest in Spanish America until these concerns were to be resolved at the Council of Valladolid (Hanke 1959; Losada 1971; Williams 1990; Veiteberg 1994).

Disputation about the nature and rationality of indigenous peoples

What Lewis Hanke denominates as 'the Intellectual and Religious Capacity' (Hanke 1974) of American indigenous peoples, represented the central matter for the disputation at the Council of Valladolid. The nature and rationality, and

[1] As the Holy Roman emperor (1519–56) he is designated as Charles V.

thus accordingly the humanity, of '*Los Indios*' were questioned through a formal inquiry. The concept of humanity is intimately related to the concepts of dignity and rights. A person who is not understood to possess rationality is not acknowledged to be human, and consequently has no dignity and no rights. The controversy was fundamentally a philosophical and moral debate on the supposed inferiority of non-European or non-Christian cultures as compared to the Christian so-called 'civilized' European nations. The humanity of the indigenous peoples of America was discussed on the background of Catholicism and European philosophy based upon previous and contemporary thinking and schools in law, philosophy and theology (Williams 1990). The disputation at Valladolid not only represents two philosophical models within the history of European ideas since antiquity, but also generates a considerable aftermath in the colonial and post-colonial period (Hanke 1959; Hanke 1974; Pagden 1982): 'Sepúlveda and Las Casas still represent two basic and contradictory responses to the question posed by the existence of people in the world who are different from ourselves' (Hanke 1959: 95).

The debate on the nature or rationality of American indigenous peoples took place between two members of the Dominican Order: Juan Ginés de Sepúlveda (1489–1573) and Bartolomé de Las Casas (1484–1566). Sepúlveda was a philosopher, lawyer and theologian. Written in Latin, the dialogue *Democrates Alter* or *Democrates Secundus sive de justis causis belli apud Indos* (1544?) ('A Second Democritus: on the Just Causes of the War with the Indians') contain his arguments of the later disputation at Valladolid (Sepúlveda 1951). As friar and Bishop of Chiapas of southern Mexico, Las Casas was not an academic but interested in the practice of law and politics towards indigenous peoples. Las Casas' Latin *Apologética Historia* (1547) argues against *Democrates Secundus*, whereas his later treatise, 'Aquí se contiene una disputa' in *Tratados* (Las Casas 1966) outlines the debate at Valladolid. The same book contains *Argumentum Apologiae*, which also contests Sepúlveda's theories from *Democrates Alter* (Hanke 1959; Hanke 1974; Losada 1971; Veiteberg 1994).

Associated with the subject of the nature and rationality at the disputation of Valladolid was the Aristotelian concept of 'natural slavery' and the justification of war against the indigenous peoples of America. In defending the war, Sepúlveda forwarded four arguments followed by the reply of Las Casas (Losada 1971: 282–306). Just war can be waged against peoples whom Sepúlveda classifies as 'barbarians' or inferior *homunculi*. According to Sepúlveda, the indigenous people were 'savages' observing non-Christian practices against nature. He compares indigenous American and European institutions, science, cultures, customs, laws and religions, in all of which the Europeans were deemed superior. Sepúlveda maintains that since the indigenous peoples have no culture and are not rational human beings, there is a natural condition making them suitable for slavery. He refers to Aristotle's theory of 'natural slavery' (*servitutem naturae*) as defined in Book I of *Politics* (Aristotle 1998). Sepúlveda contends that people with no reason or rational faculties practising barbaric customs are disposed to slavery. Moreover, he claims that 'idolatry' is a sin against nature, which justifies war. Since they are not rational human beings, indigenous peoples can only be converted by violence and conquest. By contrast, Las Casas argues that the theory of Aristotle of natural slavery is not applicable in the case of the indigenous peoples (Las Casas 1967; 1974; Pagden 1987: 27–56). Instead, he asserts that they are rational and moral human beings living in advanced societies and accordingly can be disposed for Christianity. He argues that the indigenous peoples possess universal and individual rights under natural law. The only 'barbaric' characteristic of indigenous peoples, according to Las Casas, is the fact that they are so-called 'heathens' – but this does not in itself make them natural slaves. Moreover, he claims that 'idolatry' and 'savage' religious practises are deplorable and demonstrate a lack of knowledge. Las Casas vehemently maintains the possibility to convert indigenous Americans through peaceful persuasion and not by violence (Hanke 1959; Hanke 1974; Losada 1971).

Aristotle, the Bible, Church Fathers, Christian theological writings and natural law theories guide the arguments of Sepúlveda. Contrary to Las Casas who had spent many decades in the Americas, Sepúlveda had no first-hand knowledge of indigenous philosophies and in addition no experience of indigenous cultures and languages. His information on the indigenous peoples has its source in the writings of the Spanish historian Fernández de Oviedo. Las Casas is known as 'Protector de los Indios'. In defending the rights of the American indigenous peoples he argued against the Spanish brutal colonization. Las Casas' arguments were inspired by the ideas of the School of Salamanca and in particular the Spanish Dominican professor of theology, Francisco de Vitoria (or de Victoria) (1480–1546), from the University of Salamanca (Vitoria 1989; Williams 1990: 96–108).

Las Casas influenced the papal bull, *Sublimis Deus* (1537), by Pope Paul III. This bull established the status of the indigenous peoples as rational beings, who were not to be enslaved, were to be recipients of the Catholic faith and capable of the possession of private property (Hanke 1959; Hanke 1974: 17–22; Losada 1971; Veiteberg 1994). Despite his emphasis on tolerance and respect for human beings of another ethnicity and culture, the anthropology of Las Casas suffers a quite important moral weakness: people are categorized as 'barbarians' if they do not adhere to Christianity.

The dignity of the practices of indigenous religions

Las Casas claims that indigenous peoples were to some extent superior to many Christian settlers (Losada 1971: 287, 292–9). Furthermore, he apparently supports the posterior Article 1 of the United Nations Universal Declaration of Human Rights (1948). But this principle does not apply to non-Christian religious peoples.

Both Sepúlveda and Las Casas establish their view of the humanity of indigenous peoples upon the conception of natural law developed by Thomas Aquinas (*c.*1224/5–1274) in *Summa Theologica* (Veiteberg 1994: 64). The law of nature is 'nothing else than the rational creature's participation in the eternal law of the Christian God' (Aquinas 2006: I-II.94). Although both claim to base their position on natural law tradition after Aquinas, Sepúlveda denies indigenous peoples the capability to possess dignity but, as Las Casas emphasizes similarity, he ascribes them a form of human dignity, although only as Christians. Indigenous people have the *potential* of becoming dignified after converting to Christianity. Las Casas here represents an early example of the mentality of many missionaries of the twentieth and twenty-first centuries; indigenous peoples were conceived not as heretics but as pagans, who until now had not enjoyed the privilege of knowing the Christian religion (Losada 1971: 300; Las Casas 1974: 44). As a representative of a 'developed' people, he perceives his role as a peaceful intervener assisting an 'underdeveloped' people to convert (Losada 1971: 296–8) to the only 'true' religion.

Human beings who are not Christians belong to what Las Casas names the 'fourth category of barbarians' (Pagden 1982: 134–5; Losada 1971: 285). Founded upon the words of St John Chrysostom, Las Casas has the following concept of the nature of human beings (Hanke 1974: 96):

> Just as there is no natural difference in the creation of men, so there is no difference in the call to salvation of all of them, whether they are barbarous or wise, since God's grace can correct the minds of barbarians so that they have a reasonable understanding. (Las Casas 1974: 271)

Las Casas operates from the theoretical foundation of Catholic theology as divine truth.[2] His argument with Sepúlveda was principally over the methodology of conversion from indigenous religions to Christianity (Lunenfeld 2011). But Las Casas maintains that there is no humanity in the faith and practice of a non-Christian religion. It is evident that Las Casas has made a great contribution to the acknowledgment of and regard for indigenous peoples, and in this respect the legacy of the Council of Valladolid is important. But Las Casas fails to recognize the worldview and intellectual heritage of indigenous peoples of the Americas, which represents their interconnected collective and individual dignity.

The doctrine of discovery and the dignity of self-determination

The failing of primarily Sepúlveda and to a lesser degree Las Casas at the Council of Valladolid to recognize the dignity of the belief and practice of a non-Christian religion has repercussions in the politics and law concerning indigenous peoples today. In the post-colonial period, nation states had a limited respect for the right of self-determination of the territories belonging to non-Christian indigenous peoples.

An inalienable right to *dominium rerum* or property could only apply to rational human beings created in the image of God (*imago dei*) according to

[2] Cf. Victoria/Vitoria's three fundamental arguments (Williams 1990: 97–108).

Thomistic humanist natural-law principles of the relations between humans and nations (Pagden 1987: 80–90). At the Council of Valladolid, it was disputed whether indigenous peoples were capable of self-determination of territory. As opposed to de Vitoria and Las Casas, Sepúlveda argued that indigenous peoples lacked civilization violating and abusing the laws of nature and therefore did not have this right (Pagden 1987: 90–2).

The theoretical position of Sepúlveda disclaiming indigenous peoples a right to self-determination of land has prevailed in the colonial and contemporary (post-colonial) periods through the judicial-theological 'doctrine of discovery'. Papal bulls[3] of the fifteenth century (also known as 'doctrine of Christian discovery') gave Christian explorers the 'right' to claim territories they 'discovered', i.e. any land that was not inhabited (*terra nullius*) by Christians, i.e. devoid of human beings. The Spanish principle of 'just war' or a violent 'right' to occupy indigenous land was accordingly upheld. The doctrine of discovery is a concept of law in various countries of the Americas undermining the right and dignity of indigenous peoples.

References

Aquinas, T. 2006. *Summa Theologia: Latin Text and English Translation, Introductions, Notes, Appendices and Glossaries/St Thomas Aquinas*, ed. T. Gilby. Cambridge University Press

Aristotle. 1998. *Politics*, trans. C. D. C. Reeve. Indianapolis, IN: Hackett

Hanke, L. 1959. *Aristotle and the American Indians: A Study in Race Prejudice in the Modern World.* Bloomington, IN: Indiana University Press

1974. *All Mankind Is One: A Study of the Disputation Between Bartolomé de Las Casas and Juan Ginés de Sepúlveda in 1550 on the Intellectual and Religious Capacity of the American Indian.* Northern Illinois University Press

Las Casas, B. de. 1966. *Tratados.* 2 vols. Fondo de Cultura Económica, Mexico

1967. *Apologetica histora sumaria.* 2 vols. Universidad Nacional Autonoma de Mexico, Instituto de investigaciones historicas, Ser. de historiadores y cronistas de Indias No. 1, 'México'

1974. *In Defense of the Indians*, trans. S. Poole, C. M. DeKalb. Northern Illinois University Press

Losada, A. 1971. 'The Controversy Between Sepúlveda and Las Casas in the Junta of Valladolid', In J. Friede and B. Keen (eds.), *Bartolomé de Las Casas in History: Toward an Understanding of the Man and His Work.* Northern Illinois University Press, 279–307

Lunenfeld, M. 2004. 'Las Casas, Bartolomé de' (1474–1566), in *Europe, 1450 to 1789: Encyclopedia of the Early Modern World*, www.encyclopedia.com (visited 9 November 2011)

Pagden, A. 1982. *The Fall of Natural Man: The American Indian and the Origins of Comparative Ethnology.* Cambridge University Press

[3] www.doctrineofdiscovery.org.

1987. 'Dispossessing the Barbarian: The Language of Spanish Thomism and the Debate over the Property Rights of the American Indians', In A. Pagden (ed.), *The Languages of Political Theory in Early Modern Europe*. Cambridge University Press, 79–99

Sepúlveda, J. G. de. 1951. *Demócrates Segundo o de las Justas causas de la Guerra contra los indios*, ed. A. Losada. Madrid: Consejo Superior de Investigaciones Cientifícas, Instituto Francisco de Vitoria

Veiteberg, A. 1994. *Erobring og menneskesyn: Ein idéhistorisk studie av Bartolomé de Las Casas og Juan Ginés de Sepúlveda og deira syn på indianarne i kjølvatnet av den spanske erobringa av Amerika*. Hovudfagsoppgåve i idéhistorie. Universitetet i Oslo

Vitoria, F. de. 1989. *Doctrina sobre los indios (Los Dominicos y America)*. Editorial San Esteban

Williams, R. A. 1990. *The American Indian in Western Legal Thought: The Discourses of Conquest*. Oxford University Press

8

Martin Luther's conception of human dignity

OSWALD BAYER*

Martin Luther's notion of human dignity is, in line with the entire Christian tradition, identical to the notion of humankind as the image of God (Gen. 1.26f). This at once determines the horizon within which Luther – critically – engages the corresponding notions of humankind as the image of God in scholasticism and mysticism, Renaissance philosophy and humanism (cf. Trinkaus 1970; Ebeling 1975: 320–4). With respect to his understanding of the idea of humankind as the image of God, Luther's most prominent document is the *Disputatio de homine* (1536), which discusses this understanding in light of the dispute between philosophy and theology (WA 39 I: 175–7).[1] As becomes clear from a glance at thesis 20, the very first thesis announces how fundamentally controversial the basic anthropological notion is: 'Philosophy, human wisdom, defines human beings as endowed with the gift of reason, with senses and with corporeality' (WA 39 I: 175.3f).[2] Following this classical determination of the human being as 'rational animal' or '*zoon logon echon*',[3] which stems from the Aristotelian tradition, theses 2–19 contain a critical engagement with philosophical anthropology. According to Luther, theology, on the ground of its universal claim to truth, cannot restrict itself to moving within a religious domain nor can it simply integrate and subject itself to philosophical standards. As such, then, it is the nature of theology as an academic discipline – as critical reference to other universal claims to truth – to engage in conflict and dispute.

Thesis 20, contrasting itself to this flawed philosophical understanding, states: 'Theology, on the contrary, defines, from the fullness of its wisdom, humans as whole and perfect.' Luther offers – and this is the point of his understanding of human dignity – a doctrine of humankind that is grounded in the theology of justification through and through, and is defined by the core statement (thesis 32): 'In Romans 3[:28], "For we maintain that a person is justified by faith apart from the works of the law", Paul briefly summarizes the definition of humankind

* Translated by Naomi van Steenbergen. References to Luther are to the page numbers in the Weimar edition of his collected works ('WA'). Details of English translations are given in the bibliography at the end of the chapter.

1 A magisterial commentary on this disputation is Ebeling 1982.

2 The original Latin has been translated throughout this chapter.

3 Aristotle, *Politics* I 2, 1253a 1–3; a 9f.

in the statement that humankind is justified by faith (*hominem iustificari fide*).' This means that humankind – any human without exception – is, without any merit or any worth that he could grant himself or expect from other humans as recognition, unconditionally and absolutely recognized and valued by his creator, redeemer and perfecter. This means that he has an inviolable and indestructible dignity. Since this dignity is not conferred on him by any human person, no human being can deny it to him.

This definition of human beings and their dignity, grounded in the theology of justification presupposes and implies that humans cannot be spoken of only in an abstract and isolated manner in terms of the theology of creation, but must be considered in three irreducible respects. Humans are first of all creatures; second, they are those who have corrupted their creation and have – of their own accord, yet not in the eyes of God! – invalidated and lost their dignity altogether (Romans 3:23);[4] and, third, they are those who have been redeemed by Jesus Christ from the corruption of their creation. Theses 21–23, which in the Latin original form one single sentence, correspond to these three aspects, expressing their threefold trinity: 'The human is God's creation, consisting of flesh and living soul, from the outset made in God's image without sin, destined to rear offspring and rule over the created things and never to die.' This creature 'has, however, after Adam's fall, become subject to the power of the devil, subject to sin and death – both evils that cannot be conquered by his power, and that are eternal'. This creature 'can only be saved and gifted eternal life by the Son of God, Jesus Christ (insofar as he or she believes in Him)'.

The same state of affairs is emphasized in Luther's understanding of human dignity, under the heading of 'freedom', in two other prominent documents: the treatise 'On the Freedom of a Christian' (1520) and in its companion piece and complement 'On the Unfreedom of the Will' (1525), the great polemic pamphlet against Erasmus and his conception of human dignity. Both writings can be very briefly summarized in the following way: Luther's eminent interest in human freedom is a general anthropological interest insofar as what is at stake applies to the constitution and dignity of every human being. As such, it is, however, a deeply soteriological interest: it addresses salvation and doom, the gaining or loss of life. The human being is perceived as a sinner: as a creature that controverted its original freedom by abusing it and therefore – of his accord – forfeited and lost his likeness to God (Romans 3:23). In this radical sense his will is unfree, a *servum arbitrium*. He regains and receives his freedom only through Jesus Christ, who grants and conveys it to him in a new creation; it is the new, definitive freedom 'that Christ has secured for him and given him', that is, nothing but Christian freedom (WA 7: 20.26f; cf. 29.13–18).[5] For this reason, the freedom of humans is concretely the freedom of a Christian. He who is not

[4] On this matter, see Johannes von Lüpke's (2010) exceedingly rich and astute 'Ebenbild im Widerspruch'.

[5] 'Von der Freiheit eines Christenmenschen' (On the Freedom of a Christian/On Christian Freedom), 1520.

a Christian is, with respect to the will in the roots of his existence, unfree. He lives in contradiction to his destination, yet still, in the eyes of God, has not lost his likeness to God and his dignity as creature, and is recognized by the Law and the Gospel. In the domain of secular justice, the *iustitia civilis*, even the sinner can serve the law if he uses his reason – which in this domain is not a 'whore' (cf. Bayer 2008: 160, n. 17) but 'almost something divine' (WA 39 I: 175.9f)[6] – 'as if no God existed' (WA 15: 373.3).[7]

According to the central thesis 32 of the *Disputatio de homine*, what makes humans human is the fact that they require justification of their existence through faith – this need is their dignity. The dignity of humans, their being, is their fundamental dependence on life and on what is necessary for life being bestowed anew in every second 'against all danger' (Bekenntnisschriften der evangelisch-lutherischen Kirche 1998 511.1f)[8] – something they cannot maintain even for a moment in and for themselves. The ontological depth and breadth of being justified through faith, then, is: living an existence that is not deserved, but merely owed. Luther summarizes this central point of the theology of creation and its anthropology in his explanation of the first article of the creed in a way that explicitly refers to the theology of justification: 'I believe that God created me together with all creatures . . . without any merit or any dignity in me' (Bekenntnisschriften der evangelisch-lutherischen Kirche 1998 510.33–511.5). He has, as it were, created me into a dignity without dignity. Anyone who acknowledges this expresses for himself and on behalf of the entirety of creation that all creatures owe their existence to causeless benevolence and mercy, entirely undeserved: *ex nihilo*, from nothing and nothing again – without any dignity in and of themselves. The dignity of human beings and their environment is not intrinsic, but – as unconditionally and absolutely bestowed and maintained – extrinsic. It is not a quality that inheres in humans and their world, but a relational notion: it exists only by virtue of and with respect to their creator, redeemer and perfecter. The dignity of human beings is conferred and guaranteed only by the triune God.

While, for Luther, human beings have their dignity first and foremost *amongst* their fellow creatures,[9] Luther makes very clear that humans also *differ from* them, by virtue of their gift of language and reason, through which they are 'most distinguished from other animals' (WA DB 10/I: 101, 14f).[10] This has its basis in the duty of stewardship (Genesis 1.26–8) with which humankind as the image of God is intrinsically connected. Luther cannot praise this gift of

[6] Ratio as 'divinum quiddam'. Cf. LW 34: 37 (thesis 4).

[7] Exposition of Psalm 127, for the Christians at Riga in Livonia, 1524.

[8] *Small Catechism*, explanation of the first article of the creed.

[9] This observation would have to be the starting-point of an explanation of the way in which non-human creatures have dignity as well. In any case, it is impossible for a theology of creation such as Luther's to simply affirm the Kantian privileging of humans, and view, for instance, animals as 'things' without dignity. Cf. Bayer 2007: 44–56: 'Human Life in the Midst of Life that Loves Living', 55f.

[10] Second Preface to the Psalter, 1528.

language and reason granted to humankind highly enough. Despite sin, reason functions as the 'inventor and guide of all [liberal] arts, of medical science, jurisprudence and all that humans in this life have in terms of wisdom, power, competence and glory' (WA 39 I: 175, 11–13).[11] For 'even after Adam's fall, God did not take away, but rather affirmed this majesty', the duty of stewardship (*ibid.*: 20f).[12] In the secular realm, the reason gifted to and expected of humankind is 'a sun and a sort of divine power, given in this life to govern all of these things [medical science, jurisprudence, etc.]' (*ibid.*: 18f).[13] Here, reason is the 'inventor', indeed the 'guide' (*ibid.*: 11),[14] ruler, queen – much as the rational human being who rules over the world remains a needy and receiving child *vis-à-vis* his creator: child and king in a personal union (Psalm 8). The human autonomy is grounded in the interweaving of fundamental passivity and subsequent activity, being loved and recognized from the outset. Within the boundaries of mere *iustitia civilis*, reason is aware not only of its limits, but also of its regal power and, not in the last place, of its ability to be a danger to itself. Relying like children upon their creator, redeemer and perfecter, humans are liberated from absolutisms, and thus enabled to have a sober sense of what is possible and necessary within this world and within history.

In this domain of the *iustitia civilis*, humans have – in contrast to the domain of *iustitia dei* – a free will, a *liberum arbitrium*: the freedom to choose, decide and act, to which the Augsburg Confession devotes an entire article (Article 18): 'On the free will'. 'The free will is taught in such a way that humans do in a certain respect have a free will in order to live a life that is outwardly respectable and to choose amongst the things that are understood by reason' (Bekenntnisschriften der evangelisch-lutherischen Kirche 1998 73.1–5) – amongst the things that are 'subordinate' to it:[15] the organization of relationships in marriage, family, economy, education and culture, law and state.

Luther's distinction between *iustitia dei* and *iustitia civilis*, as well as the distinction between *servum arbitrium* in relation to God and *liberum arbitrium* in relation to the secular affairs, corresponds to the distinction between God's spiritual and secular rule gained from his transformation of Augustine's doctrine of the two *civitates*. Luther's standpoint is classically expressed in the 1523 treatise 'On Secular Authority, How Far the Obedience Owed to It Extends' (WA 11: 245–81).[16] This distinction characterizes Luther's conception of human dignity and points out its social-ethical significance, which cannot be overestimated. If the dignity of human beings depends only on and is conferred only by their creator, redeemer and perfecter, then it is detached from any human

[11] Disputatio de homine, thesis 5. [12] Thesis 9. [13] Thesis 8. [14] Thesis 5.

[15] *Ibid.*: 'De libero arbitrio [ecclesiae apud nos] docent, quod humana voluntas habeat aliquam libertatem ad efficiendam civilem iustitiam et deligendas res rationi subiectas.'

[16] Cf. LW 45: 81–129 ('Temporal Authority: To What Extent It Should Be Obeyed'). Cf. Bayer 2008: 313–18.

disposition – not in the last place from the mandate of secular authority. The task of the secular authority, the state, is therefore to respect and protect the undeserved dignity of humans that is apprehended by faith (or, which is the same, through the freedom of conscience). Nobody can be forced to believe, for faith is a free endorsement of the heart inspired by inner spirit. 'Since in this case', the second part of the treatise on authority reads, 'it is up to every individual's conscience how he believes or doesn't believe, and [since] this does not derogate secular power, [the secular authority] should be contented and attend to its [own] task and allow people to believe this or that, whatever they can and want to, and not pressure anyone with violence. For faith is a free work, to which nobody can be forced.'[17]

This in no way means though, that faith is a private affair, which it understandably became in modern times (cf. Bayer 2007: 138–55). Since it stems from the 'word that is flesh' (Bekenntnisschriften der evangelisch-lutherischen Kirche 1998 58: 12f),[18] the word – and thus faith – must have room and be protected in the public sphere established by the state. If the state, as happens in situations of totalitarianism, interferes with this sphere that is constituted by word and faith, with God's 'spiritual' regimen, it should be – passively – resisted. The competencies and powers of the state are clearly limited; for this reason, it should be asked and heeded 'to what extent' the state is owed obedience. For 'we must obey God rather than man' (Acta 5.29).[19] In this way, Luther's ingenious distinction between God's 'spiritual' and 'secular' regimens functioned as an antidote against later absolutism and against the totalitarian systems of the twentieth century[20] and became one of the roots of the modern basic right to freedom of religion and conscience.[21] The modern distinctions between both religion and politics and morality and right, cultural achievements whose value can hardly be over-estimated, are not conceivable without Luther's distinction between God's spiritual and secular rule and the corresponding limits on state power for the sake of religious freedom on the one hand and, on the other, limits on the powers of the church and clergy in the public sphere for the sake of

[17] 'Temporal Authority' (see note 16 above), WA 11, 264.16–20 (including context). That 'nobody can' (or ought to) 'be compelled to Christianity' was already argued by Augustine (*Epistolae*, libr. II, ep. XCIII). Unfortunately neither Augustine nor Luther was consistent in heeding this insight.

[18] Augsburg Confession, Art. V.

[19] Art. XVI (Bekenntnisschriften der evangelisch-lutherischen Kirche 1998 [70f], 70.23–26).

[20] A prominent example in which the element of authority critique of Luther's two regiments doctrine is drawn upon for legitimating resistance to a totalitarian regime is the Norwegian Church Conflict 1942. Cf. Bayer 2008: 312f.

[21] Against Georg Jellinek's (1895) thesis, which attributes freedom of religion directly and solely to the English reformation, see the convincing argument in Heckel 1987. Heckel shows that the current distinction between religion and politics is essentially derived from Luther.

a reasonable secularity in the realm of civil society and state action. In the fifth thesis of the Barmen Declaration (1934), this inheritance is expressed clearly: 'We reject the false doctrine that the state should or could, beyond its specific task, become the single and total order of human life and thus fulfil the task of the church as well. We reject the false doctrine that the church should or could, beyond its specific task, take up the manner, tasks and worth of the state and thus become an organ of the state itself' (Burgsmüller and Weth 1983: 38).

According to Luther, human dignity, which is identical with the nature of humans as the image and likeness of God, is warranted only by the triune God: the creator, redeemer and perfecter of humans and the world around them. The explicit recognition of this warranty cannot be presupposed in a pluralistic society and in a religiously neutral state. It can, however, anonymously, become a placeholder (one that can and must be interpreted) for the absoluteness and unconditionality expressed in Article 1, paragraph 1, of the German Constitution as the criterion for any positive right: 'The dignity of human beings is inviolable.' An indication of the hidden theological ground of this criterion may be found at the start of the Preamble to the German Constitution: 'Conscious of their responsibility before God . . . '.

References

Aristotle. [350 BCE]. *Politics*

Augustine. 1930. *Saint Augustine: Select Letters*, trans. J. H. Baxter. Cambridge, MA: Loeb Classic Library

2004. *The Works of Saint Augustine, a Translation for the 21st Century: Part 2 – Letters*, trans. B. Ramsey. Hyde Park, NY: New City Press

Bayer, O. 2007. *Freedom in Response: Lutheran Ethics: Sources and Controversies.* Oxford University Press

2008. *Martin Luther's Theology: A Contemporary Interpretation.* Grand Rapids, MI: Eerdmans

Bekenntnisschriften der evangelisch-lutherischen Kirche. 1998. Göttingen: Vandenhoeck & Ruprecht

Burgsmüller, A., and Weth, R. (eds.). 1983. *Die Barmer Theologische Erklärung: Einführung und Dokumentation.* Neukirchen: Neukirchener Verlag

Ebeling, G. 1975. 'Das Leben – Fragment und Vollendung: Luthers Auffassung vom Menschen im Verhältnis zu Scholastik und Renaissance', *Zeitschrift für Theologie und Kirche* 72: 310–36

1977, 1982, 1989. *Lutherstudien*, 3 vols. Tübingen: Mohr Siebeck

Heckel, M. 1987. 'Die Menschenrechte im Spiegel der reformatorischen Theologie', in *Gesamtausgabe*, vol. 2, ed. K. Schlaich. Tübingen: Mohr Siebeck, 1122–93

Jellinek, G. 1927. *Die Erklärung der Menschen- und Bürgerrechte: ein Beitrag zur modernen Verfassungsgeschichte.* Leipzig: Duncker & Humblot

1982. *The Declaration of the Rights of Man and of Citizens: A Contribution to Modern Constitutional History*, trans. M. Farrand. New York: H. Holt

Luther, M. 1883–1966. *Martin Luthers Werke, Kritische Gesamtausgabe*, 73 vols. Weimar: Verlag Hermann Böhlaus Nachfolger (WA)

1955–76. *Luther's Works*, ed. J. Pelikan and H. T. Lehmann. St Louis, MO: Concordia Publishing House

The Book of Concord: The Confessions of the Evangelical Lutheran Church. 2000. trans. and ed. by R. Kolb, T. J. Wengert and C. P. Arand. Minneapolis, MN: Fortress Press

Trinkaus, C. 1970. *In Our Image and Likeness: Humanity and Divinity in Italian Humanist Thought*, 2 vols. London: Constable

Von Lüpke, J. 2010. 'Ebenbild im Widerspruch: Menschenwürde und Menschenrechte im Spiegel der Erzählung vom Brudermord (Gen 4.1–16)', in *Der Mensch als Thema theologischer Anthropologie: Beiträge in interdisziplinärer Perspektive*, ed. J. van Oorschot und M. Iff. Neukirchen: Neukirchener Verlag, 114–45

9

Natural rights versus human dignity: two conflicting traditions

PAULINE C. WESTERMAN

'All human beings are born free and equal in dignity and rights.' In the famous first article of the Universal Declaration of Human Rights (UDHR), human dignity is mentioned in the same breath as human rights. But what exactly is the relationship between dignity and rights? Are we to endow human beings with dignity because human beings possess certain inalienable rights, or is it the other way round: are we to guarantee people their rights because of their inherent human dignity; an indefinable quality that is proper to human beings alone and by which they are elevated above other natural beings? The relation between the two remains close but obscure. Furthermore, and more importantly: what exactly are we asked to *do*? It seems that the reader is only presented with a certain state of affairs. Human dignity is presupposed to 'exist', and all we have to do is to 'understand', to 'acknowledge' and to 'recognize' it. But, if so, we may ask, with Dylan: where do we find it? Isn't it true that we can only hope to find dignity as a *result* of the way we treat people? Why are we admonished to *begin* with dignity as a starting-point? Why aren't we simply told that human dignity is a desirable result; an aim to strive for? Aren't we running in circles by pretending that something is there which should still be realized?

In order to shed some light on these perplexities, it is instructive to take a look at the developments that took place in seventeenth-century natural law theories, which contributed to the vocabulary and style of the UDHR. First, I will briefly sketch the stage on which seventeenth-century natural law thinkers had to play. Then, I will analyze the role of the notion of human nature in the theories of Hugo Grotius and John Locke and its relation to the formulation of natural rights. It will be shown that the formulation of those rights is in no way dependent on the assumption of human dignity. Matters are, however, different for Samuel Pufendorf. In his theory, the notion of human dignity is central. As will be shown, this dignity is God-given and consists in the capacity to understand God's will. But nature does not play a decisive and informative role here and a theory of natural rights is not developed. The conclusion can be drawn that in the seventeenth century the concepts of 'dignity' and of 'rights' seem to point in opposing directions.

The stage

In order to appreciate the theoretical innovations that were carried out by seventeenth-century natural lawyers, it is important to know a bit more about the key assumptions shared by earlier natural law thinkers and the problems they faced. What did the stage look like when Grotius and Pufendorf entered the debate?

It is important to realize that underlying a host of differences and disagreements of the various thinkers who set out to develop a natural law theory, there is a set of assumptions shared by all. The first of these concerns the aim of such a theory: natural law theory sets out to develop criteria for the moral evaluation of law and society. Natural law is not meant as a tool for the explanation of social institutions, but as a means to justify or to criticize existing arrangements. It is further assumed that these criteria can be found in nature. Thinkers may disagree about how nature should be understood and conceptualized, but they all share the view that nature is the hard and solid foundation on which our normative judgments rest. And, finally, all thinkers within the natural law tradition are committed to the view that it is possible for human beings to discover those principles by the use of reason. We have access to the fundamental moral distinctions, that distinguish good from bad society and that tell the difference between just and unjust law.

It is obvious that not just every concept of nature lends itself easily to the aims of natural law theory. Nature should be thought of as something that is a worthy moral foundation; as a model to be copied or imitated, or at least as a harmonious order. However, no one with eyes to see can fail to notice that treason, bloodshed and murder are frequent natural phenomena, far removed from a practice that we might want to copy in human society. So the problem all natural lawyers have to cope with is: how can we represent or conceptualize nature in such a way that it can be used as a starting-point for the derivation of fundamental moral principles?

A well-known solution to this problem is to focus on nature not as it is in actuality, but as an order which is dynamic and which perpetually strives to realize ends. Aquinas' famous teleological version of natural law theory starts from the inclinations of plants to preserve themselves, the inclinations of animals to procreate, and the inclinations of human beings to live sociably together and to gain knowledge about God. (Aquinas 1964: I, II, 94, 2). Empirical observations of people destroying rather than building social life can then always be countered by saying that these people act against their true natural inclinations. What counts as 'nature' does not consist in ignoble actions but in noble ends. Nature is like a cathedral, designed by the divine Architect, in which every element has to fulfil a definite function.

For a number of reasons that I have analyzed elsewhere (cf. Westerman 1998: Chapter III), this teleological framework was gradually undermined. From the sixteenth century onwards, maybe even earlier, the concept of nature changed.

It was no longer seen as something that was eternally striving towards the realization of ends, but as something that simply and statically *is*. God was no longer conceived of as the Architect who, by the very building that he had designed, could be assumed to have indicated the functions of its elements. God was increasingly seen as Lawgiver who had to make explicit the do's and don'ts that he had in mind for His creatures. Created nature had to be coupled with explicit legislation in order to inform us about the principles and criteria we should cherish.

The combination of creation and legislation generated two problems, that were both hard to tackle. The first seems to endanger the enterprise of natural law as such. For if nature needs to be supplemented by an explicit command, why then should we look into nature at all? If God's legislation is needed anyway, it seems more efficient to turn to God's word directly than by investigating God's creation.

This question is accompanied by a second one, which refers to the relation between creation and legislation. How does God's explicit command relate to nature? Is nature created as a result of God's will? Or is there an indwelling rational order to be found in nature, which is binding on even God Himself? Is something good because He had willed it, or is something commanded because it is inherently good? The former solution risks to render natural law theory superfluous; whereas the latter option risks to turn God into a superfluous entity. The problem was fiercely debated by 'voluntarists' and 'intellectualists' and was never resolved.

A new starting-point

This was the sorry state natural law theory was in when people like Grotius, Locke and Pufendorf turned to natural law theory in order to find an answer to the questions that were put on the agenda by the increasing centralization of power in the young Western European nation-states of the seventeenth century: what is the scope and aim of governmental power? How can it be justified? And how to draw its boundaries?

That these thinkers turned to natural law theory is no small wonder and can only be accounted for by the strong appeal of natural law to provide for a truly universal conceptual framework. Natural law theory promised to overcome the pitfalls of theories, such as the *droit divin* in its many forms, which leaned too heavily on religious assumptions to be acceptable to the many religious denominations that had emerged in the previous era.

But, and this is important to realize, natural law could only live up to its universalist claims if it did not degenerate into endless disputes concerning God's free will, and the relation between God and nature. I think that this is at least one of the reasons why these thinkers emphasized the centrality of human nature as the basis of natural law. In seventeenth-century natural law theory, not nature as a whole, but specifically *human nature* is the basis and the foundation of our moral principles and distinctions. As Grotius writes in his *De jure belli ac pacis*: 'The very nature of man, which even if we had no lack of anything would lead us into the mutual relations of society, is the mother of the law of nature' (Grotius 1952: prol. 16). Of course, even with human nature as a starting-point, it is still possible to fight over the traditional question whether God was free to create human nature as he saw fit, or whether he was bound by some higher rule of reason. But it does not really *matter* anymore. This debate was not resolved but simply made irrelevant. That is why Grotius was able to write: 'God was free not to create man. But man having been created, that is, a nature using reason and being eminently sociable, he necessarily approves of actions in harmony with such a nature and disapproves of the opposite' (quoted in Besselink 1988: 38).

And it is echoed by Locke, who twenty years later wrote in his *Essays on the Law of Nature*:

> It seems to me that certain essential features of things are immutable, and that certain duties arise out of necessity and cannot be other than they are. And this is not because nature or God (as I should say more correctly) could not have created man differently. Rather, the cause is that, since man has been made such as he is, equipped with reason and his other faculties and destined for this mode of life, there necessarily result from his inborn constitution some definite duties for him, which cannot be other than they are. (Locke 1954: 199)

In order to change natural law, God should change human nature first. Since nobody would deny the possibility that God can change human nature as He sees fit, His freedom is not endangered. But this freedom does not turn natural law into an arbitrary affair, inaccessible to the human intellect. If He changes human nature, we human beings are the first to know and we would still have access to the principles that are derived from it. By turning human nature as a starting-point, it seems that uncontested ground has been reached on which universal and timeless principles could be erected.

A bodiless figure

The emphasis on human nature may be applauded as a welcome break from the traditional debates concerning the relation between creation and legislation, but it did not solve the other problem with which seventeenth-century natural lawyers had to cope: the problem that nature had to be considered as worthwhile of copying. If man naturally 'approves of actions in harmony with this nature', and if we would like to treat this natural approval as the foundation of our moral distinctions, we should indeed conceive of human nature as something inherently good and dignified and we should *not* regard man as immoral, depraved, weak and selfish. Yet, this is exactly how human nature is conceived of in Protestant circles. And Grotius, more than anyone else, was aware of the evil side of human nature.

The solution that is proposed by Grotius is to abstract from reality. In order to serve as a reliable standard, human nature should be presented in an idealized form. 'Essential' traits in human nature should be distinguished from 'accidental' or 'inessential' characteristics. Now, as we have seen, this solution was in fact also adopted by Aquinas, who also differentiated between 'true' nature and mere observable characteristics. But in Aquinas' case 'true' nature consisted in the ends that are pursued. This option was not open to Grotius. To seventeenth-century writers, nature, as well as human nature, is immutable and unchangeable.

So rather than focusing on ends, Grotius regards human nature as consisting of a set of eternal and immutable character traits. According to Grotius, human nature is self-interested, sociable, reasonable and capable of speech. No further arguments are adduced, for they are taken to be self-evident. The traits of human nature are compared to the properties of a 'figure abstracted from a body' (d'Entrèves 1971: 56). Human nature serves as a self-evident starting-point from which several principles of natural law can be deduced. We see this view echoed in the works of Locke and countless more minor figures who assert that from human nature alone certain immutable principles can be deduced, in the same way that from the existence of a triangle alone the indubitable proposition can be deduced that its three angles are equal to two right angles. Such statements, although they are inspired by the ambition to create a science of morals with the same degree of certainty as that of mathematics, never led to full-scale deductions. But they do indicate the need for a concept of human nature that could adequately perform its function as the sole foundation of natural law. For indeed, a triangle is a triangle if and only if its three angles can be equated to two right angles. In a similar vein, man is human if and only if he is self-interested, social and rational.

However, a closer analysis of these character traits reveals that self-interest is dominant in the writings of Grotius and Locke. For why does man seek society? Because he is so weak that he cannot preserve himself without society. What does his rationality amount to? Reason tells him to seek his long term (self-)interest rather than immediate satisfaction. All characteristics can eventually be traced back to self-preservation alone. This is, however, not openly conceded. Time and again, Grotius scorns the scepticists for having maintained that man is only driven by considerations of expediency. Expediency is starkly contrasted with the immutable dictates of natural law, which are derived from man's essential and dignified nature.[1] References to dignity merely serve here to mask the conception of man as essentially self-interested, a feature that does *not* set

[1] Cf. Grotius 1952: Prol. 5–6. In his earlier *De jure praedae*, however, Grotius is even closer to the scepticist position.

man apart from the rest of nature, but which inevitably turns him into a natural being, part of the natural world.

Natural rights

Which are then the four natural principles that Grotius derives from man's essential nature? These tell us (a) to abstain from that which is another's, (b) to restore to another anything of his which we may have, (c) to make good a loss incurred through our fault, to inflict penalties upon men according to their desert (Grotius 1952: prol. 8) and (d) to fulfil promises. We may regard the first three laws as principles of what is commonly called 'restorative justice'. Restorative justice consists of redressing the balance: the compensation for losses aims at the *restoration* of the original situation that was disturbed. Restorative justice does not answer the question whether the original situation was a just one but consists in undoing what was done.

The principles (a), (b) and (c) are therefore dependent on an existing framework of social institutions. They can only be put into operation once private property is instituted. Whether that institution itself is justified is not a question that is addressed by these principles of natural law. They do not tell us whether private property is a justifiable human institution; they do not even tell us anything on how property should be distributed. They only tell us how to proceed in a society where property is instituted and organized.

The main question, therefore, that is left unanswered by these natural laws is: do we think that a society should introduce private property? To Grotius, *that* question was entirely left to the consent of mankind. It is here that the last precept about the promises comes into play (Grotius 1952: prol. 15–16). And, in Grotius' theory, these promises may have drastic consequences. He who once consented to enslave himself, is bound by that consent (Grotius 1964: I, III, VIII, 1). Whether that consent itself was a reasonable one is no longer informed by a substantial account of natural law.

Matters are different in Locke's account of natural law. Like Grotius, Locke conceived of human nature as a bodiless figure: man is only man if he preserves himself in a rational way; i.e. if he is guided by long-term self-interest. But then he went on to develop his famous theory of property, in order to justify the institution of private property itself. Man, as the master of his own life and limbs, had to be the master of all that which was acquired by means of this life and limbs (Locke 1970). This was exactly the link in the chain that had been missing in Grotius' account. It gave at least a reason why people *should* consent to a certain kind of society (and at the same time a reason for no longer being bound by that consent). The legal formulas (a) to (c) were no longer dependent on an existing framework of human institutions. They could be – and were – turned into full-blown natural rights now they were erected on the overarching assumption that man has a right to property.

Depraved but dignified

Both Locke and Grotius took as their starting-point man's essential character-trait: enlightened self-preservation. That implied that man was not conceived as essentially elevated above the rest of nature. The only difference with animals is that man's inclination to self-preservation is enlightened, i.e. capable of the perception of *long-term* interest.

In order to find references to dignity in seventeenth-century natural law theory, we now turn to Samuel Pufendorf. Pufendorf is usually regarded as Grotius' successor, but he clearly and openly deviates from his famous predecessor on his view of human nature.

In the first place, Pufendorf did not conceive of man's self-interest as enlightened and rational. To Pufendorf, mankind is even more wicked than animals: 'A craving for luxuries, ambition, honours, and the desire to surpass others, envy, jealousy, rivalries of wit, superstition, anxiety about the future, curiosity, all these continually trouble his mind, none of which touch the senses of the brutes' (Pufendorf 1934: 6).

In the second place, Pufendorf could not see uniformity in human nature. He lacked the belief that 'underneath' appearances some 'essential' characteristics could be found. Man's desires were manifold and unbounded: Men are not all moved by one simple uniform desire, but by a multiplicity of desires variously combined' (Pufendorf 1991: 35). And, finally, Pufendorf is impressed by the diversity of cultures. He devotes many pages to the variety of customs that can be found all over the world: 'The Persians married their mothers, and the Egyptians their sisters' (Pufendorf 1934: 8). So where Grotius exerted himself in proving that 'beneath' or 'beyond' this multitude of customs and ways of life there is a universal hard core to be found in the essential nature of man, Pufendorf seems to abandon this search for uniformity. If there is something 'universal' to be found, it is that human nature is universally passion-ridden, variable, diverse and multi-faceted.

But this view implies that human nature by itself cannot be the foundation of natural laws or natural rights. The diversity of passions and desires points to the necessity of an external ordering principle. In this view, natural law does not *agree* with man's nature, but it should *constrain* and *counterweigh* man's nature. This is the background of the metaphor in which Pufendorf sketches the human condition:

> Now the more voices there are, the more dreadful and unpleasant the sound in the ear, unless they unite in harmony. In the same way the greatest confusion would have prevailed among men, were not their dissimilarity of customs and appetites reduced to a seemly order through laws. And yet this variety in another way yields man a remarkable grace and reward, since out of it, if properly guided, *a marvellous orderliness and beauty may arise, which could not possibly have come from complete uniformity.* (Pufendorf 1934: 7, emphasis added)

True harmony is polyphony; it arises out of differences and contrasts, not uniformity. Clearly, Pufendorf did not regard harmony as the outcome of an organic development. It should be 'properly guided'. Harmony does not grow naturally and of itself; it should be brought about by an external ordering principle. This ordering principle cannot be positive law, for positive law is nothing but codified custom. It is therefore the law of God which should order our passions.

In view of Pufendorf's realism and pessimism, one might expect him to be even further removed from the image of human dignity than Locke and Grotius were. Strangely enough, that is not the case. Although Pufendorf views man as more wicked than other animals, he at the same time emphasizes that man has been endowed by God with noble faculties, such as an immortal soul and dignity, by which mankind is elevated above the beasts.

The dignity of man's nature, and that excellence of his in which he surpasses other creatures, required that his actions should be made to conform to a definite rule, without which there can be no recognition of order, seemliness, or beauty. And so man has that supreme dignity, the possession of an immortal soul, furnished with the light of intellect and the faculty of judgment and choice and most highly endowed for many an art (Pufendorf 1934: 5). These noble faculties should be developed, since God gave them 'not for nothing' (*ibid.*).

At first glance, Pufendorf seems to contradict himself. How can man's nature be understood as corrupted and as noble and dignified simultaneously? I think we should keep in mind here what I noted above: Pufendorf's natural law is not derived from nature, but is meant to counterweigh nature. In itself, nature is uninformative. It is impossible to find harmony in nature. It is only by means of God's intervention, as a conductor, that harmony can arise. But His instructions do not flow from nature. They flow from His free will alone. In other words, morality is not a natural phenomenon, but is imposed or superadded by God. It is clear, therefore, that the kind of dignity Pufendorf has in mind is not linked to self-preservation. Rationality is not reduced to the capacity to know what is in one's best – long-term – interest as it is in Grotius' and Locke's theory. For Pufendorf, rationality is the capacity to God's law and we discern good from evil. Nature in itself is no more than an aggregate of shrill voices, untempered by any ordering principle. Order, beauty and harmony can only be brought about by a divine conductor. But only man can understand His instructions. And that is the core of man's dignity.

Conclusion

The juxtaposition of human dignity and rights that can be found in the UDHR seems to be inspired by two different, even mutually exclusive, kinds of theories. According to the theory held by Grotius and Locke, man is endowed with rights which directly flow from his unchanging nature. Here, man only distinguishes himself from other animals by the fact that he is better able to see how to ensure self-preservation: reason tells him to live in society and to prefer long-term interest over short term satisfaction. Man is bearer of natural rights but he is not a very dignified creature. Exactly the opposite is maintained by Pufendorf. In his theory, man's only salvation lies in making use of his Reason (with a capital R) to understand God's will and God's law. The dignity of man's nature lies in his capacity to follow God's law. Here, human dignity is central, but man is denied as having certain natural rights. According to Pufendorf, rights and (more importantly) duties can only flow from a prior law issued by a divine legislator (*ibid.*: 6). A divine law that can be called 'natural', not because it is deduced from human nature, but because we can understand its contents by our natural rational judgment.

It seems, then, that, at least in the seventeenth century, dignity and natural rights point in different directions. If we start from natural rights, we don't find dignity. Since rights flow directly from enlightened self-interest, dignity is a superfluous notion. But if we start from dignity, we don't find natural rights. All we can find then are rights and duties that flow from an external law issued by God.

References

Aquinas, T. 1964. *Summa Theologiae*, ed. T. Gilby *et al.* London: Blackfriars

Besselink, L. 1988. 'The Impious Hypothesis Revisited', *Grotiana* 9: 3–63

d'Entrèves, A. P. 1971. *Natural Law: An Introduction to Legal Philosophy*. London: Transaction

Grotius, H. 1952. *De Jure Belli ac Pacis Prolegomena*, trans. A. Dirkzwager and A. C. Nielsen. 's Gravenhage: Nijhoff

1964. *De Jure Belli ac Pacis Libri Tres*, trans. F. W. Kelsey. New York: Oceana

Locke, J. 1954. *Essays on the Law of Nature*, ed. W. von Leyden. Oxford University Press

1970. *The Second Treatise of Government: An Essay Concerning the True Original Extent and End of Civil Government*, ed. P. Laslett. Cambridge University Press

Pufendorf, S. 1934. *De Jure Naturae et Gentium Libri Octo*, in *The Classics of International Law*, trans. C. H. and W. A. Oldfather. Oxford: Clarendon Press

1991. *On the Duty of Man and Citizen According to Natural Law*, ed. J. Tully, trans. M. Silverthorne. Cambridge University Press

Westerman, P. 1998. *The Disintegration of Natural Law Theory: Aquinas to Finnis*. Leiden: Brill

10

Rousseau and human dignity

THEO VERBEEK

Any discussion of Rousseau (1712–78) in connection with the notions of 'human dignity' and 'human rights' runs up against two problems. First of all, Rousseau rejects the idea that man would have an exalted place in nature – in fact, even primitive man is in a way disadvantaged as compared to other animals. The second problem is that Rousseau rejects the traditional notion of 'natural right' as an ideological ploy to protect the rich against the poor. These two problems are of course intimately connected, dignity, as conferred by reason and language, being since Grotius (1583–1645) the feature that serves as the basis of natural right. Nonetheless – and this is the real puzzle – the shadow of Rousseau hovers over any modern debate on human rights.

Man's natural condition

Many modern representatives of the natural right tradition make use of the idea of a state of nature, basically in two different ways. Either they postulate that in their 'natural state' men are driven by egoistic passions and engaged in a continual war of all against all, or they believe that by his very nature man is guided by the rule of reason and that he seeks a relation with his fellow men that corresponds to his specific dignity. In both cases, the creation of a civil society and a body politic would be a deliberate break with the past, which would be motivated either, as in Hobbes (1588–1679), by man's natural inclination to preserve his own being; or, as in Grotius and Locke (1632–1704), by the wish to protect and consolidate values of which man is naturally aware. Although therefore civil society is an artifact and in many respects constitutes a break with 'nature' it is in a way also 'natural', either because it embodies values inherent in human nature (the rule of reason), or because it is the prolongation, albeit with different means, of individual action; the enactment of a natural obligation or the best way to protect our own interests. In either case, we would sacrifice some of our 'natural' freedom but have something better in return, like safety, prosperity and culture.

Rousseau also makes use of the notion of a natural state. Although the state of nature as interpreted by him has some things in common with the state of nature as we know it from Hobbes, Grotius and Locke, it is also fundamentally different. Like Hobbes, Rousseau believes that primitive man is not by nature a social being; but unlike Hobbes he believes that there is no confrontation with other men either: man as he is produced by nature lives a solitary life – even the family is not a natural phenomenon, except for the protection of the very young. Accordingly, there is no war of all against all if only for the trivial reason that primitive man does not come across other human beings. Moreover, given the fact that ideally there is enough of everything, if he would meet other human beings, these would not primarily be rivals – the only reason why they could be of interest is as candidates to fulfil his sexual desires, which for that matter are neither as violent nor as permanent as in cultured man. Finally, natural man is compassionate and has feelings of pity with other sensitive beings (not just humans), so would not voluntarily engage in a war of all against all. Rousseau's most fundamental objection to all pictures of the state of nature, however, is that they present primitive man as if he would be modern man living under different conditions. Neither Hobbes nor Locke and Grotius would have understood that society – in fact, any form of social life – fundamentally changes the nature of man; that cultured man is different from primitive man, not just in degree but in kind. More particularly, primitive man would not have the use of reason and language; he would have no sense of good and evil; and he would in all respects be self-supportive. Accordingly, primitive man would have none of the qualities authors like Hobbes, Grotius and Locke see as inherently human.

Of course, this view of man's natural state also reflects on Rousseau's view of society. Whereas according to Hobbes even in the state of nature man constantly anticipates the desires and reactions of other men and plans his future in terms of those anticipations, Rousseau's primitive man lacks the power of reason and abstract thinking; he hardly anticipates the future, has no knowledge of the laws of nature, and never comes across situations in which the laws of nature could be applied had he known them. Accordingly, the civil society cannot be the result of a mental process in which the advantages and disadvantages of the present state are calculated and weighed against those of an imagined future; nor can it be seen as the fulfilment of a natural need or the enactment of a natural obligation. According to Rousseau, primitive life is essentially undynamic – given the fact that primitive man lacks the occasion to compare his own predicament with that of others and lacks the imagination to compare it with other possible conditions his natural state could have continued indefinitely. Inversely, the undeniable fact that eventually primitive life was replaced by a different type of life can be explained only as an historical accident – the result of a natural disaster presumably, an inundation or a volcanic eruption, which forced men either to migrate to a different climate or to suffer the intrusion of others who fled their own habitat. Social life, however, brought with it new needs, new dangers, perhaps also a new scarcity, and in any case new faculties. The use of language and as a result the birth of imagination and reason affected human relations in a profound and irreversible way, not to mention the passions, which, according to Rousseau, are not natural (the only strictly natural desires being those of survival and reproduction) but are a product of culture, and which, especially under the influence of the imagination (and language), become a destructive force and a source of unhappiness.

It is clear that *primitive man* as pictured by Rousseau has normative rather than explanatory value: man as he is produced by nature is perfect *because* he has not all the needs and faculties which social life demands and which civilization encourages him to develop. The only thing the idea of natural man *explains* is the uneasiness some people (Rousseau himself in the first place) experience in society. Accordingly, 'natural man' is a static and eternal norm, or ideal, meant to show that man as we know him is in fact produced by an 'unnatural' condition; that the conditions under which he has been forced to live turned him into a different animal, as different from natural man as a cat and a dog from a lion and a wolf. Moreover, by putting up this norm as an ideal, Rousseau suggests that, if man could manage to retain, or retrieve, certain essential features of his original condition he would restore some of primitive man's original nobility or dignity – his present condition on the other hand would be more akin to that of a slave. What are those essential features?

Human dignity

As it developed in the West the notion of 'human dignity' was based on the idea that man has an exalted place in nature; that he has certain essential and unique properties, like reason and freedom, which differentiate him from the rest of nature; and that this difference brings with it certain rights and duties, which, given the fact that they follow from human nature, are 'natural'. In this view, man shares many properties with other animals without being himself just an animal – properties which, despite the fact that he is much better than animal, still allow him to behave like an animal. This is wrong and the fact that it is wrong is shown by feelings like shame and remorse. A man should neither behave like an animal nor be treated as an animal. His proper 'humanity' therefore and as a result his specific 'dignity' or 'excellence' would express themselves in his power to restrain what is properly animal in him, namely, the passions. As a result, 'dignity' would not be a static property; it would be something one can lose by behaving like an animal, but also something one deserves; it imposes duties but also confers rights. This ideal is eminently incorporated in the Stoic, or Neo-Platonic, or Christian Sage who after a long struggle, against the passions and against social conventions, acquires a state of perfection.

None of this could be the case according to Rousseau given the fact that what is said to be properly human (reason and language) is according to him the artificial product of an unnatural situation, whereas what would be properly animal (the passions) is in fact properly human (even though it is not part of human nature). Even so, Rousseau's primitive man has almost all the properties the Stoics ascribe to their Sage, more particularly, independence (autonomy) and imperturbability, except that primitive man does not have to acquire those properties in a struggle against the passions (which he has not), or against social conventions (which do not apply), but has them by his own nature. To that extent one could say that Rousseau's primitive man has a certain dignity; that he is the eminent instantiation of human nature. However, man has lost that condition and, according to Rousseau, there is no way to return to it no more than there is for a cat to return to the condition of the lion or the puma; even if there would be a place where 'natural' conditions still obtain (Africa, the American forests), we are too far removed from our own nature to be able to survive under those conditions. The challenge therefore is not to restore man's natural dignity but to retrieve as many as possible of the features defining man's original dignity under conditions which are not 'natural'.

Again, despite the fact that primitive man is physically fit (Rousseau tends to see illness and disease as consequences of civilization and even of medicine), he lacks reason and language, which accordingly cannot be what conferred dignity. However, even primitive man has some properties which differentiate him from other animals. Whereas these are guided by their natural instinct, man has no natural instinct but has the power to learn by imitating other animals – his disadvantage with respect to other animals is compensated by the possibility to perfect himself. Even so, that property is not the reason why Rousseau speaks of primitive man in glowing terms – indeed, according to him primitive man has no need to perfect himself. All one can say therefore is that perfectibility helped man to survive under conditions that, being not 'natural', were new for him. His real 'nobility', however, lies in the fact that he is independent; that he has no business with other people; that he does not need anything or anyone; that he can do whatever he wants to do without worrying about the reactions of others. In a word, his nobility consists in the fact that he completely is what he appears to be – that he is completely transparent. People living in society, however, are always characterized by a dissociation between what they appear to be and what they really are – a dissociation made possible by reason and language and made necessary, not only by the passions, which more often than not make it necessary to hide our true motives, but also by economic and social pressure. The introduction of property – the fact that, as Rousseau formulates it, at some point someone claims a piece of land as his own and that others are stupid enough to believe him – but also the emergence of specialized trades and competences – the blacksmith – create dependence and inequality, which in turn force us to hide our true selves and betray our true feelings, so much so that many people are not even aware of the misery of their own being. They like it and defend the civil society and the law – they find their advocates in the natural right theorists, whose role accordingly is purely ideological. In Rousseau's view, it is no coincidence that they all start with a theory of property.

Authenticity

Can the natural properties in virtue of which primitive man had a certain nobility and dignity be reproduced under unnatural conditions? In other words, can natural dignity be restored without returning to the original condition of mankind? Even more fundamentally perhaps, in what way can this notion of the original nobility of man serve as the basis for the deduction of a system of justice, given the fact that the traditional deduction is a fraud? Finally, can the progressive degradation of civilized man and the corresponding erosion of moral values be stopped? In sum, is the notion of primitive man simply a nostalgic ideal, which definitively belongs to the past, or can it provide moral and political guidance?

Again, according to Rousseau the evils of society and civilization are numerous. Apart from the fact that social ties are an emotional and psychological burden, there are basically two factors which make life in even a relatively primitive society morally problematic: (1) human relations lack sincerity – people are not what they appear to be; (2) human relations are characterized by mutual dependence – people depend on each other, not only for their material goods, but also insofar as they wish to be confirmed in their values and opinions. These two factors are intimately connected: dependence creates inequality; inequality creates duplicity; duplicity is made possible and is reinforced by the faculties developed in society (reason and language). In other words, dependence not only leads to a loss of dignity, but also creates a moral problem. But what if dependence cannot be avoided?

Rousseau does not have a single solution and in any case none of his suggested solutions are perfectly convincing. The first is education. The system proposed in *Emile* (1762) rests on the idea that education must help the child to discover, consolidate and fortify its own self. Indeed, given the fact that authenticity is no longer given, it must be learned and if learned fortified and protected. However, it can be learned only in complete isolation, out of reach for the harmful influences of society and civilization and under the guidance of a tutor who, unlike ordinary human beings, has managed to remain himself authentic. Another solution could be found in the personal strategies adopted by Rousseau himself and described in his autobiographical writings: one can avoid other people and withdraw in a 'wilderness' – usually a large house with a large garden. In fact, autobiography as such, provided it is done with humility, sincerity and integrity, can be a way of recovering authenticity. Apart from everything else, all these 'solutions' are primarily individual. They aim either at the preservation and consolidation of an original self or at a 'conversion' – it is no coincidence that the title given to Rousseau's main autobiographical book (the *Confessions*, published after Rousseau's death in 1782 and 1789) is that of the story of a conversion (Augustine's *Confessiones*). Although therefore they address authenticity as a psychological challenge, they ignore what seemed to make the loss of authenticity inevitable, namely, the various forms of dependence and inequality (economic, social, intellectual, emotional) created by society.

The solution described in the *Contrat social* (1762) on the other hand, which is primarily political, rests on the assumption that we can achieve authenticity by unconditionally and unreservedly identifying with a community. If our individual will were to be indistinguishable from the general will, whatever we do in conformity with the general will would by definition be an expression of our true and authentic self. Accordingly, Rousseau's *social contract* is not, as it is for Hobbes, a contract in the juridical sense of the word, that is, a voluntary agreement by which we promise to give up something (freedom) in exchange for something else (safety and prosperity) – if only because, according to Rousseau, freedom is not a commodity that can be exchanged. By entering it we do not create a new *Leviathan* in order to pursue our individual goals more successfully (that is the reason why the general will is not necessarily identical with the will of the majority), but we give ourselves new goals, which in turn will turn us into a new kind of human being. In fact, the *social contract* is best compared with the creation of a mystic body which allows us to transcend our own individuality and achieve a higher level of humanity.

Even Rousseau would probably admit that this is no more than an abstract theoretical model based on the perfectly abstract argument that, as soon as there is no longer any distinction between our will and the general will, 'obedience', that is, the subordination of an individual will to the will of another individual (or other individuals), becomes logically impossible. In its abstract form, moreover, the argument seems to amount to a sophism – as if to cease being a slave all the slave would have to do is to see the will of his master as his own will. However, it is not as simple as that. The general will is *general*, not only as to its *subject*, which is the collective body of men from which it emerges, but also as to its *object*. The object of the general will is by definition not limited to the interest of an individual or even of the majority of the individuals that compose a community but extends to the community as such; indeed, it is perfectly conceivable that the individual interests of all members of that community are sacrificed to the common good as it is willed by the general will. Accordingly, even though the general will can be interpreted by an individual for the rest of the community – as Robespierre (1758–94) would believe he did – it is never his own individual will that he speaks nor his own individual interest that he considers. Inversely, the various forms of dependence and inequality created by society are an objective evil only insofar as they entail an individual's obedience to the will of another individual or a group of individuals; they are eliminated by replacing that particular dependence and that particular obedience by a general will to which all willingly conform, not because they must or because it is in their interest, but because they understand that in doing so they achieve a higher form of humanity. As a result, it would be possible to retrieve our original nobility by a reform of society such that all forms of individual obedience are eliminated and replaced by a general will with which all can identify and in which all equally participate.

It seems then that dignity does not reside in a static attribute of mankind, in virtue of which man would be radically different from the rest of nature, but is an effect of man's relation with his fellow men. According to this view, an individual man *has* dignity in the state of nature only because it is only then that he is completely independent and completely autonomous. He loses that dignity as soon as he becomes social and has to adapt to other people. In fact, most people have no dignity at all, given the fact that, with a mind and a body deformed by society and civilization, they cannot even imagine that their lives lack authenticity. Individually or collectively, they can try and regain some of their original dignity but in this they depend, again, on the willingness of others to do the same. These two features constitute a radical departure from the traditional view of human dignity. Dignity is no longer a status in virtue of which an individual has rights and duties but something which to a large measure depends on others: it is through the mere presence of others that we lose it and it is only with others that we can regain it.

Again, Rousseau rejects the traditional foundation of natural right – the notions of right and justice have nothing to do with the natural condition of man but are at best, like reason and language, tools designed to cope with an essentially unnatural condition. It must be presumed that, as long as the society which produced them is not reformed in the sense of the *contrat social*, they must be a travesty of true justice. It is only against the backdrop of the social contract that it becomes possible to speak of rights and duties – indeed, these can be defined and respected only by the general will. And, although Rousseau frequently protests that the general will by definition operates in conformity with virtue and that, if it does not, it would cease to be a truly general will, the only rule he provides is that the object of the general will must be general, that is, that it must never be directed at the promotion of some particular or individual interest. This means that there is nothing by which an individual could *judge* the general will; on the contrary, by judging it and even by being willing to judge it, one dissociates from it and shows that, as yet, one has not attained a superior level of humanity. Accordingly, there is nothing above the general will; it is only through the general will that moral principles can be discovered. Nor is it clear what must guide the interpreter of the general will, that is, the government. Although it is unlikely that Rousseau would have approved the government of Robespierre, there is little in his system that prevents a Robespierre from proclaiming himself the interpreter of the general will as long as he finds a population which in his words and deeds recognize the expression of the general will.

The same problem returns on a more individual level. Even if it is granted that duplicity is wrong, it is not clear in what sense an authentic life is always *morally* better. The uninhibited *mafioso* may be more 'authentic' than the man who wants to kill his wife but is restrained by the law, but he is not necessarily 'better'. Moreover, we do have passions and feelings which may cause conflicts with the general will. Do we know at all what it means to be 'authentic'? Paradoxically, Rousseau himself seems to be aware of that problem. In *Julie ou la nouvelle Héloïse* (1761), he relates the sad story of Julie, who cannot marry the man she loves and by whom she is loved (Saint-Preux), and is forced to marry the nobleman to whom she was promised (Baron de Wolmar). Wolmar in turn marries her to save her from ignominy; he respects and honours her but he is not in love with her; he knows of her passion for Saint-Preux but is confident that eventually it will be over; and he even considers the possibility of engaging Saint-Preux as the governor of his children. Naturally, the situation creates unhappiness and distress in Julie as well as Saint-Preux. However, their moral suffering is in marked contrast with the equanimity and wisdom of Wolmar, who is not only a perfect husband but also the perfect manager of his estate. In all respects this is an ideal place, where even the servants are happy. Economically self-sufficient, it serves clearly as the model of an ideal commonwealth, in which all parties have only one goal, namely, the common good. This makes the story characteristically hard to interpret. Does it mean that it is wrong to sacrifice one's feelings to social conventions (which is where it all starts); or on the contrary that personal feelings should be sacrificed to the greater good of the community; or does it mean perhaps that the passion of love is wrong and unnatural and that Julie and Saint-Preux should have been wiser? Whose life is the more 'authentic' – that of Julie, of Wolmar, or of Saint-Preux? And to what extent is their authenticity conditioned by society? Is Wolmar, who never leaves his estate and seems to lack all curiosity for the world outside, more authentic than Saint-Preux, who travels more or less permanently in a restless bid to forget his love? Is Julie less authentic than her cousin Claire who, although she has nice feelings for Saint-Preux, refuses to marry him because she is not really in love or is she more authentic because, without forsaking her duties as a wife, she is true to her feelings of love? Or is the message simply that, given the 'unnaturalness' of our present condition, tragic conflicts like this are inevitable and that we will be freed from them only gradually and after the necessary reforms are in place?

Conclusion

The aim of Rousseau's political theory is neither to explain the working of government, nor to reconstruct the rights and duties of the citizens, but to solve an essentially anthropological problem, namely, that we can never entirely 'be ourselves'. The question is, not only whether that problem admits of a political solution, but also what exactly it would mean 'to be ourselves'. The injunction 'be yourself' is empty as long as one does not know what 'self' means – knowledge which is probably denied to people living under the perverted conditions of civilization. The only way Rousseau can demonstrate what he means is to imagine a man who has no real needs because he does not have the means to imagine what he is missing, and who is stripped of everything which, according to most people, would make him properly human: reason, language and the passions. Rousseau's real point therefore seems to be that those are not original features of mankind; that they are produced by an 'unnatural' condition; that the reason why people are miserable is that they have those faculties. Again, according to Rousseau dignity is not a status which could invariably be ascribed to mankind. Whether an individual has or does not have it depends on the kind of society he lives in. Accordingly, an individual is never entirely free to live in accordance with his original dignity. Indeed, there would be more reason to speak of an original indignity given the fact that we are born into a society which like most societies is still in want of reform. As long as that reform is wanting authenticity will be a rare virtue. As a result, the dream of authenticity is projected into a mythical and utopian future. These are innovative aspects of Rousseau's theory which ever since the end of the 18th century have been part of the discourse on human dignity and natural rights.

Moreover, although the version of it presented by Rousseau himself is pathological, the uneasiness he describes as being inherent to social life is familiar. It is the uneasiness caused by the fact that social, political and economic realities constantly demand compromises; that in many situations many people (including politicians) do not know what to do or to think; that most people have their life lived for them. Rousseau not only addresses those feelings but also suggests that there is a political solution; that by a reform of society people will finally be able 'to be themselves'. That, too, is a familiar feature of the modern discourse on natural rights and perhaps of modern political discourse generally. However, Rousseau describes that reform in a formal way only as a condition in which the individual wills that compose a specific body of men spontaneously merge into a general will, thus giving rise to a society which replaces dependence and inequality with 'authenticity'. What kind of structural reforms that entails cannot be said before the general will is in place and has found competent interpreters; nor is it clear in what way life after such a reform will be different from life now, except that it will be different. It was left to the political movements of the nineteenth and twentieth centuries to provide a more precise and, in most cases, a more sinister, meaning.

References

Jellinek, G. 1901. *The Declaration of the Rights of Men and Citizens: A Contribution to Modern Constitutional History*, trans. M. Farrand. New York: Holt (online edition, http://oll.libertyfund.org/index)

Rousseau, J. J. 1994. *Discourse on the Origin of Inequality*, trans. F. Philip. Oxford University Press

2004. *The Social Contract*, trans. M. Cranston. London: Penguin

Scott, J. T. (trans.). 2012. *The Major Political Writings of Jean-Jacques Rousseau*. Chicago University Press

11

Human dignity and socialism

GEORG LOHMANN*

Conceptual clarifications: general overview

The concepts of human dignity and socialism are both extremely indefinite and should here be understood in a broad sense. I will only briefly indicate how the concept 'human dignity' is here used (Lohmann 2013). Historically, social conceptions of a *particular* dignity and honour (for example, of a position, of a class, due to special achievements) can be differentiated from conceptions of *general* dignity accorded to all humans (for different reasons: for example ontological position in the cosmos, capacity to reason, creation in the image of god). Since the new beginning of international law after the Second World War, *universal* human dignity has been tied to the possession of human rights. Human dignity as a 'basis' of human rights is a morally grounded norm enacted as nationally and internationally applicable law through the shaping of political will. To respect, protect and guarantee these rights are in the first instance duties of the respective state, second of all states, and by means of a 'horizontal effect' of all humans as well. The content of 'human dignity' refers to the capabilities of humans for free, reflected self-determination, to their equal legal recognition and self-recognition and to the conditions of a minimum subsistence level which allow a *life worthy of human dignity* (in German, *menschenwürdiges Leben*).

'Socialism' is an equally encompassing concept applicable to different conceptions of society which aspire to a social organization of the economy, of ownership structures, of society and/or of the state in criticism of capitalism and its associated individualism. Historically, the concept first appears as a category of philosophy of law (*sozialismo*, A. Buonafede, 1798), following Hugo Grotius and Samuel Pufendorf, in order to establish natural law on the basis of sociability against catholic views (Schnieder 1984). In England, the concept has been used only since 1837 for the designation of Robert Owen's visions of society (Cole 1962). The development of socialist movements and corresponding conceptions range from early socialism (or, in Engels' terms, 'utopian socialism', 1789–1848) in France, Marx' scientific socialism and numerous variations (anarchistic socialism, state socialism, reform socialism, market socialism,

* Translated by Joana Rancine.

democratic socialism etc.), the creation of labour unions and socialist, communist or social democrat parties in Europe to the present (Schnieder 1984; Wildt 2008). The different conceptions of socialism have highly differing normative ideas and demands. Not all, but particularly those standing in the tradition of Marx may be regarded as a protest against violations of dignity and of life worthy of human dignity. In the following I shall reconstruct the implicit role of the concept of dignity in the justification and articulation of socialist notions. I shall argue that the idea of 'a life worthy of human dignity' served to justify demands for social rights, in the German history of the labour movement in particular.

Human dignity as (implicit) motive for the demands of the socialist labour movement

Socialist models of society spring from two sources: social utopias and natural law. Ernst Bloch formulated their peculiarities and relations in a concise manner: 'Social utopias predominantly are about happiness, at the least to elimination of destitution and circumstances that maintain and produce it. Theories of natural law . . . predominantly are about dignity, to human rights, to juridical guarantees of human security and freedom, to categories of humane pride' (Bloch 1961: 234). In the course of history of socialist ideas, both demands intertwine: 'There is no human dignity without end of destitution, but also no human happiness without end of old or new subservience' (*ibid.*: 237). These developments, however, occur mostly without the term of human dignity explicitly playing a role. At most, it fulfils a marginal role in formulating demands of the labour movement or in conceptually determining and justifying norms or policies from the viewpoint of theoretical reflection.

The starting-point of early socialism is the affirmation of the radical declarations of human rights of the French Revolution, in which individual liberty rights are rejected as inadequate or too abstract and must be supplemented by general political rights (universal passive and active suffrage) and social rights ('social liberty') in order to realize equality and overcome misery (Bödeker 2004). As we also find with the American and French declarations of human rights, the term 'human dignity' does not at first play an explicit role. However, it does seem as if historically and systematically many demands and ideas of the socialist movements may be understood as a battle for the recognition of equal dignity for all humans (Habermas 2010), now expanded to include the battle against destitution and misery, in particular of course of the labour force.

In these battles, three (mostly implicit) references to dignity can be distinguished. First, the concept of *dignity of social class* is important since the 'fourth estate' – the labour force – now demands the same legal and political status, the same civil rights, as the victorious 'third estate'. Second, Kant's moral philosophical concept of 'universal dignity' plays a role, in that circumstances are (negatively) criticized in which workers are made into a means and are denied free self-determination. Third, a life 'worthy of human dignity' (in German, *adjectively* '*menschenwürdiges Leben*') is demanded; enabling a life without hardship and destitution and without insult and debasement, for the worker as for all humans through the achievements of his labour. All three aspects are 'contained' ('*aufgehoben*' in a Hegelian meaning of the word) in the concept of human dignity after 1945; the third encompassing aspect however characterizes socialist conceptions until today in particular.

Marx: violations of human dignity and critique of human rights

Marx' relationship to morality and law was ambivalent, as is well known. His critical view on morality and law, which he increasingly understood only as instruments for the assertion of class interests, is explicit and dominant. Human rights also appear to him 'as nothing else than' an expression of the self-centred interests of the bourgeoisie: as 'antiquated, empty phrases'[1] that only affirm capitalist domination (Lohmann 1999). He also rejects as mere moralization the moral appeal to human dignity, for example in an overly harsh polemic against a rival in the socialist movement, Karl Heinzen (Marx 1959: 344f). But, in contrast to Marx' self-interpretation, his critique of capitalist conditions should be reconstructed normatively. And the normative standards of his critique, understood rightly, are to all intents and purposes moral categories such as freedom, equality, justice, autonomy, self-realization or indeed also human dignity (Peffer 1990: 119f). His critique may therefore be understood much more accurately as if he had seen it as a demand for the universal respect of human dignity and as a realization of human rights. In this critical reading of Marx, the concept of human dignity obtains an accentuating and encompassing role in his criticism of capitalism. This appears in three respects.

Degradation ('Entwürdigung') as an encompassing category of the critique of capitalism

In his revolutionary critique, the early Marx formulates as his 'categorical imperative': 'To overthrow all conditions in which man is a debased, enslaved, forsaken, contemptible being!' (Marx 1972: 385f). This can be read as a negativistic designation of the complex, moral, but also legal and political standards of the critique which could have been explicated positively by reframing it in terms of 'conditions of life worthy of "human dignity" and "human rights"'. For the Marxist critique is not simply directed against destitution, deprivation, exploitation and unjust disadvantaging of the working classes, against poverty, misery and lack of freedom forced upon them, but also against degradation (*Entwürdigung*); deprivation of rights and political disempowerment, which their material and intellectual situation as a working class forces on them. These

[1] www.marxists.org/archive/marx/works/1875/gotha/ch01.htm.

are, as the scathing polemic Marx formulates: 'conditions which can hardly be better described than by the exclamation of a Frenchman when it was proposed to introduce a tax on dogs: "Poor dogs! They want to treat you like humans!"' (Marx 1972: 385). This means, positively formulated, that the Marxist critique directs itself against conditions where humans are treated like animals (dogs), i.e. where they are deprived of rights and dignity (Margalit 1996; Schaber 2003).

Dignity, indirectly addressed through the criticism of *violations* of dignity, constitutes the *encompassing* normative standard of the Marxist critique of capitalism. Marx first criticizes immanently the self-legitimization according to natural law (principally going back to Locke); and, interwoven with this, second, the farther-reaching violations of more comprehensive normative values like 'social freedom' and justice. Marx only indirectly refers to these values by expounding, in the historic passages of the *Capital* book, the political, moral and legal contradicting argumentations of the workers against their appropriation and repression ('subsumption' is Marx' corresponding term) (Lohmann 1991: 39–80). Asking oneself if these aspects of Marx' critique can be subsumed under one concept, the concept of 'degradation' appears suitable. With this, the concept of dignity, addressed only negatively, remains in the background but allows the understanding of the individual aspects of Marx' critique as moments of a concept of dignity, which then also co-determines the development of socialist ideas as a background concept.

Kantian influence: dignity as an end in itself and degradation as instrumentalization

Central to this position is the extensive use Marx makes of Kant's moral prohibition of treating human beings as a *mere* means. This is, according to Kant, a violation of human dignity because his autonomy (which is the foundation for the imperative of treating human beings always also as an end in themselves) is not respected. In this the young Marx operates still very (and perhaps too) broadly with a general prohibition of instrumentalization, which at times does not observe the Kantian 'merely', and simply rejects human beings becoming a means (Von Magnis 1975: 173f).

Marx advances an even explicitly positive relationship towards dignity in an article against the death penalty. He rejects a deterrence theory of the penalty because with it the individual human is misused as a means, and with Kant and Hegel he advocates a retaliation theory: 'From the point of view of abstract right, there is only one theory of punishment which recognizes "human dignity", in the abstract, and that is the theory of Kant, especially in the more rigid formula given to it by Hegel' (Marx 1973: 507). Important for Marx' reference to Kant is that he retains the normative, equal recognition of the dignity of every human being, but that he at the same time criticizes the Kantian conception of every human being's equal dignity, which Kant grounds in the absolute value of the 'free will' as too abstract and one-sided. Marx therefore attempts, on the basis of a positive reference to Kant, to put in place of the 'abstraction of free will' – which he regards as 'one among the many qualities of man' – the entire human being, 'man himself', 'the individual with his real motives, with multifarious social circumstances pressing upon him' (*ibid.*: 508), i.e. with needs and social relationships. This expansion of the concept of dignity also marks the manner in which Marx makes use of the Kantian prohibition of instrumentalization in the *Capital.*

Marx does indeed heed the Kantian 'merely' in the *Capital*: the wage labourer makes himself into a means, reifies his life and labouring capacity in selling them as his labour power. He does not, however, thereby make himself entirely *merely* into a means for the ends of his labour power's buyer, of the capitalist; he simultaneously sustains himself as a free person and is recognized as a free legal entity on the labour market. Marx' stance on human rights is ambivalent: on the one hand, he only talks ironically and defamatorily of this 'very Eden of the innate rights of man' (Marx 1974: 172), but on the other hand he emphasizes the *epochal* significance of this recognition: with the basic (and abstract) recognition of the wage labourer's dignity, insofar as he is recognized as a legal entity, 'a world's history' (*ibid.*: 167) is made. Only on this basis is the class of free labourers formed, which, by asserting their 'right as sellers' (*ibid.*: 225) – for example in the 'determination of what is a working-day' (*ibid.*: 225) – make concrete what respect for their dignity comprehensively requires. One can therefore say in accordance with Marx not only that 'there enters into the determination of the value of the labour-power a historical and moral [*sic*!] element' (*ibid.*: 168), but also, now going beyond Marx, that this element enters into the determination of the respect of human dignity. Marx refers only negatively, via their violations, to these historic and moral elements of dignity. Increasingly, Marx invokes historical documents in which such violations of dignity are recorded (Lohmann 1991: 75f). These violations are, like the protest and battle against them, gradual, and in the historical documents an appropriate interpretation and demarcation of this 'merely as a means for alien ends' is disputed. The battle for an improved protection of dignity therefore unfolds as a historic battle over labourers' rights, for example in English Factory Acts extensively dealt with by Marx (Marx 1974: 264f). Wage labourers fight to no longer be treated merely as a means, i.e. as *arbitrarily replaceable* labour forces, but demand that the formal recognition of their legal status as free labourers is combined with social security *for every individual* which applies to all equally (hence the battle for free unions and against female and child labour).

Labour and life worthy of human dignity

The Kantian conception of dignity is based on intellectual autonomy; Marx is expanding this, as he sees it, 'abstract' dignity by arguing from an extensive anthropology. His anthropological starting-point has its ground in the philosophical tradition of Aristotle, Feuerbach and Schelling, which emphasizes the sensually *needy nature of humanity*; which affirms that human beings' capacities may only be developed in the context of the community. When Marx therefore demands social conditions of production and commerce, in which humans work 'under conditions *most* favourable to, and *worthy* of their human nature' (emphasis added);[2] and on this basis ('realm of necessities') the 'development of human energy which is an end in itself' ('realm of freedom') 'can blossom forth' (Marx 1966: 828), then he demands a life worthy to a human nature understood as encompassing. Dignity is therefore not, as with Kant, grounded merely in the intellectual capabilities of humans and related to these alone but comprises the entire human being; his corporeality and his social and intellectual needs and capabilities. A *life worthy of human dignity* in accordance with an encompassing human nature does then not just extend to the respect for his capacity of autonomous self-determination but also to the fulfilment of immediate material necessities of life. Neither does it merely extend to the functional handling, rational control and social organization of the human metabolism with nature to be carried out through work, but also to the development of capabilities as ends in themselves and social relationships, which realize by full self-realization and self-enjoyment liberated ends and values in the process of historic civilization.

We can therefore, departing from Marx' determination of human nature, differentiate between three aspects of a life worthy of human nature: (1) the aspect of conditions for the sustainment of human life, which are to be generated by work and must be suitable for the material as well as intellectual human nature (subsistence); (2) the aspect of the abilities necessary for the satisfaction of intellectual and social needs and cultural requirements (social-political, good life); and (3) the aspect of self-realization of the human being through free abilities directed at play, art and self-enjoyment (self-realization). These aspects are not clearly separated but rather interwoven: needs are always culturally embedded; individuality is always social and politically imparted, and the whole is aligned along the end-in-itself character of 'teleological' and 'experimental self-realization' (Lohmann 2011). A life worthy of human dignity, then, is a life in which these three elements of human existence are accommodated.

Marx sees this life according to human dignity as realized through labour. However, Marx thereby over-extends the concept of labour because every human activity appears to be labour, and therefore labour alone appears as guarantee and execution of life worthy of human dignity. One can reverse this hypostatization of the concept of labour by defining 'labour and interaction' (Habermas 1969) as the ways in which a life worthy of human dignity may be realized. But Marx' insight is to be kept; namely, that a life worthy of human dignity encompasses the human mind *and body* and that it is achieved and ensured through labour and interaction. Out of this expansion of the classic

[2] A more direct translation: 'under conditions which correspond to and are *most fitting for* to a life according to *human dignity*'.

concept of dignity (compared for instance to that of Kant) new areas appear of what should be protected by human rights. Not only the classic liberty rights, but also social rights, which relate to economy, culture and social relationships, should be protected.

Life worthy of human dignity and the right to work

Further references to the demand of life worthy of human dignity through labour are added to the ideas of utopian socialism or early socialism and Marx' mostly negative reference to human dignity by the labour movement. Ferdinand Lassalle demands on 12 April 1862 that 'the sorrowful and plight-laden condition of the working classes' should be improved through work (through 'more abundant and secure employment') and that only as such the working classes may 'be helped towards a life truly worthy of human dignity ("menschenwürdiges Dasein")' (Lassalle 1919: 173). This demand was endorsed more generally and led to a battle for the 'right to work' (Gardner 2002: 257–91). In the Weimar Constitution of 1919, the labour movement's demand was formulated as follows: 'The economy has to be organized based on the principles of justice, with the goal of achieving life in dignity for everyone.'[3] Finally, in particular in response to pressure from the communist states, a series of social rights were included in the Universal Declaration of Human Rights. These are, according to the catalogue of the Universal Declaration of Human Rights, so-called 'claim rights': individual rights to welfare, work, housing, education and cultural life. In international law, they have been institutionalized since 1966 in the International Covenant on Economic, Social and Cultural Rights.

Human dignity and social human rights: a socialist legacy?

In contemporary conceptions of socialism, especially on the view of market socialism, the concept of dignity does not play a visible role. Social-liberal theories of society, as well as social rights, relate to human dignity only hesitantly. In John Rawls' *A Theory of Justice*, explicit reference is made neither to the Kantian nor to the socialist conception of dignity. Nevertheless, concepts and reflections central to Rawls' position may be reconstructed in this tradition; above all, the idea of the difference principle, of the just 'value of freedom' and the concept of self-respect (Rawls 1971: 204f, 440ff). Social human rights, following Rawls and in particular the ground-breaking book by Henry Shue (1980), are justified by justice (Gosepath 2004). Thereby the concept of human dignity plays an interesting, but also disputed, role in recent debates. I give two examples.

Critically against Rawls' one-sided list of fundamental resources and explicitly in reference to Marx (and Aristotle), Martha Nussbaum establishes a list of fundamental capabilities: 'All citizens are entitled to a threshold level of these ten capabilities because, I argue, all ten are necessary conditions of *a life worthy*

[3] Weimar Constitution, Art. 151, I. 1.

of human dignity' (Nussbaum 2008, emphasis added). In accordance with Marx and the socialist tradition, she demands, contrary to the stoic, Kantian view, 'that it is quite crucial not to base the ascription of human dignity on any single "basic capability" (rationality, for example)' (*ibid.*). Instead, she attempts to demonstrate with her anthropological approach that '[t]here is dignity not only in rationality but in human need itself and in the varied forms of striving that emerge from human need' (*ibid.*). Also, Jürgen Habermas advances the thesis that there existed from the very beginning, historically and systematically, a close relationship between human dignity and human rights (Habermas 2010: 344), because human rights may be understood as constituting protection against specific violations of human dignity. He thereby not only methodically adopts Marx' negativistic approach, but also sees, as in the above interpretation of Marx, 'human dignity as a 'moral source' from which spring the contents of all fundamental rights' (Habermas 2010: 345). For him, 'the experience of violated human dignity... [has] a function of discovery', which leads to and can lead to the justification (establishment?) of rights and the 'construction of *new* fundamental rights'. Thus, for him, as in the socialist tradition, the indirect reference to human dignity becomes the source of social fundamental rights as well: 'The experiences of exclusion, destitution and discrimination teach that the classic fundamental rights only then receive "the same value" (Rawls) for all citizens, when social and cultural rights *are included*' (*ibid.*: 346). With this approach, according to which 'human dignity... founds the *indivisibility* of fundamental rights' (*ibid.*: 347), Habermas then argues against one-sided and narrowing versions of human rights, as they can at present frequently be observed.

Both authors are examples of the socialist legacy in which the concept of human dignity plays an increasing role in arguing, not only for social human rights, but also for an encompassing list of all human rights. In this philosophical struggle, it still indeed remains to be shown that human dignity possesses this authenticating and establishing power.

References

Bloch, E. 1961. *Naturrecht und menschliche Würde*. Frankfurt am Main: Suhrkamp

Bödeker, H. E. 2004. 'Der europäische Frühsozialismus und die Menschenrechte', *Mitteilungsblatt des Instituts für soziale Bewegungen* 31: 23–42

Cole, M. 1962. 'Socialism', in *The Encyclopedia of Philosophy*, ed. P. Edwards. New York: Macmillan Company and Free Press, 467–70

Gardner, M. 2002. 'Das Recht auf Arbeit', in *Grund- und Menschenrechte: Historische Perspektiven – Aktuelle Perspektiven*, ed. M. Gardner *et al.* Vienna: Oldenburg

Gosepath, S. 2004. *Gleiche Gerechtigkeit*. Frankfurt am Main: Suhrkamp

Habermas, J. 1969. 'Arbeit und Interaktion', in *Technik und Wissenschaft als Ideologie*. Frankfurt am Main: Suhrkamp, 9–47

2010. 'Das Konzept der Menschenwürde und die realistische Utopie der Menschenrechte', *DZPhil, Akademie Verlag* 58(3): 343–57

Lassalle, F. 1919. 'Arbeiter Programm', in *Gesammelte Reden und Schriften*, vol. II. Berlin: Bernstein

Lohmann, G. 1991. *Indifferenz und Gesellschaft: Eine kritische Auseinandersetzung mit Marx*. Frankfurt am Main: Suhrkamp

1999. 'Karl Marx' fatale Kritik der Menschenrechte', in *Politisches Denken: Jahrbuch 1999*, ed. K. Graf Ballesstrem, V. Gerhardt, H. Ottmann *et al.* Stuttgart, Weimar: Verlag J. B. Metzler

2011. 'Experimentelle Selbstverwirklichung: Von Marx bis heute', in *Philosophie in Experimenten: Versuche explorativen Denkens*, ed. G Gamm and J. Kertscher. Bielefeld: Transcript, 259–82

2013. 'Menschenwürde als "Basis" von Menschenrechten', in *Menschenwürde und Medizin: Ein interdisziplinäres Handbuch*, ed. J. C. Joerden, E. Hilgendorf and F. Thiele. Berlin: Duncker & Humblot, 179–94

Margalit, A. 1996. *The Decent Society*. Cambridge, MA: Harvard University Press

Marx, K. 1959. 'Die moralisierende Kritik und die kritisierende Moral: Beitrag zur Deutschen Kulturgeschichte', in *Marx Engels Werke*, vol. 4. Berlin: Dietz Verlag

1966. *Das Kapital*. 3 vols., in *Marx Engels Werke*, vol. 25. Berlin: Dietz Verlag

1972. 'Zur Kritik der Hegelschen Rechtsphilosophie: Einleitung', in *Marx Engels Werke*, vol. 1. Berlin: Dietz Verlag

1973. 'Die Todesstrafe – Herrn Cobdens Pamphlet – Anordnungen der Bank von England' (article from the *New York Daily Tribune* dated 18 February 1853), in *Marx Engels Werke*, vol. 8. Berlin: Dietz Verlag

1974. *Capital*, vol. 1. London: Lawrence & Wishart

Nussbaum, M. 2008. 'Human Dignity and Political Entitlements', in President's Council on Bioethics. 2008. *Human Dignity and Bioethics: Essays Commissioned by the President's Council on Bioethics*. Washington, DC, http://bioethics.georgetown.edu/pcbe/reports/human_dignity/chapter14.html (accessed 21 April 2013)

Peffer, R. G. 1990. *Marxism, Morality, and Social Justice*. Princeton University Press

Rawls, J. 1971. *A Theory of Justice*. Oxford University Press

Schaber, P. 2003. 'Menschenwürde als Recht, nicht erniedrigt zu werden', in *Menschenwürde: Annäherung an einen Begriff*, ed. R. Stoecker. Vienna: Oestreichischer Bundes Verlag, 119–31

Schnieder, W. 1984. 'Sozialismus', in *Geschichtliche Grundbegriffe: Historisches Lexikon zur politisch-sozialen Sprache in Deutschland*, ed. O. Brunner *et al.* Stuttgart: Ernst Klett, 923–96

Shue, H. 1980. *Basic Rights: Subsistence, Affluence, and US Foreign Policy*. Princeton University Press

Von Magnis, F. 1975. *Normative Voraussetzungen im Denken des jungen Marx (1843–1848)*. Freiburg im Breisgau, Munich: Karl Alber Verlag

Wildt, A. 2008. 'Sozialismus', in Stefan Gosepath, Wilfried Hinsch and Beate Rössler (eds.), *Handbuch der Politischen Philosophie und Sozialphilosophie*, vol. 2. Berlin: Walter de Gruyter, 1219–25

12

Human dignity in the Jewish tradition

YAIR LORBERBAUM

The Hebrew counterpart to the expression 'human dignity' – *kevod ha-adam* – hardly exists in classical Jewish sources. This expression entered the Hebrew language and Jewish-Israeli culture in modern times due to the influence of modern European structures of thought. Thus, for example, Israel's Basic Law: Human Dignity (*kevod ha-adam*) and Freedom (*ve-heruto*) was enacted by the Israeli parliament (Knesset) in 1992.

The term '*kavod*' appears in the Hebrew Bible several hundred times, and even more so in Talmudic literature. Its root is probably in the word '*kaved*', 'heavy', which also means substance (or concrete/physical presence). The core meaning of the term '*kavod*' is social honour or dignity, but it may also mean wealth, glory, greatness and splendour. Thus, the Hebrew Bible uses it to signify God's presence or substance (*kevod YHWH*, for example Exodus 16:7), or there are such Rabbinic sayings as: 'All that God created in His world He did not create but for His own glory (*li-khevodo*)' (*m. Avot* 6:11).

In classical Judaism, from early Rabbinic literature on, one finds the expression '*kevod ha-beriyot*', denoting the honour or dignity of people (literally, creatures). Like the term '*kavod*', the expression '*kevod ha-beriyot*' sometimes means the intrinsic value of each and every human being (i.e. dignity), but in many cases it connotes an acquired social or political status (i.e. honour). Though the latter is defended in some halakhic rules (see for example *b. Bava Metsi'a* 30a), there were Talmudic sages who rejected it as a worthy personal goal. Thus, for example, R. Eli'ezer ha-Kappar says: 'Jealousy, lust, and honour (*kavod*) remove a person from the world' (*m. Avot* 4:21). The rejection of *kavod* as social status is sometimes contrasted to the honour due to God: '... for how long do you put aside the honour of God and occupy yourselves with the honour of human beings' (*b. Kid* 32b).[1]

Kavod in the sense of dignity is probably best conveyed in the saying: 'So great is the dignity of creatures (*kevod ha-beriyot*) that it displaces a prohibition of the Torah' (*b. Ber* 19b). Though this saying seems to attribute significant

[1] Ironically, this saying is brought into the Talmudic discussion so as to argue that God's honour is to serve human beings.

weight to human dignity, it was narrowed, limited and almost neglected by later halakhists (both amoraic and medieval) (Blidstein 1982–3: 9–10).[2]

In classical Judaism, the intrinsic-universal value of human beings – i.e. what is referred to today by the term 'human dignity' – is embedded in the biblical notion of man being created in God's image (hereinafter, the Hebrew phrase *Tzelem Elohim*, simply *Tzelem* or *Imago Dei*). *Imago Dei* is a central notion in the Jewish Tradition. Its point of departure is the first chapter of the Hebrew Bible which, in the account of the Creation, brings together God the Creator and humankind. Though it seems to almost disappear from the subsequent chapters and books of the Hebrew Biblical corpus, it re-emerges with great force in the first and formative layer of classical Rabbinic literature in the homilies of the *tanna'im* (Jewish Palestinian Sages, first to third centuries CE). The idea of *Tzelem Elohim* emerged once again and with great force in the High Middle Ages, both in Jewish philosophy and in early Kabbalah (Jewish mysticism). From then on, at least in the realm of Kabbalah, it has always remained a central doctrine.

The importance of *Imago Dei* within classical Judaism is due, not only to its centrality as a theological conception, but also to its normative-legal (i.e. halakhic) implications and ramifications, particularly in its formative stage of early Rabbinic literature. The notion of *Tzelem Elohim* was reinterpreted in almost every period of the Jewish tradition. Due to limitations of space, I shall confine myself here to four literary corpora: the Book of Genesis, Talmudic literature, the writings of Maimonides and those of Nahmanides.

The Bible and the Talmud are the canonical texts of Jewish tradition. Biblical literature is the point of departure for every later layer in the Jewish tradition; while tannaitic literature is the first and formative layer of Talmudic literature. Both intertwine legal (halakhic) and non-legal ('aggadic' – i.e. narrative, vision, poetic) material. Maimonides is well known both for his famous philosophical treatise, *The Guide of the Perplexed*, the most important and influential philosophical treatise in the Jewish tradition, and for his legal code, *Mishneh Torah*, a seminal work in halakhah. Nahmanides, a prominent Jewish scholar of the Middle Ages, is known as both a central figure in early Kabbalah and as an innovative interpreter of the Pentateuch and the Babylonian Talmud.[3]

The most striking and fundamental element in the account of Creation in the first chapter of Genesis is the creation of man in God's image and likeness. Genesis 1: 26–7 states: 'And God said, "Let Us make man in our image, after Our likeness; and let them have dominion over the fish of the sea, and over the fowl of the air, and over the cattle, and over all the earth and over every creeping

[2] For a contemporary effort to make *kevod haberiyot* a central halakhic principle, see Sperber 2007.

[3] Among Nahmanides' writings are his interpretation of the Pentateuch, in which he incorporated enigmatic yet highly influential Kabbalistic allusions, as well as treatises and homilies that combine theology, Kabbalah and Halakhah.

thing that creepeth upon the earth".' The creation of humanity in the opening chapter of the Hebrew Bible consists of four closely intertwined elements: image and likeness; dominion; male and female; procreation. The first element governs them all. The synonyms 'image' (*Tzelem*) and 'likeness' (*demut*) entail presence: human beings are God's icons, hence the latter is present in the former in a way similar to that in which the gods, in ancient times, were believed to dwell in their statues and images. According to Genesis 1:26–8, human beings represent God not in one quality alone (for example, their intellect); the *Tzelem* rather encompasses all their features, both corporeal and mental. As extensions of the divine, human beings are granted authority and dominion over Creation. In order to govern the Earth they need to procreate; therefore they were created male and female, blessed by God, and thus they multiply the divine image.[4]

The biblical view regarding the notion of *Tzelem Elohim* originated in the ancient Near East, *inter alia* in sources relating to the status of the monarch, in Mesopotamia and in Egypt.[5] Mesopotamian sources identify the king and his offspring alone as being made in the image of God; hence his authority to rule. In contrast, Genesis 1:26–8 emphasize that man – every man – is made in the image of God (Loewenstamm 1958: 798). As Moshe Weinfeld wrote: 'In Israel there was a democratization of an idea that had previously been applied to the king alone' (1968: 114).[6] This ancient Near-Eastern royal theology, which provided the basis for the 'metaphysical'–political status of the king (whose core lasted into early modernity), is transformed in the opening chapter of the Hebrew Bible to 'the glory of the human race' (Loewenstamm 1958: 798).

The biblical *Tzelem* theology, or rather anthropology, has legal-normative implications. Thus, as stated in Genesis 9:6: 'Whoso sheddeth man's blood, by man shall his blood be shed; for in the image of God made He man.' Genesis 9:6 stands at the heart of the covenant concluded between God and Noah after the flood, a covenant which structures the post-diluvian world. This verse provides the basis for Biblical criminal law. As Moshe Greenberg noted:

> That man was made in the image of God is expressive of the peculiar and supreme worth of man. This view of the uniqueness and supremacy of human life has yet another consequence. It places life beyond the reach of other values. The idea that life may be measured in terms of money or other property and *a fortiori* the idea that persons may be evaluated as equivalences of other persons, is excluded . . . The guilt of the murderer is infinite because the murdered life is invaluable. An absolute wrong has been committed, a sin against God which is not subject to human discussion. (Greenberg 1960: 15–16)

If, as the Book of Genesis teaches, human life is infinitely valuable, then the practical-legal consequence of this conception is that a murderer must be

[4] See also Genesis 5:1–3.

[5] An echo of the view that the Mesopotamian king is divine appears in the harsh polemics directed against the Babylonian king in Isaiah 14:13–14; cf. Psalm 89: 7.

[6] Cf. Westermann 1994.

put to death. This legislation is not grounded exclusively in considerations of deterrence which might be overridden by other, economic or utilitarian considerations – as was indeed the case in most ancient Near-Eastern codes of law. In cases of murder, for example, these codes sometimes granted discretion to the victim's family to substitute capital punishment with pecuniary compensation. The verse in Genesis 9:6 thus gives concrete normative expression to the concept of the immeasurable value of human life. Given that human life cannot be quantified, only the ultimate punishment – death – is commensurate for he who takes a life away.

Furthermore, as mentioned above, *Imago Dei* implies the rejection of royal theology. If not only the king, but the entire human race is made in the image of God, the ground is pulled out from the basis upon which royal theology, or more broadly political authority, rests. It is no longer possible to base the authority of the king on any special relationship with God as this relationship is the heritage of every human being. Thus, political authority must rest on a different approach. Hence Deuteronomy 17 places limitations upon the king's powers, creating a scheme of separation of political powers (*ibid.*: 18).[7]

The *Tzelem* theology occupied a central place in early Rabbinic literature. In Talmudic literature, the biblical notion of *Imago Dei* was given a strongly iconic interpretation. God's icons are His dwelling in the mundane realm. According to this structure of thought, the creation as a whole is instrumental for the creation of man. In light of the conception of image as presence, the creation of man in tannaitic literature is perceived as 'the need' of the divine. God's desire to expand Himself motivated Him to create humanity in His own 'image and likeness' ('for His own glory').

The Talmudic idea that God is immanent in humanity has far-reaching normative-legal ramifications. Among the laws that were designed by the early rabbis (*tanna'im*) in light of the *Tzelem* theology are the rules for criminal procedure, including the forms of execution; a genuine and bold approach to capital punishment; the replacement of the biblical *lex talionis* (an eye for an eye) by pecuniary compensation; and the laws concerning procreation.

Some examples: the forms of execution in Talmudic law – stoning, burning, strangling and hanging[8] – were conceived by the early rabbis in a way which refrains from harming the condemned person's body. This becomes clear when one compares the forms of execution described in the Mishnah and other related tannaitic sources to those mentioned in the Bible and in post-Biblical Jewish and foreign sources of antiquity and late antiquity. Almost all the methods of execution mentioned in the latter insist on crushing the body, and tearing or consuming its limbs. By contrast, in the forms of execution mentioned in the Talmudic sources, the court simulates what they perceive as 'death at the hands

[7] Cf. Lorberbaum 2011: 26–37, 144–55.

[8] *m. San.* 6:1–3. Hanging, according to Talmudic literature, is performed in addition to some executions by stoning.

of Heaven'. According to the early rabbis, when God kills or causes the death of a sinner, he refrains from harming his body (*b. San* 46b). 'Death by Heaven', they stated, 'leaves no impression' (i.e. mark on the body). Why? It would seem that this is because God does not want to harm His image. Hence the court, for the same theological reason, imitates God and executes the condemned while keeping his body intact.

The application of *Tzelem* theology in Talmudic criminal procedure is not confined to the forms of execution and to the human body; it results in capital punishment as such, i.e. to the living human being. In light of their notion of image as presence, they considered bloodshed as harm to God. Rabbi Akiva taught: 'He who sheds blood is regarded as though he had impaired [literally, nullified or reduced] the likeness (*ha-demut* [of God]). What is the proof? "He who sheds man's blood . . . " Why? "For he made man in the Image of God"' (Genesis 9:6).[9] The iconic view of *Tzelem Elohim* conveyed here and in many other Talmudic sources led R. Akiva and other rabbis to describe murder, not only as an extreme moral transgression, but also as the ultimate religious sin; it diminishes the Divine image. Capital punishment, even when implemented by a legitimate court, is perceived as a form of murder. Hence the execution of a sinner, even a murderer, diminishes God's image. This line of thought led Rabbi Akiva and other rabbis (in the mid-second century CE) to abolish capital punishment in practice. In the first chapter of the mishnaic tractate *Makkot*, at the very end of the tannaitic discussions of criminal procedure, we find the following striking statement: 'Rabbi Tarfon and Rabbi Akiva said: If we sat in the Sanhedrin no man would ever be executed' (*m. Mak.* 1.11). The reason for their opposition to killing by the court is not given in the Mishnah, but it is clear from numerous other Talmudic sources that in their view all forms of killing, even execution of transgressors by courts, are a diminution of God's image, and therefore should not be exercised. The legal technique used by the early rabbis to undermine executions was an array of procedural obstacles that made conviction highly unlikely, if not impossible.[10]

When compared to its Biblical counterpart, that enumerates numerous transgressions deserving capital punishment, especially in the case of murder, this conclusion might seem surprising. Nevertheless, early Rabbinic halakhah portrays itself as drawing the logical conclusion from Genesis 9:6, which explains

[9] *Gen. Rab.* 34.14 (Theodor-Albeck edition, 326).

[10] Among these hindrances are: punctilious methods of examining witnesses; the rules that circumstantial evidence, confessions and self-incriminations are inadmissible; blanket rules concerning the disqualification of witnesses ('just as with two witnesses, if one of them is a relative or disqualified, their entire testimony is invalid'); the rule that the accused must be admonished by the witnesses prior to the commission of the offence; etc. Probably the most impressive collection of sayings and homilies that convey the intrinsic value of human life, together with the values of equality and individuality, is in *Mishnah Sanhedrin* 4.5, in the admonition of the witnesses in capital cases.

the decree to execute the murderer on the basis that man is created in the image of God. This reasoning seems paradoxical: is not the murderer likewise created in the image of God? Does not execution itself diminish the image? This line of thought, though resulting in a diametrically opposite conclusion, is founded on Biblical theology. It is viewed as the final conclusion embedded in Biblical theology itself.

The Talmudic *Tzelem* theology underlies the commandment to procreate and multiply as well. If the main purpose of the above-discussed laws was to protect God by preserving His image, the aim of this commandment is to expand and augment Him by duplicating his image. This notion is manifested in many Talmudic sources, such as the following:

> R. Eleazar b. Azariah taught: He who refrains from procreation is as though he impaired [God's] image. What is the proof? 'For in the Image of God made He man', followed by 'And you should be fruitful and multiply'. (Gen. 9:7) Ben Azzai taught: he who refrains from procreation is as if he shed blood and impaired [God's] image. What is the proof? 'He who sheds man's blood' etc. Why? 'For in the Image of God made He man', followed by: 'and you shall be fruitful and multiply'.[11]

Following Rabbi Akiva's saying quoted earlier, Rabbi Eleazar b. Azariah maintains that *Imago Dei* mentioned in Genesis 9:6 refers not only to murder, but also governs the reference to procreation in the following verse (9:7). As if to say: murder and procreation are two sides of the same coin; the former diminishes the image of God while the latter expands it. Ben Azzai strengthens R. Eleazar's suggestion by attributing the same moral and legal status to the commandment of procreation and the prohibition of murder. No wonder procreation became a prominent commandment in rabbinic halakhah – it represents the final, practical conclusion of the *Tzelem* theology.[12]

Maimonides, the great medieval halakhist and philosopher, had a radically different conception and interpretation of *Imago Dei.* Ignoring the Talmudic treatment of *Tzelem Elohim,* Maimonides subjected this Biblical idea to the allegorical method of interpretation and interpreted it in light of the Aristotelian philosophy of his time. Maimonides removed all anthropomorphic attributes from God. Hence, he rejected any concrete meaning of the Hebrew term *Tzelem Elohim,* identifying it instead with the intellect. At the very beginning of *The Guide of the Perplexed* (I:1), Maimonides writes:

[11] *Gen. Rab.* 34.1 (Theodor-Albeck, 326), cf. *b. Yeb.* 63b.

[12] For a comprehensive discussion of the Talmudic understanding of Imago Dei, see Lorberbaum 2004. Of course, against this universalistic approach based on the *Zelem* theology, one could find in classical Judaism (as in many other religious traditions) – in Talmudic Literature and especially in Kabbalah – particularistic approaches, that distinguish between Jews and gentiles. Yet it is not of my concern here to juxtapose these contradicting trends. My purpose in this chapter is to describe the universalistic view.

> The term *Tzelem* [image] . . . is applied to the natural form, I mean to the notion in virtue of which a thing is constituted as a substance and becomes what it is. It is the true reality of the thing . . . In man that notion is that form which human apprehension derives. It is on account of this intellectual apprehension that it is said of man: *In the Image of God created He him* . . . not their shape and configuration. (Maimonides 1963: 22)

For Maimonides, *Tzelem Elohim* is not the intellect as human potential but the intellect *in actu*. Only one whose intellect is 'in his most perfect and excellent state' is in God's image. In other words, only those who reach the highest levels of philosophical apprehension are for Maimonides in the image of God. Unlike the early rabbis, who believed that everyone is born in the image of God, Maimonides thought that the overwhelming majority of human beings are not in God's likeness.

Maimonides' intellectual conception of *Tzelem Elohim* carries legal-halakhic implications. Unlike Rabbi Akiva and his school, Maimonides approved of capital punishment, considering it a vital device for achieving law and order in society. The transgressor's deed, he argues, is an obvious proof that he is not in God's image. Maimonides developed an alternative criminal procedure, administered by the king. Unlike the criminal procedure of Mishnah Sanhedrin, this procedure enables the monarch to find a murderer guilty and execute him. Unlike the early Rabbinic halakhah, which strives to save from execution not only the innocent but also those who are guilty, Maimonides creates a procedure that could end up with finding a murderer guilty.

Furthermore, Maimonides argued for a sharp contrast between intellectual perfection (i.e. *Imago Dei*), on the one hand, and procreation, that entails sexual lust and the burden of supporting a family and raising children, on the other. The human *telos* – intellectual perfection – can be fully achieved only through the lifestyle of *vita contemplativa*. In contrast to the Talmud, which was committed to family values (seeing marriage and procreation as religious imperatives), Maimonides recommended (albeit only for the few) the ideal of philosophical contemplation, which entails freedom from the burdens of everyday life. Hence, unlike the Talmudic halakhah, Maimonides exempted those whose 'soul desires the Torah' – the few who realize their intellectual perfection (i.e. engage in philosophy, namely, the knowledge of God) – from marriage and procreation.[13]

Unlike Maimonides, Nahmanides followed the Talmud on *Tzelem Elohim*, while infusing it with the thought-structure and language of Kabbalah. Nahmanides locates the source of the human soul in the Divine–sefirotic realm of the Godhead. Its root is in the *sefirah* of *Binah*, from which it emanates 'down' to the mundane realm, to the human body (cf. Nahmanides 1976; Lorberbaum 2000). The *Sefirot*, according to many Kabbalists, Nahmanides included, are organized in a human shape. The divine soul is thus drawn down to the human

[13] *Mishneh Torah, Hilkhot Ishut* 15.1. For a full analysis of Maimonides' approach to Imago Dei, see Lorberbaum 1999; 2001.

body, according to Nahmanides, because of the isomorphism between its shape and the structure of the divine realm. It is this figurative resemblance that extends the 'Divine dwelling' to humanity.

Though Nahmanides is extremely esoteric on Kabbalistic matters, his scattered hints create the impression that his *kabbalah* (literally, tradition) on *Tzelem Elohim* is based on an iconic conception of the 'image' relation.[14] The *Tzelem* theology, according to Nahmanides, is 'a deep secret'. It (the *Tzelem*, i.e. humanity) was created 'for a great need and honourable aim'. Following the Talmudic tradition, Nahmanides maintains that God 'desires its existence' [i.e. of man, who is in his image] because it enables his enlargement and augmentation. Against the inclination of the soul (according to the Neoplatonic principle of *reversio*) to return to its source in the 'upper world' (the *sefirot*), it is drawn to the mundane realm, to its 'counterpart' in the human body. Hence human existence in the mundane realm is the need of God in heaven (*tzorech gavoha*). Thus, the commandments, according to Nahmanides, have a theurgic purpose – they 'repair' and enhance the divine realm. *Tzelem Elohim* became constitutive in Kabbalah in almost all its circles and trends through the ages. By and large, Nahmanides' view on *Tzelem Elohim* is an adequate representative of this tradition.

The modern notion of human dignity is embedded in the thought-structure of *Tzelem Elohim* in classical Judaism. Unlike religious worldviews that transcend God by emphasizing man's lowliness and vanity, the *Tzelem* theology 'utilizes' God and the notion of image as presence to empower humanity, and eventually to empower the divinity itself. It may be that, from a modern perspective, the intrinsic value attributed to humanity by the *Tzelem* theology is too strong. In the first chapters of the book of Genesis (i.e.1, 5 and 9), and to a greater extent in late antiquity Talmudic literature, *Tzelem Elohim* received an iconic interpretation, elevating humanity to a quasi-divine status. Maimonides deviated dramatically from this line of thought, which reached its peak in the High Middle Ages in numerous Kabbalistic circles, a tradition that continued to early modernity. The *Tzelem* theology, in most of its transformations, had normative-legal ramifications. The theurgic meaning attributed to the commandments by Talmudic literature, and to a greater extent by Kabbalah, based on this theology, seem alien to the norms derived from contemporary understandings of the concept of human dignity. It is nevertheless difficult to imagine a structure of thought (religious or secular) that ascribes such power and status to humanity. Some of the early rabbis and most of the Kabbalists viewed the daily, mundane commandments as fixing the divine Godhead. Closer to modern, normative applications of the concept of human dignity are the legal expressions of the *Tzelem* theology in the Bible, and particularly in Talmudic literature. To be sure, Talmudic literature did not derive human rights and freedoms in the modern sense from the notion of *Imago Dei*. Nevertheless, some

[14] See, for example *Sha'ar ha-Gemul*, in *Nahmanides' Writings*, in Chavel 1981: 305.

of the Talmudic laws are closely connected to the latter: thus, for example the biblical and Talmudic rules limiting the power of the monarch (and any other sovereign) and creating a structure of separation of political powers. Though the duty to procreate is not conceived as stemming from the modern concept of human dignity (should it not?), the abolition of capital punishment is closely connected to it. While we do not share the theological premises of R. Akiva (his bold anthropomorphism, the notion of image as presence, and so on), his homilies on *Tzelem Elohim* may be viewed as a mythic-symbolic source for the modern belief in the 'sanctity of life', which is the basis for the contemporary critique of capital punishment and for human rights in general.[15]

The book of Genesis and R. Akiva's *Tzelem Elohim* theology elevated humanity to the level of a divine image, thereby constituting the notion of the 'sanctity of life'. 'Sanctity' is first and foremost a religious concept, attributed to divinity. The *Tzelem* theology facilitated its attribution also to human beings. Roman *dignitas*, interpreted by Cicero as the intrinsic value of human beings, did not have this status and power. It would seem that, once the notion of the 'sanctity of life' was made available in the Western tradition, it became a constitutive idea, even when the theological scaffold on which it was first erected had long since been removed and forgotten.

References

Blidstein, G. I. 1982–3. '"Great Is Human Dignity" – The Peregrination of a Law', *Shenatom Ha-Mishpat Ha-Ivri* 9–10: 127–86 (Hebrew)

Chavel, H. (ed.). 1981. *Nahmanides' Writings*, vol. II. Jerusalem: Mossad Ha-Rav Kook

Greenberg, M. 1960. 'Some Postulates of Biblical Criminal Law', in *Yehezkel Kaufmann Jubilee Volume*, ed. M. Haran. Jerusalem: Magness Press, 5–28

Loewenstamm, S. A. 1958. 'Beloved Is Man Who Was Created in the Image', *Tarbiz* 17: 798 (Hebrew)

Lorberbaum, Y. 1999. 'Maimonides on Imago Dei: Philosophy and Law – The Case of Murder, Capital Punishment and Criminal Procedure', *Tarbiz* 68: 533–56 (Hebrew)

2000. 'Nahmanides' Kabbalistic Conception of "Tzelem Elohim"', *Kabbalah, Journal for the Study of Jewish Mystical Texts* 5: 287–326 (Hebrew)

2001. 'Humans Created in the Image of God and the Commandments to Procreate in the Talmud and Maimonides', *Iyyunei Mishpat* 16: 695–754 (Hebrew)

2004. *Tzelem Elohim – Halakhah and Aggadah*. Tel Aviv, Jerusalem: Schocken (Hebrew)

2011. *Disempowered King, Monarchy in Classical Judaism*. London, New York: Continuum

[15] It is worth noting that, in the early 1950s, immediately after the establishment of the State of Israel, the Knesset – explicitly inspired by *m. Mak.*1.10 and R. Akiva's sayings – abolished capital punishment (inherited from British Mandate law) in virtually all criminal cases. The legislation was supported by almost all parties, including the secular majority, and since then has never been changed.

Maimonides. 1963. *The Guide of the Perplexed*, trans. Shlomo Pines. Chicago University Press

Nahmanides. 1976. *Commentary to the Torah*, trans. H. Chavel, vol. I. New York: Shilo, 66

Sperber, D. 2007. *The Path of Halacha*. Jerusalem: Reuven Mass (Hebrew)

Weinfeld, M. 1968. 'God the Creator in Gen. 1 and in the Prophecy of the Second Isaiah', *Tarbiz* 37: 105–32 (Hebrew)

Westermann, C. 1992. *Genesis 1–11: A Continental Commentary*. Minneapolis, MN: Augsburg

Part II

Beyond the scope of the European tradition

13

The concepts of human dignity in moral philosophies of indigenous peoples of the Americas

LARS KIRKHUSMO PHARO*

The Universal Declaration of Human Rights (UDHR) of 1948 is perceived by many cultures, in particular Western (European and American) ones, as the fundamental point of reference in interpreting and understanding the principles of inalienable universal human rights as based on the inherent dignity of all human beings. Equivalent moral decrees and ideas existed, however, in the intellectual systems of the indigenous peoples of the Americas long before the arrival of the European invaders.[1] A concept of universal human dignity remains *avant la lettre* in the thinking and practices of American indigenous peoples. Even if a notion is lacking in a language of a particular culture, the matter might be present.[2]

Various European nations – the English, Spanish, French, Dutch, Russian and Portuguese being the foremost representatives – invaded the vast continent to be known as the Americas from the beginning of the sixteenth century onwards. Despite the destructive impact the European and the later post-colonial nation-states had on the Americas, there exist different religious, philosophical, linguistic and cultural systems of the indigenous peoples. The philosophical thought of the many Native American nations is a rather poorly studied subject in Western scholarship, where many scholars have not taken the intellectual wisdom of indigenous peoples seriously. To my knowledge, no comparative and systematic research has been conducted about how the concept of human dignity is conceived among Native Americans. Because of the great variety of numerous indigenous nations of an extensive cultural-geographic region, the present chapter will mainly concentrate upon 'the Great Binding Law of Peace' (GBLP) – or 'the Great Law' (*Kayánenhsä'óna* in the Onondaga language) – of the Haudenosaunee (known by outsiders as the Iroquois) confederacy of the northeastern part of the North American continent. However, as will be indicated, this should not be taken to suggest that only the Haudenosaunee had a moral concept of human dignity.

* I should like to acknowledge the help of Oren R. Lyons and Philip P. Arnold.

1 A related document to the UDHR is the UN Declaration on the Rights of Indigenous Peoples (2007).

2 Inspired by Bleeker 1973: 66.

The GBLP, which came into being several hundred years before the European invasion,[3] contains fundamental ethical principles of universal human dignity. The Haudenosaunee – the Six Nations consisting of Cayuga, Mohawk, Oneida, Onondaga, Seneca and Tuscarora – are considered to have the oldest functioning democracy in the world (cf. Pharo n.d.).[4] The GBLP proclaims equality between human beings and genders, and peace with foreign nations – comparable to values of inherent human dignity and universal human rights much later expressed in the UDHR. The GBLP is accordingly an analogous document to the UDHR – or, more precisely, essential ideas of the UDHR resonate in the GBLP since the ethics of human dignity of the moral philosophy of the Haudenosaunee precedes the UDHR by an exceptionally long time span.

Human rights and human dignity: historical sources and methodology

Universal human rights are required for a life of dignity for every human being (Donnelly 2003: 14, 18), which signifies an inherent respect for global human worth. Humans with dignity have social, political, civil and economic rights, which is why the UDHR relates human dignity to human rights (Gewirth 1992: 10, 15).

The English term 'dignity', which originates from the Latin, *dignitās* and *dignus* ('worthy'), has two general meanings. On the one hand, it appears as a synonym for 'honour', reserved exclusively for people who have a high, elevated or honourable rank or position. On the other hand, 'dignity' is related to the state or quality of being worthy of honour or respect, self-respect, self-esteem and self-worth, as applies to each human being living within a judicial-political system that secures equal rights for all members.

In aristocratic societies, the notion of (human) dignity refers to a privilege, which only certain people merit, rather than to the belief that every individual human being has dignity. Systems of hereditary inequality have existed in all parts of the world, and of course in the Americas as well – the civilizations of the Nahua, most famous for the Aztec empire, would be a good example (León-Portilla 1990), as would the city-states of the classic Maya of Mesoamerica (Houston and Inomata 2009) and the Inka empire of the Andes in South America (Moseley 2001). These, and other American civilizations not mentioned, constituted *timocracies* (Greek: *timē*, 'honour', 'worth', 'value'; *kratia*, 'power', 'rule by'). Timocracies are societies centred on personal prestige and honour, with a juridical and political structure that reserves human dignity

[3] Before the English Bill of Rights (1689), the American Declaration of Independence (1776) and the French Declaration of the Rights of Man (1798).

[4] In 1988, The US Senate and House of Representatives passed Concurrent Resolution 331 acknowledging the influence upon the Founding Fathers and the contribution of the Haudenosaunee Confederacy in making the US Constitution of 1787 (Lyons and Mohawk 1992).

for members belonging to the elite (Houston and Inomata 2009: 43). These societies represent hierarchical value systems in which ideas about the 'naturalness' and 'correctness' of moral inequality are legitimized (Rappaport 1999: 426–7). But this does not necessarily imply that persons of lower social ranks or within other social or kin systems lacked a concept of dignity within their own group. Millions of contemporary descendants of the above-mentioned cultures of Mesoamerica and the Andes should not be perceived to endorse 'timocratic' notions of human dignity. Moreover, a pre-Christian/pre-European concept of human dignity can be found in the moral philosophy of the Aztec didactic oratorical moral texts known as *huehuehtlahtolli.* ('words of the elders'). These were *tenonotzaliztli* ('admonishments' or 'exhortations'). Taken from the Aztec pictorial manuscripts (*tlamatinime*), *huehuehtlahtolli* taught self-control, respect and tolerance for other people. There was a call for dignity and moderate behaviour – for qualities of humility, generosity, courtesy and avoidance of excess and passion (León-Portilla and Silva Galeana 1988; León-Portilla 1990: 30–2; Baudot 1995: 225–34).

The fundamental moral value of universal human dignity in the UDHR is the equal worth and respect between members within a culture and towards other human beings and nations (Donnelly 2003: 191). A methodology of identifying essential values of human dignity from the UDHR can be summarized in a simple theoretical model enquiring whether:

- a political system, where the people have sovereign power (Greek: *demos* 'people'; *kratos*, 'power');
- human dignity applies to all without regard to social status, class or gender; and
- human dignity pertains to foreign nations and cultures.

There are quite a few examples in Native American cultures that indicate concepts of human dignity derived from this model. Different people were not identified on the basis of physical appearance but by tribal adherence, kinship, clan, residence in a specific community, and by religious, social and ritual traditions (Miles and Naylor-Ojurongbe 2004: 753). Despite having a notion of uniqueness, indigenous peoples contain hospitable communities where 'stable identities accord to other communities the dignity of the distinct existence that it wishes to receive itself' (Deloria 2003: 210–11).

The Great Binding Law of Peace (kayȧneñhså̊ˀkȯna)

The GBLP contains the story about the establishment of the Haudenosaunee ('People of the Longhouse') League (Confederacy) and an outline of its rituals, laws and practices (Woodbury 1992: xi), which became the foundation of a democratic consensus system. It is told in the GBLP that the Creator sent the messenger Tekánawi̇̀taˀ ('the Peacemaker'), with a moral law so that the nations would live in peace.

European travellers and Jesuit missionaries provide the earliest written accounts of the Confederacy, which substantiate that it was created before the European invasion of the seventeenth century (Trigger 1978; Woodbury 1992: xi). The year 1142 is the earliest date at which some scholars place the formation of the Confederacy. According to indigenous tradition, it was established much earlier.[5] The Haudenosaunee became the greatest indigenous power in colonial North America, with a homeland that comprised northern New York between the Hudson and Niagara Rivers and an influence that extended from the Ottawa River to the Chesapeake Bay and from New England to Illinois.

There are several (published) versions of the GBLP (cf. Woodbury 1992: lv–lxi). *Concerning the League: The Iroquois League Tradition as Dictated in Onondaga* by John Arthur Gibson (1992) is the only complete account[6] published in one of the languages, Onondaga, of the Haudenosaunee (Woodbury 1992: x–xii). The GBLP contains values of human dignity – the ethics of universal peace, the sovereign power of the people and justice without regard to socio-political status or gender – later recorded in the UDHR.

Ethics of peace, democratic constitution, social and gender equity

The GBLP constitutes a judicial-political doctrine stating the moral value of peace in which foreign nations and individuals enjoy liberty, respect and worthiness protected by the rule of law. The GBLP was not established only for the Haudenosaunee Confederacy. It represents international law with protection of all peoples. The Peacemaker's moral principles of reason, honesty, justice and peace apply to every human being.

Tekánawi̇̀ta' promotes an ethics of peace between people that states it is evil to be unkind or disrespectful towards other human beings. He announces the Good Message (*kaihwíyóh*), the Power (*ka'shástehsæ'*) and the Peace (*skeňoň*) to everyone. Peace and health shall prevail and thereby unite people, as they share equal worth (Woodbury 1992: xx; xxvii; Gibson 1992: 14–15, 27–33, 37–41, 304). The GBLP provides a universal ethical model of freedom based upon a balance of responsibilities in an egalitarian system. Peace is recognized as something that is built upon law and on the basis of justice practised between people and nations (Wallace 1998: 32, 34).

The GBLP outlines an ideal of human social and political relations based upon the values of equality and freedom. All human beings, genders and communities have an equal part in Creation. Tekánawi̇̀ta' proclaims not only the constitution of the confederacy, he delineates the foundation of the central concepts of

[5] www.onondaganation.org/aboutus/timeline.html.

[6] The GLP is memorized with *wampum*, which is a common name for small, white or dark violet, cylindrical seashell pearls. This mnemonic technique is practised by the Haudenosaunee and Algonquian nations in the northeastern part of North America.

the Great Law, the organization of the Confederacy Council, the ideal Commonwealth, the democratic procedures of the Council and a consensus system (Woodbury 1992: xxvi; Gibson 1992: 251–63). This democratic system secures human dignity and human rights for every member of society. After receiving the GBLP from the Creator, the Five Nations established a democratic system of government led by the Grand Council consisting of *Hoyane* (*sachems* or chiefs) from each nation. The GBLP outlines and advances a secure and balanced system with the possibility for each nation to use a veto. When a decision by the Council was passed, it came with the backing of all chiefs and was said to be 'Of One Mind' (Woodbury 1992: xxv, n. 50; Gibson 1992: 38–40).

Rules for decision-making and in addition laws for peaceful relations between the nations are put forward in the GBLP (Woodbury 1992: xxix; Gibson 1992: 440–6). This came into effect when the Tuscarora were invited to join the Confederacy at the beginning of the eighteenth century. The principle and moral value of human rights and dignity cannot be said to be restricted to native people of the Americas, since the Peacemaker conveys the philosophy of a constitution that warns against discriminating against people of a different culture, ethnicity, religion or language. Besides outlining the laws of unity within and between the Five Nations, the GBLP characterizes a supranational constitution that expresses unity in diversity and in which the rights, traditions and identities of every human being are secured.

The GBLP constitutes a protection of the rights of individual beings by freedom from fear and want. There is no private ownership but individual liberty (Woodbury 1992: xxix: Gibson 1992: 41–2, 457–60). All human beings – men, women and children – are related (Gibson 1992: 38–9).[7] A philosophy of dignity that affects every member of a society without regard to socio-political status, class or gender is delineated in the GBLP through the establishment of the representative political consensus system. The democratic governmental organization is based on the principle of equality and freedom of speech with a balance of responsibilities between women and men founded on the matrilineal clan system. The fifty chiefs are selected by the Clan Mothers, and each works with his Clan Mother and clan. In Council, the chiefs, who all have an equal say, represent the people, and work to ensure the preservation and well-being of all people (Woodbury 1992: xxviii–xxix; Gibson 1992: 418–22, 460–4). Once a man is selected to be a *Hoyane*, he holds that position for life. But, if a leader does not fulfil his responsibilities to the nation and the clan, he can be removed. It is the clan mothers who control the rules of conduct of the chief and warriors (Woodbury 1992: xxix; Gibson 1992: 450–7), securing rights and respect for every human being without regard to gender or social or political status.

[7] Sally Roesch Wagner (2001) outlines how the gender ideology of the Haudenosaunee, where women live with equal status and authority, later influenced the women's rights movement in North America in the nineteenth century.

Fundamental ethical values of universal human dignity from the UDHR can therefore be established to have existed in Haudenosaunee moral philosophy long before contact with European colonies.

Indigenous American philosophies of human dignity

In the philosophical argument of Tekánawìta', there is a logical interdependence between peace, democracy, justice, equality with connection to the natural world and the dignity of *all* beings. Indigenous peoples have an intimate relation to nature where all life and every being are equal. There is a value of 'one dish, one spoon' where humans are responsible in a moral eco-philosophy of equity (Oren R. Lyons, personal communication, 26 September 2010). The universal value of dignity connected to nature is not expressed in the UDHR.

In this brief chapter, I have not taken into account the philosophies of the many other Native American civilizations. For instance, the Lenape/Shawnee of North America has a philosophy of democracy and human dignity and rights for women and men. Tecumseh (1768–1813) was a Native American leader of the Lenape/Shawnee and of a great tribal confederacy that opposed the United States during the War of 1812. He was constantly exposed to warfare; nevertheless Tecumseh spoke about respect for all people, not only his own: 'Abuse no One and Nothing' (Newcomb 2008: 135–6; Schaaf 1990). Furthermore, the Mixtec (Ñuu Savi) of southern Mexico philosopher, Ignacio Ortiz Castro, has outlined a moral philosophy based upon the ancestral traditions of the Mixtecs, emphasizing values of universal human dignity: hospitality (*na kundeku tnaae*), solidarity (*na chindee tna'ae*) and communality (*da'an*) (Ortiz Castro 2006). These ethical principles also apply to other indigenous communities of the Americas.

Because of restricted space, I have only in a few words presented examples of how human dignity was conceived among selected indigenous nations, and proposed a quite superficial description of the GBLP as representing the highly sophisticated philosophy and complex judicial-political system of the Haudenosaunee. Future research through equal collaboration and discussion with indigenous peoples that analyzes similarities and differences in concepts of human dignity in the philosophies of the indigenous cultures of the Americas is needed because nation-states continue to undervalue indigenous peoples. Instead of extrapolating Euro-American ideas, Panikkar advises a methodology of a search for the 'homeomorphic equivalent' where the various cultures identify a mutual language and common ground (Panikkar 2008: 179–80).

References

Baudot, G. 1995. *Utopia and History in Mexico: The First Chronicles of Mexican Civilization, 1520–1569*. Niwot, CO: University Press of Colorado

Bleeker, C. J. 1973. 'Man and His Salvation in the Ancient Egyptian Religion', in E. J. Sharpe and J. R. Hinnells (eds.), *Man and His Salvation: Studies in Memory of S. G. F. Brandon*. Manchester University Press, 65–74

Deloria, V., Jr. 2003. *God is Red: A Native View of Religion*. Golden, CO: Fulcrum Publishing

Donnelly, J. 2003. *Universal Human Rights in Theory and Practice*. Ithaca, NY: Cornell University Press

Gewirth, A. 1992. 'Human Dignity as the Basis of Rights', in M. J. Meyer and W. A. Parent (eds.), *The Constitution of Rights: Human Dignity and American Values*. Ithaca, NY: Cornell University Press, 10–28

Gibson, J. A. 1992. *Concerning the League: The Iroquois League Tradition as Dictated in Onondaga by John Arthur Gibson*, trans. and ed. H. Woodbury, R. Henry and H. Webster. Winnipeg: Algonquian and Iroquoian Linguistics

Houston, S. D., and Inomata, T. 2009. *The Classic Maya*. Cambridge World Archaeology. Cambridge University Press

León-Portilla, M. 1990. *Aztec Thought and Culture: A Study of the Ancient Nahuatl Mind*. Civilization of the American Indian Series. Norman, OK: University of Oklahoma Press

León-Portilla, M., and Silva Galeana, L. 1988. *Huehuehtlahtolli: testimonios de la antigua palabra/estudio introductorio, Miguel León-Portilla; versión de los textos nahuas, Librado Silva Galeana*. Mexico: Comisión Nacional Conmemorativa del V Centenario del Encuentro de Dos Mundos

Lyons, O. R., and Mohawk, J. C. (eds.). 1992. *Exiled in the Land of the Free: Democracy, Indian Nations and the US Constitution*. Santa Fe, NM: Clear Light Publishers

Miles, T., and Naylor-Ojurongbe, C. E. 2004. 'African-American Indian Societies', in W. C. Sturtevant and R. D. Fogelson (eds.), *Handbook of North American Indians*, vol. 14. Washington, DC: Smithsonian Institution

Moseley, M. E. 2001. *The Incas and Their Ancestors: The Archaeology of Peru*. London: Thames & Hudson

Newcomb, Steven T. 2008. *Pagans in the Promised Land: Decoding the Doctrine of Christian Discovery*. Golden, CO: Fulcrum Publishing

Ortiz Castro, I. 2006. *Acercamiento a la filosofía y la ética del mundo mixteco*. Colección diálogos. Pueblos originarios de Oaxaca. Veredas. Conaculta. Culturas populares e indigenas. CNCA-DGCP/Secretaría de Cultura del Gobierno de Oaxaca. Oaxaca de Juárez, Oaxaca. Mexico

Panikkar, R. 2008. 'Is the Notion of Human Rights a Western Concept?', in R. Falk, H. Elver and L. Hajjar (eds.), *Human Rights: Critical Concepts in Political Science*, vol. 1. London, New York: Routledge, 178–99

Pharo, L. K. n.d. 'Democracy of the "New World": The Great Binding Law of Peace and the Haudenosaunee Confederacy', in H. Jordheim and E. Sandmo (eds.), *Conceptualizing the World*. New York: Berghahn Books

Rappaport, R. A. 1999. *Ritual and Religion in the Making of Humanity*. Cambridge University Press

Roesch Wagner, S. 2001. *Sisters in Spirit: Haudenosaunee (Iroquois) Influences on Early American Feminists*. Summertown, TN: Book Publishing Company

Schaaf, G. 1990. *Wampum Belts and Peace Trees*. Golden, CO: Fulcrum Publishing

Trigger, B. G. 1978. 'Early Iroquoian Contacts with Europeans', in B. G. Trigger (ed.), *Handbook of North American Indians*, vol. 15. Washington, DC: Smithsonian Institution, 344–56

Wallace, P. A. W. 1998. *The White Roots of Peace*. Iroqrafts. Iroquois Reprints. Ohsweken (Ontario): Iroquois Publications

Woodbury, H. 1992. 'Introduction', in *Concerning the League: The Iroquois League Tradition as Dictated in Onondaga by John Arthur Gibson*, trans. and ed. H. Woodbury, R. Henry and H. Webster. Winnipeg: Algonquian and Iroquoian Linguistics, xi–lxi

14

Human dignity in the Islamic world

MIKLÓS MARÓTH

Human dignity is a new concept which was unknown in antiquity and the early Middle Ages when Christendom and Islam appeared around the Mediterranean Sea. Consequently, when discussing traditional religions and cultures, scholars have to look for the various elements of these religions and cultures in various sources, and try to present them as a unified theory.

First, human dignity is not at the centre of interest of any religion, but man, through his relationship to God, comes to the fore. His partnership with God sets a high value on him. It is quite comprehensible that religions have to elaborate a concept of man, due to the fact that man is the other party in this relationship, and, as a consequence, they have to grant some kind of dignity to human beings as partners of God. Thus, the cultures created by various world religions are necessarily concerned with human beings, but their prevailing concept of human beings largely depends on their religious convictions. All this is valid for the Islamic religion too. Islam has a special view of human beings, and consequently, of human dignity too.

Second, the religion of Islam, like Judaism, is mainly concerned with the revealed divine law. The Islamic divine law known as *Shariʿa* contains the obligations of human beings towards God and towards each other, i.e. one's fellow men. All this implies that the legal prescriptions of the *Shariʿa* want to regulate primarily the conditions of private life. In the Islamic countries, everyday life in society has always been regulated by the ruler and his secular legal system (*siyasa*), which was rational and necessarily compatible with the *Shariʿa* (*siyasa sharʿiyya*). This second legal system, parallel to the first, is usually called *qanun* or *tanzimat*.

From these introductory words, it should be clear that, in examining the concept of human dignity in Islam, one has to see the problem from the point of view of the *Shariʿa* as well as from the point of view of the *qanun*, even if any kind of contradiction between them is precluded.

Human dignity in the Shariʿa

The Arabic expression equivalent to 'human dignity' is *karamat al-insan*. Various forms of the root *krm* turn up in many Quranic verses in various contexts.

The basic meaning of the root is 'to bestow honour upon' or 'to venerate' or 'to treat with deference'. According to the Quranic dictionary, its meaning is equivalent to *faḍḍala*, which in turn means 'to like better' or 'to give preference to' (*Muʿjam alfāẓ al-Qur'ān* 1990: 962–4).

In Sura 17, one can find the word in its basic meaning, when we read that Allah commanded the angels to prostrate to Adam, which they did. The only one who protested was Iblis (Satan): 'Shall I prostrate myself along with one whom Thou hast created of clay? Tell me, Lord, can I submit to this one whom Thou hast honoured above me (*karramta ʿaleyya*)?' In this sentence, the meaning of the word is simply 'venerate' (Quran 17, 62).

In another passage of the same Sura, we read the following words: 'We have indeed honoured the children of Adam (*karramnā banī Adam*), and provided for them means of transportation in land and sea, and given them wholesome food and exalted them high above the greater part of Our creation' (Quran 17, 70). Here, the words 'to honour' imply that Allah provides for human beings with everything they need for a comfortable life. A similar meaning of the word turns up in many other passages. For example, in Sura 89, one can find the word '*karrama*' parallel to the word '*naʿʿma*' in the same sentence. The latter word has the meaning 'to provide with a life of ease'. The sentence is translated into English as follows: 'It is characteristic of man that when his Lord tries him and bestows honours (*akrama-hu*) and favours upon him (*naʿʿma-hu*), he boasts: etc.' Commenting the passage in Quran 17, 70 quoted above, al-Qurṭubī writes that man's privileged position (*karamat*) in creation is manifested in his tall stature and beautiful form, and in his ability to move equally well on land and water. This privilege was given to Adam's children only (Belhaj 2009: 196). All these quotations clearly indicate that God is the only source of *karam*, he it is who bestows *karam* on human beings. To put it in other words: *karamat* is not an inherent quality of man; it is a special gift of Allah.

In this case, one has to raise the question: who will be given *karam* by God? The answer is not surprising: 'Verily, the most honoured among you in the sight of Allah is he who is the most righteous among you' (Quran 14, 49). The word '*atqā*' in the text was translated here as 'most righteous', although the correct meaning of the expression is 'most pious', 'most God-fearing'. Thus, God gives *karam* to all human beings, but some of them will get less, some of them more of it, corresponding to one's devotedness. This is what contemporary Muslim writers refer to by the expression *al-takrim al-ilahi li-'l-insan* (Belhaj 2009: 196; al-Qurṭubī (undated): 125–6).

The next problem of *karam* is its meaning. As the previous quotations indicate, *karam* refers to an elevated position, special treatment, the result of which is a comfortable life. This conclusion will be confirmed by a quotation, in which one can read about the expulsion of sinners from the abundant region of Egypt: 'Thus we drove them forth out of gardens and springs, and treasures and pleasant abodes' (Quran 26, 58–9). Another passage runs as follows: 'They left behind many a garden and spring, and cornfield, and comfortable dwelling, and luxury in which they delighted' (Quran 44, 26–8). The expression *maqam karīm* is translated in the first quotation as 'pleasant abodes', in the second one as 'comfortable dwelling'. Howsoever, the expression clearly implies a life in security, free of harm, in well-being and comfort. This is what a pious man deserves from God as a human and God-fearing creature.

The elevated position (*maqam karīm*) of human beings implies free will. This means that in various situations of life human beings are free to decide whether they do something or not. In this respect, there is a serious difference between human beings and angels. The latter are only servants without any freedom in taking decisions. In the Quran, one can read about angels as follows: 'To Him belongs whosoever is in the heavens and in the earth. Those who are in His presence do not disdain to worship Him, nor do they weary of it; they glorify Him night and day, and cease not.' Or: 'Those whom they so designate are only His servants. They utter not a word more than He directs, and they only carry out His commands. He knows what lies ahead of them and what is left behind them, and they intercede not except only he whose intercession He permits and they tremble with fear of Him' (Quran 21; 19–30). The difference between the positions of angels and human beings is well represented by the story of creation, where one can read the following story of the Quran, in which Allah speaks to the angels: 'We did bring you into being, then we gave you shape, then we commanded the angels: submit (prostrate) to Adam. The angels submitted (prostrated)' (Quran 7; 12). In light of this comparison of the free human beings with Allah's servants, it is no wonder that human beings are superior to angels. This passage of the Quran indicates that God has elevated human beings, made them free from all kinds of subjection, except the subjection to Him. In turn, God charged men with duties: the first one is the worship of God, as prescribed in the *Shariʿa*; the second one is creation of culture (in all meanings of the word '*cultura*') on Earth (Belhaj 2009: 196; al-Najjar 1995: 135).

The angels do not have choice: they can only obey the commands of Allah. Man as rational being, however, always has a choice, on which his dignity depends. If he obeys Allah he will be dignified, but if he rejects Allah's commandments he will be punished. Allah's commandments revealed to his chosen creature can be found in the Quran, and, consequently, Quran gives everybody a guideline on how to attain human dignity. This idea is expressed in the symbolic language of the Quran in the following way: 'We have now sent down to you a Book which makes provision for your uplift; will you not then understand? How many a township that acted wrongfully have We utterly destroyed, and raised up after it another people? When they perceived our chastisement, they prepared to flee from it. Flee not, but return to the comforts and luxuries in which you exulted so that you may be interrogated. At this they exclaimed: "Alas, we were indeed wrongdoers. They continued thus to bewail till We moved them down into stubble"' (Quran 21, 11–16).

Persons obeying Allah's commandments are elevated to the rank of His representatives (*khulafāʾ*) on Earth (Belhaj 2009: 196; ʿOthman 1983: 62).

This summary means that the Quran speaks of human dignity usually in terms of morals, and not in terms of law (Belhaj 2009: 196; Bielefeldt 2000: 109).

Pious men will be dignified; the impious ones will be humiliated. This essential truth was summarized by Izzeddeen al-Khateeb al-Tameemi, the chief *qadi* in Jordan, in his book about the social concepts of contemporary Islam in following words: 'So, human dignity originates from Divine Will and the immortal law of God. Hence, human dignity is inseparable from a human being whether a male or female, irrespective of colour, time, place, social position, prestige among people, age, even if still a foetus, or dead lying in his grave' (al-Tameemi 2003: 462). And later he adds: 'In other words, dignity and human beings form a syndrome that never part with each other. Dignity is an admirable value in human being's life. Human esteem does not emanate from universal declarations, international resolutions, regional agreements or inter-state conferences. Commitment to it from an Islamic standpoint is based on doctrine, not on accidental interest or temporal benefits' (*ibid.*). Thus, the real firm basis of human dignity is the doctrine of Islamic religion which has been derived from the Quran. I will now elaborate how al-Tameemi understands the concept of human dignity. The highest value is human life. The *Shari'a* of God has preserved the human lifeblood, honour, lineage and species. All these are high values adopted for safeguarding human society from violation and chaos. For this reason, God's Law has forbidden encroachment on human life. The next item of human dignity is marriage of a man and a woman. Any kind of sexual intercourse without legal marriage contract is forbidden. Such intercourse is defined as adultery, which should be abstained from under all conditions. The next constituent part of human dignity is good reputation. For this reason, calumny 'is a major sin whether done in public or in private where only God will hear it, and in this case it will be viewed as an audacity towards God' (*ibid.*: 471). And the text continues: 'Indeed, defamation is a major sin whether against Muslim or dhimmi.'

These words are thought-provoking. In the two previous cases, *dhimmis* (non-Muslims who belong to a world religion having a sacred book, i.e. Jews and Christians) were not mentioned. How shall we understand that, in the case of calumny, a special reference has been made to non-Muslims? Does it imply that in the case of murder and adultery the conditions are not extended to non-Muslims? And how shall we understand the fact that many other human beings (those who are neither Muslims nor *dhimmis* – a group to which the vast majority of humanity belongs) are not mentioned here at all? Are they excluded from the interdiction of calumny? Shall we understand human dignity as something bestowed by God mainly on Muslims, and to some degree on those living together with Muslims? These doubts, in conjunction with the words of the Quran that say that the Quran is the source of dignity, lead to the conclusion that there is an inequality in respect of human dignity between Muslims and non-Muslims, between owners of a sacred book and between members of all other religious communities.

Izzeddeen al-Khateeb al-Tameemi at any rate comes to the conclusion that 'Islamic Shari'a has banned everything that disturbs the security of society, and threatens its high values. Shari'a also prohibits anything that may endanger individuals' lives, honour, minds and property. So it has proscribed prostitution, promotion of lewdness and its printed matters, unseemly actions, rape, adultery, sodomy, lesbianism' (*ibid.*: 474). The text goes on to say that 'penal laws currently prevalent in the world, however, lean toward laxity in penalizing rape or flagrant violation of ethical codes. They often acquit those who commit such crimes or give them disproportionately low sentence . . . Wronged people therefore take the law into their hands because they are not convinced that law will do them justice or quench their anger.'

Thus, constituent elements of human dignity are security and safety in the life of society and compliance with the written and unwritten Code of Conduct in private life. Violation of the valid ethical judgment of the majority and the toleration of the deviant lifestyle of a minority forced by state authorities (in some countries) is an offence against human dignity. Security in private life and compliance with an unwritten code of conduct means, at the same time, the prohibition of 'spying, snooping, and searching for other people's defects and faults.' This rule is derived from the prophetic tradition. According to the tradition, Mohamed said to one of his followers: 'If you trace privacies of other people, you will corrupt or spoil them or you have almost done that.' Respect for privacy is thus a constituent element of human dignity, and human dignity is not separable from the dignity of the family. According to these statements, the necessary condition of human dignity is the safe and secure family life. Safe and secure family life excludes 'ill-treatment of children by their parents, laxity of upbringing, discrimination between them, and overuse of violence in dealing with them' (*ibid.*: 475). (These words imply that moderate corporal punishment is not excluded.) The author derives this claim from the following passage of the Quran: 'O you who believe, safeguard yourselves and your families against a fire whose fuel is men and stones, over which are appointed angels, stern and severe, who disobey not Allah in that which He commands them and do as they are directed' (Quran 66, 7).

So far, the following conclusions can be drawn from what has been said: human dignity is given by Allah to all those pious persons who live according to his commandments. The source of human dignity is the religion of Islam; more precisely the truth revealed by God and contained in the Quran.

Human dignity is not limited to the lifetime of individuals, because human beings deserve dignity before birth as well as after death. The embryo, the dead corpse and the living human being equally have human dignity, but the meaning of 'human dignity' is different for each of them. Human dignity excludes all kinds of behaviour that does not comply with the general rules of nature: for example, marriage between man and woman complies with the rules of nature, and, consequently, with human dignity. On the contrary, all other relationships must be regarded as not complying with the rules of nature; accordingly, they must be taken as an offence against human dignity.

As Milliot and Blanc puts it, the divine law rules the entire field of human actions (Milliot and Blanc 2001: 173). Its aim is to proclaim God's glory and to promote the comfort and welfare of people both in this life and in the afterlife. Immortality of the soul is the basis of the human dignity that was not mentioned up to now. The law will control human life in this world for the sake of one's eternal life in the world to come. The purpose of human life on Earth is to attain the degree of a perfect being, and so to attain proximity (*qurba*) to God in the afterlife. The temporary, this-worldly aim of the law is to regulate human actions in compliance with the necessities of the social life, and for this purpose the law puts restrictions on the actions of human instincts. The latter are given by God to the people to mark the fields of freedom of human actions: self-preservation and reproduction. The main task of the religious law is to ensure the welfare and well-being of people. As we understand from the previous passages, the welfare and well-being of man constitutes his dignity. Thus, the fundamental purpose of *Shari'a* is to defend human dignity. Pious people who obey the divine law will pay attention to other people's dignity, and accordingly, in a pious society, human dignity will be the main value.

One can say, in short, that, from the point of view of the Islamic religion, human dignity is the result of Allah's dignifying action (*takrim*). This action implies that man is Allah's deputy (*khalifat*) on Earth, which is proven by his outward form, his position in creation. Human dignity is thus not the result of international legal agreement, its origin is not a decision taken by humans themselves. This implies that man has obligations towards God; these are fixed in the *Shari'a*. In exchange for fulfilling obligations man was granted rights (*ḥuquq*) too, and this means mainly a secure, good life.

There is, however, one open question: does everybody have the same dignity, or is the dignity of mankind in general limited to some elements only, while some other elements are given to those only who are pious Muslims? From what has been said, various conclusions may be drawn. It seems that all human beings have the same gifts as far as man's place in the creation is concerned. This must be a matter of general agreement. It is not clear whether the other elements of human dignity (secure life and what is connected with it) are part of the dignity of all human beings.

Some Muslim authors are ready to acknowledge that human dignity as such is given to everybody, while some others exclude from human dignity everybody who is not a devoted Muslim (Belhaj 2010: 204;[1] Krämer 2004: 138).

[1] As Abdessamad Belhaj puts it: 'The sacred nature of human beings does not only apply to Muslims: it is extended to all those with whom Muslims have made peace treaties . . . or defence treaties . . . Nevertheless, certain interpretations inside the Muslim world tend to dehumanize non-believers. Unlike the mainstream interpretation that understands the concept of *karama* as being concerned with all human beings as children of Adam, these radical interpretations restrict its sense to believers who actively practise their faith.'

Human dignity in qánùn

Now let us consider the meaning of human dignity from the point of view of the generally accepted *qanun* of the Islamic countries. The document under consideration was adopted by leading politicians of the Muslim countries in Cairo.[2] The first sentence of this document in the introduction refers to what has been said in the previous part of this chapter: man is the deputy of God on Earth, and this fact defines his position: '[The Nineteenth Islamic Conference of Foreign Ministers,] keenly aware of the place of mankind in Islam as vicegerent (*khalifat*) of Allah on Earth . . . agrees to issue the Cairo Declaration of Human Rights in Islam that will serve as a general guidance for Member States in the Field of human rights.' The document, imitating Western political language, speaks of 'human rights', but this fact does not imply any contradiction: here human rights are derived from human dignity. As a matter of fact, the document starts with a doctrine that serves as the most important explanatory principle in the Islamic theory of human dignity. In the next paragraph this aim is explained in more detail. Knowing what has been said in the previous section in relation to the *Shari'a*, it will be comprehensible that the Islamic *Umma* (community of all Muslims) is taken to be the best community Allah gave to mankind, in which this life is in harmony with the life to come, knowledge is in harmony with faith. This community, on the basis of its civilization that was created by Islam and the ministers, will give a clear solution 'for all chronic problems of this materialistic civilization' in respect of human dignity. The aim of the document is further to 'affirm his [i.e. mankind's] freedom and right to a dignified life in accordance with the Islamic *Shari'a*'. The adjective 'dignified' suggests that, in speaking of human rights directly, the document speaks of human dignity indirectly. It is openly stated that the success of this aspiration cannot be achieved without taking into consideration the Islamic Law, i.e. the Islamic *Shari'a*. The two closing provisions, Articles 24 and 25, return to the same idea emphasizing the explanatory role of the Islamic *Shari'a* in everything what has been said in the previous twenty-three articles. The ambiguity of the *Shari'a*, however, is present in this secular document too. In Article 1, there are two paragraphs. The first paragraph states the following:

> All human beings form one family whose members are united by their subordination to Allah and descend from Adam. All men are equal in terms of basic human dignity and basic obligations and responsibilities, without any discrimination on the basis of race, colour, language, belief, sex, religion, political affiliation, social status or other considerations. The true religion is the guarantee for enhancing such dignity along the path to human integrity.

[2] The Nineteenth Islamic Conference of Foreign Ministers (Session of Peace, Interdependence and Development), held in Cairo, Arab Republic of Egypt, from 9–14 Muharram 1411H (31 July to 5 August 1990).

The last sentence of this paragraph seems to contradict the previous ones, depending on the explanation of the words 'true religion'. Does it mean that Islam is the source for human dignity as such, or does it mean that a sincere and deeply held religious conviction of anybody attached to any religion can be the basis of human dignity? The next paragraph seems to be as ambiguous as the first one was:

> All human beings are Allah's subjects, and the most loved by Him are those who are most beneficial to His subjects, and no one has superiority over another except on the basis of piety and good deeds.

As far as the constituent elements of human dignity are concerned, the document gives the list known from the previous section (sanctity of life, good fame, honour, secure life, etc.), except that the argumentation is different from the one we presented there.

References

al-Najjar, ʿA. ʿO. 1995. ʿAqīdat takrīm al-insan wa atharuha 'l-tarbawiyya', *al-Muslim al-Muʿaṣir* 74: 135

al-Qurṭubī, Abū ʿAbdallāh. Undated. *al-Jāmiʿ li-aĥkām al-Qur'ān*, ed. ʿAbdallāh al-Turkī. Beirut: Mu'assasat al-risāla

al-Tameemi, Izzeddeen al-Khateeb. 2003. *Islam and Contemporary Issues*. Amman

Belhaj, A. 2009. 'Karāmat al-insān – emberi méltóság', in *Az iszlám politikaelmélete; Terminológiai vizsgálat*, ed. M. Maróth. Piliscsaba: Avicenna Kiadó

2010. *Muslim Political Theory: A Comparative Terminological Investigation*, ed. M. Maróth. Piliscsaba: Avicenna Institute of Middle Eastern Studies

Bielefeldt, H. 2000. '"Western" Versus "Islamic" Human Right Conceptions?: A Critique of Cultural Essentialism in the Discussion on Human Rights', *Political Theory* 28(1)

Krämer, G. 2004. 'La politique morale ou bien gouverner a l'islamique', *Vingtieme Siecle; Revue d'histoire* 82

Milliot, L., and Blanc, F. P. 2001. *Introduction a l'étude du droit musulman*. Paris: Dalloz

Muʿjam alfāz al-Qur'ān, al-Qāhirat. 1990. ed. Majmaʿat al-lughat al-ʿarabiyya

ʿOthman, M. F. 1983. *Íuqūq al-insan baina 'l-sharīʿat al-islamiyya wa 'l-fikr al-qanūn al-gharbī*. Dar al-Shurūq

15

Hinduism: the universal self in a class society

JENS BRAARVIG

Human dignity in the Indian tradition is an immense topic; in this chapter, I will discuss some aspects of human dignity in the Hindu tradition. As a rough definition, I take Hinduism to refer to those traditions that accept the Vedic heritage (*śruti*, 'heard from the gods') as the source of truth.

I will employ three main sources for our inquiry into human dignity in the Hindu tradition: the *Upaniṣads*, the Laws of Manu and the *Bhagavadgītā*. I will discuss each of these in turn, and suggest that human dignity in Hinduism is an ambiguous and perhaps even paradoxical concept: on the one hand, all living beings (not solely human beings) are thought to possess *inherent* dignity, but on the other hand we find that in the social realm dignity appears in *degrees*.

The Upaniṣads

The *Upaniṣads*[1] are dialogues in Sanskrit which were handed down orally as part of the Veda, articulating the essentials of Vedic wisdom. These dialogues, stemming from approximately the sixth century BC, contain two central doctrines: the teachings of *ātman* and *brahman* – explaining the identity of Self and Universal Whole – and the doctrine of reincarnation or metempsychosis.

The *Upaniṣads* express a world view which is centred on the individual, but with the corollary that the self, *ātman*, is everywhere: it is really one with all things, the Whole, and as such one with *brahman* – the life power which suffuses the universe and is the ground of all material things. Material objects, phenomena, are really the projection of human experience:

> In the beginning this world was only brahman, and it knew only itself (ātman), thinking: 'I am brahman.' As a result it became the Whole. Among the gods, likewise, whosoever realized this, only they became the Whole. It was the same

[1] For the twelve oldest *Upaniṣads*, see now Olivelle 1998 with an up-to-date bibliography. The two oldest of these twelve *Upaniṣads* are the *Bṛhadāraṇyaka-upaniṣad* (BU) and the *Chāndogya-* (CU), filling almost two-thirds of the whole corpus as thus defined. The others are *Taittirīya-upaniṣad* (TU), *Aitareya-* (AU), *Kauṣītakī-* (KsU), *Kena-* (KeU) *Kaṭha-* (KaU), *Īśa-* (IU), *Śvetāśvatara-* (ŚU), *Muṇḍaka-* (MuU), *Praśna-* (PU), and the *Māṇḍūkya-upaniṣad* (MaU).

> also among the seers and among humans. Upon seeing this very point, the seer Vāmadeva proclaimed: 'I was Manu, and I was the sun.' This is true even now. If a man knows 'I am brahman' in this way, he becomes the whole world. Not even the gods are able to prevent it, for he becomes their very self (ātman). So when a man venerates another deity, thinking: 'He is one, and I am another', he does not understand. (Bu: 9–10)

So human beings, other living things and gods are not in essence distinct selves: they are unified in one entity, which is at the same time the individual and the universal. As such, the self is eternal and unchanging: *ātman* is the self that is free from evil, old age, sorrow, hunger and thirst – 'the self whose desires and intentions are real . . . When someone discovers this self and perceives it, he obtains all the worlds, and his desires are fulfilled' (CU: 7, 1). Obviously the self cannot be perceived in quite the same way human beings perceive material objects: perceiving *ātman* cannot be sensory, but is rather a form of or intuition of that which is *behind* all sensory perception;

> That which is the hearing behind hearing, the thinking behind thinking, the speech behind speech, the sight behind sight – It is also the breathing behind breathing – freed completely from these, the wise become immortal, when they depart from this world. (KeU: 1, 2)

When a human being intuits his true self – *ātman* – he becomes one with *brahman*: he manifests *brahman* as his true self, becomes one with the Universal Whole. This Universal Whole, however, is *par excellence* present in the priestly class, the *brahmin* (in Sanskrit, *brāhmaṇa*), but can also be communicated via the central institution of Vedic society: the sacrifice. In the sacrifice the cosmic qualities, the universe is brought into the sphere of the individual: the individual appears as the *projection* of the universal – exemplifying the idea that the self is identical with *brahman*, with the life power which lies 'behind' sensible phenomena.

The idea which is central to the Indian view of man, that of reincarnation, also has its origin in Vedic literature, and especially the *Upaniṣads*. The social correlate to the philosophical individualism described above appears in various ascetic movements – the ascetic, or *śramaṇa*, whose aim was a search for and realization of individual salvation from the round of eternal rebirth, *mokṣa*. Perhaps surprisingly, in the *Upaniṣads* it is not so much the (im)moral character of one's actions (*karma*) which determines rebirth or salvation, but rather the *season* in which a person deceases. If one dies in a time wherein the sun moves northwards, from winter to summer solstice, one will ascend through the various worlds towards the sun; with which one will be united and never again reborn. In this quality, the sun seems equivalent with *brahman*. Those individuals who die when the sun moves southwards, i.e. the other half of the year, will go to the realm of the deceased Fathers and from there to the Moon, where they will be food for the gods. And as the gods rain down on the Earth, these deceased will grow in the form of plants and in turn become food for men or animals. So salvation has nothing to do with *karma* in the moral sense: liberation from the round of eternal rebirth is not attained by good action but rather by the moment of death. This account of salvation, however, is balanced with another: the idea that union with *brahman* is attained by knowledge of *brahman*.

> The wise one – he is not born, he does not die; he has not come from anywhere; he has not become anyone. He is unborn and eternal, primeval and everlasting. And he is not killed, when the body is killed. If the killer thinks he kills; If the killer thinks he is killed; Both of them do not understand. He neither kills, nor is he killed. (KaU: 2, 18, 19)

The wise man is beyond good and evil, he finds liberation from the round of rebirth by the development of a supreme *knowledge* of the self, sometimes complemented with asceticism and meditation.

In the context of the question of dignity within the Hindu tradition, with respect to the *Upaniṣads* we could thus say that it is in essence an *individualistic* concept: the idea of the unification of the self with the Universal Self is an individual, in no ways social affair. Concomitantly, dignity does not hold social or legal significance.

The Laws of Manu

The *Mānavadharmaśāstra* or *Manusmṛti*,[2] which probably stems from a later period – it is notoriously difficult to date Indian texts since they were initially orally transmitted – is a story wherein the more or less mythical figure of Manu, the wise law-giver, teaches the universal laws to his pupils. These laws articulate an account of dignity which entwines the concept with social status: dignity is dependent on social class.[3]

Manu received the universal laws from the creator of the world, the 'Self-Existent Lord' (*svayaṃbhūr bhagavān*), who created four distinct social classes together with the world;

> For the growth of these worlds, moreover, he produced from his mouth, arms, thighs, and feet, the Brahmin, the Kṣatriya, the Vaiśya, and the Śudra. (I: 31)

These classes are hierarchically ordered: the priests form the class all others have to serve; the warrior aristocracy provides the king, the military and government officials; the traders and farmers come thereafter; the lowest class is made up by the servants and slaves. All classes have their own and very strict codes of

[2] For the texts on historical Indian law, i.e. the *Dharmasūtras*, see Olivelle (2000; 2005a); and, for a translation and edition of the *Mānavadharmaśāstra*, see Olivelle 2005b.

[3] On the Indian class society, see the classical work of Dumont 1966.

conduct; in particular, those of the priests and warrior aristocracy are described in detail. The wisdom of the Veda, the traditional sacrificial hymns and the foundation of all rites, is accessible to all except the lowest class; which means slaves and servants cannot partake in any socially respected activity. But it also means that those belonging to lower classes will have difficulty in achieving liberation from the round of rebirth, the unification with *brahman*: the life of the man of learning or the aristocrat is regarded as 'purer' than those of people belonging to lower classes – although *in principle* every individual possesses basic dignity, from the perspective of the social system dignity comes in degrees.

The distinction between the classes is strict, but also understood as fair and seldom questioned. The reason for this is not only that the class system was thought to have its origin in the creation of the world; the concept of *karma* explains that the class in which a person is born (if he is born human obviously; he may also be reborn as an animal, god or ghost) is his own responsibility. The situation in which a person finds himself is wholly dependent on his past actions: differences, privileges and hardships of various sorts are explained and justified on the basis of the idea that these are products of one's previous lives. This is reflected in Law and legal proceedings (*vyavahāra*). Punishments in cases of unlawful behaviour are *graded* in accordance with the social class to which a person belongs: if a brahmin and a farmer were to commit the same crime, the punishment the brahmin would receive would be milder than that of the farmer. It is important to note that both deserve punishment: although the practice of punishment is obviously in a sense meant to inspire fear in others, in the Vedic tradition it is also thought to exist for the sake of the punished. Punishment is also a form of *purification*; for instance, if a man were to steal or have illicit sexual intercourse, his sin may be purified by cutting off the relevant bodily limb.

Although this class-dependent concept of dignity is, as said above, very strict, it is balanced by a doctrine we encountered previously: the doctrine of liberation from the round of rebirth. The *Mānavadharmaśāstra* describes the path to liberation in terms of four stages in a man's life:[4] as a young man, the *ārya* (member of Vedic society) should study the Veda; starting with puberty, he should enjoy sexuality and build a family; then he must leave the family and become a 'forest dweller'; then in the last phase of his life give up all his belongings and seek truth – with the hope of finding salvation. This balances the notion of class-dependent dignity because the mendicant is always respected, regardless of which class he belongs to – although it is obviously easier for those who are purer to find liberation.

[4] In the Vedic tradition all which is said here applies to men only: a woman has no separate rights outside of her family – she follows her husband in life and is to partake in his ritual life.

Summing up, we could say that in the Laws of Manu the concept of dignity appears differently from in the *Upaniṣads*: although the ideal of liberation from eternal rebirth is retained – and in that sense so too are some of the individualistic aspects of dignity – it is countered by a very strict social notion of class-dependent or graded dignity.

The Bhagavadgītā

The *Bhagavadgītā* or 'Song of the Lord' – which is often called simply '*Gītā*', or 'The Song' – appeared quite late in the last millennium BC and, although it was a relatively small book, could be said to form the basis for later Indian religious thought. In the text, the notion of *dharma*, duty or law, is combined with the idea of liberation: the highest ideal articulated in the *Gītā* is doing one's duty for the sake of God, as a sacrifice to God. If one's actions are motivated only by devotion to God, one will become one with the divine essence of God and be liberated from the round of rebirth.

At the start of the *Gītā*, we read of a prince named Arjuna who is confronted with his own cousins on the battleground. Arjuna is saddened because he does not want to fight his cousins – slaying relatives is against *dharma* – but he is a warrior and it would be against his dignity to show the weakness of abstaining from attack. Arjuna finds himself in a moral dilemma. His charioteer, Kṛṣṇa – the incarnation of the Supreme God – speaks to him, and in this speech all the previous traditions are mentioned. The speech ends, however, with a new kind of religious message: the idea of devotion to a personal God, or the concept of self-less action. The strictly class-related notion of dignity is hereby less emphasized: indeed, the *Gītā* ascribes a form of religious dignity to everybody, not solely to the elite of monks and religious specialists – perhaps one could say the text draws upon the individualistic account of dignity one finds in the *Upaniṣads*. This notion, however, is extended in the *Gītā* in the sense that it gains a duty-related connotation: following the *dharma*, the law or duty in accordance with one's birth into a particular way of life, is extolled. What it means to do well is not, as we found in the *Mānavadharmaśāstra*, solely to be understood in terms of class-dependent norms, nor is it, as in the *Upaniṣads*, wholly unrelated to laws/duties: in the *Gītā*, we find an account of dignity which integrates the aim of unification with God and the practice of sacrifice with the concept of moral action. To become unified with God, to find salvation from the circle of rebirth, is to do one's duty as a sacrifice to God: only when one renounces all personal gain, is motivated purely by devotion to God – doing one's duty because it is one's duty – may an action be truly valuable and dignified. It is important to emphasize that this includes the aim of salvation: actions committed in order to find liberation from the circle of rebirth will not unify one with God, only those actions which are truly self-less will let the individual participate in the divine essence. Only then is one freed from all *dharmas*, duties and laws, as stated by the divine incarnation:

> Be Me-minded, devoted to Me; Worship Me, revere me; And to Me alone shalt thou go; truly to thee I promise it – (because) you art dear to me. Abandoning all (other) duties, Go to Me as thy sole refuge; From all evils I thee Shall rescue: be not grieved! (XIII: 65–6)

And eventually indeed, Arjuna is inspired by the speech of the God and decides to fight:

> Destroyed the confusion; attention (to the truth) is won, By Thy grace, on my part, O Changeless One; I stand firm, with doubts dispersed; I shall do Thy Word. (XIII: 73)

Thus, we find that the *Gītā* grants a religious identity and dignity to the individual, regardless of the class to which he (or even she; the text is written in gender-neutral terms) belongs – provided that duties are performed from pure motives, from devotion, and are not in any way inspired by personal gain.

Summing up, we can say that the concept of dignity is given shape differently in these three main sources of Hindu thought. In the *Upaniṣads*, we find that dignity is related to the individual self who should strive for unification with the Universal Self, where dignity lacks a social or moral connotation. In the *Mānavadharmaśāstra*, the social dimension of dignity is strongly emphasized in the sense that the concept becomes class-dependent: although in principle all who achieve liberation from the circle of rebirth command respect, the concept is in a sense elitist because *karma* and the concomitant notion of radical responsibility legitimizes the class system and morally favours those belonging to the higher classes over others. It is only in the *Gītā* that dignity becomes something resembling an egalitarian moral concept: dignity is related to selfless action and in that quality is independent from class. As such, the religion of the *Gītā* has historically been the ground for the ascription of religious rights to each individual. On the other hand, however, the religion also refutes dignity as a concept: especially in the ninth chapter, the *Gītā* emphasizes that God is the basic power in the Universe; human existence as a feeble fact compared to the truly divine.

All in all, we can say that, in the Hindu tradition, dignity appears as an ambiguous and even paradoxical concept; sometimes it appears as an inherent attribute of the individual, sometimes it is dependent on social class, and sometimes a concept related to moral action but is in that quality strongly religious. Taking these traditions together, we see that a type of accentuated individualism coexists with a social system which is programmatically unequal, showing us that a particular anthropology, which ascribes dignity to humans and animals alike, does not necessarily create social conventions that promote the principle of inherent and equal dignity for all human beings.

References

Dumont, L. 1966. *Homo Hierarchicus: Essai sur le système des castes*. Paris: Gallimard

Olivelle, P. 1998. *The Early Upaniṣads: Annotated Text and Translation*. Oxford University Press

2000. *Dharmasūtra Parallels: Containing the Dharmasūtras of Āpastamba, Gautama, Baudhāyana and Vasiṣṭa*. Delhi: Motilal Banarsidass

2005a. *Dharmasūtras: The Law Codes of Āpastamba, Gautama, Baudhāyana and Vasiṣṭa*. Delhi: Motilal Banarsidass

2005b. *Manu's Code of Law: A Critical Edition and Translation of the Mānava-dharmaśāstra*. Oxford University Press

16

Buddhism: inner dignity and absolute altruism

JENS BRAARVIG

In Buddhism, as in the Hindu tradition, the concept of dignity appears in different and paradoxical qualities. As in Hinduism, in Buddhism there exists a tension between dignity which is inherent to all living beings and socially embedded dignity which appears in different gradations. In this chapter, I will focus primarily on dignity in classical and Mahāyāna Buddhism.[1]

'Since beginning-less time' man is imprisoned in the round of rebirth, and whether he is born as an animal, spirit, human in a high or low class, in hell or even as a divine being, is entirely dependent on *karma*: action understood as a cause which explains a being's (way of) existence. This is reflected in the idea that the individual is completely responsible for his own existence: what one is depends wholly on one's previous actions – in this life and the ones preceding it. Indeed, in Buddhism we find a type of radical individualism: one's (well)being and fate is in a very fundamental sense an individual affair. This is a basic premise shared by nearly all Indian philosophical and religious traditions, but where Buddhism differs from the others is that it understands existence to be characterized by impermanence and emptiness – everything perishes the moment it comes into existence. This also means that there is in the strict sense no such thing as 'the self': beings, like all other things, *lack essence.* Insight in the nature of existence, combined with concentrational and meditative practices, may allow the individual to realize the end of his own suffering/disquietude: the end of further rebirth, the extinction of the self in *nirvāṇa.* Thus, in Buddhism, the individual is absolutely responsible for his own existence: his past actions are the cause of his direction towards good or bad or towards the final freedom one may seek by adopting a monk's life and isolating himself from society – solely focused on his individual salvation.

[1] For a general introduction to Buddhism with a representative bibliography, see Freiberger and Kleine 2011. What we call Classical Buddhism corresponds roughly to *Theravada*, the Buddhism of southern Asia today. *Mahāyāna* Buddhism is in recent centuries and today present in the countries of northern Asia.

Classical Buddhism

The anthropology of classical Buddhism is characterized by its ascribing to each human being an existential freedom or autonomy: every human, male or female, is at liberty to find salvation from the circle of eternal rebirth. As already suggested, this is conceptualized in a radically individualistic fashion: salvation wholly lacks a social connotation, but is rather described in psychological terms – as processes of perception, reflection etc. – which are all done away with in reaching *nirvāṇa*, the absence of disquietude. Although in a strict sense there exists no 'self', one could say that in classical Buddhism nonetheless we find a notion of dignity grounded precisely in the freedom of individuals to liberate themselves from the suffering which the circle of eternal rebirth causes them. However, this philosophical notion of dignity was not reflected as social/moral dignity: persons did not hold individual rights. This is not very surprising; the idea that happiness – absence of suffering – lies *beyond* the eternal process of reincarnation gives Buddhism a flare of unworldliness; or rather, it explicitly states that worldly matters should be shunned. In fact, part of the monastic code (the *Vinaya*) is the issue that monks should not engage in politics or economics; they should focus on the search for freedom *from* – not in – this world. We could say that Buddhist ideology is non-social: it has no interests in law and political power. The codes of conduct which follow from the tradition are rules which specify actions that would produce bad *karma*; they are not in any way motivated by a drive to protect the individual in the realm of social and political practices. Codes of conduct exist for the sake of the individual: they are aimed at preventing *him* from producing bad *karma*, and are not inspired by ideals of social justice.

This does not mean that the notion of dignity is in no way reflected in the social realm. If we take a closer look at the term '*arhat*' – the Buddhist counterpart of 'dignified' which the word directly denotes – we notice that it could not be applied to everybody: the status of '*arahts*' was reserved to persons who practiced Buddha's teachings on insight and meditation, to those who would reach *nirvāṇa* upon death. Indeed, the word is perhaps best translated as 'Saint'; the *arhats* were usually depicted in Buddhist iconography as Buddha's five hundred closest disciples. Thus, dignity as *arhat* was applicable only to monks and formed an unattainable ideal for laymen. Naturally, this inequality *qua* religious status translated to a form of social inequality: the monastic community was also socially superior to the lay community. So in classical Buddhism 'dignity' was a concept that was not universally attributed to all individuals equally, but only to the monastic elite.

According to Buddhist views, the world of phenomena is essentially impermanent: open for change, transformation – unreliable. The same holds for us: we lack a self, a constant, we are ultimately self-less, *anātman*, and our grossest misunderstanding is to cling to an illusory self. Combined, these ontological concepts form the ground for the Four Noble Truths. The first states that life is suffering, *duḥkha*: our existence is impermanent, sometimes we are happy but happiness always perishes – living beings are in a 'state' of disquietude. The second says that the cause of this suffering (*samudaya*) is craving, desire; the third that there exists a way out (*nirvāṇa*) of this suffering; the fourth specifies the 'eightfold path' (*aṣṭāṅgamārga*) by which this cessation may be achieved. This path consists of prescripts regarding knowledge, ethics and practices of concentration and mindfulness. This impermanence, and 'floating state of things', may well open up for a lack of legal protection for, *in case*, human rights, as dignity is seen as very much dependent on the individual, who is always a product of his own actions (*karma*) since 'beginning-less time' and thus completely and solely responsible for what he is. But, by the practice of the Buddhas teachings, he can attain the status of an *arhat*, sainthood, or rather *dignity*, and reach *nirvāṇa* at death. We can say, then, that classical Buddhism teaches *inner* dignity, that can be attained by religious practice, but it is not an *inherent* dignity. This kind of dignity, though, we would argue can be found in Mahāyāna Buddhism.

Mahāyāna Buddhism

The religious ideal of classical Buddhism did not remain without opposition: the so-called 'Mahāyāna Buddhism' paved the way for a more egalitarian conception of dignity. In parts of Mahāyāna Buddhism, we find a view that attributes dignity to all living things equally: not only human beings, but also gods, animals, spirits and the inhabitants of Hell participate in the 'Buddha-nature' or the 'nature of the Awakened'.

Mahāyāna Buddhism, which had its origin around the beginning of Western chronology, was a reaction to what was conceived as the incomplete interpretation of Buddha's words. It thus was a critical and in some parts strongly rhetorical attack on its predecessor; it framed the position of classical Buddhism as *hīnayāna* – the 'small way' – and its own ethics as *mahāyāna* – the 'great way'. Mahāyāna Buddhism argued that its aim was to save all living beings rather than narrowly focus on personal liberation; the aim of Buddha's teachings is to commit oneself to save all other beings before oneself. This tradition thus propounded a radical ethical altruism and accentuated egalitarian ideology, and criticized the *arhat* as an illusion or social construct unconnected with spiritual maturity. The religious ideal thus moves away from the monk and the disciple striving to be an *arhat*, towards the ideal of *bodhisattva* – the person who has vowed to give all living beings happiness and spiritual maturity, and is reborn in every cycle of the universe to help those who suffer before thinking about himself. '*Bodhi*' means 'awakening' (the Buddha), '*sattva*' means 'living being': the *bodhisattva* is thus the person who has adopted the vow of awakening for the sake of all living beings. Instead of aiming to become an *arhat*, those following the teachings of Mahāyāna Buddhism thus aim to become a compassionate Buddha.

The ethics of Mahāyāna Buddhism has its ground in two ontological concepts: emptiness and impermanency. Although we perceive things as having essences, as separate objects distinct from us as subjects, in reality every 'thing' is empty: the subject–object distinction is an illusion, everything is void of substance. This also holds for Buddha; Buddha and all living beings are essentially the same. But obviously we do not perceive it as such: what we see is a *world* created by our own 'conceptual filter', a *fata morgana* or echo which hinders our true perception of the emptiness of reality. A world of phenomena which are essentially impermanent: open for change, transformation – unreliable. The same holds for us: we lack a self, a constant, we are ultimately self-less, *anātman*, and our grossest misunderstanding is to cling to an illusory self. This view is shared with classical Buddhism, but the Mahāyāna view would add that *everything* is empty (*śūnya*), not only the idea of the *self*. On this ontological basis was built a new form of ethics, which was socially directed. Ethics are for the sake of transcending the illusory 'self and other dichotomy' by social virtue, as differing from the *Hīnayāna*, which is criticized for being only interested in the personal salvation, and thus nothing but a more subtle form of self-seeking. In this way, the ethics of purity and meditation of classical Buddhism is transformed, and specified in a list of 'six perfections': generosity, morality, tolerance, vigour, meditation and insight into the true nature of reality, where the first four are typically social virtues. Thus, also compassion and respect for life become essential. As already mentioned, the task of the *bodhisattva* is not understood as an individual or personal affair: he should aim to cultivate the 'omnipresent Buddha-nature' in all living things by his great compassion and selflessness – thus he transcends the dichotomy of self and other by sharing the life with every living being. Obviously, this is quite a lofty ideal, since it simply cannot be reached: the altruism prescribed by this tradition of Buddhism extends so far that nobody will be able to live up to this standard. In contrast with classical Buddhism therefore, in Mahāyāna Buddhism we find a concept of dignity with social or moral substance: all living things possess dignity because they participate in the Buddha-essence, and as such should be respected in the sense that others have the duty to support them in striving to end suffering. In this way, all beings have an unborn Buddha within, the *tathāgatagarbha*, a seed that can be developed into full buddhahood, and every being should be respected as a Buddha. Dignity thus appears as something which is to be equally ascribed to all, and commands that others respect the dignified person (or animal, god or spirit, etc.) in their actions. Indeed, in some of the texts, the exemplars are laymen – explicitly *not* members of the monastic class. In the *Mañjuśrīvikrīḍita* for instance, we read about a prostitute who, sharing in the dignity inherent in all, appears as a grand *bodhisattva*; setting forth the idea that all social roles are mere constructs, and that all personalities are essentially the same as *bodhi* – the awakening of the Buddha.

Emperor Aśoka

These ideas are not merely philosophical: they have been practiced as political doctrines also, for instance under the rule of emperor Aśoka. Aśoka ruled over much of what constitutes India today from 269 to 232 BC and is reckoned the military and political leader who created the first Indian empire.

Emperor Aśoka, as we are told by the Buddhist legends, was incredibly evil when he conquered his empire, but in his remorse became a devout Buddhist and piously committed himself to doing good. Aśoka's inscriptions primarily make the welfare of people and religious tolerance a political issue: he promoted rights and freedoms, especially freedom of religion. He appears to have done so on the basis of an egalitarian concept of dignity ascribed to humans and animals; *brahmin*, the poor, the chiefs, the soldiers and the elderly alike – no one should suffer harassment or humiliating treatment. In the inscriptions he left all over northern India he gives instructions on how his kingdom should be ruled by his officials.[2]

> Truly, I consider the welfare of all to be my duty, and the root of this is exertion and the prompt despatch of business. There is no better work than promoting the welfare of all the people and whatever efforts I am making is to repay the debt I owe to all beings to assure their happiness in this life, and attain heaven in the next. (6r)

And indeed, Aśoka not only promoted religious freedom negatively; he made explicit that the existence of not one but several religions was a good; there are many ways to understand truth, and interaction between religions would only contribute positively:

> Beloved-of-the-Gods, King Piyadasi, honors both ascetics and the householders of all religions, and he honors them with gifts and honors of various kinds. But Beloved-of-the-Gods, King Piyadasi, does not value gifts and honors as much as he values this – that there should be growth in the essentials of all religions. Growth in essentials can be done in different ways, but all of them have as their root restraint in speech, that is, not praising one's own religion, or condemning the religion of others without good cause. And if there is cause for criticism, it should be done in a mild way. But it is better to honor other religions for this reason. By so doing, one's own religion benefits, and so do other religions, while doing otherwise harms one's own religion and the religions of others. Whoever praises his own religion, due to excessive devotion, and condemns others with the thought 'Let me glorify my own religion', only harms his own religion. Therefore

[2] The translations are based on those of Dhammika 1993, with some changes. All the quotations are from the Rock edicts (r). For a general treatment and complete bibliography, see Falk 2006.

> contact (between religions) is good. One should listen to and respect the doctrines professed by others. Beloved-of-the-Gods, King Piyadasi, desires that all should be well-learned in the good doctrines of other religions. (12r)

The Arthaśāstra

We have chosen to treat the *Arthaśāstra*[3] under the heading of Buddhism as it is traditionally ascribed to Cāṇakya Kauṭilya ('the Crooked One'), who is supposed to be the minister of Candragupta, Aśoka's grandfather. Parts of the *Arthaśāstra* were certainly composed somewhat later, probably at the start of the Common Era. Often Cāṇakya has been called the 'Machiavelli of India', as he articulates advice and concrete suggestions on how a ruler could stay in power by any means necessary. The main task of the ruler is to be 'just with the rod' (in Sanskrit: *daṇḍa*, meaning 'authority' and 'strong rule'), in order to scare people and prevent them from disrupting the social order. So he should employ the rod; 'If not used it gives rise to the law of the fishes. For then the stronger swallows the weak in the absence of the wielder of the Rod. Protected by that, he prevails' (1.4.13–15). Lacking a religious foundation, the *Arthaśāstra* is pragmatic in style and aimed at the protection of the stability of the state. As such, the focus seems less to lie on the individual and rather on the *collective*: rules and laws are not based on a type of moral respect each individual commands, but rather on the question whether they safeguard the stability within the collective. Indeed, punishments potentially include all kinds of cruelties – killing and cutting of limbs, for instance – and their severity is dependent on the class to which a person belongs. Thus, in the *Arthaśāstra* we find no concept of dignity as something that is equally ascribed to each individual.

Conclusion

The concept of dignity appears in various forms in the Buddhist tradition. In classical Buddhism, dignity is a strongly individualistic notion and ascribed only to the *arhat*; only he will reach nirvāṇa – the absence of disquietude – after death. In Mahāyāna Buddhism, precisely this individualism and elitism is criticized: the ideal is no longer the *arhat* but the *bodhisattva*, he (or she) who manifests radical altruism in the quality of attempting to liberate the suffering of all others before thinking about oneself. In this form of Buddhism, dignity becomes an egalitarian moral notion: it is ascribed to all humans (although obviously not only to humans) and leads to a duty in others. That these are not merely philosophical concepts is shown by the example of emperor Aśoka, who tried to effectuate an egalitarian notion of dignity through political precepts – of which freedom of religion is perhaps the most prominent. But that social conditions do not necessarily reflect philosophical and religious ideas, is shown

[3] 1965. trans., ed. and commented, R. P. Kangle, vols. 1–3, Delhi: Motilal Banarsidass.

by the *Arthaśāstra*: the collective; the stability of the state became central and the individual was not in a moral sense relevant – let alone inherently dignified. So all in all we can say that dignity appears in the Buddhist tradition in many interesting but fundamentally different ways.

Buddhism, with its lofty ideals, has diffused East Asian societies throughout millennia, and rulers have supported Buddhism with surely many kinds of motivations. The Buddhist monastic communities, with their formalized rules for conduct, being the backbone and basis of the historical continuity of Buddhism, do not seem to have had much formal influence on general law-making that would implement the Buddhist ideals of tolerance, compassion, respect and peace, and to protect the dignity embedded in them. Thus, it remains always dependent on the historical context to what extent Buddhist ideals were important for the societies at large, or only for elitist groups. However, the ideals, as described above, are shared by Buddhists on the whole, even though what we have termed 'classical Buddhism', at least in the last five hundred years, have dominated the South Asian countries, such as Thailand, Burma and Sri Lanka; and the Mahāyāna has been influential in China, Tibet, Japan, Vietnam, Korea., etc., since the introduction of Buddhism to these countries after the beginning of the Common Era.

References

Arthaśāstra. 1965. trans., ed. and commented, R. P. Kangle, vols. 1–3. Delhi: Motilal Banarsidass

Dhammika, Ven. S. 1993. *Edicts of King Asoka*. Kandy: Wheel

Falk, H. 2006. *Aśokan Sites and Artefacts: A Sourcebook with Bibliography*. Mainz am Rhein: von Zabern

Freiberger, O., and Kleine, C. 2011. *Buddhismus: Handbuch und kritische Einführung*. Göttingen: Vandenhoeck & Ruprecht

17

Human dignity in traditional Chinese Confucianism

LUO AN'XIAN

The core of Chinese Confucianism concerns personhood: it addresses questions as to how to conduct oneself and what kind of person one should be. The basic notions of Chinese Confucianism are benevolence, righteousness, ritual, wisdom and integrity. The Confucian concept of human dignity is deeply interwoven with these core concepts of Confucianism. Human dignity in Confucianism addresses core questions of Confucian convictions such as how to deal with life and death, honour and disgrace, loyalty etc. This chapter will present central doctrines to these questions of the main representatives of Confucianism and attempt to disclose how human dignity may be conceived in this tradition.

Confucius: human dignity and benevolence

Although Confucianism affirms that all human life is valuable, in case of conflict, in cases wherein one has to risk his life in order to uphold benevolence and righteousness, the latter take priority over life itself. 'Benevolence' in Confucianism indicates care for other people and social groups. Fan Chi, a student of Confucius, once asked his master as to the meaning of benevolence.[1] The master responded that benevolence means to love people: benevolence means to love genuinely or authentically, to desire the well-being of others without seeking to profit from their well-being oneself. The virtue of benevolence is what makes life valuable: a life without benevolence is a life not worth living. Thus, Confucius claims that 'for gentlemen of purpose and men of benevolence, while it is inconceivable that they should seek to stay alive at the expense of benevolence, it may happen that they have to accept death in order to accomplish benevolence' (Confucius 2008: 15: 9). In circumstances wherein a specific person does not live in accordance with the requirements of benevolence or even acts in opposition to these, his life is no longer valuable: a life without benevolence is a life without *dignity*. Hence, even in the tragic situation wherein the act of benevolence

[1] Confucius (551–479 BCE) lived in what is known in Chinese history as the 'Spring and Autumn Period'. He was the founder and the most important exponent of Confucianism.

would entail death, Confucianism holds that benevolence is morally overriding because the alternative – an undignified life – is hardly a life at all. However, benevolence cannot be externally enforced; Confucius says that 'the practice of benevolence depends on oneself alone, and not on others' (Confucius 2008: 12: 1).[2] To live in accordance with dignity depends wholly on the individual person: benevolence can only have its ground in free choice. As the true manifestation of character and personality, benevolence is not something one person can force upon another. People have the right to choose for themselves how they live and die, and it is up to them to choose death in order to retain their dignity. The moment of choice so conceived represents the dignity of life. Although the acceptance of death for the sake of benevolence appears as a denial of life, it is in fact a true symbol of dignity. Though life is precious, a life without dignity is meaningless and worthless, and therefore people – whether they are of high or low social status – should live with dignity even if that entails embracing death in some circumstances.

Mencius: human dignity and righteousness

Where Confucius emphasizes benevolence, Mencius[3] attaches more importance to righteousness. Mencius said: 'I like life and I like righteousness. But if I have to choose between them I will let go of life and take righteousness' (Mencius 2003; Kao Tzu, 1: 10).[4] Righteousness is an absolute and unconditional 'should' and an expression of responsibility. Confucians believe that human existence is a kind of social existence. As social beings, all humans play a different role in society and have different social responsibilities. Members of society should strive to carry out their own social responsibilities and realize their particular destinies – this is what Confucians understand by 'righteousness'. Life and righteousness are both cherished by people; however, people should 'let go of life and take righteousness' whenever the two cannot coexist righteousness is more valuable than mere survival. Mencius said: 'I want life, but there are things more important to me than life. Therefore there are things that I won't do simply to stay alive. I hate death, but there are things that I hate more than death, and thus there are certain kinds of suffering that I won't avoid' (*ibid.*). Also, for Mencius, there are things more precious than life. So, again, only a life with dignity – in this case understood in terms of righteousness – is understood as a life worth living: without righteousness, life is mere animal-like subsistence.

[2] The *Analects of Confucius* is a collection of aphorisms attributed to Confucius, thought to be written down by his followers. The *Analects* consists of twenty sections or books, each divided in subsections. References in this chapter provide book number and subsection.

[3] Mencius (372–289 BCE) was a representative of the Confucian School. His status is only slightly lower than Confucius'.

[4] The Kao Tzu is the sixth book of the works of Mencius. It consists of two parts, divided into several chapters; references here are provided likewise.

While Confucius connects dignity to benevolence, Mencius conceives it in terms of righteousness. In the Confucian tradition, these two approaches have become integrated into an ideal of personal conduct: into a comprehensive and multifaceted account of what it means to lead a dignified life. In the Chinese tradition, such ethical ideals are not developed in the analytical style characteristic of many Western ethical positions; they are rather exemplified in narratives like short stories and aphorisms. I mention one: Wen Tianxiang, the prime minister of the Southern Song Dynasty, was captured by the Yuan Dynasty rulers. He was tortured and tempted by the rulers with various means. However, Wen Tianxiang refused the high official position and salary offered and withstood the cruel torture; he would rather die than surrender. Wen chose to die calmly and left behind famous and compelling lines of poetry: 'None since the advent of time have escaped death, may my loyalty forever illuminate the annals of history'; 'I would rather sacrifice my life for integrity than to eke an ignoble existence, may the integrity and righteousness shine and last forever.' Wen chose benevolence and righteousness over survival, died with dignity and lived a glorious life. As such, Wen became an exemplary model of a dignified person, his story provides guidance for others in attempting to live a dignified life.

Dignity and integrity

In a different way, dignity is strongly tied to integrity. Integrity refers to fortitude and steadfastness: possessing integrity means that one maintains his personality or character, especially in situations in which he is put to the test – as for instance in circumstances of calamity or life-threatening danger. Confucius said: 'The Three Armies can be deprived of their commander, but there is no way a common man can be deprived of his purpose' (Confucius 2008: 9: 26). This means that people cannot be forced to give up their own personality and conduct or the guidance for their own lives. Mencius points this out more clearly: 'If wealth and honour do not dissipate you; poverty and low status do not make you move from your principles; authority and might do not distort you: [t]hen you can be called a "great man"' (Mencius 2003: T'eng Weng Kung, 2: 2).[5] A man who will neither be confused by wealth and honour, nor change his behaviour when he is poor and low, nor thwart his principles in the face of power is a man with dignity, a 'great man'. Xun Zi[6] said: '[T]he exigencies of time and place and considerations of personal profit cannot influence him, cliques and coteries cannot sway him, and the whole world cannot deter him. He was born to follow his principles, and he will die following them: truly this can be called "being resolute from inner power"' (Xun zi, in Knoblock 1988: 1: 14). Whether one lives or dies, no matter what kind of power or hardship one faces, nothing must change one's ambition or conduct – dignity lies precisely in steadfastness.

[5] The T'eng Weng Kung is the third book of the Mencius.

[6] Xun Zi (313–238BC) is a representative of the Confucian School.

Let me rehearse another short story to exemplify this: Su Wu, the minister of the Han Dynasty, was seized by the potentates of the Huns during his diplomatic mission on behalf of the Han Dynasty. The potentates of the Huns tried various means to force or tempt Su Wu to betray the Han Dynasty in order to serve the Huns as an official. Su Wu just refused to yield, and was exiled to a deserted Siberia where he spent a long nineteen years alone. However, Su Wu kept his faith without wavering and refused to betray his motherland. In this way, Su Wu not only safeguarded his own dignity, but also that of his motherland, thus becoming a typical Confucian 'great man' who cannot be dissipated by wealth and honour, cannot be made to move from his own principles by poverty and low status, and cannot be corrupted by authority and might. So where benevolence and righteousness are virtues that give content to the notion of a dignified life in the form of ethical principles, integrity refers rather to the formal quality of steadfastness: to stand one's ground and stick to the principles one affirms, regardless of the circumstances.

Let me illustrate this with another few aphorisms. Mencius once said: 'When a bowl of rice or a cup of soup lies between life and death, and you offer it in a nasty way, even a beggar in the street will not accept it. If you kick it at him with your feet, even a beggar will not take it' (Mencius, Kao Tzu, 1: 10). People should maintain their dignity even in the cold, even when hungry. Alms accepted when given with a contemptuous attitude would damage the human dignity of recipients and thus will be refused by them, even by beggars. *The Book of Rites*[7] records that, one year, the state of Qi suffered a severe famine. A rich man named Qian Ao put some food at the roadside, waiting for the hungry to pass by. A horrendous-looking man who was shading his face with his sleeve and wore a pair of broken shoes staggered close to the food. After seeing the poor man, Qian Ao picked up the food with his left hand and held the soup with his right hand, and arrogantly yelled: 'Hey! Eat it!' The hungry man raised his head and glared contemptuously at him: 'I would rather be hungry than to take this handout' (Legge 2003: 2: 3). Qian Ao realized his impolite tone was a bit too much and apologized to the poor hungry man, but the man refused to eat and eventually starved to death at the roadside. The man's refusal to accept the food offered to him was an act that preserved his dignity, but also reflects the requirements of the Confucian theory of benevolence in that it symbolizes the limits that should be respected if one person is to respect another's dignity. Confucianism states thus that the dignity of the individual human being should be respected and not offended. Subject to the influence of Confucian ideology and culture, many traditional intellectuals risked their power and lives to protect their own human dignity. As a last story: Xi Gang was a painter of the Qing Dynasty. When the Emperor Qian Long made a journey in Zhejiang Province, the palace in which he lived lacked any murals. The prefect of Hangzhou City

[7] *The Book of Rites* is one of the Chinese Confucian literature collections of the pre-Qin Dynasty. References here specify book number and part.

summoned Xi Gang and ordered him to paint a mural. Xi Gang refused by saying: 'You can cut my head off, but you cannot get the mural.' Not even a prefect or emperor can force a person to lose his dignity: human dignity has its ground in the individual freedom of action.

As these stories show, in Confucianism benevolence, righteousness and integrity form a notion of human dignity that functions as an ethical ideal/code of conduct and explains what it means to live a dignified – a fully human – life: to care for one's fellow people without desiring anything in return, to accept the responsibilities related to one's particular social role and to act on these, and to endorse these ethical ideals even – or especially – in situations in which the strength of one's character is put to the test.

Conclusion

In Confucianism, human dignity plays a very important role: a life without dignity is not a life worth living. The Confucian notion of human dignity shows similarities to various Western traditions. First, it resonates strongly with reflections on human dignity in Greek antiquity: especially in the Stoic tradition we find similarities with the Confucian emphasis on righteousness and integrity, the idea that one should retain character and poise regardless of the perils and hardships that destiny or fortune unfolds. Second, the virtue of benevolence and the right to have one's dignity respected obviously have connections with Kantianism: both traditions affirm that people have a duty to treat other human beings in a way that respects their dignity. The Confucian concept, however, also has many differences to contemporary Western accounts of human dignity; the most fundamental of which perhaps is that in Confucianism human dignity is not conceived as inalienable. When an individual lacks steadfastness and acts contrary to his principles out of cowardice or even personal gain, he will lose his dignity: by acting in an animal-like fashion, he will no longer be a human being in the full sense of the word. This is a very profound difference, and it gives rise to the question if and how the Confucian account of human dignity and the one articulated in the Universal Declaration of Human Rights could be seen as compatible. In any case, I would suggest, this question is important and we need to answer it if we are to formulate a global concept of human dignity.

References

Confucius. 2008. *The Analects of Confucius*, trans. D. C. Lau. Beijing: Zhonghua Book Company

Knoblock, J. 1988. *Xun Zi: A Translation and Study of the Complete Works*. Stanford University Press

Legge, J. 2003. *Li Chi: The Book of Rites*, vol. 1. Whitefish: Kessinger

Mencius. 2003. *Mencius (Selections)*, trans. C. Muller. Tokyo: Tōyō Gakuen University

18

Dignity in traditional Chinese Daoism

QIAO QING-JU

'Dignity' (尊严, zūn yán) is, in the contemporary Chinese language, both a foreignism and a native term. As a foreignism, many scholars conceive the main function of dignity to be the communication of modern European ideas of human dignity, especially that of Kantian philosophy, to contemporary China which is thought to lack such ideas. Thus, in the *Ci-Hai* (辞海, literally a 'sea of terms'), one of the few comprehensive Chinese dictionaries, the second definition of this word is: 'The recognition and affirmation of the moral and social value of an individual or a social organization; The acknowledgment of the value of human life as the most fundamental dignity of human beings' (Ci-Hai 2000: 2300). The *Ci-Hai* mentions nothing of the Chinese tradition of the concept, as if it does not play a role in Chinese philosophy. This would be a misunderstanding: a notion of dignity is central in both Confucianism and Daoism. The Confucian concept of dignity is similar to the one we find in Kantian philosophy: dignity is understood as *human* dignity and strongly related to *action*. In the Daoist tradition, 'dignity' functions very differently, but this does not mean, I will suggest, that it is of no interest to our understanding of the concept. Quite the contrary: the Daoist conception of dignity could contribute to the global discussion of the concept precisely because it offers a different perspective.

I will first briefly attempt to outline the general features of the idea of Dao, and second discuss the substance and role of dignity in Daoism.

Dignity in Daoism

In Daoism, the two most important concepts are Dao (道, the way), the concept after which the school is named, and De (德), a term referring to where Dao or part of it dwells. Literally, Dao refers to the way one takes to a destination. There is a certain necessity about the concept of the way: it is not an arbitrarily chosen path in the sense that one could have chosen another and reach the same destination, the way is rather the principle that guides one's movements. The way is, in the *Lao-zi*, not merely the way of the human being, but also that of everything else in the world. It embraces the ongoing process of the whole universe: it is the highest principle to be followed, even for Heaven and Earth.

One could wonder whether, like every other way, the Dao also has a starting-point. Being the highest principle, it is impossible that anything existed prior to the Dao; there would either be no principle upon which such an existence could be founded, or something would have to exist outside Dao – both cases contradict the concept of Dao as the highest principle. Nor is it possible to say that in the beginning there existed a void wherein the Dao dwelled, or that there exists a ceaseless flow of time in which the Dao moves; such imaginations too contradict the concept of Dao. Since at the beginning there is only the Dao, it must follow that Dao is the beginning itself: it is the Dao that produces everything. In the words of *Lao-zi*: 'Dao produced the One. The One produced the two. The two produced the three. And the three produced the ten thousand things' (Chan 1973: 160). Thus, as it was the Dao that produced everything, it cannot be only a principle: it needs to hold a material component; something immaterial cannot bring forth something material. The *Lao-zi* states that Dao is constituted by form and essence, and says 'there was something undifferentiated and yet complete' – in short Dao is made up of both material and spiritual elements.

The Dao, it is said in the *Lao-zi*, also 'clothes and breeds' everything: 'The Great Dao flows everywhere. It may go left or right. All things depend on it for life, and it does not turn away from them' (Chan 1973: 157). Dao's clothing and breeding refers to the idea of bringing things forth and letting things develop as they are, without interference; the Dao has no desire of its own, it is not a principle that dominates or forces things. The characteristic of the principle of Dao is described as 'self-so', 'self-ness' or the 'as-it-is-ness' that is essential to all that is. Nature is self-so: it develops self-determinately, not guided by power from without but naturally. This holds for everything: for rivers, trees, cats and human beings – everything is brought forth and developed by Dao is a forceless, self-so way; 'Man models himself after Earth. Earth models itself after Heaven. Heaven models itself after Dao. And Dao models itself after the self-so' (Chan 1973: 153, with my revision).

The part of Dao obtained by a thing is called 'De': De is the 'dwelling place of Dao' (Li 2002: 770), the presence of Dao in individual things. Accordingly, things – human beings included – are actually and directly guided by De.

Having briefly sketched an outline of the Daoist framework, let me now turn to the concept of dignity. Daoism proclaims that, ultimately, only Dao is dignified: things have dignity only insofar as De is present in them. Dignity is described in the *Lao-zi* in terms of respectability and nobility: 'the myriad things respect the Dao and honour De. The respectability of Dao and the nobility of De emerge naturally without anyone's command' (Chen 1984: 261). Since Dao is the source of dignity, the question regarding whether a human being is dignified is intimately related to that person's relation to Dao: dignity is possessed by those who pursue Dao and embody it in themselves – 'He who pursues the Dao is identified with the Dao' (Chan 1973: 151–2). The *Lao-zi* further demands that one should accumulate De. Accordingly, to ask what it means to have dignity is the same thing as asking what it means to have accumulated De. How, then, does one accumulate De, and what is the state of a person who has successfully done so?

First, the *Lao-zi* offers a method of 'valuing or appreciating one's own body', which means not to indulge oneself in the enjoyment of worldly pleasure, but to be content with a minimum of material goods. 'The five colours cause one's eyes to be blind. The five tones cause one's ears to be deaf. The five flavours cause one's palate to be spoiled' (Chan 1973: 161). One should ultimately, in order to embody De, attempt to diminish one's desire for worldly pleasure, material goods and even fame. The *Lao-zi* asks: 'Which is more intimate to one, fame or one's body?' (*ibid.*). No doubt the answer should be the latter. Also knowledge should be abandoned: 'Abandon sageliness and discard wisdom; Then the people will benefit a hundredfold. Abandon humanity and discard righteousness; Then the people will return to filial piety and deep love. Abandon skill and discard profit; Then there will be no thieves or robbers' (*ibid.*: 149).

Second, the *Lao-zi* states that one should not compete with others but rather strive to act in their benefit: 'The best (man) is like water. Water is good; it benefits all things and does not compete with them . . . It is because he does not compete that he is without reproach' (Chan 1973: 143). And: 'It is precisely because he does not compete that the world cannot compete with him' (*ibid.*: 151). According to the *Lao-zi*, not competing is not only a kind of De, but also the heavenly Dao; furthermore, it proposes a way to win: 'The Way of Heaven does not compete, and yet it skilfully achieves victory' (*ibid.*: 173). In other words, persons who are good, respectable and noble are those who do not strive to excel by contrasting themselves with others, but rather those that strive to be in harmony with their environment.

The perceptive reader may have noticed that the path to dignity taught by the *Lao-zi* is one of negative or passive virtue: it is the path of abstinence rather than the path of action. Daoism proposes a perspective wherein dignified action is understood passively: if we would understand it in terms of movement, the path Daoism proposes is one of reversion rather than extension. The best way to live is not to continuously strive for more possessions, more power, but to reduce one's desires so that he is least in conflict with his environment. The best kind of action, then, is 'non-action': action that is not grounded in a desire for worldly things nor competition, action that is not even motivated by knowledge or ethical precepts – non-action is action that is completely natural, like the river that follows its course. 'The pursuit of Tao is to diminish day after day. It is to diminish and further diminish until one reaches the point of taking no action. No action is undertaken, and yet nothing is left undone' (Chan 1973: 162). Thus, being dignified means having identified oneself with Dao: a state in which one is not troubled by profane desires but in harmony with the world. Becoming dignified, however, is not a path of intentional action: one should refrain from goal-oriented action, and rather attempt to act naturally – to 'let action happen', as it were.

The relevance of the Daoist conception of dignity

The Daoist conception of dignity is very different from the Kantian understanding and also from the Confucian point of view. I will here emphasize two essential differences and elaborate on the potentially positive political import the Daoist perspective can be taken to have.

First, Daoism entails a kind of non-anthropocentrism: it does not restrict the ascription of dignity to human beings. As said above, Dao is the source of dignity but also the ground of all that exists; everything thus possesses dignity. 'There is not a single thing without the Dao', it even exists in 'excrement and urine' (Chan 1973: 203). This might at first sight seem in tension with what was said before – that one may attempt to accumulate De and thus become more dignified: if one can become more dignified, there seem to exist gradations of dignity, which seems to conflict with the idea that everything has dignity. But this, from the perspective of Dao, would not be correct: the idea that there is not a single thing without Dao should not be taken to lead to the conclusion that everything is in an ethically relevant sense equal, but rather that everything is *unique*: everything that exists possesses unique value. For instance, if a man sleeps in a damp place, he will have a pain in his loin; but an eel will surely not. If a man lives in the top of a tree, he will be frightened and tremble, but a monkey will surely not. 'Of these three who knows the right way of habitation?' (Fung 1952: 230). Accordingly, the *Zhuang-zi* claims: 'From the standpoint of Dao, there is nothing which is valuable or worthless, whereas from the point of view of things, each holds itself as something valuable and other things as of no account' (Fung 1952: 234, with my revision). The *Zhuang-zi's* conclusion is: 'From the point of view of Dao, what is noble and what is humble? They all merge into one' (Chan 1973: 206).

Second, the path to dignity – the accumulation of De – is a path of negative virtue or non-action. This contrasts with Kantianism and Confucianism in the sense that the latter two could be conceived as prescribing positive virtues or the preconditions of the development of these. The essence of the difference lies therein that from a Daoist perspective, it is impossible to articulate positively the path to dignity: what it means to be identified with Dao is not something that can be taught. The *Lao-zi* states: 'I take no action and the people of themselves are transformed. I love tranquillity and the people of themselves become correct. I engage in no activity and the people of themselves become prosperous' (Chan 1973: 166–7). So, unlike the Kantian perspective from which it is possible to articulate standards that may evaluate whether an action is in concord with dignity and the Confucian position in which virtues may be distinguished that determine whether one is dignified or not, the Daoist viewpoint on dignity entails that it is necessarily left to individuals to become one with Dao – one person's action cannot inspire another to non-action.

These two points on which the Daoist perspective differs from Kantian and Confucian give us interesting material to reflect upon in attempting to conceive a global notion of dignity. From a Daoist viewpoint, animals and nature are ethically relevant: like human beings, they possess unique value because they all have their ground in Dao. In political debates on ecology, Daoism thus could provide an interesting source for claiming that we should adopt a respectful attitude towards non-human forms of existence in a sense that Kantian doctrines do not easily seem capable of doing. Also, the ineffability of what it means to live a dignified life has some interesting consequences in reflecting upon the relation between state and individual: it gives rise to the thought that governmental policy has its limits. The government should be careful to interfere in citizens' lives: excessive interventions will lead to imbalance or even disorder in the individual state of being, and potentially infringe upon his path to dignity. This provides food for thought in thinking the relationship between dignity and rights: from a Daoist perspective, it is not self-evident that all policies aimed to protect human rights in fact protect that on which human rights are often thought to be based.

Daoism is a perspective that is very different from Kantian and Confucian approaches, and I hope to have explained that this does not mean it could not have relevance for the global discussion on dignity: it rather gives us material to reflect upon, and in that quality perhaps helps us to better understand the concept.

References

Baird Callicott, J., and Ames, R. T. (eds.). 1989. *Nature in Asian Traditions of Thought: Essays in Environmental Philosophy*. Albany, NY: State University of New York Press

Chan, Wing-tsit. 1973. *A Source Book in Chinese Philosophy*. Princeton University Press

Chen, Gu-ying. 1984. *Annotation and Translation of the Lao-zi with Comments*. Beijing: Zhonghua Book Company

Ci-Hai (辞海). 2002. Shanghai: Shanghai Dictionary Press

De Bery, Theodore W, and Tu, Wei-ming (eds.). 1998. *Confucianism and Human Rights*. New York: Columbia University Press

Fung, Yu-lan. 1952. *A History of Chinese Philosophy*, trans. D. Bodde. Princeton University Press

Li, Jing-de. 1986. *Classified Conversations of Zhu Xi* (朱子语类), Beijing: Zhonghua Book Company

Li, Xiang-feng. 2002. *Collations and Annotations of Guan-zi* (管子校注). Beijing: Zhonghua Book Company

Mou, Zong-san. 1985. *On the Highest Good*. Taipei: Student Book Company

Reihman, G. 2006. 'Categorically Denied: Kant's Criticism of Chinese Philosophy', *Journal of Chinese Philosophy* 33: 51–65

Ruan, Yuan (ed.). 1980. *Commentaries and Subcommentaries to the Thirteen Classics*. Beijing: Zhonghua Book Company

Su, Yu. 1992. *Justifications of the Meanings of Luxuriant Gem of the Spring and Autumn Annals* (春秋繁露义证). Beijing: Zhonghua Book Company

Wang, Xian-qian. 1988. *A Collection of Explanations of the Xun-zi* (荀子集解). Beijing: Zhonghua Book Company

Wang, Xiao-yu. 1988. *A Collection of Cheng Brothers' Works* (二程集). Beijing: Zhonghua Book Company

Zhu, Xi. 1986. *A Collection of Comments on Four Books* (四书章句集注). Beijing: Zhonghua Book Company

Part III
Systematic conceptualization

19

Social and cultural presuppositions for the use of the concept of human dignity

GESA LINDEMANN

From a sociological point of view, human dignity is to be grasped as a societal phenomenon, the analysis of which is concerned with identifying the historical circumstances for the emergence of the concept of human dignity. The assumption that every living human being is 'born free and equal in dignity and rights'[1] is understood as a normative social institution. In other words, from a sociological perspective, human dignity is conceived as a structural feature of modern societies, which are characterized by functional differentiation. The latter is either defined by an advanced division of labour (Durkheim 1930), or by the idea that there are diverse thematic fields of communication such as science, politics, law, economy, family etc., that are all assumed to be structured by different patterns of action/communication (Luhmann 1997). Functional differentiation requires that human beings recognize each other as individuals who are able to follow different patterns of action/communication. As individuals they are expected to be able to act not only as a scientist, but also as a mother, a shareholder or a member of a political party etc. The role of expectations within different realms of action are diverse and even contradictory and it is up to the individual to manage this complexity. Emile Durkheim (1950) argued that such societies first evolved in the eighteenth and nineteenth centuries in Europe and North America, a thesis that was subsequently developed further by Niklas Luhmann (1965). According to Durkheim and Luhmann, the structure of functional differentiation demands that there be individuals whose dignity is recognized. This idea forms the current basis of sociological reasoning on human dignity (Verschraegen 2002; Joas 2008; Lindemann 2010a).

If each single member of the human family is assumed to be born free and equal in dignity and rights, identifying someone as a member of the human family serves as a generally valid criterion for delimiting the circle of those beings that have to be recognized as beings with dignity. Two questions arise with regard to this premise: (1) Do sociological accounts offer a description of how the subject of human dignity is identified? In other words, how did the idea of one human family consisting of equal members arise? (2) How does sociology understand the meaning of the predicate 'human dignity'? In other

[1] Universal Declaration of Human Rights, Art. 1.

words, what does it mean to say that each member is equally endowed with inalienable human dignity?

Human dignity as cult of the individual in a society based on the division of labour

The French sociologist Emile Durkheim (1858–1917) was the first to develop a theory of human dignity in relation to social structures. According to Durkheim, although it is the interactions of human beings that produce society, 'society' has to be grasped as a unit in itself, independent of individual actors. Law and customs express a 'societal collective consciousness', which is external to the consciousness of actors and which exerts power over individual consciousness. This power is legitimate, because it is society that gives humanity its characteristic features. Society turns biological human beings into beings with the capacity to think and to use abstract categories (Durkheim 1912: 439f), and it is society that makes biological human beings into beings with the ability to follow moral rules (Durkheim 1924: Chapter II). Humans therefore have reason and morality only on ground of living in society.

If society is the precondition of reason and morality, human beings do not have dignity as such but only under particular societal conditions. In order to develop this Durkheimian idea, we need to look at the difference between modern and pre-modern societies. Pre-modern societies understand themselves in religious terms. The social order, which transcends the individual consciousness, is grasped as a sacred order. Moral rules, which are part of the societal collective consciousness, are conceived as sacred rules – guaranteed by transcendent beings like gods, demons and the like (Durkheim 1912). Modern societies are different: there are no transcendent beings at the centre of the moral order; the individual human person rather becomes a 'sacralized entity'. A 'cult of the individual' emerged due to the evolving 'division of labour in society' (Durkheim 1930: 407).

Durkheim describes pre-modern societies as segmentarily differentiated. This means that such societies consist of equally structured sub-units (for example, family clans) in which the relevant social labour is performed. Individual human beings are included more or less completely into such societal units; i.e. an individual normally belongs only to one unit. There is no significant division of labour among sub-units (Durkheim 1930). Such societies develop more or less clear-cut role expectations. Since role expectations are believed to be willed by God/gods, actors feel strongly obliged to follow the respective moral rules. The individual is a part of society as a whole, which itself has moral priority over the individual. (Durkheim 1950: Chapter V).

If a division of labour emerges and becomes a decisive feature of a society's structure, the situation changes fundamentally. Individuals are no longer included into only one sub-group or only into one form of labour. Instead, individuals are engaged in the division of social labour by being a family member and acting accordingly, by being a member of a professional group and acting accordingly, and so forth. Since individuals are no longer totally included in one sub-group, they can participate in different groups and different forms of labour. Birth no longer determines the work an individual has to perform. The daughter of a farmer may become a professor or a banker.

In advanced forms of the division of labour, individuals participate in social labour in different ways and belong to different social sub-groups. Nevertheless, the diversity of modern societies' moral obligations have a common basis. It is always assumed that human beings are capable of following different moral obligations in different situations. The more advanced the division of labour is, the more a society is dependent on individuals being capable of performing different kinds of labour in different sub-groups. It is the individual that has to handle diverse role expectations in an individual manner. Therefore, the notion of the individual person becomes a structural necessity for modern society. In this way, the individual human being comes to hold dignity.

It is important to keep in mind here that it is not the individual as a biological nor as a rational being who has dignity, but rather the individual as an emergent normative structural necessity of a functionally differentiated society. The concrete biological, individual human being has dignity as long as she/he obeys the basic normative necessities of functional differentiation. Since the basic normative feature of modern society is the concept of the dignified individual, an assault on the individual is an assault on the holy centre of modern society. Those who perform such an assault endanger their own status as dignified beings. Durkheim states explicitly that human beings whose behaviour is unworthy can even lose their dignity. Committing suicide or killing another human being are among the most severe assaults on the centre of the moral order of modern societies (Durkheim 1897: 391). Durkheim thus conceptualizes a performance-based concept of dignity, not a concept of an inalienable dignity.

Dignity as an individual accomplishment

The German sociologist Niklas Luhmann (1927–98) is the founder of the theory of autopoietic social systems (Luhmann 1984; 1997). Luhmann's basic idea is that society does not consist of human beings, and instead is composed of communications. Therefore, every social phenomenon has to be understood as the result of communication. In order to define communication, Luhmann uses the analytical concept of double contingency between actors he refers to as ego and alter. Within this framework, ego and alter are conceived as selves. As such, ego and alter perceive their environment and act accordingly, i.e. they mediate perceiving and acting. The point of departure for Luhmann's analysis of the social order is that ego and alter make themselves mutually conditional upon each other in a highly complex fashion. From the perspective of ego, we could say that ego incorporates the behaviour of alter into her or his own behaviour by expecting that alter expects ego to make her or his own behaviour dependent upon alter. A double uncertainty emerges. Since ego and alter are different subjects, they cannot know definitively from each other how the other will behave. It follows that, if ego tries to accord his or her actions with the expected expectations of alter, ego will not definitively be able to know the future behaviour of either alter or ego. This uncertainty exists for ego as a phenomenon of practical relevance. The same holds true for alter. In order to mark out this highly insecure and complex relationship, Luhmann uses the term 'double contingency' (Luhmann 1984: Chapter 3).

In order to establish certainty, actors have to communicate how they make themselves dependent on the actions of others. Communication is the means by which ego and alter create a social order, i.e. social order is an emergent phenomenon created by ego and alter in order to solve the problem of double contingency. Society is understood as a cognitive as well as a normative order. Luhmann understands the creation of general categories guiding the perception of the external and internal world and of normative institutions guiding particular actions as a basic achievement of societal processes. Like Durkheim, Luhmann assumes that reason and morality are societal achievements that cannot be understood by looking at isolated individuals.

Different forms of societal differentiation indicate the various ways in which the problem of double contingency can be solved. Luhmann – like Durkheim – distinguishes between modern functionally differentiated society and pre-modern societies. Luhmann describes the latter as either segmentarily or stratificatorily differentiated. He understands segmentary differentiation similarly to Durkheim. Stratificatorily differentiated societies, according to Luhmann, are made up of sub-units – social strata structured in a variety of ways. These strata are distinguished by wealth and/or political or religious power. It is within such a society that elementary forms of functional differentiation can emerge. In medieval Europe, for example, the different status positions of clergy, nobility and common people (farmers, craftsmen) indicate not only that actors occupy different positions in a hierarchy, but also that they contribute to the existence of society in different ways. Individuals are nevertheless totally included in their respective social status group. As members of different status groups, individuals have different freedoms and obligations, different forms of honour and dignity, etc. Within a stratificatorily differentiated society, ego and alter solve the problem of double contingency by communicating to each other to which social stratum they belong. Society is produced as a stable order by continuously reproducing legitimate forms of hierarchical inequalities (Luhmann 1997: 678f).

Functional differentiation describes another solution to the problem of double contingency. Here, societal communication is structured thematically, following the various needs of a modern society. There is a need for producing binding decisions, that is satisfied by politically specified communication; the need for the production of goods is satisfied by the economic sub-system, and so forth. Luhmann does not assume that there is a universal set of societal needs that have to be satisfied. Instead, he conceives of the emergence of societal sub-systems as unforeseen ways of providing contingent solutions to the general problem of double contingency (Luhmann 1984: Chapter 3). Functional differentiation has to be grasped as an open process.

The basic precondition of functional differentiation is that an individual as a whole does not belong to only one sub-system. Instead, ego/alter should have the possibility of participating in different sub-systems. This is guaranteed by fundamental rights, the institutionalization of which enables functional differentiation in a variety of ways. Freedom means that individuals have, in principle, the equal right to be included into every societal sub-system and can act economically, politically, as a family member and so forth (Luhmann 1965: Chapter 4). Individuals have dignity insofar as they are able to present themselves to others as a coherent personality, in which diverse communicative obligations of different societal sub-systems are integrated in a way that is consistent but specific – unique – to the individual. A personality should not only be able to act as a family member, a sales person or as a member of a political party and so on, but should also be able to communicate that he or she does so as an individual in his or her particular way. Presenting oneself as a personality thereby solves the problem of double contingency. Ego/alter have to display to each other that they are accountable, individual personalities. If they trust each other's communicative performance, they are able to establish a societal order with the individual personality as its nexus. It is the individual that integrates the diversity of functionally differentiated role expectations. The individual personality thereby becomes a structural feature of modern society. As such, the individual personality has to be generally respected. A human being has dignity because he or she presents his or herself as a personality (Luhmann 1965: Chapter 4). In a functional respect, we must distinguish from these general institutions (freedom, dignity) specific rights, which should rather be understood as institutional conditions for individual functional domains. Particularly prominent here is, for example, the right to property, which institutionally safeguards the differentiation of the functional domain of the economy (Luhmann 1965: Chapter 6).

Luhmann describes functional differentiation as a potentially self-destructive process, because sub-systems have a tendency to expand their particular pattern of communication such that a single pattern becomes the generally binding pattern of all societal communication. The development of functional differentiation is accompanied by the danger of de-differentiation. Luhmann regards the political system in particular as potentially dangerous: 'the danger of de-differentiation, of the politicization of the entirety of communication, arises when the political system is socially emancipated and autonomized' (Luhmann 1965: 24; my translation). This means that every communication can potentially be treated as politically relevant. This renders the autonomous functioning of the other sub-systems (science, economy, education, etc.) impossible, because everyone must assume that her or his actions will cause a negative sanction by those in political power. Luhmann considers constitutions to be an evolutionary achievement by means of which the political system restricts itself from politicizing society as a whole.

Since, according to Luhmann, human dignity is an accomplishment, individuals can either succeed or fail to present themselves as a consistent personality. If they fail, they fail to reproduce the modern solution to the problem of double contingency. In that case, individuals endanger their recognition as competent communication partners and thereby their dignity status (cf. Luhmann 1965: 69).

Dignity of the living human being as precondition of functional differentiation

Durkheim and Luhmann argue that functional differentiation is up to now the only social order which gives the individual human being moral priority over transcendent entities (God, gods, demons etc.) or society as a whole. This argument treats the emergence of human dignity and individualization as closely interconnected. I suggest to combine especially Luhmann's theory of functional differentiation with the idea that it is open to question which entities should be conceived as social actors. Authors working in anthropology and sociology have shown that it is a particular feature of modern, i.e. functionally differentiated, societies that there is a clear boundary between nature and culture and between human beings and other entities (Luckmann 1970; Descola 2005; Lindemann 2010b). There are many societies without functional differentiation, in which animals, plants, demons, spirits and other beings are treated also as legitimate social actors. The lesson to be learned from these analyses is that the borders of the social world are historically changing. This indicates that every society has to solve the problem how to distinguish legitimately between social actors and other beings. I call this the problem of the 'contingency of the shared world' (Lindemann 2010b: 283).

If we take into account that the borders of the social world are subject to historical change, the analysis of Durkheim and Luhmann should be expanded. They argue that it is due to functional differentiation that the individual gains moral priority over society as a whole. But they take it for granted that only living human beings are social actors, and therefore only living human beings can become individuals with a moral priority over the whole. But this cannot be taken for granted, if we assume that the borders of the social world are open to historical change. It has to be described as a feature of a functionally differentiated society that only human beings are legitimate social actors, and therefore subjects of dignity.

Non-modern societies are characterized by a diversity of locally heterogeneous understandings of which entity has to be treated as a legitimate actor. In different local environments one can identify different kinds of actors: humans, animals, demons, spirits or gods, the deceased etc. (Descola 2005). Even within the legal systems of pre-modern Europe it was unclear for centuries, whether animals can commit a crime out of a free will and should therefore be prosecuted and sentenced to death (Evans 1906; Lindemann 2009: Chapter 3). The medieval and early modern forms of identifying legitimate social actors seem to be characterized by two features: on the one hand, not only humans but also animals or other-worldly beings (like demons) could be treated as social actors, and, on the other, there was hardly any recourse to a general criterion – valid across time and space. To give an example from the sixteenth century: the vineyards of Julien (France) were infested several times by weevils. First, the local episcopal court at St Jean-de-Maurienne decided that the weevils were sent by god to punish the local population. Thirty years later, weevils came back. Now the episcopal court decided that the weevils had come out of free will. Each party (local farmers and local weevils) had a lawyer and the court had to find a decision how to solve the conflict of interests between weevils and farmers (Evans 1906: 38f).

The emergence of functional differentiation in the eighteenth and nineteenth centuries led to a new solution to the problem of the contingency of the shared world. An entity is to be recognized as a social actor, if it can be identified as a living human being. This criterion is claimed to be universal, it is valid across time and space. Here, local varieties of potential actors (animals, other-worldly beings, humans, etc.) were reduced to one kind of actor: human beings. These are assumed to be an open potential for communication, i.e. individual human beings are assumed to be in principle able to participate in diverse functional realms. The only restriction is that each individual human has to fulfil the requirements of a particular functional domain. To participate in the economic domain, an actor needs money or something to sell. To contribute to scientific communications requires actors who are educated enough and to display rational arguments.

The communicative structure of functional differentiation is characterized by a two-step mechanism of homogenization. Social actors address each other as human beings, i.e. as an open potential for communication (first step); additionally social actors are addressed according to the relevancies and particular role expectations of a functional realm. In the latter case, social actors treat each other mutually as a means to an end defined by what matters in a particular functional realm (second step). Within the economic realm, actors treat each other according to economic rationality and so forth.

On these grounds, it becomes possible to tell a slightly different story about functional differentiation and human dignity. Human dignity is the quality a being has as a generally recognized social person open to participation in diverse forms of communication. As a human being, a person has dignity because he or she is not only a means to an end within functionally specified communication, but also a human being beyond particular ends. As such, the human being within the context of functional differentiation is an end in him or herself. As an open potential for further communication, the human being is him or herself the precondition for an open process of functional differentiation (Lindemann 2010a).

While Luhmann sees the consistent presentation of individual personality as a nexus of the social order, here the crucial point is the openness for further communication. The criterion for being recognized as someone with human dignity is the sheer fact of being alive (Lindemann 2004). Such recognition does not require the exacting qualities of personal performance; on the contrary, such a requirement would be dysfunctional. Communication along the lines of particular sub-systems demands an exacting presentation of the self as a personal actor capable of calculating rationally (economic system), arguing consistently (science), etc. If such exacting performances were made relevant for recognizing someone's dignity status, it would make it impossible for forms of communication to occur that do not require such exacting qualities. Tying recognition to specifically defined forms of personal performance would endanger the fundamental openness of the communicative differentiation of society (Lindemann 2010a). One can describe this as the liberal threat to functional differentiation.

Conclusion

From a sociological perspective, the idea that there is one human family with equal members who have dignity has to be grasped as a modern achievement. Nevertheless, this achievement cannot be restricted to a particular cultural or religious tradition. Although the historical development indicates that this achievement has Christian roots, the notion of the this-worldly living human being having dignity transcends Christianity as well as every other religious or cultural foundation. Functional differentiation is in principle compatible with different religious and cultural traditions as long as these traditions are able to cope with the this-worldly living human being endowed with dignity.

Whereas Durkheim and Luhmann unfold performance-based concepts of human dignity, I proposed a different sociological concept of human dignity. Functional differentiation is described as a social order, which is in need of a general factual criterion of identifying social actors. Historically, this was achieved by institutionalizing the criterion 'living human being'. Each living human is endowed with dignity, because it transcends the ends of actual communications within particular societal domains. In this understanding, dignity can be lost only when the human being dies. It is a normatively required structural feature of the social order of functional differentiation that living humans are endowed with an inalienable dignity.

Nevertheless, functional differentiation is also a potentially self-destructive process, which itself can become a threat to the normative institution of human dignity. Luhmann has described this primarily with respect to the political realm, but other functional domains can also become potentially destructive. One even has to take into account a liberal threat to functional differentiation that would tie recognition as a person with dignity to a particular personal performance – for example the performance of the rational actor following his or her own self-interest that is demanded in the economic sphere. In this case, human dignity would be threatened by a dominance of the functional domain of the economy.

References

Descola, P. 2005. *Par-delà nature et culture.* Paris: Gallimard

Durkheim, E. 1897. *Le suicide: Etude de sociologie.* Paris: Alcan (trans. J. A. Spaulding and G. Simpson, 1951. *Suicide: A Study in Sociology.* Glencoe, IL: The Free Press)

1912. *Les formes élémentaires de la vie religieuse: le système totémique en Australie* (trans. J. W. Swain. 1915. *The Elementary Forms of the Religious Life.* London: Allen & Unwin)

1924. *Sociologie et philosophie.* Paris: Alcan (trans. D. F. Pocock. 1953. *Sociology and Philosophy.* London: Cohen & West)

1930. *De la division du travail social* (trans. G. Simpson, 1964. *The division of Labour in Society.* New York: The Free Press)

1950. *Leçons de sociologie: Physique des moeurs et du droit.* Paris: Presses Universitaires de France (trans. C. Brook. 1958. *Professional Ethics and Civic Morals*, Glencoe, IL: The Free Press)

Evans, E. P. 1906. *The Criminal Prosecution and Capital Punishment of Animals.* London: Faber & Faber

Joas, H. 2008. 'Punishment and Respect: The Sacralization of the Person and Its Endangerment', *Journal of Classical Sociology* 8(2): 159–77

Lindemann, G. 2004. 'Menschenwürde und Lebendigkeit', in E. Klein and C. Menke (eds.), *Menschenrechte und Bioethik, Schriften des MenschenRechtsZentrums*, vol. 21. Berlin: Berliner Wissenschafts-Verlag, 146–73

2009. *Das Soziale von seinen Grenzen her denken.* Weilerswist: Velbrück

2010a. 'Moralischer Status und menschliche Gattung – Versuch einer soziologischen Aufklärung', *Deutsche Zeitschrift für Philosophie* 58(3): 359–76

2010b. 'The Living Human Body from the Perspective of the Shared World (Mitwelt)', *Journal of Speculative Philosophy* 24(3): 275–91

Luckmann, T. 1970. 'On the Boundaries of the Social World', in M. Natanson (ed.), *Phenomenology and Social Reality: Essays in Memory of Alfred Schutz.* The Hague: Nijhoff, 73–100

Luhmann, N. 1965. *Grundrechte als Institution.* Berlin: Duncker & Humblot

1984. *Soziale Systeme: Grundriß einer allgemeinen Theorie.* Frankfurt am Main: Suhrkamp

1997. *Die Gesellschaft der Gesellschaft*, 2 vols. Frankfurt am Main: Suhrkamp

Verschraegen, G. 2002. 'Human Rights and Modern Society: A Sociological Analysis from the Perspective of Systems Theory', *Journal of Law and Society* 29: 258–81

20

Is human dignity the ground of human rights?

GOVERT DEN HARTOGH

Many venerable legal documents suggest that human dignity is the ground of human rights. The German Constitution (1945) opens in Article 1 with the captivating declaration: 'human dignity is inviolable', and goes on in Article 2 to state: 'The German people *therefore* acknowledge inviolable and inalienable human rights as the basis of every community, of peace and of justice in the world' (emphasis added).[1] The Helsinki Accords (1975) even more explicitly claim that human rights 'derive from the inherent dignity of the human person'. On this view human beings have rights *because* they have dignity. On an even stronger view, which is also quite common in constitutional law, it is the very function of those rights to protect the dignity of human beings. In that case, all human rights are specifications of one fundamental right: the right to have one's dignity (or the dignity of the human species?) respected.

At the other end of the spectrum of possible views we find the sceptical idea that all appeals to human dignity are entirely vacuous: they can be made for any specific claim about human rights whatsoever, they are routinely being made for opposing views, for example about euthanasia, and have no argumentative, but only rhetorical, force. 'Dignity is a useless concept . . . and can be eliminated without any loss of content' (Macklin 2003).[2]

I shall argue that both views are mistaken. Appeals to human dignity have a proper role in human rights discourse, but it is not a foundational and also in some other respects a limited role.

The meaning of dignity

One common argument for the view that the appeal to human dignity is empty is that the very term 'dignity' is hopelessly vague and equivocal. For example, as a human being you have dignity; supposedly you cannot lose it as long as you exist. But you also have the right not to be subjected to humiliating treatment and the harm this right protects you from seems precisely to be the loss of your dignity.

[1] Repeated in the Charter of Human Rights of the European Union (2000), but without the 'therefore'. For the standard interpretation of the relation between dignity and rights in the German constitution, see for example Maunz and Dürig 2013.

[2] This editorial has evoked much discussion, for example in Schulman 2008.

I believe that the concept of dignity has a tolerably clear meaning: it is an elevated status in a status-ranking, the status of some being which makes a deferential attitude to that being appropriate. A being can have one such status and lack another, hence have dignity in one respect and lack it in another. That doesn't make the concept polysemic. A mayor can have dignity because of his function and lack it because of his behaviour. Obviously, the relevant statuses can be ordered in many ways, and it makes no sense to have a controversy about 'the' proper ordering.[3] Two important categories are the following.

(1) According to Cicero, '*dignitas est alicuius honesta et cultu et honore verecundia digna auctoritas*'.[4] In hierarchical societies, dignity is the prerogative of the higher estates, for example the nobility and the church, because the members of those estates have legal power over others. And it is still a position of institutionalized authority, especially in the public domain, which is deemed to make its occupants worthy of deferential treatment. If you have dignity because of your role, you have it to the same degree as all other occupants of that role.

(2) Dignity can also be a personal characteristic which people have in general to different degrees and can individually display to different degrees on particular occasions. A normally dignified person can occasionally behave in an undignified way. Dignity in this sense is normally seen as a function of a person's condition and his comportment.

These two categories should be distinguished from a third one:

(3) The dignity you have as a person or as a human being. This notion first occurs in some Stoic texts, in particular in Cicero's *De officiis* (Book I: §§ 105–7), it gets a theological interpretation (*imago Dei*) in the work of influential fathers of the church like Augustine, and a classical exposition in Pico della Mirandola's *Oratio de hominis dignitate* (1486). A passage in Kant's *Grundlegung zur Metaphysick der Sitten* (1785) is commonly considered to contain the canonical expression of its fundamental ethical importance.

By distinguishing these grounds of dignity, we can easily dispel some confusions without supposing that the term is equivocal. Recently, a young Muslim lawyer in the Netherlands refused to stand up in court on the entering of the judges, because on his view Islam teaches us that all human beings have equal dignity. Surely they have equal dignity as human beings, but in addition some may have special dignity as judges, and to deny that comes dangerously close to denying their authority. And, if human dignity is the foundation of human rights, it is because of your inalienable dignity as a human being that your personal dignity should not be alienated.

[3] Cf. Nordenfelt 2004 and comments on that paper.

[4] The honourable authority of someone worthy of worship, honour and reverence. *De inventione* 2.166, quoted by Van der Graaf and Van Delden 2008.

Human dignity and human rights

If this is what dignity means, and if human beings have dignity as such, it is easy to see why human dignity is so often considered to be the ground of human rights. Because human beings have dignity, they are worthy of respect, and of respectful treatment. What could be a better way of showing respect than by recognizing them to have rights and deferring to those rights? The relevant class of rights, human rights, are to be classified as such precisely because they are possessed by every human being as such, and not dependent on an institutional role of authority, or on a person's condition and behaviour.

It is controversial which goods exactly are to be protected by human rights. But all such goods, whatever they are, should be seen as good to the person who bears the rights. Rights are assets; that is why, if in any particular case you turn out to be the worse for having them, you can normally waive them. Why are you entitled to this benefit? Why should the fact that some things are good for you be a reason for other people to take them into account, to respect or even to promote them? A plausible answer to this question seems to be: because you have a special value yourself. It is this special, incomparable value or preciousness which is supposed to be designated by the term 'dignity' or 'worth'. 'Your interests matter because you matter' (Velleman 1999; 2006: 40–4; 2008a).[5] This argument has often been ascribed to Kant and something like it has been expressed by many Kantian authors. But it can also be found in the theological tradition from Augustine on: when God created the Earth, he gave Man a special status, and that is why Man's interests count.

In order to evaluate this argument, let me start from a different but analogical issue. Suppose you see someone helping an old lady cross a busy street. You ask him why he does it, and he answers, somewhat pompously: that is my duty. There is something wrong with that answer. We might have hoped that he did what he did in order to help someone who needed help. If he did it instead because it was his duty, that seems a clear case of the moral mistake of 'having one thought too many' (cf. Williams 1981). More plausibly, he did not give you any answer at all. By saying that it was his duty, he did not really specify his reason, but only restated that he had one, adding, perhaps, a characterization of the nature of his reason, for instance as a compelling moral one. In that case, his reference to a duty was, as Thomas Scanlon calls it, a 'buck-passing' one (Scanlon 1998: 95–8).[6]

[5] Inspired by Anderson (1993: 26–30). Cf. Korsgaard 1996, Chapter 4; 2004: 93; Wood 1999: 115, 132–9; McMahan 2002: 242. Sensen 2009 shows that it is a mistake to ascribe this view to Kant. That he denies moral status to animals is not because they do not have dignity but because on his view they have no freedom, and hence no capacity for moral action.

[6] Cf. the placeholder view discussed by Kagan 1991: 60. On my view duty is a buck-passing concept in some cases but not in others (professional or legal duties for example). It depends on the relevance to the validity of the duty of the existence of a pattern of legitimate mutual expectations; cf. Den Hartogh 2002: Chapters 1–2.

There are many other moral concepts besides duty of which we can ask whether or when they are buck-passing, whether and when they specify a reason or only characterize it. It is a wonderful way to economize in ethics. Examples are the concepts of a right, of virtue, of equality, and of value. As for the concept of 'a right', for example, by asking that question we can perhaps distinguish between a proper and a merely inflationary use.[7] As for 'value', as Scanlon suggested it is clearly a buck-passing concept. '(T)he badness of a toothache . . . does not add a further reason to the reasons for going to the dentist that are already given by the nature of the toothache, its painfulness' (Dancy 2005: 37).[8]

Is dignity also a buck-passing concept, or isn't it? Does it specify the ground of human rights, or does it only refer to that ground, whatever it is? Do your interests really matter *because* you matter, or do both statements express the same truth? If the first view is correct, two consequences follow both of which I will deny, the first in this section, the second in the next. The first consequence is that it is possible for another being to have similar interests which do *not* matter, because that being has no 'dignity'. This is the traditional view of the moral standing of animals which Kant shared.[9] According to Kant it is morally objectionable to cause suffering to animals, because it tends to erode your sensitivity to the suffering of humans. In contrast to Descartes' view,[10] Kant does not deny that animals are capable of suffering, but for him this fact has no independent moral significance, because animals are no 'ends in themselves'. This seems morally problematic, another case of having one thought too many. If different beings have the same interests, these interests should count equally, that does not depend on any further fact which makes these interests count. Rocks don't have rights, not because they are a morally inferior type of entity, but because they have no interests that we could possibly protect.

My argument is not only an appeal to moral intuition. Suppose we have ascertained that a being has the characteristics that qualify it for having certain rights, whether it is the possession of certain interests, or the capacity of self-government or whatever. Then, in order to decide whether that being really has those rights, we need not ask: but does it have dignity? For that question can only be answered, positively, by reference to the very same characteristics. Dignity doesn't sort out the proper rights-bearers from all beings that have the relevant characteristics. This shows that they have those rights because they have those

[7] The proper use of 'a right' isolates a claim that normally excludes being weighed against competing claims.

[8] Dancy, however, does not conclude that value is merely buck-passing but rather that value and reasons supervene on the same facts. On dignity I argue for a similar position for different reasons.

[9] *Metaphysik der Sitten, Tugendlehre*, § 17; cf. Kant 1997: 212–13, 434–5, and an excellent discussion by Korsgaard 2004. In the context of his time, Kant's views should be seen as enlightened, because he at least condemned cruelty to animals and even specifically their use in experiments for purely speculative reasons.

[10] Explicitly rejected in the *Kritik der Urteilskraft* § 90 1. Anm.

characteristics, not because, in addition, they also have dignity (Feinberg 1980: 151; Griffin 2008: 66).[11]

These same characteristics, however, also make them worthy of respect, and this can be expressed by saying that, as human beings, they have dignity. That is a separate claim, and not a redundant one.

The practical relevance of the issue

When human dignity is seen as the ground of human rights, this mistake has a second unfortunate consequence. Because of both these consequences the issue is not of merely academic interest. It has great practical relevance.

If human rights are 'derived' from human dignity, our first duty is to respect human dignity, and refraining from intruding on human rights is only a way of doing so, possibly one way among others. Hence, if the duty to respect human dignity and the duty to recognize a particular human right conflict with each other, the former duty, being the foundational one, wins out. Protecting human dignity is therefore normally a good reason for constraining the exercise of human rights.[12]

This is a common view of constitutional law in many countries, and the constraining results are evident in many domains, but in particular in the area of bioethics (for example, Beyleveld and Brownsword 2001; Sulmasy 2008). Actions forbidden as violations of human dignity by the Council of Europe's Convention on Bioethics (1997), by UNESCO's Universal Declaration on Bioethics and Human Rights (2005) and by similar national legal instruments, include the selling of organs from dead and living persons, surrogate motherhood, cloning, producing hybrids or chimaeras, creating embryos for research, medical experiments on brain-dead people, and selecting an embryo by pre-implantation diagnostics on its fitness for donation of its marrow to a sibling with Fanconi anemia.

I do not deny that, to the extent that the ground of human rights, whatever it is, is also deserving of a deferential attitude, there is a moral reason for expressing that attitude. Neither do I deny that this reason can conflict with the duty to respect some particular human right. But it is a mistake to think that what fundamentally matters is expressing the attitude, and that respecting human

[11] Luban 2009 plausibly suggests that human rights instruments refer to 'dignity' as a placeholder for whatever the ground of the rights is, precisely because they don't want to commit themselves to any specific view of that ground. Cf. Glendon 2001 on the history of the Universal Declaration of Human Rights.

[12] Some Kantian authors argue that, because autonomy is the basic capacity of human beings which requires us to acknowledge their incomparable value, that acknowledgment can only result in empowering them to exercise that capacity, not in constraining its exercise. Beyleveld and Brownsword 2001. But should or should we not then protect choices, for example for palliative sedation, that imply the destruction or reduction of that capacity? Cf. Velleman 1992; 1999; 2007.

rights is only one way of doing that. The appeal to human rights protects us against harm and interference, the appeal to dignity against offense. We should clearly distinguish between these considerations before weighing them when they conflict. When we do, it appears that the appeal to dignity, whatever its rhetorical force, need not be decisive.

This is underlined by the following consideration. What is to be considered to express respect or disrespect is often a matter of convention. Hence if you think that what fundamentally matters is expressing the attitude of respect, you are in danger of overestimating symbolic values and, perhaps, even of being prepared to sacrifice to them the very real values they symbolize. Joel Feinberg calls this a form of sentimentality, but it could also be called a kind of idolatry. Feinberg's example is refusing post-mortem donation of one's organs because one thinks that this involves an instrumentalization or commodification of the human body (Feinberg 1985: 75). Similarly, it could be argued that, if we could provide a sufficient number of post-mortem organs for transplantation to patients of organ failure by allowing these organs to be bought and sold, and could not provide them in any other way, we should allow such a market, even if we share the common feeling that such a market fails to do justice to the symbolic value the human corpse derives from its association with the human person.

The Sabbath is there for men, not men for the Sabbath.

The relevance of the appeal to human dignity and its limits

I have not argued that the appeal to human dignity is vacuous, but only that it does not have the foundational importance often claimed for it. Correspondingly, I have not denied that considerations of human dignity are morally relevant, nor even that, exceptionally, the exercise of human rights can be constrained because of such considerations. That the status of a slave, even if voluntarily accepted, is incompatible with the respect properly due to human beings, may be one good reason to consider acts of voluntary self-enslavement null and void.[13] I have only contended that we will tend to over-value considerations of human dignity when they conflict with considerations of human welfare or autonomy protected by human rights, if we conceive of appeals to human rights as, basically, appeals to human dignity themselves.

There is another reason for considering the force of such considerations to be limited. Even when human dignity is not held to be the proper specification of the ground of human rights, whatever it is, the appeal to it suggests that it is appropriate to characterize that ground as something which deserves to be responded to by an attitude of respect. I want to suggest that this view, while not false, is one-sided. For the ground of human rights does not only consist in honorific properties like our capacity for self-government, which give us an

[13] Note that in that case the relevant value is not only a symbolic one: it is not a mere matter of convention that slaves lack dignity.

exalted place above most other animals, it also consists of properties like our basic needs and our vulnerability, which we share with many other animals. A proper response to these properties does not consist in a deferential attitude like honour and respect, but rather in compassion, albeit compassion without condescension.[14]

Take, for example, the right not to be tortured. It is clearly true that an essential part of the evil of torture is that it humiliates its victim. Putting the point in a paradoxical way which I have already explained: it violates the inalienable dignity of the victim by causing him to lose his personal dignity, by destroying the very basis of his self-respect. But another essential part of the evil of torture is simply that it *hurts*, that it causes excruciating pain and/or severe mental suffering from fear, shame or disgust. Cats can be tortured because they can suffer. It could be objected that even the suffering from physical pain still has a characteristic human aspect, because it involves much more than the pain itself, for example the sense of utter helplessness. Torture denies its victim any option of coping with the circumstances that cause the suffering, and thereby threatens the core of his self (cf. Cassell 1991; Velleman 2008b). And surely the human ability to cope, to manage not only one's actions but also one's emotions in the face of adverse circumstances, is a proper cause for respect. Hence even by causing physical pain the torturer fails to properly respect his victim. I do not deny that, but only maintain that he also fails to properly care for him. It is not one single attitude which is *the* proper response to the facts that invoke a human rights claim.

Human dignity is not the ground of human rights. And even as a mere characterization of the ground of human rights it is incomplete. The Germans should change their unchangeable constitution.

References

Anderson, E. 1993. *Value in Ethics and Economics.* Cambridge, MA: Harvard University Press

Beyleveld, D., and Brownsword, R. 2001. *Human Dignity in Bioethics and Biolaw.* Oxford University Press

Cassell, Eric J. 1991. *The Nature of Suffering.* Oxford University Press

Dancy, J. 2005. 'Should We Pass the Buck?', in T. Rønnow-Rasmussen and M. J. Zimmerman (eds.), *Recent Work on Intrinsic Value.* Dordrecht: Springer, 33–44

Feinberg, J. 1980. 'The Nature and Value of Rights', in *Rights, Justice, and the Bounds of Liberty: Essays in Social Philosophy.* Princeton University Press

1985. *Offense to Others, The Moral Limits of the Criminal Law*, vol. II. Oxford University Press

Glendon, M. A. 2001. *A World Made New.* New York: Random House

Griffin, J. 2008. *On Human Rights.* Oxford University Press

[14] I owe this expression to a lecture by Raimond Gaita.

Graaf, R. Van Der, and Van Delden, J. J. M. 2009. 'Clarifying Appeals to Dignity in Medical Ethics from an Historical Perspective', *Bioethics* 23: 151–60

Hartogh, G. Den. 2002. *Mutual Expectations: A Conventionalist Theory of Law.* The Hague: Springer

Kagan, S. 1991. *The Limits of Morality.* Oxford University Press

Kant, I. 1997. *Lectures on Ethics*, trans. Peter Heath, ed. Peter Heath and J. B. Schneewind. Cambridge University Press

Korsgaard, C. M. 1996. *Creating the Kingdom of Ends.* Cambridge University Press

2004. 'Fellow Creatures: Kantian Ethics and Our Duties to Animals', in G. B. Peterson (ed.), *The Tanner Lectures on Human Values.* University of Utah Press, vols. 25/26; see www.TannerLectures.utah.edu

Luban, D. 2009. 'Human Dignity, Humiliation and Torture', *Kennedy Institute of Ethics Journal* 19: 211–30

Macklin, R. 2003. 'Dignity as a Useless Concept', *British Medical Journal* 327: 1419–20

Maunz, T., and Dürig, G. 2013. *Kommentar zum Grundgesetz*, 67th edn, Munich: C. H. Beck

McMahan, J. 2002. *The Ethics of Killing.* Oxford University Press

Nordenfelt, L. 2004. 'The Varieties of Dignity', *Health Care Analysis* 12: 69–81

Scanlon, T. M. 1998. *What We Owe to Each Other.* Cambridge, MA: Harvard University Press

Schulman, A. (ed.). 2008. *Human Dignity and Bioethics: Essays Commissioned by the President's Council on Bioethics.* Washington, DC: US Independent Agencies and Commissions

Sensen, O. 2009. 'Kant's Conception of Human Dignity', *Kant-Studien* 100: 309–31

Sulmasy, D. P. 2008. 'Dignity and Bioethics: History, Theory, and Selected Applications', in *Human Dignity and Bioethics: Essays Commissioned by the President's Council on Bioethics.* Washington, DC: US Independent Agencies and Commissions

Velleman, J. D. 1992. 'Against the Right to Die', *Journal of Medicine and Philosophy* 17: 665–81 (revised version (2007) available at SSRN: http://ssrn.com/abstract=1006992)

1999. 'A Right of Self-Termination?', *Ethics* 109: 606–28

2006. 'A Brief Introduction to Kantian Ethics', in J. D. Velleman, *Self to Self: Selected Essays.* New York: Cambridge University Press

2008a. 'Beyond Price', *Ethics* 118: 191–212

2008b. 'The Gift of Life', *Philosophy and Public Affairs* 36(3): 245–66

Williams, Bernard. 1981. 'Persons, Character, and Morality', in *Moral Luck.* Cambridge University Press

Wood, A. 1999. *Kant's Ethical Thought.* Cambridge University Press

21

Human dignity: can a historical foundation alone suffice? From Joas' affirmative genealogy to Kierkegaard's leap of faith

CHRISTOPH HÜBENTHAL

Among the manifold attempts to provide the idea of human dignity and the related human rights practice with a historical foundation, Hans Joas' 'affirmative genealogy' is surely one of the most innovative and striking methodological approaches being presented during the last few years. If one wishes to analyze the advantages and disadvantages of this foundational type in general, Joas' account undoubtedly offers an excellent example of how to do this. For the purpose of such an examination, however, it is necessary first to examine the underlying argument motivating Joas' methodological decisions.

For Joas, somewhere in the eighteenth century a major cultural shift took place whereby the human person progressively became a sacred object. The outcome of this process was the emergence of an ethical value that Joas designates as the *sacredness of the person.* Different codifications of human rights and the establishment of a related human rights practice can be seen as a significant consequence of this value appearance. Though Joas constantly emphasizes the historical contingency of value emergences, he is well aware that values do not appear from nowhere but have a specific history or, as he puts it, a *genealogy.* In case of the sacredness of the person, it was the traumatic experience of violence, oppression and misrecognition that led to the emergence and experience of this value. Nowadays, however, the sacredness of the person seems to be endangered. 'Even in the core area of the West', Joas complains, 'there can be no talk of a secure consolidation of the sacredness of the person' (Joas 2011: 104). Likewise the meaning of this value threatens to become abstract, dogmatic or purely conventional so that it is in danger of being deprived of its affective power and the related human rights practice will lose its motivational basis. For Joas, it is exactly this endangering and threatening situation that generates the need for an affirmative genealogy. 'Affirmative genealogy' can thus be delineated as a method to revitalize original value experiences by means of a historical or narrative iteration of their genealogy. The revitalization, in turn, is necessary to motivate, encourage or even to extend the human rights practice. 'Value judgements', Joas says, 'point at stories. We make plausible – and in doing that we also defend – our value commitments by narrating how we have arrived at them and what will happen when they are offended' (*ibid.*: 259).

In a nutshell, Joas' systematic argument can thus be spelled out as follows: a value historically emerged, bore a corresponding practice, is now in danger and must therefore be re-affirmed through an affirmative genealogy. If we equate the sacredness of the person with human dignity (which Joas himself occasionally does), we are entitled to state that for Joas human dignity is to be affirmed by a narrative repetition of its historical genesis. Moreover, Joas is convinced that an affirmative genealogy *alone* can serve as cogent justification of human dignity, for which reason other justificatory methods might be of additional worth, but are not necessary. In the remainder of this chapter, I will, by contrast, try to show that any attempt to affirm a value by narrating its history unavoidably requires another justificatory step which, then, is to be seen as the actual foundation of human dignity.

A problem with the affirmative genealogy

Joas introduces the sacredness of the person as an ethical value; and of such values he explicitly says: 'It is these ethical values that historically arise and elapse' (*ibid.*: 156). From this we can, at least, conclude that human dignity is possibly a transitory value. This corresponds perfectly with the aforementioned observation that the sacredness of the person is a threatened and endangered value. Consequently, we have no guarantee that of all things human dignity will prevail, since it might be the case that the sacredness of the person will lose its affective binding forces and will cease to be an ethical value.

The question, then, is why should we revitalize this value by affirmatively iterating its genesis, that is, by employing an affirmative genealogy? Joas might probably respond that otherwise the human rights practice would also disappear. But again we could ask: why should we be interested in maintaining a particular practice when the underlying value is out of fashion and does not fascinate us anymore? If we cannot experience the value, why should we continue the practice?

Kierkegaard's analogous problem

Most notably, the challenge just identified in Joas is far from being new. None other than Søren Kierkegaard already struggled with an analogous problem and developed, as will be seen, a sophisticated answer simply by offering a thorough analysis of what it means to affirm a historical value.

In his *Philosophical Fragments* and the *Concluding Unscientific Postscript to Philosophical Fragments*, Kierkegaard raises the question of how a 'follower at second hand' can get access to the historical truth of Christianity because later generations obviously cannot be taught by the original teacher. So Kierkegaard supposes the historic emergence of a particular truth that the contemporaries experienced as ultimately valuable; and the problem for him is how later generations can get access to this truth. To have such access is for Kierkegaard of decisive relevance since it is this truth that gives shape to the entirety of life.[1] Accordingly, Kierkegaard is also interested in the affirmation of a historic value for the sake of a current practice; and so it seems not entirely odd to state a crucial similarity between his and Joas' problem. But there is also a difference. Whereas Kierkegaard is interested in *how* we can affirm a historic value, Joas has no sufficient answer to the question *why* we should affirm such a value. Of course, this is not a negligible difference. By looking at how Kierkegaard resolved his how-problem, however, we can also get a clue how Joas probably might meet his why-challenge.

Kierkegaard's solution

In the *Philosophical Fragments*, Kierkegaard's central question is whether eternal happiness can be based on historical knowledge (Kierkegaard 1992: 15). For the purpose of answering this question, Kierkegaard introduces the aforementioned 'follower at second hand'. It is this follower who is interested in affirming a truth by which she can achieve eternal happiness. Interestingly, however, Kierkegaard makes extensive efforts to demonstrate that any utterance of a historic truth is merely an *approximation*. First, this is due to the epistemological fact that no historic episode or person can ever be reconstructed comprehensively. More important, however, is the axiological fact that even the most comprehensible reconstruction of a historic episode or person cannot, purely by itself, enforce the affirmation of its own truth. We must not assume, Kierkegaard says, that 'if only the objective truth has been obtained, appropriation is an easy matter; it is automatically included as part of the bargain and *am Ende* [in the end] the individual is a matter of indifference' (*ibid.*: 22). Apparently, for Kierkegaard the affirmation of a historical truth is impossible without a subject actively capturing and appropriating it. Historic truth, in other words, cannot impose itself upon the individual, but can become existentially relevant only on the condition that the subject freely decides to adopt it. However strong, affective or convincing a truth may be, without free and active adoption by the subject herself it cannot become the subject's truth.

As is well known, Lessing once wrote that 'contingent historical truths can never become a demonstration of eternal truths of reason', and elsewhere he said that 'the transition whereby one builds an eternal truth on historical reports is a leap' (*ibid.*: 93). Kierkegaard who quotes these statements, ironically ignores

[1] In a diary entry from 1 August 1835, Kierkegaard writes: 'What I miss, is to come to terms with myself on *what I ought to do*, not on what I ought to cognize, except insofar as cognition precedes action... It is necessary to find a truth that is *true for myself*, to *find the idea for which I will live and die*' (Kierkegaard 1962: 16) (English translation by the present author).

Lessing's critical undertone and endorses the utterances without reservation. He even emphasizes that the affirmation of historical truth is a leap, is a *μετάβασις εἰς ἄλλο γένος* (i.e. shifting from one genus to another), is a decision and an act of faith (*ibid.*: 98, 102).[2] Elsewhere Kierkegaard also holds that faith can be gained 'only in freedom, by an act of will' (Kierkegaard 1985: 82). From this we may conclude that for Kierkegaard any truth, however valuable it may be, cannot accomplish its own affirmation. There is no specific *axiological condition* that can cause the value's appropriation by the subject. A comparable thing applies to the current situation. In order to leap, the subject cannot be conditioned by the historical context in which the decision is to be made. So there is neither an *axiological* nor a *historical condition* that causes the decision. Rather the chain of conditions must be interrupted, as it were, to make the decision possible. Kierkegaard uses different metaphors to express this lack of causation. He speaks of the 'transition from "not to be" to "to be"' (*ibid.*: 20), or he uses terms like 'moment' (*ibid.*: 43),[3] 'birth' or 're-birth' (*ibid.*: 21) to give utterance to the *unconditionedness* of the decision. Consequently, we cannot avoid taking notice of Kierkegaard's emphatic plea for the absoluteness of the deciding act by which a historic truth is affirmed. Each affirmative act, therefore, necessarily implies a spontaneous, unconditioned activity of the subject and cannot be explained solely by the historical circumstances or the attractiveness of the value affirmed.

At this point, it is of paramount importance to notice that exactly this absoluteness of the individual at the very moment of making her affirmative decision accounts for the *subject's dignity*. In *Either/Or* Kierkegaard writes: 'A human being's eternal dignity lies precisely in this, that he can gain a history. The divine in him lies in this, that he himself, if he so chooses, can give this history continuity, because it gains that, not when it is a summary of what has taken place or has happened to me, but only when it is my personal deed in such a way that even that which has happened to me is transformed and transferred from necessity to freedom' (Kierkegaard 1987: 250). This quotation convincingly shows that for Kierkegaard the construction of our own historicity presupposes the ability to distance ourselves from all historical givens in order to freely appropriate them. And it is this freedom, this unconditionedness, this absoluteness that accounts for the human dignity. Consequently, the human person is worthy and sacred precisely because she has the faculty to affirm what is valuable. She is neither conditioned by the value that is to be affirmed (*axiological conditionedness*), nor by the situation in which the affirmation is to be performed (*historical conditionedness*). Hence we can conclude that the

[2] 98: '. . . precisely because the leap is a decision . . . '; 102: 'Although, as frequently noted, the leap is a decision . . . '.

[3] 43: 'Yet this letting go, even that is surely something; it is, after all, *meine Zuthat* [my contribution]. Does it not have to be taken into account, this diminutive moment, however brief it is – it does not have to be long, because it is a *leap*.'

person is worthy and sacred because she is the *unconditioned condition of every value's validity.*

The solution of Joas' why-problem

As has been said before, Kierkegaard's phenomenology of *how* to affirm a historical value can help us to understand *why* we should or – even stronger – why we *ought* to affirm both human dignity and the related human rights practice. Human dignity or the sacredness of the person is not one ethical value among others. It is the unconditioned condition of every value's validity. Hence, in affirming the ethical value of the sacredness of the person we likewise affirm the *human faculty to affirm values at all.* As long as we believe something to be valuable (and, as practical beings we cannot cease to believe this) we are committed to affirm the dignity of the person. Hence the concluding answer to the question why we ought to affirm the sacredness of the person is that this value is not a historical value but the necessary condition of all historical value affirmation. If, moreover, the human rights practice is the practice intended to protect this value, we are also committed to affirm this practice.

Possible objections

So far it has been shown that any attempt to apply Joas' affirmative genealogy necessarily entails an unconditioned decision by which the value in question is affirmed. And it is the faculty to take such a decision that accounts for human dignity. The appropriate method of justifying this value, therefore, is not the affirmative act in itself but the uncovering of its unconditioned condition. Yet, from Joas' point of view at least two objections can be made against this solution of his why-problem.

First, at several places Joas asserts that the type of argument being employed here suffers from a serious problem: it applies only to human persons who have the mental or cognitive skills to make existential decisions, but it excludes a great number of human beings as, for instance, babies, severely mentally disabled, or comatose. This objection can be called the *objection from exclusion.*

A second challenge is related to the concept of values Joas has been putting forward in several publications. In his view, the encounter with values is an overwhelming experience of subjective evidence, for which reason the experience itself cannot be subjected to the influence of the will. 'When we experience a value', Joas says, 'we experience it as valid in itself. And when we experience it as valid in itself we are committed to its recognition' (Joas 2011: 192). A value is thus affectively intense and in that respect much closer to the person than a cognitive truth which might be perceived as indifferent and distant fact. Therefore, Joas could say that it makes no sense to presuppose an additional decision by which the value is affirmed; the experience of a value alone involves an affirmative attitude towards it. We might call this difficulty the *objection from experience.*

Though each of these challenges makes a good point, one can still doubt whether they are cogent. The *objection from exclusion*, for instance, does not prove what it intends to. Of course, initially it is the other person's ability to make existential decisions that compels us to recognize her dignity. But this by no means entails that the possession of such an ability is a *necessary condition*. There may be other reasons (and in fact there are) to attribute dignity to human beings and, in doing this, to expand the group of persons who are protected by the human rights practice.

The *objection from experience* said that values can be so appealing that their affirmation does not necessarily involve an intentional decision. But can values be that strong? To answer this question, another look at Kierkegaard may help. In *The Sickness unto Death*, he sketches the scenario of a person who is offered eternal friendship with God. This person, Kierkegaard says, 'exists before God, may speak with God any time he wants to, assured of being heard by him – in short, this person is invited to live on the most intimate terms with God! Furthermore, for this person's sake . . . God comes to the world, allows himself to be born, to suffer, to die, and this suffering God – he almost implores and beseeches to accept the help that is offered to him!' (Kierkegaard 1980: 85). On Kierkegaard's view, this person experiences the most appealing value ever. And yet, she still is free to reject the offer. Kierkegaard's famous definition of sin virtually emphasizes this possibility. 'Sin', he says, 'is – after being taught by a revelation from God what sin is – before God in despair not to will to be oneself or in despair to will to be oneself' (*ibid.*: 96). The possibility of sin entails the possibility of rejecting what one has experienced as the ultimate and most appealing value. Consequently, the affirmation of this value implies a free decision and cannot exclusively be explained by the value's attractiveness. Hence, the objection from experience also doesn't work.

Conclusion

Summing up, we can conclude that Joas is absolutely right when he states that the human rights practice must be based on motivational value experiences. Otherwise, it is doomed to disappear. Accordingly, an affirmative genealogy can make a worthwhile and presumably even indispensable contribution to the establishment, the continuation, and the expansion of the human rights practice. However, we still have to recognize that an affirmative genealogy neither can *justify the moral necessity* of the human rights practice nor can it *enforce the affirmation* of human dignity as the underlying value. Just as God in Kierkegaard's latter example, the affirmative genealogist can only implore, beg, entreat and beseech her addressees to appropriate this value by a free decision. By no means can she substitute this decision or make it redundant. Affirmative genealogy, therefore, is a sort of a 'summons' (*Aufforderung*), as Fichte once called it: an urgent appeal to leap into the recognition of the other's sacredness and dignity.

References

Joas, H. 2011. *Die Sakralität der Person: Eine neue Genealogie der Menschenrechte.* Berlin: Suhrkamp

Kierkegaard, S. 1962. *Die Tagebücher*, trans. E. Hirsch, vol. 1. Düsseldorf, Cologne: Diederichs

1980. *The Sickness unto Death: A Christian Psychological Exposition for Upbuilding and Awakening*, trans. H. V. Hong and E. H. Hong, in *Kierkegaard's Writings*, vol. XIX. Princeton University Press

1985., *Philosophical Fragments*, trans. H. V. Hong and E. H. Hong, in *Kierkegaard's Writings*, vol. VII. Princeton University Press

1987. *Either/Or: Part II*, trans. H. V. Hong and E. H. Hong, in *Kierkegaard's Writings*, vol. IV. Princeton University Press

1992. *Concluding Unscientific Postscript to Philosophical Fragments*, vol. 1, trans. H. V. Hong and E. H. Hong, in *Kierkegaard's Writings*, vol. XII.1. Princeton University Press

22

Kantian perspectives on the rational basis of human dignity

THOMAS E. HILL, JR

Immanuel Kant (1724–1804) made the dignity of humanity central in his moral philosophy, and his idea has been interpreted and extended in many ways. Here, I sketch a broadly Kantian understanding of his position, noting occasionally alternative interpretations. The main questions are these: (1) What is human dignity? (2) By virtue of what do human beings have dignity? (3) Why believe in human dignity? (4) What are the practical implications?

Kant's main themes were these (Kant 2002: 214–45):[1] all persons, regardless of rank or social class, have an equal intrinsic worth or dignity. Human dignity is an innate worth or status that we did not earn and cannot forfeit. Rather, we must strive to make our individual choices worthy of this moral standing, which elevates us above animals and mere things. A fundamental principle of reason and morality, the Categorical Imperative, tells us to treat humanity in each person never merely as a means, but always as an end in itself. We must act as if we were both law-makers and subjects in an ideal moral commonwealth in which the members, as ends in themselves, have *dignity* rather than mere *price*. In contrast to market price and other values that are dependent on our personal attachments, Kant calls dignity 'an unconditional and incomparable worth' that 'admits of no equivalent'. Human dignity is based on the prior thesis that 'the moral law', an unconditional command of reason, has an absolute dignity and authority that everyone must respect. This moral law requires respect for human dignity because all human persons, good or bad, must, from the standpoint of practice, be presumed to have the capacities and predispositions of rational autonomy. In treating humanity as an end in itself and following the moral principles of an ideal moral commonwealth, we will be giving appropriate recognition to the autonomy of each person and shaping our lives by general policies that we can rationally regard as permissible for anyone to follow. The fundamental moral law that affirms human dignity has practical implications for both law and individual ethical choices. Legal institutions must interpret, apply and coercively enforce the innate right to freedom of every person, and

[1] [6: 412–245]. All bracketed numbers refer to Kant 1903/11, except where otherwise stated.

individuals must respect themselves and others as persons with equal standing under the moral law.

What is human dignity?

As scholars have noted, there is a long history of the general concept of dignity understood as a distinguished social standing that is elevated above others (Hruska 2006; Sensen 2009). Some have dignity associated with their office, for example, as judges, senators, bishops or queens. Ordinary people are supposed to show special respect for these 'dignitaries', in various appropriate ways, in honour of their elevated standing, and the office holders are expected to behave in a manner worthy of their position. Aristocracies and caste systems divide human beings into hereditary classes that require special honours for members of the higher classes whether or not the higher ranked individuals have the responsibilities of public office. The ancient Romans considered Roman citizenship as a status worthy of honour and gradually extended citizenship widely even to former 'barbarians' for service in their armies. Rousseau gave modern expression to the equal dignity of all citizens of an ideal republic, and Kant, drawing also from Christianity and Stoicism, extended Rousseau's political ideal into a moral ideal of all of humanity united by common principles. As members of a universal moral commonwealth, even ordinary human beings have a dignity independent of office, social class and political citizenship.

Although we may speak of dignity as a 'worth' or 'value' that humanity and individual persons have, it is important to resist the contemporary assumption that all values are weights on a scale whereby we can determine what 'on balance' we should do. In contrast to values based solely on what is useful or desired, to have dignity is to have an 'unconditional' status of worth or value. This implies that dignity is independent not only of office, social class and citizenship, but also of ethnic heritage, religious affiliation, gender, race, sexual orientation and any other factor except the basic human capacities and dispositions necessary to being a rational and autonomous person. Kant shared some common prejudices of his time about the capacities of women and non-European 'races', but his mature works repeatedly affirm the equal dignity of any person with the essential capacities to be a moral agent. By doing wrong we do not forfeit our fundamental status as human beings, even though by criminal acts we may forfeit various civil rights. Even those who make the 'evil' life-governing choice to subordinate the moral law to self-interest (Kant 1998: 55–61)[2] must be respected as human beings assuming that, despite their bad choices, they have the basic rationality and freedom necessary for being moral agents. No one with these basic capacities can altogether escape rational and felt recognition of the authority of the moral law and consciousness of his or her capacity to choose to conform, for the basis of this recognized authority is not

[2] [6: 32–9].

tradition, self-interest, human sentiments, external powers or Platonic forms, but the common practical reason of each person exercised from a standpoint of autonomy.

Kantian dignity is not only 'unconditional' but 'incomparable' and 'without equivalent.' (Kant 1996: 187, 209; 2002: 235–6)[3] This contrasts sharply with Hobbes' definition: 'The value, or WORTH of a man is, as of all other things, his price: that is to say, so much as would be given for his power.'[4] According to Kant, dignity is 'above all price': it is not to be sacrificed for things the value of which depends solely on utility and personal preferences. What has dignity is also, in a sense, inviolable and irreplaceable. We cannot decide what we should do by assigning a 'dignity-value', even an equal dignity-value, to each human being and then calculating – two are worth more than one, three more than two, and so on (cf. Cummiskey 1996: 110–22). If, tragically, we must choose to let some die to save others, this calls for justification by principles that appropriately respect each person, which cannot be *simply* a matter of calculating the numbers. Each life matters, but respect for human dignity is not just about preserving lives.

The Kantian thesis that the moral law and humanity have an unconditional and incomparable value does not mean that judgments of moral right and wrong are ultimately based on a prior intuition of a value that is independent of the moral law. In an important sense, for Kant the right is always prior to the good. To attribute dignity to the moral law and therefore to humanity is to express in a concise and forceful way that we must appropriately respect and honour both in our attitudes, choices and conduct. What we must do to comply, more specifically, must be determined by the content of the moral law as expressed in the Categorical Imperative, and Kant defends this, not by appeal to a prior independent value, but by complex arguments about the presuppositions of rational moral judgments.

By virtue of what is dignity attributed to human beings?

The basic Kantian answer is that human beings have dignity by virtue of their rationality and freedom, but this has been interpreted in different ways, for example, as the capacity to set ends, as pragmatic and technical predispositions, as a good will, and as all rational capacities (for example, Korsgaard 1996: 106–32; Hill 2002: 39–41; Dean 2006; Wood 2008: 85–105). Arguably, the most plausible interpretation takes the key feature to be 'humanity' – when understood as our nature as rational beings with autonomy of the will.[5] The core of this complex Kantian idea is that persons have the capacity and disposition to recognize as authoritative and to follow both principles of instrumental

[3] 1996: [6: 436]; [6: 462]; 2002: [4: 434–6].
[4] Hobbes 1994: Part I, Chapter 10, para. 16.
[5] This includes what Kant calls 'personality'.

rationality (hypothetical imperatives) and principles of rational morality (categorical imperatives). Autonomy of the will is not the existentialist's freedom from rational constraints or a rational egoist's freedom to do whatever most effectively advances his or her interests. Autonomy is also not any particular right, for example, a right to have one's informed consent be respected in medicine, though it underlies arguments for such specific rights. Kantian rational autonomy, rather, is the general capacity and disposition to govern oneself by rational and reasonable principles that are justifiable to all insofar as they take up a common point of view in which everyone counts as an equal co-legislator of specific moral principles.

In more ordinary terms, this means that, at least as competent adults, human beings implicitly understand themselves to be bound not merely by concerns of prudence and efficiency, but also by potentially overriding constraints entailed by recognizing others as moral equals. Although they may come from different cultures and disagree about specific issues, they are presumed to be aware of the most basic requirements of morality and to think and feel that they should live accordingly even if they often fail to do so. They cannot persistently and consistently dismiss 'the moral law within' as merely an external demand or simply the product of cultural conditioning.

The Kantian thesis that human beings have dignity by virtue of their rationality and autonomy has been repeatedly challenged on the ground that it devalues animals, children and mentally incompetent human adults, making them subject to treatment merely as means. Controversy continues, but at least we should note that the thesis that ordinary competent adult moral agents have dignity by virtue of their rational autonomy does not imply that *only* they have moral value or standing. Moral principles are constraints and guides that ordinary competent agents *would* follow *if* they were fully rational and autonomous. The question is how such principles direct morally competent agents – those with the active capacities and dispositions of rational autonomy – to treat young children whose moral capacities remain latent, demented adults who have lost them, and animals that lack them. Arguably, these moral principles would require us to extend a kind of dignity to human beings who have lost or not yet developed moral capacities and also (despite what Kant says) to regard animals as more than mere means to our ends.

Why believe in human dignity?

The Kantian attributes dignity to persons by virtue of their having rational autonomy, but, focusing now just on competent adults, why believe (a) that rational autonomy confers dignity and (b) that human beings have rational autonomy? For Kantians, these are questions for practical, not theoretical, reason. That is, they call for vindication from the standpoint of deliberation and choice, not scientific or metaphysical proofs. Practical reason, however, cannot rest content with appeals to self-interest, sentiments, tradition, alleged intuition, theology, tradition or merely pragmatic considerations (Kant 2002: 240–5).[6]

First, why accept that rational autonomy entitles one to the elevated status of dignity? Kant's texts defy brief summary, but a main line of argument attempts to show that our common idea that we are bound by moral duty presupposes that there is a categorically rational imperative, expressible in several (supposedly) equivalent forms that tell us to act only on universalizable maxims, to treat humanity in each person as an end in itself, and to act as if each person is a rational autonomous legislator of moral laws (*ibid.*: 214–40).[7] Together these entail that we must act as if we are authors and subjects of laws in a commonwealth ('kingdom') of ends, in which we treat each other with the restraint and regard encapsulated in the idea of dignity. The conclusion here is conditional: if we believe in moral duty and rational autonomy (its basis), then we must believe in human dignity (*ibid.*: 245).[8]

Setting aside specifics, the point is that to accept that we are under *moral* constraints is to understand that we must restrict our choices by basic principles that are permissible for anyone to follow, that attribute to every person an equal and respect-worthy status, and that would be accepted by all reasonable persons as justifiable from this common standpoint. So those who accept that they are under moral constraints thereby accept that they must treat all persons with the restraint and concern (dignity) accorded them under such principles.

The second question remains – why attribute rational autonomy to (at least competent adult) human beings? What is at issue is not whether human beings have the capacity for instrumental rationality but whether we must accept that we are all under the implicitly acknowledged rational authority of principles that we would accept from a common mutually respectful standpoint. The Kantian answer cannot appeal to self-interest, moral sentiment, divine command or metaphysical intuition. Our attribution of rational autonomy to human beings implies that it is *rational* for us to accept and follow principles from a common moral standpoint, and this rationality claim is neither an empirical claim nor self-contradictory to deny.

Nevertheless, Kant presents considerations to heighten our awareness that in our thinking and practice we are in fact deeply, and unavoidably, committed to fundamental moral principles as rational constraints on our attitudes and choices. For example, one argument challenges us to acknowledge that we cannot help but regard *ourselves* as more than a mere means for the use of others, and that we regard ourselves in this way for the same reason that everyone else does – namely, we take ourselves to be free and rational persons (*ibid.*: 229).[9] He argues further that insofar as we are rational human beings we cannot act or even engage in theoretical investigations without taking ourselves to be 'free' as persons operating under rational standards, such as the moral law, that are not merely instrumental. Later, Kant proposes that we are conscious of moral duty,

[6] [4: 440–4]. [7] [4: 412–40]. [8] [4: 444–5]. [9] [4: 229].

which presupposes rational autonomy, as 'a fact of reason', evident in examples such as whether to bear false witness leading to the execution of an innocent person (Kant 1997: 27–8, 41).[10]

In effect, Kant calls for honest reflection on our deepest moral commitments and their implications. His arguments ask us to reflect on how we conceive of ourselves as moral agents, and then to act consistently on the practical implications. He offers no theoretical proof either that rational autonomy confers dignity or that human beings have rational autonomy. Instead, the Kantian response to 'Why believe?' is 'Examine yourself clearly and honestly – do you not already (inevitably) believe?' In other words, 'can you not recognize that these moral ideas are deeply imbedded in your own practical thinking and that you cannot consistently dismiss them as irrational prejudices, false empirical hypotheses, or mere empty metaphysical speculations?' This mode of argument will not satisfy everyone, and some Kantians attempt to offer strengthened versions.

What are the practical implications?

Kant's earlier ethical works are focused on the *duties* of individuals, but they also provide background to his later theory of *rights* (1996: 1–138).[11] For both rights and duties, Kant's ultimate standard is ('pure') practical reason. The context of questions about rights, state authority and justice is a world of embodied agents in a limited world-space who cannot help but limit each other's ('external') freedom. The questions are not about morally worthy acts and motives but rather about when a person may rightfully interfere with another, what counter-force is permissible, and why a legitimate state with coercive power is needed. The starting-point regarding these issues is the universal principle of justice: 'Any action is right if it can coexist with everyone's freedom in accordance with a universal law, or if on its maxim the freedom of choice of each can coexist with everyone's freedom in accordance with a universal law' (*ibid.*: 24).[12] This expresses the core of an innate right of freedom and equality attributed to everyone as a basis for and limit on state authority. Institutions as well as individuals must avoid treating persons simply as means, even to socially desirable ends.

From these fundamental ideas and general facts about the human condition Kant attempts to derive more specific rights – *juridical rights* to be instituted and enforced within states, standards of *international right* to be affirmed through a federation of states, and *cosmopolitan rights* of individuals independent of national borders. From a Kantian standpoint, specific human rights, such as those in the United Nations' charter, are not self-standing but must be justified by broader principles that appropriately respect human dignity. Like others who object to free-floating rights-claims that lack institutional enforcement,

[10] [5: 30–1, 47]. [11] [6: 203–372]. [12] [6: 231].

Kantians generally agree that theoretically backed ought-to-be rights can only be fully determinate, binding and effective when they are defined and enforced through political states or international institutions. Some, however, extend Kant's ideas to advocate a broader understanding of cosmopolitan rights, global duties, and promoting justice through institutions other than nation-states (O'Neill 2000: 115–202).

The idea of human dignity is also a basic standard for personal relations. Kant expresses the first principle of a system of 'ethical' principles for individuals as follows: '[A]ct in accordance with a maxim of *ends* that it can be a universal law for everyone to have. In accordance with this principle a human being is an end for himself as well as for others, and it is not enough that he is not authorized to use either himself or others merely as means (since he could still be indifferent to them); it is in itself his duty to make man as such his end' (Kant 1996: 157).[13] Here, the idea of humanity as an end is affirmed as a standard for the basic attitudes, aims and choices that we adopt as individuals. Kant repeatedly appeals to the dignity of humanity – or the ideal rational person within each of us – in support of his ethical principles, especially the duty to preserve and improve oneself as a rational being and the duty to respect other persons (*ibid.*: 176–97, 209–13).[14]

References

Cummiskey, D. 1996. *Kantian Consequentialism.* Oxford University Press

Dean, R. 2006. *The Value of Humanity in Kant's Moral Theory.* Oxford: Clarendon Press

Hill, T. 2002. *Human Welfare and Moral Worth.* Oxford University Press

Hobbes, T. 1994. *Leviathan*, ed. E. Curley. Indianapolis, IN: Hackett Publishing Co.

Hruska, J. 2006. 'Kant and Human Dignity', in *Kant and Law*, ed. B. S. Byrd and J. Hruska. Aldershot: Ashgate Publishing

Kant, I. 1903/11. *Kants gesammelte Schriften*, herausgegeben von der Königliche Preussische Akademie der Wissenschaften. Berlin: Walter de Gruyter

1996. *The Metaphysics of Morals*, ed. M. Gregor. Cambridge University Press

1997. *Critique of Practical Reason*, ed. M. Gregor. Cambridge University Press

1998. *Religion within the Boundaries of Mere Reason*, ed. A. Wood and G. di Giovani. Cambridge University Press

2002. *Groundwork for the Metaphysics of Morals*, ed. T. E. Hill, Jr and A. Zweig. Oxford University Press

Korsgaard, C. 1996. *Creating the Kingdom of Ends.* Cambridge University Press

O'Neill, O. 2000. *Bounds of Justice.* Cambridge University Press

Sensen, O. 2009. 'Kant's Conception of Human Dignity', *Kant-Studien* 100, 309–31

Wood, A. 2008. *Kantian Ethics.* Cambridge University Press

[13] [6: 395]. *Being an end in itself* is at least a central aspect of *dignity*, though some think that for Kant they are not identical. See Wood 2008: 86–8.

[14] [6: 421–47, 462–8].

23

Kantian dignity: a critique

SAMUEL J. KERSTEIN

No philosophical discussion of dignity influences current debate more than Immanuel Kant's. Interwoven with central tenets of his ethics, this discussion admits of various interpretations. According to a prominent one, Kant defends the view that dignity is an unconditional and incomparable value possessed by all persons and only persons.[1] This chapter assesses the philosophical plausibility of this view, arguing that, although it has attractive features, it suffers from serious flaws.

Kant's discussion of the dignity of humanity is centred in the *Groundwork of the Metaphysics of Morals* (Kant 1996a) and the *Metaphysics of Morals* (Kant 1996b). Kant uses 'humanity' interchangeably with 'rational nature' (Kant 1996a: 439). In his view, having rational nature involves having certain capacities, including the capacity to set and to pursue ends as well as the capacity to act autonomously (Hill 1992: 38–41). To have the capacity to act autonomously, that is, to conform to self-given moral imperatives purely out of respect for these imperatives, is to have a distinctive kind of freedom, according to Kant. A being has dignity if and only if it possesses rational nature, he suggests. If there are any human beings who do not possess rational nature, then they do not have dignity. But any being, human or not, who does possess rational nature has dignity.[2] Let us call any being who possesses rational nature a 'person'. Rational nature is a threshold concept, in Kant's view. If a being has the capacities that are constitutive of rational nature, it has rational nature, regardless of how well- or ill-developed those capacities may be.

To say that humanity has dignity is to say that it has a special value or, equivalently, worth. This value has three main features.[3] First, it attaches to

[1] This sort of view has been defended, for example, in Hill 1992; Paton 1967; and Schönecker and Wood 2003.

[2] This point is controversial. Some scholars defend the view that, according to Kant, dignity is possessed not by all beings with a rational nature, but rather only by those who have a good will (Dean 2006). Roughly speaking, a person has a good will if she has a disposition to conform her actions to the moral law and to do so on the ground that this law is authoritative for her will.

[3] For a very different interpretation of what Kant means by dignity, see Sensen 2009 and 2011.

something that exists rather than to something that does not but that might be brought about. An appropriate response to a value of the sort humanity has is to honour, cherish or preserve it, rather than to create more of it. Second, the worth of humanity is unconditional (Kant 1996a: 428). Something has unconditional worth in Kant's sense only if it is good no matter what the context of its existence is. As unconditionally good, humanity is valuable no matter how it came to exist or what the effects of its existence may be. Moreover, if something is unconditionally valuable in Kant's sense, then neither what it affects nor what happens to it can at all diminish its goodness (Kant 1996a: 393–4).

Finally, to say that humanity has dignity is to say that it has incomparable worth: it has no equivalent for which it can be legitimately exchanged (Kant 1996a: 434–6; Kant 1996b: 434–5, 462). Humanity can never be legitimately sacrificed for or replaced by something with mere price. Not even all the diamonds in South Africa would truly compensate for the killing of one person. Moreover, since humanity possesses incomparable worth, it cannot even be legitimately sacrificed for or replaced by something else with such worth (Hill 1992: 47–9). It makes no sense to say that in some context one or more persons have more or less value than one or more other persons. In Kant's view, everything that lacks incomparable worth, including human happiness and well-being, has mere price. In sum, all and only extant beings who possess rational nature possess dignity: unconditional and incomparable value.

Kant seems to invoke the special value of rational nature when he expresses what he takes to be the supreme principle of morality (the Categorical Imperative): 'So act that you treat humanity, whether in your own person or in the person of any other, always at the same time as an end, never merely as a means' (Kant 1996a: 429). Treating humanity as an end, as this 'Formula of Humanity' (FH) commands, seems to amount to treating it as something that has dignity. On one prominent interpretation of this principle, the Formula of Humanity amounts to an imperative always to act in a way that expresses respect for the worth of humanity, in one's own person as well as that of another (Wood 1999: 141). Let us call this principle RFH, since it is a specification of Kant's Formula of Humanity that invokes the notion of expressing *respect* for humanity's value, that is, for its dignity. Any action that fails to express respect for humanity's value does so at least in part by suggesting an inaccurate message regarding what this value is. So, for example, an account of what makes (or purportedly makes) an attempt at suicide wrong would necessarily include the notion that it expresses a false message, namely, that some person, presumably the one trying to kill himself, does not have dignity. Moreover, if an action expresses such a message, then it expresses disrespect for the value of humanity and is morally impermissible.

The Kantian account of dignity has several features many of us find attractive. For example, an individual's dignity does not on this account vary with his wealth, social status, or achievements. Any being who has the capacities requisite for possessing dignity has no less (and no more) dignity than anyone else.

Moreover, RFH seems to capture a core of ordinary moral thinking. It would forbid an action that aimed to maximize the preservation of dignity by killing one innocent person who wants to go on living in order to preserve the lives of two others. For such an action would suggest that persons have comparable value. Finally, the Kantian account seems to cohere with and might even provide a foundation for some appeals to dignity in international law. For example, the International Covenant on Economic, Social and Cultural Rights (ICESCR) suggests that the human rights set forth in the Universal Declaration of Human Rights (UDHR) 'derive from the inherent dignity of the human person'.[4] Some of the rights specified in the UDHR might be anchored in the Kantian account. For example, Article 4 articulates a right not to be held in slavery. Holding a person in slavery would express disrespect for her dignity: it would send the message that she had mere price.

But the Kantian account faces serious difficulties. Most of us grant that persons have a special value. Yet why should we conclude that they have incomparable or unconditional value, as Kant defines it? Contemporary philosophers have interpreted Kant to unfurl or at least to suggest sophisticated arguments for this conclusion. The arguments have the following general structure: unless you are willing to give up some very plausible, general belief regarding your agency, you are rationally compelled to hold that persons have dignity (or at least unconditional value). But the arguments incorporate dubious claims like the following: if you believe that you have the capacity to determine which ends are good, then you are rationally compelled to embrace the view that you yourself are good (Wood 2008: 90–2; Korsgaard 1996: 122–3). Proponents of such claims leave unexplained why your believing the former would commit you to the latter any more than your believing that you have the capacity to determine which ends are bad would commit you to the view that you yourself are bad (Kerstein 2001: 33–4). Of course, the failure of abstract philosophical arguments for the Kantian account of the dignity of persons would not necessarily leave it devoid of support.[5] It might gain credibility by capturing better than alternative accounts the dictates of reflective common sense on the worth of persons and what that worth implies. But, as discussed below, it is questionable whether it does.

One oft-remarked difficulty that surrounds the Kantian account of dignity concerns the status of some beings who seem not to have rational nature, for example, non-human animals and very young children (Warren 1997: 101–4). If these beings indeed fail to have rational nature, then they have mere price, according to the account. But how, then, is our treatment of them subject to moral constraints?

[4] ICESCR, Preamble.

[5] For a further critique of arguments that purport to show that we are rationally compelled to hold that persons have dignity as defined in the Kantian account, see Christiano 2008.

Kantian philosophers have tried to reply to such questions (O'Neill 1998; Denis 2000). Allen Wood insists, for example, that we do not manifest proper respect for rational nature unless we treat some beings who are not persons just as if they were persons (Wood 2008: 97). For, he says, our treatment of beings who are not persons sometimes expresses disrespect for persons. It would, for example, express disrespect for rational nature not to help it to grow to maturity in a child in whom it has already started to develop.

But this last point is questionable to say the least. It would not show disrespect to the *child's* rational nature to refrain from furthering its development; for by stipulation the child does not possess rational nature. Perhaps refraining from furthering the child's development would express disrespect for the rational nature of others, namely, those who aim to promote his thriving. But what if, unfortunately for the child, no one has this aim? Of course, not furthering the child's development might express disrespect for the child's *capacity to develop* rational nature. But that capacity, which is presumably possessed by human embryos, is obviously not the same thing as rational nature itself, which is presumably not possessed by them. And it is not clear that expressing disrespect for the capacity to develop rational nature amounts to expressing disrespect for rational nature itself.

In any case, perhaps embracing all of the premises Kant or some Kantians invoke in support of the conclusion that persons have dignity would entail holding that non-persons have mere price. But it is worth noting that, taken in itself, the idea that beings with rational nature have dignity seems perfectly compatible with the notion that some beings devoid of it nevertheless have a value that transcends that of mere things.

There are, however, further difficulties with the Kantian account of dignity. It generates normative verdicts that are at odds with considered judgments held by many of us. (If philosophical arguments rationally compelled us to embrace the account, then we might have to give up these judgments. But, as stated above, it is doubtful whether they do.)

Consider first cases of what many of us take to be heroic self-sacrifice. A United States soldier, Private First Class (PFC) Ross McGinnis, was awarded posthumously a military honour, the Silver Star. PFC McGinnis was manning the machine gun on a combat truck when someone threw a grenade towards it. He tried to deflect the grenade, but it went down the vehicle's top hatch. The narrative accompanying the military honour continues as follows:

> When an average man would have leapt out of the gunner's cupola to safety, PFC McGinnis decided to stay with his crew. Unhesitatingly and with complete disregard for his own life he announced 'the grenade is in the truck' and threw his back over the grenade to pin it between his body and the truck's radio mount. When the grenade detonated, PFC McGinnis absorbed all lethal fragments and the concussion with his own body, killing him instantly. His early warning allowed all four members of his crew to position their bodies in a protective posture to prepare for the grenade's blast. As a result of his quick reflexes and heroic

> measures, no other members of the vehicle crew were seriously wounded in the attack. His gallant action and total disregard for his personal well-being directly saved four men from certain serious injury or death. (Arlington National Cemetery website)[6]

Many of us believe that PFC McGinnis' action was not only morally permissible, but also morally admirable. Yet RFH implies that it was wrong. According to the narrative, PFC McGinnis' action of throwing his back over the grenade showed 'total disregard for his personal well-being' and 'complete disregard for his own life'. The narrative implies that McGinnis intentionally allowed himself to be killed in order to save his comrades, or at least that in order to save them, he did something which, as he was aware, would have as a virtually certain consequence the elimination of his own humanity. Either way, his action failed to express respect for the incomparable worth of his humanity. It sent the message that its value was not as great as the value of that of the four other soldiers taken together. So, according to RFH, PFC McGinnis' action was wrong.

A second case also shows that the Kantian account delivers implausible results. Suppose that a law-abiding journalist has discovered widespread financial improprieties in a large company. He has a well-grounded suspicion that a security officer employed by this company aims to kill him in order to keep him from revealing what he knows. The officer follows him into an enclosed alley and approaches him with knife raised. The journalist tries, to no avail, to reason with him. He then takes out a gun and yells at the officer to stop. But he continues to move forward, now just a step away. The journalist reflects in a flash that the officer is a former special forces soldier and an expert in hand-to-hand combat. He concludes, very reasonably, that if he doesn't shoot to kill, he is very unlikely to escape from the situation alive. If the journalist intentionally kills the officer in this case, he acts in self-defence and his action is morally permissible, or so many of us believe. But, in shooting and killing the officer, the journalist would not express respect for the officer's humanity.

In order to see this, consider first a case of intentionally killing (and thus destroying the humanity of) an innocent, non-threatening person who wishes to remain alive. Doing so would express disrespect for the value of her humanity. It would convey a message that her humanity falls short of having unconditional and incomparable value. But now note that the value of the security officer's humanity neither disappears nor at all diminishes when he acts as a malicious aggressor. That it maintains its full value is just part of what it means to say that it has unconditional value in the Kantian sense. In destroying the officer's humanity, the journalist is destroying something no less valuable than the humanity of an innocent, non-threatening person. If someone's killing the innocent person expresses disrespect for the value of her humanity, then

6 Arlington National Cemetery website, 'Ross A. McGinnis: Specialist, United States Army', arlingtoncemetery.net/ramcginnis.htm (accessed 20 July 2010).

the journalist's killing the officer expresses disrespect for the value of his. So, according to the respect-expression view, the journalist's shooting and killing the officer in self-defence is morally impermissible.

A final example illustrates a further implausible implication of the Kantian account. We have one indivisible life-saving drug and two patients who desperately want and need it: a twenty-year-old and a seventy-year-old. It is our job to allocate the drug. Each person has a claim on it in the relatively weak sense that it would be wrong for us not to give it to her on morally arbitrary grounds (for example, because we did not like her home town). Finally, neither patient is morally responsible for her need of the drug in any way that would affect her claim on it. The patient who does not get the drug will die. If the younger person gets the drug, she will thrive for decades; if the older person gets the drug, she will thrive for a couple of years but then die of natural causes.

Many of us are convinced that the younger patient should get the drug. One might suggest that she should get it on the grounds that the older patient has already had a full human life, that is, her 'fair innings'. But giving it to her on that basis would send a message contrary to the notion that humanity has dignity. For it would suggest that an instance of rational nature that has endured long enough to constitute a full life has less value than an instance that has been around for a shorter time. But this suggestion contradicts the Kantian notion that the value of humanity is unconditional.

The self-sacrifice case tries to illustrate implausible implications that Kant's account has by virtue of its holding that persons have incomparable value. The drug allocation and self-defence cases attempt to demonstrate implausible implications it has by virtue of holding that persons have unconditional value. Of course, defenders of the Kantian account might try to show that it does not have these implications.[7] Or they might contend that the implications are not implausible after all. Finally, they might acknowledge that the account has implausible implications but argue that it has fewer than any rival accounts. But that the Kantian account of dignity appears to clash with widely held judgments of reflective common sense is a difficulty with it that needs to be addressed.

It is worth keeping in mind that accounts of dignity different from the one we have examined can also find inspiration in Kant (Cummiskey 2008). For example, one might interpret or reconstruct Kant's notion of dignity to invoke fundamentally not a value, but rather a set of prescriptions that we are rationally compelled to use in deliberations regarding policies on permissible or impermissible ways of behaving (Hill 2003; 2012). The prescriptions are higher level principles that govern decisions regarding which lower level principles to adopt. According to one such account, these prescriptions include, but are not limited to, the following: first, we 'must treat persons only in ways that we could in principle justify to them as well as to all other rational persons

[7] For a far more detailed defence of the conclusion that RFH indeed has implausible implications in the self-sacrifice and self-defence cases, see Kerstein 2009a.

who take an appropriately impartial perspective' (Hill 2003: 25). Second, the value of persons is not commensurable, so we must not compare or weigh the value of one against that of others. And, third, persons have a moral status that limits how we may use them, even to realize good ends (Hill 2003: 25). The normative implications of these prescriptions are far from obvious. But they seem to be problematic in some of the sort of cases we have examined. Consider a principle that would permit, but not require, a person to voluntarily kill himself (for example, by jumping on a grenade) in order to maximize the preservation of persons. It seems as if this principle would run afoul of the second prescription; for it treats the value of persons as commensurable. But perhaps further development of this rational prescription approach to dignity would show how it could allow for principles permitting self-sacrifice.

There might be yet other ways of reconstructing a Kantian notion of dignity. Inspired by the Formula of Humanity, one might-hold that dignity is a special status held by persons, according to which they ought not to be treated merely as means, but ought to be treated as having a special worth.[8] This worth might in part be defined as *transcendent*, rather than as incomparable (Kerstein 2013). To treat persons as having transcendent value would be to treat them as having a value that transcends that of non-persons: a value that no amount of anything that is not a person can equal. A requirement to treat persons as having transcendent value would be consistent with saving more persons rather than fewer on the grounds that more have greater value than fewer. Such an account of dignity might be consistent with what many of us take to be warranted conclusions, for example, that PFC McGinnis' action was heroic, not wrong. Of course, even if the account harmonizes with reflective common sense in this case, it might clash with it in a whole range of others. Far more work would need to be done in order to defend the view that the account was worthy of acceptance.[9]

References

Christiano, T. 2008. 'Two Conceptions of the Dignity of Persons', *Jahrbuch für Recht und Ethik* 16: 101–26

Cummiskey, D. 2008. 'Dignity, Contractualism and Consequentialism', *Utilitas* 20: 383–408

Dean, R. 2006. *The Value of Humanity in Kant's Moral Theory*. Oxford University Press

Denis, L. 2000. 'Kant's Conception of Duties Regarding Animals: Reconstruction and Reconsideration', *History of Philosophy Quarterly* 17: 405–23

Hill, T., Jr. 1992. 'Humanity as an End in Itself', in *Dignity and Practical Reason in Kant's Moral Theory*. Ithaca, NY: Cornell University Press, 38–57

[8] It is not obvious what the notion of treating another merely as a means amounts to. For specifications of the notion, see Kerstein 2009b and 2013.

[9] I try to make progress on this task in Kerstein 2013.

2003. 'Treating Criminals as Ends in Themselves', *Jahrbuch für Recht und Ethik* 11: 17–36

2012. *Virtue, Rules, and Justice*. Oxford University Press

Kant, I. 1996a. *Groundwork of the Metaphysics of Morals*, trans. M. Gregor, in *Immanuel Kant: Practical Philosophy*. Cambridge University Press (the page numbers given in the text above refer to Kant [1902–] volume IV)

1996b. *The Metaphysics of Morals*, trans. M. Gregor, in *Immanuel Kant: Practical Philosophy*. Cambridge University Press (the page numbers given in the text above refer to Kant [1902–] volume VI)

Kerstein, S. 2001. 'Korsgaard's Kantian Arguments for the Value of Humanity', *Canadian Journal of Philosophy* 31: 23–52

2009a. 'Death, Dignity, and Respect', *Social Theory and Practice* 35: 505–30

2009b. 'Treating Others Merely as Means', *Utilitas* 21: 163–80

2013. *How to Treat Persons*. Oxford University Press

Korsgaard, C. 1996. 'Kant's Formula of Humanity', in *Creating the Kingdom of Ends*. Cambridge University Press, 106–32

O'Neill, O. 1998. 'Kant on Duties Regarding Nonrational Nature II', *Aristotelian Society: Supplementary Volume* 72: 211–28

Paton, H. J. 1967. *The Categorical Imperative*. New York: Harper & Row

Schönecker, D., and Wood, A. 2003. *Immanuel Kant 'Grundlegung zur Metaphysik der Sitten': Ein Einführender Kommentar*. Paderborn: Verlag Ferdinand Schöningh

Sensen, O. 2009. 'Kant's Conception of Human Dignity', *Kant-Studien* 100: 309–31

2011. *Kant on Human Dignity*. Berlin: Walter de Gruyter

Warren, M. A. 1997. *Moral Status*. Oxford University Press

Wood, A. 1999. *Kant's Ethical Thought*. Cambridge University Press

2008. *Kantian Ethics*. Cambridge University Press

24

Human dignity and human rights in Alan Gewirth's moral philosophy

DERYCK BEYLEVELD

The Preamble to the International Covenant on Civil and Political Rights 1966 (ICCPR) states that the rights proclaimed by the Universal Declaration of Human Rights 1948 (UDHR), some of which the ICCPR aims to give effect to, 'derive from the inherent dignity of the human person'. It is because human persons have dignity that they have human rights. The Preamble to the UDHR further states that human rights are 'inalienable rights of all members of the human family', possessed equally by all members of this family, all of whom have 'inherent dignity'.

Alan Gewirth argues that agents (those with the capacity and disposition to pursue purposes voluntarily) must, on pain of contradicting that they are agents, accept and comply with the 'Principle of Generic Consistency' (PGC), which requires them to respect the 'generic rights'[1] of all agents (Gewirth 1978: 53–8). Consequently, the PGC is a principle with which all rational action must comply. In Gewirth's terminology, the PGC is 'dialectically necessary', which is to say that the requirement for an agent to assent to it follows purely logically from a premise that no agent can coherently deny, namely, the claim of the agent that he, she or it[2] is an agent.

Assuming that the argument is sound, does it justify the rights recognized by the UDHR? More specifically, does it justify: (1) the claim that all members of the human family equally have (or must be accorded) inherent dignity, in consequence of which they all equally have (or must be accorded) inalienable rights; (2) the specific rights granted by the UDHR?

[1] These are rights to 'generic conditions of agency', which are conditions/capacities that must be satisfied if an agent is to be able to act at all or with general chances of success, regardless of the purposes being pursued. The generic conditions are made up of 'basic needs' (lack of which impacts on the capacity to act at all), such as life, mental equilibrium, health, food, shelter and freedom from coercion; 'non-subtractive needs' (required to maintain one's ability to achieve one's purposes), such as accurate information; and 'additive needs' (required to improve one's abilities to achieve one's purposes), such as 'higher education'.

[2] I will refer to 'it', unless referring directly to male or female agents, as agents are neither necessarily biologically human nor gendered.

The argument provides answers to three fundamental questions of moral philosophy: (a) the distributive question, 'Who has moral rights?'; (b) the substantive question, 'What is the content of (these) rights?'; and (c) the authoritative question, 'Why must (these) rights be granted?' (see Gewirth 1978: 3).[3] The direct answer to (a) is 'All agents', to (b) 'The generic conditions of agency', and to (c) 'Because it is dialectically necessary for agents to do so'.

After outlining the argument for the PGC, I will elucidate the formal nature of the generic rights it secures and the conception of dignity as the ground of these rights that it implies. I will then consider whether this conception of dignity can be seen as the ground of human rights *per the UDHR*. I present my personal views concerning what the argument for the PGC logically entails, which differ in some important ways from Gewirth's own opinions. Consideration of the extent to which the specific rights recognized by the UDHR may be viewed as rights to generic conditions of agency is beyond the scope of this chapter.

The argument, the generic rights, and dignity

The argument in outline

The argument has three stages.[4] According to Stage One, I (who might be any agent) must (on pain of contradicting that I am an agent) accept that I ought (*instrumentally* for the sake of *my* purposes, *whatever these might be*) to pursue and defend my possession of the generic conditions of agency, because they are needed for me to pursue/achieve any purposes by my own actions. According to Stage Two, I similarly must (i.e. must, on pain of contradicting that I am an agent) consider that I have both positive and negative rights to the generic conditions of agency. This is because the proposition that I have these rights is logically entailed by the proposition that I categorically (i.e. simply by virtue of being an agent, regardless of my purposes) instrumentally ought to pursue and defend my having the generic conditions. According to Stage Three, it follows purely logically[5] that I similarly not merely *must consider that I have* the generic rights (from which it follows purely logically that each other agent must consider that it has the generic rights on pain of contradicting that it is an agent), but that I similarly *must consider that it is simply because I am an agent that I have the generic rights*. From this it follows purely logically that I similarly must consider that all agents have the generic rights; and, from this, it follows logically that every agent must (on pain of contradicting that it is an agent)

[3] Note that Gewirth poses the substantive question and the distributive question in terms of interests rather than rights.

[4] This construction is spelled out fully and defended systematically in Beyleveld 1991. It received Gewirth's endorsement (Beyleveld 1991: XIV; Gewirth 1996: XI).

[5] This is by the 'Argument from the Sufficiency of Agency' (Gewirth 1978: 110). See also Beyleveld 1991, especially Chapter 8 and 377–82; and Beyleveld and Bos 2009: 7–16.

consider that all agents have the generic rights. The PGC, 'Act in accord with the generic rights of all agents', in being dialectically necessary, is categorically binding on all agents.

The formal nature of the generic rights

The argument entails that:

(1) The generic rights are positive, as well as negative, rights not only to non-interference with possession of the generic conditions, but also to assistance in securing them when the needy agent cannot secure them by its own efforts. This is because agents need assistance as much as non-interference when they cannot secure the generic conditions by their own efforts.

(2) The generic rights are rights under the 'will' or 'choice' conception of rights: i.e. agents may waive the benefits of their generic rights by releasing other agents from their correlative duties. This is because the value they must attach to their possession of the generic conditions is not intrinsic but instrumental (albeit categorically so). My negative generic rights are inalienable, but are rights not to be interfered with *against my will*, while my equally inalienable positive generic rights are rights to be assisted *if I so wish*. This, as I explain further below, entails that agents cannot have perfect duties *to themselves* to protect and pursue their possession of the generic conditions.

(3) For it to be mandatory for an agent A to be granted the generic rights, it is *sufficient* that A have the essential properties attributed to agents in the argument. These properties are:

   (i) An ability and disposition to pursue purposes voluntarily. The first step in Stage One involves inferring from my claim to be an agent (by definition, the claim that I do something X voluntarily in order to achieve some purpose E) that I necessarily attach a value to E sufficient to motivate me to take steps to achieve E. This presupposes that agents at least *feel* that *they* choose their purposes, whether or not they actually have freewill (in being first-causes of their purposes). This, in turn, supposes that they have a sense of self-identity, which requires them to possess a concept of the future and an ability to appreciate minimal logical rules.

   (ii) Perception of the need to do something in order to achieve one's purposes and that pursuit/achievement of one's purposes can be frustrated by the absence of necessary conditions. This presupposes the ability to reason instrumentally (Beyleveld and Bos 2009).

(4) Because only agents with these essential properties can waive the benefits of the generic rights, only they can be held to possess the generic rights. Thus, being such an agent is not only the sufficient, but also the *necessary* ground for mandatory attribution of the generic rights.

Dignity as the ground of the generic rights

If possession of dignity is the reason why a being has (or, strictly, must be accorded) rights, then it is possession of the essential properties of agency attributed in the argument that constitutes possession of such dignity in relation to the generic rights. Human *agents* possess these essential properties. Since it is by virtue of possession of these properties that beings are inherently subject to hopes and fears related to their existence, well-being and projects, dignity as the ground of agents' rights may be said to inhere in agents' capacity to hope and fear. This capacity is rooted in the phenomenology of human agency, which is characterized, on the one hand, by a sense (deriving from an inability to infallibly predict what will be presented to one's senses) that one inhabits a material world operating under mindless laws of cause and effect (or failing that, chance). This sense posits the possibility that human agents *might* themselves be wholly part of such a world, and hence have no ultimate value. On the other hand, human agents inherently have a sense of being the first causes of their own actions, which suggests the idea that they *might* not be wholly part of a material world existing independently of their senses, and have an inherently meaningful existence. I have argued, elsewhere (Beyleveld 2009) that both belief in freewill (suggested by the phenomenology of agency) and belief in determinism (suggested by the phenomenology of sense-experience) are antithetical to morality conceived of as a categorical imperative, and that morality so conceived is only intelligible in application to beings with the capacity to hope for freewill and transcendence of a wholly material world coupled with the fear that everything is wholly material and ultimately meaningless.

Because the argument grounds the generic rights under the will-conception, it entails a conception of dignity as the ground of rights that empowers agents to act in accordance with their own will against the will of others subject only to their actions not violating the more important rights of others. This idea of 'dignity as empowerment' is in accord with Kant's (Kant 1998: 4:429) prescription that every agent must always be treated 'as an end, never merely as a means', *provided that* it is understood that agents are not merely empowered to resist interference with their generic interests by others but also to act and to permit action against their own generic interests.

The generic rights, human rights and human dignity

Not all human beings – *if being human is defined biologically* – for example the unborn, very young children, adults with extremely severe mental disabilities, and those with very severe brain damage or in a permanent vegetative state, display the capacities of agents. Therefore, unless to be human is to be an agent *by definition*, showing that all agents must be granted the generic rights, does not show that all human beings must be granted the generic rights. Without more, the foundational argument for the PGC does not provide a foundational argument for human rights *per* the UDHR.

However, Gewirth claims that the generic rights are possessed by potential agents and beings with some but not all of the capacities of agency (whether or not they are biologically human), in proportion to the degree to which they approach being agents (Gewirth 1978: 140–5). He claims that this follows by the 'Principle of Proportionality' (PP): 'When some quality Q justifies having certain rights R, and the possession of Q varies in degree in the respect that is relevant to Q's justifying the having of R, the degree to which R is had is proportional to or varies with the degree to which Q is had.'

But, as Gewirth himself emphasizes, 'in relation to the claim to have the generic rights, actually being a prospective agent who has purposes he wants to fulfil is an absolute quality, not varying in degree' (Gewirth 1978: 123).

It therefore follows, as Hill claims (Hill 1981: 186), that the PP merely entails that non-agents approach having the generic rights in proportion to how closely they approach possession of agency, not as Gewirth claims that they possess the generic rights to the degree that they approach being agents (and specifically that they have those rights to things that they can possess and do without endangering their own and others' purpose-fulfilment) (Gewirth 1978: 123 and 141–2). Similarly, potential agents only potentially have generic rights.

Considering such objections, Gewirth claims that possession of agency is only necessary for having the generic rights *in full* (1978: 141; 1981: 225–7). But this does not answer the objection that the PP requires Q to be capable of varying in degree, when possession of agency is an all-or-nothing condition, so the PP cannot secure generic rights to a degree for non-agents on the basis of possession of a degree of agency.

Gewirth seems to be thinking in the following way. The generic rights correspond to generic interests (conditions) of agency. Some non-agents have generic *life or behavioural* interests in things that are generic conditions *of agency* for agents. Suppose that agent A claims 'I have a right to X, Y and Z because X, Y and Z are generic conditions of my agency'. Suppose, also, that non-agent B has life-interests in Y and Z though not in X, because X is a generically necessary condition for action but not for life and B lacks the capacity to act. According to Gewirth, A must grant B the generic rights to Y and Z, though not to X.[6]

The problem is that to characterize B's interests in Y and Z as generic rights of the kind secured by the argument to the PGC is a category mistake. The generic rights are, as justified, rights for certain interests not to be interfered with or to be assisted with *according to the will of an agent*. Some of these rights do correspond *in content* to interests that can be had by non-agents, but *in form* they are *essentially* the interests of agents. As such, they are only capable of being possessed by agents. Consequently, Hill's claim that Gewirth is guilty of 'the fallacy of disparateness' must be upheld (Hill 1981: 190). Gewirth's reasoning

[6] This is very much the way Gewirth presents the matter in the unpublished, unfinished manuscript on *Human Rights and Global Justice* he left at his death, which is stored in the Archives of the Regenstein Library, University of Chicago.

can only be sound if agents are required to value their lives and some other generic conditions of their agency intrinsically and not merely as categorically instrumentally necessary conditions of agency, when the argument for the PGC provides no basis for such a requirement.[7]

Alongside this, it is significant that Gewirth contends, despite himself recognizing the waivability in principle of the benefits of the generic rights *by agents*, that agents can have perfect duties to themselves to protect their generic interests. He presents the objection to perfect duties to oneself succinctly:

> [I]f a person has duties to himself, then, because of the correlativity of duties and rights, he also has rights against himself. But any right-holder can always give up his right and thereby release the respondent of the right from his duty. On the other hand, no person can release himself from a duty. Hence the notion of duties to oneself is contradictory, since it implies that a person both can and cannot release himself from his duties to himself. (Gewirth 1978: 334)

Nevertheless, he considers that the objection is not fatal to the idea of perfect duties to oneself. He claims that (i) agents have perfect duties to obey the PGC that they cannot waive; and (ii) it is possible to distinguish *within oneself* between the rights-holder and the duty-holder by viewing (a) my present self as owing duties to my future selves; or (b) my 'lower self' as owing duties to my higher self; or (c) my freedom or well-being as having rights not to be overpowered by the other (Gewirth 1978: 335–8).

But, re (i), an agent's duty to obey the PGC, which *is* unwaivable, is not a moral duty, but a purely rational requirement not to incur self-contradiction, while moral rights and duties are duties *under* the PGC. Re (ii:a), the fact that my future selves develop from and are extensions of my present self means that my present selves cannot hold my past selves to account for wrongs done to them. (ii:b) is untenable because it does not model the problem unless my higher selves can waive their rights against my lower selves, in which case the problem recurs. As regards (ii:c), this implies that I have an intrinsic duty to integrate various aspects of my psyche as an agent, which implies that I have an intrinsic duty to be an agent, for which the argument for the PGC provides no justification. Furthermore, it is wholly untenable to regard aspects of my agency as agents without altering the definition of an agent.[8]

However, it does not follow that agents do not owe duties under the PGC not to harm or to protect the life or behavioural interests of apparent non-agents. This is extremely important, because, for the PGC to justify *human* rights *per* the UDHR, it is not necessary for these rights to be viewed as the generic rights *of agents under the will conception of rights*. It is only necessary for the PGC to generate perfect duties not to interfere with or protect inherent interests

[7] For a detailed critique of Gewirth's use of the PP, see Beyleveld and Pattinson 2000.

[8] See further Beyleveld and Brownsword 2001: 105–10, which also examines Kant's similar attempts to rescue the idea of perfect duties to oneself.

of all 'members of the human family' equally, some of which duties might be correlative to rights under the interest conception of rights.

There is a relatively uncontroversial way in which the PGC can generate duties of non-interference/protection *in relation to* apparent non-agents (whether human or not). For example, agent A can have a duty not to kill apparent non-agent B because B (say, a dog) is the property of agent C; or because B (say, an unborn child) is very important to its agent parents; or if torturing apparent non-agents 'brutalizes' agents and makes them less sensitive to the suffering of agents. However, any such duties are vicarious. They are not owed to the apparent non-agent because of inherent properties of the apparent non-agent alone, but because of the contingent relationship between the apparent non-agent and an agent or agents. The duties are owed directly to the agents concerned, being protective of their generic rights, not to the apparent non-agent, and they depend on contingent relationships between the agent and the apparent non-agent. Consequently, such arguments cannot be used to establish that agents owe duties to human apparent non-agents solely because of the inherent qualities of the latter, correlative to which it may be said that human apparent non-agents have inherent rights (under an interest conception of rights) to interests they inherently have as members of the human family.

But, for this, another argument is available.[9] Its starting premise is that only agents can be certain that they are agents. This is because the essential properties of agents include what are intrinsically mental properties. I know for certain that I am an agent. I do not know for certain that other beings that behave like agents (i.e. apparent agents) are agents. This suggests that I might, *in practice*, legitimately reject the idea that I am categorically bound to comply with the PGC. For, while I must grant all other agents the generic rights, may I not hold that I am not categorically bound to treat any being other than myself as an agent? The answer is 'No!' This is because the fact that I cannot prove that there are any agents other than myself does not show that I am not required to treat apparent agents as agents. In fact, if I assume that apparent agent B is not an agent, and act accordingly, but I am (unknowably) wrong, then I violate the PGC, whereas if I assume that B is an agent, and act accordingly, but I am (unknowably) wrong, then I do not thereby violate the PGC. Hence I must treat all apparent agents as agents.[10]

Now, just as I cannot know for certain that apparent agents are agents, I cannot know for certain that apparent non-agents are not agents. It is possible that apparent non-agents (whether biologically human or not) are in fact agents.

[9] This argument was originally presented in Beyleveld and Pattinson 2000. For further clarification in response to criticisms from Holm and Coggon 2009, see Beyleveld and Pattinson 2010.

[10] It should be noted that, in order to behave like an agent, a being does not have to be living in the biological sense. Androids with the sophistication of those in films like *Blade Runner*, or *I Robot*, are cases in point.

If I assume that an apparent non-agent is not an agent, act accordingly, but I am wrong, then again I violate the PGC. On the other hand, if I make the opposite assumption, act accordingly, but I am wrong, then I do not thereby violate the PGC. From this, I have argued that while apparent non-agents cannot be granted any generic rights because these are rights under the will-conception, the PGC renders it necessary to recognize duties to apparent non-agents in proportion to how closely they approach being apparent agents, the degree of approach being measured essentially by the life and behavioural interests they have in content that correspond to the generic interests of agents. As far as rocks and tables are concerned, no duties will be incurred simply because it is not possible to relate their existence to that of agents in a way that makes it intelligible to identify appropriate interests. But, whenever we are confronted with living organisms or those capable of behaviours that mimic mental operations, then a linkage can be made. Precisely how strong these duties are is a complex matter, which need not occupy us here.[11] However, it is worth noting that the practical effect is, in principle, identical to that secured by Gewirth's unsound mode of argumentation. The proper description of the result, however, is not that apparent non-agents have a degree of generic rights, but that agents owe duties to apparent non-agents in proportion to the degree to which they approach being apparent agents.

In this way, the PGC does justify *inherent* rights of all members of the human family (biologically defined). These rights comprise two categories: (a) generic rights of human apparent agents (under the will-conception of rights); and (b) duty generating interests of human non-apparent agents (which can be seen as rights under an interest conception of rights).

Ontologically, the argument to the PGC grants dignity to agents and only to agents. But, *in application of* the PGC, the generic (will-conception) rights of (apparent) agents are to be seen as grounded in their (apparent) dignity in (apparently) being subject to hopes and fears. So, in what idea of dignity are the (interest) rights of human apparent non-agents grounded? Dignity, here, cannot consist of actual possession of the essential properties of agency that ground being subject to hopes and fears. It also cannot consist in mere possession of life and behavioural interests that correspond to the generic interests of agents. Human (interest) rights are granted because of the epistemic possibility that human apparent non-agents *might be* agents despite not appearing to be so, given the absolute requirement to act in accordance with the generic rights of agents. The importance of the interests in life and non-agency behavioural interests that correspond to agency-interests is two-fold. On the one hand, the more of these an apparent non-agent has, the closer it becomes to being an apparent agent, and the more plausible it becomes to entertain that it might, despite appearances to the contrary, in fact be an agent. On the other hand,

[11] For some preliminary analysis and remarks, see Beyleveld and Brownsword 2001: 122–6 and 225–58.

possession of such interests is necessary for it to be intelligible to take steps to protect what might be the rights of an agent. In *this* way, dignity as empowerment remains the ground of both will-conception and interest rights recognized in its application by the PGC, and the ground of any human rights justified by the PGC.

Conclusion

There remains a problem. This is that the UDHR not only proclaims that all members of the human family have inherent rights. It says that they are equal in the rights that they have. However, the logic of the precautionary reasoning by which the PGC generates duties to apparent non-agents implies that, all things being equal, the will rights of apparent agents take precedence over the corresponding interest rights of non-apparent agents, on the ground that an apparent agent is more probably (plausibly) an agent than a non-apparent agent. Furthermore, the entire logic of this approach rests on the idea that apparent agents can have additional interests to those of non-apparent agents, which is to say that apparent agents can have some will rights that non-apparent agents do not have even interest rights to. Can this problem be overcome?

Article 1 of the UDHR states: 'All human beings are born free and equal in dignity and rights. They are endowed with reason and conscience and should act towards one another in a spirit of brotherhood.' One way of tackling the problem is to read this as requiring being human to be defined as being an agent (and all human rights to be viewed as will-conception rights). However, it must be noted that the UN Declaration on the Rights of Mentally Retarded Persons 1971 holds that the subjects of the Convention have the same rights as other human beings 'to the maximum degree of feasibility', which implies that all human beings do not have equal rights. From this, it follows that either the 1971 Declaration is inconsistent with the basic Human Rights Framework, or else *all* Framework statements to the effect that all humans have equal rights must be read as saying that all humans have equal rights *to the maximum extent of feasibility*.

So read, there is no problem viewing Gewirth's argument for the PGC as justifying human rights as conceived by the Human Rights Framework.

References

Beyleveld, D. 1991. *The Dialectical Necessity of Morality*. University of Chicago Press

2009. 'Morality and the God of Reason'. Inaugural Professorial Address Utrecht University 30 March 2009. Faculty of Humanities, Utrecht University

Beyleveld, D., and Bos, G. 2009. 'The Foundational Role of the Principle of Instrumental Reason in Gewirth's Argument for the Principle of Generic Consistency: A Response to Andrew Chitty', *King's Law Journal* 20: 1–20

Beyleveld, D., and Brownsword, R. 2001. *Human Dignity in Bioethics and Biolaw*. Oxford University Press

Beyleveld, D., and Pattinson, S. D. 2000. 'Precautionary Reasoning as a Link to Moral Action', in M. Boylan (ed.), *Medical Ethics*. Upper Saddle River, NJ: Prentice-Hall, 39–53

2010. 'Defending Moral Precaution as a Solution to the Problem of Other Minds', *Ratio Juris* 23: 258–73

Gewirth, A. 1978. *Reason and Morality*. University of Chicago Press

1981. 'Replies to My Critics', in E. Regis, Jr (ed.), *Gewirth's Ethical Rationalism*. University of Chicago Press, 225–7

1996. *The Community of Rights*. University of Chicago Press

Hill, J. F. 1981. 'Are Marginal Agents "Our Recipients"?', in E. Regis, Jr (ed.), *Gewirth's Ethical Rationalism*. University of Chicago Press, 180–91

Holm, S., and Coggon, J. 2009. 'A Cautionary Note Against "Precautionary Reasoning" in Action Guiding Morality', *Ratio Juris* 22: 295–309

Kant, I. 1998 [1785]. *Groundwork of the Metaphysics of Morals*, trans. M. Gregor. Cambridge University Press

25

Human dignity in the capability approach

RUTGER CLAASSEN

The capability approach is a broad normative approach which has been developed from the 1980s onwards, most prominently by economist Amartya Sen and philosopher Martha Nussbaum. In the philosophical context, the main use of the approach is to assess the justice of social arrangements: societies are just to the extent that they guarantee each citizen an entitlement to his or her basic capabilities. In more recent years, Nussbaum has emphasized the fact that the capability approach is a human rights approach, and has begun to ground her version of the approach in a specific concept of human dignity. In this chapter, I will first briefly summarize the main concepts used in the capability approach, and then present Nussbaum's concept of dignity as a grounding of that approach. Finally, I will criticize this way of using the concept of dignity and raise some questions.

The capability approach

The capability approach is used by social scientists, lawyers and philosophers, in a variety of contexts, for descriptive, evaluative and prescriptive purposes. What all these uses share is only a rather minimal conceptual apparatus: namely, a stress on 'capabilities to functionings' as the favoured focus for research.

Functionings are defined by Amartya Sen as 'parts of the state of a person – in particular the various things that he or she manages to do or be in leading a life' (Sen 1993: 31). Functionings are 'doings' and 'beings' then, like eating, riding a bicycle, walking, working, sleeping etc. Later, Sen also described functionings as 'the various things a person may value doing or being' (Sen 1999: 75) or as the 'things he or she has reason to value.' (Sen 2009: 231). This value-laden definition of the notion of functionings builds the normative criterion for deciding which functionings are valuable into the concept itself: Sen's later definition makes individuals themselves the judges over which functionings are valuable. In Nussbaum's version of the capability approach, whether a functioning is valuable is not decided by the person herself, but by an ethical procedure of evaluation, in which dignity comes to play a role (see the next section). Arguably, then, Sen's and Nussbaum's different definitions of functionings represent different interests in using the approach (as a welfare economic theory versus a political-ethical theory).

Capabilities are derived from functionings. In Sen's use, 'The capability of a person reflects the alternative combinations of functionings the person can achieve, and from which he or she can choose one collection' (Sen 1993: 31). In contrast to this usage of 'capability' in the singular, Nussbaum uses it in the plural. For every functioning, there is a capability to function in that way. A capability is an ability or opportunity to choose a specific functioning. If one has a 'capability to ride a bicycle', one can choose whether or not to go for a ride. The concept of choice is central: it is up to the person herself to decide whether or not to realize a certain capability in her life (Nussbaum 2000: 88). Capabilities, then, are freedoms to achieve something and functionings are these achievements.

Nussbaum uses this conceptual apparatus in philosophical theorizing about justice to say that a society is just to the extent that every citizen has constitutionally guaranteed entitlements to a list of basic capabilities. This does not mean that in every situation it is only important that people are given capabilities. Sometimes it may be necessary to be more paternalist and promote people's functionings directly, bypassing their own choices (Nussbaum 2000: 89–96; 2006: 171–2; Claassen 2013). However, these cases remain exceptions to the rule. The main focus on capabilities makes the capability approach a liberal approach, which respects the choices of persons to function as they want.

The main attraction of the capability approach is that it presents an alternative to approaches which identify a society as just when persons have rights to certain resources, or when utility is maximized. The capability approach posits itself between resourcism and utilitarianism. Resources (goods and services) are important only because people can do something with them, i.e. function in a certain way. And since some persons may need more resources to get to the same functionings level as others, it is misleading to focus on bundles of resources (Sen 1990; Pogge 2002; Anderson 2010). On the other hand, one may think that what really matters for justice is not how people are able to function with a given bundle of resources, but what pleasure or utility they derive from their functioning. However, if two persons with equal capability levels experience different levels of utility, they should remain themselves responsible for that difference. A just society is not responsible for people's happiness, only for the opportunities to make themselves happy.

The crucial question now is how to select a list of basic capabilities. Sen has always refused to select such a list, preferring to keep the approach open for several uses and referring to processes of public and democratic deliberation to make selections of basic capabilities (Sen 2009). However, Nussbaum has argued against Sen that a theory of justice needs to take a stance on this issue (Nussbaum 2003). There are good reasons to agree with Nussbaum, at least if one's ambition is to have a theory of justice which fulfils an action-guiding and critical function. It is more respectful of democratic deliberation to offer a concrete list as a proposal, which is up for deliberation and adoption in a political community, than to refuse giving any input to the democratic process (Claassen 2011).

If we agree with the need to reflect philosophically on a list of basic capabilities, then the next question is what the normative criterion for such a selection might be. In earlier work Nussbaum relied on an intuitive idea of what makes a life a fully human life. This is an appeal to human nature, where that notion is itself treated as an evaluative one: that which makes a human life a good one (Nussbaum 1990; Nussbaum 1995). Arguably, such a notion is too vague to do the work of selection: humans have many morally bad, cruel abilities (Claassen and Düwell 2013). The introduction of the notion of dignity in Nussbaum's later work may be seen as a way to strengthen her approach and make the criterion that is used to select basic capabilities more strongly normative.

Nussbaum's concept of dignity

Nussbaum makes three uses of the concept of dignity: as a general notion to ground her capability list, as a concept that grounds animal entitlements and as an argument for focusing on functionings in some cases.

First, the central idea of Nussbaum's capability theory now is that 'all human beings ought to acknowledge and respect the entitlement of others to live lives commensurate with human dignity' (Nussbaum 2006: 53). She acknowledges that this is an 'intuitive notion that is by no means utterly clear' and rejects the idea that one can use it 'as if it were an intuitively self-evident and solid foundation for a theory that would then be built upon it' (Nussbaum 2011: 29). Instead, she maintains that dignity gets its importance by being related to a set of other notions. Three stand out. Dignity is related to *respect* – beings with dignity demand respect from others. Dignity is also related to *agency* – one focuses on what people are able to do, not on their passive satisfactions. Dignity is related, finally, to *equality*: it is that in respect of which we are all equal (Nussbaum 2011: 30–1). How does this help us to make a list of basic capabilities? Nussbaum argues that, with these connected notions in mind,

> [W]hat must happen is that the debate must take place, and each must make arguments attempting to show that a given liberty is implicated in the idea of dignity. This cannot be done by vague intuitive appeals to the idea of dignity all by itself: it must be done by discussing the relationship for the putative entitlement to the other existing entitlements, in a long and detailed process – showing, for example, the relationship of bodily integrity inside the home to women's full equality as citizens and workers, to their emotional and bodily health, and so forth. (Nussbaum 2011: 32)

Second, Nussbaum uses the notion of dignity to extend capability entitlements to those humans with (severe) disabilities and to non-human animals. Up to this point, 'dignity' has referred to human dignity. This concept raises Kantian associations that Nussbaum explicitly rejects. She maintains, invoking Aristotle, 'that there is something wonderful and wonder-inspiring in all the complex forms of life' (Nussbaum 2006: 347). Animals, then, have their own type of dignity. As for humans, it is related to the type of functionings that they are capable of and the flourishing that they can derive from these functionings. Dignity, functioning and flourishing exist in animals as much as in humans. But since dignity is not only related to functioning and flourishing, but also to respect and rights/entitlements, this means that animals now also deserve respect and get rights to a set of capabilities. Obviously, this leads to many controversial questions about animal ethics, that I cannot go into here (Cripps 2010; Ilea 2008; Hailwood 2012).[1]

These two uses of the concept of dignity are the main ones. However, for the sake of completeness, we must also mention that Nussbaum uses the notion of dignity in a third way, in the more restricted context of her discussion of when to promote functionings instead of capabilities.[2] We should prohibit choices people make to humiliate or debase themselves (Nussbaum 2000: 91; 2006: 172). Unfortunately, Nussbaum does not give much elaboration of this use of the concept, neither does she mention examples where we should prohibit people's choices out of a concern for her dignity (it also seems problematic: dignity is first used to lie in individuals' capacity to choose their own functionings, and later dignity justifies prohibitions on choice; one could wonder whether this is a consistent use of the term). In the following, then, I leave this third use out of consideration and concentrate on dignity as the ground for human and animal entitlements.

With this general overview in place, I will now focus on the only article in which Nussbaum has given a more elaborate account of her concept of dignity (Nussbaum 2008), relating to the first two uses discussed above: to ground a list of human basic capabilities and extend this to animals.

Nussbaum draws an opposition between a Stoic–Kantian notion on the one hand, and an Aristotelian–Marxian notion on the other hand. The Stoic notion rests on a respect for the rational powers of human beings. The fact of possessing reason makes all human beings equal (universalism), and this is the ground for our moral respect for all humans. Rationality and morality are thus closely connected: the fact of possessing reason justifies treatment as an end-in-itself, not as a mere instrument to the purposes of others (Nussbaum 2008). Nussbaum accepts the idea of dignity as deserving respect for creatures as ends. She has

[1] For an elaborate discussion of these questions, see Chapter 60 by Heeger and Chapter 61 by Schaber in this volume.

[2] Nussbaum also uses the term 'dignity' in her description of one specific capability, namely, affiliation: 'having the social bases of self-respect and nonhumiliation; being able to be treated as a dignified being whose worth is equal to that of others' (Nussbaum 2006: 77). Here, the same, more narrow sense, seems to be indicated: as a prohibition of certain types of treatment, not as a concept underlying all capabilities.

two main problems with the Stoic account. The first I have already mentioned: that the focus on rational capacities as the ground for being ascribed dignity excludes animals, with their non-rational capacities.

The second problem deserves more elaboration. The Stoics believed that human dignity cannot be violated. Thus, 'it turns out that dignity, radically secure within, invulnerable to the world's accidents, doesn't really need anything that politics can give' (*ibid.*: 355). This leads to a quietistic attitude to the outside world. Other people cannot violate my dignity by withholding important goods from me, and even enslaving me is not a violation of my dignity. The radical consequence is that any theoretical statement of the sort 'respect for dignity requires x' (where x refers to a certain treatment) is now inconsistent. It is not open to the Stoic account to claim that inhumane or indecent treatment violate one's dignity, since on the same account one's dignity cannot be violated. The reason for this stance, Nussbaum believes, is that the Stoics believed that 'in order to give human dignity its due reverence they had to show it to be radically independent of the accidents of fortune' (*ibid.*).

Nussbaum's Aristotelian–Marxian alternative rejects this independence from the external world. Human dignity does not only rest on an inviolable independence from the world. We are also vulnerable and needy beings, and require help from others in many respects: 'human beings have a worth that is indeed inalienable, because of their capacities for various forms of activity and striving. These capacities are, however, dependent on the world for their full development and for their conversion into actual functioning' (*ibid.*: 357). If we try to take the various components apart, dignity fulfils three roles. First, dignity is ascribed to humans and animals because of their *potentiality* to develop certain capabilities. This attribute cannot be lost, the potential is always there. Second, the ascription of dignity gives us the reason why humans should be treated with *respect*. In reality, the potential can fail to be developed (people's vulnerability to the natural and social world). Dignity is the ground for judging that, when other people thwart the realization of our potential, they violate a moral command. Third, respect for dignity takes the form of protection of human *rights* to the development of these capabilities (at least, rights to the 'social basis' of such development). Capability-based human dignity requires law and politics to implement a series of rights.

Dignity as a motivation for respecting capabilities?

If one believes that the capability approach is more attractive than its direct competitors (resourcism, utilitarianism) in giving an account of a just society, then one will expect that it is able to give a more convincing account of dignity as well. Ascriptions of dignity always need a grounding in one or more features of the dignity-bearing creature; there must be something about that creature that makes it dignified. It is plausible to think of these features as capabilities: as potentials to function in a specific way. All theories which ascribe dignity on the basis of rationality in this sense are also capability theories, since rationality is one of human beings' capabilities. This may sound surprising, but it is a logical consequence of the concept of 'capability'. Nussbaum's theory is different only because it happens to defend a broader set of capabilities, going beyond our rational capacities.

Despite these attractions, there are also problems with Nussbaum's use of the concept of dignity in the context of her capability theory. First, one could wonder what theoretical work the concept is actually doing. Nussbaum's capability list was drawn up in a series of articles in the 1980s and 1990s which made no use of the concept of dignity. Later, she revised the capability list slightly, but these revisions had little to do with the introduction of dignity. So either Nussbaum thinks with the benefit of hindsight that dignity as an invisible hand had been implicitly guiding her selection process all along (this seems unlikely), or that the work the concept is doing lies not in the selection of basic capabilities, but rather in motivating why these capabilities deserve respect at all. This last option seems more plausible. Dignity is meant to give normative force to a list which itself remains selected on the basis of the Aristotelian question 'What is it to flourish for a human being?' In terms of the three parts of dignity mentioned at the end of the previous section, the main function of dignity for Nussbaum is that it gives us a reason to respect the capabilities of humans and animals.

This does raise a follow-up question however. For how does dignity motivate an attitude of respect? As we saw, Nussbaum refers to the Aristotelian notion that there is something 'wonderful and wonder-inspiring' in complex forms of human and animal nature. Elsewhere she elaborates on this in the following passage:

> The idea of dignity has broad cross-cultural resonance and intuitive power. We can think of it as the idea that lies at the heart of tragic artworks, in whatever culture. Think of a tragic character, assailed by fortune. We react to the spectacle so assailed in a way very different from the way we react to a storm blowing grains of sand in the wind. For we see a human being as having worth as an end, a kind of awe-inspiring something that makes it horrible to see this same person beaten down by the currents of chance – and wonderful, at the same time, to witness the way in which chance has not completely eclipsed the humanity of the person. As Aristotle puts it, 'the noble shines through'. Such responses provide us with strong incentives for protecting that in persons that fills us with awe. (Nussbaum 2000: 72–3)

Despite the rhetorical power of this passage, I think we need to remain critical of the idea that 'wonderful' and 'awe-inspiring' things justify our attitude to respect those things. We should never forget that respect is meant in the specific sense in which it in turn leads to the protection of a series of rights. Now I can judge many things wonderful without thinking that these things deserve respect. I judge my iPad to be a wonderful, even awe-inspiring piece of technology.

Nevertheless, I do not think that my iPad has individual rights that deserve protection. Similarly, I may find a landscape awe-inspiring without thinking that it deserves this kind of rights-protecting respect. Awe and wonder seem to be different attitudes than respect, and there is no easy way to get from one to the other. But if this is so, and if dignity is related to awe and wonder, than it is a deficient basis to ground an attitude of respect.

It is important to mention that before Nussbaum took the turn to the wonder-inspiring concept of dignity, she grounded her capability list in a method she called 'internalist essentialism'. The general idea there was to enquire for oneself which functionings are defining of one's human nature by asking which functionings one is willing to give up. Functionings like affiliation and practical reason, Nussbaum argued there, cannot seriously be given up, because the cost of doing so is too high (Nussbaum 1995: 110; see also the discussion in Claassen and Düwell 2013). She called this the use of 'self-validating arguments': the procedure of asking such questions validates the answers one gives to these questions. The respect-motivating force of the capabilities, according to this method, then, does not have its ground in what we think inspires awe and wonder, but in the consideration of what is essential to be able to lead our own lives. If Nussbaum would have upheld this method, then dignity would have been – more credibly, in my opinion – something ascribed to (1) ourselves, because we have capabilities that are vulnerable to violation or underdevelopment, and (2) other human beings, because they also have the same capabilities (given that they belong to the same species as me). The capabilities essential to lead our own life are also those essential to lead a 'human life' in general. The deep wound that *we* would feel if our capabilities were violated is what motivates us to respect the capabilities of similarly placed others.

This brings us most naturally to the question of the extension of dignity to animals. On Nussbaum's theory any creature that is able to function in a certain way would deserve to have its own type of dignity recognized. The problem with this is that it would seem to set no limit at all to the extension of dignity. Plants also function in certain ways, and maybe ecosystems do so as well – plants can flourish or perish, ecosystems can be stable or degrade. To set a limit, Nussbaum first considers adopting the utilitarian criterion of sentience, but then turns to her own capability approach, and holds that any creature with one of her capabilities qualifies. This she calls a 'disjunctive approach';

> [I]f a creature has *either* the capacity for pleasure and pain or the capacity for movement from place to place *or* the capacity for emotion and affiliation *or* the capacity for reasoning, and so forth (we might add play, tool use, and others), then the creature has moral standing. (Nussbaum 2006: 362)[3]

As she notes just after this passage, possession of one of these capabilities normally coexists with sentience: 'Aristotle reminds us that this is no accident: for

[3] Similarly Nussbaum 2008: 363.

sentience is central to movement, affiliation, emotion, and thought' (Nussbaum 2006: 362). For practical purposes, the capability approach and utilitarianism converge on this point.

I will grant that the disjunctive approach would give Nussbaum a workable criterion to distinguish creatures with moral standing from other natural phenomena. The problem is that this answer is unavailable on Nussbaum's own theory. For she restricts the disjunctive approach to the ten capabilities she has defined as central to *human* life. Given the animal basis of human life, unsurprisingly this also works well enough to include animals in the moral realm. Both animals and humans eat, walk around, use senses, etc. However, plants and ecosystems are also functionally organized natural phenomena, i.e. they have *other* types of functionings (which, incidentally, are not accompanied by sentience), and it seems arbitrary to exclude these from the disjunction. So far, then, Nussbaum has given no argument why these should be excluded. Her argument is circular: first she defines a list of capabilities shared by humans and animals, and then she concludes that human and animals (but not plants and ecosystems) fit the bill.

This problem is related to the previous one, and it can also be solved by my suggestion to use Nussbaum's earlier self-validating method as the basis of dignity-ascriptions. For it is not arbitrary to ascribe dignity to humans and animals if one starts with a method which reflects on which capabilities are essential to lead one's own (and, by extension, a human) life. Such a method leads, unsurprisingly, to human dignity. It also leads to animal dignity because humans also have an animal nature. Humans must recognize the value of capabilities in themselves (like play, or nourishment) that animals also have. If we base respect for the capability for play in others on the judgment that we ourselves would not want to do without play in our lives, then there seems no good reason to restrict the extension of this respect to *human* others only; animal others then also come into the picture. This reasoning then grounds Nussbaum's extension to animals while not leading to dignity and respect for plants, ecosystems and material objects.

There is one potential objection to this line of reasoning. This is that the human capability for play (and all the other capabilities that we share with animals) only deserve respect because they are instantiated in a being which *also* has rational capacities. This Kantian objection, then, is that what ultimately grounds respect remains rationality; and the 'animal capabilities' in humans are merely worthy of protection because they help make possible the attainment of a rational life. I think this objection is mistaken. Nussbaum is right to claim that 'animal capabilities' in humans are valuable for their own sake, not merely as a necessary precondition for our rational capabilities. This comes out most clearly when thinking about humans who are incapable of rationality (like severely mentally disabled persons). However, given the fact that Kantians will in such cases ground respect in complicated extensions of rationality means that I cannot here give a full refutation of this objection. At least Nussbaum's position here is worth considering. It is mirrored, moreover, by similar extensions of dignity to animals in the Kantian tradition (Korsgaard 2004).

In conclusion, I have argued that Nussbaum's earlier self-validating method (or a similar method) is better able to ground respect for a set of rights to human capabilities, and their extension to animals, than an appeal to human dignity, at least when the latter is based upon intuitive judgments of whatever in nature inspires us with awe and wonder. This does not preclude the possibility that the concept of dignity could be used to describe the status of those beings that the self-validating method selects as worthy of respect. Whether the ascription of the status of dignity would then be doing any real normative work, is a question that I will have to leave for another day.

References

Anderson, Elizabeth. 2010. 'Justifying the Capability Approach to Justice', in H. Brighouse and I. Robeyns (eds.), *Measuring Justice: Primary Goods and Capabilities*. Cambridge University Press, 81–100

Claassen, R. 2011. 'Making Capability Lists: Philosophy Versus Democracy', *Political Studies* 59(3): 491–508

2013. 'Capability Paternalism', *Economics and Philosophy*' (forthcoming)

Claassen, R., and Düwell, M. 2013. 'The Foundations of Capability Theory: Comparing Nussbaum and Gewirth', *Ethical Theory and Moral Practice* 16(3): 493–510

Cripps, E. 2010. 'Saving the Polar Bear, Saving the World: Can the Capabilities Approach Do Justice to Humans, Animals and Ecosystems?', *Res Publica* 16: 1–22

Hailwood, S. 2012. 'Bewildering Nussbaum: Capability Justice and Predation', *Journal of Political Philosophy* 20(3): 293–313

Ilea, R. 2008. 'Nussbaum's Capabilities Approach and Nonhuman Animals: Theory and Public Policy', *Journal of Social Philosophy* 39(4): 547–63

Korsgaard, C. 2004. 'Fellow Creatures: Kantian Ethics and Our Duties to Animals', Tanner Lectures on Human Values

Nussbaum, M. 1990. 'Aristotelian Social Democracy', in R. B. Douglas, G. M. Mara and H. S. Richardson (eds.). *Liberalism and the Good*, New York: Routledge, 203–52

1995. 'Aristotle on Human Nature and the Foundation of Ethics', in J. E. J. Altham and R. Harrison (eds.). *World, Mind and Ethics: Essays on the Ethical Philosophy of Bernard Williams*. Cambridge University Press, 86–131

2000. *Women and Human Development: The Capabilities Approach*. Cambridge University Press

2003. 'Capabilities as Fundamental Entitlements: Sen and Social Justice', *Feminist Economics* 9(2/3): 33–59

2006. *Frontiers of Justice*. Cambridge, MA: Belknap Press of Harvard University Press

2008. 'Human Dignity and Political Entitlements', in President's Council on Bioethics. 2008. *Human Dignity and Bioethics: Essays Commissioned by the President's Council on Bioethics*. Washington, DC, http://bioethics.georgetown.edu/pcbe/reports/human_dignity/chapter14.html, 351–80

2011. *Creating Capabilities: The Human Development Approach*. Cambridge, MA: Harvard University Press

Pogge, T. 2002. 'Can the Capability Approach Be Justified?', *Philosophical Topics* 30(2): 167–228

Sen, A. 1990. 'Justice: Means Versus Freedoms', *Philosophy and Public Affairs* 19(2): 111–21

1993. 'Capability and Well-Being', In M. Nussbaum and A. Sen, *The Quality of Life*. Oxford: Clarendon Press, 30–53

1999. *Development as Freedom*. Oxford University Press

2009. *The Idea of Justice*. Cambridge, MA: Belknap Press of Harvard University Press

26

Human dignity in Catholic thought

DAVID HOLLENBACH, SJ

In the years since the Second Vatican Council (1962–5) the Roman Catholic community has emerged as a vigorous global advocate of human rights. The recent social teachings of popes and bishops, as well as the social engagement undertaken by individual Catholics and by Catholic associations, have increasingly been formulated in terms of human rights. Catholic thought and advocacy grounds its appeal to human rights in an affirmation that human dignity is the most basic standard to which all personal behaviour and social institutions are accountable. Pope John XXIII affirmed that the modern Catholic tradition of social thought is controlled 'by one basic theme – an unshakable affirmation and defence of the dignity and rights of the human person' (1964: 233). This commitment has led the Catholic community to become a significant force for the promotion of human dignity and human rights in Latin America, former Warsaw Pact countries such as Poland, Asian nations like the Philippines and South Korea, and increasingly in African countries. Because of these developments the late Samuel Huntington concluded that the post-Second Vatican Council Catholic church had become one of the strongest worldwide forces for human dignity, human rights and democracy (Huntington 1991).

Shifts in Catholic thought

This is a remarkable development. In the nineteenth and early twentieth centuries, Catholicism was a significant source of opposition to both human rights and democracy. For example, in 1832, Pope Gregory XVI argued against the fundamental right to freedom of conscience, declaring it to be a form of 'insanity' (in Latin, *deliramentum*) (Neuner and Dupuis 1998: No. 1002). Just over a century later, the Second Vatican Council affirmed that 'the right to religious freedom has its foundation in the very dignity of the human person, as this dignity is known through the revealed word of God and by reason itself' (1965a: No. 2). More broadly, the Council committed the Catholic community to support for the full array of human rights by declaring that, 'by virtue of the gospel committed to it, the Church proclaims the rights of the human person' (1965b: No. 41).

This dramatic shift was occasioned by the way Catholic experience in the twentieth century led the church gradually to recognize that the promotion of human rights was increasingly a precondition for the protection of the dignity of the person called for by the church's religious mission. From the time of the French Revolution into the mid-twentieth century, church leadership had seen freedom of conscience and freedom of religion as linked with a secularizing agenda that sought to marginalize the church from active engagement in public life. Indeed, the church's identification with the *ancien régime* had given eighteenth-century liberal thinkers good grounds for maintaining that the social change they sought required reducing the public influence of Catholicism. In a parallel way, some socialist thinkers of the nineteenth century, especially Marx and Lenin, saw the Catholic conviction that humanity's ultimate hope lay beyond history as reducing believers' commitment to struggle for economic justice (religion as the 'opium of the people'), and as an impediment to the revolution they sought. Thus, the church adopted a defensive stance against both liberal and socialist revolutions. In fact, some forms of French liberalism, such as those manifest in the 1790 Civil Constitution of the Clergy and the Third Republic's 1905 law of separation of church and state, explicitly sought to reduce the church's public influence and even to subordinate the church to the state. Soviet Marxist-Leninism also set out to reduce the influence of religion. Thus, Catholicism had good reasons for seeing some aspects of eighteenth-century liberalism and nineteenth-century socialism as its adversaries. The result was the church's suspicious stance towards key elements of the democratic and economic transformations of eighteenth- and nineteenth-century modernity, which led to its opposition to key parts of the modern human rights agenda.

Nevertheless, there were also aspects of the Catholic response to modernity that brought to the surface the Catholic tradition's deeper commitment to human dignity, thus opening the way for the strong support for human rights developed much more fully at the Second Vatican Council. Pope Leo XIII recognized that the Catholic resistance to the subordination of church to state that had emerged in French liberalism and Soviet Marxism could best be expressed by affirming that the human person transcends control by the institutions of government. In Leo's words, 'man precedes the state' (1891: No. 7). He argued, therefore, that governmental and legal institutions are to be assessed in light of their respect for the freedom and dignity of persons. The power of the state, including the power of the majority in a democratic state, should be limited by its duty to respect the free exercise of religion and to provide space for an active church role in public life. Leo XIII's desire to protect the freedom and self-interest of the Catholic community, therefore, overlapped with his insistence on a limited state, with his insistence that the dignity of the person transcends the power of the state, and thus with an incipient argument for the human rights of the person (Murray 1953).

Similarly, Leo XIII responded to the threats that Marxist socialism was raising for the church by proposing an alternative approach to securing justice for the working class and for the poor. In doing so, he launched what has become the modern Catholic approach to arguing that the justice or injustice of economic decisions are to be evaluated in light of their impact on the dignity of persons. Economic institutions as well as the power of those who control them are accountable for their impact on the dignity of all those they affect, especially for their effects on the dignity of the most vulnerable members of society. In Leo's words, 'No man may with impunity outrage the dignity which God Himself treats with great reverence' (1891: No. 40). Indeed, employers have a responsibility not to treat workers as 'mere instruments for money making' but to respect their dignity by paying them a living wage and by recognizing their right to organize labour unions (Leo XIII 1891: No. 42; see Nos. 43-47). Thus, the dignity of workers is at the root of twentieth-century Catholicism's significant support for the labour movement and for the rights of working people. These initiatives of Leo XIII were carried forward by Pius XI in his 1931 encyclical, *Quadragesimo Anno*, which took them to a deeper level in light of the economic crisis that had begun in 1929. They led to the development of what has come to be called 'social Catholicism' – a tradition that appeals to human dignity as the basis for its strong commitment to social justice (Hollenbach 1979: 41–106).

Basis of human dignity in recent Catholic thought

The articulation of human dignity as the foundation of the Catholic tradition's commitment to justice and human rights became most fully explicit at the Second Vatican Council. *Gaudium et Spes*, the Council's Pastoral Constitution on the Church in the Modern World, grounds the overarching vision of recent Catholic social teaching in the themes of the dignity of the human person, the importance of the vocation to community in solidarity, and the religious significance of this-worldly activity. Each of these themes is supported both by distinctively Christian theological warrants as well as by secular warrants based on reason.

Human dignity is theologically supported by the biblical teaching in the book of Genesis that human beings are created in the image and likeness of God (Genesis 1:26). Persons possess a worth that deserves to be treated with the reverence shown to that which is holy. As made in God's likeness, human beings possess a sacredness analogous to the holiness of God. When we look upon the face of a human being we stand in the presence of the sacred. Thus, mistreating a human person is a kind of sacrilege. In the thirteenth century, Thomas Aquinas carried this biblical argument a step further when he affirmed that human beings are the only creatures God has created as valuable in themselves. They alone in all the universe are 'governed by divine providence for their own sakes' (Thomas Aquinas 1956: 116). This theological affirmation comes quite close to Kant's philosophical argument that persons are ends in themselves and never to be treated only as means to the attainment of the purposes of others or of society as a whole. Further, Christian revelation affirms that, because human beings are redeemed and recreated in Christ, believers are called to esteem human dignity even more highly (John XXIII 1963: No. 10; Vatican Council II 1965b: No. 22). Thus, the church's mission to defend human dignity and rights flows from the heart of Christian faith.

At the same time, human dignity can be recognized by all human beings, and makes claims upon all, both Christian and non-Christian. The Second Vatican Council offered several secular warrants for its affirmation of the dignity of the person, very much in line with Catholicism's long-standing, natural law-based conviction that fundamental ethical responsibilities can be grasped by human reason and by philosophical reflection on what it is to be human. First, the Council affirmed that the dignity of the human person is discernible in the transcendent power of the human mind. Through the intellect, human beings transcend the material universe, and the mind's capacity to share in divine wisdom gives humans a worth analogous to God's. Second, human dignity is manifest in the capacity of the human conscience to search for moral truth and to adhere to it when it has been found. Obedience to the dictates of conscience – which is the deepest core and sanctuary of a person – 'is the very dignity of the human person'. Third, dignity is also evident in the excellence of human liberty. Freedom is 'an exceptional sign of the divine image within the human person'. The dignity of freedom requires that persons act in accord with their free choice and that they seek to direct their freedom through knowledge of the true good (Vatican Council II 1965b: Nos. 15–17).

These three secular warrants for human dignity – the transcendence of the mind, the sacredness of conscience, and the excellence of liberty – are all aspects of the power of human reason which is a prime manifestation of the likeness of humans to God. They lead to what has been called a *substantialist* interpretation of the image of God in the human person. They are called 'substantialist' because they are aspects of the very substance of the person and inherently present within the person. This can be contrasted with interpretations of the image of God that have been called 'relational' and 'functional', which are also affirmed in Catholic thought (Middleton 2005). The *relational* interpretation sees the image of God in persons as a reflection of the fact that the God in whom Christians believe is a Trinitarian union of three persons – each related with the other divine persons in mutual love. The God of Christian faith is not a monadic being isolated in sublime solitude. The One God of monotheistic Christian faith is simultaneously a Trinity of related persons. Since God is thus radically relational, so are human persons. As the Council put it, 'God did not create the human being as a solitary . . . For by his innermost nature the human being is a social being, and unless he relates himself to others he can neither live nor develop his potential' (Vatican Council II 1965b: No. 12; International Theological Commission 2004).

This theological understanding of human dignity as a relational reality also has secular warrants. For example, the Council cites Thomas Aquinas' appropriation of Aristotle's philosophical defence of the 'social nature' of the human person, which implies that the development of the person and the advance of society 'hinge on each other' and that each person 'stands completely in need of social life' (Vatican Council II 1965b: No. 25). Thus, on both theological and secular grounds the dignity of the person can only be achieved when persons enter into fraternity and solidarity with each other. Human dignity is not realized by persons acting autonomously on their own but only through collaboration and solidarity. An individualistic ethic is thus inadequate in light of Catholicism's relational understanding of human dignity. Protection of human dignity and realization of the common good go together. Neither personal flourishing nor communal well-being can be secured without the other.

This relational understanding of the image of God and of human dignity has important practical implications, particularly for the way human rights are understood. During the Cold War, the West was inclined to conceive human rights largely in individualistic terms and to give priority to the civil and political rights: to freedom of belief, speech, and association, as well as due process of law. The negative rights not to be interfered with often took primacy in the West in its ideological struggle with the Soviet bloc. In contrast, Eastern bloc nations and some in the Southern hemisphere adopted ideologies stressing social interdependence and the priority of community provision over individual initiative. This led to granting priority to social and economic rights such as those to adequate food, work and housing.

The simultaneous Catholic affirmation of both the substantialist and relational understandings of dignity, however, denies the legitimacy of both poles of this conflict. Neither individualistic understandings that see human rights primarily as rights to be left alone nor collectivist approaches that subordinate persons to the community in a totalitarian way are adequate. The Catholic tradition holds that opposition between individual freedoms on the one hand and mutual solidarity in society on the other is a false dichotomy. Persons can live in dignity only when they live in a community of freedom – a community in which both personal initiative and social solidarity are valued as essential aspects of human dignity. The give-and-take of dialogue is an intellectual manifestation of such a linkage of personal initiative and social solidarity. This linkage also has institutional dimensions; it will be realized only when persons have both political space for action (civil and political rights) and the material and institutional prerequisites of communal life that make such action possible (social and economic rights). Thus, both civil-political and social-economic rights are required if human dignity is to be respected in its multiple aspects.

Third, the image of God in persons has been given a *functional* interpretation. Just as God has brought the world of nature into being and sustains and governs it, human beings as images of God also exercise a creative, sustaining and governing role in the world. The book of Genesis speaks of the human person as being given a role of dominion analogous to God's dominion over creation. In the face of contemporary environmental and ecological challenges, however, it is important to note that recent biblical scholarship sees this dominion as a responsibility to care for and sustain the created order, not to dominate or, much less, to destroy it. Humans are in God's image by being delegated by God to exercise the kind of care for creation that God's love for all creatures leads to.

This understanding of the *imago Dei*, and thus human dignity, should therefore lead to a strong sense of the interconnection between humans and the natural world and of responsibility to protect the well-being of the entire biosphere. Contrary to some interpretations of the implications of Christian thought for environmental issues, commitment to the distinctive worth of human persons ought to lead to a strong ethic of ecological responsibility (Benedict XVI 2010a: No. 6). Recent Catholic discussions of human dignity, particularly those of Pope Benedict XVI, have picked up on this theme and adopted a notably 'green' orientation. These discussions lead to an understanding of human dignity that supports 'third-generation' human rights such as the right to 'an environment of a quality that permits a life of dignity and well-being', and a 'responsibility to protect and improve the environment for present and future generations'.[1]

This support for environmental integrity and sustainability as a requirement of human dignity implies that the person who possesses dignity is a bodily, biological as well as spiritual, being. Recent Catholic discussions of human dignity have stressed that the biblical understanding of the person rejects mind–body dualism. The dignity of the person is not simply the dignity of a spiritual soul or of what Kant would call a 'noumenal' self, transcending empirical and bodily existence. Human bodiliness, including the reality of human sexuality, is an aspect of the image of God in the human person. Respect for the dignity of the person thus calls for respect for the person's biological needs such as those for food, shelter and healthcare. It also requires respect for the sexual differentiation of male and female, including the equality of man and woman (International Theological Commission 2004: Nos. 26–38).

A living tradition

All these considerations show that the Catholic understanding of human dignity exists within a living tradition that is open to development and change. In earlier stages of this tradition, social practices such as restrictions on religious freedom and even slavery and torture were accepted. The Catholic tradition and its official representatives regarded such practices as legitimate and even morally necessary for the defence of human dignity. Today, however, Catholic thought judges these practices to be fundamental violations of human dignity and human rights, and thus to be gravely immoral (Vatican Council II 1965b: No. 27; Noonan 2005).

[1] United Nations Environment Programme, Declaration of the United Nations Conference on the Human Environment, Stockholm, www.unep.org/Documents.Multilingual/Default.asp?DocumentID=97&ArticleID=1503&l=en (accessed 6 July 2010).

These developments in Catholic thought have occurred as a result of a living interaction between the normative sources of Catholic identity, including the Bible and key doctrinal beliefs, and the ongoing social experience of the Catholic community reflected upon by practical reason. For example, the church's lived experience of the denial of religious freedom by the Soviet state under Stalin led Popes Pius XII and John XXIII to re-examine the tradition's earlier conclusion that support for religious freedom was part of a secularizing agenda that threatened the church's role in public life. Practical reflection on the experience of denial of religious freedom then led the Second Vatican Council to recognize that the freedom to express one's religious convictions in public is an essential condition for the protection and realization of human dignity. Thus, through a sort of back-and-forth movement between normative Catholic beliefs and lived experience, notable developments have occurred in both the more theoretical Catholic understanding of human dignity and in more practical Catholic commitments to protect human rights.

In this way, Catholicism has come to be a participant in what John Rawls has called an 'overlapping consensus' on a public philosophy of human dignity and human rights. In such a consensus, people from diverse religions or cultures reach agreement on the ethical standards for the institutions that structure their lives together. They discover within their own particular traditions adequate grounds for affirming a set of basic moral principles that persons from other traditions can also affirm for their own reasons. Such a consensus was attained in the practical agreement reached by the drafters of the Universal Declaration of Human Rights.

It can be asked, however, whether this agreement on human rights, and Catholic participation in it, was in fact simply a fortuitous convergence occasioned by the experience of the grave abuses of Nazi genocide and the violence of the twentieth century's world wars. A consensus that arises fortuitously could equally well evanesce if the circumstances that occasioned it were to change. The Universal Declaration did not rest on a philosophical agreement on why human rights should be supported or a metaphysical agreement about the meaning of human dignity (Maritain 1949: 9). This leaves open the question of whether agreement to the Declaration, including agreement by the Catholic community, might disappear if historical conditions become sufficiently different from those that led to its drafting.

To address this question it is important to distinguish between a chance convergence of Catholic thought with other traditions and an experience-based agreement on the moral demands of human dignity shaped by the conclusions of practical reason. 'Practical reason', of course, can mean several things. On one level it could be an instrumental calculus of self-interest. Understood this way, practical agreement to the requirements of human dignity and rights would mean that the Catholic community has become convinced that the self-interests of the church will be best achieved under a human rights regime. Such an interest-based practical agreement would disappear if it became clear that human rights challenge some significant Catholic interests or important aspects of Catholic self-understanding. Practical consensus of this type is simply an expression of what the particular tradition involved already believes. On the other hand, a second form of practical reason goes beyond this sort of self-interest. It claims to have attained true insight into ways in which practical action will promote the genuine human good. In fact, recent Catholic thought, especially that of John XXIII and the Second Vatican Council, affirms support for human rights in this way. Human rights are not simply supportive of the practical self-interests of the church, nor are they just congenial expressions of already existing convictions of the Catholic tradition. Rather, the support for human rights at the Second Vatican Council in fact challenged existing church traditions and what had been seen as the self-interests of the church. Human rights affirmed in this way were able to challenge existing patterns of Catholic thought and life precisely because they were seen as expressing true insights into the human good. Because of the deep Catholic claim to be promoting the human good, the tradition was thus compelled to change.

This way of understanding Catholicism's entrance into the contemporary consensus on human dignity and human rights provides a way of understanding past developments in the tradition. But it also suggests that we can expect further developments in the Catholic understanding of human dignity and rights in the future. In particular, very recent church teachings on the equality of men and women are often accompanied by an affirmation of a complementarity of male and female gender roles that leads to a rejection of some of the rights claimed by persons involved in same-sex relationships. Similarly, recent church teachings reject some innovative forms of medical and technological support for human reproduction as threats to human dignity (International Theological Commission 2004: Nos. 81–94). Clearly, support for same-sex relationships and for some forms of technologically assisted reproduction would require notable departure from aspects of the Catholic moral tradition. Whether such a development in the tradition is called for cannot be determined here. But in the past, Catholic moral understandings have clearly developed and changed in a number of other domains when practical reason indicated that change would serve the human good and promote human dignity. At present, there are notable disputes concerning the appropriate direction for Catholic thought in the domain of sexuality and reproduction if it is to be supportive of human dignity in these important areas of human life. The past experience of development within the tradition suggests that change should not be ruled out in the way Catholic thought assesses the relation among human dignity, sex and reproduction. Rather, we need careful reflection on the human experience of how human dignity is being affected by new practices in these areas.

It will not be only Catholic thought and practice, of course, that will be led to change by the influence of emerging social, political and technological realities on our understanding of the requirements of human dignity. Other traditions, both religious and secular, may need to change as well. In particular, Catholicism's strong emphasis on the social nature of the human person challenges the individualistic tendencies of some approaches to human rights. For example, freedom of personal initiative in the economic sphere is a right that should be stressed if state control stifles human dignity. But markets should also be regulated when this is needed to insure that the dignity of the poor and marginal members of society is protected, especially when these markets have increasingly global reach (Benedict XVI 2010b). Human dignity thus raises ongoing challenges for all traditions of moral reflection. We can expect Catholicism to be an active participant in the efforts to respond to these challenges that lie ahead.

References

Benedict XVI. 2010a. 'If You Want to Cultivate Peace, Protect Creation', message for the World Day of Peace, 1 January 2010, www.vatican.va/holy_father/benedict_xvi/messages/peace/documents/hf_ben-xvi_mes_20091208_xliii-world-day-peace_en.html (accessed 5 July 2010)

2010b. 'Address to the Pontifical Academy of Social Sciences', 30 April 2010, www.vatican.va/holy_father/benedict_xvi/speeches/2010/april/documents/hf_ben-xvi_spe_20100430_scienze-sociali_en.html (accessed 25 May 2010)

Hollenbach, D. 1979. *Claims in Conflict: Retrieving and Renewing the Catholic Human Rights Tradition.* New York: Paulist Press

Huntington, S. 1991. 'Religion and the Third Wave', *National Interest* 24: 29–42

International Theological Commission. 2004. *Communion and Stewardship: Human Persons Created in the Image of God.* www.vatican.va/roman_curia/congregations/cfaith/cti_documents/rc_con_cfaith_doc_20040723_communion-stewardship_en.html (accessed 19 July 2010)

John XXIII. 1963. 'Pacem in Terris (Peace on Earth)', in D. J. O'Brien and T. A. Shannon (eds.), *Catholic Social Thought: The Documentary Heritage.* Maryknoll, NY: Orbis Books [1992], 131–62

1964. 'A Preview of Mater et Magistra', in The Staff of the Pope Speaks Magazine (eds.), *The Encyclicals and Other Messages of John XXIII*, Washington, DC: TPS Press

Leo XIII. 1891. '*Rerum novarum* (On Capital and Labor)', www.vatican.va/holy_father/leo_xiii/encyclicals/documents/hf_l-xiii_enc_15051891_rerum-novarum_en.html

Maritain, J. 1949. 'Introduction', in UNESCO (ed.), *Human Rights: Comments and Interpretations*, New York: Columbia University Press

Middleton, J. R. 2005. *The Liberating Image: The Imago Dei in Genesis 1.* Grand Rapids, MI: Brazos Press

Murray, J. C. 1953. 'Leo XIII: Separation of Church and State', *Theological Studies* 14: 145–214

Neuner, J., and Dupuis, J. (eds.). 1998. *The Christian Faith in the Doctrinal Documents of the Catholic Church*, 6th revised and enlarged edn, New York: Alba House

Noonan, J. T. 2005. *A Church That Can and Cannot Change: The Development of Catholic Moral Teaching.* Notre Dame, IN: University of Notre Dame Press

Thomas Aquinas. 1956. *Summa contra gentiles*, trans. V. J. Bourke. New York: Doubleday

Vatican Council II. 1965a. 'Dignitatis humanae (Declaration on Religious Freedom)', in W. Abbott and J. Gallagher (eds.), *Documents of Vatican II*, New York: America Press [1966], 675–96

1965b. 'Gaudium et spes (Pastoral Constitution on the Church in the Modern World)', in W. Abbott and J. Gallagher (eds.), *Documents of Vatican II*, New York: America Press [1966], 199–308

27

Jacques Maritain's personalist conception of human dignity

PAUL VALADIER*

> If civilization is to be salvaged, the new age of civilization will have to be an age of theocentric humanism. Today, human dignity is trampled under foot far and wide. Even worse, it collapses from the inside, for guided by the pure perspective of science and technology we are at a loss when it comes to discovering the rational foundations of the dignity of the person, and to believing in these.
>
> (Maritain 1990: vol. IX, 363)[1]

This text, uneasy, written at the end of the Second World War as bolshevist totalitarianism spread over large parts of Europe, clearly marks the twofold character of Maritain's approach to dignity: rooted in a lucid and bemused view of historical actuality, it calls for philosophical, metaphysical and even theological steps towards finding an adequate response to the challenges of the present; challenges which science and technology are incapable of meeting. As such, Maritain the metaphysician (and theologian) is inseparable from Maritain the political watchdog – and even agent, since he was one of the indirect architects of the 1948 Charter of the United Nations on account of his membership of a UNESCO enquiry commission on human rights. His concern for human dignity, therefore, does not ignore the diversity of conceptions and practices made manifest to him by his experience with the preparation of the Charter. Yet, at the same time, the philosopher is convinced that, without a strong metaphysical foundation, the concept of dignity risks being effaced from the human consciousness. It is with this metaphysical and historical background in mind that Maritain's philosophy of dignity ought to be approached.

Dignity and natural law

We believe we have a good sense of what human dignity comprises, and we feel the same way about the concept of a person. It seems self-evident that there is shared and general consensus on these notions. In Maritain's eyes, however, there is no such thing. In fact, the pseudo-self-evidence of a universal agreement on the content and meaning of dignity is extremely dangerous. Contrary

* Translated by Lin van Steenbergen and Naomi van Steenbergen in collaboration with the author.

[1] Maritain 1953: 102.

to popular opinion, the distinction between individual and person 'is a distinction that is difficult to grasp, and that requires an exercise of metaphysical spirit which is rather uncommon in contemporary thought' (Maritain 1990: vol. IX, 169).[2] It does therefore not suffice to declare oneself a 'personalist' in order to reach agreement on the concept of dignity, for 'there is not one doctrine of personalism, but personalist aspirations and a good dozen personalist doctrines, which at times have nothing more in common than the word "person", and of which some to a greater or lesser degree tend towards one of the opposing errors between which they situate themselves' (*ibid.*: IX, 170).[3] For there are personalist philosophies which justify individual anarchism, and others which justify dictatorship or which in the name of society or community are prepared to legitimize totalitarian regimes, thus subordinating the person to the social Whole. Only, in Maritain's eyes, a personalism inspired by the thought of Thomas Aquinas is capable of steering clear of those excesses, which deplete dignity of any content actually respectful of the human person.

It is for this reason that the concept of dignity must be grounded in an appeal to the traditional expression of 'natural law'. In our day, to be sure, this expression is not much cared for, rejected even. But the concept has a very long philosophical tradition, which must be revisited in order to give it all its lustre and pertinence. In order to meet the metaphysical requirements of the idea of dignity, it must be understood that the natural law is by no means a written code, but that 'there is, in virtue of human nature even, an order or disposition that can be discovered by human reason, and according to which human will must act in order to align itself with aims that are essential and necessary for the human being'. Thus, reason can discover 'the standards of its operation', 'a watershed between what is appropriate and what is not appropriate', which one can agree either to follow or not to follow. This law is both *ideal*, since it is prescribed by the intelligible necessities of the human essence, and *ontological*, since it is engrained in the structure of human concerns. But one must not forget the historicity of such a law, at least when it comes to its progressive and slow discovery by people in history and in the diversity of cultures.

To this first *ontological element*, we must add a second *gnoseological element*, through which people discover little by little what it takes to avoid evil and to act according to the good. *Understanding through inclination*, says Maritain (adding to the doctrine of Thomas Aquinas – inspired, no doubt, by Bergson, who was an early mentor to him), and not purely rational knowledge: knowledge that is obscure, vital, non-systematic, knowledge that advances through sympathy, for the intellect 'hears and consults the kind of song that is produced in the subject by the vibrations of its inner tendencies' (Maritain 1990: vol. IX, 585–6). This explains why knowledge of the good thing to do and the evil to avoid (natural law) has progressed in correspondence with the maturation of the moral consciousness of the peoples, that it has fluctuated, even gone astray

[2] Maritain 1946: 30. [3] *Ibid.*: 31.

depending on their cultural, political, social or religious 'horizons' or 'climates'. This also explains the diversity in the content given to this same natural law by different cultures, a diversity which must evidently be appreciated in conjunction with its fundamental ontological element. Such a diversity is to be understood according to the thomist doctrine of analogy, which appeals to a diverse application of one single principle depending on time and culture. This approach anticipates the possible ways in which consciousness can develop and allows for mutual questioning between different epochs and cultures. Such a progressive understanding is the source of human rights, which are its modern expression, codified in our constitutions or in charters, modern rights, perhaps, but fruits of a process of maturation, and of the development of consciousness. But 'these dynamic formulas of moral rules' are grounded in a 'transcendent' law, the natural law, itself 'participating in the eternal Law', that is to say 'in the order of Wisdom', since such a law can be obliged only if one discerns in it the trace of divine Reason or of Wisdom. It must be acknowledged by reason, and thus by the freedom reflected in this infinitely complex reality that man and society constitute.

It is advisable, therefore, to keep these two elements of the natural law together, yet distinguish them. The ontological element grounds the dignity of every human being (to which we could add a theological argument that Maritain used to cite often, according to which every human being is made in the Creator's image, and thus participates in a truly sacred dignity), and, for this reason, dignity does not depend on any internal sensation, nor on individual psychological appreciation, nor on the verdict of society or another; it is not measured by subjectivity, nor can it be effaced; 'in reality, the privilege connected with the dignity of the person is inalienable, and human life involves a sacred right. Whether to rid society of a useless member or for *raison d'état*, it is a crime to kill an innocent man' (*ibid.*: IX, 212).[4] The two elements, ontological and gnoseological, support each other: what of human rights, and first and foremost of the dignity of each person, if the *intrinsic* worth and dignity of man were denied? What is the use of charters multiplying into infinity if the person himself is not granted a 'sacred' dignity? At the same time, though, it is impossible to deny the newness of certain rights (or of the abolition of certain practices, such as slavery), and here 'the proper achievement – a great achievement indeed – of the eighteenth century has been to bring out in full light the *rights* of man as also required by natural law' (Maritain 1990: vol. IX, 589).[5] History thus plays its part through 'the development of the moral and social experience', to the point, even, that Maritain writes: 'what at any rate has been gained for the secular conscience, if it does not veer to barbarism, is faith in the march forward of humanity' (Maritain 1990: vol. VII, 854), but, and this mitigates the optimism displayed in the previous quotation, its role can be negative, too, if 'ideological errors' have come to taint these discoveries

[4] *Ibid.*: 445. [5] Maritain 1951: 94.

(individualist–anarchist or collectivist interpretations of rights or dignity) – errors that have not remained in the realm of ideas, but that have marked totalitarian regimes denounced by Maritain since the 1930s. This evidently calls for permanent vigilance on the part of the citizen and philosopher.

Political scope

The insistence on the dignity of every human may give rise to the impression that Maritain professes an individual personalism, one that is non-relational and ignores social and political life; it may make it seem that he concentrates his attention on isolated monads, valued only in and for themselves. Nothing could be further from the truth. For '[t]here is a correlation between this notion of the person as social unit and the notion of the *common good* as the end of the social whole. They imply one another. The common good is common because it is received in persons, each one of whom is as a mirror of the whole . . . The end of society, therefore, is neither the individual good nor the collection of the individual goods of each of the persons who constitute it . . . The end of society is the good of the community, of the social body.' 'The common good of the city . . . is the good *human life* of the multitude, of a multitude of persons; it is their communion in good living. It is therefore common to both *the whole and the parts* into which it flows back and which, in turn, must benefit from it. Unless it would vitiate itself, it implies and requires recognition of the fundamental rights of persons' (Maritain 1990: vol. IX, 200).[6] It is not the relation between person and community that signifies the particularity of Maritain's 'personalism' here, for the person is not understood in his relation to a communal life. Rather, the concept of a person is to be understood in relation to the common good, in terms of their reciprocal development. In no way 'communitarian', as we would say today, Maritain rather insists on the dignity of the people (*peuple*), and he employs this old usage of 'people', which seems a bit outmoded, without batting an eyelid, and wholly endorses it. This concept is essential for his political philosophy (Maritain 1990: vol. VI, 443).[7]

In fact, 'under the inspiration of the Gospel at work in history, the secular conscience has understood the dignity of the people and the common man . . . The people are not God; the people do not have infallible reason and virtues without flaw; the will of the people or the spirit of the people is not the rule which decides what is just or unjust. But the people make up the slowly prepared and fashioned body of common humanity, the living patrimony of the common gifts and the common promises made to God's creature – which are more profound and more essential than all the additional privileges and the social distinctions – and of the equal dignity and the equal weakness of all as members of the human race' (Maritain 1990: vol. VII, 733). While the theological tone is already striking here, many more passages can be found in which

[6] Maritain 1946: 436–7. [7] Maritain 1973: 130.

Maritain heavily factors in the 'populace' (*commun du peuple*), always affirming the evangelical origin of his confidence in the people, for he refers to the 'people of the poor to whom the promise of the Beatitudes has been made and who enjoy an "eminent dignity" in the community of saints' (Maritain 1990: vol. IX, 379).[8] He does, incidentally, provide a rather firm 'definition' of 'people': 'the people are the multitude of human persons who, united under just laws, by mutual friendship, and for the common good of their human existence, constitute a political society or a body politic. The notion of body politic means the whole unit composed of the people... Nay more, since the people are human persons who not only form a body politic, but who have each one a spiritual soul and a supratemporal destiny, the concept of the people is the highest and noblest concept among the basic concepts that we are analyzing' (Maritain 1990: vol. IX, 510–11).[9]

His insistence on the dignity of the people results in the idea of fraternity and that of pluralism. Fraternity is even seen as the 'primordial "myth" giving direction to common life', or as the 'essential dynamic principle' of democratic life (Maritain 1990: vol. VI, 520–1).[10] In Maritain's eyes, the concept has a clear Christian origin, and does not only call for fraternity within communities, but also for fraternity between peoples, for attention to a shared humanity, or a humanity common to all of us, compelled by the dignity this humanity contains. The people, in turn, is not a compact mass, an undifferentiated multitude, a fuzzy and vague reference, convenient for all demagogies (Maritain 1990: vol. IX, 381).[11] It is formed in the course of a history, has known painful, tragic or happy experiences which are part of its heritage and its memorized values. It is therefore 'pluralistic', composed of 'social groupings and structures, each of them embodying positive liberties' (Maritain 1990: vol. VI, 477).[12] It is, therefore, apposite to insist on 'The pluralist principle in democracy' (the title of Chapter 4 of *The Range of Reason*). This democratic regime, which, according to Maritain's stated preference, should be pluralistic, 'the society of tomorrow'; 'of men belonging to very different philosophical or religious creeds and lineages could and should co-operate in the common task and for the common welfare of the earthly community, provided they similarly assent to the charter and basic tenets of a society of free men' (Maritain 1990: vol. IX, 421).[13] For Maritain also values the idea of a 'democratic credo' or of a fundamental charter wholly dedicated to human rights: his experience with UNESCO made him understand that it is necessary to both respect the irreducible diversities regarding conceptions of humanity and religion, and promote a common ground on which to find each other in order to develop solutions to problems common to all of humanity. Yet respect for this diversity does not imply that fundamental agreements are impossible. 'Men possessing quite different, even opposite metaphysical or religious outlooks, can converge,

[8] Maritain 1953: 123. [9] Maritain 1951: 26. [10] Maritain 1973: 204.
[11] Maritain 1953: 125. [12] Maritain 1973: 164. [13] Maritain 1951: 109.

not by virtue of any identity of doctrine, but by virtue of an analogical similitude in practical principles, toward the same practical conclusions, and can share in the same practical secular faith, provided that they similarly revere, perhaps for quite diverse reasons, truth and intelligence, human dignity, liberty, brotherly love, and the absolute value of moral good' (Maritain 1990: vol. IX, 611).[14] We can see that, well before John Rawls, Maritain proposed such a charter as a sort of 'overlapping consensus': as long as parties can agree on certain values, such as human dignity, it should be possible to arrive at common practical conclusions, notwithstanding fundamental convictions, which can legitimately separate them. Democratic life must in some way or another disregard these ultimate references, rather extending itself to 'points of practical convergence' or basing itself on a 'unity of friendship' between citizens.

Still, it does not suffice to profess 'communal values', and inscribe these in constitutions or statutes. Where Maritain uses the term 'faith', which at this point we can consider out of place, then the point is to engage with these values, not only proclaim them intellectually, honour them verbally or include them in statutes. Granted, this 'faith' has a secular character, not supernatural, 'yet even a secular faith implies the commitment of the whole man and his innermost spiritual energies, and draws its strength, therefore, from beliefs which go far beyond scientific method' (Maritain 1990: vol. IX, 435).[15] No democracy is worthy of its name, therefore, without the engagement of each and every person. No purely procedural 'democracy' which could result in the justification of any decision, even unjust ones, could follow from an honestly conducted debate. For a democracy implies citizens who engage in shared values and who gauge potential costs (those of the resistance against oppression, against traditions or against public opinion). Maritain does not support the idea of a sort of schizophrenia that proposes on the one hand communal beliefs and on the other parenthesized superior philosophical or religious principles. For 'the fact remains that democratic faith – implying as it does faith in justice, in freedom, in brotherly love, in the dignity of the human person, in his rights as well as in his responsibilities, in that power of binding men in conscience which appertains to just laws, in the deep-rooted aspirations which call for political and social coming of age of the people – cannot be justified, nurtured, strengthened, and enriched without philosophical or religious convictions . . . which deal with the very substance and meaning of human life' (*ibid.*: IX, 426).[16] Another politically and philosophically essential consequence: it is in the name of his confidence in the people who 'remain the great granary of vital spontaneity and non-pharisaic living force' (*ibid.*: IX, 381),[17] and the value accorded to pluralism that Maritain criticizes *the concept of the sovereignty* of the state. Such a concept is 'intrinsically illusory', for it presupposes that 'the people have absolutely deprived and divested themselves of their total power in order to transfer it

[14] *Ibid.*: 111. [15] Maritain 1953: 168. [16] *Ibid.*: 169. [17] *Ibid.*: 124.

to the sovereign' (Maritain 1990: vol. IX, 519).[18] Now, the people cannot rob itself of what they are entitled to *ipso jure*, namely, the right to govern itself and to decide for itself. Presuming such a thing were possible for the benefit of a sovereign state results in the intrinsic dignity of the people – which lies in the fact that it is perfectly capable of governing itself – being ridiculed. Sovereignty strips the people of its rights; reduces it to the rank of a passive servant and, most of all, grants the state apparatus a 'separate and transcendent' power, which is a usurpation. Hence the sharp criticisms aimed at Bodin and Hobbes for having defended what Maritain considers a 'heresy'. Hence the repetition of one of Saint Augustine's theses in *City of God*: 'no human agent, nor any human institution, possesses by virtue of its own nature the right to govern men' (cf. *ibid.*: IX, 530).[19] A claim which leads in no way to anarchism if we admit that every right to power 'is possessed only' to the extent that a person or an institution are 'in the body politic a *part* at the service of the common good, a part which has received this right, within certain fixed bounds, from the people exercising their fundamental right to govern themselves' (*ibid.*: IX, 530).[20] Maritain thus endorses Lincoln's definition, according to which democracy is the government of the people, by the people and for the people. Instead of surrendering oneself to a state which is supposed to situate itself above society, it is important to enliven the driving forces and the inherent group dynamics, count on the propensity of each and every person to strive for the good, and draw resources once more from the dynamics inherent to the people. The state has thus only an 'instrumental' role, in the service of and subordinate to the people and its capacity to govern itself as much as possible by itself. The dignity of the people, incidentally, is such that anti-democratic ideologies eliminate it, in favour of illusory and dangerous sovereignties (states, parties, charismatic chefs).

It should be self-evident that such a promotion of the people and of democracy by no means signifies a blind and demagogical exaltation of popular aspirations. The people must let itself be oriented and guided by the democratic charter, that is to say, by human rights and certain fundamental values of liberty, dignity, equality or solidarity (fraternity). The people is not a fully autonomous and independent whole; it doesn't find itself in a universal will which would infallibly guide it. It is bound to truth, and thus to the rational and patient search for this truth. 'But the body politic as such has an obligation to the truth to which the people themselves, the citizens who constitute the body politic – adhere in conscience. The body politic does not know another truth than that which the people know' (*ibid.*: IX, 675).[21] A strong and almost excessive statement, if it were not embedded in the social philosophy mentioned above, and in a religious conception which opens the people towards a transcendence where it finds its dignity and its legitimacy.

Maritain's wager for the new civilization he hopes for is risky, for the initiation of democracy does not flow from an irrefutable logic that develops ineluctably

[18] Maritain 1951: 34. [19] *Ibid.*: 43. [20] *Ibid.*: 43–4. [21] *Ibid.*: 166.

towards democratic modernity. Rather, the ever difficult formation of democracies depends largely on the people's education, on their insight into the dignity of each human being and their own dignity, and thus on their morality and religion. Now, like other basic moral values, dignity is by no means secured once and for all. The people can deny itself; it can be seduced to accept slavery by the siren song of mendacious ideologies, as we have witnessed all too often in the reign of totalitarian Nazi or bolshevist regimes, or in crude dictatorial and tyrannical forms, but no less in the 'bourgeois' faux democracies which Maritain denounced in the 1930s. The philosopher, incidentally, had been contemplating the importance of general education for a long time already (Maritain 1990: vol. VI), and on the political level insisted on the role of 'prophetic shock minorities' – 'prophets' or 'sages' who shake up the passivity of the people, reveal the lack of awareness of serious matters or denounce the injustices not perceived or justified by the ideologies. It is worth noting that Maritain himself took up such responsibilities when he judged the dignity of persons or peoples to be spurned (Spain under Franco, denunciation of anti-Semitism in the 1930s, refusal to collaborate with the regime of Marshal Pétain in Vichy in 1940 etc.).

In this light, we can understand his insistence on the role of Christian religion for cultivating informed and alert moral consciences. It is no longer appropriate for the Churches to subordinate themselves as in the times of medieval Christianity, an era which Maritain considers lost. Their place is now to recollect the 'primacy of the spiritual', for it is in the awareness of its transcendent vocation and its supernatural dignity that man can resist positivisms and determinist thoughts which ruin its sense of its own proper dignity. Hence also the evangelist connotation of his confidence in the people. 'I believe', he writes, 'that the concept of the people as understood today . . . is derived from Christian and, so to speak, "parochial" sources. The idea of "the little people of Our Lord", or of the people of the poor to whom the promise of the Beatitudes has been made and who enjoy an "eminent dignity" in the communion of saints', which has 'contributed to the formation of the concept, this time an ethical–social one, of the working people – which is neither antiquity's rather civic and national idea of the *populus* nor yet its idea of the *plebs*' (Maritain 1990: vol. IX, 379–88).[22] It should be added that, these days, this 'faith' in the people calls for anticipating a 'political unification of the world', since, for a variety of reasons (preventing wars, distributing the goods of the planet as fairly as possible), 'the community of peoples must form *one* people, even taking into account the qualifications to which such a pluralist unity would be subject' (Maritain 1990: vol. IX, 728).[23] Here, once again, in the name of the 'conquest of dignity', people should be able to gain awareness of the imperative of this task, an imperative that cannot be ordained from far and above. 'Now, if a world political society is some day founded, it will be by means of freedom. *It is by means of freedom that the peoples of the earth will have been brought to a common will to live together*' (*ibid.*: IX, 725,

[22] Maritain 1953: 123. [23] Maritain 1951: 209.

emphasis in original).[24] Here, again, the appeal to liberty respects the meaning of the dignity of peoples: if they are aware of their communal dignity even given their differences, they will be able to also want such political unification. But, still, they need to want it, and thus they will have to be convinced of their liberty and their dignity in order to betake themselves to a path that will be difficult and that will require sacrifices, for 'living together' implies 'suffering together', too (*ibid.*: IX, 727–8).[25]

For Maritain, then, dignity is not merely a concept attached to a single person. Dignity radiates onto the peoples themselves, and thus onto their being-together, either in nations, or, for the future, in a society that has become global. But how to ignore the fact that the awareness of this dignity depends largely on the philosophical and religious convictions which persons and peoples place ahead of an eminent value that lives in them and transcends them?

References

French originals

Maritain, J. 1990. *Œuvres completes.* 17 vols. Fribourg: Editions Universitaires, Paris: Editions Saint-Paul (vol. VI, *Humanisme intégral*; vol. VII, *Pour la justice*; vol. VII, *Pour une philosophie de l'éducation*; vol. IX, *La personne et le bien commun*; vol. IX, *L'homme et l'Etat*; vol. IX, *Raison et raisons*)

English translations

Maritain, J. 1939. 'Integral Humanism and the Crisis of Modern Times', *Review of Politics* 1(1): 1–17

1946. 'The Person and the Common Good', trans. J. J. FitzGerald, *Review of Politics* 8(4): 419–55

1951. *Man and the State.* University of Chicago Press

1953. *The Range of Reason.* London: Geoffrey Bles

1972. *Christianity and Democracy*, trans. D. C. Anson, reprinted edn, London: Ayer Publishing

1973. *Integral Humanism*, trans. J. W. Evans. Notre Dame, IN: University of Notre Dame Press

Several translations can also be accessed on the website of the Jacques Maritain Center, University of Notre Dame, http://maritain.nd.edu/jmc/etext

[24] *Ibid.*: 206. [25] *Ibid.*: 207.

28

Scheler and human dignity

ZACHARY DAVIS

Within the human rights discourse of the twentieth century, dignity has come to assume a central and pivotal role. Nowhere has this been made more apparent than in the Preamble to the 1948 Universal Declaration of Human Rights, where dignity is understood as the foundation of 'freedom, justice and peace in the world'. The validity and legitimacy of universal human rights has consequently shifted and now rest in the supposed dignity of all persons. Yet, if dignity is the ground or basis for human rights, what is the ground or basis of dignity?

In his *magnum opus*, *Formalism in Ethics and Non-Formal Ethics of Values*, Max Scheler takes the question concerning the ground of human dignity as a primary motivation. As suggested by the subtitle of the work, *A New Attempt Toward the Foundation of an Ethical Personalism*, Scheler's task is to provide a new grounding, a phenomenological rather than rationalistic grounding, for the human being as a person and, consequently, a new grounding for the dignity of the person. For Scheler, any purely formal or rationalistic account of dignity leads to the depersonalization of the human being. The ground of dignity, rather, is the absolute value of the individual person given in the act of love, an act that reveals the other as a wholly unique and irreplaceable person.

Despite his criticisms of Kant, Scheler's approach still remains within the Kantian tradition of a search for an ethical *a priori* or universal axiology. This approach stands in sharp contrast to more recent attempts to formulate a post-metaphysical ethics and understanding of human dignity, attempts that reject an ethical *a priori* or universal notion of the person in light of the tremendous diversity that is covered under the international scope of human rights.[1] Grounded in the absolute singularity of each and every person, Scheler provides an account that secures the universality of human rights without assuming a fixed or universal definition of the person.

[1] The view I have in mind here is perhaps best expressed by Michael Ignatieff. He writes, 'Pragmatic silence on ultimate questions has made it easier for a global human rights culture to emerge' (2001: 78).

Scheler's value personalism and critique of formal (rational) ethics

Despite the centrality that the dignity and value of the person have in Scheler's ethical thought, the term 'dignity' (*Würde*) is sparingly used by Scheler throughout his work. Its most frequent occurrence is in Scheler's *Formalism*, but, even here, Scheler makes little explicit mention of it. The task for Scheler was not to provide a new definition, but to reformulate the ground or basis of the dignity of the person.

The definition of dignity Scheler assumes is the one given by Kant in the *Groundwork of the Metaphysics of Morals*. In his discussion of the third formulation of the categorical imperative, the imperative understood within the context of the kingdom of ends, Kant writes: 'What has a price can be replaced by something else as its *equivalent*; what on the other hand is raised above all price and therefore admits of no equivalent has a dignity' (1996a: 4:434). Scheler makes reference to this definition of dignity only in his critique of Kant. Yet, without making any explicit reference to the notion of dignity or Kant, Scheler makes use of this distinction between that which has a price and that which is above all price when he distinguishes between relative and non-relative (or absolute) value. In the *Metaphysics of Morals*, Kant also speaks of dignity as 'an inner absolute worth' and places it within the context of treating oneself and others always as an end in itself and never merely as a means (1996b: 6:435). Scheler and Kant are in complete agreement on this point, namely, that the person is of absolute value and worth. Any action that would compromise the absolute value of a person, any action that would treat the person as if his or her worth were relative to some good or other end is evil. This shared understanding of dignity as an inner absolute worth by both Kant and Scheler is the sense of dignity that serves as the basis for much of the discourse concerning the universality of human rights.

Where Scheler parts ways with Kant is the grounds or justification of this absolute value of the person. When Kant introduces the notion of dignity in the *Groundwork for the Metaphysics of Morals*, he does so by first speaking of the dignity of all rational beings and declares that the dignity of the rational being is found in the obedience to only those laws which the rational being gives to itself (1996a: 4:435). Kant concludes his discussion of dignity in the *Groundwork* by writing that '*autonomy* is the ground of the dignity of human nature and of every rational nature' (1996a: 4:436). Both the identification of the person as a rational being and the grounding of dignity in autonomy are, for Scheler, direct consequences of Kant's strictly formal, i.e. purely rational, approach to ethics, and are expressions of the type of depersonalization present in a formal ethics. By depersonalization Scheler means the process by which a concrete individual person is treated or regarded as merely a formal category. To define the person as a rational person means 'that the person is basically nothing but a logical subject of rational acts, i.e. acts that follow these [moral] laws' (Scheler 1973: 371). There is nothing in particular about the individual human being that makes him or her a person other than the fact that he or she is 'some X of rational activity'.

In order to overcome the depersonalization of the human being, Scheler rejects the assumption that only a formal ethics is able to found the dignity of the human being and demonstrates that the experience of value ultimately grounds both the objectivity of ethics (the ethical *a priori*) and the dignity (absolute value) of the person. For Scheler, all that is given in the experience of value is not necessarily relative to the subject. The content of value experience transcends the subject to reveal both an objective ordering of value and the absolute value of person.

All experience is, according to Scheler, value-latent. Value is the most primordial relation we have to the world (1966: 40). Before the world is perceived or known, it is valued (1963: 77–98). Evidence of this primordial relation is the allure the world has upon us. The world entices us to perceive and know it and as such is given in a type of relief. Things in the world bear value as they bear sensible qualities such as colour and taste. According to Scheler, we see the beauty or pleasantness of the landscape as we see its bright hues (1966: 41).

Values are grasped immediately and are intuitively given in the act of feeling. Scheler rejects the traditional, philosophical prejudice that takes feelings as mere psychological states. Feelings are, for Scheler, intentional acts, exhibiting their own inherent logic (1966: 261). The two most primordial feelings are love and hate. Love, for Scheler, is an intentional act that discloses originally positive values; hate is the act wherein negative values are disclosed. As Brentano had earlier shown, there are so-called axioms, purely essential relations, that are co-given with the disclosure of positive and negative values. Positive values are given as that which ought to be, while negative values are given as that which ought not to be (1966: 100). These axioms pertain to the essence of the value and are thus not subject-relative, but objective, relating to the nature of value itself.

The distinction between positive and negative values introduces a further element of the givenness of value, namely, the act of preferring. It is with this aspect of preferring that we discover the material *a priori* that grounds Scheler's value ethics. All feelings, and love and hate in particular, are an act of preferring. Love is the preferring of positive value to negative, while hate is the reverse. Among the positive values, Scheler distinguishes among five value modalities: pleasure, utility, life, spirit and the holy. Exhibited in the act of love is a preferring of the higher values to the lower, or, as Pascal would say, an *ordre du coeur*. Love is the movement towards ever higher value, while hate is the movement towards lower value (1973: 160). The five value modalities have an essential and thus objective rank ordering. Utility is preferred to pleasure; life to utility, spirit to life and holy to spirit. What may be considered to bear the value of life or the holy is culturally relative. Yet, that the holy is to be preferred and of higher value than life is not culturally relative. It is an objective rank ordering of value, a material *a priori* that is given in the experience of value.

The ground of dignity

Dignity, understood as the absolute value of the person, remains the highest of the values (1966: 495). The values of spirit and the holy are personal values, but these are simply distinctive value modalities and are quite different from speaking of the value of the individual person. As is also the case with Kant, persons are of absolute value. The difference for Scheler is that this absolute value is given in experience. Relative and absolute are qualities of value given immediately and intuitively (1966: 116). That is, we experience a bearer of value as either relative or absolute. In contrast to a formal account, the absolute value of the person is, according to Scheler, given as absolute in the experience of the other person. By absolute, Scheler means that which has no equivalent value. What is of absolute value is, strictly speaking, not a thing or object, nothing that could in principle be represented by something else. Any attempt to objectify the person is necessarily an act of degradation, a compromise of a person's absolute value.

The only act wherein the absolute value (dignity) of the person is given is in the act of love (1966: 480). As such, dignity is immediately and intuitively grasped. There is no proof of the dignity of the person other than that which is self-evident in the act of loving another person. Furthermore, the value and dignity of the person is wholly unique (1966: 508). Though every person is of absolute value, no value is the same. No one can take the place of another person or absolute value. The absolute value of the person is given in a unique manner to the person, to the loving of the individual. Scheler's notion of dignity is a highly personalized notion. Each and every person has his own unique dignity. We as persons may all be of absolute value, but no one person is the same or of the same value. There is, in this respect, a value inequality. The dignity of all persons ought to be respected. Yet, the manner in which we love and respect the other person is unique to that person.

It is, thus, not a formal category, but *radical singularity* that grounds the dignity of the person. The conception of the person as unique follows directly from Scheler's correction of the Kantian definition of the person as rational being. For Scheler, the person indeed commits rational acts, but the being of the person is not reducible to its being rational. A rational act is just one among a host of intentional acts a person executes, acts such as loving and hating. The whole person is 'contained' in every one of his or her acts, but is yet irreducible to any one of these acts or the summation of the total acts of a lifetime (1966: 385). The person is non-objectifiable, cannot be represented by any particular act or class of acts.[2] Scheler defines the person as 'the concrete and essential unity of being of acts of different essences' (1966: 382). By 'unity', Scheler means the peculiarity or distinctiveness in which the individual person executes and lives

[2] In his later works, Scheler defends the non-objectifiability of the person with respect to his concept of *Geist*. See Scheler 1976: 39.

in his or her acts (1966: 386). Hence, the being of the person is not a substance, but a particular style, a unique style in which the individual loves, thinks and wonders – a style of one's own. The dignity or absolute value of the person is inseparable from the uniqueness of the person. It is always the dignity of this person that is given in the act of love, not the dignity of persons in general. There is no love of humanity or love of the dignity of the human being.[3] Love is always directed to the being and value of the individual person and it is in this act that the unique and absolute value of the person is given.

Although love is considered by Scheler to be a radically singular act directed at a particular person, there is a universal element in the experience of the other person as absolute value. This universal element is crucial for any concept of human rights which assumes some type of respect for all human beings. For Scheler, given in the experience of the other human being as person is the meaning of person itself. The other is given as person, as a being of absolute value, a being who shall never be treated in a manner that compromises his or her dignity. Hence, the meaning of person is co-given in the love of the other and as such the obligation to respect the dignity of all persons is also co-given. Scheler indeed rejects any general love of humanity, but demonstrates how the love of another assumes the love of all persons, a universal respect for the dignity of each and every human being. Universal human rights would, for Scheler, be one way in which to articulate the moral and political responsibility entailed in the meaning of person.

Solidarity and human rights

The final aspect of Scheler's notion of dignity concerns the distinction between self-love and love of others. This distinction follows that between the respect of one's own dignity and the respect for the dignity of others. For Scheler, the love of others is wholly distinct from but equally primordial to self-love (1966: 489). The dignity and absolute value of the other has its own distinctive means of givenness from that of one's own dignity. As a consequence, a distinctive sense of responsibility is implied in the dignity of others from that of the self. Not only am I wholly responsible for my own actions and how my actions respect the dignity of others, I am also co-responsible for all persons and their actions. This sense of co-responsibility does not mean that I take responsibility from the person who has committed the act of evil. Every person is fully responsible for his or her actions. Yet, because of the genuine love of the other, I share responsibility for the degradation of the person. When a person is degraded I am called to act for that person, not because I was the cause, but because I love the other. Scheler calls this dual sense of the responsibility the principle of solidarity. There are different levels of depth in solidarity, of the scope and sense of co-responsibility. Dignity is operative at the deepest level of solidarity,

[3] For Scheler's critique of modern humanism, see Scheler 1955: 96–113.

a moral community of love. The scope of this sense of solidarity is infinite, not limited by cultural or political borders.[4]

Scheler has very little to say as to how his notion of solidarity rooted in the wholly unique dignity of the person relates to the notion of human rights. In general, he is sceptical of any suggestion of a universal responsibility and has great reservations concerning modern humanism. Any human rights discourse that begins with a reduction of the individual person to a universal category or substance leads ultimately to a depersonalization of the dignity of the person, resulting in practices that disregard the utter uniqueness of each and every person. In order to rescue human rights discourse from this danger, human rights would have to be articulated, according to Scheler, within the context of solidarity and the distinctive sense of responsibility rooted in the love of the other. Rooted in the principle of solidarity, human rights discourse becomes personalized, comes to be directed to the particular, individual person.

Due to his premature death (1928), Scheler was unable to complete his major work on politics, *Politik und Moral* (*Politics and Morality*). In this work, there is at least the promise of clarification on the relation between solidarity and the growing campaign for an international recognition of universal human rights. This is an avenue of Scheler's thought that has been under-developed.[5] Nevertheless, Scheler is unequivocally clear that the task of both morality and politics is the realization of the deeper personal values such as dignity, and, at the most profound level of human solidarity, all persons are called to act for the abolition of any degradation of the individual person or community of persons. While Scheler has relatively little to say on what this call to act on behalf of a person's right means in practice, he remains committed to the idea that this call springs from nothing other than the absolute singularity of each and every human being.

References

Blosser, P. 1995. *Scheler's Critique of Kant's Ethics.* Athens, OH: Ohio University Press

Brunkhorst, H. 2005. *Solidarity: From Civic Friendship to a Global Legal Community*, trans. J. Flynn. Cambridge, MA: MIT Press

Ignatieff, M. 2001. *Human Rights as Politics and Idolatry*, ed. Amy Gutman. Princeton University Press

Kant, I. 1996a. *Groundwork of the Metaphysics of Morals*, in *The Cambridge Edition of the Works of Immanuel Kant: Practical Philosophy*, trans. M. Gregor. Cambridge University Press

[4] For a more detailed treatment of Scheler's notion of the life-community, see Ranly 1966.

[5] In his work, *Solidarity: From Civic Friendship to a Global Legal Community*, Hauke Brunkhorst has provided the fullest and most cogent account of the relation between solidarity and human rights. However, this work does develop this relation with respect to Scheler's notion of solidarity or dignity.

1996b. *The Metaphysics of Morals*, in *The Cambridge Edition of the Works of Immanuel Kant: Practical Philosophy*, trans. M. Gregor. Cambridge University Press

Ranly, E. W. 1966. *Scheler's Phenomenology of Community*. The Hague: Martinus Nijhoff

Scheler, Max. 1966. *Der Formalismus in der Ethik und die Materiale Wertethik: Neuer Versuch der Grundlegung eines Ethischen Personalismus*, in *Gesammelte Werke*, vol. II, ed. M. Scheler. Bern: Francke Verlag

1955. *Das Ressentiment im Aufbau der Moralen. Vom Umsturz der Werte: Abhhandlungen und Aufsätze*, in *Gesammelte Werke*, vol. III, ed. M. Scheler. Bern: Francke Verlag

1963. 'Liebe und Erkenntnis', *Schriften zur Soziologie und Weltanschauungslehre*, in *Gesammelte Werke*, vol. VI, ed. M. Scheler. Bern: Francke Verlag

1973. *Wesen und Formen der Sympathie: Die Deutsche Philosophie der Gegenwart*, in *Gesammelte Werke*, vol. VII, ed. M. S. Frings. Bern: Francke Verlag

1976. *Die Stellung des Menschen im Kosmos. Späte Schriften*, in *Gesammelte Werke*, vol. IX, ed. M. S. Frings. Bern: Francke Verlag

29

Dignity and the Other: dignity and the phenomenological tradition

PETER ATTERTON

A fundamental claim of phenomenology is that the meaning of something is not given to us in the manner of abstract theoretical knowledge but arises out of our *concrete*, non-theoretical dealings with the world. Phenomenology rejects the idea that we need to find *a priori* or metaphysical grounds to justify what, by remaining faithful to our deepest experiential evidence, we in a certain sense already know to be true. It carefully attends to the nature of consciousness as actually experienced, not as represented by the tradition or abstract philosophizing or scientific theory. This leads to a method in philosophy: the careful description of things or their meanings as they *appear* to a 'transcendentally reduced' (Husserl 1991: 34 *passim*) consciousness, i.e. minus all prejudices and theoretical assumptions, while taking their very manner of appearance into consideration. But how does phenomenology shed light on something like the meaning of human dignity? If human dignity is not something I have to infer but something directly intuited in experience, how is it that human beings inhabit my experience in such a way that they present themselves to me as beings worthy of respect, possessing certain rights and generating correlative duties and obligations, which are essential components of their recognition?

Emmanuel Lévinas' *phenomenological ethics* suggests the possibility of an answer to these questions by grounding the idea of human rights and dignity in the relationship with the other person he calls 'the Other' ('*Autrui*'). Lévinas takes the position that dignity and rights are attributes that persons could not fail to have *as human persons*, and that those attributes present themselves to me in the concrete and immediate encounter he calls 'the face-to-face'. His view is not simply reducible to the claim that as a rational agent I am forced to recognize the rationality of others. He holds, for instance, that the respect for universal rights would be impossible *but for a prior attachment to the Other that precedes reason and autonomy*, and which is made possible by the *demand* that comes from the Other, a call on me to set aside my self-preoccupations and to concern myself with the Other instead. Lévinas' endorsement of the rights of man goes hand in hand with his theory of responsibility for the Other. Roughly put, this is the theory that I, as an ethically motivated individual, find myself responsible for taking care of the needs of the Other prior to consciousness and choice. If Lévinas is correct in his claim that 'the Rights of Man are originally the rights of the other man' (Lévinas 1999b: 149), then this has startling and far-reaching consequences, not only for global justice and politics (overseas development, aid, etc.) but also for the classic Enlightenment problem of the justification of human rights and the meaning of human dignity. These are sufficient reasons for us to take Lévinas' 'phenomenology of the rights of man' (Lévinas 1994: 125) very seriously.

Phenomenology of human dignity and rights

For Lévinas, what separates phenomenology from traditional philosophy and science is its enormous potential for recognizing the distinctly *human*: 'No one combated the dehumanization of the Real better than Husserl [the father of phenomenology], the dehumanization which is produced when one extends the categories proper to mathematized matter to the totality of our experience... Phenomenology has not only permitted the "de-thingifying", the "de-reifying" of the human being, but also the humanizing of things' (Lévinas 1998c: 131–2). If phenomenology is to show how it is that we can come by a 'de-reified' conception of human being, it must meet two demands: (1) It must describe concrete human phenomena while 'bracketing' antecedent misconceptions stemming from ideological or scientific prejudices about what human beings *must* be like in theory; and (2) it should also teach us how *another human being* can at least be thinkable or putatively recognized. For Lévinas these are the same demands insofar as the proper meaning of the human lies not in its showing itself to me as an object of knowledge but implicitly refers to the first-hand experience of the other human being in a relationship 'face-to-face'. For Lévinas, the fundamental recognition of the humanity and dignity of the Other just is the *recognition* that he or she *has a face*. The central problem of Lévinas' philosophy is that of explaining how the face is able to signify the presence of the other human being outside of knowledge and comprehension. This requires one to adopt the first-person perspective of one who stands *within* the face-to-face encounter with another human being rather than the position of a neutral third party who stands outside the relationship looking in. For Lévinas the interpersonal face-to-face constitutes a relationship not of perception or knowledge but one of ethics and responsibility. Lévinas is not trying to explain how ethics is possible by appealing to a preliminary awareness of the others: the term 'ethics' is but a label for accomplishment of the relationship with the Other insofar as 'the very significance of the face and of the original speaking that asks for me, holds me in question and awakes me or gives rise to my response or my responsibility' (Lévinas 1998a: 167).

When Lévinas explicitly defines what it is that the face 'says' to provoke responsibility, what emerges is the assertion of an original 'right' *against me* of the right to life: *Thou shalt not kill.* This fundamental right to life comprises more than simply the negative right of non-interference; it comprehends also positive duties, including the positive obligation to *maintain* the other's life.

Lévinas clarifies its meaning thus: '"Thou shalt not kill" – means then "Thou shalt cause thy neighbor to live"' (Lévinas 1999a: 127) ('"*Tu ne tuera point*" – *cela signifie donc "tu feras vivre le prochain"*'). Thus, for Lévinas, the presence of the Other's face is the first condition for the possibility of recognizing the right of the Other to the material means of his or her existence. As Lévinas says in his *magnum opus, Totality and Infinity* (1961):

> This regard that supplicates and demands – that can supplicate only because it demands – deprived of everything because having a right to everything and that one recognizes in giving . . . this regard is precisely the epiphany of the face as face. The nakedness of the face is destituteness. To recognize the Other is to recognize a hunger. To recognize the Other is to give. (Lévinas 1969: 75)

When confronted with the face of a fellow human being who is hungry (or in need), I immediately feel morally constrained to feed, clothe, etc. him or her. This sense of moral constraint is not in virtue of some rational decision process or procedure whereby I recognize that I must give adequate consideration to others if I am to act on principles that all autonomous rational beings as such could adopt. Indeed, I do not *act on* principle at all; rather, my will is already predisposed to act in response to the hungry Other prior to rational acceptance. This is how *phenomenologically* I experience the Other's face, not as a perceptible thing, but as a *demand* put to me in the form of an urgent requirement to take care of his or her welfare needs.

The paradox of 'equal dignity'

It is interesting to compare what Lévinas says about the face of the Other being 'deprived of everything because having a right to everything' ('*privé de tout parce que ayant droit à tout*') with the first sentence of Article 1 of the Declaration: 'All human beings are born free and equal in dignity and rights.' The latter is usually taken to mean that *all* human beings are born with equal rights and freedoms because of their inherent dignity. But, if Lévinas is correct, then the Other would appear to have more rights than I have – 'a right to everything' no less – precisely insofar as we stand in a relationship with each other face-to-face.

Lévinas' exposition is very informal but it is clear that it is merely a variant of the argument enshrined in the Declaration. The difference is that Lévinas does not pretend to derive the dignity of the Other from his or her species membership. This becomes apparent once we take note of the paradox that lies implicitly at the basis of the Declaration, namely, that the human rights that all people have *by virtue of their humanity* are also meant to express the absolute uniqueness of each and every human being. As Lévinas puts it in an important essay appearing in 1985 entitled 'The Rights of Man and the Rights of the Other':

> The rights of man manifest the uniqueness or the absolute of the person, despite his or her subsumption under the category of the human species, or because of that subsumption. This is the paradox, or mystery, or novelty of the human being. (Lévinas 1994: 117–18)

According to Lévinas, humans are distinctive among beings by virtue of the fact that, while it is possible to view them in purely *ontological* terms as mere instances of a universal ('human being'), in which their 'singularity vanishes' (Lévinas 1969: 59), it is not possible *ethically* to do so, which requires them to be viewed and treated as unrepeatable and incomparable individuals in their own right. Lévinas is at pains to demonstrate that a human person always exists in the mode of a *concrete* humanity as something that is uniquely and irreducibly hers and not to be confounded with the humanity of her neighbour. What is fundamental to individuals, and which cannot be made common to others of the same species, is precisely interiority or *subjectivity*. Lévinas writes: 'We have always known that it is impossible to form an idea of the human totality, for men have an inner life closed to him who does, however, grasp the comprehensive movements of human groups' (Lévinas 1969: 58). The human person does not have subjective interiority as something over and above his or her humanity, but rather as something that *is* the person and nothing else besides. It is because there is no Being of the person that may go un-actualized in subjectivity that each and every individual is unique in the sense of '*the only one* of his kind' (Lévinas 1994: 117). Each person, then, is her own species, and thus the only possible member of the species, and not a mere specimen of humanity. While it might still strike us as puzzling how Lévinas can still speak of a 'human species', the point to bear in mind is that Lévinas is persuaded that being human – or what he is inclined to refer to in French in the form of a non-anaphoric nominalized adjective '*l'humain*' (for example, Lévinas 1998a: 166) – can only be realized by *individuals* existing separately from one another, each in the context of his or her own subjective existence.

The Enlightenment thinker Kant we know likewise described 'dignity' ('*Würde*') as 'infinitely above all price, with which it cannot be brought into reckoning or comparison without, as it were, a profanation of its sanctity' (Kant 1983: 96). However, dignity, for Kant, resides not in the unique personal status of the person, but in the capacity to impose lawlikeness on one's actions by adopting principles that *any and all persons* can act on, which is why 'all respect for a person is properly only respect for the law... of which that person gives an example' (Kant 1983: 67n). For Lévinas, by contrast, the inherent dignity of persons resides in the putatively 'pathological' factor of their wills that Kant invoked to explain their 'unconquerable disinclination' (Kant 1983: 65) to submit to the authority of reason. Lévinas asks rhetorically: 'Is it so certain that the entire will is *practical reason* in the Kantian sense? Does not the will contain an incoercible part that cannot be obligated by the formalism of universality? And we might even wonder whether, Kant notwithstanding, that incoercible spontaneity, which bears witness both to the multiplicity of humans and the uniqueness of persons, is already pathology and sensibility and "ill will"' (Lévinas 1994: 122). Lévinas thus takes the position that something in *addition* to 'practical reason' is required to account for the difference between human beings, that reason is not the sole origin or justification for human rights, and that it is insufficient to qualify one for membership in the human family with all the rights and *duties* it entails. The 'human aspect of human rights'[1] presupposes on the part of every member of the human family not only reason but compassion, sympathy and a sense of duty, the absence of which makes such membership of the human family questionable.

This is not to suggest that the dignity that Lévinas argues is at the base of human rights has no connection with reason, or that reason is dispensable when it comes to fully respecting and defending those rights. He speaks of 'science' and 'technology' as 'the first conditions for the factual implementation of the respect for the origins of the rights of men' (Lévinas 1994: 119). He harshly criticizes the influential Heideggerian critique of technology, which 'has become a comfortable rhetoric, forgetful of the responsibilities to which a "developing humanity" more and more numerous, calls and which, *without the development of technology, could not be fed*' (Lévinas 1998b: 9). And he is the first to admit the moral superiority of 'the egalitarian and just State, in which man is fulfilled (which is to be set up, and especially to be maintained)' (Lévinas 1981: 159). But Lévinas is more prepared than his predecessor to expose what he sees as the negative consequences of a total and exclusive reliance on standards of reason. What worries Lévinas is the same 'dialectic of Enlightenment' that worried Horkheimer and Adorno, namely, the propensity of reason itself to turn against the rationally emancipated individual. 'In a totally industrialized society or in a totalitarian society', writes Lévinas, 'the rights of man are compromised by the very practices for which they supplied the motivation. Mechanization and enslavement!' (Lévinas 1994: 121). The development of science and technology that was supposed to liberate human beings from nature and lead to human freedom brings with it 'inhuman requirements' 'that make up a new determinism, threatening the free movements that it was said to make possible' (Lévinas

1 This phrase was used by Peng Chung Chang, part of the eight-member Drafting Committee of the UDHR, when he argued that 'stress should be laid upon the human aspect of human rights. A human being had to be constantly conscious of other men, in whose society he lived' (Angle and Svensson 2001: 207). Indeed, it was Chang who successfully argued for the inclusion of the Confucian concept of 'mindfulness of the other person' or 仁 (pinyin: rén) – translated as 'conscience' – in Art. 1 of the UDHR ('All human beings are born free and equal in dignity and rights. They are endowed with reason and conscience and should act towards one another in a spirit of brotherhood.'). This was seen as a way of complementing the reference to *reason*, and striking a balance between rights and duties by underscoring that human beings should act with consideration for their fellow human beings (Angle and Svensson 2001: 209; see also Lindholm 1999: 43–4).

1994: 121). History has shown over and again that in the absence of an ethical counterweight the state has a propensity to subordinate the individual, using physical force if necessary, to increasing government and bureaucratic control. Hereby it ultimately destroys the conditions of its own legitimacy, namely, the protection of the individual: 'An end soon lost in the deployment of means brought to bear. And in the eventuality of a totalitarian state, man is repressed and a mockery made of the rights of man, and the promise of an ultimate return to the rights of man is postponed indefinitely' (Lévinas 1994: 123).

If modern forms of instrumental (or institutionalized) rationality, including politics and the state, are by themselves incapable of protecting human rights this is not because of any formal deficiencies, but because, according to Lévinas, 'the defense of the rights of man corresponds to a vocation *outside* the state, disposing, in a political society, of a kind of extraterritoriality... a vigilance totally different from political intelligence, a lucidity not limited to yielding before the formalism of universality, but upholding justice itself' (Lévinas 1994: 123). This 'extraterritoriality' is not to be construed literally to mean the famous Lockean state of nature preceding the state and presided over by a divine law that declares that all individuals should refrain from causing harm to each other's life, liberty, health, and property. *It is a phenomenological claim about how rights appear to me as one who is 'endowed with reason and conscience and should act towards one another in a spirit of brotherhood'.* Rights do not appear to individuals possessed of reason alone ('To be I and not only an incarnation of a reason is precisely to be capable of seeing the offense of the offended, or the face' (Lévinas 1969: 247)), and are at risk of being repressed by the very political necessities for which they provide a justification. Rather, they appear in the ethical relation with the Other that Lévinas calls 'fraternity' – 'in which the responsibility of one-for-the-other is affirmed, and through which the rights of man manifest themselves *concretely* to consciousness as the rights of the other, for which I am answerable. Their original manifestation as rights of the other person and as the duty for an *I*, as my fraternal duty – that is as the phenomenology of the rights of man' (Lévinas 1994: 125).

The obligation to help the needy

One crucial article in the Declaration that is worth examining in this connection is Article 25, which states that persons who cannot, through their own capacities, secure the conditions of an adequate livelihood have a right to social security:

> Everyone has the right to a standard of living adequate for the health and well-being of himself and of his family, including food, clothing, housing and medical care and necessary social services, and the right to security in the event of unemployment, sickness, disability, widowhood, old age or other lack of livelihood in circumstances beyond his control.

The article fits well enough with the framework that seeks to outline those positive ('welfare') rights whose recognition is indispensable for the dignity, life and agency of persons. But the article does not tell us how this is to be ensured. When someone has a right to something then some agent or agency must have a corresponding duty to provide it. Whose duty then is it to ensure that someone has an adequate standard of living: food, clothing, housing, medical care and social services?

The Preamble to the Declaration makes it clear that 'Member States have pledged themselves to achieve, in co-operation with the United Nations, the promotion of universal respect for and observance of human rights and fundamental freedoms'.[2] This implies that obligations to meet the dignity-threatening needs of rights-holders are originally *unallocated*, positive obligations awaiting the allocation of agents (or agencies) to recipients by the state and the international community as a whole through a process of institutionalization. Notably, Article 22 underscores that: 'Everyone, as a member of society, has the right to social security and is entitled to realization, *through national effort and international co-operation and in accordance with the organization and resources of each State*, of the economic, social and cultural rights indispensable for his dignity and the free development of his personality.'[3] Under human rights law, then, the state and the international community have the responsibility of providing for the individual who lacks the resources to provide for him- or herself. But what happens when states fall short of their pledges or become disorganized? What are we to do in a society that prefers to ignore its poor and least advantaged, and values lower taxes over a commitment to welfare?

In Lévinas' ethics, obligations to help the needy, in particular an obligation to feed the hungry, are not merely institutionalized welfare obligations awaiting allocation by the state to agents or agencies. While it is doubtlessly the case that in modern societies the obligation to help the needy is often best fulfilled at the institutional level in the form of the welfare state, Lévinas is clear that *the fundamental obligation to help the needy is neither chosen nor allocated*: 'Prior to any act, I am concerned with the Other, and I can never be absolved from this responsibility' (Lévinas 1989: 290). This pre-contractarian and pre-constitutional obligation, is according to Lévinas ineluctable and inalienable and, most importantly of all, *rests with me in particular*. To use an idiom from Dostoyevsky's *The Brothers Karamazov* that Lévinas never tires of quoting: 'every one of us is responsible for everyone else in every way, and I most of all' (Dostoyevsky 1984: 339; quoted by Lévinas 1981: 146 *passim*).

To be sure, this 'most of all' makes little sense from the point of view of logic according to which guilt and responsibility are of a fixed amount that is divided among individuals. If we all have responsibility for each other, then is it not the case that we have it *equally*? But, if someone reneges on his or her responsibility to the needy, Lévinas suggests, I now find myself with more responsibility than

[2] UDHR, Preamble, para. 6. [3] UDHR, Art. 22.

I had before, namely, my original responsibility *plus* the responsibility of the one who reneged (cf. also Singer 2000). What this suggests is that responsibility multiplies rather than divides, leading to the apparently illogical result that I can be *fully* responsible, say, for the death of someone notwithstanding that others in the same circumstances who did not do their 'fair share' can also be held at least *partially* responsible. Of course, it is frequently pointed out that, while we have a duty to help save the starving, no one of us could possibly save all the starving people in the world. There are simply too many indigent and needy, and none of us has the resources. Therefore, *I personally* cannot be under an obligation to help all those who have a right to be fed. But Lévinas' ethics does not traffic in abstract duties and generalities. There is no *perfect* obligation to meet a universal demand for help for those whose agency is under threat. Speaking in *Totality and Infinity* of the power of the Other's face to summons me to respond with 'an infinite responsibility', Lévinas asserts: 'The infinity of responsibility denotes not its actual immensity, but a responsibility increasing in the measure that it is assumed; duties become greater in the measure that they are accomplished. The better I accomplish my duty the fewer rights I have; the more I am just the more guilty I am' (Lévinas 1969: 244).

The 'infinity' of responsibility is not mathematical but refers to the impossibility of discharging completely a duty to save *this* person whom I could help but didn't. It should be mentioned, if only in passing, that, in living the normal affluent way of life we have come to expect in the West, we can never be certain that we have not unthinkingly, without realizing it, deprived someone of some means to life. For example, when we purchase goods made of cash crops imported from people in the developing world, do we not fail to discharge our responsibilities to the very people we ought to be helping? Lévinas puts it even more strongly: 'When we sit down at the table in the morning and drink coffee, we kill an Ethiopian who doesn't have any coffee' (Lévinas 1988: 173).

Self-worth and moral dignity

But why is it the case that the 'better I accomplish my duty the fewer rights I have'? Do I not have equal dignity and a face too? And do I not therefore have the same rights as other members of the human family? Perhaps the most radical aspect of Lévinas' ethics, the part that is most difficult to swallow by those who attempt to ground the notion of dignity and rights in reason alone, is the priority that Lévinas cedes to the rights of the Other over my rights. It is essentially this point made in *Totality and Infinity* where Lévinas writes: 'What I permit myself to demand of myself is not comparable with what I have the right to demand of the Other' (Lévinas 1969: 53). Freedom here ('what I permit myself to demand of myself') is the freedom that is required to exercise an obligation, not the freedom to claim a right for myself. Unlike the traditional view on the rights of man, in which my rights are seen as competing with those of my neighbour, whereby my right to freedom can always be exercised at the expense of the rights of the other (say, the right to life), Lévinas underscores the sense in which the rights of the other have priority over my own. This indeed is how they appear *phenomenologically*: 'In their original *mise-en-scène* there is also the affirmation, as a manifestation of freedom, of the rights of the obligated person, not only as the result of the simple transference and . . . generalization of the rights of man as they appear in others to the obligated person' (Lévinas 1994: 125). For Lévinas, rights *appear* in the first instance as the rights of the other. My own dignity and (positive) freedom, understood as the capacity to transcend my natural impulses is necessarily hidden from me as long as it is exercised solely in the service of spontaneity and enjoyment. As Lévinas states: 'My consciousness of my ego reveals no right to me. My freedom shows itself to be arbitrary' (Lévinas 1990: 17). It is only when I am confronted with Others' needs that the *non-arbitrary* exercise of freedom is made manifest to me, in whose name my own call for recognition and respect, which derive from my responsibility to the Other as an investing of one's own freedom, becomes justified for the first time. Lévinas is perhaps the only philosopher who has sufficiently appreciated how much my dignity is bound up with the defense of the rights of others, in the form of responsibility for the Other, which 'is not something constructed by philosophy; it is the unreal reality of men persecuted in the daily history of the world, whose dignity and meaning metaphysics has never recognized, from which philosophers turn their faces' (Lévinas 1987: 150).

References

Angle, S. C., and Svensson, M. 2001. *The Chinese Human Rights Reader: Documents and Commentary*, 1900–2000. New York: East Gate Book

Dostoyevsky, F. 1984. *The Brothers Karamazov*, trans. D. Magarshack. London: Penguin

Husserl, E. 1991. *Cartesian Meditations*, trans. D. Cairns. Dordrecht: Kluwer

Kant, I. 1983. *Groundwork of the Metaphysics of Morals*, trans. H. J. Paton. London: Hutchinson

Lévinas, E. 1969. *Totality and Infinity*, trans. A. Lingis. Pittsburgh, PA: Duquesne University Press

1981. *Otherwise Than Being or Beyond Essence*, trans. A. Lingis. The Hague: Martinus Nijhoff

1987. 'No Identity', in *Collected Philosophical Papers*, trans. A. Lingis. The Hague: Martinus Nijhoff

1988. 'The Paradox of Morality Interview', *The Provocation of Lévinas*, ed. R. Bernasconi and D. Wood. London: Routledge

1989. 'Ethics and Politics', in *The Lévinas Reader*, trans. S. Hand. Oxford: Blackwell

1990. 'A Religion for Adults', in *Difficult Freedom*, trans. S. Hand. Baltimore, MD: Johns Hopkins University Press

1994. 'The Rights of Man and the Rights of the Other', in *Outside the Subject*, trans. M. B. Smith. Stanford University Press

1998a. 'Notes on Meaning', in *Of God Who Comes to Mind*, trans. B. Bergo. Stanford University Press

1998b. 'Secularization and Hunger', trans. B. Bergo, *Graduate Faculty Philosophy Journal* 20(2)–21(1): 3–12

1998c. 'The Permanent and the Human in Husserl', in *Discovering Existence with Husserl*, trans. and ed. R. A. Cohen and M. B. Smith. Evanston, IL: Northwestern University Press

1999a. 'The Prohibition Against Representation and "The Rights of Man"', in *Alterity and Transcendence*, trans. M. B. Smith. London: Athlone Press

1999b. 'The Rights of the Other Man', in *Alterity and Transcendence*, trans. M. B. Smith. London: Athlone Press

Lindholm, T. 1999. 'Article 1', in *The Universal Declaration of Human Rights: A Common Standard of Achievement*, ed. G. Alfredsson and A. Eide. The Hague, Boston: Martinus Nijhoff Publishers

Singer, P. 2000. *Writings on an Ethical Life*. New York: The Echo Press

30

Dignity, fragility, singularity in Paul Ricœur's ethics

MAUREEN JUNKER-KENNY

Both in his approach to ethics and in his treatment of concrete cases as matters of 'practical wisdom', Paul Ricœur has developed a distinctive position towards grounding and specifying what is called 'human dignity' in Kant. It appears in references to what is 'above all price', using Kant's term for indicating what is not at our disposition since it is the foundation, not the object of our autonomy (Ricœur 2005: 237).[1] The reference to dignity is not made explicit, but is present in examples of its denial which give rise to the moral feeling of 'indignation', and in identifying the limit of tolerance in what is 'intolerable' (Ricœur 1996: 198–9).[2] While it does not belong to the terms that are subjected to an analysis of the philosophical problems contained in them, such as 'autonomy' and 'imputability', it is given a place of immediate evidence:

> [I]n Kant himself, the subjective side of imputation relies on moral feelings that constitute what he called the rational motives of action. Only one motive, only

[1] 'History showcases the ever-increasing defeat of what is without price, driven back by the advances of a commercial society . . . The question then arises: Do any non-commercial goods still exist? . . . Conversely, perhaps we can find the gift in every form of what is priceless, whether it is moral dignity, which has a value but not a price, or the integrity of the human body, and the non-commercialization of its organs' (Kant 1964: 102–3). Kant states: 'In the kingdom of ends, everything has either a *price* or a *dignity*. If it has a price, something else can be put in its place as an *equivalent*; if it is exalted above all price and so admits of no equivalent, then it has a dignity. What is relative to universal human inclinations and needs has a *market price* . . . but that which constitutes the sole condition under which anything can be an end in itself has not merely a relative value – that is, a price – but has an intrinsic value – that is, *dignity*.'

[2] 'The occasions to be indignant present themselves in dispersed order: what is there in common between the disgust sparked by the crime of a paedophile, the horror that continues to inspire the stories of deportation and extermination camps, the contempt ignited by vicious attacks of rampaging slander directed against an honest man, the revolt against the manifestations of racism, against the disguised returns of slavery, against the extreme inequalities, against the politics of exclusion? . . . If then it were possible to recognize in indignation, an eminently reactive feeling, a positive motivation, it would be the responsibility with regard to the fragile in its multiple forms.'

> one reason is considered by Kant: respect. One of the tasks of moral philosophy today would be to enlarge, to expand, the field of moral feelings concerning shame, courage, admiration, enthusiasm, veneration, indignation. These feelings have to do with dignity, a kind of immediate recognition of the dignity of a moral subject. (Ricœur 2002: 287)

As his interest in the feelings that express the human capability for morality shows, Ricœur sees the need to elaborate the connection between Kant's formal concept of freedom and its concrete appearance; he treats the capabilities of speaking, acting and narrating as components of a self-understanding that reaches a normative level in 'imputability'. He seeks to align Kant's foundational concept of the 'good will' with the Aristotelian starting-point of each individual's motivation to lead a flourishing life. Beginning with 'solicitude', the moral dimension is no longer a demand isolated in its contrast to inclination, but is linked to an anthropology of human striving 'to live with and for others in just institutions' (Ricœur 1992: 72). The content of autonomy, respect for the moral law and for the other, is reinterpreted as being 'a wish before it is an imperative' (Ricœur 2007: xv).[3] Reworking Kant's approach in light of Aristotle's, Ricœur emphasizes the *intention* of morality both at its starting-point and in concrete judgments; he explores the motivation for moral action, and its application within the specific domains in which 'equitable' solutions have to be found that honour both the singularity of persons and the universal norm. Before turning to the spheres of law, biomedical ethics, and memories of violence and forgiveness in which the concrete meaning of dignity has to be specified, I shall outline the framework established for ethics by his philosophical anthropology and hermeneutics of action.

Capable, fragile and striving: self and agency in Ricœur's anthropology and ethics

In his analysis of core human capabilities that lead up to 'imputability', the hermeneutical philosopher is careful to outline the transitions from one course of enquiry to another. Beginning with a 'minimal definition of capability as the power to cause something to happen' (Ricœur 2006: 18), he develops the capabilities to speak, act and narrate as competences which allow agents to experience their power of initiative but which need supporting conditions to be realized concretely (discussed in the first subsection). With 'imputability', a form of self-recognition arises that brings in a different dimension, a reversal from mastery to need, as well as an ethical reflection on what is good, right and equitable (discussed in the second subsection).

[3] 'Justice, in this reading, is an integral part of the wish to live well . . . the wish to live in just institutions arises from the same level of morality as do the desire for personal fulfilment and the reciprocity of friendship. The just is first an object of desire, of a lack, of a wish. It begins as a wish before it is an imperative.'

Capabilities and the need for institutions to enable concrete realizations of freedom

The specifically human capabilities of speaking and acting spontaneously receive a reflective turn in the ability to narrate which constitutes the possibility of biographical and moral identity. In narrating its story, the self is characterized by a dialectic between two aspects: continuity and sameness on the one hand, and spontaneity on the other, the first designated as *idem*, the second as *ipse*. New departures and self-definitions can be worked out by taking a stance to what is given and inherited, by reviewing courses of action and reconceiving goals. It takes effort to construct the 'narrative unity of a life', as Ricœur calls it (with Alasdair MacIntyre), and it faces temptations for easy solutions, such as self-serving and ideological rationalizations.

> The successive questions – who speaks to whom? Who acts with or against other agents? Who tells stories about himself or herself and about strangers held as friends or enemies? – find a kind of culmination in the question: who is capable of imputation? (Ricœur 2006: 20)

This culmination, however, does not mean that the prior self-expressions can be superseded. Imputability as the ultimate designation that unites them in a different register depends on the continued availability of the first three capabilities. The insight that there is no imputability without the prior experience of competence in speaking, acting and narrating will affect the concrete interpretations of dignity that will be examined below. The juridical sphere of criminal law, based on the necessary assumption of a generic accountability, has to seek to understand individual circumstances in concrete cases of judgment.

Being designated as author in the use of one's capabilities moves the analysis into a different territory: from a 'descriptive' to a 'normative' framework (Ricœur 2006: 18, 22). The 'rights' that some theorists, among them Amartya Sen and Martha Nussbaum, seek to develop in connection with capabilities, are identified as belonging to a different order, which reveals a need that assumes interaction with others. Rights have to be granted, or can be disputed, they do not follow automatically from the existence of specific capabilities. With a primary interest in the concrete historical realization of rights, not in the Kantian emphasis on duties as their counterpart, Ricœur analyzes them as a matter of 'creative conflictuality' (Ricœur 2006: 23) that has already made the step to conceive negativity as a moment within a process of recognition. At stake is the choice between two paradigms in interpreting the conflicts that arise between humans: in terms of a fundamentally negative attitude to otherness which is seen as threatening the survival of the self, or from a 'normative motivation' whereby the social bond is constituted by recognizing and negotiating requests. In this framework, the key need is not conceived as a Hobbesian struggle for survival, but as a quest for *recognition* as an equal. The motivation to mutually grant each other such a status is a moral one, rather than naturalistic and compelled by fear (Ricœur 2005: 170). At this stage of the debate, in his analysis of the necessary steps to link the anthropological concept of capabilities to the legal concept of rights, Ricœur remains at the level of legality, of the creation of institutions in which the key term of Kant's deontology, 'respect', can be translated into juridical structures that underpin the 'historical actualization of freedom' (Ricœur 2006: 22). This level is about equality in terms of rights, as Ricœur's quote from Joel Feinberg makes clear: 'What we call "human dignity" is nothing else than the recognized capacity to require a right' (Ricœur 2006: 24).[4] This definition operationalizes dignity as recognizing the quest for new rights in the interest of new subjective capabilities; their refusal is experienced as contempt. As in the global discrepancy between 'the equal *ascription* of rights and the unequal *distribution* of primary goods', also in the sphere of symbolic recognition 'a negative motivation is a powerful factor of social change'. Ricœur adds as conditions two factors that belong to the sphere of ethics – 'self-respect' and a 'will' to engage in political action – for this motivation to be successful: 'under the condition of a parallel increase of self-respect and of the will to play a role in the enlargement of the sphere of subjective rights' (Ricœur 2006: 24).

What needs to be analyzed now is the way in which Ricœur interprets this quest for recognition in the shape of rights; it is in terms that presuppose an intrinsic understanding of dignity, not merely the form it takes in political struggles.

> [R]ecognition in the juridical sense (of each person as free and equal) adds to the basic capabilities considered in our first part under the aegis of self-recognition the new capabilities proceeding from the conjunction between the universal validity of the norm and the singularity of the persons. (Ricœur 2006: 24)

By contrasting 'universality' and 'singularity', he introduces a limit also to the norm, proposing a radicalized version of Kant's notion of respect for human beings as ends in themselves: in cases of conflict between duties, the ultimate point of reference is not the universal rule but the individual as an end in herself.[5]

[4] Quoting from Feinberg 1980.

[5] In the section entitled 'Respect and Conflict' in Ricœur 1992: 262–73, the author elaborates on the hidden contradiction in the famous humanistic formulation of the Categorical Imperative: 'a fine dividing line tends to separate the universalist version of the imperative, represented by the idea of humanity, from what can be called the pluralist version, represented by the idea of persons as ends in themselves. According to Kant, there is no opposition here, to the extent that humanity designates the dignity *by reason of which* persons deserve respect, despite – so to speak – their plurality. The possibility of conflict arises, however, as soon as the otherness of persons, inherent in the very idea of *human* plurality, proves to be, in certain remarkable circumstances, incompatible with the universality of the rules that underlie the idea of humanity. Respect then tends to split up into respect for the law and respect for persons. Under these conditions, practical wisdom may consist in

The tension between 'universal' and 'singular' is mirrored in the architecture of Ricœur's ethics which will be explained in the following subsection. It will investigate how dignity in the intrinsic sense appears at each of its levels.

Ethics as solicitude, moral norm, and singularity in practical wisdom

Prior to analyzing the distinctive feature of each level in the sequence of self-reflection on the ethical and moral dimensions of agency, the field of practical reason has to be characterized.

From imputability to attestation

In the preceding reflections offered by Ricœur as clarifications towards the efforts of some fellow-theorists, 'imputability' has been identified as a turning-point to a normative analysis. It takes acts as having individuals as their authors and thus opens up their qualification not just as socially given, but as claiming 'validity'. However, the question of imputability belongs to the sphere of theoretical discourse in which the Kantian antinomy between freedom and determination by natural laws is under debate (Ricœur 2006: 19, 21). In the sphere of practical reason, by contrast, the challenge of opposite interpretations is not in terms of cosmological, but of existential truth.[6] In ethics, imputability becomes the claim to autonomy which is a matter of 'attestation'; its opposite is 'suspicion', as opposed to a theoretical questioning of its status (2006: 18). A contestation of freedom in the practical sense of agency cannot be refuted by theoretical reasons but only resisted in a living proof.

The following analyses spell out a position that clearly indicates where it takes up and where it parts company with classical and contemporary approaches to social ethics. Its well-known combination of two approaches that are usually understood as opposites – an Aristotelian ethics of striving for a flourishing life and a Kantian analysis of the human experience of moral self-reflection – will be discussed only insofar as it provides a framework in which human dignity is situated: seeking its foundations in a desire that already includes the aspiration towards just structures also for anonymous others; exploring the need in view of human violence to rise to the obligation to respect the other as a limit to the self's wishes; and conceiving a third level, 'practical wisdom', in which the faculty of judgment is dedicated to combining the critically examined insights of the first two. Ricœur argues for the possibility of seeking convergences between the two historically opposed approaches. The first decisive move is to interpret Aristotle beyond the limits of the *polis*, effectively broadening a communitarian

giving priority to the respect for persons, in the name of the solicitude that is addressed to persons in their irreplaceable singularity' (Ibid.: 262). Cf. also *ibid.*: 222.

6 The distinction and the relationship between theoretical and practical truth claims is discussed in Ricœur 2007: 58–71.

framework into a cosmopolitan one, and to take Kant's foundational concept of the 'good will' as an indication of the originating benevolence human beings desire to extend to each other. Ricœur highlights not only the shared symbolic world in which the individual's quest for existence takes place and the distancing ability[7] required in relationships, but also analyzes the self in its quality as an 'other'.

Three levels of ethics emerging in self-reflection on agency

Ricœur approaches the self in its ethical dimension from the way in which it perceives its agency. Understanding the whole realm of action as oriented towards the anticipation of being able to evaluate the ultimate unity of one's biography as a flourishing life, Ricœur identifies the elements belonging to this aim (*visée*) as 'living well, with and for others, in just institutions' (Ricœur 1992: 172). The good thus consists, as Christof Mandry has observed, both in a formal goal, namely, the narrative unity of a life, and in a substantive one, albeit expressed without naming specific goods, as the capability to act.[8] Already this level contains a normative dimension, in perceiving and agreeing that the 'others' one lives 'with and for' have the same desire and should have the same opportunity to access resources for action. The capability for morality on which human dignity is based for Kant can be seen to find an initial expression in the spontaneous benevolence called 'solicitude.'

On the one hand, against Kant's dichotomy between inclination and duty, Ricœur highlights the continuity present in the 'good will' extolled by Kant as the only thing that can be 'taken as good without qualification'.[9] On the other hand, he equally spells out the distinct character of the second, moral level in its formality and universality. The metaphor for this type of reflection on one's action, 'sieve of the norm' (Ricœur 1992: 170), indicates an act of critical discernment between maxims or intentions that either respect or violate the other. If 'self-esteem' was based on the awareness of one's capability to act, 'self-respect' is won by going against some possibilities of action and by recognizing the other also as a limit to one's own agency. Here, the previously defended continuity between the inclination to benevolence and duty is interrupted by the call of conscience which Ricœur identifies as one form of otherness in the

[7] Ricœur 2006: 23, as distinct from a 'fusional attachment'.

[8] Mandry 2002: 219–20: 'The "good" contains a hidden double function . . . a teleological goal orientation . . . towards the integrating good of the flourishing life . . . [O]n the other hand, however, a content determination, even if only in its formal shape', resulting in a 'connection between striving for the "good" and the self-esteem which has its foundation in being able to act (*Tun-Können*)' (translation by the present author).

[9] The opening sentence of Kant's *Groundwork of the Metaphysic of Morals* reads: 'It is impossible to conceive anything at all in the world, or even out of it, which can be taken as good without qualification, except a *good will*' (BA 1).

self (Ricœur 1992: 341–55). The ability for independent, principled judgment is also highlighted against the historical experience of the need to resist the pull towards conformity and to stand up against corrupted institutions, as in the National Socialist state and other totalitarian regimes in the twentieth century. Such opposition can be seen as historical examples of intrinsic dignity, as the concrete capability to discern and defend what is morally relevant also at a cost to oneself.

Most of all, however, dignity is identified with singularity in the conflict that erupts between regard for the rule and doing justice to the individual. It is the reason why a third level, 'practical wisdom', is introduced: it has the task of judging in conflicts of duties which course of action is relatively the best to protect persons as ends in themselves, in their irreducible plurality, also from rigoristic applications of norms. These need to be tested not only for their universalizability, but also for their equity in relation to agents in their particularity. This level will allow questions to surface that could not be known at the theoretical level of constructing the architecture of ethics: about the self, who is more than the sum of his (successful or failed) acts; about the role of asymmetry, of love in relation to justice, and of the gift as a unilateral initiative; about religious and cultural traditions that can reinvigorate their own heritage of supporting dignity by addressing their unkept promises.

Dignity in concrete interpretations by practical wisdom

We have seen from the preceding account that the premises on which Ricœur establishes the foundations for an ethics of justice are fundamentally different from contract theories. Their pattern of strict reciprocity is absent, and a readiness to engage in one-sided, asymmetric action uncertain of any return is implied: the wish for a flourishing life includes living with and for others; the capability for morality is evidenced at the second level where decisions against one's self-interest are taken, rising to what the agent's conscience urges; and at the third level the needs of human beings in their singularity, not in their contract obligations, are key. What follows is the exploration of processes of judgment on how to concretize dignity as an absolute value under finite, culturally particular conditions. It is to be expected that Ricœur's interest will not be whether specific liberty rights are being violated, but how to do justice to the normative core of any rights-based system of governance. This is where both Kant and he differ from a liberal emphasis on rights. It is not just the state that is asked to deliver but also the citizens; they are seen first and foremost as solicitous and moral beings. It is true that all they can be committed to externally is legality in the sense of outward observance of the law; yet this qualification is to protect freedom of motivation and conscience and does not absolve citizens from their sense of morality. The one-sided readiness to respect even the hostile other challenges an understanding of ethics that can be fulfilled by mere reciprocity. As the counterpoint to a mere 'logic of equivalence' Ricœur introduces religious motives, namely, '*agape*', nourished by 'superabundance' and an 'economy of the gift' (for example, Ricœur 1995).

However, beyond Kant's idea that the guiding principle – to honour humanity in one's own person and in that of every other – is self-explanatory, the hermeneutical philosopher points out a double need for interpretation: both of the principle, and of the situation and individuals in question (Mandry 2002: 221). In the three domains to be examined now, (1) criminal law, (2) intellectual and mental disability, and (3) memories of histories of violence, it has to be specified how 'dignity' can be recognized and safeguarded through adequate conceptual analyses, institutions and policies.

The dignity of the offender in criminal law

The approach Ricœur takes in his article, 'Autonomy and Vulnerability', is that of a philosophical anthropology in which the 'paradox' of autonomy and vulnerability is uncovered (Ricœur 2007, 72–3). What now becomes decisive is the connection established before between the four capabilities of speaking, acting, narrating and being imputable: 'Let us say therefore that a subject capable of leading his or her life in agreement to an idea of narrative coherence is an autonomous subject' (Ricœur 2007: 80). Yet, what about those who have not acquired the narrative capacity to evaluate their deeds against their intentions and motivations? Here, Ricœur alerts lawyers to the possibility that:

> jurists run the greater risk of having to deal with individuals who are incapable of constructing a narrative identity, of identifying themselves not only through some history but with some history... The handling of one's own life, as a possibly coherent narrative, represents a high level competence that has to be taken as one of the major components of the autonomy of a subject of rights. (Ricœur 2007: 79–80)

When it comes to the institutional level of a court case, a discrepancy is noted: 'what the codes disavow are violations of the law – but what the courts punish are persons' (Ricœur 2004: 489). These persons, however, are being identified as authors in senses they may not experience themselves. Society's task is to institutionalize ways in which the failure of early processes of inclusion and participation can still be turned around: 'Punishment has two ends, a short-term one, which is the protection of society as regards a threat to public order, and a long-term one, which is the restoration of social peace. Every measure of rehabilitation, in our penal system, is meant to serve this ultimate end' (Ricœur 2007: 230). The social bond has been broken not only by the perpetrator. What needs to find symbolic expression in penal institutions, is the equal value of each fellow-citizen:

> [M]oral philosophy has always underscored the connection between justice and equality... This model of distributive justice presupposes a more radical form of equality, equality in the value of every agent. The formula for this basic

> kind of equality is: your life is as important, as significant, as valuable as my own. (Ricœur 2007: 224)

The goal and standard for evaluations of penal systems is their ability to reintegrate the person who has become guilty in front of the law and against specific fellow-citizens:

> We are confronted with the absence of a practical alternative to such a loss of liberty through imprisonment. Admitting this is equivalent to admitting a collective failure on the part of our society... What remains is the duty to preserve for those detainees the possibility of their reinscription into the community of free citizens... to put an end to the physical and symbolic exclusion which is imprisonment. (Ricœur 2007: 230)

The goal of the judicial system is to 'transfer conflicts from the plane of violence to that of language and discourse' (Ricœur 2007: 221). In each case, practical wisdom conducts a double interpretation of the narratives of the incident and of the specific laws in question violated by the offense. What links these agents to the next group is a fragility that appears in their lack of articulacy and integration into the symbolic world of a society. The question arising with regard to mentally and intellectually disabled fellow-humans is how to arrive at an adequate analysis of their difference while equally highlighting the shared condition of fragility and mortality.

Respect as a response to the difference and vulnerability of intellectual disability

In this essay, the task of translating the absolute value of dignity is directed both to structures and to relationships. It is about laying 'the basis for respect – and, beyond such respect, for the friendship – we owe to the physically and mentally handicapped, as well as to all others struck by infirmities' (Ricœur 2007: 187–97, 187). Ricœur analyzes how a medical deficit model underrates capacities and feeds into an additional social rejection based on an attitude of possessing health as an asset. The alternative model is to see all human life as capable of perception and initiative in its environment, and to encourage an understanding of shared vulnerability that does not have to be the opposite of happiness.[10]

Distinguishing (with Georges Canguilhem) a biological, a social and an existential sense of the pathological, he opposes the negative reading in which 'the pathological signifies a deficit or deficiency' with a positive one in which 'it signifies another, an *other* organization, one that has its own laws' (Ricœur

[10] Ricœur (1992: 269) refers to 'the proper use of solicitude, when it moves in the narrow space where it remains true that there is no ethics without happiness, but where it is false that happiness excludes suffering'.

2007: 190). The existential level of an encounter with 'this other way of being-in-the-world, with its own values' gives rise to 'respect' (*ibid.*: 190). This analysis presupposes a capability that Ricœur had identified also in other contexts, namely, the possibility to enter into a different world, to actively attempt to understand difference between humans in their aspirations. In his discussion of different spheres of valuation, the underlying ability identified is one of crossing borders.

> [W]e can develop a typology of the types of criticism directed by one world to another . . . the most interesting issue . . . lies in the capacity to awaken the actors of one world to the values of another world . . . A new dimension of personhood is thereby revealed, that of understanding a world other than one's own, a capacity we can compare to that of learning a foreign language to the point of being able to appreciate one's own language as one among many. (Ricœur 2005: 209)

This awareness of a foundational likeness, comparability and translatability is at the basis of recognizing dignity in diversity, even if the difference is one of disease. It is a matter of 'recognition of positive values attached to any disease . . . something other than a deficiency, a lack, a negative quantity. It is another way of being in the world. It is in this sense that the patient has dignity, is an object of respect. The value of the disease and of the patient remains even within the shadow of madness' (Ricœur 2007: 197).[11] The task for physicians, carers and friends is to compensate for lost functions, without, however, extinguishing the other's own initiative that remains crucial for their self-esteem:

> How are we to reach, beyond the disease, the patient's still-possible resources of the will to live, of initiative, of evaluation, of decision? . . . [S]elf-esteem . . . also includes within itself an expectation of approbation coming from these others. In this sense, self-esteem is both a reflexive and a relational phenomenon, where the notion of dignity unites the two faces of such recognition. (Ricœur 2007: 194, 196)

'Reflexivity' relates to the awareness of one's power to act, which is thus taken in an existence-related rather than a cognitive sense. Ricœur concludes the article that is dedicated to Jean Vanier, the founder of the Arche communities for people with intellectual disabilities, with a reflection on the basic human condition:

> It is important for the supposedly healthy individual to discern in the handicapped individual those resources of conviviality, of sympathy, of living with and suffering with that are bound expressly to the fact of being ill or handicapped. Yes, it is up to those who are well to welcome this proposition regarding the meaning of

[11] In Ricœur 2007: 194, he observes that the 'threat of madness, along with the fear of social retribution, replaces the fear of hell'.

> illness and to allow it to aid them in bearing their own precariousness, their own vulnerability, their own mortality. (Ricœur 2007: 197)

Histories of violence and forgiveness as a gift

A high regard for spontaneity, for agency as a quest for existence, for trust in fellow humans and a 'fiduciary connection' (Ricœur 2007: 100, 105) rather than defence of one's negative rights, has become evident in Ricœur's reconstructions of basic human capabilities and pursuits. However, agency does not completely define the self. In his reflections on forgiveness after the monumental histories of violence that have marked the twentieth century, he identifies as the crucial move the willingness and ability to release an agent from her acts by first distinguishing between self and act. 'Everything, finally, hangs on the possibility of separating the agent from the action' (Ricœur 2004: 490) through a 'liberating word . . . you are better than your actions' (*ibid.*: 493). Forgiveness is the only way in which the sources of good agency can be reopened. 'Under the sign of forgiveness, the guilty person is to be considered capable of something other than his offenses and his faults' (*ibid.*). He is 'rendered capable of beginning again: this would be the figure of unbinding that commands all the others' (*ibid.*: 490).

However, this liberating act must remain a prerogative that may also not be granted. It belongs to the dignity of the victims that they can choose either course of action. Unlike other types of agency, forgiveness cannot be turned into an institution, as Ricœur insists in his sharp critique of an amnesty sought at the cost of victims in order to establish a superficial truce. Forgiveness remains a gift, and thus reveals something priceless that cannot be converted into calculable equivalence.

By giving a lead role to practical wisdom in its mediating function between universality and singularity, the hermeneutical philosopher shows confidence in the resources from which humans draw to deal with incompatibilities, tensions, and tragic choices. His vision for democracy is one of multiple traditions in search of political authority that can be legitimated within a public sphere of which they are co-founders. Among them are the religious traditions that keep open the thought of an ultimate, gracious Other and the possibility of understanding and leading life as received in an economy of the gift. Dignity can draw from resources that pose a limit to marketability and self-objectification. A final sign for the respect accorded to singularity is the guarantee for radical critics and anarchists to decline participating in this venture shared between 'heterogeneous traditions'. While they seek to convince each other's members that they are creditable and that their resources, 'reinvigorated and driven by their unkept promises', are worthy of consideration, they should concede:

> Finally . . . a place has to be reserved for dissensus and for the right to respond to the offer of creditability on the part of any authorities in place by a refusal to grant credit to them. This calculated risk, which should be recognized as

having a supporting marginal role, is, after all, part of the very idea of 'credit', of accrediting. (Ricœur 2007: 105)

References

Feinberg, J. 1980. *Rights, Justice, and the Bounds of Liberty: Essays in Social Philosophy.* Princeton University Press

Kant, I. 1964. *Groundwork of the Metaphysic of Morals*, trans. H. J. Paton. New York: Harper

Mandry, C. 2002. *Ethische Identität und christlicher Glaube: Theologische Ethik im Spannungsfeld von Theologie und Philosophie.* Mainz: Grünewald

Ricœur, P. 1992. *Oneself as Another*, trans. K. Blamey. Chicago: University of Chicago Press

1995. 'Love and Justice', in *Figuring the Sacred: Religion, Narrative and Imagination*, trans. D. Pellauer, ed. M. Wallace. Minneapolis, MN: Fortress, 315–29

1996. 'The Erosion of Tolerance and the Resistance of the Intolerable', in P. Ricœur (ed.), *Tolerance Between Intolerance and the Intolerable.* Oxford: Berghahn, 189–201

2002. 'Ethics and Human Capability: A Response', in J. Wall, W. Schweiker and D. Hall (eds.), *Paul Ricœur and Contemporary Moral Thought.* London, New York: Routledge, 279–90

2004. *Memory, History, Forgetting*, trans. K. Blamey and D. Pellauer. Chicago: University of Chicago Press

2005. *The Course of Recognition*, trans. D. Pellauer. Cambridge, MA: Harvard University Press

2006. 'Capabilities and Rights', in S. Deneulin, M. Nebel and N. Sagovsky (eds.), *Transforming Unjust Structures: The Capability Approach.* Dordrecht: Springer, 17–26

2007. *Reflections on the Just*, trans. D. Pellauer. Chicago: University of Chicago Press

31

Human dignity as universal nobility

CHRISTIAN NEUHÄUSER AND RALF STOECKER

The concept of human dignity, despite its growing importance in legal texts and declarations in the last decades, is notoriously contested in moral philosophy and legal theory. There is no agreement either on what human dignity is or whether one should care much about it. We will show how these questions could be answered given the assumption that the expression 'human dignity' is to be read literally, as dignity of humans, where 'dignity' is understood as *dignity proper*, i.e. dignity as it is usually ascribed outside of legal contexts. Dignity proper has played an important role in the history of mankind. It is sometimes also called 'social dignity' because it is bound to social relations, or 'contingent dignity', on the assumption that having dignity proper is due to contingencies of life and one's own behaviour (in contrast to human dignity as an essential feature of humankind). Dignity proper therefore depends on being treated with respect by others and on being able to present oneself as being of equal dignity in various practical contexts.

Dignity proper is part of an extended conceptual space of evaluative terms which are important in moral life, including, among others, decency, nobility, rank, honour, respect, esteem, grace, decorum, merit, self-respect, coolness, offence, humiliation, degradation, shame. It is obvious, historically, that the concept of dignity proper must have played some role in the development of the concept of human dignity. There are a number of good reasons, however, that speak for a sharp distinction between human dignity and dignity proper:

(1) Most importantly, dignity proper is fragile, it has to be earned and can be lost, it is unequally distributed and perhaps also bound to conditions like social status, birth etc. Human dignity on the other hand is usually regarded as innate, inviolable, and equally shared by all men and women.
(2) Despite its prevalence in everyday moral talk, reference to dignity proper is apparently rather old-fashioned. Only a minority of people would regard dignity proper as being of utmost value, compared to other values like well-being, health, leading one's life as one chooses etc. Human dignity on the other hand is believed to be the most fundamental and powerful value.
(3) Human dignity is strongly debated in an area of bioethics where dignity proper evidently is not an issue at all: with regard to the way human embryos

should be treated. Thus, it seems, either this debate has been off target from the outset, or human dignity is very different from dignity proper.

On the other hand, though, there are a number of considerations which point into the opposite direction and therefore encourage attempts to explain human dignity in terms of dignity proper:

(1) Although disrespect of dignity proper usually does not amount to a violation of human dignity, violations of human dignity at least frequently seem to be humiliating as well. This has to be accounted for.
(2) While the expression 'dignity' apparently is somewhat outdated and of minor importance in most people's lives, other elements from the *conceptual family of dignity*, like decency, self-respect, offence, humiliation, shame, make up a large part of the fabric of everyday moral considerations. Therefore, the 'idea of dignity' plays a much more important part in modern life than one might expect from the restrained usage of the word. It indicates a realm of moral evaluation beyond rights, duties and utility that is of philosophical interest in any case, and as a whole may pile up to something essential like human dignity.
(3) The importance of dignity proper for everyday evaluations is confirmed by the observation that elements of its conceptual family figure prominently in many different issues of applied ethics.
(4) Finally, the historical roots of the concept of human dignity suggest its interpretation in terms of dignity proper.

Since it is our aim to explore the promises of an account of human dignity in terms of dignity proper, we will take up item (3) first and provide an overview on the role of dignity proper in different areas of practical ethics. We will then formulate three challenges that dignity proper has put forward to philosophy historically, before we take up the original question again and outline three different possibilities of connecting dignity proper with human dignity leading finally to the idea of human dignity as universal nobility that we take to be the most attractive proposal yet.

Dignity proper in applied ethics

Dignity proper plays an important role in a surprising variety of different areas of applied ethics.

Nursing ethics

In 2009, English nursing ethicist Ann Gallagher started her editorial for an issue of the journal *Nursing Ethics* as follows: 'It might be said that dignity is the new autonomy. Autonomy has been the focus of western bioethics for some three decades. Now the ethical turn is towards dignity' (Gallagher 2009: 145). According to her, what went wrong in hospitals in the last decades was not so much that patients' autonomy was violated, but that their dignity was not sufficiently respected. As she, among others, has shown in the last years, patients as well as nursing staff frequently complain about indignity in healthcare facilities (for example, Franklin, Ternestedt and Nordenfelt 2006; Gallagher, Li, Wainwright, Jones and Lee 2008; Jacobson 2009). These complaints may be roughly grouped into three different categories. First, the patients' privacy is endangered by the way hospital wards are constructed and organized as well as by irresponsible behaviour of the nurses, who put the patient in his or her weakness, nakedness and plight on display to other people. Second, there is a tendency, in the special asymmetric bedside situation, to ignore the rules of normal civilized interaction and to switch either to a patronizing or a parade-ground attitude towards the patients, or simply to *act upon* them instead of *interacting with* them. Third, the patients' weaknesses and disabilities easily lead to a paternalistic tendency on the side of the nurses to take over control instead of supporting self-control, and hence deprive the patients of their means of leading their lives despite being ill.

Psychiatric ethics

Although respect for the patients' dignity is a universal demand in medical ethics, it is of special importance with regard to patients who are particularly vulnerable: psychiatric in-patients. When in 1793 the French physician Phillipe Pinel unchained the inhabitants of the Parisian hospital Bicêtre and initiated the practice of giving patients therapeutic treatment instead of merely keeping them behind bars, he was described as restoring their dignity. In the 1950s, the American sociologist Erving Goffman spent some time as a visiting scholar in a mental hospital, which resulted in his famous study, *Asylums*, where he described in painstaking detail the mechanisms of humiliation in psychiatric institutions (Goffman 2007). Although today the situation has changed considerably, it is still very much debated whether the patients' dignity is sufficiently respected in psychiatry. It seems that the peculiar features of interaction between mentally disturbed patients and the hospital staff is particularly prone to violations of dignity. This is most obvious in situations where the patient is treated involuntarily and under physical constraint. Moreover, there is the difficult question whether and how far the therapists are obliged to guard the patient's dignity against the patient herself or himself, for example in the case of mania.

Dying with dignity

Another area of bioethics where dignity plays a prominent role is the debate on euthanasia. Interestingly enough, proponents of both sides refer to the traditional idea of dying with dignity. They differ, however, in what it is that makes death dignified. Defenders of a right to euthanasia emphasize the importance of being in control of one's path through life instead of being at the mercy of fate, and moreover they point to the undignified concomitants of the last stages of death (pain, anxiety, mental disorientation etc.) that might be avoided by euthanasia. Opponents of a right to euthanasia, on the other hand, usually react in (at least) one of three ways: either they emphasize the advanced facilities of modern palliative medicine and care which make it unnecessary to have oneself killed, or they point out the particular dignity of facing the evils of dying and death with courage (Kass 2002), or finally they claim a fundamental incompatibility between dignity and killing that morally forecloses euthanasia (although it might be argued that what is supposed in this third claim is not dignity proper).

Punishment

In the ethics of punishment, there are three somewhat interlocking discussions about dignity proper. First, it is discussed in how far the authorities are obliged to take care that while punishing offenders they also minimize violations of their dignity. Prison sentences usually lead to a social degradation of the prisoner, but one can still arrange the situation in jail in a more or less dignified/humiliating way. The crucial question here is, whether there is any moral obligation for the state to respect the offender's dignity (Whitman 2005).

Second, it is debated whether *capital punishment* violates the convict's dignity proper. It is evident that the way capital punishment is executed in many countries is deeply humiliating. It is less clear, however, whether this is necessarily so, and moreover whether such an offence to dignity proper would entail that the death penalty is incompatible with human dignity.

The topic of the third discussion is the moral assessment of so-called 'shame punishment'. For the whole history of punishment humiliation and degradation have been intentionally employed as punitive measures. Under the influence of philosophers and legal theorists of the eighteenth and nineteenth centuries, however, shame punishment was progressively banned from the penal codes of more and more developed countries. Some twenty years ago, however, it made a comeback in the United States, leading to a fresh interest in the moral assessment of shame, humiliation and hence of dignity proper (for an overview, see Harvard Law Review 2003).

Discrimination

In a newspaper interview, an American pop singer of Italian origin, Tony Bennett, told a story from mid-1950s Florida where he and the famous black jazz musician Duke Ellington had performed at the opening gala of a fancy hotel; Bennett was accommodated in the hotel, but Ellington had to stay somewhere else. Obviously, various kinds of degradation and disrespect make up the fabric of all kinds of discrimination – racism, sexism, discrimination on the basis of religion, sexual orientation and disability – besides the coarse girders of unequal rights and physical suppression. And today still, even from the univocal intention not to discriminate, there are a number of problems concerning how to avoid humiliation and offence, for example with respect to terminology or for instance in job applications.

Living conditions

One of the first occurrences of the notion of human dignity in legal documents is to be found in the Constitution of the Weimar Republic, which came into effect in 1919. Article 151 of the Constitution demands that the economic order must serve the aim of establishing a '*menschenwürdiges Dasein*' for everybody. This claim is not surprising, since there had been repeated complaints about the undignified life of the working class during the nineteenth century, for example by Friedrich Engels. In the history of the labour movement, class struggle is frequently described as being based on the dignity of the suppressed workers (Bloch 1985; Appiah 2010). Today, there are still many areas where people have to work in undignified conditions, for example because the work is so excruciatingly hard or because it forces workers into particularly degrading situations as in the sex industry. Moreover, there are many conditions in which people have to make their living that hardly qualify as labour but are all the more deplorable because they are so deeply humiliating, for example digging for something edible in garbage dumps or trying not to starve on a trail of refugees. The ethical debate on global exploitation, new forms of slavery, poverty and hunger would be utterly inadequate if it did not mention the degrading aspects of living under such poor conditions (cf. Schaber 2011).

Torture

Although torture was prevalent during the whole of the twentieth century, there was a span of time by the end of the century when torture was univocally banned by moral philosophers and legal theorists. In the wake of 9/11 this ban started to crumble again and new discussions on possible justifications for torture set in. Obviously, torture is somehow related to dignity proper; this became vivid at the pictures of Abu Ghraib. For understanding the relationship between dignity proper and human dignity, however, it is important to shift the focus from possible justifications of torture to the question why univocally vile cases of torture are so disgusting and abhorrent.

In this respect, the blood-soaked history of the twentieth century has provided moral philosophy with ample material, for example in autobiographical reports by survivors of concentration camps and gulags (Des Pres 1980). Obviously, the evil in how these victims were treated has many faces. Every moral right or claim they had was constantly trampled upon. It is revealing that for them and also in the eyes of their tormentors, what constituted essential elements of their ordeal were the permanent, deliberate attacks against their dignity proper. As Terence Des Pres put it: 'The survivor preserves his life, but also his humaneness, against a situation in which, at every turn, decency seems stupid or impossible' (*ibid.*: 45). Yet, the tormentors took great pains to break their victims' resistance. The reports Des Pres has collected describe the variety of attacks on the dignity of the victims, for example the omnipresence of dirt, the hellish stench, the constant plight of urinating and defecating, the assaults by lice and other vermin, the loss of all personal belongings, the total helplessness against insults and maltreatment, the pains of hunger, illness, fatigue and despair.

Daily life

The importance of dignity proper in exceptional situations, in hospitals, prisons and concentration camps, should not lead one into underestimating its role in daily life. As William Ian Miller has vividly shown in his book, *Humiliation*, modern social life has inherited much of the concept and many mechanisms that can already be found in early honour-based cultures (like the culture of saga Iceland) (Miller 1993). Respect and offense, recognition and disdain are at least as prevalent in daily social interaction as the obeying and ignoring of rules and rights. And they raise ethical issues, for example whether only individual persons are to be respected or if states, nations or genders can have a claim to respect as well (Neuhäuser 2011). Moreover, in the context of daily life the question that was already touched upon in relation to euthanasia becomes more important: namely, if dignity proper gives rise to moral obligations to oneself (see Hill 1991).

Historical roots of dignity proper

The list of issues in applied ethics raising questions of dignity proper shows that any moral philosophy which intends to stay close to our life–world morality has to say something about the role and value of dignity proper and its conceptual relatives. But dignity proper has also played a more general role in the history of philosophy that may not be evident at first sight, but should be taken seriously in order to gain a better understanding of the relationship between dignity proper and human dignity. In what follows, we will distinguish three different (though interrelated) challenges of dignity proper to philosophy.

The ethical challenge

Ethics in the original sense of the term is the art of leading a good life; and in the ethical philosophy of antiquity dignity plays an important role. The first famous treatment is to be found in Aristotle's reflections on magnanimity (NE 1123), but perhaps the most prominent text about the importance of dignity proper for a good life is Cicero's *De officiis*, where he describes in minute detail how to lead one's life appropriately, and in particular how to keep one's decorum as an essential part of one's life conduct. Cicero's work was not only important because of his claim that one has to take great care for one's dignity but also in his elaboration on the facets of dignified behaviour that mirror more or less the rules of honour of the Roman aristocracy: gravity, solemnity, self-mastery. Both questions (regarding the ethical value of dignified behaviour and its characteristic components) run through the history of ethics, they are for example found in Kant's treatment of servility in his *Metaphysics of Morals*. And John Stuart Mill, who faced the problem that the utilitarian focus on hedonism seems to lead to a philosophy for 'happy pigs', drew upon 'a sense of dignity, which all human beings possess in one form or other . . . and which is so essential a part of the happiness of those in whom it is strong, that nothing which conflicts with it could be, otherwise than momentarily, an object of desire to them' (Mill 1998: 57). Today, this topic is discussed under the heading of *self-respect*, where self-respect is understood as a person's concern about his or her dignity proper (cf. Dillon 1995).

The metaphysical challenge

It was a central question for stoic philosophy of how to maintain one's dignity under unfavourable external circumstances. Seneca, Epictetus and other Roman authors recurrently explained how to act in a dignified way even under extremely hostile conditions, for example as a captive or slave. In this respect, they laid the foundation for a distinction of remaining importance: between *external* and *internal* dignity or honour. 'Internal' is to be read as independent of appraisal or respect by others, whilst 'external' refers to a type of dignity that is dependent precisely on others' recognition. The stoic Sage paradigmatically rendered his dignity immune against the uncertain chances of social life in the Roman Empire, so that he could not lose control over things important for him and thereby be degraded and humiliated.

This very practical and reasonable concern about the conditions of dignity under uncertain and harsh political conditions, however, led to a much more detached, philosophical concern about dignity proper: the question whether the metaphysical conditions of human life are per definition humiliating. There seem to be several good reasons to assume they are, as often expressed in poetry: the uncertainties of destiny seem to pre-empt human claims of power and control, almighty divine beings annihilate any human ambition, the overwhelming size and lifespan of the everlasting cosmos apparently reduces the individual human being to wormlike nothingness, the inevitability of death threatens to destroy all future aspirations. Philosophers' concern with the metaphysical conditions of human life frequently culminated in worries about the status of man under these potentially degrading circumstances; and many prominent anthropological claims could be read as attempts to meet this challenge and find a way of retaining dignity for humans, typically with recourse to a special relationship to God (being created in God's image), freedom of choice (for example, Pico della Mirandola), reason (for example, Pascal), morality (for example, Kant) or even the last resort of leading an absurd revolt (for example, Camus). Others, like B. F. Skinner, tried to bite the bullet and to accept that in a determined world there is no place for keeping one's dignity (Skinner 2007).

What is remarkable about these attempts is that the contemporary idea of degradation still rests on the ancient aristocratic concept of dignity: power, self-mastery, standing upright.

The moral challenge

Dignity proper always combined normative constraints of the dignified person herself (self-respect) with constraints regarding the way others had to treat this person (respect). While the former constraints played an important part throughout the history of philosophy (that is, the ethical challenge), the latter constraints came into focus comparatively late, only by the end of the eighteenth century, when political philosophers started to wonder whether there are basic constituents of respect that are owed not only to certain dignitaries but to everyone. Thomas Paine, for example, defended the French revolutionaries against Edmund Burke's attempts to ridicule the idea that everybody has to be treated as a person with dignity. In contemporary moral philosophy, this idea seems to be more of a widely shared background condition than a topic of explicit theoretical concern. John Rawls, for instance, in *A Theory of Justice*, describes self-respect as 'perhaps the most important primary good' (Rawls 1999: 386), but he is not merely interested in self-respect as part of leading a good life (i.e. as a response to the ethical challenge) but also as something that has to be secured by the way in which the basic structure of society is organized. Joel Feinberg relies on dignity proper when he defends a right-based moral theory against a duty-based moral theory. He illustrates this distinction by a fictional society, Nowheresville, where everybody obeys his or her duties towards their comrades and hence all demands of duty-based ethical theories are fulfilled. Nonetheless, Nowheresville is a deeply inhuman society because in order not to violate the dignity of its members it is not enough that people are treated properly out of duty, it is necessary that they are treated properly because they have moral claim rights to be respected by others (Feinberg 1970). Again, dignity proper in its traditional dependence on power and self-mastery is considered as fundamental to the extent it even allows for a decision between two basic moral approaches. Similarly, Harry Frankfurt has argued that equality as such has no value at all, but gains its fundamental appeal from the humiliating character of being treated unequally (Frankfurt 1999). And Avishai Margalit, in his influential book, *The Decent Society*, explicitly contrasted a decent society 'whose institutions do not humiliate people' (Margalit 1996: 1) with the usual political ideal of a just society. In a more recent book, Margalit emphasized the importance of dignity proper for political philosophy in distinguishing, within the realm of non-decent societies, between those which are merely non-decent in that institutions *sometimes* humiliate people, and regimes like Nazi Germany where it is part of their *nature* to be cruel and humiliating. With the latter, according to Margalit, no compromises should be made, because such compromises would always be rotten (Margalit 2010).

Dignity proper and human dignity

At least part of the topics sketched so far might also show up in presentations of the concept of human dignity instead of dignity proper, for example torture and poverty, the ideas of Pico della Mirandola and Skinner, equal dignity for everybody and the merits of the decent society. It is therefore time to pick up the question of the very beginning of how dignity proper and human dignity are related.

Human dignity as dignity as a human

In light of the historical sketch of the importance of dignity proper, one can distinguish three ways in which human dignity and dignity proper might be connected. The first way is to be found as early as in the writings of Cicero. In *De officiis*, Cicero did not merely describe the ways a person has to behave as a member of a particular social class or as the holder of a certain office. Cicero also emphasized that people have dignities just by being humans and not mere brutes. As beings able to reason and gain knowledge they are obliged to behave accordingly; otherwise they would disrespect their dignity as humans, in short: their human dignity. One way to connect human dignity to dignity proper is to assume that in addition to the various social roles people play they also occupy a role just by sharing human nature which (like the other roles) entails duties to behave in certain ways.

This proposal fits well with the metaphysical challenge, i.e. the threat that human nature confines us to an undignified, disgraceful and miserable existence. It also fits well with the proposal from the eighteenth century that as a human everybody shares a kind of inborn nobility that has to be respected by his or her fellows. However, just some kind of residual dignity that every person shares, no matter how dignified or undignified she is in other respects, would hardly justify the high esteem which is usually conferred to human dignity.

Human dignity as universal rank

At this point, a lesson from the Christian understanding of dignity might fit in, according to which human dignity, since it is conferred by God, is of infinitely higher value and rank than any possible social dignity could be. Compared to the shared status of human dignity, all other differences in dignity between people vanish. This second line of thought was emphasized in recent publications by James Q. Whitman and Jeremy Waldron. As Waldron writes: 'once associated with hierarchical differentiations of rank and status, "dignity" now conveys the idea that all human persons belong to the same rank and that rank is a very high one indeed, in many ways as high as those that were formerly regarded as ranks of nobility' (Waldron 2007: 201). This is the position of human dignity as universal rank, which is employed by Whitman as a possible explanation of the different roles that considerations of dignity proper play in the legal systems in the United States and in middle Europe, for example in Germany and France: while in the United States there is a certain tendency to deny rank to everybody, Europeans traditionally confer it equally even to defendants and prisoners (Whitman 2005).

The proposal to regard human dignity as universal rank is very attractive historically as well as systematically. It is for instance spelled out in Stephen Darwall's (1977) influential proposal to distinguish between recognition-respect that is owed to all humans and appraisal-respect that is owed to particular human beings for their achievements. The emphasis here lies on the categorical priority of recognition-respect. Yet, the idea of universal rank also raises at least two severe difficulties. First, it remains an open question how to justify the claim that human beings have such a high rank. Offhand, it appears to be a blunt instance of speciesism. Second, it is not clear why characteristic features of dignity proper, namely, that it can be gained and lost, are not shared by human dignity.

Human dignity as universal nobility

At this point, it is important to consider another approach to human dignity that goes back to the sociologist Niklas Luhmann (Luhmann 1965). His proposal is based on the assumption that modern societies have changed the traditional role structure in such a way that everybody has to fulfil different roles at the same time. In order to succeed, people have to build up another role besides and above those special roles: the role of an individual person. The modern concept of dignity is bound to this individual role. Persons have to be respected, not necessarily in their social roles nor in their role as human beings (whatever this may be), but in their role as individuals who construct and uphold an individual personality with certain idiosyncratic features and preferences.

Luhmann was a sociologist, not a normative moral philosopher. His proposal, however, allows for an amendment of the idea of universal rank. According to this third line of thought, what has happened in the past 200 years was not merely a kind of generous upgrading of everybody into a high rank but also an *individualization* of these high ranks. While at the time of the French Revolution people had a rather traditional conception of which kind of behaviour is dignified and which is not, people today live in a variety of different ways with different conceptions of decency. Moral philosophy is rather reluctant to prescribe the ways people should lead their lives within the loose boundaries of what is morally acceptable, yet almost everybody is aware that building up and maintaining an individual personality presupposes a hospitable or at least a non-hostile climate of respect and support.

During the 1930s and 1940s many people all over the world had to suffer a radical loss of respect in this sense. It therefore is not surprising that after the Second World War the universal claim to respect of one's dignity that already was influential outside of legal systems (for example, in novels and political statements) entered the new declarations and constitutions. And it was not unexpected either that in the post-war period the victims of suppression and persecution all over the world complained about violations of human dignity.

Human dignity, according to the third proposal, is not a special kind of dignity proper, it rather stands for the general value of having dignity proper respected and supported in modern societies. Since it is not a dignity in itself it obviously cannot be diminished or forfeited, in this sense it is inborn and inviolable. In order to emphasize the close connection as well as the difference to the second proposal we suggest calling it: the idea of human dignity as universal nobility (Stoecker 2011).

References

Appiah, A. 2010. *The Honor Code: How Moral Revolutions Happen.* New York, London: W. W. Norton

Bloch, E. 1985. *Naturrecht und menschliche Würde.* Frankfurt am Main: Suhrkamp

Des Pres, T. 1980. *The Survivor: An Anatomy of Life in the Death Camps.* Oxford University Press

Dillon, R. S. 1995. *Dignity, Character, and Self-Respect.* New York: Routledge

Feinberg, J. 1970. 'The Nature and Value of Rights', *Journal of Value Inquiry WINT* 70(4): 263–7

Frankfurt, H. 1999. 'Equality and Respect', in Harry Frankfurt (ed.), *Necessity, Volition, and Love.* Cambridge University Press, 146–54

Franklin, L. L., Ternestedt, B. M., and Nordenfelt, L. 2006. 'Views on Dignity of Elderly Nursing Home Residents', *Nursing Ethics* 13(2): 130–46

Gallagher, A. 2009. 'Dignity as a Virtue: Appreciating Ambiguity', *Nursing Ethics* 16(2): 145–6

Gallagher, A., Li, S., Wainwright, P., Jones, I. R., and Lee, D. 2008. 'Dignity in the Care of Older People – A Review of the Theoretical and Empirical Literature', *BMC Nurse* 7: 11

Goffman, E. 2007. *Asylums: Essays on the Social Situation of Mental Patients and Other Inmates.* New Brunswick, NJ: Aldine Transaction

Harvard Law Review. 2003. 'Shame, Stigma, and Crime: Evaluating the Efficacy of Shaming Sanctions in Criminal Law', *Harvard Law Review* 116(7): 2186–207

Hill, T. E. 1991. *Autonomy and Self-Respect.* Cambridge University Press

Jacobson, N. 2009. 'Dignity Violation in Health Care', *Qualitative Health Research* 19(11): 1536–47

Kass, L. 2002. *Life, Liberty, and the Defense of Dignity: The Challenge for Bioethics.* San Francisco: Encounter Books

Luhmann, N. 1965. *Grundrechte als Institution.* Berlin: Duncker & Humblot

Margalit, A. 1996. *The Decent Society.* Cambridge, MA: Harvard University Press

2010. *On Compromise and Rotten Compromises.* Princeton University Press

Mill, J. S. 1998. *Utilitarianism.* Oxford University Press

Miller, W. I. 1993. *Humiliation: And Other Essays on Honor, Social Discomfort, and Violence.* Ithaca, NY: Cornell University Press

Neuhäuser, C. 2011. 'Humiliation: The Collective Dimension', in P. Kaufmann, H. Kuch, C. Neuhäuser *et al.* (eds.). *Humiliation, Degradation, Dehumanization.* Dordrecht: Springer, 21–36

Rawls, J. 1999. *A Theory of Justice.* Cambridge, MA: Belknap Press of Harvard University Press

Schaber, P. 2011. 'Absolute Poverty', in P. Kaufmann, H. Kuch, C. Neuhäuser *et al.* (eds.). *Humiliation, Degradation, Dehumanization.* Dordrecht: Springer, 151–8

Skinner, B. F. 2007. *Beyond Freedom and Dignity.* Indianapolis, IN: Hackett

Stoecker, R. 2011. 'Three Crucial Turns on the Road to an Adequate Understanding of Human Dignity', in P. Kaufmann, H. Kuch, C. Neuhäuser *et al.* (eds.). *Humiliation, Degradation, Dehumanization.* Dordrecht: Springer, 7–17

Waldron, J. 2007. 'Dignity and Rank', *European Journal of Sociology* 48(2): 201–37

Whitman, J. Q. 2005. *Harsh Justice: Criminal Punishment and the Widening Divide Between America and Europe.* Oxford University Press

32

Dignity in the ubuntu tradition

THADDEUS METZ

What the '*ubuntu* tradition' in the title of this chapter refers to is the conception of how one ought to live that was prominent among pre-colonial societies below the Sahara desert and that continues to inform much moral reflection among black Africans in the region. '*Ubuntu*' literally means humanness or personhood among speakers of Zulu, Xhosa and Ndebele in southern Africa, and it has cognates in many other African languages, for example '*botho*' in Sotho-Tswana, '*hunhu*' in Shona and '*utu*' in Swahili (Broodryk 2002: 14, 31). The term '*ubuntu*' is often used to concisely sum up a particular view of what is morally fundamental, roughly, to live a genuinely human way of life or to become a real person.

As one would expect of a large and diverse region such as sub-Saharan Africa, conceptions of what (genuine) humanness or (real) personhood consists of are far from uniform. Nonetheless, there are certain ideas associated with talk of '*ubuntu*' and related terms that one encounters recurrently, and they are what I focus on here, particularly insofar as they bear on the value of dignity as the ground of human rights articulated in the Universal Declaration of Human Rights of 1948.

I treat the *ubuntu* tradition philosophically and not anthropologically, meaning that my primary aim is not to *reflect* in detail the beliefs of a particular African people or group of them. I draw on ideas commonly advocated by adherents to *ubuntu* in order to spell out and sometimes *construct* understandings of human dignity that are worth taking seriously by professional ethicists, moral philosophers, jurisprudential scholars and constitutional courts anywhere in the world today. In particular, I seek to articulate a theory of dignity grounded on sub-Saharan values that could serve as a genuine rival to the influential Kantian conception that currently dominates most intellectual reflection on the topic.

The morality of ubuntu

A large swathe of sub-Saharan thinking about ethics is summed up with phrases usually translated as 'a person is a person through other persons' or 'I am because we are'. These are overly literal renditions that convey little to English speakers unfamiliar with sub-Saharan worldviews. All they connote, on the face of it, are sociological claims about individuals always being part of a society or children needing adults in order to survive. In fact, they are also often meant to convey a certain moral ideal.

Implicit in the claim that a person is a person through other persons is the judgment that one ought to develop one's personhood or humanness, where these come in degrees. From a scientific or descriptive standpoint, anyone who is self-aware and reflective in certain ways counts as a person, and any individual that is a member of *Homo sapiens* is a human being. However, when thinking normatively, terms such as 'personhood', 'humanness' and the like in the *ubuntu* tradition refer to finally *valuable* aspects of our nature, *virtues* that can be exhibited to a greater or lesser extent. One's basic aim as a moral agent should be to become a *complete* person or to live a *truly* human life.

Contemporary philosophers would name this kind of perspective a 'self-realization' or '*eudaemonist*' ethic, according to which one's fundamental goal should be to develop the facets of one's human nature that are good for their own sake. Failure to do so would mean that one is living an 'inhuman' life or is 'not a person', and, indeed, sub-Saharans often call those who particularly fail to manifest *ubuntu* 'animals' (Pearce 1990: 147; Bhengu 1996: 27). Of course, these pejorative labels are meant metaphorically; it is not as though one who lacks virtue is literally no longer a human being. Rather, he is simply not a *real* human being, in the way that a jalopy is not a real car, for failing to function as it should (Gaie 2007: 33).

So far, I have discussed the first half of the maxim that sums up an *ubuntu* ethic, 'a person is a person through other persons'; the claim that a person is a person is a prescription to develop one's personhood. It is the second half of the phrase, about how to do so, where considerations of dignity arise. The way in which one becomes a real person is 'through other persons', and this, in much African thinking, means through a communal relationship with others. As Augustine Shutte, a South African who was one of the first professional philosophers to publish a book on *ubuntu*, sums up the basics of the ethic: 'Our deepest moral obligation is to become more fully human. And this means entering more and more deeply into community with others. So although the goal is personal fulfilment, selfishness is excluded' (Shutte 2001: 30). Who are the 'others' with whom we are to commune in order to exhibit *ubuntu*? The answers to this question are *prima facie* attractive conceptions of human dignity: one obtains humanness or virtue by prizing communal relationship with the most important beings in the world.

Three sub-Saharan conceptions of dignity

For beings to have dignity is basically for each of them to be objectively good for their own sake to an equally superlative degree that entitles them to respectful treatment (Metz 2012: 20–1). In other words, beings with dignity have the highest non-instrumental value such that they must be treated as having *that* kind of value. If a being has dignity, then one morally must treat it neither as though it has a merely instrumental value, i.e. merely as a means, nor as though it has less value than another such being.

These ideas are familiar from the Western, and specifically Kantian, moral tradition, according to which persons have a dignity in virtue of autonomy, and human rights violations are serious forms of disrespect for this capacity. When referring to this perspective in what follows, I do not have in mind Immanuel Kant's own ideas, but rather views typical of theorists inspired by him, such as John Rawls, Ronald Dworkin and Onora O'Neill. Unlike Kant himself, they tend to think of autonomy as an ability to deliberate and decide that is part of the natural world, but that makes us higher than animals, which lack it. For these thinkers, treating an individual as dignified because she has that ability means according her equal rights to choose for herself. Negative human rights violations such as authoritarianism, slavery and torture are conceived as interference with self-governance, whereas positive human rights violations, such as not fighting poverty, are often thought of as failures to enhance people's ability to choose their own ways of life.

The Kantian idea of self-determination as the source of our dignity and the ground of human rights is currently the most influential conception, at least in the West and often in international human rights documents. In what follows, I discuss three sub-Saharan conceptions of dignity, in search of one that provides serious reason to question whether the Kantian view is most justified.

Spiritual nature

Here is one account of with whom to commune in order to develop *ubuntu* that is standard among pre-colonial sub-Saharan societies and also accepted by several contemporary African philosophers: beings with a certain *supernatural essence.* God and ancestors, persons who are alive but not visible, are relevant others with whom to enter into community, as are human beings because they have a spiritual nature that has its source in God. African texts that address human rights often suggest that it is in virtue of having a 'divine spark' that human beings have a dignity of a sort that is capable of grounding human rights (for example, Wiredu 1996: 157–71; Ramose 1999: 49–64, 138–45, 163–95; Ilesanmi 2001; Deng 2004: 501). Since human beings have something akin to a soul, an immaterial substance that will survive the death of their body, they are the most special things on the planet and hence deserve respect in the form of universal entitlements to life, liberties, resources and the like.

Although appeal to a spiritual element is the most common idea of what grounds human dignity in African thought, I do not think it is promising. For one, there are notorious philosophical difficulties in seeking to ground values on supernatural properties. For another, an appeal to the spiritual is unlikely to entail or well explain certain human rights. Infringements of core rights do not seem to consist fundamentally of degradations of an individual's *soul* or other spiritual property. Nor do they all even appear necessarily to be degrading of the body as what houses the soul.

It would be much more philosophically appealing to ground such rights on a Kantian view of dignity as inhering in our capacity to make voluntary or reasoned decisions. Dictatorship, segregation and slavery are more plausibly understood to be degradations of people's autonomy than of their soul or the like. I therefore suggest moving on to critically explore some other sub-Saharan conceptions of dignity, in order to find one that can truly compete with the Kantian one.

Liveliness

The *ubuntu* tradition occasions awareness of two other ways to conceive human dignity, i.e. two additional conceptions of the most special beings with whom to commune so as to realize one's humanness. One of them appeals to a certain understanding of human life as being more important than anything in the animal, vegetable or mineral kingdoms insofar as it has a greater capacity for 'life-force'.

Among many traditional African societies, the universe is understood to consist fundamentally of an invisible, vital energy that has come from God, with rocks having a low degree of it, plants having more than rocks, animals having more than plants, and humans having more than animals. Although the origins of the idea of life-force are thickly metaphysical, the concept can be of use when shorn of the supernatural. That is, one can plausibly understand in purely physical terms what it is for a thing to be intrinsically valuable by virtue of its vital energy, which I call 'liveliness'. African philosophers who prize vitality often characterize it in terms of health, strength, growth, reproduction, generation, creativity, vibrancy, activity, self-motion, courage and confidence, with a lack of life-force being constituted by the presence of disease, weakness, decay, barrenness, destruction, lethargy, passivity, submission, fear, insecurity and depression (Dzobo 1992; Kasenene 1994; Magesa 1997; Iroegbu 2005a; 2005b). Consider the view that those beings with the former, physical properties to a sufficiently great degree have a superlative inner worth, a dignity.

Thinking of substantial liveliness, or the capacity for it, as constitutive of human dignity avoids the problems facing the spiritual conception. The vitality theory entails that we can have dignity in a world that is entirely physical, and it does a plausible job of accounting for the human rights where the spiritual one could not; forced labour, whether by virtue of segregation or enslavement, would inhibit people's liveliness, and, as John Stuart Mill argued long ago, people who participate in democratic governance tend to be more independent, active and self-reliant than those who live under autocratic regimes.

However, the vitality conception of human dignity does face some serious objections (see Metz 2012 for the ideas that follow). One problem is that it is unclear that violating, for instance, the right to informed consent is best understood as a degradation of liveliness. For example, if a physician believed that a given treatment would be most effective for curing a patient, then the latter's consent would be irrelevant from the standpoint of a demand to respect her *vitality*. This would be especially true if the doctor believed that the treatment would be marginally less effective if the patient knew why and how she were being treated.

The at hand reply is that liveliness would be gravely impaired if patients found out that they had not been informed of a given medical intervention. If patients discovered that their physician had not told them of their treatments, they would be less likely to adhere to the required regimen and hence would tend not to become as healthy. Furthermore, patients would feel violated upon discovering the lack of truth-telling on the part of doctors, and such a violation of trust could be expected to reduce a person's exuberance and self-esteem.

The reply appears to misfire, though, in that its logic suggests that what constitutes the violation of the human right would be the *failure to keep secret* the lack of informed consent. Liveliness would be impaired only upon a patient's awareness that medical professionals had not fully informed her of the nature of the intervention; it would not be the lack of informed consent *per se* that would be the culprit. Hence, this rationale oddly entails that a medical practice of deception that is successful, or perhaps likely to be successful, would not be a human rights violation.

For another case of a human right that seems poorly captured by considerations of liveliness, consider one concerning criminal justice. Citizens have a human right not to be punished if they are innocent, or at least if a fair procedure has not judged them guilty (UDHR, Article 11). Even if framing and punishing a person known to be innocent would alone prevent more harm to innocents, say, by convincing a bloodthirsty mob not to riot, it would constitute a human rights violation if a magistrate were to do so. However, it does not appear degrading of a person's *liveliness* as such to treat him so.

One might wonder why not, and reply that punishing an innocent would surely count as a human rights violation since doing so would reduce his vitality. However, such a rationale counter-intuitively forbids the use of *all* punishment and coercion, even when directed against aggressors as needed to save innocents. A similar point applies to the reply that it is degrading to reduce one person's liveliness for the sake of protecting that of others; for those suffering from ethnic cleansing have a right that the state impair the vitality of aggressors when doing so would save that of innocents. Sometimes vitality-impairing coercion is justified, and sometimes it is not.

Obviously, the guilt and innocence of the parties largely determines when the use of punishment and other force is justified, but the liveliness conception does not distinguish fundamentally between aggressors and non-aggressors, who are both alive. Here, again, the Kantian view appears to do better. It is straightforward to maintain that punishing an innocent degrades his capacity for decision-making, whereas punishing a guilty party does not. Treating a person's ability to make decisions as special means responding to the way he has exercised it, such that it need not be degrading of autonomy to reduce one person's autonomy in response to her using it to reduce someone else's. In addition, failure to inform patients of their medical treatment is widely viewed to be a degradation of their capacity for autonomy. The next conception of dignity grounded in sub-Saharan values, I will suggest, provides the strongest challenge to the Kantian one.

Communal relationship

A third conception of human dignity that has a recognizably African pedigree is the idea that we are more special than rocks, plants and animals in virtue of our capacity for communal relationship. When it is said that a person is a person through other persons, we have seen that this means that one should develop one's personhood or virtue, something one does insofar as one enters into community with others. The relevant others with whom to commune, according to the present theory of dignity, are those who in principle are the *most capable of communing* (Metz 2011, 2012, from which the following paragraphs borrow; for different communitarian views, which focus on membership, often in a spiritual realm, see Cobbah 1987: 323–31; Bujo 2001: 88; Cornell 2011: 327, 331).

What is it, then, to be capable of a communal relationship? Much African thought about the nature of community can be analytically clarified by understanding it as the combination of two logically distinct relationships, *identity* and *solidarity*. Identification is, at the core, a matter of thinking of oneself as a 'we', that is, as a member of a group, and of engaging in joint projects with its members. Exhibiting solidarity is basically a matter of helping others for their sake, often out of sympathetic emotional reaction to what it is like to be them. So stated, these are not one and the same thing. A good example of identity without solidarity is the relationship between workers and management in a capitalist firm; employees think of themselves as members of the same company as employers and coordinate their behaviour with the latter, but do not usually go to work out of sympathy for employers or for their sake. Conversely, one can find a relationship of solidarity without identity when anonymous donations are made to a charity.

Now, the combination of identifying with others, or sharing a way of life with them, on the one hand, and exhibiting solidarity towards them, or caring for their quality of life, on the other, is what most people mean by 'friendship' or a broad sense of 'love' (cf. Tutu 1999: 34–5). So, one way to understand the claim that dignity inheres in our capacity for communal relationship is to say this:

we are more special than anything else on the planet because we are capable of being part of a friendly or loving relationship in a way that nothing else is.

Human rights violations, from this perspective, are ways of degrading people's capacity for loving relationship (both to love and be loved), which are often a matter of acting in seriously unloving ways towards them. What genocide, slavery, systematic rape, human trafficking, apartheid and totalitarianism arguably have in common is, in large part, that those who engage in these practices treat people in an extremely unfriendly way, namely, by thinking of others as separate and inferior, greatly undermining others' ability to pursue their own goals, seeking to grossly impair their quality of life, and exhibiting emotions such as *Schadenfreude* as well as motives of power-seeking.

Such an Afro-communitarian conception of dignity as applied to human rights avoids the problems facing the views previously discussed. Unlike the spiritual nature theory, it is secular and intuitively accounts for the human rights not to be subjected to segregated employment, slavery or a dictatorship. These practices are plausibly understood to consist of failures to honour others' communal nature, in part because they are unlikely to be good for others or done out of sympathy with them, but most clearly because they are failures to share a way of life with them, i.e. to enjoy a sense of togetherness and to cooperate.

Furthermore, the communal relationship view appears to be more attractive than the vitality one in that the former can ground human rights that the latter does not underwrite with ease. For a physician not to inform his patient of the treatment she is undergoing is to fail to share a way of life with her, which requires transparency about the terms of their interaction. And the reason it is wrong to punish or otherwise harm an innocent person, even when it would save more innocent lives, is that it fails to treat him in accordance with the way he has exercised his capacity for community. Roughly, if someone has been friendly, then he warrants friendliness in response, whereas if someone has been unfriendly, then he warrants unfriendliness, at least when it would protect the victims of his unfriendliness. That principle explains not only why it is wrong to punish an innocent for the sake of the greater protection of innocents, but also why the state should use violence against aggressors who threaten to harm innocents. It does not treat a person's capacity for friendliness in a degrading way to treat him in an unfriendly way as necessary to counteract his own unfriendliness.

Conclusion: ubuntu and cross-cultural theorization

For all that has been said in this chapter, the Afro-communitarian theory of human dignity and the Kantian conception appear to be on a par. Both do a fair job of entailing and explaining a wide variety of human rights that we intuitively have. I lack the space to explore which is more defensible, but note that this project is worth undertaking. It is not obvious that human rights violations are fundamentally to be understood as degradations of our autonomous nature, the standard view in the West, as opposed to degradations of our communal nature, in line with the philosophical interpretation of the *ubuntu* tradition.

Defenders of the Kantian conception of dignity take it to be applicable universally, not merely to those in the West, where the view originated. After all, human rights are by definition understood to apply to (nearly) all human beings, and so it is to be expected that a view of dignity, as what grounds human rights, is going to be true of humans wherever they are on the planet. Pluralism with regard to what people *believe* about dignity is consistent with there being a monistic fact about the actual nature of human dignity, or so Kantians think. The Afro-communitarian conception articulated here may be seen as aiming for a similarly universal scope, that is, for the displacement of the Kantian view. Which conception of dignity is likely to gain greater assent across the globe? Even if no actual intercultural consensus were forthcoming, which view could be demonstrated philosophically to cohere with other judgments that are widely accepted, at least by those who have reflected with the most care on moral matters? I hope the reader agrees that such questions merit careful answers.

References

Bhengu, M. J. 1996. *Ubuntu: The Essence of Democracy*. Cape Town: Novalis Press

Broodryk, J. 2002. *Ubuntu: Life Lessons from Africa*. Pretoria: Ubuntu School of Philosophy

Bujo, B. 2001. *Foundations of an African Ethic*, trans. B. McNeil. New York: Crossroad Publishers

Cobbah, J. 1987. 'African Values and the Human Rights Debate', *Human Rights Quarterly* 9: 309–31

Cornell, D. 2011. 'A Call for a Nuanced Constitutional Jurisprudence: South Africa, Ubuntu, Dignity, and Reconciliation', in D. Cornell and N. Muvangua (eds.), *Ubuntu and the Law*. New York: Fordham University Press, 324–32

Deng, F. 2004. 'Human Rights in the African Context', in K. Wiredu (ed.), *A Companion to African Philosophy*. Malden, MA: Blackwell, 499–508

Dzobo, N. K. 1992. 'Values in a Changing Society', in K. Wiredu and K. Gyekye (eds.), *Person and Community*. Washington, DC: Council for Research in Values and Philosophy, 223–40

Gaie, J. 2007. 'The Setswana Concept of Botho', in J. Gaie and S. Mmolai (eds.), *The Concept of Botho and HIV/AIDS in Botswana*. Eldoret, Kenya: Zapf Chancery, 29–43

Ilesanmi, S. 2001. 'Human Rights Discourse in Modern Africa', *Journal of Religious Ethics* 23: 293–322

Iroegbu, P. 2005a. 'What Is Life?', in P. Iroegbu and A. Echekwube (eds.), *Kpim of Morality Ethics*. Ibadan: Heinemann Educational Books, 435–9

2005b. 'Right to Life and the Means to Life: Human Dignity', in P. Iroegbu and A. Echekwube (eds.), *Kpim of Morality Ethics*. Ibadan: Heinemann Educational Books, 446–9

Kasenene, P. 1994. 'Ethics in African Theology', in C. Villa-Vicencio and J. de Gruchy (eds.), *Doing Ethics in Context*. Cape Town: David Philip, 138–47

Magesa, L. 1997. *African Religion*. Maryknoll, NY: Orbis Books

Metz, T. 2011. 'Ubuntu as a Moral Theory and Human Rights in South Africa', *African Human Rights Law Journal* 11: 532–59

2012. 'African Conceptions of Human Dignity', *Human Rights Review* 13: 19–37

Pearce, C. 1990. 'Tsika, Hunhu and the Moral Education of Primary School Children', *Zambezia* 17: 145–60

Ramose, M. 1999. *African Philosophy Through Ubuntu*. Harare: Mond Publishers

Shutte, A. 2001. *Ubuntu: An Ethic for the New South Africa*. Cape Town: Cluster Publications

Tutu, D. 1999. *No Future Without Forgiveness*. New York: Random House

Wiredu, K. 1996. *Cultural Universals and Particulars: An African Perspective*. Bloomington, IN: Indiana University Press

33

Posthuman dignity

MARTIN G. WEISS

The notion of 'posthuman dignity' first appeared in a paper entitled 'In Defense of Posthuman Dignity', which Nick Bostrom published in 2005 in the Journal *Bioethics*. In this paper, he stresses that neither means nor ends of enhancement technologies advocated by the exponents of the transhumanist or posthumanist movement endanger human dignity or the fundamental human rights derived from it (Bostrom 2005).

As the concept of 'human dignity' as well as that of 'enhancement' are controversial and the answer to the question of whether radically enhancing human nature violates human dignity depends on the definition of these two notions, in the following I will try to clarify these key concepts in the context of the enhancement debate. Whereas the notion of enhancement is relatively well defined by its proponents, the different argumentations put forward to explain human dignity will lead us to the question of human nature and its moral status.

In the context of posthumanism and transhumanism, the notions 'nature' and 'human nature' are crucial, as posthumanism and transhumanism challenge both meanings of nature, i.e. 'biology' as well as 'essence', by questioning the relation between human nature in the sense of essence and human nature in the sense of the biology of the human being. Is human nature (its biology) a normative boundary, which one has to preserve in order not to harm human dignity? Or is the will to transform the nature of humans (their biology) a genuine expression of the very essence of man and therefore of his constitutive freedom, which again is the fundament of human dignity.

The first section of this chapter deals with the basic concept of posthumanism, i.e. its notion of enhancement, and very briefly with its links to Renaissance Humanism and the Enlightenment.

The following sections discuss three different accounts of human dignity put forward in the debate on the ethical permissibility of human enhancement, in order to explore their compatibility with posthumanism. Whereas personism conceives human dignity as an absolute concept – meaning that there are no grades of personhood – and therefore concludes that enhancement has no impact on human dignity as long as it does not compromise personhood, naturalistic conceptions of human dignity, which identify dignity with a given natural feature of the person – its 'genetic asset' (Fukuyama), 'natural origin' (Habermas) or 'openness to the unbidden' (Sandel) – condemn enhancement technologies as hubristic manipulation of human nature.

As this naturalistic critique of posthumanism re-echoes the well-known religious argument which stresses that enhancing technologies equal to 'playing god', the penultimate section deals with the theological notion of 'Co-Creation', i.e. with the idea that enhancing technologies may not be a form of hubristic manipulation, but the expression of man's likeness of God.

Finally, the conclusion suggests that posthumanism implies an unspoken mind–body dualism, because the enhancement of human nature/biology can be conceived as liberation only if there is something which needs to be liberated from nature/biology: free subjectivity (i.e. human nature/essence). Paradoxically, this dualism, which is at the origin of enhancement technologies, is foiled by these very technologies, because the alleged liberation of the subject through domination of its nature/biology, leads to the deeper insight that the subject is caught in its body, i.e. *is* its body.

What is posthumanism?

In the words of Nick Bostrom, Director of the Future of Humanities Institute at the University of Oxford:

> Transhumanism is a loosely defined movement that has developed gradually over the past two decades, and can be viewed as an outgrowth of secular humanism and the Enlightenment. It holds that current human nature is improvable through the use of applied science and other rational methods, which may make it possible to increase human health-span, extend our intellectual and physical capacities, and give us increased control over our own mental states and moods.
>
> (Bostrom 2005: 203)

As Bostrom himself stresses in this passage, the core concept of 'posthumanism' dates back to Renaissance humanism and the ideals of the Enlightenment. In his *Oration on the Dignity Of Men*, a sort of humanist manifesto published in 1486, the Italian philosopher Pico della Mirandola wrote:

> The Great Artisan . . . made man a creature of indeterminate and indifferent nature, and, placing him in the middle of the world, said to him 'Adam, we give you no fixed place to live, no form that is peculiar to you, nor any function that is yours alone. According to your desires and judgment, you will have and possess whatever place to live, whatever form, and whatever functions you yourself choose. All other things have a limited and fixed nature prescribed and bounded by our laws. You, with no limit or no bound, may choose for yourself the limits and bounds of your nature . . . '. (Pico della Mirandola 1990: 4)

This 'humanistic' approach defines man, as Immanuel Kant puts it, as '*animal rationabile*', that is: as an animal that is able to 'achieve' humanity.

In Kant, the main figure of eighteenth-century enlightenment, the transformation of the human animal into man, which is the history of civilization, is conceived as 'emancipation' from nature. Humanity here is identified with rationality as the result of the emancipation from nature, which moreover is largely identified with the body.

Until recently, despite all efforts at educating humankind and controlling their souls and bodies, no one really questioned the stability of humanity's biological basis. Until the rise of pharmacology, genetics and prosthetics, human nature was thought to be unchangeable. To speak of something's nature meant to speak of its eternal given essence. Now this last line of objectivity is gone. Humans have definitively lost their essence. Since the work of Sigmund Freud at the latest, we are aware of the fact that our soul and subjectivity are nothing we can rely on; due to the astonishing achievements of biotechnologies, we are also forced to accept that nothing is given in our biological nature and objectivity. There is no natural boundary for what humans can be, no intrinsic essence of humanity, neither in the human soul nor in human biology. Thus, biotechnology carries the promise of finally transforming the human animal into the free being the Renaissance dreamed about. To reach this goal, posthumanism advocates the enhancement of three human 'central capacities':

(1) *healthspan*: the capacity to remain fully healthy, active, and productive, both mentally and physically;
(2) *cognition*: general intellectual capacities, such as memory, deductive and analogical reasoning, and attention, as well as special faculties such as the capacity to understand and appreciate music, humour, eroticism, narration, spirituality, mathematics, etc.;
(3) *emotion*: the capacity to enjoy life and to respond with appropriate affect to life situations and other people (Bostrom 2008: 107).

Without going into detail, troubling questions arise, because, whereas the meaning of an enhanced health-span seems sufficiently clear, posing only the question of whether we want to live in a world without 'nativity' (Arendt 1998) and the freshness of the youth – as a society of health-span-enhanced people would have to agree to limit reproduction to a minimum – it seems much more difficult to define what it would mean to enhance cognition, emotion and behaviour. Do we really want to remember everything? What consequences would a generally increased IQ generate? What kind of society would a society of Mr Spocks be, in which everybody has complete control over his impulses and moods? And, finally, what would an enhancement of our spirituality consist of?

Bioethicists inclined towards posthumanism and liberalisms deem the improvement of these central characteristics of the human being as desirable. These features represent in their view not 'positional goods' – 'whose goodness for those possessing them depends on other subjects not possessing them' (Bostrom and Savulescu 2009: 11) – but all-purpose-remedies, which do not prejudice individual choices of good life, but empower the subject to realize his own version of good life.

Hence, although it may be good for posthumans to be posthuman, the question we have to answer first is whether it is good for us to become posthuman, as it is us who have to decide whether we want to embrace enhancement technology or ban it. In his paper, 'Why I Want To Be a Posthuman When I Grow Up' (Bostrom 2008), Nick Bostrom tries to argue that posthuman values are actually human values and that we have some sort of moral obligation to become posthumans, but as humans. Bostrom maintains that enhancement is a dispositional good. A good that we can anticipate, that we would value if we were perfectly acquainted with it. 'The claim is that for *most* current human beings, there are possible posthuman modes of being such that it could be good for these humans to become posthuman in one of those ways' (Bostrom 2008: 108). In the words of Nicholas Agar: 'Consider a music lover who has never listened to Bach's B-minor Mass. The Mass may be among his musical values if it were the case that he would enjoy it were he to be acquainted with it. The dispositional account enables Bostrom to say that posthuman values that seem beyond our comprehension may nevertheless fall within the ambit of our current dispositions' (Agar 2007: 15). Against Bostrom's attempt to demonstrate that posthuman values are human values, Agar stresses the importance of 'local values': 'Local values are high on the list of those that contribute meaning to our lives . . . You wouldn't swap your child for another child, even if that child were manifestly smarter and better at sport . . . I value humanity because I'm human. I wouldn't trade my humanity for posthumanity even though I recognize that posthumans are objectively superior' (Agar 2007: 16). According to Agar, even if we accept that posthuman values are dispositional goods, this does not imply any moral obligation to embrace enhancement. Whereas Agar thus sees no obligation to become posthuman, George Annas, one of the most outspoken opponents of posthumanism – famous for his equation of enhancement technologies with 'weapons of mass destruction' (Annas 2000: 773) – is much more sceptical. Annas even launched a campaign for an international convention to ban posthumanist 'species alteration', as this may endanger human nature and dignity:

> There are limits to how far we can go in changing our human nature without changing our humanity and our basic human values. Because it is the meaning of humanness (our distinctness from other animals) that has given birth to our concepts of both human dignity and human rights, altering our nature necessarily threatens to undermine both human dignity and human rights. With their loss, the fundamental belief in human equality would also be lost.
>
> (Annas 2000: 773)[1]

[1] Cf. Silver 1997.

Enhancement and human dignity

The concepts of human nature and human dignity, emphasized by Annas and other 'Bioconservatives', as Bostrom labels them, are fundamental to the debate on enhancement.

Although human dignity is a very controversial concept (Resnik 2007), it plays a key role in debates on bioethics and is adduced as the basis of several important legal treatises and conventions. Among the numerous interpretations of 'human dignity' put forward, three have been most influential: the Kantian, the naturalistic and the religious (Judeo-Christian).

All three approaches to human dignity mentioned share the notion of human dignity as an expression of the exceptional moral value of the human being, forming the basis for its undeniable rights:

> Human dignity is the idea that human beings have inherent moral value or worth. The 18th century German philosopher Immanuel Kant, who has developed the most influential view of human dignity, distinguished between two types of things in the world: things with a price and things with a dignity. Things that have dignity have a moral value that cannot be measured in terms of a price . . . According to Kant, dignity entails special treatment: one should not treat humanity (whether in one's own self or in another person) as having only an instrumental (market) value but always as having inherent, moral worth . . . Moral duties towards human beings imply moral rights: human beings have rights to life, liberty, property, due process and so on. (Resnik 2007: 215)

For Kant, the basis of human dignity is human autonomy. It is important, however, to underline that by autonomy Kant does not mean arbitrariness of individual decisions, but the insight into the natural laws of morality given with rationality. The subject of dignity, the 'person' in Kant's terminology, is autonomous insofar as she finds in herself ('*autos*') the norm of morality ('*nomos*') as a given 'fact of reason'. However, the feature of personal autonomy in the sense of free choice or freedom according to Kant can be indirectly deduced (albeit only as a regulative principle) from human morality, because the appeal expressed by the categorical imperative makes sense only under the condition that the moral subject is actually free. But what is more important in our context is the track record of Kant's concept of personhood, largely accepted as the dominant explanation for the exceptional moral status of human beings 'in terms of their capacity for self-consciousness and rationality' (Savulescu 2009: 215).

Personism

Michael Tooley and Peter Singer are the most famous or infamous proponents of personism. They argue that what matters morally is not being a member of the species *homo sapiens*, but some property of human beings – rationality and self-consciousness – which characterizes us as persons: 'It is wrong to kill persons because they can conceive existence into the future. Non-persons do not have such preferences. It is the frustration of these preferences that is wrong. Being human [in contrast to being a person] is merely having the property of being able to interbreed or having a certain chromosomal structure. These facts are not in themselves of normative significance' (Savulescu 2009: 221). What the naturalistic approach instead maintains will be discussed in more detail below.

In the context of the enhancement debate, a personist position is held by Allen Buchanan. He claims that human dignity refers not to the biological species but to the moral status of the person, as personhood in his view represents a 'threshold concept' and not a 'scalar one', so that once *homo sapiens* has acquired the features of personhood (namely, self-consciousness and rationality), to boost these traits would not augment the moral status of the enhanced person.

Although posthuman persons could thus not claim a higher moral status than human persons, Buchanan warns of the danger that non-enhanced persons might have to face serious constrictions of their rights: 'Given the history and persistence of racism, there is a serious risk that the enhanced would treat the unenhanced as if they had a lower moral status, even if they do not. Even if enhancements did not create beings with a higher moral status, or a mistaken perception of unequal moral statuses, this might result in a conflict of legitimate interest between the enhanced and the unenhanced, and a just accommodation of these conflicting interests might involve restrictions of some of the rights of the unenhanced' (Buchanan 2009: 350), similar to the restrictions now in place for the seriously mentally disabled.

Naturalism

Whereas the exponents of a personalistic approach to human dignity thus do not reject enhancement in principle but express doubts concerning the possible legal consequences for the unenhanced, the proponents of the naturalistic model of human dignity try to maintain the concept of human nature as some sort of unchangeable norm, although the arguments often differ considerably. Whereas Francis Fukuyama's position, for instance, is openly naturalistic, Jürgen Habermas' criticism of liberal eugenics focuses more on the consequences that manipulating the human genome may create on the social level.

Fukuyama's naturalistic approach is revealed in his definition of human nature. In *Our Posthuman Future*, he states, 'human nature is the sum of the behaviour and characteristics that are typical of the human species, arising from genetic rather than environmental factors' (Fukuyama 2002: 130).

Fukuyama identifies human nature with the specific genetic assets that determine our interaction with the environment, especially our emotional reactions. This pattern of emotional response encoded in the genome of the human species and transmitted from generation to generation represents for Fukuyama a sort of safe haven, as on his view our emotional reactions are the common ground of human behaviour and therefore the basis of all social interaction. According to Fukuyama, emotion – and not reason – is the ground of social interaction and politics. Emotions rather than arguments guarantee the peaceful co-existence between humans, or at least between members of the same ethnic group to which one feels viscerally attached 'by nature'. Interference in this relatively well-functioning system of instinctive behaviour could lead to disastrous consequences. Strangely enough, for Fukuyama the possible victory of the mind over the body, represented by biotechnologies, carries a risk of ending in a situation of general violence, a violence that today is restrained because of our inherited instincts.

A second problematic outcome of genetic enhancement picked up by Fukuyama is the danger that it allegedly poses to democracy, as it threatens to undermine the basic equality of humans. Fukuyama fears that the genetically modified 'will look, think, act, and perhaps even feel differently from those who were not similarly chosen, and may come in time to think of themselves as different kinds of creatures' (Fukuyama 2002: 157).

Jürgen Habermas, the elder statesman of German philosophy and last heir of the Frankfurt School, shares this fear. For him, the great difference between genetic inequality and all other possible inequalities (economic, social and political) between people is, that, in contrast to all of these traditional inequalities, genetic inequality is not reversible. Whereas all social and political differences are contingent – because at least in theory the relationship between master and slave can be reversed – the relationship between the 'enhanced' and the 'naturals' is irreversible. For Habermas, the problem with liberal eugenics is that it threatens to fix power relations once and for all.

A second problematic consequence of genetic enhancements in Habermas' focus concerns the image that genetically modified people may have of themselves. According to Habermas, a genetically modified person who is aware of her condition, would no longer be capable of seeing herself as solely responsible for her actions, as she would always have in mind that perhaps she acts the way she does only because someone else made her that way. According to this argument, a genetically modified person would be incapable of conceiving of herself as an autonomous subject and therefore also as someone capable of making responsible decisions. From this, Habermas concludes that with any but a natural origin – the German word Habermas uses is '*Naturwüchsigkeit*' – no person would be able to conceive of herself as an equal and autonomous individual. Thus, according to him, biotechnologies risk undermining the two most important pillars of liberal democracy: equality and autonomy. According to Habermas, a manipulated individual who becomes aware of the aims her parents pursued with her creation will lose the capacity to see herself as an autonomous and equal individual: 'We cannot rule out that knowledge of one's own hereditary features as programmed may prove to restrict the choice of an individual's life, and to undermine the essentially symmetric relations between free and equal human beings' (Habermas 2003: 23).

As liberal democracy is possible only as an association of autonomous and, at least theoretically, equal citizens, germline interventions, according to Habermas, therefore endanger the very foundations of our liberal democracies.

Similar to Habermas, Michael Sandel also fears that enhancement technologies 'may cause . . . loss of openness to the unbidden' (Bostrom and Savulescu 2009: 6). And, like Habermas, Sandel also stresses that the liberal approach to enhancement, expressed by Nozick's famous plea for a 'genetic supermarket' (Nozick 1974) is not essentially different from the old fashioned state-organized eugenics: 'What, after all, is the moral difference between designing children according to an explicit eugenic purpose and designing children according to the diktats of the market?' (Sandel 2009: 85).

But the most interesting point in Sandel's criticism of human enhancement perhaps consists in his thoughts about the possible consequences that it may have for the notions of personal responsibility and solidarity:

> If bioengineering made the myth of the 'self-made man' come true, it would be difficult to view our talents as gifts for which we are indebted, rather than as achievements for which we are responsible. This would transform three key features or our moral landscape: humility, responsibility, and solidarity . . . Suppose genetic testing advanced to the point where it could reliably predict each person's medical future and life expectancy . . . The solidarity of insurance would disappear as those with good genes fled the actuarial company of those with bad genes . . . A lively sense of the contingency of our gifts – a consciousness that none of us is wholly responsible for his or her success – saves a meritocratic society from sliding into the smug assumption that the rich are rich because they are more deserving than the poor. (Sandel 2009: 86)

Sandel's preoccupations are shared by Eric T. Juengst, who stresses that the dangers of the new technologies lie not in the alleged manipulation of human nature, but in their amplification of pre-existing social divides:

> It is the social perception of genetic difference, not the actual biological differences that fuel human rights abuses . . . To the extent that this wave of post-genomic work accentuates perceived genetic differences between human groups already socially sorted by their mutual power relations (like the 'races'), it will feed draconian 'public health' infringements on reproductive freedoms, oppressive DNA identification and data banking programs, neo-eugenic immigration policies, economic discrimination practices, and at the extreme, biological warfare strategies. (Juengst 2009: 56)

Habermas, Annas, Buchanan, Fukuyama, Sandel and Juengst, alarmed most of all by the possibly disruptive social consequences of enhancement, argue for a ban on enhancement technologies and advocate abstaining from enhancing human nature and from forgetting that, once we have the possibility to intervene in the natural lottery of genes, there is no way to escape responsibility. But, even if we decide not to manipulate our genome, we have to actively make this decision (Bayertz 1994). Once technology confronts us with the possibility of enhancing our biological features, we have lost our innocence one way or another, as we are responsible for acting in the same way that we are responsible for abstaining from acting: 'Could not a child who later became interested in a musical career, but had only the modest talents of its parents, complain that they had opted for the natural outcome and rejected it. In context, letting nature take its course is no longer a neutral response' (Coady 2009: 175).

Co-creation

Against the objections put forward by the so-called 'Bioconservatives', the 'progressive techno-euphoric' position embraces enhancement as ultimate liberation and emancipation from the biological boundaries that obstruct human freedom, which for this position is the very essence of man. On this view, the human animal represents only a transitory stage in the evolutionary history of this species, which has not yet come to an end. The human animal is not yet what it has to be, but must achieve its very essence by enhancing its proper nature.

However, in this respect, posthumanism is, as we have already seen, no different from classical humanism, which identifies man as the animal whose specific essence consists in not having a given essence at all. Man is the only being that is not what it is, but, since essentially free, has to decide for itself what to be. According to Stock, Director of the Program on Medicine, Technology and Society at the School of Medicine of the University of California in Los Angeles, if humanity is not actively pursuing the goal of genetic enhancement, the possibility will come forward as a side-effect of already widely accepted therapeutic practices: 'The fundamental discoveries that spawn these coming capabilities will flow from research deeply embedded in the mainstream, research that is highly beneficial, enjoys widespread support, and certainly is not directed toward a goal like human germline engineering. The possibilities of human redesign will arrive whether or not we actively pursue them' (Stock 2003: 40).

In agreement with Kurt Bayertz (1994), Stock points out that the very concept of a given natural nature, with which man ought not to interfere, is quite problematic, as it is based on the assumption that man himself is not part of nature. This distinction between the realm of nature (*physis*) where things develop on their own on the one hand, and man and his technical products (*technè*) on the other, dates back to Aristotle. In the latter's work, the term nature is used to designate the realm of life, the realm of the beings, which have the principle of their motion within themselves (keep in mind that Aristotle's concept of motion includes local movement as well as becoming and dying). Christianity takes on the Aristotelian distinction between *physis* and *technè*, with the difference that nature is then conceived as God's creation, seen in contrast to man and his products (technology), since, after the Fall of Man, humanity in a certain sense was no longer part of the created universe.

But there is also a different interpretation of the relationship between man and nature. The concept of being created in the image of God is generally connected with the idea that man shares with God the features of personhood and freedom which again are central to human dignity. But man, created in the image of God, has a relationship not only to the divine but also to nature. In the history of the three great monotheistic traditions (Judaism, Christianity and Islam), the relationship of man to nature has taken three main forms: domination, stewardship, and co-creation (Coady 2009), of which the latter is of particular interest in the context of the enhancement debate. Thus, for Eric Parens, 'according to Genesis, and it seems to me much of Judaism, our responsibility is not merely to be grateful and remember that we are not the creator of the whole. It is also our responsibility to use our creativity to mend and transform ourselves and the world. As far as I can tell, Genesis and Judaism do not exhort us to choose between gratitude and creativity' (Parens 2009: 189).

The idea of human co-creation, well known in Christianity (Rahner 1970), is especially important in Judaism. Here, man is seen as being as natural as everything else and therefore a fundamental part of creation. And, if man is part of created nature, his products are as well. Rabbi Barry Freundel, a consultant with the United States Presidential Commission on Cloning, states: 'If G-d has built the capacity for gene redesign into nature, than He chose for it to be available to us, and our test remains whether we will use that power wisely or poorly' (Freundel 2000: 119). Here, the idea that man is the image of God results in the conception that man, as poor as he is, has to be creative himself (Prainsack 2006).

> I do not find [human beings gaining control of their own evolution] to be any more troubling than discussing any other human capacity to alter the natural world. I take this position as a result of Judaism's teaching that human beings are the most important part of G-d's created universe... G-d has entrusted this world to humankind's hands, and the destiny of this world has always been our responsibility and our challenge. Whether or not we live up to that challenge is our calling and essential mission. (Freundel 2000: 119)

Secularizing the Judaic vision of the God–nature–man relationship, which essentially means eliminating the notion of God, Stock states: 'To some, the coming of human-directed change is unnatural because it differs so much from any previous change, but this distinction between the natural and the unnatural is an illusion. We are as natural a part of the world as anything else is, and so is the technology we create... Remaking ourselves is the ultimate expression and realization of our humanity' (Stock 2003: 197).

Hence, whereas the conservative faction tries to save a normative concept of nature, thereby risking to fall into the naturalistic fallacy that deduces norms from facts, the posthumanist – or genuinely humanist – position forgets the constitutive contingency of the human being, as this position is latently based on the idea that the human body is only the accidental substratum of the essentially free spiritual subject. This is because, if one thinks that the free subject is something different from his physical incarnation, it is possible to identify control over the body with liberation of the subject. Therefore, underlying the humanist/posthumanist position is an unconscious dualism of mind and body.

But who is this subject that gains control not only over its physical body, but even over its mental states? It is clear that Bostrom thinks of the human subject as something not only immaterial but beyond mental states. Bostrom's subject, which uses (bio)technology to liberate itself from outer and inner nature, is pure freedom, a very difficult notion to grasp.

Conclusion

The short analysis I have tried to give in the previous pages has shown that both the technophobic rejection of biotechnology and the techno-euphoric embracing of new technology are problematic. The first because it tries to maintain a normative concept of human nature comprehensible only on the grounds of extensive naturalistic presuppositions; the other because, standing in the tradition of the Enlightenment, is therefore subject to the 'dialectic of Enlightenment' described by Adorno and Horkheimer: what started as liberation from the boundaries of man's biological nature turns into reification of the entire human being (Adorno and Horkheimer 2002). In the words of Hans Jonas: 'technologically mastered nature now again includes man, who (up to now) had, in technology, set himself against it as its master' (Jonas 1985: 168).

So the pretended liberation from nature risks ending in a new form of manipulability, as the alleged liberation of the subject from its corporeal limitations finally threatens to create a new sort of oppression of man. He thus tragically learns that the body is not the grave of the soul (to quote Plato), but the only mode in which the mind exists.

The effort of biotechnology to manipulate human nature, which represents the acme of reification, thus paradoxically leads to the insight that this ultimate reification, which aims at total control of the objective nature by the human subject, is not possible. This is because the alleged liberation of the subject by means of the domination of nature (the classical programme of the Enlightenment according to Adorno and Horkheimer) shows that in biotechnology it is not a matter of a subject taking control over a mere body, but rather a human being as a whole being manipulated. The unintentional effect of biotechnology, which is based on the uncritical assumption of a dualistic model of man (defining man as the connection between objective nature and subjective *ratio*), thus consists in the demonstration that this dualistic model is no longer suitable. Having been explored as a consequence of mind–body dualism, biotechnology finally leads us to reach the conclusion that the human being is an indivisible psychosomatic unity.

References

Adorno, T. W., and Horkheimer, M. 2002. *Dialectic of Enlightenment.* Stanford University Press

Agar, N. 2007. 'Whereto Transhumanism? The Literature Reaches a Critical Mass', *Hastings Center Report* 37(3): 12–17

Annas, G. 2000. 'The Man on the Moon, Immortality and Other Millennial Myths: The Prospects and Perils of Human Genetic Engineering', *Emory Law Journal* 49(3): 753–82

Arendt, H. 1998. *The Human Condition.* University of Chicago Press

Bayertz, K. 1994. *GenEthics: Technological Intervention in Human Reproduction as a Philosophical Problem.* Cambridge University Press

Bostrom, N. 2005. 'In Defense of Posthuman Dignity', *Bioethics* 19(3): 202–14

2008. 'Why I Want To Be a Posthuman When I Grow Up', in B. Gordijn and R. Chadwick (eds.), *Medical Enhancement and Posthumanity.* New York: Springer, 107–37

Bostrom, N., and Savulescu, J. 2009. 'Human Enhancement Ethics: The State of the Debate' in N. Bostrom and J. Savulescu (eds.), *Human Enhancement.* Oxford University Press, 1–22

Buchanan, A. 2009. 'Moral Status and Human Enhancement', *Philosophy and Public Affairs* 37(4): 346–81

Coady, C. A. J. 2009. 'Playing God' in N. Bostrom and J. Savulescu (eds.), *Human Enhancement.* Oxford University Press, 155–81

Freundel, B. 2000. 'Gene Modification Technology', in G. Stock (ed.), *Engineering the Human Germline: An Exploration of the Science and Ethics of Altering the Genes We Pass to Our Children.* Oxford University Press, 119–22

Fukuyama, F. 2002. *Our Posthuman Future: Consequences of the Biotechnological Revolution.* New York: Farrar, Straus & Giroux

Habermas, J. 2003. *The Future of Human Nature.* Oxford: Blackwell

Jonas, Hans. 1985. 'Lasst uns einen Menschen klonieren', in H. Jonas, *Technik, Medizin und Ethik.* Frankfurt am Main: Suhrkamp, 162–203

Juengst, E. T. 2009. 'What's Taxonomy Got to Do with It? Species Integrity", Human Rights, and Science Policy', in N. Bostrom and J. Savulescu (eds.), *Human Enhancement.* Oxford University Press, 43–58

Kant, I. 1993. *Grounding for the Metaphysics of Morals,* 3rd edn, Indianapolis, IN: Hackett

Nozick, R. 1974. *Anarchy, State, and Utopia.* New York: Basic Books

Parens, E. 2009. 'Toward a More Fruitful Debate About Enhancement', in N. Bostrom and J. Savulescu (eds.), *Human Enhancement.* Oxford University Press, 181–98

Pico della Mirandola, G. 1990. *De hominis dignitate.* Hamburg: Meiner

Prainsack, B. 2006. 'Negotiating Life: The Regulation of Human Cloning and Embryonic Stem Cell Research in Israel', *Social Studies of Science* 36(2): 173–205

Rahner, K. 1970. 'Zum Problem der genetischen Manipulation aus der Sicht des Theologen', in F. Wagner (ed.), *Menschenzüchtung: Das Problem der genetischen Manipulierung des Menschen.* Munich: C. H. Beck, 135–66

Resnik, D. B. 2007. 'Embryonic Stem Cell Patents and Human Dignity', *Health Care Analysis* 15: 211–22

Sandel, M. J. 2009. 'The Case Against Perfection: What's Wrong with Designer Children, Bionic Athletes, and Genetic Engineering', in N. Bostrom and J. Savulescu (eds.), *Human Enhancement*. Oxford University Press, 71–90

Savulescu, J. 2009. 'The Human Prejudice and the Moral Status of Enhanced Beings: What Do We Owe the Gods?', in N. Bostrom and J. Savulescu (eds.), *Human Enhancement*. Oxford University Press, 211–50

Silver, L. M. 1997. *Remaking Eden Cloning and Beyond in a Brave New World*. New York: Avon Books

Stock, G. (ed.). 2000. *Engineering the Human Germline: An Exploration of the Science and Ethics of Altering the Genes We Pass to Our Children*. Oxford University Press

2003. *Redesigning Humans: Choosing Our Genes, Changing Our Future*. New York: Mariner Books

34

Dignity as the right to have rights: human dignity in Hannah Arendt

CHRISTOPH MENKE*

In recent years, Hannah Arendt has – with increasing frequency – been interpreted as a theorist of human dignity.[1] This frequency stands in clear contrast to the fact that Arendt herself only very rarely speaks about the dignity of human beings – in distinction, for example, from the 'dignity of the political' which she investigates and defends in many of her works (Villa 2000). The most prominent of the rare passages in which Arendt does speak of human dignity appears in the foreword to the first edition of *The Origins of Totalitarianism* (1951). Towards the end of this foreword, she writes that:

> Antisemitism (and not merely the hatred of Jews), imperialism (not merely conquest), totalitarianism (not merely dictatorship) – one after the other, one more brutally than the other – have demonstrated that human dignity needs a new guarantee which can only be found in a new political principle, in a new law on earth, whose validity this time must comprehend the whole of humanity while its power must remain strictly limited, rooted in and controlled by newly defined territorial entities. (Arendt 1958b: ix)[2]

Precisely this emphatic formulation, which links the idea of human dignity to the struggle against anti-Semitism, imperialism and totalitarianism, has, however, already 'been dropped' (Arendt 1986: 13) by the 1955 German edition of the book. In the major books that Arendt dedicated to the essence of the political – from *The Human Condition* (1958a) through *On Revolution* (1967) to *Lectures on Kant's Political Philosophy* (1982) – the question of human dignity is only addressed in passing, if indeed at all.

And yet Arendt's appeal to human dignity in the foreword to *The Origins of Totalitarianism* is the expression of a line of thought every bit as central to her understanding of the political as her understanding of the political can be helpful for a clarification of her concept of human dignity. This line of thought is contained in the famous formula from the ninth book of *The Origins of*

* Translated by Birgit Kaiser, Kathrin Thiele and Erica Weitzman.

1 Especially Isaac 1996, Helis 2008 and Parekh 2008; see also Beiner 1990 and Kateb 2007.

2 See Birmingham 2006; 2007.

Totalitarianism on the 'right to have rights' (Arendt 1958b: 296). The rationale behind Arendt's appeal to human dignity implies that human dignity *consists in* 'a right to have rights (and that means to live in a framework where one is judged by one's actions and opinions) and a right to belong to some kind of organized community' (*ibid.*: 296f). For '[only] the loss of a polity itself expels him [i.e. man] from humanity' (*ibid.*: 297).

This revealing formula, which will be cited far more often than Arendt's cursory appeal to human dignity, is also one that she never used again. The reason for this may be easily understood and is a direct consequence of the specific context in which Arendt introduces the concepts of human dignity and the right to have rights. This context is Arendt's diagnosis of the 'aporia of human rights', in other words her radical critique of the tradition of human rights from the eighteenth to the middle of the twentieth centuries.[3] For, if Arendt speaks of human dignity and the right to have rights in *The Origins of Totalitarianism*, she does this not in order to approve the tradition of the idea of human rights, but rather to *reproach* it.[4] Since this internal connection between Arendt's appeal to human dignity as the right to have rights and her diagnosis of the aporia of human rights is, however, easy to overlook (and often *is* overlooked), Arendt later abandoned this terminology. This does not mean, however, that she revised the underlying ideas.

Arendt expressed the internal connection between the appeal to human dignity and the critique of human rights most succinctly in a 1949 essay which forms the basis of the famous chapter of *The Origins of Totalitarianism*. This essay is even more interesting in view of the fact that Arendt is writing directly under the influence of the Universal Declaration of Human Rights, which was the first attempt to codify the concept of human dignity *for* the grounding of human rights in an international treaty as a response to the same experience of totalitarianism that Arendt also refers to in her own appeal to human dignity.[5] Arendt, however, asserts that the Declaration displays a strong

[3] 'The Aporias of the Rights of Man' ('Die Aporien der Menschenrechte') is the title of the last section of Chapter 9 of *Origins of Totalitarianism* in the German version (Arendt 1986). The English title speaks of 'The Perplexities of the Rights of Man' (Arendt 1958b, 290ff).

[4] See in this regard Balibar 2007 and Rancière 2004. Opposed to this are interpretations that, for a whole variety of purposes, seek to undo or refute the connection between Arendt's critique of human rights and the counter-concept of the right to have rights: while Benhabib (1996: 193ff) and Cohen (1996) attempt to return Arendt's human rights critique to an anti-universalist thematic (which can then only be overcome through a Kantian reinterpretation of 'the right to have rights'), for Agamben (2000) Arendt's critique of human rights is such a fundamental one that through it the concept of (subjective) rights may be completely repudiated. In this regard, see Menke (2007); in what follows here I use certain formulations and lines of thought taken from this text.

[5] It is, however, unclear from the text whether Hannah Arendt had access to the final version of the Universal Declaration of Human Rights while writing her essay. Arendt

conceptual confusion, one that 'invariably leads to philosophically absurd and politically unrealistic claims such as that each man is born with the inalienable right to unemployment insurance or an old age pension' (Arendt 1949: 34). For Arendt, this conceptual confusion corresponds to a blatant 'lack of reality' (Arendt 1949: 37), insofar as this latter attempt to reformulate human rights merely repeats, in both spirit and attitude, the traditional declarations which were formulated at the end of the eighteenth century without accounting for the profound crisis that befell the idea of human rights after its failure in the face of totalitarian politics. For Arendt, the tradition of human rights is not the (good) Other *opposed to* a totalitarian politics of exclusion and extermination; rather, the former is connected to the latter in complicated fashion. If this connection is not clarified, no real opposition to totalitarianism can exist. The appeal to human dignity (as the Universal Declaration ambiguously approaches it) is, according to Arendt, not only inadequate as such, it may also be dangerous if it fails to perceive the aporias or perplexities in which the idea of human rights found itself when confronted with a totalitarian politics. Understanding this critique of the tradition of human rights (first subsection below) is thus the precondition for understanding Arendt's concept of human dignity (second subsection below).

Arendt's critique of the tradition of human rights

In her critique, emphasizing the unrealistic nature of the Universal Declaration of Human Rights, Arendt takes up the 'English' critique of the 1789 *Déclaration des droits de l'homme et du citoyen*, i.e. the critique – first formulated by Edmund Burke and extended shortly thereafter by Jeremy Bentham – that human rights are 'an abstraction' (Arendt 1949: 31). When Burke calls the French declaration of human rights 'monstrous' and 'tragicomic' (Burke 1987: 9), or when Bentham calls it 'nonsense upon stilts' (Bentham 1843: 523), they mean that 'human rights' are normative demands which relinquish the conditions and forms of the very action they require for their implementation. This action is, namely, political action, or, more precisely, the act of legislation: 'rights' only exist by virtue of legislation. However, laws are only passed for particular political entities, that is, according to modern understanding, for particular (nation) states. Thus, rights 'as such' do not exist, because laws 'as such' do not exist. For Arendt, this double insight – first, that all rights depend upon laws, and, second, that all legislation is inescapably tied to a certain 'locale' – is the essence of Burke's position when he claims to prefer 'the rights of an Englishman' over those of the human being: 'According to Burke, the rights which we enjoy spring "from within the nation", so that neither natural law, nor divine command, nor any concept of mankind, such as Robespierre's "human race, the sovereign of the

speaks of a 'Bill of Rights of the United Nations', and a footnote in the German version refers to the 'drafts of the UN Commission' (Arendt 1949: 35).

earth", are needed as a source of law' (Arendt 1949: 31). There are no rights other than those like 'the rights of an Englishman', i.e. rights that derive 'from within the nation'. 'Rights of human beings', therefore, do not exist.

Arendt alludes to the English critique of the French *Déclaration* for the purpose of interpreting in its light the epochal event of the 'decline of the nation-state' in the first half of the twentieth century, which was in fact nothing less than the 'end of the rights of man'. By 'the decline of the nation-state', Arendt means what was first the erosion, then the complete shattering, of the principle that all inhabitants of a given territory are also citizens of the state that legislates over this territory (for the reason that they are all members of the same people or nation). Such an assumption was made henceforth impossible by the politics of discrimination, expulsion and expatriation in regard to minorities, Jews and refugees in Europe after the First World War. Above all, however, Arendt claims that the 'loss of national rights in all instances entailed the loss of human rights' (Arendt 1949: 31). For Arendt, the central event of the twentieth century is that anyone who ceased to count as the citizen of a particular state not only lost his or her civil rights in that particular state, but also his or her human rights: 'The conception of human rights broke down at the very moment when those who professed to believe in it were for the first time confronted with people who indeed had lost all other qualities and specific relationships, except that they were still human. The world found nothing sacred in the abstract nakedness of being human' (Arendt 1949: 31). This is due to the fact that the 'world' still understood human rights in the tradition of the French Revolution, i.e. in the sense that human rights can only come into being under the auspices of nation-states, and therefore only for these nation-states' respective members. If, however, the nation-state is effectively the only juridical authority that can acknowledge and implement human rights, there can be no human rights for all those who, as a result of expatriation and emigration, cease to belong to any nation-state. The lesson that Arendt draws from the crisis of human rights, however, is precisely the opposite of this conclusion. The link between the rights of man and the rights of the citizen that ultimately led to the loss of human rights with the decline of the nation-state does not reflect a misunderstanding of the true nature of human rights for Arendt; rather, this linkage *is* human rights' true nature.

Arendt bases this claim in the observation that all of the 'so-called Rights of Man' (Arendt 1949: 30) listed by the classical declarations – and they are many and 'of the most heterogeneous nature and origin' (Arendt 1949: 37) – are in fact not concerned with the kind of rights to which each individual human being, simply as human being, is endowed at all. As the first and paradigmatic case of human rights, i.e. freedom of religion, shows, human rights are rather 'formulas which were designed to solve problems *within* given communities' (Arendt 1949: 28). Any declaration of human rights therefore implicitly presupposes that human beings are already members of a community. What the classical declarations call 'human rights' are in fact political principles of legislation within a given community; they thus presuppose the individual's membership of that community. The 'so-called Rights of Man' are a misleading articulation of the rights of each member of a political community and thus of rights which also can *only* pertain to the members of this political community.

For Arendt, there is no way out of this conceptual dilemma (which she therefore describes as 'aporetic') in which rights are bound up with political membership. The traditional declarations of human rights sought a way out by taking recourse to the idea of nature: that is, while human rights in fact deal with problems and establish claims '*within* given communities', declarations of human rights have misrepresented themselves, claiming 'to spell out primary positive rights, inherent in man's nature, as distinguished from his political status, and as such they tried indeed to reduce politics to nature' (Arendt 1967: 104). Through this naturalization, however – which was originally meant to give these rights a concrete basis – the declarations of human rights undermine that which is the very foundation of any juridical political community: the idea of equality. For '[w]e are not born equal, we become equal as members of a group on the strength of our decision to guarantee ourselves mutually equal rights' (Arendt 1949: 33).[6] Equality is not an attribute of the natural human being, but rather one of members of a political community; the act of referring to the natural human being will therefore eventually destroy any claim to equal rights. This reversal of the natural grounding of *human* rights into the dissolution of human *rights* is the real explanation for the powerlessness of human rights in the face of totalitarianism's politics of exclusion and extermination which forced their victims to 'live outside the common world'; the victims of totalitarianism were 'thrown back on their natural givenness, on their mere differentiation' (Arendt 1949: 33). Totalitarian politics thus turned their victims into precisely those natural human beings to whom human rights were meant to refer. However, in that same moment it became clear that by being merely natural beings they were no longer potential bearers of rights because they were no longer equals. Or else it became clear that the declarations of human rights, when speaking of natural human beings, were in fact referring to members of political communities. This confusion remained (relatively) harmless for as long as (almost[7]) all human beings were members of a political community in one way or another. But when the world was confronted with masses of non-members, this confusion all of a sudden gained terrible significance. At that

[6] 'Equality . . . is not given to us' (Arendt 1958b: 301); '[n]either equality nor freedom [is] understood as a quality inherent to human nature' (Arendt 1967: 23). For a different reading of Arendt's critique of naturalization, see Agamben 1998, Part III.

[7] Given that slaves were, in certain respects, still counted as 'a part of the human community' (Arendt 1949: 30), even if Aristotle denied them the capacity of reason, it was the 'savages' of the imperial nineteenth century who were the first 'natural' human beings in whose respect this problem could have arisen (Arendt 1949: 32) – that is, had their existence been taken seriously by the European perspective as a challenge to the concept of human rights.

moment it became evident that the declarations of human rights were unable to counter the overwhelming power of the appearance of the natural human being as something essentially non-equal.

Precisely this is the aporia of human rights: there are only equal rights for political members – and thus these are no *human* rights; and there are only different needs or claims of natural human beings – and thus these cannot lead to human *rights*.

Arendt's concept of dignity

This 'aporia' of human rights emerges when the decisive question of the rights of those who have been violently turned into non-members is answered by taking recourse to the idea of the natural condition of the human being. Such an answer undermines just what it is meant to establish – the idea of equal rights. These human rights are *in fact* just that – the rights of citizens, of the members of a community. What is most urgently needed by the growing masses of non-members; by the expatriated, refugees, stateless persons who neither have nor can find a community, does not appear in the declarations of the 'so-called Rights of Man'.

Arendt's expression for what is needed is the 'right to have rights' (Arendt 1949: 30). The right *to* which non-members must have a right is that of the members of a political community, that is, the right to equality. The right *to have* this right, however, cannot be of the same order as other rights: it is not the right *of* members, but the right *to* membership – 'a right to belong to some kind of organized community' (Arendt 1949: 30). 'We know even better than Burke that rights materialize only within a given political community, that they depend on our fellow-men and on a tacit guarantee that the members of a community give to each other. But we also know that apart from all so-called human rights, which change according to historical and other circumstances, there does exist one right that does not spring "from within the nation" and which needs more than national guarantees: it is the right of every human being to membership in a political community' (Arendt 1949: 34). According to Arendt, this 'right to have rights' is, in distinction to the 'so-called Rights of Man', indeed a human right, namely, *the* ('only') human right, 'the one right without which no other can materialize' (Arendt 1949: 37).

It thus follows from Arendt's demonstration of the aporia of the tradition of human rights that 'it would be a serious error to define this one right, which was never even mentioned among the Rights of Man in the categorical framework of the eighteenth century' (Arendt 1949: 34). Instead, a radical break with that tradition would be required in order to be able to think this one truly human right to have rights. Towards the end of her essay, Arendt suggests two different, even contradictory ways of accomplishing this task.

The first way consists in structurally transforming the human right to have rights into that of a (membership) right within a political community. According to this interpretation, the human right to have rights would belong to the 'sphere of a law that is above the nations' – to international or even cosmopolitan law (Brunkhorst 1999: 93ff; 2002: 19ff). This new international law would be traceable to an act of legislation like any other law: 'This human right, like all other rights, can exist only through mutual agreement and guarantee. Transcending the rights of the citizen – being the right of men to citizenship – this right is the only one that can and can only be guaranteed by the comity of nations' (Arendt 1949: 37). This comity of nations would in turn be based upon a historical development: the 'emergence of mankind as *one* political entity' (Arendt 1949: 36).

This, then, is the first of Arendt's ways out of the aporias of human rights: the human right to have rights would be the fundamental right brought about by an international law – legally binding through 'mutual agreement and guarantee' – which would constitute mankind as a 'political entity'. However, in treating the emergence of mankind qua political entity as a mere historical fact, this solution avoids the crucial question of why such a politically unified humankind *should* exist in the first place. Understanding the right to have rights as the outcome of inter- or supra-national legislation is insufficient to answer this question. Instead, the concept of a right to have rights must provide a reason for the establishment of such legislation.

With this critique, a second way of understanding the right to have rights gains significance. Arendt articulates this alternative understanding with the term 'humanity' (or sometimes 'mankind') using it in a manner different from the two ways that we have thus far encountered, i.e. as the term either for a natural condition or for a historically developed political entity. In this context, Arendt, albeit only in passing, speaks of 'human dignity' (Arendt 1949: 30). Here, 'dignity' refers to what is prior to 'all so-called Rights of Man': 'Man, it turns out, can lose all so-called Rights of Man without losing his essential quality as man, his human dignity. Only the loss of a polity itself expels him from humanity' (Arendt 1949: 30). Arendt thus uses the term 'dignity' (or 'humanity') to designate what would be lost, *beyond* all human rights, with the loss of the status of being a member of a polity and thus with the loss of the right to have rights itself: 'Its loss entails the loss of the relevance of speech (and man, since Aristotle, has been defined as a being commanding the power of speech and thought), and the loss of all human relationship (and man, again since Aristotle, has been called the "political animal", that is, one who by definition lives in a community), the loss, in other words, of some of the most essential characteristics of human life' (Arendt 1949: 30).[8]

One can discern two argumentative moves made by Arendt which are fundamental for her understanding of the concept of human dignity. First, modern natural law founded rights upon properties which human beings are endowed with by nature: either human beings are thought to be created

[8] Cf. Enders 1977: 501f.

by God, or thought to possess capacities specific to their species, such as reason or pity. These properties form the basis of fundamental claims every human being can make. From these legitimate claims, which pertain to every human being as human being, follow claims which every human being can make with respect to others in the 'social' sphere. Arendt's concept of human dignity, on the other hand, operates in an entirely different manner from that of natural law. With reference to Aristotle, she defines the dignity of human beings by virtue of their being speaking beings, which means for Arendt by virtue of their being political beings. Human dignity is then no natural property with which human beings are individually endowed and that would only subsequently have social consequences. Rather, it consists in nothing other than their politico-linguistic existence: their speaking, judging, and acting as faculties, which they have essentially through, with, and in relation to others.

If, Arendt argues, the politico-linguistic existence of human beings is what constitutes their dignity, this also means attributing to this form of existence a privileged status: politico-linguistic existence is not just one form of life among others, it is the essentially human form. The politico-linguistic existence of human beings is the human *disposition*: 'a general characteristic of the human condition' (Arendt 1949: 30). In this first move of Arendt's argument, therefore, her use of the concept of human dignity introduces a definition of human nature that does not take recourse to the idea of the natural human being. Human dignity consists *in* politico-linguistic human existence, because human beings are politico-linguistic 'by nature': they are predetermined to develop a politico-linguistic existence. Each human being's right to membership in a political community is therefore based upon the experience of the significance of politico-linguistic existence for human beings – in other words, it is their right to that form of their existence that is the actual human condition. Or, expressed the other way around: it means that each human being's right to membership in a political community cannot be based upon attributes that are independent from human politico-linguistic existence (and that could in this sense be termed 'natural'). The foundation for each human being's right to membership in a political community cannot be found outside of or below his or her existence within such a community, but rather is located in the experience of the significance of this existence, an experience that is only available within this existence (cf. Birmingham 2006).

Second, Arendt thus no longer refers to the nature of human beings in the sense of a pre-political attribute. By referring to it as the human disposition to political existence, she distances herself from the normative design of modern natural law. Modern natural law traces juridical rights back to natural rights. Both have the same form: that is, they are both subjective rights. Subjective rights are claims by means of which a subject can obligate others. The paradigmatic case in this regard is the right to property: a possession becomes property if it is possible to obligate others to refrain from using the object in question by uttering the words 'this is mine' (or through some equivalent symbolic act). In the juridical sphere, subjective rights are rights bestowed upon the subject. 'Natural' rights, on the contrary, are considered to be non-bestowed subjective rights: while they may function like legal rights (insofar as they confer the capacity to obligate others), one 'possesses' them more or less naturally. We have already seen that Arendt agrees with the 'English' critique, which holds that such non-bestowed subjective rights are 'nonsense upon stilts' (Bentham). The consequence of this is that either the one human right, the 'right to have rights', must also be bestowed – this is the gist of the previously criticized solution to the aporias of human rights, i.e. their being merged with international law – or that, contrary to how it may appear, this one human right cannot be a subjective right (cf. Michelman 1996).

The concept of right must thus have an objective rather than a subjective sense: it no longer defines a claim that human beings are entitled to make, but instead defines what is right *for* them. Understood in a subjective sense, the right to have rights implies that human beings can make a claim to political membership, and are – via law, contract or nature, respectively – entitled to do so. Understood in an objective sense, on the other hand, the right to have rights means that *it is right* for human beings to be members of a political community, in which they – as members – have rights. The objective understanding of the right to have rights *constitutes* the subjective right to political membership, and thereby shows that what grounds subjective rights is not of the same order as these rights themselves (as modern natural law had assumed).[9] The claim of each human being to political membership is instead based on the conviction that political membership is the right thing for human beings, emerging out of the understanding of political membership as the (true) human condition.

From the crisis that befell human rights after totalitarianism's politics of exclusion, Arendt draws the conclusion that human rights must be conceived wholly different from the traditional categories of 'natural' rights. That kind of naturalization of rights is in fact an element of the crisis of human rights, if not indeed – *per* Agamben's radicalization of Arendt's critique – complicit with totalitarian politics, and in any case offers no real solution to the crisis of human rights. Arendt's concept of human dignity, on the other hand, *does* offer a solution; albeit one that does not dispute but rather presupposes the insight into the aporias of human rights. It shows that a solution to the crisis of human rights will only be found if the understanding of human rights is transformed entirely, including all its defining elements. The two (more or less implicit) argumentative moves that Arendt is able to make through her use of

[9] 'Before this [i.e. the "deprivation of a place in the world which makes opinions significant and actions effective"], what we must call a "human right" today would have been thought of as a general characteristic of the human condition which no tyrant could take away' (Arendt 1958b: 296f).

the concept of human dignity show the direction that must be taken in order to think the 'one human right' to have rights, beyond the aporias of human rights. The concept of human dignity offers a way out of the crisis of human rights only if, first, it introduces a different anthropology than that of modern natural law – specifically, an anthropology of human life forms as opposed to an anthropology of quasi-natural human 'needs' or 'interests'; and, second, if it understands the foundation of rights differently: by grounding subjective rights in the experience of what is right for human beings.

References

Agamben, G. 1998. *Homo Sacer: Sovereign Power and Bare Life.* Stanford University Press

2000. 'Beyond Human Rights', in G. Agamben, *Means Without Ends: Notes on Politics.* Minneapolis, MN: University of Minnesota Press, 15–26

Arendt, H. 1949. '"The Rights of Man": What Are They?', *Modern Review* 3(1): 24–36 (German translation: 'Es gibt nur ein einziges Menschenrecht', *Die Wandlung IV.* Heidelberg: Schneider, 754–70)

1958a. *The Human Condition.* University of Chicago Press

1958b. *The Origins of Totalitarianism.* Cleveland, New York: World Publishing Company

1967. *On Revolution.* New York: Viking Press

1982. *Lectures on Kant's Political Philosophy.* University of Chicago Press

1986. *Elemente und Ursprünge totaler Herrschaft.* Stuttgart: Piper

Balibar, E. 2007. '(De)Constructing the Human as Human Institution: A Reflection on the Coherence of Hannah Arendt's Practical Philosophy', *Social Research* 74(3): 727–39

Beiner, R. 1990. 'Hannah Arendt and Leo Strauss: The Uncommenced Dialogue', *Political Theory* 18(2): 238–54

Benhabib, S. 1996. *The Reluctant Modernism of Hannah Arendt.* Thousand Oaks, CA: Sage Publications

Bentham, J. 1843. 'Anarchical Fallacies: Being an Examination of the Declaration of Rights Issued During the French Revolution', in *The Works of Jeremy Bentham*, vol. II, Edinburgh

Birmingham, P. 2006. *Hannah Arendt and Human Rights: The Predicament of Common Responsibility.* Bloomington, IN: Indiana University Press

2007. 'The An-Archic Event of Natality and the "Right to Have Rights"', *Social Research* 74(3): 763–76

Brunkhorst, H. 1999. *Hannah Arendt.* Munich: C. H. Beck

2002. *Solidarität: Von der Bürgerfreundschaft zur globalen Rechtsgenossenschaft.* Frankfurt am Main: Suhrkamp

Burke, E. 1987. *Reflections on the Revolution in France.* Indianapolis, IN, Cambridge: Hackett

Cohen, J. L. 1996. 'Rights, Citizenship and the Modern Form of the Social: Dilemmas of Arendtian Republicanism', *Constellations* 3(2): 164–89

Enders, C. 1977. *Die Menschenwürde in der Verfassungsordnung: Zur Dogmatik des Art. 1 GG.* Tübingen: Mohr Siebeck

Helis, J. 2008. 'Hannah Arendt and Human Dignity: Theoretical Foundations and Constitutional Protection of Human Rights', *Journal of Politics and Law* 1(3): 73–8
Isaac, J. C. 1996. 'A New Guarantee on Earth: Hannah Arendt on Human Dignity and the Politics of Human Rights', *American Political Science Review* 90(1): 61–73
Kateb, G. 2007. 'Existential Values in Arendt's Treatment of Evil and Morality', *Social Research* 74(3): 811–54
Menke, C. 2007. 'The "Aporias of Human Rights" and the "One Human Right": Regarding the Coherence of Hannah Arendt's Argument', *Social Research* 74(3): 739–62
Michelman, F. I. 1996. 'Parsing "A Right to Have Rights"', *Constellations* 3(2): 200–8
Parekh, S. 2008. *Hannah Arendt and the Challenge of Modernity: A Phenomenology of Human Rights*. New York: Routledge
Rancière, J. 2004. 'Who Is the Subject of the Rights of Man?', *South Atlantic Quarterly* 103(2–3): 297–310
Villa, D. 2000. 'Introduction', in D. Villa (ed.), *The Cambridge Companion to Hannah Arendt*. Cambridge University Press, 1–24

35

Individual and collective dignity

MICHA WERNER

Is there such a thing as *collective* dignity? Does it make sense to talk about the dignity of (some of such) entities as the human species as a whole, indigenous peoples, states, religious communities, women, baseball teams or green-eyed men who get up at 7:30? Can we even conceive of dignity as something that could be assigned to collectives? There is no easy answer to these questions, since both parts of the expression 'collective dignity' are problematic even before they are combined. Obviously, dignity is a heavily contested, multifaceted and ambiguous concept; moreover, there are different ways to understand the 'collective' character of 'collective dignity'. Nevertheless, one finds a growing number of references to 'collective dignity' or 'collective human dignity' (for example, De Gaay Fortman 2011; Falk 2009: 58; Howard 1992: 84; International Law Association 2010: 40–3; Mann 2001: 34–6). However, most of them come without any effort to clarify the meaning of these terms. At the same time, the question of whether collective dignity can be warranted seems systematically relevant, at least in the context of certain branches of the human rights discourse. Let us just consider two rather obvious points. The first has to do with the discussion on 'collective rights': *if* one is of the opinion that collective human rights exist and *if* one, in addition, supposes that dignity is the normative basis or 'source' of human rights, it seems reasonable to ask whether collective human rights are also grounded in some form of collective dignity. The second point is related to one strategy of interpreting and vindicating dignity: *if* one argues that the normative basis of dignity is something like agency and *if* one, in addition, supposes that not only individuals but also collectives can be agents, it is again an obvious question whether collective dignity exists.

In what follows, I will first mention some of the most prominent uses of the term 'collective dignity' (2nd section) and then make some tentative remarks about the extent to which these uses are plausible (3rd section).

Different uses of the term 'dignity'

As is well known, the meaning of the term 'dignity' has changed significantly throughout history, and different semantic layers are still present in its current uses. In general, 'dignity' signifies a certain *normative status* of an entity; a status that is attributed on the basis of certain intrinsic or relational *properties* the entity is taken to have (for example, that it holds a certain social role or office, or behaves in a certain way, or that it is created in the likeness of God, or that it is an agent, or an autonomous or rational being) and that consists of, entails or warrants certain – more or less formalized – *rights and/or duties* of the entity who 'has' dignity. It is important to note that 'rights and/or duties' does not necessarily mean full-fledged moral or legal rights in a modern sense. They may just be some informal normative expectation, and its content may be nothing more than some emotional or social attitude. Just like other normative terms, 'dignity' is sometimes used in a derivative, non-normative way, in which case to ascribe dignity to an entity does not imply acknowledging or ascribing some normative status to the entity but mainly stating that such status is in fact assigned to it by the entity itself or by (some relevant part of) its social environment. For example, a historian may write about the specific dignity of kings in earlier times without accepting any of the normative commitments that constituted the respective conception of dignity.

Collective dignity and the duties of political collectives

A first group of references to collective dignity focuses on the moral *duties* of those to whom this dignity is attributed. A typical example can be found in Fuller (2006: 108): 'Second-class citizenship is incompatible with dignity – not only the dignity of those consigned to it, but the collective dignity of the society that tolerates the discrimination.' Sometimes, it is not (only) assumed that collective dignity constitutes certain duties, but (also) that the collective will somehow lose its dignity if it does not respect them, for example where López claims that the immigration detention system of the United States 'robs us [citizens of the USA] of our collective dignity' (2011). However, something appears puzzling here. If the dignity of *X* brings about certain duties for *X*, *and* if to neglect these duties destroys *X's* dignity, it seems all too easy for *X* to get away with his neglecting his duties: they would vanish the very moment he neglects them.[1] Hence it seems that the dignity that *constitutes* certain duties (or rights) is not the same as the dignity that one *earns by respecting* the respective duties (or that one *destroys by disrespecting* the rights) in question, though the two different forms of dignity might be related in some straightforward way. For example, in a Kantian line, one can plausibly distinguish the dignity *X* has due to his property of *being able* to respect moral laws from the dignity *X* earns by *respecting* these moral laws.

Independent of whether collective dignity is taken as the source of collective duties, or as something a collective 'earns' by respecting these duties, or both, it remains to be asked what is actually collective about it, and in what sense.

[1] A problem of the same sort arises if we assume that *Y*'s dignity or *Y*'s humanity is the source of certain rights of *Y* *and* assume that, by disrespecting these rights, we dehumanize *Y* or deprive him of his dignity.

However, before we enter this discussion, we should first consider some of the alternative uses of the term 'collective dignity'. Let us just note one obvious point: where 'collective dignity' is related to duties of the respective collective, this collective has to be seen as some sort of collective agent. In fact, most respective uses of the term 'collective dignity' are about the dignity of political entities, and are related to actions of political institutions, especially the government. Hence, any interpretation of what is collective about this type of collective dignity will be directly related to the interpretation of collective agents.

Collective dignity, the struggle for collective recognition, and collective rights

A second type of use of the term 'collective dignity' emphasizes the rights, not the duties, of the respective collectives. For example, as Cheah (2006: 73) notes, in the context of decolonization 'national self-determination' has sometimes been 'understood as a people's achievement of collective dignity so that it can participate as an equal member in democratic self-legislation on the global stage' (for example, Cabral 1972; Kiros 2001: 107; cf. Margalit and Raz 1990; Smith 1981). This understanding of collective dignity refers to the normative status of peoples or other collectives that deserve to be or actually are recognized as having a distinct identity, and the ability as well as the right to govern themselves.

Obviously, struggles for the recognition of distinct identities do not only arise on the macro-level of international relations but also within the borders of modern national states; and it is here that uses of the term 'collective dignity' or 'collective human dignity' come closest to – and potentially interfere the most with – uses of the concept of individual dignity as the source of human rights. Some authors hold that, just as individual dignity can be seen as the source of individual human rights, collective dignity should count as the source of collective (human) rights or rather group rights, like rights of minorities.

For example, Rhoda Howard argues that the claims of '[m]any indigenous groups . . . for the recognition of their collective or communal rights' do not, or at least not primarily, originate from their being 'interested in the human rights of the individual members of their collectivities'. Rather, Howard claims, 'they are interested in the recognition of their *collective dignity*, in the acknowledgement of the value of their collective way of life as opposed to the way of life of the dominant society into which they are usually "integrated"' (Howard 1992: 83f). While, in Howard's terminology, the concept of human rights always refers to *individual* human rights, human dignity can be either individual or collective (*ibid.*: 84). However, Howard's understanding of 'human' dignity does not imply the idea that one enjoys it 'merely because one is a human being'. Rather, she defines human dignity as 'the particular cultural understandings of the inner moral worth of the human person and his or her proper political relations with society' (*ibid.*: 83; emphasis omitted). In Howard's view, the normative status of human dignity is a social construct, something 'that is granted at birth or on incorporation into the community as a concomitant of one's particular ascribed status, or that accumulates and is earned during the life of an adult' (*ibid.*).

While in Howard's view there does not seem to be any fundamental difference between individual and collective (human) dignity, Christian Neuhäuser aims at a more moderate account of collective dignity within the borders of ethical individualism. According to Neuhäuser, collectives cannot have 'personal' dignity, but may still enjoy 'something like shared dignity' (Neuhäuser 2011: 22) which can be seen as the proper basis of collective rights (*ibid.*: 21, 32f). Obviously, what 'shared dignity' means in this context needs to be specified, since any form of individual dignity is 'shared' in a certain sense as soon as it is assigned to more than one individual (for example, individual human dignity is usually thought to be 'shared' by all human beings). Hence, Neuhäuser tries to clarify the specifically 'collective' or 'social' character of 'shared dignity' by pointing to three possible violations of the dignity that is shared within a group: direct, symbolic, and representative group humiliation (*ibid.*: 22, 23, 25, emphasis omitted). In the case of *direct* group humiliation, 'all members of a group are directly humiliated precisely because they are members of this group'. *Symbolic* group humiliations are acts that are directed against symbols of a group that express or are intentionally linked to a real threat against the group. *Representative* group humiliations means that 'a whole group is humiliated through the humiliation of one or more of its members' (*ibid.*: 25). This is the case, Neuhäuser argues, if '[t]he humiliation of some members of a group . . . is directed against a collectively shared part of identity', if 'this shared part of identity is constitutive for [recte: of] the self-respect of the members of this group' and if 'the humiliation is sanctioned on a social level and/or no appropriate measures against it are taken.' (*ibid.*: 30). According to Neuhäuser, these forms of group humiliations highlight an 'essentially social' or 'collective dimension of dignity' (*ibid.*: 32) which lies in-between 'dignity, on the one hand, and social honor, on the other . . . Social dignity is dignity and not only honor, because without it someone is not a fully respected member of a society. But it is social and not human dignity, because this does not necessarily mean that someone could not be a respected member in another kind of society of humans.' According to Neuhäuser, this concept of social dignity can be seen as an argument for 'group rights . . . and special policies . . . like . . . affirmative action . . . because whether a society is confronted with a humiliating discrimination or not can only be seen on a group level' (*ibid.*: 33).

As is well known, the notion of collective rights, group rights or minority rights is heavily contested (for example, Tamir 1999). Moreover, not everyone who defends collective rights or group rights shares the idea that these rights originate from something like collective dignity (cf. Kymlicka 1995; 2001; Wall 2007). Still another position is taken by Bastiaan de Gaay Fortman (2011) who regards the concept of minority rights as a 'major misconception' (*ibid.*), but suggests that the notion of collective human dignity could form the basis of a more convincing alternative.

Collective human dignity as the dignity of the human species

In a different line, collective *human* dignity is taken to signify a normative status that 'belongs to humankind' rather than to its individual members. The idea seems to be that human dignity is not only *shared* among members of the human species (so that each human being would 'own his/her share' of dignity) but that it belongs to all human beings like a common property. Accordingly, Steven Malby takes the decision of the French Conseil d'Etat 'that it was an affront to human dignity to allow the throwing (for sport) of a person selected by reason for [recte: of] his physical handicap, despite the willing participation of the dwarf involved' to draw on a notion of collective dignity (Malby 2002: 110). However, the idea that human dignity does not only warrant but also restricts the right to self-determination does not necessarily imply a notion of collective dignity. Nevertheless, references to the collective 'dignity of the human species'[2] do play a prominent role in the moral and legal discourse on biomedical issues like abortion, cloning or human enhancement. These references usually share two features: first, they emphasize that (this form of) human dignity is grounded in human nature alone and not in demanding capacities that only *some* human beings possess. Second, they take the dignity of the species to impose restrictions even on actions that do not (directly or evidently) affect the claim rights of another (already existing) person, as in the case of reproductive cloning. This idea of dignity of the species may seem self-evident to those who believe that all human life is created in the likeness of God. Some authors, however – most prominently Jürgen Habermas (2003) – try to establish a more cautious philosophical reconstruction of the idea. Habermas distinguishes between 'human dignity as guaranteed by law to every person' and 'the dignity of human life' (*ibid.*: 35f; cf. *ibid.*: 77). Whereas the former is grounded in relations of intersubjective recognition between equal persons, the latter needs to be established as part of our 'ethical self-understanding of the species' (*ibid.*: 40). While this self-understanding expresses ideas of a good life that are controversial in many respects, it is also 'closely interwoven with our self-understanding as moral persons' (*ibid.*: 67). Accordingly, the 'dignity of human life' lies in those features of the ethical self-understanding of the human species that are essential for our ability to regard ourselves as equal members within a community of all human beings. While Habermas emphasizes the difference between the dignity of human life and personal human dignity, the former is also sometimes understood as a direct object of legal protection (for

[2] Such references would find support in the formula of the end in itself of Kant's Categorical Imperative ('act in such a way that you treat humanity, whether in your own person or in the person of another, always at the same time as an end and never simply as a means': Kant 1968: 429) only if we could take the term 'humanity' ('*Menschheit*') to refer to the collective of human beings rather than to the essential quality of being human, which seems doubtful (Joerden 2005; Müller-Terpitz 2007: 331).

example, Isensee 2001) – an interpretation that is heavily contested (for example, with further references, Schlüter 2008: 113f).

Discussion

Since we now have some overview of the most common uses of the concept of 'collective dignity', let me add some tentative remarks about the extent to which these uses are plausible.

First, what I proposed as a common denominator of different interpretations of 'dignity' (in short: that it signifies a specific normative status of an entity, attributed on the basis of certain intrinsic or relational properties and consisting of, entailing or warranting certain rights and/or duties of the respective entity) surely leaves conceptual space for collective dignity. For even those who are sceptical about collective agency, identity or responsibility will probably acknowledge that collective entities can enjoy a normative status, at least insofar as we can take them as *personae fictae*, like legal persons. For example, if one takes the normative status of dignity to be nothing more than a specific right not to be humiliated (Gan 2009), the idea of collective dignity is *prima facie* just as conceptually problematic as other rights of collectives – they seem possible at least in the sense of a legal fiction. However, that it is conceptually possible, at least in the minimal sense of a legal fiction, to ascribe dignity to collectives does not yet imply that it is plausible or useful to do so. Hence we need to ask whether there are any good reasons to ascribe dignity to (certain) collectives.

As for the first type of uses we considered, we may at least guess one of the *goals* that may be served by the normative fiction of collective dignity. Appeals to the 'collective dignity' of a political community (for example, a state which treats 'illegal' immigrants in a humiliating way) can be seen as instances of a *performative use of moral language* that aims at constructing a shared identity. Accordingly, they need not presuppose an already existing collective identity, collective intentionality or collective responsibility. Rather, they may serve as attempts to prompt identification and form collective intentions in the first place – as summons to unify and take responsibility collectively.

What about those uses that link 'collective dignity' to rights, especially to group rights? To begin with, it is striking that in many of the respective uses the meaning of 'collective dignity' remains quite close to (social) honour. According to Neuhäuser, 'it is difficult to draw a clear line between social honor and human dignity' (Neuhäuser 2011: 27; see also Howard 1992: 83). If we accept this interpretation, the notion of collective dignity seems reasonable in at least the following way: insofar as our dignity refers to elements of our identity that are essentially collective (for example, certain aspects of a shared language or culture), and to the extent that the same elements also form part of the dignity of other members of a collective, our dignity may also be called collective. Against this background, it seems plausible that '[i]f a humiliation is directed against a collectively shared part of identity, the whole group is humiliated' (Neuhäuser 2011; 27). This is what Neuhäuser calls 'symbolic group humiliation'.

Paradoxically, though, it is precisely the fact that it is easy to grasp the meaning of this form of collective dignity and of group humiliation that makes it hard to understand why it should give rise to *group rights*. Note that we should distinguish between collective rights and group rights. According to De Gaay Fortman, collective rights are 'rights that by their nature can be enjoyed collectively', like self-determination or the right to a healthy environment. In the case of group rights, on the other hand, 'the legal subject is a collective entity no matter the character of the rights involved' (De Gaay Fortman 2011: 284). So in the case of group rights or minority rights, the *rights-holder* is the collective rather than a number of individuals. Given this distinction, it is easy to see why the step from collective dignity (as defined above) to group rights is not at all necessary. For one can certainly try to protect collective interests or collective values within the framework of individual rights, or 'collective' rights *sensu* De Gaay Fortman (see Griffin 2008: 260). Article 27 of the International Covenant on Civil and Political Rights is probably the most prominent exemplification of this point.[3]

Hence, additional arguments are needed in order to show that collective dignity (taken as something close to social honour) needs to be protected by group rights. As for direct group humiliations, Neuhäuser argues that, because '[i]t is by virtue . . . of being a member of this group that . . . individuals are humiliated', the 'struggle for recognition must' also 'focus on the group level and should not isolate the affected individuals' (Neuhäuser 2011: 22f); but this is not obvious. Being identified as a member of a certain group by those who take this very membership as a reason to humiliate me is no sufficient reason for me to identify with the respective group. I may rather have good reasons to resist the whole system of classification, because it is as such arbitrary and virtually humiliating. Moreover, even if I do understand myself as member of an encompassing group (cf. Margalit 1996; Margalit and Raz 1990) whose collective dignity needs to be protected, it may not be the best option to grant rights to the group rather than to each of us individually. While it is sometimes strategically useful to take measures against discrimination collectively as a group, this is not always the case. Moreover, the introduction of legal or even moral group rights creates theoretical as well as practical problems, for example concerning the proper definition of group membership (De Gaay Fortman 2011), concerning the requirements for the internal structure of groups, and, last but not least, concerning possible conflicts between group rights and individual

[3] 'This article contains a minority provision and reads as follows: "In those States in which ethnic, religious or linguistic minorities exist, persons belonging to such minorities shall not be denied the right, in community with the other members of their group, to enjoy their own culture, to profess and practice their own religion or to use their own language". It is already apparent from the wording that though this minority right has collective aspects, it is granted not to minorities as such, but to the individual members of these groups. This view is confirmed by the General Comment on Article 27, which was adopted in 1994 by the Human Rights Committee' (Galenkamp 1995: 56).

rights (Griffin 2008; Tamir 1999; for a somewhat cautious defence of the idea of group rights, see Jovanovic 2005). These challenges remain, regardless of whether we think of group rights as protections against direct, symbolic or representative group humiliation.[4]

General problems with group rights aside, one may wonder to what extent a concept of dignity that is so close to the notion of honour can be seen as the source of rights. Obviously, not all forms of honour are worthy of protection. As Neuhäuser puts it, some people 'ground their self-respect in the wrong things' (Neuhäuser 2011: 33). However, what are the criteria for 'right' forms of self-respect? For example, what distinguishes the collective dignity of a people that strives for self-determination from rabid nationalism?

This question leads to two more general challenges that those who link the notion of collective dignity to rights are faced by. As a matter of fact, these authors either take *dignity itself as a specific right* (for example, the right not to be humiliated), or, alternatively (drawing on a descriptive notion of dignity) take it as the *content of such specific right* (for example, a certain social state that needs to be protected like the social conditions of self-respect). Either way, these authors need to determine the scope and boundaries of dignity. Second, they need to vindicate the normative force of the respective right.

As is well known, one of the most prominent competing interpretations of dignity takes this concept just as the main element of a *solution* to the problem of specifying and justifying human rights. In this Kantian interpretation, human dignity is seen as the normative source and/or the governing principle of the whole human rights framework. However, the Kantian notion of dignity has rarely been used to explain the meaning of *collective* dignity, taken as a collectively 'owned' normative status of a group or collective. Even Habermas, who in general subscribes to the Kantian idea of *individual* human dignity (Habermas 2010), emphasizes the link between dignity and honour where he talks about the *collective* aspect of the dignity of human life (Habermas 2003: 37) and takes it as a matter of our collective ethical self-interpretation rather than a moral concept.[5] This may be explained by the fact that Habermas' notion of the dignity

[4] As a matter of fact, Neuhäuser himself is not completely clear about the normative standing of groups since he sometimes affirms and sometimes denies that groups as such can be humiliated (cf. Neuhäuser 2011: 31, 34, 35). Besides, if we take Neuhäuser's criterion for *representative* group humiliation seriously, it boils down to *direct* group humiliation. Since the crucial element of this criterion is that the humiliating act against a member of a group 'is sanctioned on a social level and/or no appropriate measures against it are taken', and this is tantamount to a situation wherein social protection is withheld from all members of the group, which is a case of *direct* group humiliation. The act of a representative humiliation against an individual member of the group together with the lack of adequate social reactions, are just the *epistemic* conditions that make the lack of social protection of all group members *visible*.

[5] For Habermas, the ethical use of practical reason answers questions of a good life that are subordinated to moral questions of what we owe to each other; see Habermas

of human life relates to the status of a certain (civilized) biological species, and that membership of a biological species is certainly not rationally unavoidable in the same sense as those more formal features of agency or rational nature that have been exploited by traditional Kantian justifications of dignity.[6] However, it does seem reasonable to ask whether Kant's idea of a kingdom of ends can be defended or reformulated in a plausible way, and, if so, whether this notion would warrant a specific dignity of this 'community' that is distinct from and irreducible to the dignity of its members.

References

Brune, J. P. 2010. *Moral und Recht: Zur Diskurstheorie des Rechts und der Demokratie von Jürgen Habermas.* Freiburg im Breisgau: Alber

Cabral, A. 1972. 'Identity and Dignity in the National Liberation Struggle', *Africa Today* 19(4): 39–47

Cheah, P. 2006. *Inhuman Conditions: On Cosmopolitanism and Human Rights.* Cambridge, MA: Harvard University Press

Darwall, S. L. 2006. *The Second-Person Standpoint: Morality, Respect, and Accountability.* Cambridge, MA: Harvard University Press

De Gaay Fortman, B. 2011. 'Minority Rights: A Major Misconception?', *Human Rights Quarterly* 33(2): 265–303

Falk, R. A. 2009. *Achieving Human Rights.* New York: Routledge

Fuller, R. W. 2006. *All Rise: Somebodies, Nobodies, and the Politics of Dignity.* San Francisco: Berrett-Koehler

Galenkamp, M. 1995. 'Collective Rights', Advisory Committee on Human Rights and Foreign Policy of the Netherlands', *SIM Special* 16: 53–106

Gan, S. 2009. 'Human Dignity as a Right', *Frontiers of Philosophy in China* 4(3): 370–84 (doi:10.1007/s11466-009-0024-3)

Gewirth, A. 1978. *Reason and Morality.* University of Chicago Press

1996. *The Community of Rights.* University of Chicago Press

Griffin, J. 2008. *On Human Rights.* Oxford University Press

Habermas, J. 1993. *Justification and Application: Remarks on Discourse Ethics.* Cambridge, MA: MIT Press

2003. *The Future of Human Nature.* Cambridge: Polity

2010. 'The Concept of Human Dignity and the Realistic Utopia of Human Rights', *Metaphilosophy* 41(4): 464–80 (doi:10.1111/j.1467-9973.2010.01648.x)

Howard, R. E. 1992. 'Dignity, Community and Human Rights', in A. A. A. Na'im (ed.). *Human Rights in Cross-Cultural Perspectives: A Quest for Consensus.* Philadelphia, PA: University of Pennsylvania Press, 81–102

1993: 1–18. However, insofar as Habermas assumes our 'species ethical' self-understanding as members of the human species to be constitutive for our ability to regard ourselves as equal and autonomous members of a moral community, this self-understanding seems to have moral significance as well. In the end, the status of Habermas' concept of dignity of human life remains somewhat ambiguous (for further discussion, see Brune 2010: 464f; Kaufmann and Sosoe 2005).

[6] For example, Darwall 2006; Gewirth 1978, 1996; Korsgaard 2009.

International Law Association. 2010. *Interim Report of The Hague Conference on Rights of Indigenous Peoples*

Isensee, J. 2001. 'Die alten Grundrechte und die biotechnische Revolution', in J. Bohnert, C. Gramm, U. Kindhäuser cs. (eds.) *Verfassung – Philosophie – Kirche: Festschrift für Alexander Hollerbach zum 70. Geburtstag*. Berlin: Duncker & Humblot, 243–66

Joerden, J. C. 2005. 'Der Begriff "Menschheit" in Kants Zweckformel des kategorischen Imperativs und Implikationen für die Begriffe "Menschenwürde" und "Gattungswürde', in M. Kaufmann and L. Sosoe (eds.). *Gattungsethik – Schutz für das Menschengeschlecht?*. Frankfurt am Main: Peter Lang, 177–92

Jovanovic, M. A. 2005. 'Recognizing Minority Identities Through Collective Rights', *Human Rights Quarterly* 27(2): 625–51

Kant, Immanuel. 1968. *Grundlegung zur Metaphysik der Sitten*, in *Werke: Akademie Textausgabe*, vol. 4. Berlin: Walter de Gruyter, 385–464

Kaufmann, M., and Sosoe, L. (eds.). 2005. *Gattungsethik – Schutz für das Menschengeschlecht?*. Frankfurt am Main: Peter Lang

Kiros, T. 2001. *Explorations in African Political Thought: Identity, Community, Ethics*. London, New York: Routledge

Korsgaard, C. M. 2009. *Self-Constitution: Agency, Identity, and Integrity*. Oxford University Press

Kymlicka, W. 1995. *Multicultural Citizenship: A Liberal Theory of Minority Rights*. Oxford: Clarendon Press

2001. *Politics in the Vernacular: Nationalism, Multiculturalism, and Citizenship*. Oxford University Press

López, V. 2011. 'Immigration Detention System Robs Us of Our Collective Dignity'. http://azstarnet.com/news/opinion/article_456b3110-154b-54ea-af1c-d18f666c3a9f.html (accessed 21 July 2012)

Malby, S. 2002. 'Human Dignity and Human Reproductive Cloning', *Health and Human Rights* 6(1): 102–35 (doi:10.2307/4065316)

Mann, J. 2001. 'Dignity and Health: The UDHR's Revolutionary First Article', *Health and Human Rights* 3(2): 30–8

Margalit, A. 1996. *The Decent Society*. Cambridge, MA: Harvard University Press

Margalit, A., and Raz, J. 1990. 'National Self-Determination', *Journal of Philosophy* 87(9): 439–61 (doi:10.2307/2026968)

Müller-Terpitz, R. 2007. *Der Schutz des pränatalen Lebens: eine verfassungs-, völker- und gemeinschaftsrechtliche Statusbetrachtung an der Schwelle zum biomedizinischen Zeitalter*. Tübingen: Mohr Siebeck

Neuhäuser, C. 2011. 'Humiliation: The Collective Dimension', in P. Kaufmann, H. Kuch and C. Neuhäuser (eds.). *Humiliation, Degradation, Dehumanization: Human Dignity Violated*. New York: Springer, 21–36

Schlüter, J. 2008. *Schutzkonzepte für menschliche Keimbahnzellen in der Fortpflanzungsmedizin*. Münster: LIT Verlag

Smith, A. D. 1981. *The Ethnic Revival*. Cambridge University Press

Tamir, Y. 1999. 'Against Collective Rights', in C. Joppke and S. Lukes (eds.) *Multicultural Questions*. Oxford University Press, 158–81

Wall, S. 2007. 'Collective Rights and Individual Autonomy', *Ethics* 117(2): 234–64 (doi:10.1086/511197)

Part IV
Legal implementation

36

Equal dignity in international human rights

BAS DE GAAY FORTMAN

Two genealogies of human rights

Human rights reflect a determined effort to protect the dignity of each and every human being against abuse of power through fundamental rights. Notably, in the global political idea of human rights that emerged after the Second World War, two genealogies converged: first, the fight for universal recognition and equal protection of the dignity of each and every human being; and, second, the struggle for inalienable fundamental rights as a way to protect citizens against abuse of power, in particular by their own sovereign (the state).

Strikingly, while the emergence of the basic rights idea as legal protection against abuse of power, particularly by one's own sovereign, may indeed be called a 'Western' history, the narrative of universal recognition and protection of human dignity could just as well be termed 'anti-Western' history in the sense that equal dignity had to be vindicated in *contravention* of Western ideas and powers. For instance, the idea of legal principles was already part of Roman law (*generalia iuris principia*). One of these referred to freedom as something of inestimable value (*libertas inaestimabilis res est*);[1] yet the application of this principle excluded subjugated peoples in general and slaves in particular. In fact, the whole story of the realization of universal human dignity must be understood as an ongoing political struggle. Indeed, the struggles against colonization and conquest, and the historical efforts to fight racial and ethnic hierarchy, have shaped the idea of truly *universal* human rights (Gilroy 2009).

The two genealogies meet in Article 1 of the Universal Declaration of Human Rights (UDHR): 'All human beings are born free and equal in dignity and rights. They are endowed with reason and conscience and should act towards one another in a spirit of brotherhood.' This global political confession reflects the two grand principles that underlie these paired but distinct genealogies, one of a substantive and the other of a procedural nature: *universal human dignity* and *fundamental rights*. Human rights thus have their origin in two

[1] Paulus libro secundo ad e*dictum*, *Corpus iuris civilis*, De diversis regulis iuris antiqui, D. 50, 17, 106. See also 122: Gaius libro quinto ad e*dictum* provinciale: 'Libertas omnibus rebus favorabilior est'.

distinct principles, each of which gives rise to specific problems with regard to the realization of these rights. In what follows I will discuss both principles, and highlight fundamental problems related to these. I will show, first, that there is a tension between the notion of universal human dignity and basic rights views: human dignity qualifies and connects the three basic values of liberty, equality and solidarity. On the level of fundamental rights, however, these values are often compartmentalized, which endangers the protection of universal human dignity. Second, I will argue that the effective implementation of human rights is problematic: the responsibility of enforcing rights lies mostly with individual nation-states, and in many states the notion of a 'right' as a protection against power is relatively new or even not evidently compatible with the existing legal order.

Equal dignity

The first of the two overarching principles underlying human rights, universal human dignity, refers to the inherent worth of each and every human being, simply as an innate consequence of human existence whether or not an individual person is herself convinced of that (De Blois 1998).[2] 'Inherent' is, indeed, the adjective used in the Preamble to the UDHR, meaning that human dignity is a matter of being rather than having, and hence implying that it cannot be taken away. In fact, as argued by United States Supreme Court Justice, William Brennan (1974, quoted in Wermiel 1998: 232), 'even the vilest criminal remains a human being possessed of common human dignity'.[3] Yet, although inalienable, human dignity can be violated, by the individual himself, as well as by others.

Human dignity is seen then, as the core value sustaining human rights to which three basic values relate: liberty, equality and solidarity ('brotherhood'). First, human dignity qualifies all three basic human rights values – liberty, equality and solidarity – with the adjective 'all'. Second, it connects the three values behind distinct human rights. Hence, it would be a mistake to see one specific right – freedom of expression, for example – as just linked to one value, such as liberty in this case. Equality requires in this respect that the environment in which press freedom is being exercised should be conducive to free speech for everyone, while solidarity means that such freedom is not absolute in the sense of a right disconnected from the community in which it is being enjoyed. Human dignity, in any case, is the core value against which the exercise of any human right must be tested.

Implications of human dignity tend to be primarily approached from a negative angle. Thus, Ronald Dworkin has argued that the idea of human

[2] For a full discussion of human dignity as a core principle in human rights, see Klein Goldewijk and De Gaay Fortman 1999.

[3] Not surprisingly, Justice Brennan (1990, quoted in Wermiel 1998: 233) saw the death penalty as 'wholly inconsistent with the constitutional principle of human dignity'.

dignity 'supposes that there are ways of treating a man that are inconsistent with recognizing him as a full member of the human community, and holds that such treatment is profoundly unjust' (Dworkin 1978: 198–9). In a similar vein, Avishai Margalit has focused his understanding of human dignity on its opposite, *humiliation*, which he relates to injury of self-respect: it is 'any sort of behaviour or condition that constitutes a sound reason for a person to consider his or her self-respect injured' (Margalit 1996: 9).

From an operational perspective, the public-political implications of human dignity as the core of a global 'faith' in human civilization, encompass more than good governance and the rule of law as exemplified by human rights. Notably, the idea of a universal declaration of human rights was based to a considerable extent on the thinking of the American wartime president Franklin Delano Roosevelt. His 'four freedoms' comprised freedom of speech, freedom of worship, freedom from want and freedom from fear. These are naturally interrelated, not only within the global human rights mission, but also in close connection with two other major ventures: human security, as based on FDR's freedom from fear, and human development, as tuned towards his freedom from want.

Human development, from this perspective, means that life becomes more than a mere struggle to sustain daily livelihoods; it implies, in other words, that people acquire certain options in their lives: a socio-economic perspective. Human security, then, entails protection against violence in people's lives and with that freedom from daily fears. Human rights, finally, means defence of fundamental freedoms and basic entitlements by state law, implying, indeed, a functioning state, the rule of law, and good governance.

Human development might be further interpreted in the sense of global responsibilities towards an uplifting of people's material well-being through human empowerment and the elimination of structural constraints to sustainable livelihoods. Naturally, that venture has to do with self-esteem, culture and religion, politics and other aspects of life, too. The 'product' of human development, as mentioned already, is that it provides a *socio-economic perspective* in people's lives.

The lack of a socio-economic perspective, as a result of poverty and exclusion, may be seen as a major factor contributing to intra-state violence. Indeed, the following observation from Adam Smith's *Wealth of Nations* is still applicable:

> Commerce and manufactures gradually introduced order and good government, and with them the liberty and security of individuals, among the inhabitants of the country, who had before lived almost in a continual state of war with their neighbours, and of servile dependency upon their superiors. (Smith 1900 [1776]: 214–15)

Conversely, a well-functioning economy requires protection against violence. In a broad sense, security entails safety. Safety implies protection against disaster. Security adds a dimension of prevention: a minimization of threats to human (co)existence. Consequently, it means freedom from disaster, anxiety, attack and violent disruption of what is considered a 'normal' life.

Thus, the three cornerstones of human dignity realization are substantially interlinked. However, in the international venture that took off with the founding of the United Nations in 1945, these missions were compartmentalized into three distinct projects: international security through the Security Council; international justice through distinct Charter and treaty Bodies charged with setting and supervising human rights standards; and international development through the international financial institutions and the UN development agencies. Not surprisingly, however, in the countries at the bottom of the Human Development Index ranking, as annually published in the United Nations Development Program's Human Development Report, significant weaknesses in human security and human rights are correlated. Hence, the challenge remains twofold: to integrate these three separated endeavours, and to renovate each of them in conformity with their human (dignity) dimension. It is, indeed, the intrinsic connection between those three manifestations of human dignity in a public political context – human security, human development and human rights – that constitutes the core of global universal responsibilities.

In order to achieve human security, then, a socio-economic perspective (and hence a functioning economy) is required as well as good governance and the rule of law (and hence a functioning state). For the realization of human rights, it is also important that people enjoy a socio-economic perspective in their lives while living in peace in a context of political stability. This last aspect is important for human development, too, as well as good governance based on the rule of law.

The whole idea of human dignity protection as a universal mission with interconnected implications has a great and diverse cultural backing. However, human dignity as a fundamental standard of judgment easily gets twisted into a norm applying 'to us but not to all those others', implying that the fundamental ideas of human dignity and the core values it sustains are considered inapplicable to the latter. Hence, crucial qualifications of human rights such as 'inalienable' and 'universal' tend to meet with a great deal of practical resistance.

Even more problematic than the support for protection of *everyone*'s human dignity *per se* is the way in which such protection is to be secured. With the formation of nation-states, law became the primary instrument in efforts to protect people's basic dignity. It still plays a vital role today, but the limits of its effectiveness in advancing and protecting human dignity are becoming increasingly manifest.

Equal rights

The tendency to abuse power is as old as human history; hence the incessant efforts to tie power to certain norms. Where such norms express legal protection of the fundamental freedoms and basic entitlements of each and every human being in the sense of those freedoms and entitlements that refer directly to basic human dignity, we speak of 'human rights'.

This endeavour long predates the UDHR of 1948 as well as the famous eighteenth-century documents such as the French Declaration of the Rights of Man, and is much broader in its application than mere legal protection of interests. Yet, it is precisely the connection with a fundamental rights discourse that constitutes the basis for a unique international venture to provide the global arena with a normative setting in respect of the use of power. Since here human dignity itself is at stake, claims based on such rights should normally trump other types of claims, both private and public.

Yet, reality does not conform to this ideal picture of human rights. While the UN Charter and treaty bodies for country assessments and treatment of cases of human rights violations are meant as effective institutions, there is remarkably little attention to the follow-up of cases in which evident violations of human rights were established. Thus, there is a global *human rights deficit*, manifested particularly in the following realms:

(1) impunity of state-related perpetrators of human rights abuse, such as government officials, politicians, prison officers, policemen and members of the armed forces;
(2) human rights violations committed under the cover of the 'public–private divide' such as domestic violence and abuse directed against women and children;
(3) structurally failing protection of 'minorities', giving rise to collective violence and internal and external displacement of whole groups of people; and
(4) structural non-implementation of the human rights of those living in situations of extreme poverty and marginalization.

To recall, the way in which the international human rights mission has been conceptualized in legal instruments and mechanisms has placed great emphasis on the second foundational principle of human rights: the quest for inalienable fundamental rights. The major flaws that affect implementation can be traced to this over-reliance on judicially enforceable rights as such. International mechanisms for the realization of human rights were set up as if the emancipatory struggles preceding effective implementation of the legal model had already been definitively concluded with the victory of the allied forces in the Second World War. That model is based on three stages: standard-setting, supervision through monitoring of compliance, and enforcement. Its capacity to enforce international human rights law, however, is rather weak. Indeed, the responsibility for implementing all those internationally *declared* rights still rests basically at the national and local level.

A major complication in this regard is that more than half of the global population live in socio-cultural environments in which the notion of a 'right' is of fairly recent origin (in Bantu languages, for example, there is no word for 'right'), or etymologically close to power *per se* (China, for instance, see Perry 2008). To understand this problematique, let us examine the meaning of rights as envisaged in the human rights mission.

From rights to realized claims

Rights protect freedoms and entitlements through abstract legal acknowledgment of claims based on these. Thus, they enable us, among other things, to participate in processes of production, distribution and consumption of goods and services. Economic rights represent 'the abstract acknowledgement of the legitimacy of claims to income and to participation in resource allocation' (Samuels 1974: 118). But the problem with rights is their relativity. One individual's rights are limited by another person's rights. Whether the owner's claims will, indeed, be realized, depends also on other people's interests and the possible protection of these interests through rights.

Behind different claims there are different interests. Rights legitimize claims only insofar as there are corresponding obligations on the part of others to respect these rights. This depends on the relative strengths of the respective rights. In a society that tries to settle conflict through law, the conflicting interests are weighed against one another by some institution or person not part of the conflict (a 'judge'), on the basis of norms (rules, rights) as well as the values behind these.

In this respect, law is a process of continuous change in the way in which human behaviour is ordered through making and applying rules and settling disputes. Inevitably, legal rules are imprecise, requiring a non-mechanical application. This makes it impossible, for one thing, to determine in a normative and fully predictable manner which types of loss or injury to private persons should be compensated. The compensation problem, in other words, is theoretically insoluble (Samuels 1974).

Yet, legal anthropologists have taken great trouble in efforts to describe real types of legal order in terms of different distributions of rights and duties among individuals and groups. Such attempts are, however, bound to be frustrated by the radical indeterminacy of any type of legal order. The actuality of pre-existing rights does not imply a pre-existing legality since, as was pointed out above, one person's rights may collide with another person's rights or with public interests. Hence, one might just as well take indeterminacy as the theoretical basis of social, cultural and legal relationships, an indeterminacy which individuals either try to exploit through 'processes of situational adjustment' or try to combat through 'processes of regularization' (Falk Moore 1983: Chapter 7).

Indeed, to have a title – i.e. to be *entitled* – by no means implies having one's rights actually realized. Rights are just *images* of power; to realize a concrete claim, certain action must be taken. Subjective rights, in other words, are generally *action*-oriented. This applies even more to rights of a declared nature such as human rights in general and to economic, social and cultural rights in particular.

Thus, although in international and national human rights the equal dignity line tends to be of minor significance as opposed to the strict focus on each fundamental right separately, it still plays its part as a *legal principle* in both legislative and judicial law development. But in practice the impact of human rights on actual arrangements, relations and decisions may well be much higher in their role as political standards of legitimacy.[4] It is particularly in the formation and execution of political, economic and cultural power that its impact as a *political principle* could be considerably enhanced.

References

De Blois, M. 1998. 'Self-Determination or Human Dignity: The Core Principle of Human Rights', in A. Hendriks and J. Smith (eds.), *To Baehr in Our Minds: Essays on Human Rights from the Heart of the Netherlands.* Utrecht: Netherlands Institute of Human Rights

Dworkin, R. 1978. *Taking Rights Seriously.* Cambridge, MA: Harvard University Press

Falk Moore, S. 1983. *Law as Process: An Anthropological Approach.* London: Routledge & Kegan Paul

Gilroy, P. 2009. 'Race and the Right To Be Human'. Inaugural address of 3 December, 2009, delivered on accepting the Treaty of Utrecht Chair, Faculty of Humanities, Utrecht

Griffin, J. 2008. *On Human Rights.* Oxford University Press

Klein Goldewijk, B., and De Gaay Fortman, B. 1999. *Where Needs Meet Rights: Economic, Social and Cultural Rights in a New Perspective.* Geneva: WCC Publications

Margalit, A. 1996. *The Decent Society.* Cambridge, MA: Harvard University Press

Perry, E. 2008. 'Chinese Conceptions of "Rights": From Mencius to Mao – And Now', *Perspectives on Politics* 6(1): 37–50

Samuels, W. J. 1974. 'An Economic Perspective on the Compensation Problem', *Wayne Law Review* 21: 113–34

Smith, A. 1900 [1776]. *An Inquiry into the Nature and Causes of the Wealth of Nations.* London: George Routledge & Son

Wermiel, S. J. 1998. 'Law and Human Dignity: The Judicial Soul of Justice Brennan', *William and Mary Bill of Rights Journal* 7(1): 223–40

[4] The notion of legitimacy relates to the use of power, implying simply that the rule of the rulers is acceptable to the ruled. Yet, as its meaning is to transform power into authority it relates not just to the outcome of the use of power as assessed by those affected but also to the observance of accepted principles and institutions, and to due process (Klein Goldewijk and De Gaay Fortman 1999: 118–19).

37

Is human dignity a useless concept? Legal perspectives

JUDGE CHRISTIAN BYK

If we consider that the concept of human dignity appeared only quite recently (after the Second World War) as a legal reference, we may have doubts regarding its utility. Why should we consider useful a concept which was legally non-existent since Roman legal reasoning? But we may interpret the question posed in the title of this chapter to raise another issue: what is the meaning of utility in a legal perspective? All lawyers – whether in the tradition of common law or civil law – know that the law uses concepts to create legal categories and to qualify facts and situations in order to incorporate them in the social theatre in which we all live. In that sense, the rationality of the law tends to have useful social meanings and does not need purely theoretical or metaphysical concepts because they cannot serve its main purpose: to maintain the organization of the society on the basis of legal norms. I understand that the vagueness and uncertainty of the concept of human dignity may create some trouble and disinterest in using it as a legal reference, especially for those who conceive of law as a practical exercise which aims at finding the appropriate answers to precise questions (discussed in the first section below). However, as a pragmatic lawyer, I have also to consider that the concept of human dignity is already present in international law as well as in different domestic legislation. Its appearance during the second part of the twentieth century should not be neglected in understanding the message sent by its introduction in law (discussed in the second section below).

A vague but powerful concept

The theoretical difficulties of the concept

Regarding *the definition* of the concept, dignity – *dignitas* – was associated by the Romans with the respect and honour due to a person with an important position. In this time, it had no universal meaning. The idea that humanity – the gathering of all human beings: '*hoi anthropoi*' as the ancient Greeks would have called it – could be defined by an intrinsic value simply did not exist. And for many centuries this remained the same. In particular, the 1789 Declaration of the Rights of Man and of the Citizen refers to the word 'dignity' in Article 6 to express that every citizen is eligible for all high offices. The transformation of the meaning of human dignity appeared only with the 1948 Universal Declaration of Human Rights when it states (Article 1) that 'all human beings are born free and equal in dignity and rights'. From a social distinction, dignity became an essential characteristic of each human being: what made him unique, sacred. Therefore, dignity is the founding value of the respect due to each human person, whatever his or her biological or social condition might be. I feel that many people will object to the transubstantiation of the definition of dignity. I can hear their claims: what may justify and support this idea of an intrinsic and fundamental value of each human being? To satisfy this legitimate request, we then take the risk to enter complex and controversial philosophical or theological discussion that may be far from our legal perspectives. We may refer to Plato and the Christian theology according to which the human spirit is from a divine nature (*imago Dei*). We may also believe, as the philosopher Paul Ricœur expressed, that 'something is due to each human being simply because he is human' (Raymond 1988: 236f).

Another strong criticism of the concept of human dignity concerns its *interpretation and implementation*. Depending on the philosophical roots a person holds the notion of dignity to possess, using the concept may result in opposed views. One may argue that human dignity will justify assisting a suffering person in dying, while others will say that dignity means to respect human life. Dignity is also used as a knock-down argument to fight practices viewed as unethical, such as human reproductive cloning or genetic sex selection. Reference to human dignity can be an easy way to eliminate those practices without developing further reasoning. The French administrative Supreme Court has ruled that the throwing of a dwarf during a circus performance was a violation of human dignity, even though this meant that the dwarf would have to find another job. The broad definition and opposed interpretations create legal uncertainty that may certainly prejudice the utility of the concept of human dignity as well as our trust in the legal system.

The utility of a dynamic concept in a pluralistic system of law

However, my view is that all these difficulties, although very real, are not obstacles that prevent us from benefiting from the concept of human dignity. People grew indignant at injustice and atrocities before the concept of human dignity was invented. It means that the idea of dignity is born through concrete realities of resentment, and has developed man's moral conscience. When the authors of the 1948 Universal Declaration of Human Rights unanimously agreed, after the crimes of the Nazi regime, to acknowledge that each human being had equal dignity, they upheld different political, philosophical and religious views. We need the notion of human dignity as a reminder that the perpetration of violence against others may create a negation not only of the humanity of others but of our own humanity. Although human dignity has complex origins and leads to an uncontrolled variety of applications, it is a key notion of human rights law. For some authors, it is even a 'mother principle' ('*principe matriciel*') which supports and grounds all other substantial principles in human rights including the respect of the human being and human life.

Broadly referred to as a goal or value in all international human rights documents, human dignity has also largely been incorporated since the 1990s as a reference concept in most international instruments adopted in the field of biomedicine by the Council of Europe, the European Union, the World Health Organization and UNESCO. The main reason for such an expansion in the use of the notion is the creation of a conceptual link between human rights law in general and human rights law in the biomedical field, and also the clear assertion that biomedicine and biotechnology should not transform the human person into an instrument for science. Human dignity is also a powerful concept precisely because – much like fundamental legal or philosophical concepts such as family, love, good, justice etc. – it may be interpreted in various ways and serve as a guiding value – and not a dogma – to face a changing world. Therefore, the development of the concept of human dignity has to take into account those recurrent contradictions to support public discussion and to reach a balanced view in order to define the limits which, at a given time, a society should adopt to conform its practices to its values.

Dignity is a value which defines and should guide humanity

Once again, many would argue that vagueness and ambiguity are sufficient reasons to eliminate the concept of human dignity as a legal reference. Undoubtedly, law requires certainty and predictability. Undoubtedly, human dignity is not sufficient to solve all the questions posed by the progress of science and technology. Undoubtedly, it needs to be assisted by notions which are legally more precise and that could therefore facilitate the implementation of the legal norms. But, as a guiding principle, the concept of human dignity has two major useful roles: it helps define what humanity is and it gives us the opportunity of a discussion on the limits of human power.

The 'anthropological' function of dignity: defining humanity

First, the concept of human dignity has an essentialist function: it appears anthropological, even ontological. It points out to us what we are, our humanity. At the same time, it invites us, particularly taking into consideration the development of sciences and technology, to question the transformations of the content and the perception of this humanity. It is thus not, from this viewpoint, a philosophically useless concept. It would rather be a reminder of our human condition: we are in a quest to find some transcendental origin (jusnaturalism, divine mystery etc.), but at the same time, we have to accept that man has to realize himself in a relative world.

In substantive law, the extension of the concept of human dignity to the species is already a reality. As ruled by the French Constitutional Council, respect for the principle of dignity is part of the integrity of mankind. Taking this as a starting-point, certain authors argue that – in particular after the adoption in the French Constitution (2005) of the Charter of the environment – here lie the premises of a 'radical' evolution, leading to a possible extension of the principle of dignity to future generations and the environment. In international law, the Universal Declaration on Bioethics and Human Rights – which was adopted by UNESCO in 2005 and introduces the idea of responsibility towards future generations, the protection of the world biosphere and environment – could also be understood as driven by such a prospect.

The dialectical function of dignity: a struggle for ourselves and against ourselves

We should thus admit that, on a political view, dignity is a concept which – although it certainly clarifies our understanding of the *conditio humana* – is constituted by and specified in a confrontation between our acts and our values. Dignity is thus related to the capacities for choice and responsibility because it obliges us to question ourselves, regarding the measure of our freedom, our capacities and the way in which we exert them. It is, to some extent, a recall of the awareness that, after Auschwitz, how others perceive us imposes on us a constraint: a responsibility to defend the dignity of others and safeguard humanity. The absolute character of dignity lies, then, not in the specific rules that it imposes on us. It lies rather in the lightning glance that it sheds on the world which surrounds us and the responsibilities which rise from our freedom. In that, it is a struggle for ourselves but also against ourselves. It is what makes Xavier Bioy argue that because the individual sees himself legally constrained to articulate his human condition, he becomes responsible for it (Bioy 2006).

The question of confrontation between personal freedom and dignity

Dignity, a contextual concept

The difficulty with determining the meaning of the concept of dignity does not lie in the ascribed primacy of human dignity over all other principles of human rights law, but rather in conceptualizing dignity while taking into account the singularity of specific cases. Wherein, for instance, is the dignity of the disabled person found: in his refusal to claim financial 'compensation' for his disadvantage, or, conversely, in the payment of special allowances allowing him to lead a more normal life? When is the dignity of the dwarf recognized: in the prohibition of degrading practices (dwarf-throwing) or in respecting his rational capacities to choose a line of work? Such contextualist problems are all the more stringent since the meaning of dignity evolves over time: to work is today a right, while for the nobility of the *Ancien Régime* it would have been an infringement of their dignity. They are also culture-dependent: in France, for example, prostitution is regarded as a freedom, while in many other countries it is prohibited.

Dignity, a way to moderate the excesses of individual freedom

Dignity can be thus used only to justify the interference of public authorities in controlling excesses of personal freedom, including when these excesses endanger only the person whose freedom is in question. They are 'constraints of humanity' (cf. Kant 1998). But generally, these limits must respect the rule of proportionality.

It is only when the use of the concept of dignity has an important symbolic impact, in particular in the eyes of the public, that it authorizes the establishment of absolute prohibitions, even if the coherence of those is not always obvious. (Mathieu Bertrand (2010) thus points out that human reproductive cloning undermines the principle of dignity only qua intention; the children who would be born via this method would profit from equal dignity. On the contrary, therapeutic cloning is essentially contrary to dignity since it instrumentalizes the embryo.) The appreciation of these potential conflicts, and in particular of that between dignity and personal freedom (or right to autonomy), will have to be solved keeping in mind that, in national as in international law, there is no hierarchy between human rights.

The French Constitutional Council Decision of 27 July 1994, which ranked the protection of health and the rights of the family (tenth and eleventh subparagraphs of the Preamble to the Constitution) equally to the safeguard of human dignity and personal freedom, does nothing but recall what had already been ruled by courts previously. Admittedly, international law recognizes the absolute character of certain prohibitions (torture, slavery), which find their basis in the concept of dignity, but, for the implementation of other rights (in particular the right to private life or freedom of expression), the influence of dignity must be appreciated in light of factual circumstances (see the prohibition of the Benetton campaign using an 'AIDS mark' on the skin of the models photographed).

Dignity is a primary principle. It irrigates and inspires a number of fundamental principles, but it does not institute them and does not govern legal scheduling. To preserve the 'absolutism' of dignity, it must maintain a special place. From this place, dignity can be a powerful moral fibre, breath or 'holy spirit', which animates the legal system and maintains a necessary tension between the transcendence of law and the contingent nature of standards.

Conclusion

It is normal and useful that dignity contributes to the legal debate, but it must preserve a certain autonomy since it is itself dependent on several guiding principles: coherence and legal certainty, social peace, open-ended interpretation of the provisions, the concern for human consideration and the need for allowing for, in particular in the field of private and family life, certain behaviours that may be considered as unusual by a majority of people.

However, if dignity is to contribute to our understanding regarding the fundamental principles of the law, it should not result in nourishing a 'legal fundamentalism' which would exclude from the benefit of the 'social contract' the people whose behaviours would be judged heterodox. The recognition in full and whole of the dignity of each human being supposes on the contrary, to build via democratic debate, a meaningful social standard by which to live – if possible with the support of all. It supposes that we understand that the safeguarding of humanity depends on the strength and the quality of exchanges between all men and between man, the biosphere and the environment.

References

Bertrand, M. 2010. 'La dignité, principe fondateur du droit', *Journal international de bioéthique* 21(3): 77–83

Bioy, X. 2006. 'La dignité: questions de principes', in H. Pauliat and S. Gaboriau (eds.), *Justice, ethique et dignité: cinquièmes entretiens d'Aguesseau*. Limoges University Press, 47–86

Kant, I. 1998. *Groundwork of the Metaphysics of Morals*, trans. M. Gregor. Cambridge University Press

Raymond, J. F. 1988. *Les enjeux des droits de l'homme*. Paris: Larousse

38

Human dignity in French law

STÉPHANIE HENNETTE-VAUCHEZ

As most of the contributions to this part of the handbook have underlined, human dignity certainly is a foundational concept of the Universal Declaration of Human Rights (UDHR). The UDHR however, can hardly be described as foundational – or even central – to the French legal order. Although it was signed in Paris, the technical fact that France never ratified the Declaration is quite emblematic of its actual standing within the French legal order.[1] That is to say, the human dignity concept that underpins the Declaration has a rather limited echo in French law. Although it did have a strong philosophical and political influence in the post-war decades, it remained essentially absent from legal norms; mostly, it was an a-juridical principle. When, later on, it eventually was articulated as a legal (constitutional) concept, its meaning began to be intensely debated and some of its normative uses did in fact part with its function as a basis of and premise for human rights. To this day, both the meaning and the importance of a legal principle of human dignity remain uncertain in France.

Human dignity: an uncertain concept

France prides itself on the global influence of its 1789 Declaration of Rights of Man and Citizen, and gloriously tends to speak and stand up to the world as the land of human rights. But the 1789 Declaration ignores human dignity, and the dignity of man that the UDHR promoted was mostly absent from French law until well into the 1990s (Girard and Hennette-Vauchez 2005); it remained, in other words, a concept that legal theorists and human rights activists would refer to as the ultimate justification for human rights, but that was only very marginally used in positive law.

There were, surely, traces of a legal concept of dignity prior to the last decade of the twentieth century, but in their vast majority these were (and remain) heirs to an ancient concept of *dignitas*: related to social and professional statuses rather than to human nature. Regardless of the continued relevance of this particular structure of the legal concept of dignity in contemporary French law

[1] The UDHR was published in the *Journal officiel* on 9 February 1949, but was never ratified. Consequently, it is not technically included within the national legal order and thus cannot be judicially invoked.

(Hennette-Vauchez 2009; 2011), 'dignity' in that sense certainly became increasingly less central as French society democratized and experienced a 'leveling-up process', the effect of which was a generalization of 'the respect and solicitude for dignity that was previously confined to a particular high and exclusive rank of humanity' (Whitman 2003: 245). Mostly, it became contained in nationality law[2] or the law of professions.

Progressively, however, a concept of 'human dignity' did start to appear in various branches of law, albeit in a loose and mostly inarticulate fashion. Legal rules aiming at explicitly protecting the workers' dignity emerged from the 1980s onwards (Revet 1999) – in particular, the imposition of working conditions contrary to human dignity became a criminal offence in 1992. In parallel, the elevation of socio-economic rights after the Second World War contributed to consolidating the idea that rights such as the right to work were instrumental to the flourishing and even to the respect for human dignity. However, socio-economic rights have lastingly been constructed as less binding than civil and political ones (not judicially enforceable).[3] The regulation of the freedom of expression is yet another field in which the concept of human dignity has played a role. A 1986 law states that freedom of communication can be constrained by the human dignity principle. This has led judges to examine cases in which radio stations had been sanctioned for airing talk shows during which degrading or insulting words had been proffered.[4] Other leading cases include those in which the supreme judicial court ruled that the publication of photographs of President Mitterrand on his deathbed[5] or *préfet* Claude Erignac lying dead on the street after his assassination in Corsica[6] was contrary to the human dignity principle.

The principle's fate was to change, however, in the 1990s, a decade during which human dignity became a constitutional principle.

Attempts to institute human dignity as a constitutional principle

Before turning to the transformation of the legal principle of dignity from either an old principle of *dignitas* or a scattered and largely disunited presence

[2] It is noteworthy that recurring legislative proposals amount to reactivating such mechanisms (*déchéance de nationalité*) in cases such as those of naturalized citizens convicted of criminal offences against police officers; see draft proposal: Assemblée Nationale, Projet de loi No. 2400 relatif à l'immigration, à l'intégration et à la nationalité, Art. 3bis (although it was eventually rejected; see www.assemblee-nationale.fr/13/projets/pl2400.asp, accessed 28 March 2013).

[3] On both these aspects, see the research project led by Diane Roman and related publications: http://droits-sociaux.u-paris10.fr/index.php?id=23.

[4] Conseil d'Etat, 9 October 1996, *Association Ici et Maintenant*, req. 173073; Conseil d'Etat, 20 May 1996, *Sté Vortex*, req. 167694.

[5] Cour d'Appel de Paris, 2 July 1997.

[6] Cour de Cassation, 1re ch. civile, 20 December 2000, req. 98-13875.

in French law into a new *constitutional principle of human dignity*, it must be noted that there had been previous attempts, throughout the century, to elevate the principle to the constitutional level. The first of these attempts dates back to the Vichy regime that ruled for four years after France's military capitulation in 1940, albeit on uncertain constitutional grounds and while collaborating with Nazi Germany. Unsurprisingly, the principle of dignity that it tentatively put forth, although nominally a principle of *human* dignity, did not resemble the one articulated in the UDHR.

The Vichy regime rested on uncertain grounds: not only was the constitutionality of the law of 1940[7] that put an end to the Third Republic and designated Maréchal Petain highly dubious, but also the *régime de Vichy* never adopted a new constitution, resulting in a loose and floating constitutional nature of the regime. Drafts were written, however, and they did contain several references to a constitutional principle of dignity. For instance, one draft proclaimed that 'human dignity is an intrinsic quality of the human person that she should always be able to oppose to the Nation, the State or other social groups'. Another ruled that '[t]he State respects and protects the human person, her life, her dignity, her soul' (Le Floch 2003). These are thus constitutional projects that refer to a principle of human dignity. However, they simultaneously contained rules such as the total prohibition on political parties, familial suffrage or the superiority of duties over rights. These elements suggest that, again, the human dignity principle that is referred to in those texts remains quite alien to the one that was to be proclaimed a couple of years later in the UDHR. This is interesting not only from the internal perspective of French law, but also more generally in that it reminds us that the readily positive and very human-rights-related apprehension we may have of the human dignity principle actually must be restated as the result of a social process throughout which the principle did in fact gain positive connotations – a process, however, which did not accompany the human dignity principle *ab initio*.

To be sure, French law did not stand free from exposure to the growing influence and pervasiveness of international human rights law. To a certain extent, it is then only consequent that the human dignity principle did gain in importance in France after the Second World War, as exemplified by the first draft of the constitution of the Fourth Republic, which was to be submitted to referendum. Several of its provisions referred to human dignity, in particular as a basis for social and economic rights. For instance, Article 22 read as follows: 'Every human being has rights that guarantee his full physical, intellectual and moral development, while respecting his integrity and dignity.' In a similar vein, Article 27 foresaw that 'Neither working time nor working conditions should infringe on workers' health, dignity or familial life'.[8] Finally, Article 28 referred

[7] See www.assemblee-nationale.fr/histoire/suffrage_universel/suffrage-1940_loi-constitutionnelle.asp.

[8] Translation by the present author.

to the principle according to which both men and women should earn wages that allow them to live a 'dignified life'. Significantly, though, this particular draft was not approved by the people of France in the referendum that took place on 19 April 1946 – and the human dignity principle was no longer referred to in the subsequent draft that was eventually approved and became the constitution of 27 October 1946. This, of course, should not be read as implying that the first constitutional project was rejected *because* it contained the human dignity principle; it does, however, serve as a partial explanation for the principle's absence in constitutional law in particular until very recently.

Human dignity as a principle of constitutional value

It is only since a ruling by the Constitutional Council of 29 July 1994 that the human dignity principle has been rediscovered, under the guise of a 'principle of constitutional value'.[9] The Constitutional Council had to decide on the conformity of the Law of Bioethics with constitutional provisions. It upheld the text and did so by articulating, for the first time, a constitutional principle of human dignity (by way of deduction from the very first and rather vague phrases of the constitutional Preamble that referred to the atrocities of the Second World War).[10]

Ever since this landmark decision by the Constitutional Council, the legal principle of human dignity in France has been torn between two main interpretations. On the one hand, it has served as a vector for either the foundation or the expansion of a number of human rights – especially in the field of social rights. Various pieces of legislation and judicial rulings have grounded social rights and social protection mechanisms on the principle of human dignity. A law of 1998 proclaims that 'the fight against social exclusion is a national imperative grounded on the respect of all human beings' equal dignity';[11] and the Constitutional Council ruled in 1995 that the right to decent housing was a constitutional objective that stemmed from the constitutional principle of human dignity.[12]

On the other hand, however, the principle of human dignity's dignitarian echo (as opposed to its utilitarian or human-rights-inspired dimensions, cf. Beyleveld and Brownsword 2001; Brownsword 2003; 2005) has been particularly strong, both in French law and in French legal debate. In many instances, the principle of human dignity has served to ground obligations of the individual

[9] Conseil Constitutionnel, 27 July 1994, 94-343–344 DC, Loi Bioéthique.

[10] 'In the morrow of the victory achieved by the free peoples over the regimes that had sought to enslave and degrade humanity, the people of France proclaim anew that each human being, without distinction of race, religion or creed, possesses sacred and inalienable rights.'

[11] Loi No. 98-657 of 29 July 1998 d'orientation relative à la lutte contre les exclusions.

[12] Conseil Constitutionnel, 19 January 1995, 94-359 DC, Loi relative à la diversité de l'habitat.

towards a higher instance of humanity, or towards the parcel of humanity of which he is a repository but not a proprietor. This has been true in the famous dwarf-throwing cases that have led the Supreme Administrative Court to rule that the protection of human dignity as an abstract aim could validly ground *a priori* administrative restrictions on the use of civil liberties;[13] it has also been true of restrictions on the individual right to refuse life-saving medical treatments,[14] freedom and autonomy of contract (Marella 2006) or administrative control of broadcasting.[15] More strikingly, these dignitarian uses of the human dignity principle were enthusiastically praised by large segments of French legal elites. Emblematically, the idea that those legal uses of the principle that tend to affirm it as a basis for social rights and entitlements are flawed (in that they imply a degradation of the sheer ontological superiority of the principle) found wide support over the years. In the words of a prominent constitutional scholar: 'The extension of the human dignity principle to social rights . . . leads to protecting no longer the human person, but the individual as an entity seized within the tensions and contradictions of the social world. The human dignity principle then loses its specificity; it becomes diluted, and is lowered down to the level of other social rights with which it then starts to compete' (Mathieu 1998).

Further change?

At the time of writing, it may well be that the human dignity principle's fate is changing in France. In 2008, President Nicolas Sarkozy appointed a committee of experts in constitutional law with the task of deciding whether it was necessary to change or complement the 1946 constitutional Preamble (which to this day remains the main source of constitutional human rights within the French legal order). In fact, the question was not that open, for President Sarkozy had clearly indicated his own preference for a revision of the Preamble and had insisted in particular on the necessity to give constitutional standing to the human dignity principle by means of explicit inclusion in the written basic law of France.[16] The experts' committee did not, however, follow his idea (Veil 2008). This was, first, because it chose to insist at relatively great length on the strong ambiguities inherent in the legal principle of human dignity. After explicitly

[13] Conseil d'Etat, Ass., 27 October 1995, Commune de Morsang-sur-Orge.

[14] On ambiguities of French case law on the right to refuse medical treatment, see Hennette-Vauchez 2004.

[15] In 2001, when reality shows were first broadcast on French television, the High Authority for Audiovisual Communication (Conseil Supérieur de l'Audiovisuel) issued a recommendation according to which participants in the show should not be filmed twenty-four hours a day, even if they consented to it, out of respect for the principle of human dignity. See Communiqué No. 449 of 14 May 2001.

[16] See Gomez 2008.

acknowledging the fact that these stemmed from diverging philosophical and ideological standpoints, the committee's official report opposed two of its main understandings: one in which the human dignity principle serves as a protection against aggression from and domination by other subjects, the other in which dignity constitutes a limitation on each individual's liberty (Veil 2008: 94). Subsequently, the committee insisted that as far as 'dignity' went, it could only recommend the inclusion, within the text of the Constitution, of a principle of 'equal dignity of all' – but not that of a 'human dignity principle'. The endorsement of such a clear-cut distinction between egalitarian and dignitarian understandings of the principle by an official body of experts in constitutional law was an important step in the debate that has been unfolding over the human dignity principle for a decade or so. It does seem, however, that the report is unlikely to get a concrete follow-up. To this day, no project of constitutional amendment has been drafted and the situation in which 'human dignity' is a judge-made constitutional principle and 'equal dignity' is mostly absent from norms of higher level, is likely to last.

The critical move that the committee's report sought to make *vis-à-vis* an uncritically confident embrace of the human dignity principle nonetheless did find an echo in other important legal arenas. In particular, the French Conseil d'Etat, which played a crucial role in 1995 when it upheld the human-dignity-based bans on dwarf-throwing, now seems to have distanced itself from its previous position on the issue. Indeed, it was asked at the beginning of 2010, in its advisory capacity, to give an opinion on the possible legal grounds for legislative action aimed at banning the public wearing of the *niqab* (Conseil d'Etat 2010). Since the human dignity principle had often been referred to as a relevant ground for action in the public debate that had been ongoing for some months at the time, the Conseil d'Etat gave its opinion on that particular aspect of the project. But again, one reads in the advisory opinion that the principle of human dignity is an inappropriate and indeed dangerous ground for such a ban: 'the assessment of what does or does not detract from the dignity of the person is at least potentially comparatively subjective' (Conseil d'Etat 2010: 22). Again, this particular difficulty is linked to the great ambivalence of the human dignity principle, for several opposing understandings of the principle exist: 'that of the collective moral requirement to protect human dignity, perhaps at the expense of the freedom of determination and that of the protection of self-determination as a consubstantial aspect of the human person' (*ibid.*: 21–2) – especially since, as the opinion recalls, 'the wearing of the full veil is in most cases voluntary' (*ibid.*: 22). To be sure, the government decided to ignore this advisory opinion and went ahead with the legislative draft that eventually was adopted in Parliament and upheld by the Constitutional Council albeit devoid of any reference to the human dignity principle. These episodes have, however, considerably weakened the dignitarian approach of the human dignity principle – or, at least, they have made its dangers more conspicuous.

References

Beyleveld, D., and Brownsword, R. 2001. *Human Dignity in Bioethics and Biolaw*. Oxford University Press

Brownsword, R. 2003. 'Bioethics Today, Bioethics Tomorrow: Stem Cell Research and the Dignitarian Alliance', *Notre Dame Journal of Law, Ethics and Public Policy* 17: 15–51

2005. 'Stem Cells and Cloning: Where the Regulatory Consensus Fails', *New England Law Review* 39: 535–71

Conseil d'Etat. 2010. 'Etude sur les possibilités juridiques d'interdiction du port du voile integral', www.conseil-etat.fr/cde/media/document/RAPPORT%20ETUDES/etude_voile_integral_anglais.pdf (in English) (accessed 22 April 2013)

Girard, C., and Hennette-Vauchez, S. 2005. *La dignité de la personne humaine: Recherche sur un processus de juridicisation*. Paris: Presses Universitaires de France

Gomez, M. 2008. 'La constitution pourrait s'ouvrir à la bioéthique', La Croix, 9 January 2008

Hennette-Vauchez, S. 2004. 'Kant contre Jehovah? Refus de soins et dignité de la personne humaine', *Recueil Dalloz* 3154–60

2009. 'Une dignitas humaine? Vielles outres, vin nouveau', *Droits. Revue française de théorie juridique* No. 48, 59–85

2011. 'A Human Dignitas? Remnants of the Ancient Legal Concept in Contemporary Dignity Jurisprudence', *International Journal of Constitutional Law* 9(1): 32–57

Le Floch, E. 2003. 'Les projets de constitution de Vichy (1940–1944)', PhD dissertation. Université Paris II Panthéon Assas

Marella, M. R. 2006. 'The Old and New Limits to the Freedom of Contract in Europe', *European Review of Contract Law* 2: 257–74

Mathieu, B. 1998. *Constitution et ethique biomédicale*, N. Lenoir, B. Mathieu and D. Maus (eds.). La Documentation Française, 50–1

Revet, T. 1999. 'La dignité de la personne humaine en droit du travail', in M. L. Pavia and T. Revet (eds.), *La dignité de la personne humaine*. Paris: Economica

Veil, S. 2008. *Redécouvrir le Préambule de la Constitution: Rapport au President de la République*. Paris: La Documentation Française

Whitman, J. Q. 2000. 'Enforcing Civility and Respect: Three Societies', *Yale Law Journal* 109: 1279–1398

2003. 'On Nazi "Honor" and New European "Dignity", in C. Joerges and N. S. Ghaleigh (eds.), *Darker Legacies of Law in Europe: The Shadow of National Socialism and Fascism over Europe and Its Legal Tradition*. Oxford: Hart Publishing

39

Human dignity in German law

HORST DREIER

Human dignity is a concept that affects much more than the field of law, not only in Germany, but also in other countries. In Germany, it found its first written embodiment in the legal system in Article 1, paragraph 1, of the German Federal Constitution (*Grundgesetz*) of May 1949, which corresponded to the Universal Declaration of Human Rights of December 1948. From that point began the triumphant development of human dignity, finding also expression in Article 1 of the Charter of Fundamental Rights of the European Union. Today, human dignity constitutes a central point of reference in practically every moral and legal discourse around the world.

In this chapter, I will examine, first, the exceptional position of human dignity in the constitutional order of the Federal Republic of Germany. The subsequent sections analyze the difficulties in interpreting this fundamental notion of law. The next section demonstrates how human dignity influences in different ways the current (statutory) law (private law, criminal law, public law). This will demonstrate that the absoluteness and imponderable nature of human dignity can only be preserved if its application is limited to a small but absolutely undisputed and generally accepted number of factual situations. The assumed triumphant development of human dignity, however, produces the result that this exceptional principle becomes trivialized and thus ultimately loses significance.

Human dignity as the supreme rule of constitutional law

Article 1, paragraph 1, of the German Constitution states: 'Human dignity shall be inviolable. To respect and protect it shall be the duty of all state authority.'[1] This norm has become absolutely outstanding and increasingly dominating in the legal order of the German Federal Republic (Geddert-Steinacher 1990; Enders 1997; Dederer 2009; Teifke 2011). Besides the symbolic position of being first on the list of fundamental rights at the beginning of the Constitution, its outstanding role is confirmed by general characterizations of the norm by highly respected German scholars. Thus, Konrad Hesse attached to human

[1] Inter Nationes translation: see www.iuscomp.org/gla/statutes/GG.htm#1.

dignity 'immense importance as the normative foundation of this historically concrete polity' (1995: 55); Hasso Hofmann called it the 'essence of the German federal state' ('*Sinn bundesrepublikanischer Staatlichkeit*') (1993: 357). The German Federal Constitutional Court has always characterized human dignity as the 'highest value' and 'central constitutional principle' and sometimes as the 'fundamental rule' of the Constitution.[2] This remains the case today: human dignity represents the 'highest legal value';[3] it is the 'fundamental principle and highest value'[4] of the Constitution. This indicates that Article 1, paragraph 1, of the Constitution is neither a solemn proclamation nor a mere political manifesto, but an applicable legal principle binding all public authorities.[5] The expression 'inviolable' is not intended to be descriptive, but prescriptive. It is certainly correct that an outlawed, tortured or otherwise inhumanely victimized person does not lose his human dignity so that this dignity truly remains inviolable – a thought which can ultimately be traced back to stoic philosophy (Margalit 1999). If a person can therefore never be deprived of his or her human dignity, the right to have that dignity respected, which arises from the right to dignity, can nevertheless be infringed upon; violations of this kind are held to be unconstitutional under Article 1, paragraph 1, of the Constitution.

The inviolability of human dignity is reflected in its high and exceptional normative status. What is granted or at least intended is an absolute guarantee, which has neither exceptions nor legitimate restrictions. All other fundamental rights – including those referred to in the Constitution as 'inviolable' (Articles 4, 10 and 13) can and may be restricted under certain conditions. An intrusion into the scope of a protected fundamental right (*Schutzbereich*) does not necessarily constitute a violation of this right, but rather may be legally justifiable. Any such possibility of balancing or compromising between competing constitutional rights or values (*Verfassungsgüter*) is impossible under Article 1, paragraph 1, of the Constitution. Every intrusion upon human dignity is inevitably a violation of the Constitution.[6] Accordingly, the Federal Constitutional Court has repeatedly confirmed that human dignity can never be relativized or balanced against some other constitutional right or constitutional value.[7]

Any such violation of this constitutional principle – and this shows once again the exceptional status of the right of human dignity – could not even be made permissible by amending the Constitution. The reason for this is that Article 1 of the Constitution comes under the protective scope of the so-called 'eternity clause', namely, Article 79, paragraph 3, of the Constitution, which prohibits the

[2] BVerfGE (German Federal Constitutional Court Decisions) 5 (1956) 85 (204); 50 (1979) 166 (175); 27 (1970) 344 (351).

[3] BVerfGE 117 (2006) 71 (89).

[4] BVerfGE 109 (2004) 279 (311); as well as BVerfGE 115 (2006) 118 (152).

[5] Dreier 2013: para. 44 with further references.

[6] This is the dominant view in the literature. For references, see Dreier 2013: para. 46; of course, there are an increasing number of opponents of this view: see Baldus 2011.

[7] BVerfGE 93 (1995) 266 (293); 107 (2003) 275 (283f).

amendment of the principles included in Articles 1 and 20 of the Constitution. Certain acts, which would be considered violations of human dignity, are thus normatively prohibited for all eternity. Article 79, paragraph 3, of the Constitution declares restrictions impermissible. If certain practices or technologies, for example in human genetics, were found to encroach upon human dignity, their licensing in Germany would be completely impossible for all time. Human dignity arguments are 'winner arguments' (Bayertz 2010). This explains to a large extent the strong interest in how Article 1, paragraph 1, is interpreted within the discussions of bio-political issues, which are highly controversial not only due to their legal, but also their theological and philosophical aspects.

Conflicts, consensus and concepts

It is in this by no means ended debate that opposing positions have clashed with particular force. The one side held and still considers embryo research, pre-implantation genetic diagnostics (PID) and therapeutic cloning to be flagrant violations of the right to human dignity, whereas the other holds these practices to be readily justifiable, for example by the freedom of research and the freedom to have children as well as other fundamental rights.[8] However, it must not be overlooked that the lack of agreement here is only or at least essentially about the question of whether the un-individuated, not-yet-successfully-implanted pre-embryo is bearer of human dignity (*Träger der Menschenwürde*).[9] Here, the clash between contrary positions continues, each resorting to elaborate argumentational strategies. For example, whilst advocates of embryo research and PID may point out that during the pre-implantation phase there still exists no individuated life, but only a species-specific one (*human life*, but not *a human being*) (Dreier 2013: paras. 82f), opponents insist that only the protection of life and human dignity from the very beginning avoids an arbitrary cut-off point (Höfling 2011: paras. 59f). There has been an undisputed consensus that the practices referred to above would be absolutely impermissible on living human beings after birth. This would constitute experimentation on humans or the arbitrary destruction of human life, which by general conviction would be as reprehensible as torture, stigmatization, human trafficking or slavery. This is at the same time also a list of some of the most obvious examples of the violation of human dignity.[10] In more abstract terms, Article 1, paragraph 1, of the Constitution protects against the most serious violations of the fundamental freedoms and the equality of all individuals.

It is a salient feature of these groups of cases that they are defined by an obvious violation of human dignity, and precisely because of their overwhelming

[8] Representing the pro and contra positions in the various opinions of the German National Ethics Council (see German National Ethics Council 2003; 2004; 2007).

[9] References for both opinions: Dreier 2013: paras. 82f.

[10] References in Dreier 2013: paras. 60f, 138.

plausibility are supported by a broad consensus. To a certain extent human dignity is defined negatively by the establishment of a violation applying generally accepted criteria in the presence of relevant facts. So construed and narrowly defined, the legal principle of human dignity secures a generally accepted area of protection. The clear and narrowly defined scope of application guarantees the absolute nature of the right and the certainty of firm and clear boundaries.

This certainty is quickly shattered if one attempts to deduce general criteria for the existence of a violation of human dignity using the so called 'object formula'. According to this formula, human dignity is violated whenever the 'specific human being is degraded to an object, to a mere instrument, to a replaceable entity' (Dürig 1956: 127). This formula can be traced back to Kant's prohibition of the instrumentalization of human beings. Its vagueness is, however, an easy gateway for partisan or subjective evaluations (Hilgendorf 1999: 146f; Dreier 2013: para. 55).

The differences become much sharper if one attempts to determine positively the meaning of the term 'human dignity' (rather than listing violations to define it negatively). Performance theories, for example, conceive human dignity not as something substantially existing but rather as something to be attained (Luhmann 1965: 68f). According to communication theories, human dignity is generated through a process of social recognition and reveals human solidarity as its core idea (Hofmann 1993: 364, 368).

Extension, inflation, trivialization: banalizing a rule intended for exceptional situations

Largely without extensive recourse to any of the approaches sketched out above, the concept of human dignity has been widely extended more than anywhere else in the jurisdiction of the Federal Constitutional Court. When Article 1, paragraph 1, was included in the Constitution of 1949 it was primarily understood as a protest against the 'unspeakable atrocities committed against humans by the totalitarian powers of the 20th century' (Hasso Hofmann), but in the meantime this right has developed further in a wide variety of ways. Aimed to apply in the most exceptional circumstances, and as an obvious bulwark against the totalitarian disregard of the rights of the individual, human dignity has become a right of almost ubiquitous application. It is applied to a wide variety of factual situations widely removed from the totalitarian disregard of human rights reflected in the massive violation of human dignity during the National Socialist and Stalinist periods. It is only a slight exaggeration to speak now of the tendency towards a universal application of human dignity. Three developments deserve particular attention.

First, the Federal Constitutional Court has in several decisions encouraged the idea that special fundamental rights written into the Constitution are all to be understood as concrete examples of the right to human dignity; human dignity constitutes the 'root of all fundamental rights'.[11] The systematic relationship which exists between human dignity and the other fundamental rights, as reflected in the tiered structure of the three paragraphs of Article 1, is misunderstood in this way as describing a derivation of the various rights from this right. Moreover, the idea of a root suggests some mistaken conception that all fundamental rights in the Constitution are somehow connected to the right to human dignity. Similarly, the widespread ideas in the literature regarding an inalienable central value or core of human dignity contributing to all fundamental rights raise altogether more questions and problems than they answer (for critical analysis, see Dreier 2013: paras. 162f).

A different and much older train of thought which has likewise been strongly promoted by the Federal Constitutional Court is the creation of combined fundamental rights by linking a fundamental right to human dignity. The most important and indeed best known example of this is the general right of personality, derived from Article 1, paragraph 1 (human dignity), taken together with Article 2, paragraph 1, of the Constitution, which has appeared in a wide variety of different concrete expressions.[12] It is noteworthy that the main problem of this and other combinations of rights is that human dignity, as an absolute right, is here linked to other rights which are subject to constitutional restrictions. Nobody is able to say exactly where the boundary is to be drawn between the absolutely protected core value (Article 1, paragraph 1) and the surrounding area (Article 2, paragraph 1) which is subject to restrictions. Court decisions in this area are quite diverse and are hard to predict because of the element of balancing of interests, sometimes going in one direction, sometimes the other, as reflected in the *Diary Entry Case* and the *Eavesdropping Case*.[13] As a result, the absolute character of the right to human dignity is evaporating in favour of a balancing procedure, as is frequently employed for other fundamental rights. Thus is exemplified the high price to be paid for human dignity finding its way into the everyday practice of law.

A third trend intensifies the extension to the point where it becomes an inflation. It bears the scars of trivialization when citizens start court proceedings to protect their right to human dignity in utterly insignificant cases of state interference or legal requirements such as the need to submit receipts for expenses, or wear a certain work uniform, subsequently going on to one or several appeals.[14] It bears the scars of hasty recourse to human dignity by the courts themselves, when, in concrete cases requiring a balancing of rights,

[11] BVerfGE 93 (1995) 266 (293); 107 (2003) 275 (284). Approved in BGHZ (German Federal Supreme Court Civil Cases) 149 (2001) 247 (262f).

[12] See the numerous citations of cases in Dreier 2013: paras. 76, 140.

[13] BVerfGE 80 (1989) 367; 109 (2004) 279; for a critical evaluation of the reasoning in both decisions, see Baldus 2011: 537f; for a discussion of the *Diary Entry Case*, see Dederer 2009: 114f.

[14] For this and other examples, including references, see Dreier 2013: paras. 49, 50.

they abruptly resort to the highest constitutional value to decide the disputes. At the Federal Administrative Court (*Bundesverwaltungsgericht*) this applies particularly to the Senate dealing with cases coming from the armed forces (*Wehrdienst*), which has undoubtedly held in a particularly excessive manner that disciplinary measures for misconduct qualify as violations of human dignity. Furthermore, in the notorious *Peep-Show Case*,[15] the court first set aside the relevant provisions of the trading regulations before abruptly holding that the human dignity of the performers had been violated. In a very similar way, the highly criticized civil decision of the Federal Supreme Court (*Bundesgerichtshof*) in the *Living Wills Case* of 2003[16] held that many private law rules are derived from general constitutional rights such as human dignity. Similar examples of hasty recourse to Article 1, paragraph 1, of the Constitution can also be found in criminal cases.[17] Altogether, the impression becomes increasingly clear that the right to human dignity is used as a justification, or even in place of a justification, in order to give more force to one's own conclusions, potentially based on completely different arguments, to make the decision seem to have no alternatives because the highest constitutional principle to a certain extent governs or even requires the decision. Thus, the proud first clause of the Constitution threatens to become 'small change' in the day-to-day work of lawyers because of its ubiquity, universal application and omnipresence. Human dignity is in jeopardy of being used in a random fashion. The ever more frequent references to human dignity represent a threat to both its exceptional status in the legal order as well as its claim to prevail over all other rules. As elsewhere, inflation results in devaluation.

Human dignity is pervasive in the German legal system: private law, criminal law, and administrative law

These few examples of potentially exaggerated and not always legally well-founded references to Article 1, paragraph 1, of the Constitution should not be misunderstood as implying that the right of human dignity does not extend beyond the area of constitutional law. Although it may arguably be in need of stronger methodological control, it has very wide effects in Germany at the level of ordinary law, exerting itself over the entire legal system. This is due to the widely accepted constitutional doctrine of 'radiating effect' (*Ausstrahlungswirkung*), together with the legal maxims of 'interpretation in conformity with the Constitution' (*verfassungskonforme Auslegung*) and 'constitutionally oriented interpretation' (*verfassungsorientierte Auslegung*). Thus,

[15] BVerwGE 64 (1981) 274. There was very heavy criticism of this decision; for references, see Dreier 2013: para. 149 (also for subsequent case law changes).

[16] BGHZ 154 (2003) 205.

[17] OLG Frankfurt (Higher Regional Court Frankfurt) NJW 1997, 1647 (1648): 'Violation of human dignity via the administration of emetics to drug dealers'.

for example, sometimes ordinary laws are interpreted in light of human dignity; in many instances, human dignity is simply an element of the ordinary legal rule; and, finally, important dogmatic concepts are enriched by the idea of human dignity or are supplied with enhanced legal justifications. In the various fields of law the resulting picture differs significantly, as will be shown below.

In civil law, it is settled in both the case law and the legal doctrine which follows from it that (particularly) the general clauses (*Generalklauseln*) of the Civil Code (*Bürgerliches Gesetzbuch*, BGB), may function as gateways for judgments that are made on the basis of constitutional law. This also applies in principle to human dignity, which has been used as the reference point for determining what is *contra bonos mores* under § 138 BGB, has helped define what is 'good faith' (*Treu und Glauben*) under § 242 BGB, and has largely been used for determining whether behaviour amounted to intentional damage contrary to public policy (*vorsätzliche sittenwidrige Schädigung*) under § 826 BGB. Of course, the civil law's claims to autonomy are so strong that human dignity can hardly be found as a heuristic tool in legal treatises in this area. Nevertheless, use of the previously mentioned combined fundamental right of the general right of personality, with its almost incomprehensibly vast range of interpretations, is expanding. In the *Benetton Advertising Cases*, the Supreme Court stuck firmly to its assessment, holding that so called 'shock advertising' violated human dignity and was therefore *contra bonos mores* in the context of competition law.[18] In the recent past, the most effective references to the right of human dignity were made, significantly, on a highly disputed ideological battlefield: the issue is referred to as 'child as damage'. This includes both *wrongful birth* and *wrongful life*.[19] It was in this context that a very rare public disagreement between the two chambers of the Federal Constitutional Court played out.[20]

Criminal law has proved to be an area of law which has always been strongly influenced by the principle of human dignity (Prittwitz and Manelodakis 1998). From the specification of certain acts as criminal offences, including justifications for criminalizing those acts, to the imposition of punishments, and then further to the implementation of sentences, human dignity has always played a pivotal role (Lagodny 2005; Dreier 2013: paras. 139f). It is considered to be one of the most important factors in the perception of the nature of criminal punishment and the relationship between guilt and atonement. The doctrine *nulla poena sine lege* has its place not only in the principle of *rule of law* and in Article 2, paragraph 1, of the Constitution, but also, or perhaps foremost, in the

[18] BGH (German Supreme Court) decision of 6 July 1995 – I ZR 180/94 = NJW 1995, 2492; BGHZ 149 (2001) 247 (259f). The German Federal Constitutional Court held repeatedly that there was no violation of Art. 1, para. 1, of the Constitution: see BVerfGE 102 (2000) 347 (366f); 107 (2003) 275 (283f).

[19] For an overview, see Dreier 2013: paras. 158f.

[20] See BVerfGE 88 (1993) 203 (204) on the one hand, and BVerfGE 96 (1997) 375 (399f) on the other.

right to human dignity. The prohibition on compulsory self-incrimination (*nemo-tenetur-Grundsatz*), although not included in the actual text of the Constitution, is sometimes considered to be derived in part from Article 1 paragraph 1. One finds human dignity among the elements of some offences in the German Criminal Code (*Strafgesetzbuch*, StGB), for example § 130 StGB (incitement to hatred, *Volksverhetzung*) and § 131 StGB (dissemination of depictions of violence, *Gewaltdarstellung*). It also plays a role in laws on the protection of minors and in § 22 of the German Code of Military Justice (*Wehrstrafgesetz*, WStG). Furthermore, the term 'public morals' (*gute Sitten*) in § 228 StGB is a reference to Article 1, paragraph 1. Finally, the law on the enforcement of punishments, with its highest goal being rehabilitation, is thoroughly imbued with the concept of human dignity. The details of the implementation of punishment are governed, among others, by the consideration 'that the conditions for a dignified existence by the prisoner must continue to exist while he is held in custody and that the State is obliged to take the necessary steps to realize that objective'.[21]

The protection of human dignity is also one guiding principle for Germany's strong and sophisticated Social Law. This becomes particularly obvious when looking at the social security system which provides unemployment insurance benefits, welfare benefits and nursing care for the infirm, with the aim of giving the persons concerned the opportunity to lead a life 'consistent with the dignity of a human being'. Precise financial quantifications can, of course, not be derived from the text of Article 1, paragraph 1, of the Constitution. Precise financial figures can similarly not be derived from the 'fundamental right to a decent minimum income', which the Constitutional Court held to exist under Article 1, paragraph 1, taken together with the principle of the social welfare state (*Sozialstaatsprinzip*) under Article 20, paragraph 1, of the Constitution.[22] The absoluteness of these social guarantees has suffered to a certain extent because the amount of benefits granted is ultimately contingent both on economic factors as well as on social conditions (Bayertz 2010).

Public law, in particular special administrative law (*Besonderes Verwaltungsrecht*), presents itself as an extremely varied area of law in Germany. It is in this area of law that some of the most spectacular and always highly disputed cases, like the *Peep-Show Case* or *Dwarf-Tossing Case*,[23] have come to court. The main issue in the litigation of these cases is the construction of the general clause on public policy in the trade laws, more specifically *bonos mores* (*gute Sitten*) which is a gateway with a huge potential for involving daring

[21] BVerfGE 45 (1977) 187 (228); citation from BVerfG (decision of 13 November 2007, 2 BvR 939/07, para. 12). Compare the reasoning in BVerfGE 109 (2004) 133 (149f).

[22] BVerfGE 125 (2010) 175. For more detail, see Egidy 2011.

[23] On the *Peep-Show Case*, see note 15 above. On the *Live Dwarf Tossing Case*, see VG Neustadt NVwZ Administrative Court 1993, 98; see also Teifke 2011: 84f, for additional critical comments.

displays of one kind or another. Similarly, 'public order' (*öffentliche Ordnung*) in risk prevention law (*Gefahrenabwehrrecht*) is a concept interpreted in light of human dignity. Examples of this are the *Körperwelten Case*[24] (Body Worlds) which involved the public exhibition of plastinated cadavers and the *Laserdrome Case*[25] and similar cases which dealt with death games. There were particularly intensive discussions of the right to human dignity in connection with tasteless television formats such as *Big Brother* and *Dschungelcamp*. One of the most difficult issues in all these cases proved to be whether participation by the subjects was really 'voluntary' (Dreier 2013: para. 149).

One has to remember that the quality of being 'tasteless' is not in itself automatically a violation of the right of human dignity under Article 1, paragraph 1, of the Constitution, even if the show's participants engage in ridiculous, self-degrading behaviour. It would be a misconception both of the deep historical and philosophical core of the right to human dignity as well as its exceptional nature to conceive of it simply as the highest normative substrate of paternalistic social morality or as a fixed pattern of social order. The danger always exists of misinterpreting human dignity as an objective value concept, pitting it against its actual foundations, namely, individual autonomy and self-determination over one's own life and the way the life is lived. It then mutates from a promise of freedom and equality for all persons into a rule giving the state the power to intervene in people's lives. This would lead to the opposite of what was intended.

Concluding remarks

Human dignity has a prominent and exceptional status in the legal order of the Federal Republic of Germany. It is exactly because of the absoluteness of its guarantee and the normative safeguard in Article 79, paragraph 3, of the Constitution (the 'eternity clause') that it is not only a wrong, but also a dangerous, strategy to apply the human dignity clause (Article 1, paragraph 1, of the Constitution) as extensively as possible and to establish it as the decisive factor in court decisions in as many cases as possible. From the point of view of the 'rule of law', such use of human dignity as a 'perfect example of good order with universal application' (Christoph Enders) would lead to a dubious unsettling of settled areas of law. It would be equally intolerable if human dignity were taken to be the 'universal solution' (Rainer Wahl) suitable for dealing with all epochal developments like biotechnology and other processes of great social transformation. One should not fall victim to the dangerous belief that the

[24] For the *Körperwelten Case*, see BayVGH (Bavarian High Administrative Court) NJW 2003, 1618 (1619f).

[25] The Federal Administrative Court (*Bundesverwaltungsgericht*) viewed this as a violation of human dignity: BVerwGE 115 (2001) 189 (199f); BVerwG (decision of 13 December 2006, 6 C 17/06 para. 25). This has justifiably been viewed rather critically in the literature (Teifke 2011: 83f, with additional references).

solutions to complicated legal problems in commercial law or the clarification of urgent problems of the future always and only lie in a proper understanding of the inviolable Article 1, paragraph 1, of the Constitution. That would overrate the constitutional principle and underrate the capacity of a free, pluralistic society for individual and collective self-determination.

References

Baldus, M. 2011. 'Menschenwürde und Absolutheitsthese', *Archiv des öffentlichen Rechts* 136: 529–52

Bayertz, K. 2010. 'Menschenwürde', in H. J. Sandkühler (ed.), *Enzyklopädie Philosophie*, new edn, 3 vols., vol. II. Hamburg: Meiner, 1553–8

Dederer, H. 2009. 'Die Garantie der Menschenwürde (Art. 1 Abs. 1 GG): Dogmatische Grundfragen auf dem Stand der Wissenschaft', *Jahrbuch des öffentlichen Rechts* 57: 89–124

Dreier, H. 2013. 'Art. 1 Abs. 1 GG', in H. Dreier (ed.), *Grundgesetz-Kommentar*, 3 vols, vol. I. Tübingen: Mohr Siebeck, paras. 1–168

Dürig, G. 1956. 'Der Grundrechtssatz von der Menschenwürde', *Archiv des öffentlichen Rechts* 81: 117–57

Egidy, S. 2011. 'Casenote – The Fundamental Right to the Guarantee of a Subsistence Minimum in the Hartz IV Decision of the German Federal Constitutional Court', *German Law Journal* 12: 1961–82

Enders, C. 1997. *Die Menschenwürde in der Verfassungsordnung – Zur Dogmatik des Art. 1 GG*. Tübingen: Mohr Siebeck

Geddert-Steinacher, T. 1990. *Menschenwürde als Verfassungsbegriff: Aspekte der Rechtsprechung des Bundesverfassungsgerichts zu Art. 1 Abs. 1 Grundgesetz*. Berlin: Duncker & Humblot

German National Ethics Council 2003. 'Genetic Diagnosis Before and During Pregnancy', www.ethikrat.org/archive/national-ethics-council/opinions/opinions?set_language=en (accessed 9 February 2012)

2004. 'Cloning for Reproductive Purposes and Cloning for the Purposes of Biomedical Research', www.ethikrat.org/archive/national-ethics-council/opinions/opinions?set_language=en (accessed 9 February 2012)

2007. 'Should the Stem Cell Law Be Amended?', www.ethikrat.org/archive/national-ethics-council/opinions/opinions?set_language=en (accessed 9 February 2012)

Hesse, K. 1995. *Grundzüge des Verfassungsrechts der Bundesrepublik Deutschland*. Heidelberg: C. F. Müller

Hilgendorf, E. 1999. 'Die mißbrauchte Menschenwürde – Probleme des Menschenwürdetopos am Beispiel der bioethischen Diskussion', in B. Sharon Byrd *et al.* (eds.), *The Human Analyzed, Jahrbuch für Recht und Ethik 7*, Berlin: Duncker & Humblot, 137–58

Höfling, W. 2011. 'Art. 1 GG', in M. Sachs (ed.), *Grundgesetz-Kommentar*. Munich: C. H. Beck, paras. 1–112

Hofmann, H. 1993. 'Die versprochene Menschenwürde', *Archiv des öffentlichen Rechts* 118: 353–77

Lagodny, O. 2005. 'Menschenwürde im Strafrecht – am Beispiel der grundrechtlichen Legitimation staatlichen Strafens', in M. Fischer (ed.), *Der Begriff der Menschenwürde: Definition, Belastbarkeit und Grenzen*. Frankfurt am Main: Peter Lang, 65–77

Luhmann, N. 1965. *Grundrechte als Institution*. Berlin: Duncker & Humblot

Margalit, A. 1999. *Politik der Würde: Über Achtung und Verachtung*. Frankfurt am Main: Fischer

Prittwitz, C., and Manoledakis, I. (eds.). 1998. *Strafrecht und Menschenwürde: Deutsch-Griechisches Symposium, Thessaloniki 1995*. Baden-Baden: Nomos

Teifke, N. 2011. *Das Prinzip Menschenwürde*. Tübingen: Mohr Siebeck

40

Human dignity in US law

CARTER SNEAD

A comprehensive analysis of the uses of 'human dignity' in American law would be an extraordinary undertaking. To do so responsibly would require a systematic discussion of a massive array of sources of law. It would also require exploration of a diverse expanse of legal disciplines.

The aspiration of the present chapter is more modest. It aims to offer a brief survey of how 'human dignity' has (and has not) gained purchase in the American legal landscape. To that end, first, the chapter will offer a necessarily cursory reflection on the contested definition of 'human dignity.' Next it will follow a discussion of how human dignity has made its way into American law. This discussion will examine those subject-matter areas that feature human dignity as a legal concept, and will identify possible legal conceptual analogues in the American system (for example, liberty and equality).

Which sense of 'dignity'?

It is necessary briefly to identify two of the principal competing definitions of 'human dignity' in order to better understand its usage in American law. A useful way to divide the manifold approaches to human dignity is to distinguish those conceptions that treat dignity as a *contingent* human quality from those that regard it as an *intrinsic* attribute of human beings.

The contingent approach to human dignity ascribes it only to those individuals whose actions (or active capacities for certain actions) satisfy a predetermined set of criteria. One species of this approach holds that human dignity is properly attributable to 'a person whose actions, thoughts and concerns are worthy of intrinsic respect because they have been chosen, organized and guided in a way that makes sense from a distinctly individual point of view' (cf. Davis 2008). Thus, human dignity is equated with an activity, namely, the exercise of autonomous choice. Under this dignity-as-autonomy model, certain actions – even certain kinds of lives – are dignified or not (or dignified to greater or lesser degrees) depending on how the individual conducts himself. Dignity is an attribute that ebbs and flows – it can be acquired or lost. Human dignity can be diminished by restraints on autonomous choice wrought by disease, disability or coercion (whether in the form of restrictive laws or private violence). Lives characterized by radical dependence and vulnerability would, according to this view, be undignified. People who lack the cognitive capacity for free choice – young children, the mentally disabled and individuals suffering from dementia – do not possess human dignity in any measure. Conversely, those individuals who have the strength, intelligence and resources to exercise robust free choice possess human dignity in abundance.

By contrast, human dignity has also been conceived as an *intrinsic*, inalienable, absolute property of individuals simply by virtue of their status as human beings. This understanding of dignity holds that all human beings – regardless of their characteristics (such as size, strength, wealth, independence or social standing), actions or circumstances – are equal in dignity and thus entitled to at least a minimal standard of moral respect and care. Here, dignity is understood to be a pre-political quality that is not conferred by others, and cannot be taken away. Under this intrinsic conception of human dignity, the individual is inviolable and entitled to moral concern as well as the protection of the law.

The foregoing is merely a rough sketch of the variable approaches to human dignity, and could surely be refined, deepened and improved. But it is adequate for present purposes as a tool to negotiate the usages of human dignity in American law.

Human dignity in American law

'Dignity' is a relatively new juridical concept. In American law, the term was first used to denote the proper esteem owed to governmental entities.[1] For example, in *Federalist* 55, James Madison notes that the requirements for membership in the federal judiciary are meant to ensure the work of the courts be conducted with 'utility and dignity' (Rao 2008: 239). In the same spirit, in some of its opinions articulating the law of sovereign immunity, the US Supreme Court has asserted: 'Federalism requires that Congress accord States the respect and dignity due them as residuary sovereigns and joint participants that is consistent with their status as sovereign entities.'[2]

However, outside of the US, largely in response to the Nazi atrocities of the Second World War, 'human dignity' as a juridical concept was introduced and applied in a personal sense, to ground the inviolable worth of all members of the human race. A wide array of nations and intergovernmental bodies integrated human dignity prominently into their legal instruments.

The American legal system did not follow this path of introducing human dignity as a formal concept in its law.[3] But human dignity did eventually appear

[1] Judith Resnik and Julie Suk have offered a survey and discussion of the history of the term 'dignity' in US Supreme Court jurisprudence (Resnik and Suk 2003); see also Rao 2008 and Goodman 2006.

[2] *Alden* v. *Maine*, 527 US 706, 714–15 (1999).

[3] Several state constitutions reference 'dignity', and two (Louisiana and Montana) include assertions that there is a right to individual dignity.

on the American legal landscape, albeit indirectly. Indeed, appeals to dignity are widespread in American law, though not as a first-order enforceable principle. Human dignity is instead invoked rhetorically to bolster the normative force of other recognized juridical concepts – for example liberty, equality, and due process. In this limited, indirect form, 'human dignity' has been invoked in both its intrinsic and contingent iterations.

Intrinsic human dignity in American law

Since the 1940s, every branch of American government has invoked 'human dignity' as a personal concept expressing the esteem owed to all human beings. The term has been introduced in multiple fields of law, including criminal law, civil rights law, disability and elder law, and, more recently, in public bioethics.

Criminal law and procedure

Substantive and procedural criminal law is replete with references to intrinsic human dignity as a personal concept. This is particularly true in the law governing the investigative process and criminal punishment.

Justices of the US Supreme Court have invoked 'human dignity' to add rhetorical force to their arguments regarding constitutional limits on the authority to investigate crime. The Fourth Amendment to the US Constitution (which forbids 'unreasonable' searches and seizures) is meant to safeguard the privacy interests of individual citizens, while allowing the government to investigate crime. 'Privacy' is thus a juridical principle with some direct force. To underscore the importance of privacy, some Justices have made an appeal to human dignity. For example, the US Supreme Court has asserted that '[t]he overriding function of the Fourth Amendment is to protect personal privacy and dignity against unwarranted intrusion by the State'.[4] In this case and others like it, the Court invoked dignity not as a first-order principle, but as part of a rhetorical strategy to underline the importance of another recognized Fourth Amendment value, namely, privacy.

The Fifth Amendment (among other things) protects individuals from being compelled to be a witness against themselves in a criminal trial. The goods underlying this provision are at least twofold, namely, to protect the criminally accused from unfair coercion, and to sustain the character of the US criminal justice system as primarily accusatorial rather than inquisitorial. To shore up support for these established goods, the US Supreme Court has invoked the concept of human dignity. In the iconic decision of *Miranda* v. *Arizona*, wherein the Supreme Court held that suspects subject to custodial interrogation must first be advised of their rights (to remain silent and to counsel), the Court

[4] *Schmerber* v. *California*, 384 US 757 (1966).

held that 'the constitutional foundation underlying the privilege [against self-incrimination] is the respect a government – state or federal – must accord to the dignity and integrity of its citizens'.[5] Thus, here (as with the Fourth Amendment) human dignity is invoked to bolster a claim on behalf of other well-recognized normative goods, namely, freedom from improper coercion at the hands of law enforcement.

Apart from the investigative phase of the criminal process, human dignity as an intrinsic personal concept has been cited widely (as a secondary principle) in the law governing punishment. The Eighth Amendment to the US Constitution prohibits 'cruel and unusual' punishment. In this context, more than any other, the Supreme Court has invoked the concept of intrinsic human dignity as a crucial animating principle: 'By protecting even those convicted of heinous crimes, the Eighth Amendment reaffirms the duty of the government to respect the dignity of all persons.'[6] The Court has asserted: '[T]he basic concept underlying the Eighth Amendment is nothing less than the dignity of man.'[7] Thus, the Supreme Court has held that the death penalty may not be imposed on those defendants who are categorically incapable of the moral culpability warranting the ultimate punishment (for example, mentally disabled defendants[8] and defendants who were under the age of eighteen at the time of the capital offense[9]). Also, the Supreme Court has held that holding prisoners in degrading and inhumane conditions can constitute 'cruel and unusual' punishment.[10] *En route* to these conclusions, the Court repeatedly appealed to the intrinsic human dignity of all people – including convicted felons. In each case, intrinsic human dignity was deployed as a normative good to anchor the Court's analysis, though it did not constitute the applicable legal standard itself.

Aside from the jurisprudence of the US Supreme Court, intrinsic 'human dignity' has been invoked in the criminal context by the US Congress. The federal statute establishing certain rights for victims of federal crimes provides that: 'A crime victim has . . . [t]he right to be treated with fairness and with respect for the victim's dignity and privacy.'[11]

Civil rights/anti-discrimination law

Intrinsic 'human dignity' has been invoked as a normative grounding for laws against discrimination based on race, sex and disability. Here, human dignity is not itself the legal standard, but rather offers a grounding for the juridical principle of *equality*. In many instances, courts and other governmental officials have asserted that discrimination violates intrinsic dignity by failing to respect

[5] *Miranda* v. *Arizona*, 384 US 436, 460 (1966).

[6] *Roper* v. *Simmons*, 534 US 551, 560 (2005).

[7] *Trop* v. *Dulles*, 356 US 86, 100 (1958).

[8] *Atkins* v. *Virginia*, 536 US 304 (2002).

[9] *Roper* v. *Simmons*, 543 US 551 (2005).

[10] *Estelle* v. *Gamble*, 429 US 97, 104 (1976); *Hope* v. *Pelzer*, 536 US 730 (2002).

[11] 18 USC 3771(a)(8).

the fundamental equality possessed by all people by virtue of *who they are* as members of the human family. Dissenting from the notorious Supreme Court decision in *Korematsu* v. *US* (which upheld President Roosevelt's internment of Japanese Americans into 'relocation camps' during the Second World War), Justice Murphy condemned the majority opinion as 'adopt[ing] one of the cruelest of the rationales used by our enemies to destroy the dignity of the individual'.[12] Similarly, in an iconic decision of the Supreme Court upholding the constitutionality of the public accommodations provisions of the Civil Rights Act of 1964, the Court cited approvingly the purposes of the law: 'The primary purpose of [the Civil Rights Act] ... is to solve ... the deprivation of personal dignity that surely accompanies denial of equal access to public establishments.'[13] The Court has also argued that discrimination on the basis of sex 'deprives persons of their individual dignity'.[14]

More recently, the Supreme Court has employed the language of 'human dignity' to denote the respect owed to all people – including those adults who choose to engage in intimate sexual relations with members of the same sex. The Court held that a state law criminalizing 'homosexual conduct' violated liberty interests protected by the Due Process clause of the Fourteenth Amendment.[15] The first-order juridical principle affirmed by this decision was liberty or autonomy. But, in advancing the case for liberty, the Court appealed to the equal dignity of all persons.[16]

Relatedly, the US Congress has adopted the language of intrinsic 'human dignity' in the legislation aimed at ensuring the equality of the disabled and the elderly. For example, one section of the US Code ('Developmental Disabilities Assistance and Bill of Rights') directs that 'services, supports, and other assistance [offered pursuant to this law] should be provided in a manner that demonstrates respect for individual dignity'.[17] Also, in the Special Olympics Sport and Empowerment Act of 2004, Congress recognized the 'dignity and value the giftedness of children and adults with an intellectual disability'.[18] Similarly, in the Housing and Recovery Act of 2008, Congress declared that one purpose of the law was to 'enable elderly persons to live with dignity and independence by expanding the supply of supportive housing'.[19]

Public bioethics/global health

The conception of intrinsic human dignity is frequently deployed in American public bioethics – the governance of science, medicine and biotechnology in the

12 *Korematsu* v. *US*, 323 US 214, 240 (Murphy J dissenting).

13 *Heart of Atlanta Motel Inc.* v. *US*, 379 US 241, 250 (majority opinion) and 291–2 (1964) (Goldberg J concurring).

14 *Roberts* v. *US Jaycees*, 468 US 609, 626 (1984).

15 539 US 558 (2003).

16 *Ibid.*: 567.

17 42 USC 15001(c)(4).

18 Pub. L. 108-406: Special Olympics Sport and Empowerment Act of 2004 § 2(a)(2) (30 October 2004).

19 12 USC 1701q(a).

name of ethical goods. A few examples will suffice for purposes of illustration. Those public officials who regard the use and destruction of living human beings at the embryonic stage of development as a grave injustice frequently invoke human dignity. In vetoing a congressional effort to liberalize his stem cell research funding policy (which authorized funding only for those forms of stem cell research that did not create material incentives for future destruction of living human embryos[20]), President Bush cautioned against 'temptations to manipulate human life and violate human dignity'.[21] In opposing embryonic stem cell research, Congresswoman Virginia Foxx invoked human dignity even more explicitly:

> Those embryos are human beings and should not be treated as research subjects. We would never kill to harvest body parts because of the principle of human dignity. We do not even do this with our most heinous criminals. We do not treat them as things. We treat them with dignity until the time that they die . . . All human beings have profound human dignity.[22]

In the Executive Order directing the National Institutes of Health to pursue research involving alternative (i.e. non-embryonic) sources of pluripotent cells, President Bush declared that 'it is critical to establish moral and ethical boundaries to allow the Nation to move forward with medical research, while also maintaining the highest ethical standards and respecting human life and human dignity'.[23]

In the related context of abortion, those public officials who advocate legal protection for the unborn routinely use the language of human dignity. The Partial Birth Abortion Act of 2003 banned a particular method of abortion involving the partial delivery of a living foetus prior to piercing or crushing its skull.[24] In describing the purpose of the statute, the US Supreme Court noted that 'the Act expresses respect for the dignity of human life'. In support of the new law, Congresswoman Ileana Ros-Lehtinen declared that 'this is a barbaric act that is a grave attack against human dignity and justice'.[25]

Finally, in the context of global health, President Bush specifically invoked intrinsic human dignity as the grounding good for his policies to address disease in the developing world. For example, President Bush defended his Malaria

[20] Such forms included research on adult and alternative sources of pluripotent cells, as well as research involving only those embryonic stem cell lines derived before the announcement of the policy on 9 August 2001.

[21] Veto Letter from President George W. Bush to Congress (19 July 2006).

[22] 66 Cong. Rec. H3552 (daily edition. 18 May 2005) (statement of Representative Foxx).

[23] George W. Bush, 'Expanding Approved Stem Cell Lines in Ethically Responsible Ways', Exec. Order No. 13,435, 72 Fed. Reg. 34951 (20 June 2007) (revoked by Barack Obama, 'Removing Barriers to Responsible Scientific Research Involving Human Stem Cells', Exec. Order No. 13,505 (9 March 2009)).

[24] 18 USC 1531.

[25] 149 Cong. Rec. 10, 13790 (2003).

Initiative (PMI) as grounded in the truth that 'every human life has inherent dignity and matchless value'.[26]

Contingent human dignity in American law

To a lesser extent, some American public officials (particularly jurists) have variously invoked 'human dignity' in its contingent sense. Such officials have embraced the dignity-as-autonomy conception noted above. This usage of human dignity is most evident in the context of American public bioethics. Specifically, contingent human dignity has been invoked in connection with the laws touching and concerning abortion and end-of-life decision-making.

In defending the constitutionally protected liberty interest in abortion (pursuant to the Due Process clause of the Fourteenth Amendment), some jurists have suggested that the dignity of women depends on their capacity to freely choose to terminate a pregnancy without interference from the state.[27]

The US Supreme Court has recognized a protected liberty interest in declining unwanted medical treatment (including life-sustaining measures). No constitutional right to physician-assisted suicide exists, though a few states have legalized it. Defenders of a robust right to terminate life-sustaining measures, and even the right to physician-assisted suicide, invoke the notion of 'death with dignity'. On this view, autonomy makes dignity possible. That is, a life characterized by agonizing pain or radical dependence on others is, in an important sense *un*dignified – an unworthy state of affairs that individuals should have the right to choose against. Choosing to die in the face of the threat of radical dependency and cognitive decline is dignified in two senses: first, it involves the exercise of free choice in the most intimate and existential context, and, second, it evades (or ends) a life bereft of human dignity. This contingent view of dignity is expressed by Justice O'Connor in her concurrence in *Washington* v. *Glucksberg*:

> This freedom embraces not merely a person's right to refuse a particular kind of unwanted treatment, but also her interest in dignity, and in determining the character of the memories that will survive after her death . . . Avoiding intolerable pain and the indignity of living one's final days incapacitated and in agony is certainly 'at the heart of [the] liberty . . . to define one's own concept of existence, of meaning, of the universe, and of the mystery of human life'.[28]

In both the beginning- and end-of-life contexts discussed above, contingent human dignity is invoked as a normative principle amplifying the moral force of a first-order juridical principle, namely, the liberty to make choices in intimate matters. But, unlike the above-discussed examples of intrinsic dignity (where

[26] George W. Bush, 'Malaria Awareness Day, 2008', Proclamation No. 8246, 73 Fed. Reg. 23063 (25 April 2008).

[27] *Planned Parenthood* v. *Casey*, 505 US 833 (1992); *Gonzales* v. *Carhart*, 550 US124 (2007).

[28] *Washington* v. *Glucksberg*, 521 US 702 (1997).

human dignity was the grounding and justification for liberty, equality and privacy), here human dignity *depends on* and is *defined by* the exercise of autonomy. A woman's dignity depends on her freedom to choose abortion. A patient's dignity depends on his freedom to decide against a life marked by radical dependency on others. The incapacity to freely choose in these circumstances (because of coercive laws or debilitating disease) destroys the possibility of human dignity.

Conclusion

The foregoing discussion has briefly explored the various constructions of 'human dignity' in American law. It is a term that is used both to denote an intrinsic characteristic entitling all human beings to at least a bare minimum of respect and protection, and, alternatively, a contingent quality that is premised on the capacity to exercise autonomous choice. As a legal concept, it has had a limited direct impact. It has not, for example, been recognized by the Supreme Court as a constitutionally protected interest to the degree that liberty, equality, or even privacy have. It has not been enshrined in positive law as a doctrinal principle directly applicable to regulate conduct. It is, however, often invoked by courts and officials in the political branches alike to amplify the moral claims made pursuant to more commonly recognized principles of American law, such as equality, liberty, privacy and justice.

References

Davis, D. 2008. 'Human Dignity and Respect for Persons: A Historical Perspective on Public Bioethics', in President's Council on Bioethics. 2008. *Human Dignity and Bioethics: Essays Commissioned by the President's Council on Bioethics.* Washington, DC, http://bioethics.georgetown.edu/pcbe/reports/human_dignity/chapter14.html

Goodman, M. D. 2006. 'Human Dignity in Supreme Court Constitutional Jurisprudence', *Nebraska Law Review* 84: 740

Rao, Neomi. 2008. 'On the Use and Abuse of Dignity in Constitutional Law', *Columbia Journal of European Law* 14: 201

Resnik, J., and Suk, J. 2003. 'Adding Insult to Injury: Questioning the Role of Dignity in Conceptions of Sovereignty', *Stanford Law Review* 55: 1921

41

Human dignity in South American law

CLAUDIA LIMA MARQUES AND LUCAS LIXINSKI*

The aim of this chapter is to explore the ways in which human dignity has been used as a legal concept across South American countries. The concept has high value, and has been central to (at least Western) legal thinking since the approval of the Universal Declaration of Human Rights (UDHR) in 1948 (Cançado Trindade 2008: 11). As all South American constitutions currently in force were established after the UDHR, we suggest that human dignity plays a central role in those constitutions as well, and thus in the legal orders of all countries on the South American continent.

In order to support this claim, this chapter will focus primarily on comparative constitutional law, but it will also look at selected examples of uses of the notion of dignity in other legal contexts. Our central contention is that the concept of human dignity has evolved as an axiological (as a core value or fundamental principle) and normative foundation (as a fundamental right or rule) of the legal systems of South American countries, and that, even though theoretically under-developed, the notion has been used extensively by lawyers and judges.[1] This 'under-comprehension' of the concept, however, has led to the reduction of its normative value and even threatens to nullify it altogether, at least before the eyes of society at large (cf. Lorenzetti 1998: 166).

The chapter is structured in two sections: first, we will look at 'dignity clauses' in South American constitutions (that is: constitutional law and theory), and, second, examine the extra-constitutional role of the notion of human dignity.

Dignity in South American constitutions

The centrality of dignity in Kantian thought has readily seeped into South American constitutions, in no small part due to the German influence in the drafting of South American constitutions during transitions from authoritarian

* We are highly indebted to A. Michel, C. Perrone, P. Baquero, S. Schwager and V. Garbini for the research assistance in collecting the comparative case law. All errors remain the authors'.

[1] See, for Mexico, Novoa Monreal 1997: 22; for Argentina, Mosset Iturraspe 1994: 10; and, for Brazil, De Moraes 2003: 113.

regimes to democracies (Sarlet 2004: 61).[2] As such, human dignity became the very cornerstone of legal orders across the continent.

Curiously enough, South American law has developed its own version of how dignity should be used. Instead of looking at dignity as a baseline that, if impinged upon, automatically invalidates legislation, South American law looks at dignity as yet another fundamental right, but one that cannot be defined and thus in this quality is unfortunately used as a clause with the power to 'patch up' legal reasoning when a justification based on another norm cannot be articulated by the judge. In other words, human dignity has become more of a rhetorical tool in legal (particularly judicial)[3] reasoning than a well-structured, carefully used legal mechanism. Case law on the Universal Declaration of Human Rights follows along the same lines, using references to dignity in the UDHR as an additional rhetorical device to stress a point, but attributing to the idea of dignity enshrined in the document a very indirect function.[4]

The UDHR's dignity clause has been used as an additional argument by a Brazilian court in stating that essential utility services, such as the provision of water, could not be suspended in case of non-payment, precisely because of their essential character for the realization of human rights and human dignity as protected by the Declaration.[5] The UDHR and its construction of dignity have also been invoked as the basis for a 'principle of humanity' with regard to the treatment of persons deprived of liberty, particularly mental health patients.[6] Another case involves the use of human dignity in the Universal Declaration as implying a general ethics of human rights protection so as to uphold the right of a transsexual to change names.[7]

Most South American constitutions[8] (with the notable exceptions of Uruguay's 1997 Constitution, last amended in 2004,[9] and Argentina's 1994

[2] One must also take into consideration the Mexican Constitution of 1917, written before the German Weimar Constitution of 1919.

[3] Dignity has been used especially in connection with family law, rights of the accused and of persons deprived of liberty, *habeas corpus*, among others. The case law is, however, largely a repetition of the (non-)articulation of human dignity in constitutional texts, and examples in this chapter will be sparse, mostly due to space constraints.

[4] For an analysis of this case law in Brazil, see Lima Marques and Lixinski 2009: 155–6.

[5] State Court of Appeals of Rio de Janeiro, *Interlocutory Appeal (AI) 2001.002.11382*, judgment of 9 May 2002.

[6] State Court of Appeals of Rio de Janeiro, *Criminal Appeal (ApCrim.) 1995.050.00066*, judgment of 27 June 1995.

[7] State Court of Appeals of Rio Grande do Sul, *Civil Appeal (ApCív.) 70013909874*, judgment of 5 April 2006.

[8] French Guyana has been excluded, as it is still a French territory. The country therefore uses the same legal system as France, including the French notion of dignity.

[9] But the Uruguayan Constitution does mention the protection of rights 'inherent to human personality' (Art. 72).

Constitution) recognize human dignity and its importance. The uses of dignity in constitutional texts can be of three different types.

First, there are countries which attribute moral value to dignity, but fall short of turning it into a positive legal rule. One example of this is the 1980 (with reforms in 1996) Constitution of Guyana, which mentions the protection of human dignity, in its Preamble, as a historical legacy and as a pledge for the future. It does not, however, mention dignity in the actual constitutional text. Because 'dignity' is found in the Preamble, it is clearly a moral commitment of the nation and influences the way the actual Constitution is applied, but, because it is not in the text, it falls short of being a legal – not to mention enforceable – rule.

The second category is comprised of the vast majority of countries which place dignity at the very centre of the positive legal order. For instance, the 1988 Brazilian Constitution does include human dignity not in the list of fundamental rights, but as one of the very pillars of the republic (Article 1.III). Apart from this, there are no references to human dignity or dignity in the list of fundamental rights, and the only references are found in the articles of the Constitution that refer to the protection of children (Article 227), elderly persons (Article 230) and families (Article 226).

A similar situation occurs in the Paraguayan Constitution (1992), which recognizes human dignity as a foundation of the state (Article 1). Subsequently, dignity is mentioned in connection with the rights to honour, privacy and family life (Articles 23 and 33), the right to equality (Article 46) and the right to health (Article 68). Regarding the right to health, 'dignity' is mentioned in relation to sanitary law, operating as a limitation to the state's power to enact and enforce legislation in the area. The same idea of dignity as a gatekeeper lies behind the reference in the article that refers to compulsory military service: military service is compulsory unless it impinges upon a person's dignity (Article 129).

Venezuela's 1999 Constitution also mentions human dignity as a foundational value of the state (Article 3). Other provisions associate dignity with the protection of personal liberty (Article 46), protection of the elderly (Article 80), disabled persons (Article 81) and the right to fair wages (Article 91). Dignity has a gatekeeper function in the right to privacy by serving as a limit to judicial orders determining search and seizure (Article 47). It plays the same role in determining the extent to which force may be used by the police (Articles 55 and 332).

In Colombia's 1991 Constitution, dignity performs the function of a foundational norm of the state as well (Article 1). 'Dignity' is mentioned in connection with the protection of honour (Article 42), the protection of labour contracts and relations (Article 53) and the several distinctive cultures that compose the Colombian nation (Article 70). This reference to dignity in the context of culture is a prelude to a trend that is much more tangible in later constitutions, such as that of Bolivia.

The Bolivian 2009 Constitution also attributes to human dignity the condition of a foundational norm of the state and the legal order (Article 8.II). It also acknowledges dignity as an important component of several fundamental rights, including the right to honour and privacy (Article 21) and as a corollary to liberty (Articles 22, 23 and 73). But in this constitutional text dignity gains a new dimension, already hinted at in the Colombian Constitution: while hardly ever explicitly stated, there is the presumption that dignity is something that relates to the individual, as it is also conceptualized in the UDHR. However, the Bolivian Constitution speaks of the dignity of persons, nations, peoples and communities (Article 9.2), adding an important collective dimension to human dignity. This reflects a shift we find in recent Latin American constitutionalism from the liberal focus on the protection of individual rights to a more collectivist emphasis on the recognition of group rights and multiculturalism (particularly indigenous peoples, but also other traditional groups and communities).

In the latter case, 'dignity' appears as a term which signifies all fundamental rights protected by the constitution, since, if the legal order is founded on dignity, all norms must be interpreted as taking dignity into account. There is no right to dignity, but dignity is instead the source and ultimate purpose of all rights (cf. Rolla 2002: 471–2).

The third group is comprised of countries that do not recognize human dignity as an autonomous norm, but rather as an accessory rule to the protection of fundamental rights. One such example is Suriname's 1987 Constitution (with 1992 reforms), which mentions dignity only in the context of an article protecting personal liberty and safety, determining that people deprived of their liberty shall be treated with dignity (Article 16.3). And the Chilean Constitution of 1980 only speaks of dignity in the context of the protection of equality (Article 1), although it makes this reference in the title of the Constitution referring to the foundations of the country, and uses a language very similar to that of Article 1 of the UDHR.

Instances like these suggest that the reference to dignity is but a safeguard to guarantee the evolutionary interpretation (that is, interpretation that takes into account present-day values and circumstances – in opposition to finding an 'original meaning' to a provision) of the clause (cf. García Ramírez 2008: 355). That is to say, whenever dignity is mentioned in connection with another right, it has been suggested that this means dignity plays a role of leaving the door open for evolutionary interpretations that can respond to changes in the social and legal fabrics, while still maintaining the effectiveness of the constitutional text's commitment to the protection of fundamental rights (García Ramírez 2008: 468–9).

Naturally, these categories are not watertight, as most countries which attribute to dignity the value of a foundational norm also associate it with specific fundamental rights. One similarity between the second and third categories, however, is that dignity is not a right on its own. In other words, these constitutional texts do not formulate dignity as a *right*; dignity is either a foundational norm of the state, or a value to be taken into account when considering specific fundamental rights. In this sense, South American constitutions seem to have moved away from German constitutional law's explicit use of dignity as a right.

But obviously dignity does not play a role only in constitutional law: in law outside the constitutional realm one also finds many references to dignity. The following section will look at some of these uses.

Dignity in extra-constitutional law

The first type of use of dignity that is worth analyzing in this section is the protection of human dignity in the Inter-American System for the protection of human rights. Even though this is an international system, its influence on South American countries is undeniable (for example Garcia-Sayán 2005): the status of the American Convention on Human Rights in national legal orders is not uniform across the continent: some countries (Argentina and Brazil most notably) grant it the status of a constitutional norm, whereas others still look at the American Convention as being on a lower legal level than the domestic constitution. In other words, for some countries the American Convention will have the same weight as their domestic constitutions; for others, it will have the weight of ordinary legislation, and cannot modify the constitution. Regardless of the status in municipal legal orders, the fact remains that the American Convention and other instruments of the system have been important in shaping law across the continent, and make reference to human dignity.

For instance, the American Declaration on the Rights and Duties of Man (1948), which in fact preceded the UDHR, already mentions the protection of dignity in its Preamble, and then again in connection with property and private life (Article XXIII). The American Convention (1969, also known as the Pact of San José) mentions 'dignity' in connection with personal integrity (Article 5), the prohibition of slavery (Article 6) and private life and reputation (Article 11). To be more specific, Article 11 articulates a right to dignity, but as a synonym for the protection of honour and reputation. This has been articulated by the Inter-American Court of Human Rights in one of its cases, but there is very little case law concerning the protection of dignity as such.[10]

Regarding other instruments in the system, the Inter-American Convention to Prevent and Punish Torture also mentions 'dignity' in its Preamble, as does the San Salvador Protocol on Economic, Social and Cultural Rights, the Inter-American Convention on Enforced Disappearances and the Inter-American Convention on the Rights of People with Disabilities. The Inter-American Convention Against Violence Against Women (Belém do Pará Convention) mentions that all women have a right to dignity (Article 4.e), in connection with the

[10] Inter-American Court of Human Rights, *Ricardo Canese* v. *Paraguay*. Merits, Reparations and Costs. Judgment of 31 August 2004, Series C No. 111, para. 101.

protection of families. The uses of dignity in the Inter-American instruments thus reflect to a large extent the uses in constitutional law: it does not articulate dignity as a right, but uses it as a moral imperative which permeates all human rights protection.

It is interesting to note that, in the Inter-American system of human rights protection, dignity generally loses its central dimension, gaining almost a 'ceremonial' role. It is nevertheless still important, much in the way dignity is important when mentioned in the Preambles to constitutions. This is so at least to the extent that references to dignity reassert or 'narrate' the values from whose perspective the entire instrument is to be interpreted.[11]

Besides international human rights law, human dignity is also a relevant concept in both criminal and civil law, particularly when it comes to the protection of honour and reputation, privacy, and even freedom of expression.[12] Human dignity also plays a very important role in the affirmation of the legal category of 'personality rights' in private law,[13] and in the protection of consumers' rights across the continent. Consumer law in South America has evolved in response to the need to protect the dignity of human beings as market agents, as opposed to more traditional understandings of dignity, which usually focus on dignity within the private realm of honour and family protection.[14]

But the fact of the matter remains that in none of these instances does there exist an autonomous right to dignity; instead, dignity is used as a means to reinforce rules, having more of an axiological-inspirational than normative value. It is nevertheless a role which cannot be disregarded, and perhaps ultimately the role that dignity, as a very open-ended and practically indefinable term, can play.

Concluding remarks: the pervasiveness of an 'underdeveloped' concept

Human dignity has evolved into a central norm of South American law. But it has done so not through the articulation of a 'right to dignity'; instead, dignity pervades the entirety of South American countries' legal orders by acting as an inspirational norm, either by being mentioned as one of the foundations of the state in several constitutions, or simply through other references, constitutional or not.

Perhaps this is precisely the strength of human dignity. To the extent that dignity is not a fully enforceable right, it cannot be combated; at the same time, because it is mentioned in all places, it cannot be ignored. The subtle power of human dignity in South American law is thus great, and praiseworthy.

[11] On narration as a phenomenon of post-modern law, see Jayme 1995.

[12] For a collection of examples of such uses, see Rolla 2002: 478–85.

[13] On the Brazilian case regarding personality rights, see Lixinski 2006.

[14] On the protection of consumer dignity, see Lima Marques (forthcoming).

References

Cançado Trindade, A. A. 2008. *Evolution du droit international au droit des gens*. Paris: Pedone

De Moraes, C. B. 2003. 'O conceito de dignidade humana', in I. W. Sarlet (ed.), *Constituição, Direitos Fundamentais e Direito Privado*. Porto Alegre: Livraria do Advogado

García Ramírez, S. 2008. 'Recepción de la Jurisprudencia Interamericana sobre Derechos Humanos en el Derecho Interno', *Anuario de Derecho Constitucional Latinoamericano* 353–76

García-Sayán, D. 2005. 'Una Viva Interacción: Corte Interamericana y Tribunales Internos', in *La Corte Interamericana de Derechos Humanos: Un Cuarto de Siglo*, ed. Inter-American Court of Human Rights, 323–84

Jayme, E. 1995. 'Identité culturelle et intégration: le droit international privé postmoderne – Cours general de droit international privé', *Collected Courses of the Hague Academy of International Law* 251: 11

Lima Marques, C. Forthcoming. 'Protection of the Weaker Party in Private International Law (Consumers, Small Business and Non-Profit-Making Activities)', *Recueil des Cours*

Lima Marques, C., and Lixinski, L. 2009. 'Treaty Enforcement by Brazilian Courts: Reconciling Ambivalences and Myths?', *Brazilian Yearbook of International Law* 4(1): 138–69

Lixinski, L. 2006. 'Considerações acerca da inserção dos direitos de personalidade no ordenamento jurídico brasileiro', *Revista de Direito Privado* 201

Lorenzetti, R. 1998. *Fundamentos do Direito Privado*. São Paulo: Revista dos Tribunais

Mosset Iturraspe, J. 1994. *Visión Jurisprudencial del Valor de la Vida Humana*. Buenos Aires: Rubinzal Culzoni

Novoa Monreal, E. 1997. *Derecho a la Vida Privada y Libertad de Información*. Buenos Aires: Siglo XXI

Rolla, G. 2002. 'El Valor Normativo del Principio de la Dignidad Humana: Consideraciones en Torno a las Constituciones Iberoamericanas', *Anuario Iberoamericano de Justicia Constitucional* 6: 463–89

Sarlet, I. W. 2004. *Dignidade da Pessoa Humana e Direitos Fundamentais*. Porto Alegre: Livraria do Advogado

42

Human dignity in South African law

ANTON FAGAN

In no legal system does human dignity play a greater role than in the South African one. The South African Constitution accords everyone 'the right to have their dignity respected and protected'.[1] It also recognizes human dignity as one of three values (the others are equality and freedom) upon which the Republic of South Africa was founded and which the South African Bill of Rights affirms.[2]

Dignity as a right and as a value in South African law

Inconsistency with the *right* to dignity (like inconsistency with any other right in the Bill of Rights) is ground for a court to declare invalid a legal rule, whether it be a statutory, common-law or customary rule.[3] Which legal rules are inconsistent with the right to dignity depends upon the scope of its application. That is: it depends upon whom the right binds. According to the Constitution, every one of the rights in its Bill of Rights, and thus also the right to dignity, binds the state.[4] The Constitution does not, however, say whether the right also binds private persons. As with all the other rights in the Bill of Rights, the question whether the right to dignity binds private persons is left to the courts to determine, 'taking into account the nature of the right and the nature of any duty imposed by the right'.[5] Though this is not entirely clear, the South African Constitutional Court seems to have accepted that the right to dignity does bind private persons.[6]

The South African courts have declared a number of legal rules invalid on the ground of their inconsistency with the right to dignity. Most of the rules have been statutory, such as a provision in the Criminal Procedure Act permitting the death penalty to be imposed for murder,[7] a provision in the same

[1] The Constitution of the Republic of South Africa, 1996, s. 10.

[2] *Ibid.*: ss. 1 and 7(1). [3] *Ibid.*: s. 172(1). [4] *Ibid.*: s. 8(1).

[5] *Ibid.*: s. 8(2). [6] *NM* v. *Smith* 2007 (5) SA 250 (CC).

[7] *S* v. *Makwanyane* 1995 (3) SA 391 (CC), *per* Mahomed J, Mokgoro J and O'Regan J.

Act allowing for corporal punishment of juvenile offenders,[8] provisions in the Aliens Control Act dealing with applications by foreign spouses of South African citizens for immigration and work permits[9] and a provision in the Black Administration Act regulating intestate succession in the case of black South Africans.[10] However, inconsistency with the right to dignity has been the ground for declaring invalid at least one common-law rule, namely, the rule criminalizing sodomy.[11] And it has been the ground for declaring invalid a rule of African customary law, namely, the rule of male primogeniture as applied to intestate succession.[12]

As a *value*, human dignity is explicitly given two roles by the South African Constitution. The Constitution requires a court to promote the value of human dignity (along with those of equality and freedom) whenever it interprets the Bill of Rights.[13] And it requires a court to consider the value of human dignity (again along with those of equality and freedom) when determining whether the limitation of a right in the Bill of Rights by a legal rule is 'reasonable and justifiable', and thus constitutionally permitted.[14]

The South African Constitutional Court has frequently employed the value of human dignity in the first of these roles. So, for example, the Court invoked the value of human dignity when interpreting the right not to be subjected to cruel, inhuman or degrading treatment or punishment,[15] the right to freedom and security of the person,[16] the right against unfair discrimination,[17] the right to have access to adequate housing,[18] the right to privacy,[19] the right to have access to social security,[20] the right to culture[21] and even the right to a fair

[8] *S* v. *Williams* 1995 (3) SA 632 (CC).

[9] *Dawood, Shalabi and Thomas* v. *Minister of Home Affairs* 2000 (3) SA 936 (CC); *Booysen* v. *Minister of Home Affairs* 2001 (4) SA 485 (CC).

[10] *Bhe* v. *Magistrate, Khayelitsha* 2005 (1) SA 580 (CC).

[11] *National Coalition for Gay and Lesbian Equality* v. *Minister of Justice* 1999 (1) SA 6 (CC).

[12] *Bhe* v. *Magistrate, Khayelitsha* 2005 (1) SA 580 (CC).

[13] The Constitution of the Republic of South Africa, 1996, s. 39(1).

[14] Ibid.: ss. 36(1) and 8(3)(b).

[15] *S* v. *Makwanyane* 1995 (3) SA 391 (CC), *per* Chaskalson P; *S* v. *Dodo* 2001 (3) SA 382 (CC).

[16] *Bernstein* v. *Bester* 1996 (2) SA 751 (CC), *per* O'Regan J.

[17] *Prinsloo* v. *Van der Linde* 1997 (3) SA 1012 (CC); *President of the Republic of South Africa* v. *Hugo* 1997 (4) SA 1 (CC); *Harksen* v. *Lane* 1998 (1) SA 300 (CC); *National Coalition for Gay and Lesbian Equality* v. *Minister of Justice* 1999 (1) SA 6 (CC).

[18] *Government of the Republic of South Africa* v. *Grootboom* 2001 (1) SA 46 (CC); *Occupiers of 51 Olivia Road and 197 Main Street, Johannesburg* v. *City of Johannesburg* 2008 (3) SA 208 (CC).

[19] *Investigating Directorate: Serious Economic Offences* v. *Hyundai Motor Distributors* 2001 (1) SA 545 (CC).

[20] *Khosa* v. *Minister of Social Development* 2004 (6) SA 505 (CC).

[21] *MEC for Education, Kwazulu-Natal* v. *Pillay* 2008 (1) SA 474 (CC), *per* O'Regan J.

trial.[22] The value of human dignity has also been employed in the second role, but more rarely. There are two rights whose limitations have been found to be reasonable and justifiable, and thus constitutionally permitted, on the ground that the limitations served the value of human dignity. They are the right to freedom of religion (limited by a statute prohibiting corporal punishment in all schools, including private religious ones) and the right to freedom of expression (limited by a statute criminalizing various acts to do with child pornography and by the common-law rules imposing tortious liability for defamation).[23]

According to the Constitutional Court, the Constitution by implication gives the value of human dignity four further roles. The basis for these implied roles is the Constitution's express imposition, on the courts, of an obligation to 'promote the spirit, purport and objects of the Bill of Rights', first, when interpreting a statute, second, when developing the common law, and, third, when developing customary law.[24] The Constitutional Court has held, reasonably enough, that the obligation to promote the spirit, purport and objects of the Bill of Rights when engaged in any one of these three activities, entails an obligation to promote the value of human dignity (as well as the values of freedom and equality).[25] Consistent with this, the Court relied upon the value of human dignity to justify its interpreting the word 'spouse' in two statutes to include parties to a Muslim marriage.[26] Less reasonably, the Court has held that the second of these obligations, that is, the obligation to promote the spirit, purport and objects of the Bill of Rights *when* developing the common law, entails the further and very different obligation *to develop* the common law whenever it falls short of the spirit, purport and objects of the Bill of Rights.[27] According to the Constitutional Court, therefore, the Constitution accords the value of human dignity a primary, and not merely a secondary, role in the common law's development. The value of human dignity is to serve as an independent ground for developing the common law, alongside the rights in the Bill of Rights, and not merely as a tie-breaker when one or more of those rights already justify

[22] *Bothma* v. *Els* 2010 (2) SA 622 (CC).

[23] *Christian Education South Africa* v. *Minister of Education* 2000 (4) SA 757 (CC); *De Reuck* v. *Director of Public Prosecutions, WLD* 2004 (1) SA 406 (CC); *Khumalo* v. *Holomisa* 2002 (5) SA 401 (CC).

[24] The Constitution of the Republic of South Africa, 1996, s. 39(2).

[25] *Investigating Directorate: Serious Economic Offences* v. *Hyundai Motor Distributors* 2001 (1) SA 545 (CC); *Daniels* v. *Campbell* 2004 (5) SA 331 (CC); *Masiya* v. *DPP, Pretoria* 2007 (5) SA 30 (CC).

[26] *Daniels* v. *Campbell* 2004 (5) SA 331 (CC).

[27] *Carmichele* v. *Minister of Safety and Security* 2001 (4) SA 938 (CC); *S* v. *Thebus* 2003 (6) SA 505 (CC); *K* v. *Minister of Safety and Security* 2005 (6) SA 419 (CC); *Masiya* v. *DPP, Pretoria* 2007 (5) SA 30 (CC); *Barkhuizen* v. *Napier* 2007 (5) SA 323 (CC).

some development of the common law, but are indeterminate as to the precise form which that development should take.[28]

The concept of dignity in South African law

Notwithstanding the many occasions on which human dignity has been invoked by the South African courts, South African law has yet to develop a *concept* of human dignity capable of explaining the multiple roles accorded it by the South African Constitution. It is true that the South African Constitutional Court, in a number of judgments over a number of years, has endorsed the following more-or-less Kantian set of propositions about human dignity:

> (1) Human dignity is the value inherent in every human being (the value every human being has simply by virtue of being human). (2) This value is infinite and consequently incomparable with other values. (3) This value, since it is both inherent and infinite, is equal for all human beings, regardless of their character or conduct. (4) Human beings, as objects of value, deserve respect. (5) Human beings, as objects of equal value, deserve equal respect. (6) Human dignity, so understood, is the foundation of most (possibly all) of the rights in the Bill of Rights.[29]

However, the Court's use of this Kantian concept of human dignity to explicate the value of, and right to, dignity in the South African Constitution is not without difficulty. The second proposition above states that human dignity (the value inherent in human beings) is infinite and incomparable. But how could the value of human dignity, so understood, play the second of the roles which the Constitution explicitly accords it, namely, to help determine whether the limitation of a right is reasonable and justifiable? For that, as the Constitutional Court has accepted, may require a court to balance the value of human dignity against (and thus compare it to) the right being limited.[30] A similar problem arises with respect to the right to dignity, if it is given a Kantian content along

[28] Why an obligation to develop the common law whenever it deviates from the objects of the Bill of Rights cannot be inferred from an obligation to promote those objects when developing the common law is explained in Fagan 2009: 181–4; 2010.

[29] *S* v. *Makwanyane* 1995 (3) SA 391 (CC), *per* Chaskalson P at 423A, 451C–D, *per* O'Regan J at 507A–C; *S* v. *Williams* 1995 (3) SA 632 (CC) at 655B; *Ferreira* v. *Levin* 1996 (1) SA 984, *per* Ackermann J at 1013F–G; *Bernstein* v. *Bester* 1996 (2) SA 751 (CC), *per* O'Regan J at 816C–E; *Prinsloo* v. *Van der Linde* 1997 (3) SA 1012 (CC) at 1026D–G; *President of the Republic of South Africa* v. *Hugo* 1997 (4) SA 1 (CC) at 22H–23A, 23F; *National Coalition for Gay and Lesbian Equality* v. *Minister of Justice* 1999 (1) SA 6 (CC) at 28C–E; *Dawood, Shalabi and Thomas* v. *Minister of Home Affairs* 2000 (3) SA 936 (CC) at 961G; *S* v. *Dodo* 2001 (3) SA 382 (CC) at 404D; *S* v. *Jordan* 2002 (6) SA 642 (CC), *per* O'Regan J and Sachs J at 670H.

[30] *Christian Education South Africa* v. *Minister of Education* 2000 (4) SA 757 (CC); *De Reuck* v. *Director of Public Prosecutions, WLD* 2004 (1) SA 406 (CC); *Khumalo* v. *Holomisa* 2002 (5) SA 401 (CC).

the lines suggested by the propositions above. Understood as the right to the respect owed to one by virtue of one's inherent, infinite and incomparable value, the right to dignity must be an absolute right. For to accord a person any less respect than that would be to deny his humanity. And nothing could possibly justify that. However, the Constitution does not preclude the possibility that the constitutional right to dignity may be justifiably and reasonably limited. More than that, the Constitutional Court has explicitly held that '[l]ike all constitutional rights, [the right to dignity] is not absolute and may be limited in appropriate cases'.[31]

There is a further difficulty with the idea that the Kantian concept of human dignity can explain dignity in the South African Constitution. Human dignity, so conceived, certainly is capable of playing the foundational role which the Constitutional Court ascribes to it (in the last of the propositions above). However, it is possible that the contribution of human dignity to the justification of rights, though indispensible, is purely formal. It may be that we have reason to care about others' interests only because they have human dignity. If so, human dignity is essential to the explanation of others' rights against us. It does not follow, however, that human dignity has any role to play in the identification and elucidation of those rights. For it may be that, in order to determine and give content to the rights others have against us, it is enough that we consider their (and our) interests. (There may be doubts that something can have an essential, yet formal, role to play in the justification of a norm. But imagine that, after a mother has instructed her son to obey the babysitter, the babysitter commands him to go and blow his nose. Without the mother's instruction, the babysitter's command would impose no duty. The instruction is thus essential to the existence of the duty. But it has no role to play in the determination of the content of that duty: that depends entirely on what the babysitter has commanded.)

This presents a problem for the Constitutional Court's attempt to cast dignity in the South African Constitution in a Kantian mould. For it would appear to be incompatible with the Constitution's explicit instruction that the value of human dignity is to guide the interpretation of the rights in the Bill of Rights. And it would appear to be incompatible with the Constitutional Court's assumption that the value of human dignity is to guide the interpretation of statutes, as well as the development of common and customary law. If the role of human dignity in the justification of rights is a purely formal, albeit essential, one, human dignity could not possibly discharge these tasks (no more than the

[31] *Dawood, Shalabi and Thomas* v. *Minister of Home Affairs* 2000 (3) SA 936 (CC) at 970E–F. See also *S* v. *Makwanyane* 1995 (3) SA 391 (CC), *per* O'Regan J at 509–10; *S* v. *Williams* 1995 (3) SA 632 (CC) at 649–58; *National Coalition for Gay and Lesbian Equality* v. *Minister of Justice* 1999 (1) SA 6 (CC) at 30–1; *S* v. *Mamabolo* 2001 (3) SA 409 (CC) at 431A–B; *Bhe* v. *Magistrate, Khayelitsha* 2005 (1) SA 580 (CC) at 616, 622–3.

mother's instruction to her son could help him to decide what the babysitter meant when she ordered him to blow his nose).

References

Fagan, Anton. 2009. 'The Confusions of K', *South African Law Journal* 126: 156

2010. 'The Secondary Role of the Spirit, Purport and Objects of the Bill of Rights in the Common Law's Development', *South African Law Journal* 127: 611

43

The Islamic world and the alternative declarations of human rights

ANN ELIZABETH MAYER

Since the appearance of the Universal Declaration of Human Rights, various human rights declarations have been proposed that purport to set forth alternative Islamic principles on human rights. How Islam pertains to human rights remains contested, and none of the proposed Islamic human rights declarations can be taken as a definitive statement of Islamic human rights. The Islamic heritage is diffuse and complex, and trends in contemporary Islamic thought vary widely. Moreover, the rationale for producing Islamic alternatives is challenged by Muslims who embrace the UDHR as consonant with their faith along with the concept of dignity that is linked to the human rights that it sets forth.

The idea that Islam possesses its own distinctive version of human rights has been promoted by conservative forces in Muslim societies that seek to uphold rules of Islamic law, or *Shari'a*, that are in conflict with the UDHR. In league with some of these conservative forces, governments of Muslim countries have sponsored alternative declarations and resolutions that rely on Islamic elements to rationalize non-compliance with the UDHR, eliminating some UDHR rights and circumscribing others. Where the concept of dignity figures in such declarations, because it accommodates inequality and restrictions on rights, it takes on colourations unlike those of dignity in the UDHR.

As the years have passed, the 1990 Cairo Declaration on Human Rights in Islam,[1] which was put forward by the Organization of the Islamic Conference – renamed in 2011 the Organization of Islamic Cooperation (OIC), the organization to which all Muslim majority countries belong – has outstripped other Islamic declarations in terms of international prestige. Enjoying observer status at the UN, the OIC has vigorously promoted its positions on human rights in the UN, presenting the Cairo Declaration as the definitive statement of Islamic human rights. Working to coordinate its members' strategies on human rights, the OIC has managed to influence the UN to move towards treating the Cairo Declaration as a legitimate Islamic alternative to the UDHR. The Cairo Declaration was included in the UN documents issuing from the 1993 World Conference

1 Cairo Declaration on Human Rights in Islam, 5 August 1990, UN GAOR, World Conference on Human Rights, 4th Session, Agenda Item 5, UN Doc. A/CONF.157/PC/62/Add.18 (1993) (English translation).

on Human Rights in Vienna and was published by the Office of the UN High Commissioner for Human Rights.[2] The fact that the Cairo Declaration has won a level of acceptance in the UN human rights system has enhanced the confidence of OIC member states in defending it against charges that it conflicts with the UDHR. At the same time, it has been vigorously critiqued by respected human rights NGOs and by Muslims who are committed to upholding human rights according to international standards, who note the striking deficiencies in the rights protections that it offers.

In issuing the Cairo Declaration, the OIC member states were emulating the method that had been used in drafting the UDHR. They acted on the assumption that a human rights declaration should be endorsed by national governments, in this case governments linked by the religious affiliation of the majority of their citizens. In so doing, the OIC members disregarded the fact that, in terms of Islamic jurisprudence and theology, governments of contemporary Muslim countries possess no authority whatsoever to declare Islamic doctrine on dignity or any other subject. Despite these problems, the endorsements of OIC member states did buttress the credibility of the Cairo Declaration in UN forums.

The terminology of the Cairo Declaration is confusing, at least in part because it is simultaneously seeking to serve OIC members' agendas by establishing an Islamic counter-model to the UDHR that places curbs on rights while also attempting to obscure how significantly it deviates from the UDHR. For this Islamic counter-model to be plausible and to win acceptance in the UN, it had to borrow many aspects of the format and terminology of the UDHR, including terms like 'dignity'. However, dignity in the Cairo Declaration must be understood in relation to provisions that stipulate that all human rights are subordinated to Islamic law, as indicated in Article 24, which states: 'All the rights and freedoms stipulated in this Declaration are subject to the Islamic Shariʿah', and in Article 25, which states: 'The Islamic Shariʿah is the only source of reference for the explanation or clarification to any of the articles of this Declaration.' Because these superimposed Islamic criteria are fundamentally at odds with the egalitarian foundations of the UDHR, one should not be misled into thinking that the intent is to replicate dignity as conceived in the UDHR.

The term dignity appears four times in the Cairo Declaration, and a prohibition of subjecting people to 'indignity' and a right to 'a dignified life' also appear. The Cairo Declaration does not explicitly stipulate that dignity is afforded only subject to Islamic criteria, but it does articulate a closely related proposition. The Preamble treats what it calls a 'right to a dignified life' not as a secular or universal principle but as one that is to be configured according to the rules

[2] *Human Rights: A Compilation of International Instruments*, vol. II, *Regional Instruments* (New York, Geneva: Office of the High Commissioner for Human Rights, 1997), 475–6.

of Islamic law. It asserts that OIC member states '[wish] to contribute to the efforts of mankind to assert human rights . . . and to affirm his freedom and right to a dignified life in accordance with the Islamic Shari'ah'.

When assessing the parameters of dignity, scholars have appreciated that dignity is an ambiguous term, one that can be used both to affirm equality and to ratify hierarchy. Taking advantage of the ambiguity, the Cairo Declaration treats dignity as being congruent with the inequalities mandated by versions of Islamic law that are favoured by conservative Muslim opinion that subordinates women and non-Muslims. Dignity in this sense is at odds with the UDHR, which in its proclamation effectively repudiates hierarchy when it underscores its 'recognition of the inherent dignity and of the equal and inalienable rights of all members of the human family' and notes the reaffirmation in the UN Charter of 'faith in fundamental human rights, in the dignity and worth of the human person and in the equal rights of men and women'.

The Cairo Declaration effectively repudiates the crucial linkage in the UDHR of dignity with equality in rights, and, more specifically, eliminates wording linking dignity to equal rights for men and women. Scrutiny of the language in Article 1(a) of the Cairo Declaration uncovers significant deviations from Article 2 in the UDHR, which indicates that 'everyone' is entitled to the rights and freedoms that it sets forth 'without distinction of any kind, such as race, colour, sex, language, religion, political or other opinion, national or social origin, property, birth or other status'. In lines that appropriate some of this UDHR language but also introduce religious considerations, the Cairo Declaration in Article 1(a) stipulates: 'All human beings form one family whose members are united by submission to God and descent from Adam. All men are equal in terms of basic human dignity and basic obligations and responsibilities without any discrimination on the grounds of race, colour, language, sex, religious belief, political affiliation, social status or other considerations. True faith is the guarantee for enhancing such dignity along the path to human perfection.'

It is striking that, amidst the obvious borrowings from Article 2 of the UDHR, when the Cairo Declaration speaks of 'all men' being 'equal in terms of basic human dignity' in Article 1(a), this is not paired with any stipulation of equality in rights and freedoms. Instead, equality in 'basic human dignity' is paired with equality in 'basic obligations and responsibilities'. No indication is offered regarding what falls within the categories designated by the adjective 'basic', but presumably discrimination is allowed outside these categories. Article 1(a) of the Cairo Declaration does not clarify what is meant by the affirmation that 'basic human dignity' is to be afforded 'without any discrimination' on the named grounds. A ban on discrimination in obligations might suggest that, because obligations can be seen as the obverse of rights, this amounts to an innocuous variation on the equality in rights stipulated in the UDHR. However, the Cairo Declaration's concept of equality in obligations cannot equate to equality in rights, because scrutiny of other provisions reveals that it is designed to accommodate discriminatory rules that deprive women and non-Muslims of rights. In switching from the UDHR's ban on discrimination affecting rights and freedoms to a ban on discrimination affecting dignity, Article 1(a) breaks with the logic of the UDHR.

Political calculations are the likely reason for the way that Article 1(a) of the Cairo Declaration diverges from its UDHR counterparts. Intending to leave space for retaining laws discriminating in rights based on gender and religion, the countries involved in shaping the Cairo Declaration substituted 'equality in basic human dignity' – a formulation that was devoid of precise legal significance – for the equality in rights and freedoms stipulated in Article 2 of the UDHR. Establishing any principle guaranteeing rights and freedoms without discrimination had to be avoided, because it would expose the legitimacy of their own discriminatory domestic laws, many of which claimed Islamic authority, to challenges. The relatively vague concept of 'equality in basic human dignity' presented itself as an expedient substitute for the original UDHR wording. Since dignity figures prominently in the UDHR, by incorporating the term dignity in Article 1(a), the Cairo Declaration managed to convey at least a superficial impression that it was showing solicitude for the UDHR principle of human dignity and that it was therefore in synchrony with ideals in the UDHR. A careful appraisal of the Cairo Declaration shows that the insertion of dignity and the omission of the UDHR ban on discrimination affecting rights and freedoms is part of a pattern of obfuscation that is designed to leave space for rules conflicting with the UDHR while simultaneously trying to minimize the appearance of conflicts.

The notion that there should be no discrimination with regard to dignity is not coherently elaborated. In fact, the last sentence of Article 1(a) of the Cairo Declaration suggests that its authors believe that there are gradations in dignity, because it indicates that dignity is a quality that is susceptible to enhancement via 'true faith'. Because the entire declaration has a pronounced Islamic bias, with Article 10 positing that 'Islam is the religion of unspoiled nature', the natural inference is that belief in Islam constitutes the 'true faith' that enhances human dignity. This suggests that Muslims have advanced further along what Article 1(a) calls 'the path to human perfection' and thereby benefit from enhanced dignity. This in turn correlates with the idea expressed in the first lines of the Preamble to the Cairo Declaration, in which the authors refer to the concept of Muslims belonging to one community based on religion, the *umma*, and assert that they are '[r]eaffirming the civilizing and historical role of the Islamic Ummah which God made the best nation'. Article 1(a) therefore can be fairly read to say that Muslims possess superior dignity *vis-à-vis* non-Muslims, with the consequence that non-Muslims are only entitled to an inferior level of dignity, a level that might be what is envisaged as falling into the category that the Cairo Declaration calls 'basic human dignity'. The notion that dignity has gradations would account for the decision to establish what seems to be an inferior, restricted category of dignity, designating it by the otherwise peculiar qualification 'basic'.

In addition to the features of the Cairo Declaration already mentioned that elevate Islam and its adherents to a superior status, Article 10 admonishes after it singles out Islam as the religion of unspoiled nature that '[i]t is prohibited to exercise any form of compulsion on man or to exploit his poverty or ignorance in order to convert him to another religion or to atheism.' This reveals the authors' assumption that other religions are inferior and that apostasy from Islam results from coercive tactics or the exploitation of a Muslim's poverty or ignorance. The possibility that a rational Muslim not afflicted by poverty might freely elect to convert to another religion or to embrace atheism is not conceded. In practice, the principle in Article 10 will be used to justify the common pattern in Muslim countries of criminalizing apostasy from Islam while welcoming and encouraging conversions to Islam. This correlates with a central premise of the Cairo Declaration, that Islam ranks above other religions – with the corollary that its adherents also rank above adherents of other religions.

In Article 1(a) of the Cairo Declaration, human beings are depicted as submitting to God, which correlates with the philosophy of the Cairo Declaration that Islamic law, viewed as God's law, must be observed. Significantly, the Cairo Declaration contains no provision whatsoever protecting freedom of religion or freedom of conscience, nor does it offer language equivalent to the UDHR provision in Article 1 that all human beings 'are endowed with reason and conscience'. Therefore, whatever dignity it does provide cannot imply any duty to respect the freedom of individuals to act according to their reason and conscience; instead, all are deemed to be bound to defer to Islamic law. If the recognition that human beings are endowed with reason and conscience is deemed to be foundational for human dignity, the Cairo Declaration can be fairly viewed as repudiating an essential component of human dignity.

When dignity appears in Article 22(c), it is in the context of a provision that belongs not in a human rights document but in a criminal code and that aims to prohibit expression that offends the dignity of prophets. In context these can only be prophets honoured by Islam. It states: 'Information . . . may not be exploited or misused in such a way as may violate sanctities and the dignity of Prophets.' The rule requiring respect for the dignity of Islamic prophets is a product of political concerns at the time when the Cairo Declaration was prepared, which occurred during a meeting of OIC foreign ministers in Tehran, Iran, in December 1989. The OIC was then confronting the international controversy created when Iran's leader, Ayatollah Khomeini, issued a death edict in February 1989 targeting the British novelist Salman Rushdie for allegedly offending Islam in his novel, *The Satanic Verses*, which featured a fictional pseudo-prophet who in some ways resembled the Prophet Muhammad. Responding to Iran's efforts to obtain backing for Khomeini's position, the authors of the Cairo Declaration tried to craft a version of human rights that would support criminalizing insults to the Prophet Muhammad like the ones allegedly contained in Rushdie's novel. One can see that, in prohibiting the violation of the dignity of prophets, Article 22(c) deploys a version of dignity that indirectly legitimizes Ayatollah Khomeini's death edict – with corresponding negative implications for freedom of expression.

An illustration of how the authors of the Cairo Declaration treat the term dignity as a vessel that can accommodate hierarchical ideas at odds with the UDHR can be found in Article 6(a), which provides: 'Woman is equal to man in human dignity, and has rights to enjoy as well as duties to perform.' (Inconsistent wording seems troubling in this connection, because Article 1(a) had earlier referred to 'all men' having equality in dignity and obligations.) Casual readers could miss the significance of the disparity between Article 6(a) and the UDHR principle that human beings are 'equal in dignity and rights'. By dropping the stipulation that all are equal in rights, the Cairo Declaration deliberately seeks to create space for Muslim countries to continue their long-standing pattern of imposing discriminatory laws affecting women, many of which are justified as reflecting Islamic requirements, and treating women as inferior beings subject to patriarchal control. Laws in a few Muslim countries essentially reduce women to the status of chattel, often in the guise of upholding Islamic law and morality. In deliberately avoiding guaranteeing women equality in rights, the Cairo Declaration obviously contemplates maintaining the *status quo*, affording a version of dignity that accommodates men's privileges and women's subordination. The rhetorical endorsement of women's equality in dignity in Article 6(a) demonstrates how the Cairo Declaration deploys dignity as a device to obscure its aim to construct a system that allows for maintaining a hierarchical order and the attendant restrictions on women's rights.

In Article 5 of the Cairo Declaration, the consequences of simultaneously upholding the superior status of Islam and the inferior status of women are manifest. In order to accommodate the Islamic rule that bars a Muslim woman from marrying a non-Muslim, in enumerating what kinds of restrictions on the right to marry are impermissible, the article deliberately fails to prohibit restrictions on marriage based on religion. It provides: 'Men and women have the right to marriage, and no restrictions stemming from race, colour or nationality shall prevent them from enjoying this right.' Because in Islamic law wives are subordinated to their husbands and are obligated to obey them, a Muslim woman marrying a non-Muslim man is seen as an affront to the dignity of Islam. Conversely, a Muslim man is allowed to marry a non-Muslim woman, because his superior rights as a husband accord with the superior dignity that should be accorded to Islam.

Once scrutinized, dignity as used in the Cairo Declaration is revealed to be a concept that embraces inequalities. It presupposes the superiority of Islam over other faiths and the retention of traditional understandings of Islamic law, viewed as mandating a hierarchy granting male Muslims superior rights and subjecting women and non-Muslims to discriminatory treatment.

References

Johnston, David. 2007. 'Maqāsid al-Sharī a: Epistemology and Hermeneutics of Muslim Theologies of Human Rights', *Die Welt des Islams* 47: 149–87

Mayer, Ann Elizabeth. 2012. *Islam and Human Rights: Tradition and Politics.* 5th edn, Boulder, CO: Westview Press

44

The protection of human dignity under Chinese law

PERRY KELLER

While the protection of human dignity figures prominently in the laws of the People's Republic of China, it is no simple task to reconcile contemporary liberal democratic discourse regarding human dignity with the exercise of power through law in China. Since its establishment in 1949, the government of China has determinedly rejected liberal democratic models of the state, including the constitutionalization of fundamental rights (Loughlin 2010: 47). China's rise towards the heights of global economic and political power has moreover strengthened the confidence of Chinese Communist Party ('the Party') leaders in their domestic model. Eschewing meaningful legal restraints on the powers of government, the Party has maintained a system of political and administrative intervention in legal outcomes (Clarke 2011).

Compared to the violent persecutions of the recent past, most notably including the Cultural Revolution unleashed in 1966 by Mao Zedong, personal freedom and security are undoubtedly much improved in China today (MacFarquhar and Schoenhals 2006). Nonetheless, the Chinese Party-state's often unrestricted use of power continues to raise vital questions about the exercise of state power and the protection of human dignity under Chinese law.[1] Yet those concerns should not obscure the ways in which questions of human dignity are also at the forefront of current efforts to improve legal protections and remedies addressing harm to the integrity of the body and the mind. While these largely concern the prevention and redress of harmful acts of the state, they also include a widening sphere of private acts in China's fast-changing market economy. New communications technologies and services have, for example, transformed Chinese society and brought demands for more effective legal remedies for injuries to reputation and intrusions into privacy (for example, Yang *et al.* 2011; Wang *et al.* 2010: 45).

[1] UN Committee Against Torture, Consideration of Reports Submitted by State Parties Under Article 19 of the Convention: Concluding Observations of the Committee Against Torture: China, CAT/C/CHN/CO/4, 12 December 2008. See also, Pils 2005.

Human dignity and constitutionalized rights

Specific concerns regarding the recognition and protection of human dignity in Chinese law are situated within the broader question of whether and to what extent China will become a constitutionalized, human-rights-based state (for example, Balme and Dowdle 2009). Indeed, this question has provided the main conceptual framework for Western analysis and support for Chinese legal development since the current reform period began in 1978. More than three decades later, the Chinese legal system has acquired all the formal components necessary for the creation of a constitutionalized state. And yet, despite that panoply of legislation, it does not aspire to the protection of human dignity in ways expected under the dominant international model of independent judicial authority over fundamental rights.

The present Constitution, adopted in 1982, uses the term 'dignity' in several different contexts.[2] These include the dignity of the Constitution itself, the dignity of the socialist legal system and the personal dignity of Chinese citizens.[3] The Constitution also contains significant declarations regarding civil and political as well as economic and social rights, which ostensibly secure the liberty of citizens from the state although counterweighted by broadly phrased limitations and duties.[4] The Chinese legal system, however, contains no direct mechanism to apply these constitutional liberties and protections in legal or administrative practice. Indeed, that essential element of constitutionalism is incompatible with the basic design of the Chinese state, which is a creation of the Party and in all aspects, including its structure, organization and work, remains subject to Party authority (McGregor 2010). While the Standing Committee of the National People's Congress, China's national legislature, is empowered to interpret and supervise the enforcement of its provisions, it rarely uses these powers to create constitutional doctrine.[5] The Supreme People's Court moreover has neither the legal nor political authority to apply constitutional principles or rights to resolve legal claims and disputes (Kellogg 2009a: 215). Chinese constitutional law is therefore largely dormant.

In the past decade, the Supreme People's Court has tentatively breached and then reaffirmed those barriers to judicial constitutional review. In 2001, the Court famously intervened in a case that raised a point of constitutional law and a complex human dignity question involving the fundamental right of citizens to education (Kellogg 2009b). In this case, a student stole the college examination results of a fellow student and then falsely using her identity gained a college degree and subsequent employment at a bank. On discovering the deceit some years later, the defrauded student, named Qi Yuling, brought a

[2] Constitution of the People's Republic of China, adopted 4 December 1982.

[3] Constitution, Preamble, Arts. 5 and 38.

[4] Constitution, Chapter Two, The Fundamental Rights and Duties of Citizens.

[5] Constitution, Arts. 62 and 67. See Zhu 2010a: 625.

civil case in which she claimed damages not only for theft of identity but also for infringement of her constitutional right to an education.[6] In determining how to decide this novel claim, the provincial court sought advice from the Supreme People's Court, which directed that the defendants should pay compensation for infringing Qi's constitutional right to an education through theft of her identity.

Viewed from within Western constitutional experience, the Qi Yuling case was an unusual choice for a ground-breaking direct judicial application of the Constitution. The Supreme People's Court applied the Constitution to an instance of private interference with access to a state-supported educational resource, which in terms of human dignity is at the more contentious end of its potential application to constitutionalized rights. In a Chinese context, however, these features gave the case obvious advantages. It involved neither an alleged unconstitutional act by the state nor a restriction on a politically sensitive right, such as freedom of speech. Yet any foray into judicial constitutional review, however seemingly innocuous, is contrary to the fundamental rules of the contemporary Chinese legal and political order (Tong 2010: 669). Direct application of the Constitution opens the way to doctrinal fetters on the powers and acts of the state and with that the Party's ultimate power to determine governmental policy and to guide state administration. After allowing the case to languish without mention for several years, the Supreme People's Court quietly withdrew the Qi Yuling Reply in 2008, noting only that it was no longer applicable.

Official opposition to constitutionalism in China has not entirely blocked its development. The Party's legal reform programme, which has brought greater professionalization of judges and extensive reforms to procedural and substantive law, has created the foundations for rule-of-law-based challenges to the exercise of state power (Fu and Cullen 2008: 11; Lin 2010: 305). In a wide variety of cases, public interest lawyers, and to a lesser extent local judges, have attempted to develop constitutionalism interstitially, rhetorically invoking if not directly applying constitutional rights. These cases involve criminal defendants, environmental victims, villagers dispossessed of their land and homes and other claimants of grave and unjustifiable injury to physical and mental integrity (Fu and Cullen 2008).

Nonetheless, China's entire legal system, including the procuratorates, courts and legal profession, are thoroughly enmeshed in Party as well as state hierarchies (Liebman 2007: 620). Judges, like all other government officials, must work within Party and state policy guidelines, administrative targets and personal accountability systems (Zhu 2010b: 63). While most lawyers are not state employees, their rights to practise are nonetheless subject to annual good conduct reviews by Party-state authorities (Fu and Cullen 2008). Chinese national and local authorities consequently have ample means to discipline judges,

[6] Constitution, Art. 46.

lawyers or other individuals who attempt to develop legal rights or practice beyond current permitted boundaries, even at the cost of a more effective legal system (Minzner 2011: 935).

Human dignity and legislative reforms

While China's government has acted firmly to contain public interest lawyering (Fu 2011), legislative provisions that generally or specifically protect human dignity are a notable feature of Chinese law. These laws typically concern the protection of vulnerable classes of individuals from violations of mental or physical integrity.[7] The national Mental Health Law, for example, stipulates that the human dignity of persons with mental disorders shall not be violated.[8] In recent years, legal changes have also strengthened procedural and substantive protections for individuals suspected or accused of criminal offences. These include various changes to procedural and evidentiary rules regarding confessions obtained by torture as well as amendments to the criminal law eliminating some offences from those carrying a potential death penalty.[9]

Despite reforms of this nature, the effective protection of the individual from arbitrary or otherwise unjustified coercive acts of state authorities, including gross violation of criminal procedure laws, remains a widespread problem in China (McConville 2011). In the field of administrative rather than criminal detention, the Party's determination to retain flexibility has often outweighed arguments for the better protection of the individual. In 2003, a media and public outcry following the violent death of Sun Zhigang, a young university graduate, in administrative custody, brought about a significant change in police powers to detain vagrants (cf. Hand 2006: 117).[10] While these changes in the law may have eased the problem of arbitrary and excessive detention in one aspect of policing, the Communist Party's Central Political-Legal Committee and the national Ministry of Public Security have so far refused to allow the abolition or wholesale reform of the critically important *Laodong Jiaoyang* system (Yu and Mosher 2010: 66). Under this form of administrative detention, known as

7 See, for example, the Law on the Protection of Women's Rights and Interests of the People's Republic of China, adopted in 1992, and the Prison Law of the People's Republic of China, adopted in 1994.

8 Mental Health Law of the People's Republic of China, adopted in 2012, Art. 4.

9 Supreme People's Court, Supreme People's Procuratorate, Ministry of Public Security, Ministry of State Security, and Ministry of Justice, Rules Concerning Questions About Examining and Judging Evidence in Death Penalty Cases (2010), and Rules Concerning Questions About Exclusion of Illegal Evidence in Handling Criminal Cases (2010). Amendments to the Criminal Law of the People's Republic of China, adopted on 25 February, 2011, and amendments to the Criminal Procedure Law of the People's Republic of China, adopted on 14 March 2012.

10 The State Council Measures on Custody and Repatriation of Vagrants and Beggars in Cities (May 1982) were replaced with the State Council Measures on the Administration of Aid to Indigent Vagrants and Beggars in Cities (June 2003).

Re-Education Through Labour (RTL), local public security committees may sentence individuals to detention with forced labour for a period of up to four years.[11] Similarly, the Party continues to employ its own coercive procedures in which Party Discipline Inspection authorities may hold in custody and interrogate Party members suspected of wrongdoing (Sapio 2008: 7).

The concept of human dignity as a personal or civil right, as expressed in the Constitution, has however provided an important if controversial stimulus for the development of private law rights. In 2002, the Standing Committee of the National People's Congress issued a draft civil code, setting out a framework for existing and planned legislation (Zhang 2009: 1000). This draft was extolled for its distinctive introduction of a separate chapter on human dignity, encompassing rights to life, body and health as well as name, image, reputation and privacy. With the 2007 Property Rights Law and the 2009 Tort Liability Law safely adopted, work is currently underway on a projected national law on human dignity to fulfil this element of the 2002 draft code.[12]

Human dignity and the paternalistic state

In one dimension of human dignity, the state's responsibility to ensure the basic economic and social well-being of its citizens, China has become a global model. Since the Cultural Revolution, the Party has created the conditions for an unprecedented rise in household and personal well-being. Yet, as the Chinese government recognizes, greater efforts are needed to tackle the country's increasing differences in personal income and wealth. That, however, will require reforms to the national household registration (*hukou*) system which exacerbates growing inequalities in access to education, employment and pensions as well as medical and other key services. Under the *hukou* system, every Chinese citizen is registered as resident in a particular place, resulting in an urban–rural status division running throughout Chinese society (Wu and Treiman 2007: 415).[13] In general, if a person's *hukou* is registered in a major city, he or she will enjoy much better life chances as compared to rural-registered individuals, including those who have temporary permission to reside and work in that city as 'migrant workers' (Kam and Buckingham 2008: 582). The children of these migrant workers are frequently barred from the better quality urban state schools for lack of the proper *hukou* (Branigan 2010).[14] This occurs despite national laws that create a duty on state authorities to provide nine years of

[11] State Council Provisional Measures on Re-education Through Labour (1982).

[12] See, for example, the 2011 model 'Law of the Right to Dignity of the PRC' produced by the Research Group of the Centre for Civil and Commercial Law of Renmin University, Beijing.

[13] State Council, Regulations on Hukou Registration (1958).

[14] This is in apparent conflict with China's obligations as a state party to the International Covenant on Economic, Social and Cultural Rights (see Arts. 2(2) and 13).

compulsory education for all children.[15] Chinese policy-makers have debated radical reform of the *hukou* system for years, but fears of unleashing a flood of internal migration have meant that most rural poor do not qualify under schemes permitting change of *hukou*.

In other areas, such as the equality of women, the Party, once at the forefront of women's emancipation in China, has responded slowly to the inequalities and risks faced by women in a fast-changing, market-based society (Diamant 2000: 171).[16] Pressure from Party-affiliated women's organizations, including the paramount All China Women's Federation, has certainly helped to bring legislative change in areas such as domestic violence and sexual harassment.[17] The difficulty, characteristic of the Chinese legal system generally, has been to transform the general provisions of national law governing these issues into defined rights and duties underpinned by standards of liability and compensation that local public authorities are able and willing to enforce (Liu 2011: 6).

Conclusion

China undoubtedly has a blemished record for the protection of the physical and mental integrity of its citizens from arbitrary and excessive acts committed by state authorities. National laws that purportedly protect individuals from such harm often lack the legal specificity and the institutional capabilities necessary for enforcement, leaving state authorities free to violate the moral status of citizens without the basic justifications required by any conception of human dignity. On the other hand, improvement of this situation is a matter of debate within China in spheres that include advisory bodies within the Party as well as intellectual circles critical of the Party's abuses of power.

In these debates, perhaps the most important question is whether China can develop an alternative to the constitutionalized liberal democratic model that provides effective remedies for such abuses. That alternative, if successful, may well emerge out of China's long history of citizen–state relationships, grounded in the Confucian tradition, in which elites advance moral principles through the institutions that guide state behaviour (Balme and Yang 2007: 445). Here, for example, the basic Confucian obligation of those in positions of authority to act consistently with the concept of *Ren* (meaning benevolence or goodness) has obvious potential in relation to the achievement of higher standards of human dignity. Plainly, the Chinese government has embraced the concept of

[15] Compulsory Education Law of the People's Republic of China, adopted 12 April 1986.

[16] Marriage Law of the People's Republic of China, adopted 10 September 1980.

[17] Domestic violence is prohibited under the Criminal Law (Arts. 234, 236, and 260), the Public Security Administration Punishment Law, adopted 1 March 2006 (Art. 43), the Marriage Law (Art. 3) and the Law on the Protection of the Rights and Interests of Women (Arts. 2, 38 and 46).

fundamental human rights, and these now play an important role in public debate in China.[18] This new expectation that the realization of fundamental rights is a key measure of the legitimacy of Chinese government may, however, be satisfied primarily through political rather than legal institutions. If that were to occur, the Chinese model would prove itself to be not simply a wilful distortion of Western models for the protection of human dignity, but instead the fruit of conscious, long-running efforts to create a viable alternative to the Western version of modernity.

References

Balme, S., and Dowdle, M. (eds.). 2009. *Building Constitutionalism in China*. New York: Palgrave Macmillan

Balme, S., and Yang, L. 2007. 'The Politics of Constitutional Reform in China', *Zeitschrift für Staats- und Europawissenschaften* 5(3–4): 445

Branigan, T. 2010. 'Millions of Chinese Rural Migrants Denied Education for Their Children', *Guardian*, 15 March

Clarke, D. 2011. 'China's Jasmine Crackdown and the Legal System', *East Asia Forum*, 26 May

Diamant, N. 2000. 'Re-examining the Impact of the 1950 Marriage Law', *China Quarterly* No. 161: 171

Fu, H. 2011. 'Making Sense of the Recent Harassment and Persecution of Public Interest Lawyers in China', *East Asia Forum*, 7 June

Fu, H., and Cullen, R. 2008. 'Weiquan (Rights Protection) Lawyering in an Authoritarian State', *China Journal* No. 59 (January): 111

Hand, K. 2006. 'Using Law for a Righteous Purpose: The Sun Zhigang Incident and Evolving Forms of Citizen Action in the People's Republic of China', *Columbia Journal of Transnational Law* 45: 114

Kam, W., and Buckingham, W. 2008. 'Is China Abolishing the Hukou System', *China Quarterly* No. 195: 582

Kellogg, T. 2009a. 'Constitutionalism with Chinese Characteristics? Constitutional Development and Civil Litigation in China', *International Journal of Constitutional Law* 7(2): 215

2009b. 'The Death of Constitutional Litigation in China?', *China Brief* 9(7): 4

Li, D. 2010. 'Only Protecting Rights Can Protect Stability', *Southern Metropolitan Daily* (7 April, 2010) (translated at www.boxun.us/news/publish/index.shtml)

Liebman, B. 2007. 'China's Courts: Restricted Reform', *China Quarterly* No. 191: 620

Lin, L. 2010. 'The Rise of Rights and Protections for the Disadvantaged', in D. Cai and C. Wang (eds.), *China's Journey toward the Rule of Law Legal Reform, 1978–2008*. Leiden: Brill

Liu, M. 2011. 'Toward Legislation to Prevent Sexual Harassment in China: Practice and Experience', *Women's Watch China Newsletter* No. 68, April

[18] See, for example, Li 2010.

Loughlin, L. 2010. 'What Is Constitutionalization?', in L. Loughlin and P. Dobner (eds.), *The Twilight of Constitutional Law: Demise or Transmutation?*. Oxford University Press

MacFarquhar, R., and Schoenhals, M. 2006. *Mao's Last Revolution*. Cambridge, MA: Harvard University Press

McConville, M. 2011. *Criminal Justice in China: An Empirical Inquiry*. Cheltenham, Northampton: Edward Elgar

McGregor, R. 2010. *The Party: the Secret World of China's Communist Rulers*. London: Allen Lane

Minzner, C. 2011. 'China's Turn Against Law', *American Journal of Comparative Law* 59(Fall): 935–84

Pils, E. 2005. 'Land Disputes, Rights Assertion, and Social Unrest In China: A Case from Sichuan', *Columbia Journal of Asian Law* 19(Spring): 235–94

Sapio, F. 2008. 'Shuanggui and Extralegal Detention in China', *China Information* 22: 7

Tong, Z. 2010. 'A Comment on the Rise and Fall of the Supreme People's Court's Reply to Qi Yuling's Case', *Suffolk University Law Review* 3: 669

Wang, F. *et al.* 2010. 'A Study of the Human Flesh Search Engine: Crowd-Powered Expansion of Online Knowledge', *IEEE Computer* (August): 445

Wu, X., and Treiman, D. 2007. 'Inequality and Equality under Chinese Socialism', *American Journal of Sociology* 113(2): 415

Yang, L. *et al.* 2011. *Guide to the Application of the Tort Liability Law in Cases Involving Chinese Media*. Renmin University

Yu, J., and Mosher, S. 2010. 'From Tool of Political Struggle to Means of Social Governance: The Two Stages of the Re-education Through Labour System', *China Perspectives* No. 82

Zhang, L. 2009. 'The Latest Developments in the Codification of Chinese Civil Law', *Tulane Law Review* 93: 999

Zhu, G. 2010a. 'Constitutional Review in China: An Unaccomplished Project or a Mirage?', *Suffolk University Law Review* 43(3): 625

Zhu, S. 2010b. 'The Party and the Courts', in R. Peerenboom (ed.), *Judicial Independence in China: Lessons for Global Rule of Law Promotion*. Cambridge University Press

45

Human dignity in Japanese law

SHIGENORI MATSUI

Respect for human dignity is one of the cornerstones of the Japanese legal system. As interpreted by modern scholars, the constitutional commitment to human dignity reflects the importance of respect for human rights and, in particular, the growing recognition of the need to make space for personal autonomy. However, the articulation of human dignity in Japanese law is far from complete, clear or straightforward. In some areas, the law still lags behind the modern understanding of human dignity.

This chapter starts by sketching the constitutional significance of human dignity and the extent to which Japan has embraced international human rights commitments. Some particular applications of this conjunction of human dignity and human rights are then given, before putting these developments in the context of a society that, traditionally, has a group orientation. The chapter continues with some remarks about the relationship between human dignity and Japan's modern pacifist stance; and it concludes with an indication of how human dignity applies in private law.

Human dignity as the most foundational constitutional value

Human dignity is generally believed to be the foundation of all fundamental human rights as protected by the Constitution of Japan (enacted in 1946) and the most foundational value of the constitutional order. Although there is no specific mention of human dignity in the Constitution, Article 13 provides that '[a]ll of the people shall be respected as individuals'; and Article 24 refers to 'individual dignity' when it provides that:

> Marriage shall be based only on the mutual consent of both sexes and it shall be maintained through mutual cooperation with the equal rights of husband and wife as a basis. With regard to choice of spouse, property rights, inheritance, choice of domicile, divorce and other matters pertaining to marriage and the family, laws shall be enacted from the standpoint of individual dignity and the essential equality of the sexes.

The prevailing view among constitutional academics, represented by the late Toshiyoshi Miyazawa (1971: 213–14) and the late Nobuyoshi Ashibe (2011: 82), interprets these references as indicating the supremacy of individuals over the state or society, thus proclaiming individualism as the most fundamental constitutional principle. According to this view, these references demand that the government should respect each person as an individual human being, thus protecting human dignity as the most basic value.

The leading constitutional scholar Kouji Sato argues that every human being, having the ability to discipline himself or herself based on reason, has a right to personal autonomy. According to Sato, this right is the justification of human dignity and is the most foundational moral right that underlies all fundamental rights as protected by the Constitution (Sato 2011: 121). Despite some criticisms concerning the ambiguity of the concept of human dignity and the excessive emphasis on reason as the most important element for human dignity, Sato's work has been highly influential in shaping the prevailing view.

According to the prevailing view, the fundamental rights protected by the Constitution are to be understood as rights inherent in every human being, such rights deriving from human dignity and deserving protection even before the enactment of the Constitution. They are, thus, natural rights – not simply the creation of the Constitution – to be granted not only to Japanese citizens but also to non-citizens (subject to exceptions for voting and welfare rights).

Protection of human rights

The Constitution guarantees a range of individual rights, including the equality right, democratic rights (such as the right to vote), personal freedoms (such as freedom of thought and conscience, freedom of religion, freedom of expression and academic freedom), economic freedoms (such as occupational freedom and the right to property), social rights (such as the welfare right, the right to receive education and the rights of workers) and procedural rights (such as due process, the right of access to the courts and the rights of suspects and defendants during criminal proceedings). It is one of the most significant characteristics of the Japanese Constitution that it grants protection to social rights in addition to equality and freedoms in order to secure human dignity. The protection of social rights, especially the welfare right as provided for in Article 25, is rooted in the belief that human dignity requires that a government supports the minimum standard of healthy living.

These rights are all constitutionally protected and constrain the Diet (the national legislature), as well as all branches of government. The Diet can pass legislation restricting these rights in order to protect public welfare (see Articles 12 and 13 of the Constitution), but any restriction may be challenged before the courts, the courts having a power of judicial review to decide upon the constitutionality of the restrictions (see Article 81 of the Constitution).

Japan has also ratified a significant number of international human rights conventions, including the International Covenant on Civil and Political Rights (ICCPR), the International Covenant on Economic, Social and Cultural Rights

(ICESCR), the Convention Relating to the Status of Refugees, the Convention on the Rights of the Child (CRC), the Convention Against Torture (CAT), the Convention on the Elimination of All Forms of Racial Discrimination (ICERD), the Convention on the Elimination of All Forms of Discrimination Against Women (CEDAW) and the Convention on the Rights of Persons with Disabilities (CRPD). However, Japan has not ratified some other important conventions, such as the International Convention on the Protection of the Rights of All Migrant Workers and Members of Their Families (MWC). In line with dualist theory, it has been assumed that international treaties and domestic law belong to different legal systems, with international treaties not being automatically enforceable as national law – they are enforceable in this way only when they have been transformed into domestic law by statutes passed by the Diet or if they are otherwise self-executing. Some of the international human rights conventions are regarded as self-executing and, therefore, could be invoked by individuals before the Japanese courts. However, Japanese courts are reluctant to interpret these conventions more broadly than the Constitution,[1] as a result of which their domestic impact is limited.

Some specific applications

Article 18 of the Constitution prohibits slavery and involuntary servitude by providing that '[n]o person shall be held in bondage of any kind. Involuntary servitude, except as punishment for crime, is prohibited.' Any slavery contract will be held to be invalid under section 90 of the Civil Code, which precludes juristic acts that are contrary to public order and good morals. Moreover, abduction or illegal confinement for human trafficking, as well as human trafficking itself, is prohibited by the Criminal Code.

Article 14 of the Constitution prohibits racial discrimination by protecting equality before the law. Yet, because there is no law which discriminates against a racial minority, there is no court decision on the legitimacy of racial discrimination. The Constitution does not have any provision on aboriginal people or on the protection of rights of aboriginal people. This gap in the Constitution has impacted on the indigenous Ainu, a people with their own language and culture. Because of the assimilation policy of past governments, the Ainu language and culture have been almost totally destroyed. Although the Ainu people are not granted any special rights or privileges as aboriginals, the government, having abandoned a policy of assimilation, now attempts to preserve their distinctive culture.

Similarly, the Constitution prohibits sexual discrimination. In the past, women were not granted the right to vote and were regarded as incompetent to manage property. Yet, under the Japanese Constitution, women are granted

[1] Supreme Court, Grand Bench, 8 March 1989, 43 *Minshu* 89.

a right to vote; and, under Japanese family law, which was completely rewritten after the Second World War in order to conform to the Constitution, women also have equal rights to men in the family. There still remains some sexual discrimination, such as a waiting period of six months after divorce before a *woman* (but only a woman) may remarry, and the Supreme Court has shown itself willing to uphold such discrimination.[2]

Although the Criminal Code prohibits abortion, the Women's Body Protection Act allows an artificial termination of a pregnancy when the pregnancy will present a danger to the life or health of the woman, and this requirement has been interpreted quite loosely to allow practically any abortion during the early stage of the pregnancy. The foetus is not regarded as a human being deserving human dignity under the Constitution and, therefore, there is no argument that liberalization of abortion is unconstitutional. Given that, in practice, early stage abortions are permitted, there is no serious attempt to challenge the constitutionality of the ban on abortion as an infringement of the woman's right to autonomy.

Human reproductive cloning is prohibited by the Act on Human Cloning. The Act, which prohibits the return of an embryo created by cloning technology to a woman's body, is based on concerns about safety as well as respect for human dignity. Some of those who assume that human reproductive cloning violates human dignity see this as a violation of Article 13 of the Constitution; however, precisely why human reproductive cloning violates human dignity is not crystal clear and some argue that the prohibition is justified only for safety reasons.

Despite the protection of human dignity, the Criminal Code imposes the death penalty on defendants who have committed certain serious crimes, such as murder, and the Supreme Court has upheld the constitutionality of capital punishment.[3] While the Court conceded that '. . . life is precious [and] [t]he value of one human being is more precious than the whole Earth', Article 13 of the Constitution assumes that even a life may be restricted for the public welfare and Article 31 assumes that a life may be taken in accordance with the law. The Supreme Court thus concluded that the Constitution permits the death penalty and that this is not a cruel punishment as prohibited by Article 36. Roughly ten to twenty defendants are sentenced to death each year. The method of execution is hanging. Although it is stipulated that the sentence must be carried out within six months of the final judgment, there is usually a delay of several years – some justice ministers refusing to sign the execution papers during their terms of office – and, in several cases, death row convicts have been retried and found not guilty after more than thirty years of confinement.

By contrast, the status of the right to die with dignity, that is, the right to withdrawal of life-sustaining support from patients, is not clear. Physicians

[2] Supreme Court, 3rd Petty Bench, 5 December 1995, 1563 *Hanreijihou* 81.

[3] Supreme Court, Grand Bench, 12 March 1948, 2 *Keishu* 191.

who remove such support, based on the wishes of the patient's family, might face prosecution for murder. Assisted suicide and killing with consent are both prohibited by the Criminal Code; mercy killing is not permitted in Japan. In the past, organ transplantation was seriously limited. Brain death was not legally recognized; it was only when brain-dead patients carried an organ donation card, and with the consent of the family, that physicians could lawfully remove organs for transplant. However, the conditions for lawful transplantation of organs have been significantly relaxed and now families may assent to donation even when no donation card was carried.

Personal autonomy and Japanese society

Despite the constitutional protection of human dignity, Japan is traditionally a group-orientated society, placing more emphasis on group harmony than respect for individual autonomy. When children enter elementary school, they are taught the necessity of maintaining the harmony of the class and of observing discipline. Many public junior high schools, as well as high schools, require students to wear uniforms as well as having strict dress and hair codes. When students graduate and enter into private companies, they will be trained to keep the harmony of the workplace and to maintain loyalty to the company. In Japanese society, everyone is taught to act and to behave just as others do. Those who stand out will be criticized (the nail that sticks out will be hammered in!).

In recent years, an increasing number of scholars have challenged this traditional emphasis on group conformity, arguing that the right to personal autonomy is constitutionally recognized in the form of the right to life, liberty and the pursuit of happiness in accordance with Article 13. These scholars argue that the right to personal autonomy allows individuals to be different from one another and, therefore, the government should not force an individual to conform to the majority in private matters (Sato 2002). Most will agree that, at least, one has a right to personal autonomy with respect to private matters that are integral to personal development. However, some go further, arguing that one has a freedom to do whatever one likes so that restrictions on freedom should be judicially reviewed to assess whether they are reasonable and justified.

Human dignity and pacifism

Drawing on the experience of the Second World War, many Japanese people believe that war, with its creation of misery and inhuman deprivation of life, is the ultimate denial of human dignity. In its Preamble, the Japanese Constitution declares the necessity of world peace and it both renounces the war power (Article 9, section 1) and prohibits the maintenance of armed forces (Article 9, section 2). Many people believe that the effect of the Constitution is to prohibit government from engaging in war, even in self-defence, or maintaining armed forces for the purpose of self-defence. Human dignity, according to such a view, necessitates pacifism.

Nevertheless, when the Korean War erupted, the government was allowed to establish the National Police Reserve; and now it maintains the Self-Defence Force and allows the stationing of American military forces under the Japan–United States Mutual Security Treaty. According to the government, the Japanese Constitution never abandoned the right of self-defence as recognized in international society, from which it follows that the government is not precluded from maintaining the minimum force required to defend the country. The Self-Defence Force is such a minimum force and it does not fall within the terms of the Article 9 prohibitions.

Human dignity in private law

Article 2 of the Civil Code makes clear that private law 'must be construed in accordance with honouring the dignity of individuals and the essential equality of both sexes'. Moreover, private rights must conform to the public welfare and no abuse of rights is permitted (Article 1). Hence, any private contract that would violate human dignity would be found to violate public order and good morals (as per Article 90) and it would be held to be invalid. Any infringement of human dignity would also constitute a tort, and victims would be able to seek damages.

That said, the Constitution has been interpreted to apply only to governmental exercise of power and not to private individuals and corporations. Thus, the infringement of civil rights by a private individual or a corporation cannot be challenged as unconstitutional. Moreover, there is no comprehensive civil rights or human rights legislation that prohibits private discrimination or private infringement of civil rights – infringers can escape punishment and victims have no entitlement to civil redress. There is also no administrative tribunal or commission to regulate private discrimination or to give assistance to victims. Some of the most egregious acts of private discrimination, such as the mandatory retirement practice that forces women to retire at a younger age than men, have been found to violate public order and good morals.[4] However, more subtle acts of discrimination have been tolerated. Past attempts to enact civil rights legislation have failed and the future prospects for enactment of new legislation are unclear.

Finally, it should also be said that there is no criminal ban on hate speech in Japan. Solicitation of racial hatred or wilful promotion of racial hatred is not subject to legal prohibition or penalty.

[4] Supreme Court, 3rd Petty Bench, 24 March 1981, 35 *Minshu* 300.

References

Ashibe, Nobuyoshi. 2011. *Kenpo* [Constitution]. 5th edn, Tokyo: Iwanami shoten
Miyazawa, Toshiyoshi. 1971. *Kenpo II* [Constitution II]. New edn, Tokyo: Yuhikaku
Sato, Koji. 2002. *Nihonkoukenpo to 'ho no shihai'* [Japanese Constitution and the Rule of Law]. Tokyo: Yuhikaku
2011. *Nihonkoku kenporon* [Japanese Constitutional Law]. Tokyo: Seibundo

46

The place of dignity in the Indian Constitution

UPENDRA BAXI

While the makers of the Indian Constitution rather acutely anticipated the notion of 'human dignity as empowerment' (Beyleveld and Brownsword 2001), it is no simple task to understand the precise place of human dignity within the constitutional scheme. Moreover, for a variety of reasons, grasping the ways in which dignity as empowerment has been put to work in the sixty-plus years of the Indian Constitution remains an even more hazardous narrative.

First, India's sixty-year-long freedom struggle was premised on the idea that sustained colonial predation and subjugation constituted an epic saga of humiliation – the Other of dignity. This Indian struggle for freedom, together with the Constitution that it eventually produced, offers a becoming and befitting response to the contemporary and ahistoric 'digcrits' discourse (questioning the conceptual and normative coherence of human dignity as well as its institutional viability).

Second, the freedom movement also generates a new *telos* of dignity for the subjects of violent social exclusion constituted by the discursive formations of the Hindu *Dharma* that disacknowledged moral capacity and legal subjectivity to India's millennially humiliated peoples – the Untouchables, the indigenous peoples, and in a related yet distinct sense the masses of Indian women.

Third, the Indian Constitution composes its own idea of dignity at the very moment of the enunciation of the value of dignity by the Universal Declaration of Human Rights (UDHR) – an elementary global social fact often unacknowledged.

Fourth, the Indian Constitution's conceptions of dignity, far from being mimetic of Euro-American incarnations of the idea, offer points of departure for 'the global South'. While it may be too much to say that dignity by and in itself furnishes the leitmotif of the Indian freedom struggle, it is abundantly clear that it at least inspired many conceptions of dignity, as displayed in contrasts between the thinking of two founders, Mohandas Gandhi and Bhim Rao Ambedkar (Baxi 1994).

The place of dignity in the Indian Constitution

Dignity is the last of the four values enunciated by the Preamble to the Indian Constitution. After 'Justice, social, economic, and political', 'Liberty, of thought, expression, belief, and worship' and 'Equality, of status and of opportunity', we read 'Fraternity, assuring the dignity of the individual'. Subject to two exceptions, the Indian Constitution (with a hundred amendments) does not further elucidate this sense of dignity as a subset of the virtue or value of 'fraternity'.

The first exception is the forty-second amendment, added after the Emergency period of 1975–6. Here, the Preamble's reference to fraternity is amended by adding the phrase 'the unity and integrity of the Nation', as if to suggest that the practices of fraternity or of dignity may erode this! The second exception, one that is more amenable to the combination of fraternity and dignity, is to be found in the insertion by the same amendment of Part IV-A, entitled 'the fundamental duties' of citizens. Clause (e) speaks of the duty to 'promote harmony and common brotherhood' beyond 'religious, linguistic, and regional or sectional diversities' and in particular 'to renounce practices derogatory of women'; clause (f) speaks to the duty to 'value and to preserve the rich heritage of our composite culture'; clause (g) outlines duties of environmental preservation and of 'compassion for all living creatures'. This extraordinary elaboration of fraternity values has not remained merely hortatory because the duties in Part IV-A impose constitutional obligations on all citizens, including legislators and justices. On the basis of this, the Supreme Court of India has been able to legislate a binding law against sexual harassment in workplaces,[1] and its environmental jurisprudence draws extensively on Part IV-A duties, which also increasingly catalyze performances of legislative activism. I pursue this in what follows, but only through the question whether it may be the case that fraternity values are more apt for a language of obligations whereas dignity values remain more suited to the language of rights.

Even so, it may seem at first sight that the combination of fraternity and dignity constitutes merely an appendage to the preceding three values; further, and in the abstract, it may be thought that these three value enunciations already crystallize the core dignitarian interests. Leading treatises on constitutional law almost eliminate from view the importance of the combination of fraternity and dignity, and much the same may be said concerning a handful of judicial autobiographies (Reddy 2008 being a notable exception). And it is only with the beginnings of radical post-1975–6 Emergency judicial activism in the 1980s (for example, Baxi 1980; 2001; 2010; Fredman 2008; Sathe 2001; and Sankar 2009) that constitutional adjudication becomes oriented to the fuller development of fraternity–dignity values.

[1] *Vishakha* v. *State of Rajasthan*, AIR 1997 Supreme Court 3011.

Dignity and fundamental rights

Yet, in many a sense, the writing of Part III of the Indian Constitution (Fundamental Rights) elaborates the sense of fraternity as dignity. The right to equality is also a right against caste-based discrimination, extending beyond the state to civil society actors, networks and institutions. Article 15 forbids discrimination that enunciates statuses of indignity, in particular the caste-based ones; equally, Article 15(2) forbids caste-based discrimination limiting or denying access to 'shops, public restaurants, hotels, and places of public entertainment' and to 'the use of wells, tanks, bathing ghats, roads and places of public resort maintained wholly, or partly, out of state funds or dedicated to the use of general public'. The Indian constitutional combination of fraternity and dignity wages a war against the indignity of caste-based apartheid via a manifold and multiplex constitutional authorization of programmes of affirmative action enabling access to the rights to literacy and education, public services, and even legislative representation (Baxi 1984; Galanter 1984). Further, the provision for freedom of conscience and religion (Article 25) is constitutionally qualified by the dignity-affirming basic human rights of all citizens – especially by the 'throwing open of Hindu religious institutions of a public character to all classes and sections of Hindus', which is further elaborated as inclusive of 'persons professing Sikh, Jaina, or Buddhist religion'.

The capping stone of the combination of fraternity and dignity is Article 17, which insists that 'Untouchability' is 'abolished', its practice is 'forbidden' and the 'enforcement of any disability on the ground of untouchability shall be an offence punishable in accordance with the law'. Further, Article 35 (suspending the federal design and detail) obliges as well as empowers Parliament to enact such offences. As far as I know, no constitutional arrangement has gone as far in enacting a code of constitutional criminal law in the processes of enunciating basic human rights. The Untouchability Offences Act, later replaced by the Civil Rights Act, proscribes practices of humiliation that are ritually sanctioned or socially tolerated. Further, the remarkable Prevention of Atrocities Act makes such practices of exclusion and violence against ex-untouchables and also indigenous peoples (named Scheduled Castes and Scheduled Tribes, respectively) offences of strict as well as group liability. A constitutional authority – the Commissioner for Scheduled Castes and Scheduled Tribes – is fully empowered to take action against existent as well as potential constitutional transgressions. Even as the well-stated dichotomy between the law-in-the-books and the law-in-action persists, at times fiercely (Rao 2009; Baxi, P. 2011), the overall pro-dignity profiles of the normative and institutional apparatus present a remarkable ensemble. Further, it also remains true that new social identities and solidarities, movements and struggles, today articulate new meanings and priorities for the combination of fraternity and dignity.

Dignity: specific emergences

During nearly two-and-a-half decades of Indian constitutionalism, dignitarian interests and considerations featured rarely in the jurisprudence of Part III fundamental rights to equality – except of course in cases involving challenges to laws implementing Article 17. In these exceptional cases, the Supreme Court employed the idiom of the dignitary rights of historically vulnerable communities, as well as advancing an early judicial articulation of the right to privacy as an element of the rights to life and liberty.[2] Further, the 1973 *Kesavananda Bharathi* doctrine of the basic structure of the Indian Constitution, which identified a number of essential features that may not be amended, named 'dignity' as one such feature.

In the space available, I can only highlight the extraordinary resurgence of the idea of dignity as an integral part of the rights to life and liberty of Article 21. Even as I narrate this briefly, three caveats are necessary. First, when presented with, *inter alia*, dignity-based challenges to capital punishment, the Supreme Court sustains the constitutionality of the challenged laws even though it limits them to the 'rarest of rare cases'. Second, the Supreme Court does not regard the Medical Termination of Pregnancy Act as a violation of the dignity of foetal life forms, although it reinforces laws and policies directed against female feticide, and not necessarily in terms of any dignity-based discourse. Quite how this stands alongside judicial recourse to *Roe* v. *Wade* in the development of privacy as a component right of dignity concerning same-sex sexual orientation and conduct,[3] and even the physician-assisted termination of human life,[4] is unclear. Third, the distinct range of bioethical concerns with dignity has yet to arrive at the doorstep, or even the backstage, of Indian constitutional adjudication.

That being said, an extraordinary adjudicatory rewriting of Article 21 by *Maneka Gandhi*[5] makes possible a full-fledged discourse of dignity rights. The authors of the Indian Constitution considered and specifically rejected the ideology of the 'due process of law' and instead provided that the state shall not deprive any person of his or her life or liberty without a procedure established by law; *Maneka* substitutes this with the phrase 'due process of law' (Chandrachud 2011).

Broadly speaking, judicial engagement with Article 21 now focuses on the constitutional meaning of life. A paradigm shift occurs with Justice Bhagwati's insistence in *Mullin* that:

> the right to life includes the right to live with human dignity and all that goes along with it, namely, the bare necessaries of life such as adequate nutrition,

[2] *Gobind* v. *State of Madhya Pradesh*, AIR 1975 SC 1378.

[3] *Naz Foundation* v. *Government of New Capital Territory of Delhi*, 160 *Delhi Law Times* (2009) 277.

[4] *Aruna Ramchandra Shanbaug* v. *Union of India*, AIR 2011 SCI 1290.

[5] *Maneka Gandhi* v. *Union of India*, AIR 1978 SC 597.

> clothing and shelter and facilities for reading, writing and expressing oneself in diverse forms, freely moving about and mixing and commingling with fellow human beings. Every act which offends against or impairs human dignity would constitute deprivation *pro tanto* of this right to live and it would have to be in accordance with reasonable, fair and just procedure established by law which stands the test of other fundamental rights.[6]

This 'jurisgenerative' articulation opens up all forms of state action and conduct to full deliberative adjudicative scrutiny and in this way also marks a paradigm shift towards a near-'sovereign' role for constitutional judicial review. Initially occurring in the contexts of institutional practices of punitive as well as preventive detention, this articulation invigilates against and at times invalidates, restricts or forcefully disapproves of many a normative prescription and institutional practice – such as solitary confinement, denial of basic rights of persons in incarceration or preventive detention, handcuffing and prison irons, torture, cruel, degrading and inhumane punishment or treatment – (to extend Justice Krishna Iyer's phrase) as 'barbarity hostile to our goal of *human dignity* and *social justice*'.[7]

Soon enough, this combination moves towards a jurisprudence of normative empowerment. Rights against exploitation (Articles 23 and 24) suddenly assume visages of dignitary rights: practices not just of bonded labour but labour below the statutory minimum wages and child labour stand judicially christened as un-free, slave-like labour violating the canon of dignified life. So do many forms of domination in closed institutions, such as institutions of psychiatric care and juvenile and women's remand homes. In this way, dignitary rights assume a new form of complex juridification making regimes of custodial institutional exploitation constitutionally illegitimate. Further, even in relatively less-closed institutions such as schools, corporeal chastisement remains judicially outlawed as a violation of 'dignified life'. Dignitarian interests find an expansive endorsement in the proliferating judicial decisions concerning HIV/AIDS-affected persons. The new judicial dispensation of dignity rights is impressive indeed, extending co-equally to state as well as non-state actors and frameworks.

The reach of 'dignified life' becomes even more extensive by way of advancement of the erstwhile non-judicially enforceable socio-economic rights lumped together in Part IV of the Indian Constitution under the rubric 'Directive Principles of State Policy'. The jurisprudence of normative empowerment flourishes rather luxuriantly under the innovative auspices of dignity rights. Affirming and celebrating human dignity under the canopy of Article 21 rights – for example, the rights to healthcare, housing and shelter, literacy and education – this jurisprudence leaves open the question whether or not in actual judicial

[6] *Francis Coralie Mullin* v. *Administrator, Union Territory of Delhi and Others* (1981) 1 SCC 608, para. 8.

[7] *Sunil Batra (11)* v. *Delhi Administration*, 1980 SCR (2) 557 at 587 (emphasis added).

reasoning, rhetoric and result these decisions in fact and effect advance other primary considerations of equality or liberty rights.

'Dignity-plus'

Practices of activist constitutional interpretation, however, do not regard fraternity and dignity as free-wheeling or stand-alone virtues. With the Delhi Court's *Naz* decision,[8] reading down section 377 of the Indian Penal Code to exclude acts of same-sex adult sexual intimacy conducted in private from the sanction of the criminal law, we arrive at a fuller understanding of 'dignity-plus' logics, paralogics and languages. Earlier, as already noted, this 'plus' was 'fraternity'. With *Naz*, the 'plus' is dignity as the privacy of intimate forms of life (Baxi, U. 2011). By elaborating dignity notions that speak to *identity as difference* as the core of 'dignity-plus' full human 'personhood' rights, *Naz* places dignitarian interests and rights far above the contingency of dominant social moralities and the 'virtues' of state paternalism.

All the more remarkable is the reasoning that animates the adjudicative protection of 'dignity-plus'. I have suggested elsewhere (Baxi, U. 2011) that what remains distinctive to *Naz* is the salience of the latter consideration, now vociferously challenged before the Supreme Court by assorted public interest petitioners claiming that it vitally infringes core religious beliefs and practices. However, the constitutional morality developed by *Naz* achieves no such result; this dignity-plus reasoning does not ordain the practise of same-sex relationships by peoples of faith. Rather, it allows them to continue to practise their faith; however, this practise of faith is now within a context of interpretive pluralism in reading scriptural canons. Put another way, dignity-plus reasoning suggests that, if the state and its laws may not go so far as to criminalize conduct running against the grain of constitutional morality, neither may the custodians of faith or keepers of tradition do so. Scholarly forecasts of what Justices may do from the High Bench remain fallible; even so, it would be astonishingly unworthy of the Supreme Court to overrun this specific element of the *Naz* judgment.

A concluding remark

The remarkable aspect of dignity is that it rises above the indictment of human rights as constructs of domination. In the Indian experience, the dignity-plus constitutional conversation ineluctably suggests that taking human rights seriously remains impossible without taking human and social suffering seriously.

[8] *Naz Foundation* v. *Government of New Capital Territory of Delhi and Others*, 160 *Delhi Law Times* (2009) 277.

Lata Mani, a leading cultural and feminist theorist, suggests that such a linkage entails three ideas:

> First, that suffering leads to a loss of dignity; second, the absence of choice leads to suffering and indignity; and third, control over self and circumstance facilitates freedom from suffering and in so doing, preserves dignity. Deducible here is an ideal of mastery over self and context or at least, the ability to set limits on how one is impinged upon by social forces and more broadly, by the conditions of life. (Mani 2011: 24)

However, Mani questions whether it is not time now to restore 'dignity's autonomy from suffering' and to strive to 'liberate empathy from a near exclusive association with the understanding of suffering and open the door to a subtler notion of attunement', that may enable activist 'witness and designated sufferer' to 'meet and remake each other outside the constricting frames which structure present encounters' (Mani 2011: 25). If so, how may we further rethink the juridical idea of dignity beyond 'constraint' and 'empowerment'?

References

Baxi, U. 1980. *The Indian Supreme Court and Politics*. Lucknow: The Eastern Book Co.

1984. 'Legislative Reservations for Social Justice', in R. B. Goldman and J. Williams (eds.), *From Independence to Statehood: Managing Ethnic Conflict in Five African and Indian States*. London: Pinter, 210–24

1994. 'Justice as Emancipation: The Legacy of Babasaheb Ambedkar', in U. Baxi and B. Parekh (eds.), *Crisis and Change in Contemporary India*. New Delhi: Sage, 122–49

2001. 'The Avatars of Judicial Activism: Explorations in the Geography of (In)Justice', in S. K. Verma and K. Kumar (eds.), *Fifty Years of the Supreme Court of India: Its Grasp and Reach*. Oxford University Press and Indian Law Institute, 156–209

2010. 'The Justice of Human Rights in Indian Constitutionalism', in A. Singh and S. Mohapatra (eds.), *Indian Political Thought: A Reader*. London, New York: Routledge, Chapter 17

2011. 'Dignity In and With Naz', in A. Narrain and A. Gupta (eds.), *Law Like Love: Queer Perspectives on Law*. Delhi: Yoda Press, 231–52

Baxi, P. 2011. 'Rape as Atrocity: Notes on the Judicial Interpretation of the SC and ST (Prevention of Atrocities) Act, 1989'. Paper presented at the Kate Hamburger College, Institute of Law as Culture, Bonn, 28 June 2011

Beyleveld, D., and Brownsword, R. 2001. *Human Dignity in Bioethics and Biolaw*. Oxford University Press

Chandrachud, A. 2011. *Due Process of Law*. Lucknow: The Eastern Book Company

Fredman, S. 2008. *Human Rights Transformed: Positive Rights and Positive Duties*. Oxford University Press

Galanter, M. 1984. *Competing Equalities: Law and the Backward Classes in India*. Oxford University Press

Mani, L. 2011. 'Human Dignity and Suffering: Some Considerations', *Economic and Political Weekly* 46(36) (3 September 2011)

Rao, A. 2009. *The Caste Question: Dalits and the Politics of Modern India*. Berkeley, CA: University of California Press

Reddy, O. C. 2008. *The Indian Supreme Court: Summits and Shallows*. Oxford University Press

Sankar, S. 2009. *Scaling Justice: India's Supreme Court, Anti-Terror Laws and Social Rights*. Oxford University Press

Sathe, S. P. 2001. *Judicial Activism in India*. Oxford University Press

Part V
Conflicts and violence

47

Human dignity and war

ANDREAS HASENCLEVER

War as moral evil

War as sustained combat between political communities is a moral evil (Walzer 2006; Levy and Thompson 2010). War signals the breakdown of law and order and develops a deadly dynamic of its own. Conflicts are no longer settled by moral reasoning, legal adjudication or political negotiation, but by well-organized armed forces. War always goes along with death and destruction. Troops are moved strategically to overcome violent resistance and to defeat an enemy. As a rule, not only fighters are victimized on the battlefield, but entire societies suffer. The number of non-combatants dying from the direct and indirect consequences of sustained combat such as economic shortages, famines, displacement or disrupted healthcare and social security systems by far exceeds military casualties. Additionally, warfare goes along with the categorization, and, in most cases, dehumanization of opponents. Adversaries are no longer considered individual human beings but enemies who may be killed without further justification. Given the recent increase in ethnic conflicts, the traditional distinction between combatants and non-combatants blurs even further. War was never restricted to the battlefield, but today's wars more than ever target civilian populations. Depending on the severity of the fighting and the number of atrocities committed, it takes a generation or more to overcome the social disruptions of war and to re-establish a robust peace among former combatants and their successors.

Human dignity, by contrast, requires the peaceful settlements of disputes among as well as within societies (Gewirth 1996: 1–70; Steigleder 1999: 157–75). Individuals and groups should be treated according to established human rights standards. They are entitled to life in peace and their legitimate interests should be protected by appropriate institutions. The distribution of rights and obligations within as well as among societies should be clearly specified and generally respected. In cases of transgression, a public authority should intervene to restore justice and to punish the offender if appropriate and reasonable. As such, the settlement of conflicts by well-recognized human right standards contradicts their settlement by the use of well-organized armed forces. In fact, human dignity requires the abrogation of war.

Even though war is a moral evil and should be avoided, throughout history respected scholars and practitioners maintain that under strict conditions war might be the lesser evil (Walzer 2006; Fisher 2011). In cases of external or internal aggression, victims might have a right to collective self-defence including the use of armed forces. Additionally, under certain circumstances third parties are entitled, if not required, to intervene militarily and to advance peace and justice. To decide whether war in fact should be considered the lesser evil a number of criteria have been developed which are summarized under the heading of the so-called 'just war tradition' (Rengger 2002).

In the following, I summarize the basic principles of the just war tradition. I argue that these principles are of a formal nature and that it is necessary to link them to a substantive conception of morality. In a second step, I elaborate on the emergence of human dignity and the corresponding human rights as core values of the international system. Finally, I discuss whether warfare might be under certain conditions an appropriate instrument to protect population from large-scale and systematic human rights violations. In my opinion this is rarely the case. While respect for human dignity entitles threatened persons to be rescued under conditions of mass atrocities, military intervention more often than not is inappropriate to sustainably improve the human rights record in the target region.

Just war tradition

Originally, the just war tradition comprises the *jus ad bellum* – the justification of why wars are fought – and the *jus in bello* – the question of how wars should be fought (Orend 2006; McMahan 2009). Most recently, scholars also discuss a *jus post bellum* addressing the obligations that arise for individual states or the international community after a war has been completed.

As to the *jus ad bellum*, most scholars working in the field agree on the following six formal criteria that should guide the decision to wage war. First, any just war presupposes a just cause. Armed forces should be used in cases of very grave injustice only. Second, the primary purpose of a war must be to stop wrongdoing and to advance peace and justice. Third, war must be the last resort. All other means to stop an aggressor are exhausted or could be considered inadequate. Fourth, there must be a reasonable chance of success to advance peace and justice by the use of force. Fifth, the expected benefits of war must outweigh its foreseeable costs. Finally, the decision to take up arms must be made by a legitimate authority. Just wars are waged for the common good only and should not result from private decision-making. The *jus in bello* adds two further criteria. First, non-combatants must not be targeted. If harm is done to civilians, this has to be the unintended consequence of an otherwise legitimate military move to defeat an unjust enemy. Second, force should be proportionate to the envisaged ends.

While the formal criteria that should guide the use of armed forces are widely accepted, their material content remains contested. What counts as a sufficiently grave injustice? How benign do intentions have to be to qualify the use of force as just? When is war the last resort? What counts as successful warfare and how to make up the moral balance of military interventions given the inevitable losses of life? It is evident that questions like these are far from settled. Remarkably, however, a strong and consistent normative trend has developed in international politics that puts human dignity at the center of the deliberation on the justification of warfare in general and humanitarian interventions in particular. As a result, it is not only foreign aggression that might be a just cause for the use of military force but also the large-scale and systematic violation of human rights on foreign territories.

Responsibility to protect

The adoption of the Universal Declaration of Human Rights (UDHR) by the United Nations' General Assembly on 10 December 1948 marked the emergence of a global human rights regime based upon a strong notion of human dignity (Gewirth 1992; Donnelly 2002; Buergenthal 2006). As stated in Article 1 of the UDHR: 'All human beings are born free and equal in dignity and rights. They are endowed with reason and conscience and should act towards one another in a spirit of brotherhood.' Today, a dense and ever growing network of legal instruments and institutional mechanisms serve the protection of individual rights and liberties worldwide. As noted by the United Nations, all member states are party to at least one of the nine core international human rights treaties – the implementation of which is monitored by committees of independent experts – and 80 per cent are party to four or more. The broad recognition of the nine core treaties can be taken to indicate that human rights are firmly embedded within the normative fabric of the international community even though human rights practice is still very far from perfect.

Along with the emergence of human rights as core values of the international system, a *new understanding of sovereignty* developed (International Commission on Intervention and State Sovereignty 2001; Bellamy 2011). In cases of mass atrocities, international law no longer shields governments against outside scrutiny. By contrast, it is now widely recognized that states do have rights only insofar as they are instruments at the service of their people und do not systematically violate the dignity of the persons living under their jurisdiction. The new understanding of sovereignty is enshrined in the Outcome Document of the World Summit 2005. Accordingly, each state has a responsibility to protect its populations from genocide, war crimes, ethnic cleansing and crimes against humanity. When a state manifestly fails in this regard, the international community, through the Security Council, is entitled to use force to stop the wrongdoing should peaceful means be inadequate. Additionally, the members of the United Nations assume a responsibility to assist states after an armed conflict ends. For this purpose, the General Assembly together with the Security Council decided to create a Peacebuilding Commission in 2006.

Critics hold that the 'responsibility to protect' as articulated by the United Nations does not go far enough to make a real difference in international politics – calling it an 'R2P-lite' at best (Weiss 2007: 116–17). For instance, clear legal criteria guiding the use of force in emergency situations are still lacking. Similarly, the scope of the new principle remains highly controversial. What seems to be even more problematic is that, in its present form, the new principle is an imperfect obligation only. Although no state disputes that something should be done in case of genocide, war crimes, ethnic cleansing or crimes against humanity, there is no indication who should take the initiative. Finally, the legal authority to decide on military interventions firmly rests with the Security Council. As a political body, however, the Security Council is too often paralyzed by the national interest of member states. Does this mean that a population at risk must stay without external protection as long as Security Council decision-making is blocked?

While it is evident that the responsibility to protect is not yet a valid norm of international law, it nevertheless amounts to a guiding principle of international morality. Large-scale and systematic human rights violations are equated to international aggression, and a state brutalizing its own populations effectively compromises its otherwise legitimate claim to territorial integrity and political independence. Human rights concerns might in fact override state rights in cases of grave humanitarian emergencies, and they also structure how third parties should proceed to save endangered populations.

War for the protection of human rights?

Let us assume that a government commits mass atrocities against its own people. Let us further assume that a military intervention would stop the killing, that enough troops are available and that the UN Security Council had already sanctioned their deployment under Chapter VII of the UN Charta. To justify a military intervention from a human rights perspective, however, two further requirements must be met: the use of force clearly has to be the lesser evil and the use of force must help to re-establish peace and justice on the affected territory. As to the first requirement, since warfare always kills non-combatants, it is still an open debate how to balance the benefits of military protection against the unavoidable loss of innocent life. On the one hand, proponents of the just war doctrine answered this question with reference to the so-called 'principle of double effect' (Orend 2006: 115–18; Walzer 2006: 153). To protect a population from mass atrocities, innocent civilians might be harmed if harm occurred as the unintended consequence of otherwise legitimate and necessary military activities. The benefits of the use of force, however, must clearly outweigh the collateral civilian casualties. Additionally, we should have strong reasons to believe that the beneficiaries of the intervention do prefer the risks that are associated with the deployment of troops over the continuation of the *status quo ante*. Or, as Téson (2003: 121) has put it: 'Citizens of a state would ideally agree that humanitarian intervention should be allowed for extreme cases of injustice even at the cost of the deaths of some innocents, and even if some of those citizens will inevitably be those persons.'

On the other hand, a growing number of scholars doubt whether military necessity in fact has the power to override individual human rights even if the use of force serves to repel aggression and to restore justice (Fiala 2008; Hidalgo 2009). For them, any armed protection of endangered populations cannot be but tragic. Warfare always implies the loss of innocent life and it is hard to justify why some persons must die for other persons to be rescued. From this perspective, just war considerations ultimately rest on a consequentialist calculus even though this calculus is necessarily related to the human rights discourse and the entitlement of all persons to life in a 'community of rights' (Gewirth 1996). In cases of just wars, the creation of public goods and the defeat of a criminal government outweigh individual rights at least to the extent that the recognition and enjoyment of individual rights presuppose a well-ordered society. Therefore, it might be more appropriate not to focus on military necessity but on political necessity when it comes to decide to what extent force should be used in an emergency situation – if it might be used at all.

For the second condition to hold, warfare has to advance peace and justice. Fundamental human rights must be better protected after a just use of force than without it. While it is always possible to cite individual cases of success such as the outcome of the Second World War, most of the time warfare does not result in a decent and stable political order (Chenoweth and Stephan 2011; Wallensteen 2012). This is especially true for internal armed conflicts that represent the dominant form of contemporary warfare. First of all, recent research shows that civil resistance has a far better success record than armed struggle even under comparable conditions. Second, civil wars tend to recur. The risk of a new armed conflict after the settlement of an old one is desperately high. Moreover, the prospects of democracy after a civil war are very limited. This is also the case for military interventions with the explicit goal of advancing democracy in target countries. Similarly, military interventions tend to undermine the respect for core human rights in the target country. What is even more frustrating, the success rate of multilateral peace operations by the United Nations and other international organizations is far from satisfactory. While the prospects of stability are somewhat higher than in cases without a peace mission, the root causes of violence are rarely addressed, leading to so-called 'no war, no peace' situations (MacGinty 2010). As a consequence, not only are the odds for a new outbreaks of violence high, it also remains questionable whether the protection of human rights was enhanced to the degree necessary to justify the loss of innocent lives by the military operation.

Even though the track record of multilateral peace operations might be considerably improved by better funding and stronger leadership, until today the international community evidently lacks the political will to promote the necessary reforms. In the end, therefore, more and more scholars argue that the resources used for multilateral interventions might be better invested in development projects and the prevention of armed conflicts. By these means, the global human rights record might be better served than by the use of force. Given the tragic nature of military intervention, what counts in the end is the comparative advantage or disadvantage of the use of force for the provision of utterly needed public goods.

Conclusion

In principle, the use of armed forces to repel aggression and to protect endangered populations from mass atrocities can be morally justifiable within strict limits. The bar, however, is high if human dignity and the corresponding human rights are accepted as the guiding criteria. This is especially true for humanitarian interventions. While the genocides in Rwanda and Darfur cried for outside help that did not materialize, the experiences with those military interventions that did occur after the end of the Cold War are not encouraging. In most cases, they failed to accomplish their mission successfully. Either the civilian death toll was very high or the political situation on the ground remains unstable. Given both the prevalent reluctance among military powers to use their armed forces in clear cases of mass atrocities and the disappointing record of those missions that tried to advance peace and justice in war-torn societies, two lessons have to be drawn. First, the international community in general and the industrial countries in particular should increase their engagement for crisis prevention and the peaceful settlement of conflicts. Additionally, they should target the root cause of violence, namely, poor economic performance and bad governance. Second, the member states of the United Nations should make the world organization fit for successful military intervention when everything else has failed to protect endangered populations from mass atrocities. However, as long as there is no clear progress in both dimensions, it remains disputable whether powerful states really care for the responsibility to protect when they intervened militarily in armed conflicts beyond their borders – even if they maintain the contrary. In the final analysis, therefore, the principles of the just war tradition should be used more as a critical tool for the assessment of contemporary wars and military intervention than as an instrument to legitimize the use of force.

References

Bellamy, A. J. 2011. *Global Politics and the Responsibility to Protect: From Words to Deeds.* London: Routledge

Buergenthal, T. 2006. 'The Evolving International Human Rights System', *American Journal of International Law* 100(4): 783–807

Chenoweth, E., and Stephan, M. J. 2011. *Why Civil Resistance Works: The Strategic Logic of Nonviolent Conflict.* New York: Columbia University Press

Donnelly, J. 2002. *Universal Human Rights in Theory and Practice.* Ithaca, NY: Cornell University Press

Fiala, A. G. 2008. *The Just War Myth: The Moral Illusions of War.* Lanham, MD: Rowman & Littlefield

Fisher, D. 2011. *Morality and War: Can War Be Just in the Twenty-First Century?.* Oxford University Press

Gewirth, A. 1992. 'Human Dignity as the Basis of Rights', in M. J. Meyer and W. A. Parent (eds.), *The Constitution of Rights: Human Dignity and American Values.* Ithaca, NY: Cornell University Press, 10–28

1996. *The Community of Rights.* University of Chicago Press

Hidalgo, O. 2009. 'Der "Krieg" als Deus ex machina – ein agnostizistisches Plädoyer', in I. Werkner and A. Liedhegener (eds.), *Gerechter Krieg – gerechter Frieden: Religionen und friedensethische Legitimationen in aktuellen militärischen Konflikten.* Wiesbaden: VS Verlag, 83–109

International Commission on Intervention and State Sovereignty (ICISS). 2001. *The Responsibility to Protect: Report of the International Commission on Intervention and State Sovereignty.* Ottawa: International Development Research Centre

Levy, J. S., and Thompson, W. R. 2010. *Causes of War.* Chichester: Wiley-Blackwell

MacGinty, R. 2010. 'No War, No Peace: Why So Many Peace Processes Fail to Deliver Peace', *International Politics* 47(2): 145–62

McMahan, J. 2009. *Killing in War.* Oxford University Press

Orend, B. 2006. *The Morality of War.* Peterborough (Ontario): Broadview Press

Rengger, N. 2002. 'On the Just War Tradition in the Twenty-First Century', *International Affairs* 78(2): 353–63

Steigleder, K. 1999. *Grundlegung der normativen Ethik: Der Ansatz von Alan Gewirth.* Freiburg im Breisgau, Munich: Alber

Téson, F. R. 2003. 'The Liberal Case for Humanitarian Intervention', in J. L. Holzgrefe and R. O. Keohane (eds.), *Humanitarian Intervention: Ethical, Legal, and Political Dilemmas.* Cambridge University Press, 93–129

Wallensteen, P. 2012. *Understanding Conflict Resolution.* London, Thousand Oaks, CA: Sage Publications

Walzer, M. 2006. *Just and Unjust Wars: A Moral Argument with Historical Illustrations.* New York: Basic Books

Weiss, T. G. 2007. *Humanitarian Intervention: Ideas in Action.* Cambridge: Polity Press

48

Treatment of prisoners and torture

DAVID LUBAN

For entirely obvious reasons, the first substantive article of the Universal Declaration of Human Rights (UDHR) proclaims 'the right to life, liberty and security of person'. Nothing, we think, can be more basic. Other articles of the UDHR spell out what liberty and security mean. Article 5 declares that 'no one shall be subjected to torture or to cruel, inhuman or degrading treatment or punishment'. To most of us, this protection belongs side by side with the rights to life and liberty at the very core of international human rights. A similar clause protecting against torture appears in other human rights instruments around the world – in the International Convention on Civil and Political Rights as well as in the regional human rights conventions of Africa, Europe and the Americas.

The UDHR, like other human rights instruments, also proclaims that concern for human dignity lies at the foundation of human rights. That is a philosophical proposition, and it raises profound questions about the nature of human dignity and why human rights are rooted in it.[1] Among the puzzles is how (if at all) we can deduce particular human rights from the concept of human dignity. Why, in particular, do torture and cruel punishment violate human dignity? The evils of physical torture scarcely need philosophical explanation, and they are not specific to human beings and our dignity: torturing a dog is also evil, and it is evil for much the same reason as torturing a human. The evil lies in the infliction of pain and suffering on a sentient being, not in the affront to dignity – or so the objection might go to a human-dignity-based analysis. One could even object that focusing on the victim's dignity rather than her pain and suffering is overly refined or downright evasive. I shall argue that focusing on dignity is not at all evasive. But the connection between the evils of torture and human dignity clearly requires explanation.

Therefore, in both cases – torture and cruel treatment of prisoners – we must explain how and why they violate human dignity – in other words, what the connection is between the specific evils associated with the rights violations and human dignity. As we shall see, the connection lies in the fact that cruel

[1] For a critique of the claim that human rights practice rests on a philosophical foundation, see Beitz 2009.

practices assault basic aspects of the human personality, and do so to deny the equal dignity of the victim.

Life sentences without parole

A good place to begin is with an important 1977 decision of the German Constitutional Court, which held that life sentences without the possibility of parole are unconstitutional. The Court relied on the first two articles of the German Constitution: Article 1(1) states, '[h]uman dignity shall be inviolable', and Article 2(1) guarantees the right of free development of the personality. The Court reasoned that the two articles together impose a duty on the state to rehabilitate prisoners, and 'the state strikes at the heart of human dignity if it treats the prisoner without regard to the development of his personality and strips him of all hope of ever earning his freedom'.[2] Life without parole violates human dignity because it assumes that the prisoner is, quite literally, beyond redemption, his personality incapable of free development.

The image of human dignity embedded in the German decision focuses on the nature of the human personality. Unlike Stoics such as Cicero, who thought it is reason that endows us with human dignity, or Epictetus, who thought it is the unshakeable will, the German Constitutional Court emphasized the dynamic and changing nature of the human personality, its capacity to renew itself and make itself into something no longer cabined by its own past deeds. Only the recognition of this feature 'makes the sentence bearable in terms of human dignity'.

The psychological insight associated with this view is that, without hope of self-transformation and self-transcendence, we cannot set goals, and without goals we cannot form motivations. We would simply be serving time until death ends the sentence, and indeed static hopelessness is closely related to endlessness, the 'tedium of immortality' that the philosopher Bernard Williams famously argued would make eternal life unbearable (Williams 1973: 82–100). Lacking motivations, our personalities would stand at risk of disintegration. Plainly, not everyone sentenced to life without parole actually disintegrates. Some prisoners find ways to hold hopelessness at bay. Famously, Epictetus maintained that imprisonment cannot touch the virtuous person's dignity (Epictetus 1877: 6). Perhaps lifelong prisoners maintain themselves through some version of stoic detachment. Others do it through religious faith, angry defiance or (one suspects) stubborn self-deception. Some prisoners, on the other hand, simply deteriorate.

In addition to assaulting psychological integrity, life without parole treats the prisoner as a lesser being than his fellows, and condemns him to lifelong

[2] *Life Imprisonment Case* (1977), 45 BVerGE 187, in *The Constitutional Jurisprudence of the Federal Republic of Germany*, ed. and trans. Donald P. Kommers, 2nd edn, Durham, NC: Duke University Press, 1997, 308–9.

subordination. Importantly, the UDHR systematically ties 'inherent dignity' to 'equal rights'. Where concern about psychological integrity emphasizes a personal and existential meaning of individual human dignity, the emphasis on equality means that human dignity is the common possession of all human beings in equal measure – a relational sense of human dignity. The two go together: destroying someone's personality reduces her to a lower level, and systematic subordination assaults the personality.

Dehumanizing conditions of confinement

Conditions less drastic than lifetime confinement can also assault the personality. Long-term solitary confinement (used in the United States on an estimated 25,000 residents of 'supermax' prisons and additional tens of thousands in other facilities) can cause rapid deterioration of the personality. Psychologist Craig Haney explains:

> Some of them lose their grasp of their identity. Who we are, and how we function in the world around us, is very much nested in our relation to other people. Over a long period of time, solitary confinement undermines one's sense of self. It undermines your ability to register and regulate emotion. The appropriateness of what you're thinking and feeling is difficult to index, because we're so dependent on contact with others for that feedback. And for some people, it becomes a struggle to maintain sanity. (Kelm 2009)[3]

Other conditions of imprisonment besides life without parole and long-term solitary confinement can also assault the human personality. In its well-known *Soering* decision, the European Court of Human Rights barred the United Kingdom from extraditing a German to face a potential death sentence for a double murder. The Court found that the 'death row phenomenon' of waiting for years in the death house, literally in the shadow of death, amounts to inhuman and degrading treatment.[4] (For legal reasons, the Court could not address the death penalty itself.)

In the most extreme form of prisoner mistreatment, concentration camp conditions aim to dehumanize inmates as well as making them suffer. As explained by Avishai Margalit and Gabriel Moskin, humiliating the victims as a sign of their expulsion from the human race was an essential, not accidental, part of the Holocaust, because it made the category of 'murder' inapplicable: only a being with human dignity can be murdered (Margalit and Motzkin 1996: 70–6).

Inmates' compelled degradation forms one of the themes of Primo Levi's powerful books on his experiences in Auschwitz. With too few calories to go around, nobody could survive without stealing food from other inmates. Auschwitz became a Hobbesian hell that morally degraded those it did not kill;

[3] See also Gawande 2009.

[4] *Soering* v. *United Kingdom*, 11 ECHR (Series A) (1989).

Levi asserts that few survivors could claim innocence because the innocent did not survive – in Levi's unforgettable language, they were the drowned, and only those who found some form of special protection were the saved (Levi 1958: 87–100; 1989: 40–1)

Forcing prisoners to sacrifice moral integrity to survive is different from an attack on the personality as such, although innumerable inmates suffered lasting psychological damage. But it is an important example of a phenomenon systematically connected with degrading practices of confinement, and torture as well: degradation induces behaviour by prisoners that makes them contemptible in their guards' eyes, and their contemptible condition seemingly justifies the abuse. This vicious circle of dehumanization justifying further dehumanization is extremely important in sustaining inhuman systems. The victims themselves provide the evidence that they deserve their treatment.

The defining evils of torture

Harsh punishment and degrading treatment are closely connected with torture, and may in fact be forms of torture. Torture was, of course, a common method of punishment until its abolition in the nineteenth century.

The paradigm case of torture is physical torture, not more intangible assaults on dignity. It leads us again to the question of why the evil of inflicting so much suffering on a sentient being requires explanation through the concept of human dignity – or, indeed, any explanation at all. The answer is that the evil of torture cannot be reduced to the pain alone. Consider that women whom no one would deem irrational choose natural childbirth despite the pain; its association with a joyful event transforms excruciating pain into something they do not regard as unalloyed evil. The evil of physical torture lies in the connection between pain, fear and the horror of being wholly in the power of a malignant enemy. The Stoics recognized this. Seneca observed that even the Stoic sage loses his courage when he sees the instruments of torture displayed, and 'the spectacle overcomes those who would have patiently withstood the suffering' (Seneca 1917: 87). He observes that diseases can be as painful as torture, but

> that which shakes us most is the dread which hangs over us from our neighbour's ascendancy [lit. 'another's power', *aliena potentia*]; for it is accompanied by great outcry and uproar . . . Picture to yourself under this head the prison, the cross, the rack, the hook, and . . . all the other contrivances devised by cruelty . . . It is not surprising that our greatest terror is of such a fate. (Seneca 1917: 85)

Notably, Seneca emphasizes suffering aggravated by imagination, and he associates the horrors of torture with being in another's power and having that power put on display. Bearing these observations in mind, I shall define torture as follows:

> Torture is the assertion of unlimited power over absolute helplessness, accomplished through the infliction of severe pain or suffering on a victim in the torturer's custody or control that the victim is meant to perceive as the assertion of the torturer's limitless power and the victim's absolute helplessness.

This is a different and more complicated definition than the standard legal definition of torture as intentional infliction of severe pain or suffering. It is not intended to replace the legal definition, which serves its own purposes, which we shall examine shortly. The definition offered here means to capture the distinctive evil of torture, which lies in the connection between suffering, domination and unlimited helplessness. Torture is pain used as a communicative vehicle to let its victims know that they are wholly at the mercy of the merciless. The definition offered here makes it clear how torture violates human dignity in both senses described above: it inflicts suffering to make visible the victim's helplessness and it does so to assert absolute inequality.[5]

The definition offered here encompasses mental as well as physical torture. So long as the mental suffering is severe, and is inflicted to communicate the absolute dominance of the torturer and helplessness of the victim, it qualifies as torture.

Historically, rulers have inflicted torture for four reasons in addition to punishment: the celebration of military triumph by torturing the defeated, terrorizing subjugated people to maintain political control, extracting criminal confessions, and intelligence-gathering (Luban 2005: 1432–7). That the first two satisfy the definition of torture offered here should be clear. As for interrogational torture, its point is to replace the victim's will with the interrogator's, so that, as Jean Améry (himself a torture victim) remarks, the torturer 'is master over flesh and spirit, life and death' (Améry 1980: 35). More subtly, the philosopher David Sussman argues that the defining evil of interrogational torture lies in forcing the victim 'into the position of colluding against himself through his own affects and emotions, so that he experiences himself as simultaneously powerless and yet actively complicit in his own violation' (Sussman 2005: 4). The victim is not only humbled, but forced to betray himself. Although there is clearly something to this argument, focusing solely on the subordination of will and feeling misses what I take to be a central feature of all these forms of torture: they use pain and suffering as a medium to communicate the mastery of the torturer and abjectness of the victim.

It would be naïve to suppose that any of these practices of cruel triumph, terror, confession or interrogation has died out, but all except the last have lost any semblance of respectability. Within today's political debates, focused on defeating terrorism, only torture for intelligence-gathering still finds unashamed defenders.[6]

[5] For further explication and defence of this definition, see Luban (forthcoming), Chapter 6.

[6] A BBC poll in 2006 found that one-third of 27,000 subjects worldwide favour torture to combat terrorism, ranging from a low of 14 per cent in Italy to a high of 43 per cent

Torture, cruel treatment and the law

Officially, however, no state condones torture even for interrogation. In addition to the human rights treaties, the 1988 Convention Against Torture (CAT) has more than 150 parties. CAT makes torture an international crime, requires states to criminalize torture, licenses universal jurisdiction over torture, and categorically asserts that no war or other emergency can ever justify torture. Under current international law, torture has entered the small infernal circle of *jus cogens* crimes – violations whose prohibition no custom or treaty can undo. Other treaties reinforce this commitment by branding torture a war crime or a crime against humanity in the contexts of armed conflict or attacks against civilian populations.[7]

CAT defines torture as the intentional infliction of severe mental or physical pain or suffering (Article 1).[8] Importantly, CAT identifies a separate category of 'cruel, inhuman or degrading treatment or punishment' (CIDTP) less severe than torture. States are required to criminalize torture, but not CIDTP; instead, CAT obligates states to 'undertake to prevent' CIDTP in any territory over which they have jurisdiction.

Other legal instruments also distinguish between torture and other forms of cruelty, but without suggesting that states have lesser obligations towards CIDTP than torture. Thus, the Geneva Conventions speak of 'cruel treatment and torture' in a separate clause from 'outrages upon personal dignity, in particular humiliating and degrading treatment' (Article 3 common to all four Geneva Conventions), with no suggestion that one clause takes priority over the other. The European Convention on Human Rights treats torture and inhuman or degrading treatment together, although the European Court of Human Rights created a three-tiered hierarchy of abuse, with torture at the top, serious inhuman treatment in the intermediate position and lesser inhuman or degrading treatment at the bottom.[9] Neither the Geneva Conventions nor the European Convention suggests that torture must be criminalized, while

in Israel. BBC News, 'One-Third Support "Some Torture"', 19 October 2006, http://news.bbc.co.uk/2/hi/6063386.stm. Meanwhile, regular polling within the United States shows support for torture increasing gradually from 43 per cent in July 2004 to 53 per cent in August 2011. Pew Research Center Databank, '43% – Torture Justified', http://pewresearch.org/databank/dailynumber/?NumberID=520; Pew Research Center, 'United in Remembrance, Divided Over Policies', www.people-press.org/2011/09/01/united-in-remembrance-divided-over-policies.

[7] Rome Statute of the International Criminal Court, Arts. 7(1)(f), 8(2)(a)(ii) and 8(2)(c)(i)–(ii).

[8] CAT adds: '. . . at the instigation of or with the consent or acquiescence of a public official or other person acting in an official capacity'. Presumably the restriction to public officials appears in CAT only because treaties obligate states, not private parties. CAT's definition exempts pain or suffering 'inherent in or incidental to lawful sanctions'.

[9] *Askoy* v. *Turkey*, 23 EHRR 553, § 63 (1996).

states must only 'undertake to prevent' CIDTP. The Geneva Conventions and the European Convention leave torture undefined, and today the authoritative legal definition is the one found in CAT. Its basic formula – 'severe pain or suffering, whether physical or mental . . . intentionally inflicted' – has become canonical.

Notoriously, lawyers in the US government concluded that a dozen abusive techniques used by the CIA, including waterboarding (controlled suffocation) and sleep deprivation of up to 180 hours did not cross the 'severity' threshold into torture. One problem with CAT's two-tiered classification scheme in which torture is a crime while CIDTP is not is that it invites pettifoggery in drawing the line. It creates an opening for intelligence services to use so-called 'torture lite' techniques that leave no scars, break no bones, and do not obviously sound awful. (Of course, some forms of bloodless torture, such as electrical shocks, are incontrovertibly torture.) Historian Darius Rejali has shown that democratic regimes pioneered the push towards 'stealth' torture. Perversely, as the law moved to prohibit torture, interrogators moved towards methods that leave no evidence and, if discovered, are less likely to shock the public conscience (Rejali 2007: 405–9).

Mental torture

One crucial refinement has been the development of mental or psychological torture (Luban and Shue 2012: 823–63). An important boost came from psychological research on 'learned helplessness', which originated in experiments in which dogs, subjected to random electrical shocks unconnected with their behaviour, soon became so passive that they no longer even tried to avoid the shocks. Cold War researchers (some funded by the CIA) discovered that seemingly minor disorientations like hooding, temperature manipulation, isolation and irregular hours of being woken up could induce personality collapses in astonishingly short periods of time (McCoy 2006; Bloche 2011: Chapters 7 and 8). The same is true of physical insults and humiliations piled one on top of another, such as slapping, grabbing, forced nudity, forced grooming and sexual taunting. Cumulatively, humiliation, disorientation and 'torture lite' techniques like stress positions – none of which might independently qualify as torture – have a devastating effect on those subjected to them, reducing them to an infantile state.

By this point, it should be evident that the forms of mistreatment we have examined – life without parole, prolonged isolation, compelled moral degradation, humiliating punishments, and 'stealth' torture – have family resemblances. They attack the personality and make a mockery of human equality. Less dramatic than physical torture, they nevertheless violate human dignity in both the senses implicit in human rights norms. Seeing how they do so explains why human rights norms do indeed affirm human dignity, and why the affirmation of human dignity demands rights against torture, cruelty, degradation and humiliation at the hands of the state.

References

Améry, J. 1980. 'Torture', in *At the Mind's Limits: Contemplations by a Survivor on Auschwitz and Its Realities*, trans. S. Rosenfeld and S. P. Rosenfeld. Bloomington, IN: Indiana University Press

Beitz, C. R. 2009. *The Idea of Human Rights*. Oxford University Press

Bloche, M. G. 2011. *The Hippocratic Myth*. New York: Palgrave Macmillan

Epictetus. 1877. *The Discourses of Epictetus with the Enchiridion and Fragments*, trans. G. Long. London: George Bell & Sons

Gawande, A. 2009. 'Hellhole', *The New Yorker*, 30 March, www.newyorker.com/reporting/2009/03/30/090330fa_fact_gawande

Kelm, B. 2009. 'Solitary Confinement: The Invisible Torture', *Wired Magazine*, 28 April, www.wired.com/wiredscience/2009/04/solitaryconfinement

Levi, P. 1958. *Survival in Auschwitz*, trans. S. Woolf. New York: Touchstone

1989. *The Drowned and the Saved*, trans. Raymond Rosenthal. New York: Vintage

Luban, D. 2005. 'Liberalism, Torture, and the Ticking Bomb', *Virginia Law Review* 91: 1432–7

Forthcoming. *Torture, Power, and Law*. Cambridge University Press

Luban, D., and Shue, H. 2012. 'Mental Torture: A Critique of Erasures in US Law', *Georgetown Law Journal* 100: 823–63

Margalit, A., and Motzkin, G. 1996. 'The Uniqueness of the Holocaust', *Philosophy and Public Affairs* 25: 70–6

McCoy, A. W. 2006. *A Question of Torture: CIA Interrogation, from the Cold War to the War on Terror*. New York: Metropolitan

Rejali, D. 2007. *Torture and Democracy*. Princeton University Press

Seneca, 1917. *Epistles 1–65*, trans. R. M. Gummere. Cambridge, MA: Harvard University Press

Sussman, D. 2005. 'What's Wrong With Torture?', *Philosophy and Public Affairs* 33(1): 1–33

Williams, B. 1973. 'The Makropulos Case: Reflections on the Tedium of Immortality', in *Problems of the Self*. Cambridge University Press

49

Human dignity and prostitution

NORBERT CAMPAGNA

One of the major philosophical justifications for laws making sexual services (or the use of these) illegal is that prostitution is, intrinsically, a violation of human dignity, especially of the human dignity of women. Paying a person in order to accomplish a sexual act upon her or to have her accomplish a sexual act upon oneself is, so the argument runs, using her as a mere tool for sexual gratification, and this is so even if we suppose – what some claim to be impossible – that the person in question offers her sexual services voluntarily and without being forced or coerced. Consent may be transformative in many instances, but it cannot transform a prostitutional act into something compatible with human dignity, however well the client may treat the prostitute. Behind the humane treatment in the context of particular acts, one should always see the inhumane institution. In this sense, prostitution could be said to resemble slavery.

There is no denying the fact that prostitution as it exists nowadays is to a very large extent incompatible with respect for human dignity. Even before looking at the client who uses the prostitute for his sexual gratification, we must take account of all those people who use the prostitute as a source of revenue, keeping her under inhumane conditions, using violence against her whenever it pleases them, leaving her a very insubstantial part of what she receives from the clients, etc. Abducting a person, by force or by deceit, and then forcing her to prostitute herself is clearly contrary to human dignity and is rightly criminalized. And it can also be argued that clients who may be supposed to know that the prostitute is exploited can be criminalized.

But suppose a person – a man or a woman – freely decides to offer his or her sexual services for money. Some will object that such a person only exists in the mind of philosophers and that to evoke such a possibility will aid only those who already profit most from prostitution. For present purposes, however, the focal argument claims (1) since prostitution is contrary to human dignity and (2) since nobody is free to renounce his human dignity, then it must follow that nobody can freely decide to prostitute him- or herself.

The force of this logically valid argument depends on the strength of its premises. Its opponents may impugn either the truth of its first or that of its second premise. As to this second premise, nobody will deny the fact that we may actually do things which are contrary to our human dignity. But the premise does not state that we lack the physical possibility to do these things. It declares that we have the duty to do nothing that will give other persons the impression that we have abandoned our human dignity and, with this dignity, also the claim to have it respected. By giving him this impression, we delude the other person and ourselves by making us and him believe that we have abandoned something which we just cannot abandon – 'cannot' in a metaphysical sense.

Rather than discussing the question whether it is possible, in a metaphysical sense, to abandon our human dignity or the question whether we have a right to renounce our claim to have that dignity respected, I want to concentrate on the first premise of the argument in order to see whether prostitution intrinsically violates human dignity.

In order to answer this question, we need a definition of prostitution and a definition of human dignity. Some will define prostitution in such a way that it implicitly contains the idea of a violation of human dignity (for example, prostitution is sexual slavery), thus winning by an analytical knock-out. Defining prostitution in such a way that it does not yet contain any reference to a violation of human dignity will of course call forth the objection that one denies the facts – one does not define prostitution but something else.

Conscious that such an objection may be raised, I nevertheless want to give what I think to be a morally neutral definition of prostitution, or more precisely a definition of a prostitutional act: a prostitutional act – in the sexual sense of the word – is an act by which an individual exchanges a sexual service against something which is not sexual. In a pure prostitutional act, one person is not interested at all in her own sexual gratification. One person demands sexual gratification but is not expected to offer sexual gratification and the other person offers sexual gratification but is known not to demand it. What this other person demands must not necessarily be money, but can be such diverse things as a job, a meal, drugs, a child, a holiday, etc. What is important is that this person expects *something* in return and that this something is not sexual gratification.

At this point, one might object that prostitution is essentially a *public* phenomenon – isn't the female prostitute often called a 'public woman'? Though not denying the fact that prostitution is a social practice and thus a public phenomenon, the fundamental moral problem does not only appear at the public level. Performing prostitutional acts is not merely morally problematic when these acts are performed as a part of a public institution, but they are already problematic when performed at a private level. Performing them at a public level may add new morally problematic elements, but the fundamental problem already appears at the private level. Moreover, the very distinction between the public and the private is problematic. Having a mistress may be seen as belonging to the private sphere, but what if having a mistress is a social practice within a specific social group?

Performing a prostitutional act is not the same as becoming a prostitute, in the same way that performing a cooking act is not becoming a cook. A prostitute is a person who makes her living by engaging in prostitutional acts. In this context, one could distinguish the professional prostitute who makes her whole living by engaging in prostitutional acts and the occasional prostitute who engages in prostitutional acts only to supplement her income. According to my definition, a mistress who receives what she needs to live from her lover is a prostitute – at least if we suppose that she doesn't also expect sexual gratification from him. To be a prostitute, one need only fulfil one and a half of the elements mentioned by the Roman jurist Ulpianus: for money, without pleasure, with anybody. Having sex with anybody, i.e. not to be selective as to one's sexual partners, is called promiscuity, and though it is true that prostitutes are promiscuous, promiscuity does not, at least not in my thesis, belong to the essence of prostitution. The defining elements of prostitution are the absence of pleasure – in the sense that the prostitute does not seek sexual gratification – and receiving something non-sexual in exchange.

Is excluding promiscuity from our definition of prostitution not the trick which helps us evade the conclusion that prostitution is intrinsically a violation of human dignity? For what is a promiscuous person if not a person who accepts having sex with anybody, even with a person whom she knows will treat her like a mere thing? And is accepting being treated like a mere thing not announcing that one has renounced one's human dignity?

Promiscuity does not necessarily mean that one will perform sexual acts just with or for anybody. It just means that one does not limit one's sexual acts to one single person. A person may well be promiscuous and categorically refuse to perform sexual acts with or for a person whom she knows will treat her like a mere thing. So, even if we included promiscuity in our definition of prostitution, it would not commit us to the view that prostitution is intrinsically a violation of human dignity. It might, however, commit us to the view that prostitution is a violation of the dignity of sexuality – at least if we conceive of sexuality as an activity which is intrinsically monogamous.

A prostitutional act occurs each time a person exchanges a sexual act for something non-sexual. If we suppose that the mere fact of making oneself sexually available to another person does not yet constitute a declaration that one renounces one's human dignity – as Kant would have us suppose, at least in the absence of a valid marriage contract – the violation of human dignity must somehow be linked to the fact that one does not expect the other person to make him- or herself also sexually available to us. The ethical problem of prostitution, at least insofar as human dignity is concerned, must lie in this asymmetry.

But could it not already lie in one's making one's body available to another person? If we suppose that one's person is intrinsically linked to one's body and that making one's person available is just what constitutes a violation of human dignity, making one's body available would also constitute such a violation.

One thing to be said here is that the prostitute does not sell his or her body. It does of course happen that criminal organizations sell prostitutes in the same way slaves were sold – and are still sold in some countries. But there is a difference between a criminal who sells a prostitute to a pimp and an independently working prostitute who asks money for sexual services. The client does not buy a body, but the right to ask for sexual services from the prostitute. What some persons provide out of love, what is taken by force from some other persons, prostitutes provide for money.

Of course, in a loving relationship lovers get much more than just sexual gratification. For them, sexuality is also a means of communicating their mutual love to each other; it is one of the many ways they have to feel close to each other, etc. All these related aspects are absent from a prostitutional relationship and they are also generally expected to be absent. In this sense, one can say that prostitutional sex is an impoverished form of sexuality. But this judgment has more to do with aesthetics than with ethics, and even if we suppose that it has something to do with ethics, it belongs more to the realm of recommended ideals than to the realm of obligatory norms. We may be encouraged to pursue a richer form of sexuality, but I strongly doubt that we may be obliged to pursue it.

As was said before, the question whether prostitution intrinsically violates human dignity presupposes a definition of prostitution and a definition of human dignity. So after having said what constitutes a prostitutional act, we must now turn to the question of what constitutes human dignity. And the first thing to notice is that we are concerned with *human* dignity and not merely with *status* dignity. Yet status dignity can give us a clue as to how to find our way to a definition of human dignity. For status dignity is defined by a certain number of expectations, and the person who does not live up to these expectations shows that she doesn't merit the social status she has.

Hence the question is: what do we expect from a human being as a *human* being? It should be clear from the outset that these expectations will not just be biological expectations, but that they will refer to elements which distinguish human beings and which give them their value. If we place ourselves in the Kantian tradition (and this tradition is predominant today, at least in continental Europe), what gives us our value is our autonomy, i.e. our ability to give ourselves our own law of action. Hence Kant's categorical imperative which urges us not to treat humanity, either in ourselves or in others, merely as a means, but always also as an end in itself. This means that we should never forget that human beings can and should determine by themselves the laws which will guide their actions. And, for Kant, this capacity is linked to reason. Respecting human dignity is respecting the capacity to decide for oneself, following one's reason, how one is going to act.

For Kant, submitting oneself to the sexual desire of another is giving him to understand that one accepts being his tool for sexual gratification, so that the other stops seeing in that person an end in itself and so a being capable to decide for itself. It is as if a human being became an inflatable doll. In order to escape this fate, according to Kant, the person who submits herself to sexual intercourse must first contract with the other person, the core of the contract being that the two persons bind themselves for life, so that whatever consequences will follow from their sexual intercourse – pregnancy, diseases, etc. – they will have to bear them together, in the sense that neither can discard the other as he would discard a lemon out of which he has taken all the juice.

In the case of prostitution, the client can discard the prostitute after he has obtained his sexual gratification. No legal duty obliges him to care for the person he may have made pregnant or who may have caught a venereal disease because he was infected. And the prostitute has sold her right not to be treated like a used lemon. She has engaged in a potentially dangerous act without caring to establish any legal duties, so as to give the impression that her moral rights count for nothing. Insofar as the wife secures the respect of her fundamental moral rights by binding her husband to legal duties, nothing similar happens in the case of the prostitute. And, because he pays her, the client may get the impression that he has bought himself out of the duty to respect the prostitute. The prostitute has sold her right to be respected as a human being, and the client has bought the right not to respect her as a human being.

It may be the case that many clients think that things are like this. And the cultural and legal stigmatization of prostitution may comfort them in what they think. But there is no reason why the relation between a client and a prostitute should be interpreted in this way. The fact that nowadays many legal systems admit the legal possibility of raping a prostitute clearly shows that the prostitute should not be understood as having sold all her rights. Moreover, 'traditional' prostitutes have what may be called their own code of deontology: there are some sexual acts which they refuse to do, many never consent to be kissed on the mouth, etc. Even though these prostitutes sell a right to be made use of for the sexual gratification of another person, they do not sell all their rights, nor does the law allow the client to think that they have sold all their rights.

So, even if we suppose that a client uses a prostitute's body to obtain his sexual gratification and pays her for this, this does not necessarily mean that he treats her as a mere instrument. Whether one treats someone as a mere instrument or also as an end in itself does not depend on what one physically does to that person or have her do, but on how one considers her. The respect for human dignity does not express itself in the substance of the act, but in the modality of its accomplishment.

But aren't there exceptions and doesn't prostitution belong to these? The most obvious exceptions are genocide and torture. Even if one decides to wipe out a people without causing suffering to a single individual and if one does it with the sincere belief that it will secure the eternal salvation of those individuals, it will be hard to say that the genocidal act is compatible with human dignity. Some types of act just cannot be accomplished in a way that respects human dignity because their very substance negates it.

I do not think that prostitution belongs to these exceptions. There is no compelling reason to think that a person making use of a prostitute for his sexual gratification necessarily stops respecting her as the person she is, a person worthy of respect which one may not treat as one wishes and whom one is bound to by moral as well as legal duties. By having paid intercourse with her, one does not implicitly negate what morality exhorts us to respect. There is no contradiction in saying: 'I pay you for the sexual act and I respect you as a human being.'

Of course, if one knows or has good reasons to believe that the other person is disgusted by the idea of being paid for giving sexual gratification – something she believes she should only offer in the context of a true love affair – and that she consents to sell what according to her has no price, paying her for a sexual act can be morally condemnable. And here seems to lie the crux of the problem: while some think that any human being conscious of his human dignity *should* feel disgusted or morally horrified at the idea of selling sexual gratification, others think that a human being who does not feel disgust or moral horror at this idea may still be conscious of his human dignity. Sexuality seems to be so intimately linked to our humanity, that selling/buying sexual gratification seems to be selling/buying one essential ingredient of one's/the other's humanity and thus treating the latter as a mere means. Sexuality, some – but not Kant, of course – may be tempted to say, is an end in itself and cannot be anything but an end in itself. And, as such, it should be out of commerce. For if it is commercialized, it will be reduced to a merchandize or a service, like any other. But wasn't this kind of objection once made against the selling of philosophical knowledge?

What has been said does not exclude the possibility of condemning forced prostitution and human trafficking. As it now exists, the social institution of prostitution is highly problematic and in many instances morally condemnable. I do not deny that a large part of this institution is controlled by criminal groups and that many clients consider prostitutes as mere objects for their sexual gratification. But morally condemning the – nowadays – paradigmatic form of institutional prostitution implies neither a condemnation of prostitution as such nor the condemnation of all possible institutional forms of prostitution. The Netherlands or Germany have decided to consider prostitution as a legally recognized profession. Of course, such a legal recognition does not in itself mean that prostitutes will be respected. For this to happen, an important cultural change concerning our views of sexuality and the persons selling sexual services must occur.

One of the major moral-legal problems confronting legislators today is the following: once we admit that many prostitutes are exploited and treated as mere objects, should one, like some Scandinavian countries, make laws aimed at criminalizing the buying of sexual services – though not the selling, as prostitutes are seen as victims – or should one make laws giving more rights to prostitutes, thus officially recognizing prostitution? At a more fundamental level, two opposite views confront each other: on the one hand, the view that prostitution must disappear as it is fundamentally incompatible with human dignity. And, on the other hand, the view that only *forced* prostitution must disappear. And, among those who merely hold that forced prostitution must disappear, we find those who think that the only means to get rid of forced prostitution is to criminalize the buying of sexual services as such and those who think that one can get rid of forced prostitution without a wholesale criminalization of the buying of sexual services.

References

Assemblée Nationale (ed.). 2011. *Rapport d'information 3334: Prostitution: l'exigence de responsabilité: En finir avec le mythe du 'plus vieux métier du monde'*, Paris

Campagna, N. 2005. *Prostitution: Eine philosophische Untersuchung.* Berlin: Parerga

2008. *Prostitution et dignité.* Paris: La Musardine

De Marneffe, P. 2010. *Liberalism and Prostitution.* Oxford University Press

Jeffreys, S. 1997. *The Idea of Prostitution*, Melbourne: Spinifex

Mathieu, L. 2001. *Mobilizations de prostituées.* Paris: Belin

O'Neill, M. 2001. *Prostitution and Feminism: Towards a Politics of Feeling.* Cambridge: Polity Press

Outshoorn, J. (ed.). 2004. *The Politics of Prostitution: Women's Movements, Democratic States and the Globalization of Sex Commerce.* Cambridge University Press

Pryen, S. 1999. *Stigmate et métier: Une approche sociologique de la prostitution de rue.* Presses Universitaires de Rennes

Rossiaud, J. 2010. *Amours vénales: La prostitution en Occident XIIe–XVIe siècles.* Paris: Aubier

Zelizer, V. A. 2005. *The Purchase of Intimacy.* Princeton University Press

50

Human dignity, immigration and refugees

GÖRAN COLLSTE

The aim of this chapter is to inquire how the principle of human dignity applies to the political question of the treatment of immigrants and refugees. Human dignity is often given two related meanings: first, the intrinsic and equal value of each human being; and, second, a dignified human life, i.e. a life lived under decent conditions. Decent conditions imply for example freedom and education, as well as the absence of repression, torture and starvation. Both meanings are related to human rights; owing to her intrinsic value each human being has rights to freedom, health etc. Human dignity in the second sense informs us about the requirements for a decent human life, i.e. the content of human rights (Collste 2002).

Refugees and immigrants[1] are in a vulnerable position. They are forced to leave their homes and are potential victims of exploitation and extortion. This chapter deals primarily with the political and ethical conditions for respecting the human dignity of immigrants and refugees. How can a 'global political practice' (Heuser 2008: 71) of respecting their dignity be justified from a moral point of view? There is a link between arguments for human dignity, human rights and moral cosmopolitanism. According to moral cosmopolitanism, the individual human being is the ultimate unit of worth and entitled to equal consideration regardless of such contingencies as nationality and citizenship (Beitz 1999; Tan 2004).

I will start by reiterating some basic facts concerning immigrants and refugees in the twenty-first century. What are the numbers? Where do immigrants and refugees come from and where do they go? Then I present the moral and legal status of refugees in international politics and regulations. Primary documents are the Universal Declaration of Human Rights and the Geneva Convention of 1951. Next, I draw attention to the views of Immanuel Kant and Hannah Arendt, two philosophers who have contributed to the ethical discourse on the rights

[1] In this chapter 'immigrant' refers to economic and social immigrants, i.e. individuals who because of poverty or unjust social conditions leave their countries to get a better life elsewhere. Business people, employees, students, volunteers etc. who go abroad for other reasons are not included.

of refugees; and finally I discuss how human rights of immigrant and refugees can be protected in an age characterized by globalization.

Immigrants and refugees

The number of international immigrants has risen continuously during the last twenty years. In 1990, the total number was 155 million, and in 2013, the figure had risen to 230 million. This means that, in 2013, around 3 per cent of the world's population consisted of international immigrants. About 60 per cent of the immigrants are localized in the more developed regions and 40 per cent in less developed regions. China, India and the Philippines are the three major migrant-sending countries, whereas the US, Russia and Germany host the largest numbers of international immigrants. 'Push factors' that motivate migration are poverty, political instability and, presumably in the future, climate-related changes of the natural environment (United Nations Population Division 2013; International Organization for Migration 2010; Gibney 2004).

In 2012, there were a total of 15 million refugees and 29 million internally displaced persons in the world. Major source countries of refugees are Afghanistan, Iraq, Somalia, Syria and Congo, i.e. recent conflict zones, and the major refugee hosting countries are Pakistan, Iran, Syria and Germany. The main reason for refugees leaving their country is war, and usually they go to neighbouring countries. The vast majority of refugees stay in a host country for a shorter or longer period of time before they return to their home country, while a minority (2–10 per cent) resettles in the hosting country (United Nations High Commissioner for Refugees 2012).

Amnesty International and other NGOs continuously report on the maltreatment of refugees and immigrants. For example, in European border countries like Greece and Italy, they are often treated as criminals and detained in subhuman conditions. Since the 1990s, female refugees from war zones have been extremely badly off. In the war in the former Yugoslavia as well as in a number of African countries, rape has become a method of warfare intended not only to hurt individual women but also to undermine culture and morals (Stop Rape Now 2010; Amnesty International 2013).

International law and morals

Human rights are moral claims of particular importance. They belong to every individual human being assuring him or her equal status irrespective of nationality, race or sex. Human rights are universal and equal; no human being has more human rights than any other.

In the evolution of human rights, the Universal Declaration of Human Rights (UDHR) is of special significance. Several articles of the UDHR relate to questions of refugee status and immigration. Article 6 affirms that every individual, irrespective of citizenship, has a right to equal treatment before the law. This is a universal right valid across national borders. Article 13 deals with freedom of movement. To migrate – both within a country and across national borders – is thus a human right.

Article 14 deals especially with the questions of refugee status and asylum. According to Article 14(1): 'Everyone has the right to seek and to enjoy in other countries asylum from persecution.' Finally, Article 15 secures a right to nationality.

Someone's right presupposes someone else's obligation. The UDHR signatories are nation-states. Hence, nation-states are both the guarantors *of* and the primary agents *for* the enforcement of human rights within their borders. States have obligations to fulfil human rights. However, as regards Article 14, there is an asymmetry: refugee rights do not correspond to particular obligations of states. Refugees leave their home country due to persecution and suppression, i.e. due to the fact that their human rights are violated. Who then has the obligation to secure their rights as refugees? Does any particular nation have an obligation to guarantee refugee status to any particular refugee who happens to cross its borders? Is the obligation shared among the signatories of the UDHR? Alas, so far these questions have no positive answers.

In order to strengthen the responsibility to protect refugees, the Geneva Refugee Convention was adopted in 1951. At the time the Convention referred primarily to European war refugees, but its scope was expanded in the 1967 Protocol. Besides defining the meaning of 'refugee' (see below), the Geneva Convention also proclaims ways to protect refugees' human rights. Refugees are granted a fair hearing and permission to stay in the country while they seek asylum. The Convention explicitly prohibits the expulsion of refugees; the so-called 'non-*refoulement*' principle. The Office of the United Nations High Commissioner for Refugees (UNHCR) has the mandate to monitor the worldwide implementation of the Geneva Convention. However, the UNHCR's status is weak in relation to states due to the fact that it is not given any formal authority (Loescher 1999: 245f). Hence, unlike immigrants, refugees have some internationally recognized rights of protection. Who then is a refugee?

Who is a refugee?

Refugees are in a vulnerable situation and in need of protection. The Geneva Convention defines 'refugee' as:

> [a]ny person who, owing to a well-founded fear of being persecuted for reasons of race, religion, nationality, membership of a particular social group or political opinion, is outside the country of his nationality and is unable or . . . unwilling to avail himself of the protection of that country . . .

Reasons for being granted refugee status are persecution caused by race, religion, or nationality and persecution due to political membership and political opinion. The definition is open to different interpretations and affirms some limitations that might be questioned. What, for example, does 'well-founded fear' imply? Is it based on the individual's subjective views or on political conditions in the country of origin? What counts as a 'social group'? Why is persecution for reasons of sexual orientation not included (Carens 2003)?

One should observe that the Geneva Convention refers to 'any person' as a potential refugee. To differentiate between potential immigrants or refugees on the basis of, for example, race, religion or ethnicity would clearly conflict with the principle of human dignity (Carens 2003).

According to the Geneva Convention, individuals who leave their country of origin due to social and economic reasons are excluded from obtaining refugee status. Is this distinction between political and economic reasons for migration reasonable? Political refugees have strong reasons for needing protection. They must leave their countries because they are threatened by imprisonment or perhaps even death. On the other hand, social and economic deprivation is not – *prima facie* – less threatening for the individual than political repression. As a consequence, migration caused by severe poverty in case of a government that cannot or will not protect the basic economic rights of its citizens could also count as a moral reason for the wealthier nations to open their borders (Shacknove 1984).

Rights of foreigners

As long as the principle of human dignity is materialized in *state-centred* human rights, refugees will remain in a vulnerable position. By leaving their home country they are less protected. Immanuel Kant tried to compensate for this in his cosmopolitan treatise, *On Perpetual Peace.* The third article claims that 'The rights of men, as citizens of the world, shall be limited to the conditions of universal hospitality' (Kant 1992: 137). Notably, Kant emphasizes that hospitality is not philanthropy, i.e. dependent on the goodwill of the host, but *a right* foreigners hold. Seyla Benhabib comments that for Kant the right of hospitality occupies the space 'between the right of humanity in our person and the rights that accrue to us insofar as we are members of specific republics' (Benhabib 2004: 27).

Hannah Arendt discusses the fate of the millions of people who became stateless after the two world wars (Arendt 1951). The result, according to Arendt, was that '[t]he Rights of Man, supposedly inalienable, proved to be unenforceable... whenever people appeared who were no longer citizens of any sovereign state' (Arendt 1951: 372). The emergence of millions of refugees without rights illustrated the weakness of the metaphysical justifications of human rights and human dignity as 'inalienable' or in 'the image of God'. How, then, can the rights of every individual be guaranteed and have practical implications, asks Arendt (Arendt 1951: 378f). How can human rights of refugees be justified and guaranteed today? Arendt's problem has become even more acute in an age of globalization.

Human dignity and the rights of refugees and immigrants

In the present ethical discussion, some influential views leave refugees and immigrants without structural protection. They will instead depend on the goodwill of the decision-makers in the receiving country. One finds this situation theoretically justified in the nationalist position expressed by the political philosophers Michael Walzer and David Miller. According to nationalism, the receiving countries have the right to decide admission criteria. Walzer argues that nations are like clubs and the citizens/club members have the right to distribute membership to others according to their will (Walzer 1983: 40). Walzer's argument supporting this claim is that the integrity of a community should be protected, but the side-effect is that immigrants and refugees have no right to claim asylum. Miller argues that liberal states are entitled to close their borders to immigrants to protect their culture and control their populations (Miller 2005: 199f). Refugees belong to a different category from citizens. Although they have basic rights and deserve protection, no particular state has an obligation to admit any specific refugees. Miller hopes that states will informally agree on a fair distribution of responsibilities (Miller 2005: 203).

If we assume that each human being has equal worth and as a consequence some basic rights to protection and subsistence, both Walzer's and Miller's positions are inadequate. Their positions may imply that nationalist interests outweigh the universal principle of human dignity. Furthermore, their reference to the protection of national culture is controversial in an age of globalization and multiculturalism (Scheffler 2007).

As we saw, Article 14 of the UDHR states the rights of refugees. This indicates that human rights are not equivalent to citizen rights. How, then, can the principle of human dignity justify the rights of refugees and immigrants? And what are the political implications in an age characterized by globalization?

Let me start by discussing a Kantian approach. Duties to immigrants and refugees can be justified by both the first and the second versions of Kant's Categorical Imperative. We, who are citizens of affluent and relatively secure nation-states, can imagine situations when the political or social situation changes and we would be forced to leave our countries due to repression or poverty. In this hypothetical situation, we want protection and/or asylum and, hence, it would be irrational for us to will a law that did not provide immigrants and refugees with protection and/or asylum. Thus, it is a duty to protect immigrants and refugees. Second, to respect the rights of immigrants and refugees is to treat them as ends in themselves (Kant 1983). Thus, there is a duty to respect the rights of immigrants and refugees.

Seyla Benhabib develops the Kantian approach in a discourse-ethical direction. She articulates a 'post-metaphysical' justification for rights based on mutual respect for personal autonomy and communicative freedom. This then forms the basis for a human right to membership. The right to membership is more general and fundamental than specific political or citizen's rights. She concludes:

> In this sense, the human right to membership is an aspect of the principle of right, i.e. of the recognition of the individual as a being who is entitled to moral respect. (Benhabib 2004: 141f)

Benhabib's idea of 'the human right to membership' needs to be anchored in institutions that go beyond the nation-state. Citizenship is no longer the ultimate ground for rights. The disaggregation of citizenship is, as she writes, 'an inescapable aspect of contemporary globalization' (Benhabib 2004: 173). Cosmopolitan norms justifying the rights of immigrants and refugees should be embedded, contextualized and incorporated through 'democratic iteration' of public deliberation.

In John Rawls' theory of justice, human dignity adopts a foundational role. Rawls' idea of a contract is based on the assumption that humans are free and rational and treat each other with mutual respect as equals. The aim of a just society is to realize basic human rights and equality. How then could the rights of immigrants and refugees be granted from a Rawlsian perspective? Rawls himself is bleak when it comes to questions of immigration and refugees. The problem of immigration will, according to Rawls in *The Law of Peoples* (1999), be eliminated in a realistic utopia, i.e. in a world where a law of peoples is established.

However, it is possible to reconstruct Rawls' theory in a cosmopolitan direction. This is important today not least because the weakening of the nation-state as a result of globalization (Beitz 1979; Pogge 1989; Tan 2004).

Immigration is, as we noted, clearly an aspect of globalization. Increased knowledge of the living conditions in wealthy societies provides a pull for people in poverty-stricken nations to try to get there. Boats crossing the Mediterranean overfull with Africans wanting to go to Europe, and Latin-Americans trying to cross the border between Mexico and the US, are illustrative examples.

One way to develop a theoretical grounding for the rights of immigrants and refugees is to imagine a global contract including all persons of the world deliberating on the appropriate principles of justice behind a 'veil of ignorance'. Would a global contract justify free immigration without borders? Not necessarily. As Joseph Carens argues, if unrestricted immigration would lead to chaos and the breakdown of social institutions this is an argument to restrict the freedom of immigration (Carens 1987: 259). Second, principles of global justice might be better realized through other means than open borders. Those who are desperately poor and risk their lives in trying to cross the Mediterranean or the border between Mexico and the US would perhaps benefit more from other redistributive measures (Brock 2009: 193). And the refugees of political suppression would possibly benefit more from a democratic development in their home countries than from a right to asylum in an alien one. On the other hand, these are not mutually exclusive alternatives. Even if the ultimate goals are the realization of social equality and democracy on a global level, more liberal immigration and asylum laws admitting entrance to a larger number of immigrants and refugees would most likely in the short run be a step towards justice. Today, poor countries receive the major portion of refugees. A global contract put demands on the wealthier nations to take greater responsibility.

To sum up: the argument has focused on how the dignity and rights of immigrants and refugees could be protected. Moral cosmopolitanism maintains that each human being, irrespective of nationality and citizenship, has the same basic rights. As Kant and Arendt already observed, there is an incongruity between human rights and citizen rights, and the UDHR implicitly presupposes global institutions above nation-states with the mandate to enforce human rights when necessary. Benhabib argues for a right to membership that goes beyond national borders. Global principles of justice would imply liberal and humanitarian refugee and immigration laws. Both points of departure require more powerful global institutions that can enforce the laws. Only then will the human rights proclaimed in Articles 13 and 14 of the UDHR correspond to enforceable political obligations.

References

Amnesty International. 2010. 'Refugees and Migrants', www.amnesty.org/en/refugees-and-migrants (accessed 3 January 2013)

Arendt, H. 1951. *The Origins of Totalitarianism*, New York: Harcourt

Beitz, C. 1979. *Political Theory and International Relations.* Princeton University Press

1999. 'International Liberalism and Distributive Justice: A Survey of Recent Thought', *World Politics* 51: 269

Benhabib, S. 2004. *The Rights of Others, Aliens, Residents and Citizens.* Cambridge University Press

Brock, G. 2009. *Global Justice: A Cosmopolitan Account.* Oxford University Press

Carens, J. 1987. 'Aliens and Citizens: The Case for Open Borders', *Review of Politics* 49: 251–73

2003. 'Who Should Get In? The Ethics of Immigration Admissions', *Ethics and International Affairs* 17: 95–110

Collste, G. 2002. *Is Human Life Special? Religious and Philosophical Perspectives on the Principle of Human Dignity.* Bern, New York: Peter Lang

Gibney, M. 2004. *Ethics and Politics of Asylum: Liberal Democracy Response to Refugees.* Cambridge University Press

Heuser, S. 2008. 'Is There a Right to Have Rights? The Case of the Right of Asylum', *Ethical Theory and Moral Practice* 11: 3–13

International Organization for Migration. 2010. 'Global Estimates and Trends', www.iom.int/jahia/Jahia/about-migration/facts-and-figures/lang/en (accessed 17 August 2010)

Kant, I. 1983. 'Grounding for the Metaphysics of Morals', in *Ethical Philosophy*, Indianapolis, IN: Hackett

1992. *Perpetual Peace: A Philosophical Essay.* Bristol: Thoemmes Press

Loescher, G. 1999. 'Refugees: A Global Human Rights AND Security Crisis', in T. Dunne and N. Wheeler (eds.). *Human Rights in Global Politics.* Cambridge University Press

Miller, D. 2005. 'Immigration: The Case for Limits', in A. Cohen and C. Wellman (eds.), *Contemporary Debates in Applied Ethics*, Malden, MA: Blackwell

Pogge, T. 1989. *Realizing Rawls*, Ithaca, NY: Cornell University Press

Rawls, J. 1999. *The Law of Peoples.* Cambridge, MA: Harvard University Press

Scheffler, S. 2007. 'Immigration and the Significance of Culture', *Philosophy and Public Affairs* 35: 93–125

Shacknove, A. E. 1984. 'Who Is a Refugee?', *Ethics* 95: 274–84

Stop Rape Now. 2010. 'Stop Rape Now: UN Action Against Sexual Violence in Conflict', www.stoprapenow.org (accessed 17 August 2010)

Tan, K. 2004. *Justice Without Borders.* Cambridge University Press

United Nations High Commissioner for Refugees, Division of Programme Support and Management. 2013. '2011 Global Trends', www.unhcr.org/4fd6f87f9.html (accessed 25 November 2013)

United Nations Population Division. 2010. 'International Migrant Stock: 2008 Revision', http://esa.un.org/migration (accessed 25 November 2013)

Walzer, M. 1983. *Spheres of Justice: A Defense of Pluralism and Equality.* New York: Basic Books

Part VI
Contexts of justice

51

Human dignity and social welfare

KLAUS STEIGLEDER

The normative concept of dignity

As a strictly normative concept, dignity was introduced into moral philosophy by Immanuel Kant. It signifies an absolute value. Ultimately, a person possessing dignity must not be an offset against somebody else. She may not be sacrificed for the sake of another person or other persons. Thus, her dignity constitutes a strict limit to the actions of others. Furthermore, mutual positive duties derive from the dignity of a person. Accordingly, dignity is the basis of claim rights, since the normative concept of dignity is explicated by determinate claim rights. At the same time, one can gather from the concept of dignity how rights are to be understood as a whole, which requirements any adequate theory of claim rights must fulfil, and what the mutual duties between the bearers of dignity and rights are. The following are the four most important principles which accrue from the normative concept of dignity.

First, the normative concept of dignity is not gradable. It is impossible for one being to possess more dignity than another. Rather, all beings that possess dignity possess the same dignity and the same fundamental rights. Thus, a fundamental normative equality exists between each bearer of dignity.

Second, the normative concept of dignity implies the existence of *absolute* rights. An absolute right is a right which under no circumstances can be superseded by another right. To be sure, most of the rights that originate from dignity are not absolute rights, but some are. Under certain conditions, a more important right of one person may supersede a less important right of another person, for example the right to life may supersede the right to property. But under no circumstances may one or more bearers of dignity supersede another bearer of dignity. Therefore, each bearer of dignity possesses an absolute right to life.[1]

Third, the rights grounded by dignity are not only negative rights, i.e. rights to forbearance, but also positive rights, i.e. rights to assistance.

Fourth, dignity is inalienable insofar as an agent may forfeit certain rights, but never his dignity and therefore never all of his rights. Thus, a bearer of

[1] For a more precise determination of this right, see Gewirth 1981. See also the critique by Levinson 1982 and the reply by Gewirth 1982.

dignity who has committed a crime thereby does not lose his dignity. It follows that the criminal must always be treated as a bearer of dignity and must not be punished in a way that is incompatible with his dignity.

A moral theory whose basis is the normative concept of dignity differs from two other families of moral theories, namely, utilitarianism and libertarianism. In contrast to utilitarianism, which is interested in cumulative results and the maximization of the aggregate utility, theories which are based on the normative concept of dignity have a distributive focus. Each bearer of dignity constitutes a strict limit to the actions of others. Within rights-based theories, theories based on dignity differ from libertarian theories by recognizing genuine and original positive rights or at least original positive duties, as in the case of Kant, whereas libertarian theories only recognize negative rights but no original positive duties.[2]

The content of the rights, positive rights and the necessity of organized institutions

In the following, I will presuppose with Gewirth that through his dignity every agent possesses claim rights to the necessary conditions of his self-fulfilling agency (Gewirth 1978).[3] These consist in his freedom and the further necessary conditions enabling him to act and to act successfully at all. For instance, in order to be able to act at all, an agent needs his life and his physical and psychological integrity. Gewirth calls the rights to these preconditions *basic rights* (Gewirth 1978: 212). In order to be able to act successfully at all the agent must on the one hand be able to preserve her level of purpose fulfilment. Among the necessary preconditions for this are not being lied to nor being stolen from. Gewirth called the rights to these preconditions 'non-subtractive rights' (Gewirth 1978: 233). On the other hand, the agent must be able to enhance his level of purpose fulfilment. Among the necessary preconditions for this are self-esteem and education. Gewirth called the rights to these preconditions 'additive rights' (Gewirth 1978: 241). These rights show a certain order or hierarchy. Thus, rights can possess a situationally variable pertinence and urgency. Given certain circumstances, rights can supersede other rights. Miller's right to life may supersede Smith's property rights if Smith possesses food in abundance and Miller is starving. Moreover, basic rights may take precedence over non-subtractive or additive rights. A small, short or temporary infringement of a right may be justified if a severe, longer or dispositional infringement of a right can only be averted securely or effectively by this breach. So, to use the terminology proposed by

[2] At this point I will not seek to explain why Kant did not recognize basic positive rights. For this, see Steigleder 2002. There (Ibid.: 254–59), I have also tried to show that Kant argues in favour of positive second-order rights which today we would call rights to social welfare.

[3] For an introduction to this concept see Chapter 24 by Beyleveld in this volume.

Judith Thomson, not every infringement of a right is a (morally forbidden) violation of a right (Thomson 1986: 40–2, 51–5).

The important point to note is that moral rights based on dignity are not unconnected. For, on the one hand, they serve a common purpose or rationale, namely, to secure the necessary conditions of an agent's ability to act, to act successfully at all and thus to have the possibility to lead a self-fulfilling life. On the other hand, the agents are connected by their rights. There exists a fundamental normative equality between them. They possess the same dignity and the same rights serving the same purpose or rationale. And so the right of one agent can situationally take priority over a right or rights of other agents. It follows that we must distinguish between the fundamental and the actual scope of rights, and be aware that the equal rights of agents adapt to different conditions and circumstances. They may therefore partially differ both in content and in urgency for different agents or groups of agents. So, for example, there are differences between the rights of persons with disabilities and the rights of persons without disabilities.

As already mentioned, the rights of agents are not only negative rights, i.e. rights to forbearance, but also positive rights, i.e. rights to assistance. This is a direct consequence of the agent's rights claims being based on the normative concept of dignity. But the obligation to assist somebody affects the rights of agents in a way the obligation to forbearance does not. Thus, regardless of any prior contractual or other obligations, there can only be a rights-based obligation to help or assist somebody, (1) if a right to a necessary condition of agency is concerned, (2) if the rights-holder is unable to help herself and (3) if the possible helper is able to help 'at no comparable cost' (Gewirth 1978: 218). If Smith's life is in danger and Miller can help Smith only by endangering his own life or by undergoing substantial risks to his long-term health, then Smith will have no right to Miller's help, and Miller will have no obligation to help Smith. But, if Miller can help without endangering important rights of his own or of others, Miller will be strictly obligated to help Smith by trying to save Smith's life. The criterion of 'no comparable cost' presupposes the hierarchy of rights and follows from the equality of rights between agents. From this equality, it also follows that a necessary condition for the duty to assistance is that the person to be assisted is not able to help herself.

But the criterion of 'no comparable cost' seems to give rise to an important objection against the existence of positive rights. Since so many persons live in dire straits, the fulfilment of their positive rights would lead to an overload of duties on the part of their potential helpers. This overload would severely impair the potential helpers in their ability to lead a life in accordance with their own rights, such that they would not be able to help at no comparable cost. Therefore, the objection concludes, they do not have the obligations to help and the persons living in dire straits do not have the positive rights grounding such obligations. Still, it is important to note that the objection pertains only to the *scope* of positive rights, not to their *existence*. If they cannot help themselves, each of the persons living in dire straits has positive rights to the assistance of others, whenever those others are able to help at no comparable costs. Nevertheless, and here lies the strength of the objection, the circumstances implying a duty to assistance might be limited to certain situations which manifest a singular acute need for help. Many or most circumstances of multiple or chronic needs for help may be excluded from this duty.

The putative weight of the objection derives from the misleading assumption that it is only relevant what an agent can do on her own. But it does not follow from the fact that each single agent may not be able to help at no comparable costs that agents could not do so when acting in concert. And even if we are not obliged to provide individual help we might nevertheless be under the strong obligation to contribute to the joint fulfilment of common duties.

There is a common duty to ensure the effective protection of the rights of every agent so that his or her rights are really respected. But the implementation of common duties is highly problematic, not least because there are severe problems of coordination. The solution to these coordination problems is the establishment and arrangement of organized institutions that provide for the fulfilment of the common duties of agents. It is the task of these institutions to make sure that the rights of agents are effectively protected and respected. Thus, each agent will fulfil her part of the common duties, if she supports those organized institutions. She is therefore strictly obliged to do so.

These considerations lead to the justification of the state, but they can be applied to the establishment of international regimes and of global institutions as well. Thus, dignity also justifies second-order rights, i.e. rights ensuring that one's first-order rights are effectively secured and protected. Duties correspond to these rights. These second-order duties augment the first-order duties and can modify first-order rights. The state must fulfil both the tasks of the minimal state with legal institutions, including the establishment and implementation of a police system and a criminal law, and the tasks of the supportive or welfare state. And the state must be organized as a democratic constitutional state.

The welfare state

The welfare state is confronted with a number of complexities. But, within the confines of this chapter, I have to restrict myself to a few remarks concerning these complexities.

First, the content of the common duties is not independent of the prevalent social structures within communities. The common duties arising in agrarian societies with subsistence farming, extended families and village communities differ from the duties that have to be performed in industrial societies characterized by an extreme division of labour, big cities and nuclear families. Whereas, in agricultural societies, the loss of employment may be compensated through farming on one's own land, the loss of employment under the conditions of extreme division of labour in industrialized countries tends to amount to the loss of the means of existence (Keyssar 1986). Thus, social arrangements must be made in order to guarantee that unemployment or disability do not lead to the loss of the means of existence.

Second, in general it is the task of the welfare state to assist its citizens actively in the protection of their elementary rights. This comprises the provision of the material requirements necessary to lead a decent life should the agent be incapable of providing for himself. It also comprises the provision of adequate healthcare. A further task of the welfare state is to make sure that its citizens possess the intellectual preconditions of leading an autonomous and self-fulfilling life. Therefore, it has to provide for adequate schooling and education.

Third, it is difficult indeed to determine what a 'decent' life and 'adequate' healthcare and schooling and education consist of. These questions cannot be dealt with independently of the capacities of the society in question. Thus, it is an important societal task to provide for the wealth of the society as a whole so that the tasks of the welfare state can be fulfilled as comprehensively as possible. A functioning, productive and sustainable economy is an important public good. The possibilities for agents to lead a self-fulfilling life, the range of assistance agents are able to offer at no comparable costs and the extent of protection and advancement of rights the government can foster are all depending on it. If it is true that a functioning, productive and sustainable economy must be a market economy, which indeed is in need of regulations but cannot be planned, then the government has no direct command over that on which its abilities and the abilities of the governed are highly dependent. Therefore, questions of social justice are, on the whole, not independent from questions of efficiency. Policies which are meant to correct injustices and to implement more just regulations may turn out to be counterproductive because they have deleterious effects on the economy. The question how to establish a just and sustainable welfare state is therefore a most complicated matter. The answers to these normative questions are highly dependent on disputed, unclear or unknown factual questions, so that there probably are no ideal solutions and no single correct answer. This is one of the reasons the state must be constitutionally democratic and allow for democratic competition and decision-making processes to ensure the balance between competing convictions and possible solutions.

Fourth, the assistance of the welfare state pertains only to those who cannot help themselves. As the extent of the welfare measures is dependent on the capacities of the state and its citizens, the help must be offered according to the urgency of needs, so that the more pressing needs are given priority over the less pressing needs. One of the aims of the welfare measures must be to end dependence on and the need for assistance and to restore or enable autonomy as far as possible. This aim is required by the dignity of the beneficiaries of the help.

And, fifth, the welfare state has the task not only to provide help when help is needed, but also to assure its citizens that certain existential risks are covered by society. An important consequence of this is the elimination of fear, which may contribute to the citizens' ability to act with confidence. But, as with any insurance, such societal guarantees are confronted with moral hazard problems such as a lack of precaution and increased risk-taking on the part of the individual. There is the well-known problem that the benefits of the welfare state will influence and distort the incentives of agents and will create opportunities for misuse. On the one hand, it is important to limit the distortions of incentives and the possibilities of misuse in order to protect the welfare state. On the other hand, it is important to make sure that those countermeasures do not deprive those in need of the necessary assistance. In order to avoid this, probably some misuse has to be tolerated.

The preceding remarks are not meant as an unqualified justification of the existing forms of the welfare state in industrialized countries which are confronted with the problems of financing welfare benefits in the face of soaring healthcare costs and their aging populations. Instead, they try to provide criteria for the assessment of existing states and welfare states. For the latter, it will probably be the case that, to different degrees, they both withhold normatively required benefits and provide benefits which are not justifiable. With regard to the pressing financial shortages, the task of setting the right priorities is most pertinent. In this context, probably one of the most pressing tasks is to distinguish between those forms of healthcare the inhabitants of a country have a right to and those to which they don't have a right. The justification of general criteria does not render the meticulous and patient study of complex normative questions unnecessary. It can only supply some of the necessary normative instruments for conducting those studies.

References

Gewirth, A. 1978. *Reason and Morality*: University of Chicago Press

1981. 'Are There Any Absolute Rights?', *Philosophical Quarterly* 31: 1–16

1982. 'There Are Absolute Rights', *Philosophical Quarterly* 32: 348–53

Keyssar, A. 1986. *Out of Work: The First Century of Unemployment in Massachusetts*. Cambridge University Press

Levinson, J. 1982. 'Gewirth on Absolute Rights', *Philosophical Quarterly* 32: 73–5

Steigleder, K. 2002. *Kants Moralphilosophie: Die Selbstbezüglichkeit reiner praktischer Vernunft*. Stuttgart: Metzler Verlag

Thomson, J. J. 1986. *Rights, Restitution, and Risk: Essays in Moral Theory*. Cambridge, MA: Harvard University Press

52

Dignity and global justice

THOMAS POGGE

Dignity is not an independently existing thing, but an attribute – of human beings, for example. It is essential to our notion of dignity that it has two distinct but related meanings. Using one meaning, we say that each human being has an inherent dignity, which is inalienable and equal for all. Using the other meaning, we say that the dignity of human beings is precarious and stands in need of social protection.

We find both meanings used side by side in the Universal Declaration of Human Rights (UDHR). In the first three occurrences of the word, it is used in its first sense:

> recognition of the inherent dignity and of the equal and inalienable rights of all members of the human family is the foundation of freedom, justice and peace in the world (UDHR, Preamble, paragraph 1)
>
> the peoples of the United Nations have in the Charter reaffirmed their faith in fundamental human rights, in the dignity and worth of the human person and in the equal rights of men and women (UDHR, Preamble, paragraph 5)
>
> [a]ll human beings are born free and equal in dignity and rights (UDHR, Article 1)

In the next occurrence, 'dignity' is used in its other sense:

> Everyone, as a member of society, has the right to social security and is entitled to realization, through national effort and international cooperation and in accordance with the organization and resources of each State, of the economic, social and cultural rights indispensable for his dignity and the free development of his personality. (UDHR, Article 22)

To call these rights indispensable for dignity is to say that any person lacking in these rights also falls short in dignity. Article 22 thus suggests that dignity is both alienable and possibly unequal: those who have dignity can lose its indispensable preconditions and therefore dignity itself – and will then not be 'equal in dignity' with those who still have it.

One can clarify the link between the two senses of 'dignity' by examining how the UDHR treats the closely related notion of rights or human rights. Article 22 suggests that every human being has certain rights, but also that these rights stand in need of realization. A group of frightened children, caught in the midst of a terrible bombing campaign, do not enjoy their human 'right to life, liberty and security of person' (UDHR, Article 3), and yet they still have this right in the sense that they ought to enjoy it. Here, we might say that the realization of a human right (globally, or within some jurisdiction) involves the achievement of secure access to its object (for all human beings, or for those within this jurisdiction). To call X a human right is to say that secure access to X must be established and maintained for human beings – which imperative persists even, and especially, when the right is not realized.

Calling X a human right also implies that it is *for the sake of the human beings having this right* that secure access to its object ought to be maintained. Any responsibilities or duties we may have in regard to the realization of a human right are duties owed to those who still lack secure access to its object. Thus, those who violate human rights are wronging those whose rights they are violating – rather than merely disobeying God, for example, or disturbing the harmonious order of the cosmos.

Tying these thoughts together, to say that every human being has dignity in the first sense is to say (a) that she or he has the potential for dignity in the second sense and (b) that the realization of this potential – a life with dignity – is of great moral importance. A human being can lead such a life only if she or he has secure access to certain essentials, that is, only if her or his human rights are fulfilled. It is therefore of great moral importance to ensure such fulfilment. When a human right is fulfilled for all, then we may say that it is fully realized (worldwide, or within some jurisdiction).

There are three dimensions in which a human being may fall short of a life with dignity. The first involves greatly inferior social standing and excessive subordination to others. Many people live under such conditions of indignity: being ordered about, ridiculed, humiliated, slapped in the face, terrified, not in control of their dress or appearance (naked in front of strangers) and perhaps adapting to such conditions with servility, flattery or self-abnegation. US treatment of captives at Abu Ghraib provides a comprehensive range of examples of how people can be stripped of their dignity. Similar fates are suffered, less dramatically, by much larger numbers of people worldwide: by domestic servants, factory workers and wives in many countries, by refugees and prisoners, by people trafficked for prostitution or labour, and also by patients in hospitals and nursing homes, enlisted soldiers, and pupils unpopular with their peers.

The second dimension of (in)dignity involves care of one's physical self. This dimension is related to the first in that it is humiliating to appear in public clothed in rags, smelling of urine or covered with skin lesions or eczema. But these dimensions are separable nonetheless. Even when a person has little or no contact with others, she may take care of herself through proper personal hygiene, a healthy diet and regular physical exercise – or she may be unable or unwilling to do so and then become a fit object for pity or disgust for herself and for others.

The third dimension of (in)dignity involves a person's inner or mental life. Here, dignity is especially closely associated with self-control. It is undignified to be overwhelmed by low emotions and desires such as envy, greed, hunger, lust, anger or pride. It is undignified to lack cognitive or executive powers: to be highly forgetful, for instance, or unable to pursue mildly complex tasks. And it is undignified to be held back by laziness or weakness of the will.

There are in principle two ways in which human dignity can be protected or maintained in these three dimensions. One involves a change in human psychology such that what was perceived or experienced as indignity comes to be seen as consistent with the full dignity of human beings. Society may, for instance, be or become fully accepting of people with speech impediments, of ethnic minorities, of women, or of people with an artificial anus. This path to dignity is not always workable for either of two reasons. In some cases, psychological reactions can at best be mitigated. Thus, it may be impossible to wholly eliminate feelings of disgust in response to certain skin diseases or incontinence problems. In other cases, such a psychological adjustment of how we conceive human dignity would be morally unacceptable. Thus, even if torture could be thoroughly professionalized – administered perhaps through machines remotely operated by emotionally uninvolved technicians focused on the extraction of information – we should still have to judge it a grievous affront to the dignity of the person screaming in pain. And even if there were wide cultural acceptance of conduct driven by strong emotions of greed or lust (as has indeed existed in some societies), we should still want to maintain our judgment that this is conduct to be left behind.

These empirical and moral limits of cultural adjustment indicate our social task: to structure human life, insofar as reasonably possible, so that all human beings can live in dignity. The three dimensions of indignity suggest the indispensable presuppositions to be socially secured. First, human beings must have a protected standing within their social world that allows them to avoid excessive dependency on others and to defend themselves against humiliation and abuse. The human rights specified in Articles 3–21 of the UDHR are especially relevant to protecting this component of human dignity. Second, human beings must have the education, income and social services they need to take proper care of their bodies through adequate nutrition, clothing, shelter, sanitation, clean water, physical exercise, rest and medical care. This component of human dignity is protected especially in Articles 22–27. Finally, human beings should also have access to the ennobling achievements of humanity: to literature and music, sports and science, and to the exploration of other species and our natural environment. Here, again, appropriate education is crucial, as is access to museums, libraries, academic institutions, theatres, movies and other cultural facilities and community activities. It is through the encounter of others and their achievements that human beings reach their full potential.

Dignity is different from those many things and attributes that are valuable insofar as they are valued. Such conferral of value presupposes a certain value in the conferrer. One person's appreciation may confer value on a musical performance even while another's lust confers no value on his encounter with a prostitute. The human capacity to confer value depends on our potential for dignity. Respect for this potential requires respect for dignity – one's own and that of others. By depriving someone of dignity, one is then demeaning not merely something valuable but a precondition of value.

This complexity can be integrated into a conception of morality as aiming to maximize value by protecting human capacities to confer value and human opportunities to do so. Such a consequentialist conception might instruct us to sacrifice the dignity of some in order to enhance the capacities or opportunities of others. Typically, however, those who give a central place to dignity in their moral thinking resist such trade-offs. They deny that one may sacrifice the dignity of some for the sake of multiplying valuable activities, or even protecting the dignity, of many others. This is not tantamount to the assertion that human dignity must never be sacrificed, no matter what. It does affirm, though, that the value of dignity transcends the value it confers on human activities and that the non-violation of dignity is of greater moral importance than its promotion.

One need not take sides on this dispute to conclude that current global institutional arrangements constitute a massive and wholly unjustifiable violation of human dignity. Shaped in negotiations among the world's most affluent and powerful agents, these arrangements maintain and aggravate vast social and economic inequalities that force half of humankind to subsist in conditions of severe deprivation, as is dramatically documented in the latest statistics regarding social and economic human rights. Among 7.1 billion human beings, 868 million are chronically undernourished, 884 million lack access to safe water, 2.5 billion lack access to basic sanitation, 2 billion lack access to essential drugs, over 1 billion lack adequate shelter, and 1.6 billion lack electricity; 775 million adults are illiterate and 215 million children are child labourers. Roughly one-third of all human deaths, 18 million annually, are due to such poverty-related deprivations, easily preventable through better nutrition, safe drinking water, cheap re-hydration packs, vaccines, antibiotics and other medicines (Pogge 2010a: 11–12). Most human beings do not have 'a standard of living adequate for the health and well-being of oneself and of one's family, including food, clothing, housing, medical care and necessary social services' (UDHR, Article 25).

We see that this ongoing catastrophe is avoidable from a single figure: the poorer half of humanity has been reduced below 3 per cent of global household income. This progressive marginalization of the poor is long-standing and ongoing. Between 1988 and 2005, the richest one-twentieth of humanity has raised its share of global household income from 42.9 to 46.4 per cent, to well over nine times the global average income. The bottom half (ten times as many people) saw its share decline from 3.5 to 2.9 per cent or 1/17 of the global average income. Losses were greatest in the bottom quarter, whose share declined by one-third: from 1.16 to 0.77 per cent or 1/32 of the global average income. The eradication of all severe poverty would require a shift of no more than 1.75 per cent of global household income – half of what the richest twentieth gained in recent years.

In conjunction with such vast inequalities, extremely low incomes (in the region of US$10–30 per person per month) also undermine the civil and political human rights of those in the poorer half. To meet their most basic needs, many feel obliged to commit themselves or their children into various forms of slavery or debt bondage, into beggary or into jobs of extreme dependency, exploitation or servility. And, in most cases, the people of a 'less developed' country are politically disempowered by an oppressive and corrupt 'elite' that ignores their needs, imposes huge national debts upon them, and sells their natural resources to foreigners in exchange for the arms it needs to stay in power.

The world's affluent mostly manage to remain ignorant of the magnitude of global poverty: of the scandalous contrast between the enormous death toll and humiliation it produces and the minuscule shift in global income needed for its eradication. Those who understand the true proportions admit that they should be doing more, but most feel only slight unease in regard to their perceived moral imperfection. Few understand that the massive poverty the affluent fail to alleviate is poverty they cause and aggravate through institutional design decisions in which they prioritize their own comparatively trivial interests over the most basic needs of the majority of humankind.

The terms of the WTO Agreement reflect the pressure powerful firms in the affluent countries exert towards continued and asymmetrical protections of their markets through tariffs, anti-dumping duties, export credits and huge subsidies to domestic producers. Such protectionism greatly impairs export opportunities for the poorest countries and regions. If the WTO proscribed protectionist barriers against imports from poor countries, their populations would benefit greatly: export revenues would be higher by hundreds of billions of dollars each year, hundreds of millions would escape unemployment, and wage levels would rise substantially (Pogge 2010b: 183–4).

Powerful firms have also successfully insisted that their intellectual property rights – ever-expanding in scope and duration – must be vigorously enforced in the poor countries. Music and software, production processes, words, seeds, biological species and medicines – for all these, and more, rents must be paid to the corporations of the rich countries in exchange for (still multiply restricted) access to their markets. Millions would be saved from diseases and death if generic producers could freely manufacture and market life-saving drugs in the poor countries (Pogge 2010a: 20–1).

While the WTO requires all member states to legislate strong intellectual property protections, its rules do not constrain working conditions or labour rights and thereby engender a race to the bottom in which poor countries, to attract investment, compete by offering workers that are even more exploitable and mistreatable than those elsewhere. Hundreds of millions bear the consequences in the form of inhuman working conditions: incredibly long periods without breaks or vacations, assaulted by dust, dirt, noise, heat and pollution, and terrified by supervisors who can fine, punish, harass or fire them on a whim.

To be sure, the ruling elites of poor countries – together – could better protect their populations. They predictably fail to do this because they have more to gain from serving the interests of rich foreign firms and governments. Most have little need for domestic popularity, relying instead on an important international convention according to which rulers – merely because they exercise effective power in a country and regardless of how they acquired or exercise such power – are entitled to confer legally valid property rights over the country's resources and to dispose of the proceeds of such sales, to borrow in the country's name and thereby to impose debt service obligations upon it, to sign treaties on the country's behalf and thus to bind its present and future population, and to use state revenues to buy the means of internal repression. Such recognition accords international resource, borrowing, treaty and arms privileges to many governments unworthy of this title. These privileges are impoverishing, because their exercise often dispossesses a country's people who are excluded from political participation as well as from the benefits of their government's borrowing or resource sales. These privileges are oppressive because they give oppressors access to the funds they need to keep themselves in power even against near-universal popular opposition. And these privileges are disruptive because they provide strong incentives towards the undemocratic acquisition and exercise of political power, resulting in frequent coups and (civil) wars in the developing world.

Humanity's technological-economic capacities now easily suffice for the avoidance of all severe poverty. But global institutional arrangements keep half of humanity in continuous anxiety: oppressed and humiliated, unable to take proper care of themselves and their families, and constantly preoccupied with making ends meet. These global rules do not arise spontaneously; they are carefully designed in protracted negotiations among powerful governments, acting with the approval of their citizens, and those in a position to lobby such governments. These privileged agents do not hate the poor and wish them no harm; they merely act rationally, in a competitive game, to enhance their own power and affluence. But they knowingly deny all human beings our fundamental right 'to and social and international order in which the rights and freedoms set forth in this Declaration can be fully realized' (UDHR, Article 28). Such conduct constitutes a double denial of dignity. It denies the poor the preconditions of a life in dignity by depriving them of secure access to the objects of their human rights. And it denies that the poor have moral standing, that their unfulfilled human rights furnish reasons that must be given their due weight in the design of global institutional arrangements.

References

Pogge, T. 2010a. *Politics as Usual: What Lies Behind the Pro-Poor Rhetoric.* Cambridge: Polity Press

2010b. 'Responses to Critics', in A. Jaggar (ed.), *Pogge and His Critics.* Cambridge: Polity Press, 175–250

53

Human dignity and people with disabilities

SIGRID GRAUMANN

Concepts of human dignity gain special significance if their implications for persons with disabilities are considered. Disability activists and advocates speak about violation of the human dignity of people with disabilities with regard to involuntary institutionalization, medical treatment without consent, exclusion from education, work and social life, lack of assistance and care, risk of poverty, absence of respect for privacy, home and family, as well as the experience of disregard, disrespect and humiliation. Particularly, in the field of biomedicine and bioethics, disabled persons feel their dignity is violated due to selective abortion and end-of-life decisions based on an understanding of disability as 'wrongful life'. They identify the values and perspectives of scientists, physicians and ethicists holding such views as those of well-educated, middle-class members of society who 'prize intellect, rationality, and the goal of human health' (Ash 2001: 293). This corresponds to a negative assessment of the quality of life of people with disabilities, which in turn promotes degrading or insulting behaviour towards them (Hubbard 1997).

Human dignity is understood here not as an individual attribute or a special right but as the founding moral principle of an adequate human rights framework that is truly inclusive and universal and hence recognizes the particular needs and living conditions of people with diverse impairments. What follows is that, by stating that 'someone has dignity', what is expressed is that she or he has to be recognized as a bearer of human rights. And saying 'her dignity has been violated' indicates a systematic disregard of human rights.

Disability activists and advocates have recently been quite successful in implementing their views even in international law: in December 2006, the new Convention on the Rights of Persons with Disabilities ('the Convention') was adopted by the United Nations, that since then has been ratified by many states and has thus become part of their legal systems. In the following, I will first elaborate the concept of human dignity in the Convention, and subsequently defend it from a contemporary Kantian point of view (for example, O'Neill 1996; Wood 1999; Korsgaard 2000; Hill 2002).

Human dignity and human rights in the Convention

The Convention refers to human dignity in its very first paragraph:

> The purpose of the present Convention is to promote, protect and ensure the full and equal enjoyment of all human rights and fundamental freedoms by all persons with disabilities, and to promote respect for their inherent dignity.

With this wording, the Convention anticipates that respect for the dignity of disabled people cannot be taken for granted and therefore emphasizes the principle of inclusion in the protections defined by human rights. It is explicitly stated that *all* persons with disabilities, regardless of their individual impairment, shall be included.

Furthermore, the formulation states that people with disabilities are equals in dignity, and therefore should be treated with equal respect. In this way, the Convention takes a major step from the traditional policy of charity and welfare for disabled persons towards a new policy based on rights. The concepts of charity and welfare imply a paternalistic attitude towards disabled persons: they are connected with the idea of altruistic action and voluntary solidarity, where claim rights are not applicable and disabled people are rather expected to show gratitude for any potential aid. From a human rights perspective, alternatively, disabled persons are seen as subjects with equal rights and responsibilities, who should be given control over their own lives; heteronomy and paternalism are considered as violating human dignity and human rights (Office of the High Commissioner for Human Rights/United Nations 2002).

The Convention follows in the footsteps of other conventions protecting groups in especially vulnerable situations. It does not formulate special rights; it rather takes general human rights, and specifies and defines them in relation to the special circumstances of disabled persons. The consequences are revolutionary, not only for disability politics but also for our conception of human rights. This is further reflected in changes to and the broadening of the terminology: the Convention conspicuously forgoes a final definition of disability. It refers to the 'social model', where a disability is understood as the interaction between the person's impairment and their environment. In doing so, the Convention questions deficit-orientated definitions, where disability, according to the 'medical model', is traced back to individual functional impairments. It is also important that discrimination is understood not only in a traditional way as the arbitrary denial of equal rights, but also as a lack of support and the absence of social recognition. When formulating separate rights, the Convention is very much in agreement with other human rights treaties. However, specifications within the Convention take into account the particular hazards that disabled persons are exposed to. For example, civil liberties, such as the right to freedom and security, are defined by forbidding compulsory confinement due to disability. Moreover, the convention links civil rights to the right to access social services that actually enable disabled persons to exercise their rights. Economic, social and cultural rights have special comprehensive specifications and definitions for disabled people. They guarantee that disabled persons, including those in need of extra support, have a self-determined and independent life with full and equal inclusion in all areas of society. This includes, for example, the right to have a family of one's own even when this includes parental assistance, the right to choose how and where and with whom one wants to live, as well as the right to an accessible working environment and full employment rights. In accordance with civil liberties, economic, social and cultural rights are linked to the comprehensive prohibition of patronizing tutelage (Kayess and French 2008; Graumann 2011: 80–134).

Taking all these aspects into consideration, the concepts of human dignity and human rights have been extensively developed (Mégret 2008). In particular, on the one hand, all people with disabilities are explicitly included, and on the other hand demands for respect and for care have been interlinked throughout the whole catalogue of human rights.

The principle of inclusion in the protections defined by human rights

The principle of inclusion in the protections specified in the human rights framework means in concrete terms that also newborn babies with disabilities and people with profound cognitive or intellectual impairments should be considered as moral and legal subjects. In the debate on human dignity, however, such a kind of universality is repeatedly questioned. Some argue that this kind of human dignity is based on controversial theological or metaphysical assumptions which cannot be generally accepted in a pluralistic society and an ideologically neutral state. Others criticize an inflationary and imprecise use of 'human dignity' that leads to a trivialization of the concept of human rights. Usually, such positions explicitly restrict dignity to human persons with the capacities required for autonomous moral agency (Griffin 2008: 151–2). However, if human dignity would be rooted in the exercise of capacities, then dignity could be ascribed or withdrawn by others (cf. Kopelman and Moskop 1984; Kittay and Carlson 2010).

In such debates, disability activists and advocates are among those who defend human dignity as a truly inclusive concept. They understand human dignity as based on the assumption that all human beings deserve equal respect irrespective of achievement, rank or social standing (Wood 1999: 111–55). This notion of human dignity must be distinguished from dignity as the particular estimation of a person on the basis of office or achievement. In the latter sense, 'dignity' distinguishes a particular person and may for example serve as a justification for privileges. Such privileges are usually accessible by persons with a high social status, not by those with any sort of impairment. Therefore, it is obviously not an attractive concept of dignity for people with disabilities.

In the context of disability, 'dignity' is also sometimes used in the sense of the subjective value attached to a person's life. According to this position, severe impairments, constant suffering and loss of independence lead to the judgment that a person's life is no longer worth living (cf. Kuhse and Singer 1985; McMahan 1996). However, such judgments are always highly subjective and biased by prejudices about what it means to live a life with disability. Thus, from the point of view of disability activists and advocates they are dangerous for people with disabilities (cf. Kittay 2005).

In Kantian ethics, respect for human dignity refers to the reciprocal obligation to treat other human beings 'always as an end and never as a means only' (Kant 1974: 61). In Kant, human dignity is founded in the capacity of autonomy and thus to the capacity for moral agency. However, disability activists and advocates usually share the view that autonomy need not be realized at all times in a person's life. According to such positions, it is the *potential* for autonomy that characterizes human beings as human beings and awards their dignity. This interpretation of the Kantian concept of human dignity ensures that people with disabilities are not at risk of being deprived of their dignity and rights due to judgments about their capacities and qualities by third parties.

However, in bioethical debates it is highly contested if belonging to the human species as such is of any moral significance. Without discussing this controversy in detail, in the following I will present three arguments in favour of a truly inclusive concept of human dignity and the protections defined by human rights that don't refer to a questionable normative concept of the human species (Graumann 2011: 258–66):

(1) Considering the living conditions of people with disabilities, it is obvious that the concept of autonomy and its use in contemporary liberal moral and political philosophy is an unrealistic ideal (Nussbaum 2006: 25f). If fully developed autonomy were required for ascribing human dignity, babies and little children as well as many persons of old age or with illnesses or disabilities would lack the protections provided by human dignity and human rights. A realistic understanding instead considers autonomy as a developmental concept realized to different degrees in certain periods of life. On this understanding, not the developed capacity of autonomy of a particular person, but the potential for autonomy of the human being – regardless of the degree of individual development of this capacity – should be considered as the basis of human dignity.

(2) One could answer that at least a certain potential for autonomy should be required for the concept of human dignity to make any sense. James Griffin, for example, states that it should not be applied to 'persons deep in dementia' (Griffin 2008: 151). The same would be true, according to Griffin's view, for babies born with a very limited life expectancy or adults with profound intellectual or cognitive impairments. This would imply that a line has to be drawn between individuals with sufficient and those with insufficient capacity for autonomy. However, any evaluation of the particular potentiality for autonomy of an individual person would unavoidably be loaded

with uncertainty and arbitrariness. Moreover, it would entail that a certain group has to be authorized to judge the (potential) degree of autonomy an individual has achieved or will achieve. Such a hierarchical division of authorized persons and others would be inconsistent with the principle of equal respect articulated in the human rights framework. That should be reason enough, I think, for us to generally avoid drawing such a line.

(3) Every needy human being depends on being included in a community where others care for her well-being regardless of her individual skills and features. All human persons take part in such a 'primary moral community' long before they are able to understand themselves as autonomous agents. And some may not even come to understand themselves as such if others were not to provide the support and care they needed without being asked (MacIntyre 1999: 82f). Such positions are based on an insight into the fundamental dependency on others as part of human life, and thus consider the primary moral community as unquestionable. Rather similar to this position is Hannah Arendt's notion of the right to have rights, which likewise can be understood as a prior claim of membership (Arendt 1949; Benhabib 2004: 49f). Such arguments might not count as strictly logical deductions for the duty to include all persons with disabilities in the protections defined by human dignity and human rights; nevertheless, they show, I think, that a truly inclusive concept of human dignity is convincing. If we pose the question in what kind of society we would like to live, the answer would be, I think, that we don't want to live in a society which excludes particular persons according to the decision of third parties. And if we want to avoid that particular persons, for instance because they have an impairment, could be excluded, the inclusive primary moral community should be taken for granted.

The principle of universal respect for human rights

The inclusive notion of human dignity and the developmental concept of autonomy are in line with further developments of the concept of human rights. From the perspective of disabled persons with a high need for assistance and care in their daily life, it is obvious that a traditional concept of human rights, primarily understood in terms of negative rights, would contradict the idea of equality. Many disabled persons are only able to exercise their human rights and fundamental freedoms on an equal basis with others if access to proper support, assistance and care is ensured. This means that demands for respect and care have to be equally included in an adequate concept of human dignity and human rights (Graumann 2011: 270–91).

Some contemporary interpretations of the Kantian concept of human dignity also support this view. According to these positions, Kant's moral imperative to treat others as ends in themselves entails not only that we should not harm, exploit or patronize others, but also that we are morally obligated to actively contribute to their well-being (Korsgaard 2000: 124–8; Hill 2002: 106–24). Correspondingly, the Convention includes not only negative rights ruling out interventions in a person's life by the state or other third parties, but also the universally binding obligation to recognize positive rights to receive the social services required to enable disabled people to participate fully in society, if necessary with social support. Furthermore, respect for diversity, equal rights and opportunities means not only the absence of environmental obstacles but also the active promotion of the societal recognition of disabled persons.

However, positive rights correspond to positive duties. We can force others to respect our negative rights – to abstain from taking our life, injuring us, offending us, etc. Assuming the duty to help us, to support us or to care for us, however, requires much more personal energy and action. This is why positive duties are related to a certain degree of voluntariness: if a person were forced to assume positive duties, her own negative rights might be violated. But how should we conceptualize universally binding, positive rights if others can't be forced to help, support and care for us?

The rights of persons with disabilities to support, assistance and care and the corresponding duties of beneficence and solidarity can be justified by reference to Kant's principle of human dignity and an extended interpretation of his doctrine of justice, which, on the one hand, includes comprehensive claims for solidarity and, on the other, retains a consistent refusal of any form of paternalism. As mentioned above, Kant's concept of human dignity includes the moral obligation to promote the well-being of others. With her twofold distinction of charitable duties as complete or incomplete duties and as general or specific duties, Onora O'Neill elaborates what this means in terms of legal obligations which can be externally enforced (O'Neill 1996: 122f). As moral duties all duties of beneficence are categorically binding. However, whether and to what extent we can force these on others is conditional. Complete duties of beneficence such as emergency aid can be externally enforced. Incomplete duties of charity, however – such as helping the poor – leave space for interpretation regarding when, in favour of whom and to what extent they are exercised. Specific duties of charity are duties of beneficence in specific relationships of care. We consider them as morally and legally binding from within existing personal and professional relationships, but individuals are granted space to choose freely whether to establish and maintain such relationships. Furthermore, there are also certain limits of enforcing care in personal and professional relationships; we cannot, for instance, enforce attitudes of love and passion which are necessary for good care. If we consider the fact that many persons (not only those with impairments) depend on the help, support and care provided by others on the one hand, and the insight that charitable duties can or should only be externally enforced under particular conditions on the other, we can define the public obligations concerning the Convention more precisely. The Convention reveals the necessity to establish social and institutional conditions that are able to support personal caring relations, as well as to replace them by professional care if needed. The corresponding positive duties are not only individual obligations of beneficence but also collective duties of solidarity, for which the state is responsible on behalf of its citizens. These are universally binding because they are necessary to guarantee equal rights for all citizens and because they are not overly demanding with regard to individual persons; thus they do not infringe upon their negative liberty rights. This means that the adequate protection of human rights, particularly of weaker and more vulnerable persons, entails on the one hand the obligation to support care in familial and private relationships, and on the other hand the guarantee of good, professional assistance and care through social services. At the same time, paternalism has to be avoided.

To conclude, there are convincing arguments for the recognition of the rich concept of human dignity and how it is put forward by disability activists and advocates. Human dignity requires social conditions in which the protection, not only of negative rights but also of positive rights, is institutionally anchored. This means that help and care for weaker and dependent members of our societies should be guaranteed and a social climate which promotes a moral attitude of recognition of these fundamental rights and the individual and collective readiness to assume the corresponding positive duties has to be established. Furthermore, the social conditions that are necessary to realize a truly inclusive and universal concept of human dignity and human rights, while acknowledging the individual needs and situations of all persons with disabilities, have to be created.

References

Arendt, H. 1949. 'Es gibt nur ein einziges Menschenrecht', *Die Wandlung IV*. Heidelberg: Schneider, 754–70

Ash, A. 2001. 'Disability, Bioethics, and Human Rights', in G. L. Albrecht, K. D. Seelman, M. Bury (eds.). *Handbook of Disability Studies*. Thousand Oaks, CA: Sage Publications, 297–326

Benhabib, S. 2004. *The Rights of Others*. Cambridge University Press

Graumann, S. 2011. *Assistierte Freiheit: Von einer Behindertenpolitik der Wohltätigkeit zu einer Politik der Menschenrechte*. Frankfurt am Main: Campus

Griffin, J. 2008. *On Human Rights*. Oxford University Press

Hill, T. E. 2002. *Human Welfare and Moral Worth: Kantian Perspektives*. Oxford University Press

Hubbard, R. 1997. 'Abortion and Disability', in L. J. Davis (ed.). *The Disability Studies Reader*. New York: Routledge, 187–202

Kant, I. 1974. *Grundlegung zur Metaphysik der Sitten, in Werkausgabe*, vol. VII, ed. W. Weischedel. Frankfurt am Main: Suhrkamp, 9–102

Kayess, R., and French, P. 2008. 'Out of Darkness into Light? Introducing the Convention on the Rights of Persons with Disabilities', *Human Rights Law Review* 8: 1–34

Kittay, E. F. 2005. 'At the Margins of Moral Personhood', *Ethics* 116: 100–31

Kittay, E. F., and Carlson, L. (eds.). 2010. *Cognitive Disability and Its Challenge to Moral Philosophy.* Chichester: Wiley-Blackwell

Kopelman, L., and Moskop, J. C. (eds.). 1984. *Ethics and Mental Retardation.* Dordrecht, Boston: D. Riedel Publishing Company

Korsgaard, C. M. 2000. *Creating the Kingdom of Ends.* Cambridge University Press

Kuhse, H., and Singer, P. 1985. *Should the Baby Live? The Problem of Handicapped Infants.* Oxford University Press

MacIntyre, A. 1999. *Dependent Rational Animals: Why Human Beings Need the Virtues.* Chicago: Open Court

McMahan, J. 1996. 'Cognitive Disability, Misfortune and Justice', *Philosophy and Public Affairs* 35: 3–35

Mégret, F. 2008. 'The Disabilities Convention: Towards a Holistic Concept of Rights', *International Journal of Human Rights* 12(2): 261–77

Nussbaum, M. 2006. *Frontiers of Justice: Disability, Nationality, Species Membership.* Cambridge, MA: Harvard University Press

O'Neill, O. 1996. *Towards Justice and Virtue: A Constructive Account of Practical Reasoning.* Cambridge University Press

Office of the High Commissioner for Human Rights/United Nations. 2002. *Human Rights and Disability: The Current Use and Future Potential of United Nations Human Rights Instruments in the Context of Disability.* G. Quinn and T. Degener with A. Bruce, C. Burke and J. Castellino. New York/Geneva: United Nations

Wood, A. W. 1999. *Kant's Ethical Thought.* Cambridge University Press

54

Human dignity as a concept for the economy

ELIZABETH ANDERSON

Two roles of dignity

The Universal Declaration of Human Rights (UDHR) affirms three types of universal economic rights. One concerns secure *access to resources*: everyone has a right to property (Article 17), including intellectual property (Article 27), to a decent standard of living (Article 25), to social security in case of accident, illness, disability, unemployment, widowhood and old age (Articles 22 and 25) and free education (Article 26). A second set of rights concern *work*: everyone has a right to work, to join a labour union, to a free choice of occupation, a just wage, equal pay for equal work, decent conditions of work (Article 23), and to limited working hours and paid holidays (Article 24). A third set of economic rights *protect the vulnerable from specific injustices*: everyone has a right against slavery and servitude (Article 4) and against discrimination on the basis of their race, gender, or other social identities (Articles 2 and 23). These economic rights are supposed to be specially connected to the dignity of human beings. What conception of dignity is capable of supporting the UDHR's list of economic rights?

Any such conception must support the two roles played by dignity in the UDHR and in its implementing Covenants, the International Covenant on Civil and Political Rights (ICCPR) and the International Covenant on Economic, Social and Cultural Rights (ICESCR), which altogether comprise the International Bill of Human Rights (IBHR). First, at the start of these documents, dignity serves as a *foundation* for universal human rights in general. The UDHR only suggests this association in its Preamble (recognizing the 'inherent dignity' and 'equal and inalienable rights of all members of the human family') and Article 1 (declaring all human beings 'equal in dignity and rights'). It is explicit in the Preambles to the ICCPR and ICESCR: 'these rights derive from the inherent dignity of the human person'. Second, in later provisions of these documents, dignity figures in the *content* of specific human rights. Article 22 of the UDHR affirms that everyone has 'the economic, social and cultural rights indispensable for his dignity'. Article 23 affirms a right to a wage and other social protections sufficient for 'an existence worthy of human dignity' on the part of the worker and his family. Article 13 of the ICESCR declares that everyone has a right to an education that is 'directed to the full development of the human personality and the sense of its dignity'. This dual role of dignity – as the foundation of all human rights and as the content of some – calls for explication and justification.

Start with the foundational question. The concept of dignity refers to a kind of worth or value said to be inherent in human beings and a ground of rights. It is tempting to define a person's dignity simply as a person's being a bearer of rights. Joel Feinberg has expressed this thought as follows:

> [W]hat is called 'human dignity' may simply be the recognizable capacity to assert claims. To respect a person, then, or to think of him as possessed of human dignity simply is to think of him as a potential maker of claims. (Feinberg 1980: 151)

If dignity is simply a way of referring to the status of being a rights-bearer, then it cannot serve as a *foundation* from which all human rights can be derived. It could serve a foundational role only if it referred to whatever human features possess the sort of value that *grounds* everyone's status as a rights-bearer. I shall leave it to the authors of Part I of this volume to explore this issue.

Some philosophers argue that the characteristics that are supposed to ground this status of being a rights-bearer could generate a full and rich set of rights. For example, neo-Kantian approaches to human rights attempt to derive substantive rights from the features of rational agency – from what we must necessarily will, given that we are also animals who live on Earth (Herman 1993; Korsgaard 1996). Whatever the merits of this approach – and I have doubts about its ability to generate more than a minimal set of rights – it leaves behind the concept of dignity quickly, or appropriates the term 'dignity' to label a set of ideas about the requirements of practical reason that could get along fine without that term.

A genealogical approach to dignity

I suggest that, if we want to give the idea of dignity some real normative work in a theory of human rights, we take a genealogical approach: we can give distinctive content to the idea of dignity by considering what people originally meant by it and how current usage reflects those origins. This will facilitate reflection on whether and how it remains a compelling normative idea in modern life. Once we know what dignity demands, we can see whether those who live in societies governed by this ideal have favourable experiences of living dignified lives. Kant is a pivotal figure in the ethics of dignity. A genealogical approach to Kant suggests that his ethics of dignity is a universalized form of an ethics of honour (Anderson 2008). An honour ethic focuses on the entitlements, bearing, and regard owed to *dignitaries* – persons of high social status who occupy, or are deemed worthy to occupy, positions of command in a hierarchical society. Traditionally, these have been persons such as patriarchal heads of families, tribal and clan leaders, military officers, monarchs, aristocrats and feudal lords.

Honour or dignity denotes a superiority of status, recognition and esteem that those in command enjoy over those who are commanded (Anderson 2008: 136). Kant's moral revolution, prefigured by Rousseau (1762) was to universalize dignified standing to all human beings: to eliminate the lower ranks, and elevate all to the same entitlements as dignitaries enjoyed.

This was not a revolution in thought alone. Centuries of struggle have made it a revolution in practice. Politically, the upshot of recognizing that all are entitled to a share in command is democracy. In criminal law, European states committed to this universalizing moral vision took the entitlements granted to nobles in criminal procedure and punishment as the baseline for dignified treatment – for treatment as a dignitary or honourable person – and extended them to all (Whitman 2003). Jeremy Waldron (2009) argues that this logic generalizes across all practical domains in which the concept of dignity has figured in modern times: take as a model the entitlements and incidents of high social status, and secure for everyone whatever can be universalized on an equal basis within that model. Not just nobles, but all are entitled to 'a trial by their peers'. Every man in his home is 'a king in his castle'.

This genealogical approach to dignity must meet three challenges for it to be applicable in the economic realm. First, it must be able to account for the three types of economic rights in the UDHR. Second, it must be able to explain how dignity can serve as a foundation for rights, while also figuring in the content of certain specific rights. Third, it must answer the challenge of parochiality. It seems too culture-bound and contingent a basis for a universal system of rights to generalize from a conception of dignity and its incidents originally found in European aristocracy.

The key to addressing these challenges is to cut through the contingent expressions of dignity that are culture-bound to their general underlying normative concerns. Here, I stress three normative ideas traditionally associated with the dignity of those of high social status: authority, dignified bearing, and an entitlement to displays of respect from others. These ideas were sharpened by contrast with the normative ideas associated with those of low social status.

First, dignity involves commanding authority. To have dignity entails having the authority to command others to act or refrain from acting, and to hold them accountable for their conduct. It entails having a voice in decision-making, being entitled to speak for oneself and to demand reasons for complying with others' requests. Beings of lower rank have none of these attributes. Like animals, they might be bent to the will of others by goading or prodding. Or as servants, they may simply be ordered to do things. No reasons need be offered to get them to do what commanding authorities want them to do. Second, dignity involves dignified bearing or conduct. Dignified persons stand erect, hold their heads high, address demands to others with a confident sense of their own entitlements, and manifest pride in their appearance and conduct. Lowly persons bow and scrape, beg and wheedle, and humble themselves before their superiors. Third, dignified persons are the objects of others' respect. Others take their entitlements as normally conclusive reasons for action, address them with honourable titles, and manifest respect by obeying other norms of civility towards them. Lowly persons are treated with contempt.

It is not difficult to universalize the second and third aspects of dignity. Social norms can prescribe the same modes of dignified bearing and polite conduct for all. To universalize commanding authority, its scope must be restricted so that each person has an equivalent domain over which they can exercise it. This is the domain of universal individual *rights*. Each has the final say in matters concerning himself, may demand that others constrain their actions to respect those rights, and hold them accountable for failure to do so. By contrast, in an ideal-typical honour-based society, while dignitaries may have duties to their inferiors (*noblesse oblige*), such duties are not matched by corresponding rights on the part of inferiors to exact compliance from their superiors, or to hold their superiors accountable. The *dignity* of honourable social standing consists in such entitlements to exact compliance and hold people accountable.

This is the source of the idea that human dignity is the ground of rights in general. To have a dignified status is, in part, to be a rights-bearer, as Feinberg asserts above. One might object that such a conception of dignity as being a rights-bearer is empty in that it entails no particular rights. However, if dignity is inherent in individuals, then the moral status of being a rights-bearer is inalienable. This is incompatible with certain kinds of social status that are defined by the condition of *lacking* any rights – the slave, the outlaw, the exile, the pariah. At a minimum, then, the UDHR implies that such social statuses should be abolished. Hence, slavery must be prohibited (Article 4) and everyone recognized as a legal person (Article 6).

Dignity and economic rights

Turn now to the economic sphere. As noted above, Article 22 of the UDHR declares that everyone has 'the economic, social and cultural rights indispensable for his dignity'. This is the key to understanding the rest of the specific economic rights in the UDHR: rights to resources, rights concerning work, and protections against discrimination and servitude. Economic rights are instrumental to securing the three dimensions of dignity: being a bearer of effective rights, being able to conduct oneself in a dignified manner, and eliciting respect from others. They are, in part, responses to human social psychology. Clothing, food, shelter and the like are not merely means of subsistence. Particular types of possessions or the lack thereof mark their owners as elevated or demeaned in status. To be deprived of the right to own property at all, to have access only to food deemed within one's culture as fit for animals, to lack the privacy afforded by shelter and thus be reduced to defecating in public – such lacks mark a person as contemptible. They elicit shame and humiliation in the person suffering from them, and mockery and abuse from others. People also need resources to vindicate their other rights. Public authorities and private parties alike systematically ignore or violate the rights of the destitute, who cannot afford lawyers or other representatives to get their rights vindicated in court. This is why the level of resources guaranteed by Article 23 of the UDHR is not merely what people need to survive, but to enjoy 'an existence worthy of human dignity'. Since not everyone can attain this level of resources through work, individuals need the protections of social security in case of unemployment, disability, old age, illness and loss of a family's primary wage earner to ensure that they can maintain a dignified level of consumption (Article 25).

Work is a domain in which people are especially vulnerable to loss of dignity. In most cultures, unemployment (at least for those who are not independently wealthy) is not merely a threat to survival but a mark of shame. Hence, people need a right to work and effective access to work to be able to bear themselves with dignity and not be reduced to begging or living at the mercy of others. Since most occupations involve cooperation under the supervision of superiors, special rights are needed to ensure that workers are not treated in a contemptible manner like beasts of burden or mere tools, but are treated with respect and able to conduct themselves with the dignity that befits persons with 'reason and conscience' (Article 1). The right to join a labour union (Article 23) helps secure workers' voices over the terms and conditions of their work. The rights to enjoy safe and decent conditions of work (Article 23) and to have limited working hours (Article 24) mark their bearers as respectable human beings, not mere tools that may be used until they wear out.

Finally, the UDHR recognizes certain economic rights to protect the vulnerable against reduction to a despised, stigmatized, undignified status. Desperate people would find themselves unable to resist contracts into servitude if this were not prohibited (Article 4). Human societies tend to construct social inequalities along lines of social identity such as race, religion, ethnicity and gender, marking privileged identities as respectable and the others as contemptible. Rights against discrimination on the basis of such identities (Articles 2 and 23) are needed to prevent and dismantle such hierarchies.

Thus, the genealogical approach to dignity, once abstracted to its fundamental normative elements (normative authority to make demands on others, capacity for dignified bearing, eliciting respectful treatment from others) and universalized to all, can answer all three challenges posed to founding economic rights on the basis of dignity. First, specificity: the economic rights enumerated in the UDHR can be rationalized as necessary to enable people to vindicate their other rights, to live a dignified life and/or to elicit respectful treatment from others or deter degrading treatment. Second, parochiality: while no specific types of clothing, food and so forth are pan-culturally recognized as worthy of a dignified existence, within any society it is possible to identify a level of access to resources below which a person's ability to live in a fashion recognized as dignified is threatened. The universal right to a dignified level of resources makes room for cultural variation without tying itself to any single parochial standard. Third, dignity as both a foundation of rights in general and the content of specific rights: the most important normative idea tied to dignitaries is that they are rights-bearers; the assertion of universal dignity thus claims that whatever entitles dignitaries to such a status grounds an equal status for all and so grounds rights in general. At the same time, the economic rights *explicitly* tied to dignity in the UDHR are those connected to the second and third aspects of dignity – dignified bearing, and respectful treatment by others. Here, the specifically symbolic, expressive aspects of dignity are stressed: the importance of having command over enough resources, and enough self-command, to appear in public without shame and to elicit respectful treatment from others.

The upshot of this analysis is that the concept of dignity in the UDHR includes a plurality of normative concerns. Only so would it be able to play the rich and varied roles the UDHR makes it play in a theory of human rights. What unifies the concept of dignity is not a single normative idea, but rather a history of practice in which certain persons enjoyed a unified bundle of goods. What makes it relevant for the modern world is the possibility of extending access to that bundle of goods to all persons. What makes it normatively compelling is a set of facts: (1) that persons experience their lives as improved when they enjoy secure access to this bundle of goods; (2) that we have enough experience with forging dignitary practices to be confident that access to this bundle can be universalized; and (3) that no arguments for denying access to this bundle to subordinated groups on the basis of their supposed intrinsic inferiority survive critical scrutiny.

References

Anderson, E. 2008. 'Emotions in Kant's Later Moral Philosophy: Honor and the Phenomenology of Moral Value', in *Kant's Virtue Ethics*, ed. M. Betzler. New York, Berlin: Walter de Gruyter, 123–45

Feinberg, J. 1980. 'The Nature and Value of Rights', in *Rights, Justice and the Bounds of Liberty*. Princeton University Press

Herman, B. 1993. *The Practice of Moral Judgment*. Cambridge, MA: Harvard University Press

Korsgaard, C. M. 1996. *Creating the Kingdom of Ends*. Cambridge University Press

Rousseau, J.-J. 1762. *The Social Contract*, trans. G. D. H. Cole. Amherst, NY: Prometheus Books

Waldron, J. 2009. *Dignity, Rank and Rights*. Tanner Lectures on Human Values. Berkeley, CA: University of California Press

Whitman, J. Q. 2003. *Harsh Justice: Criminal Punishment and the Widening Divide Between America and Europe*. Oxford University Press

55

Human dignity and gender inequalities

ANNIKA THIEM

A particular challenge of considering human dignity and gender inequalities together lies in the fact that discussions about gender inequalities rarely make any reference to human dignity.[1] Another difficulty arises from the expansiveness and variegated nature of the category of 'gender inequalities'. As groups, women and gender minorities still face inequalities in many areas of daily life, but the institutional, social, material and psychological aspects of these inequalities differ greatly among various geographical, economic and cultural contexts. 'Gender' as a category of difference and a basis for unequal treatment cannot and should not be reduced to mean only women, but the debates, especially in the context of international human rights, have to date focused almost entirely on women's rights and women's empowerment, leaving gender minorities in the margins. Yet while human dignity and gender inequalities have seldom been discussed in connection with each other, the perspective of gender can offer a critical heuristic to examine how appeals to dignity might implicitly and inadvertently reinscribe norms of gender, race, class, ableness, sex and sexuality. With this critical perspective in place, dignity as a philosophical concept can be productive in a feminist context to foreground the relation among social respect, self-respect and agency as central to ongoing emancipatory struggles (cf. Cornell 2002). Laying claim to one's dignity, regardless of one's gender, can attain the force of a critical moral act, particularly in situations where individuals are socially, culturally or politically denied the freedom of enacting a moral vision of themselves and the world. Just as the full enactment and experience of one's own dignity requires social respect, social respect without self-respect remains a limited actualization of an individual's human dignity. To the extent that it is useful to approach gender inequalities as infringements on individuals' human dignity, abolishing inequalities requires social and

[1] See, for instance, Lorber 2010; Krook and Childs 2010. Exceptions are considerations of gender in discussions about biomedical ethics and violence against women, where human dignity plays an important theoretical role. However, these discussions tend to invoke dignity in the context of bodily and mental violations and integrity rather than in the context of a broader set of gender-based social, legal, political and cultural inequalities.

cultural changes alongside legal, political and economic advances. To circumscribe the relationship between human dignity and gender inequalities, this chapter will first consider key United Nations (UN) documents to trace the conceptual expansion in the treatment of gender issues from that of equal rights and the protection of individuals from violence to a broader agenda of women's empowerment. The second part of the chapter will outline the conceptual difficulties in drawing on the concept of human dignity in the struggle to overcome gender inequalities.

From universal human rights to women's empowerment: historical considerations

The development of international support for gender-specific women's human rights in the context of the UN takes as its first point of departure the Universal Declaration of Human Rights (UDHR) of 1948. Following a Preamble that grounds universal human rights in the fundamental affirmation of the inherent dignity of all humans, the subsequent articles substantiate and elaborate this commitment. The UDHR explicitly mentions men *and women* in only two articles, which address marriage and motherhood. Otherwise, discussions surrounding the formulation of the UDHR converged to agree that the category of 'the human' was sufficiently gender-inclusive and that gender distinctions should consciously not be made in the general elaboration of human rights.

In the following years, UN member states conceded that the economic and social realities of women's daily lives and the special hardships that women face were not sufficiently grasped by the gender-neutral language of the UDHR.[2] To address the gendered dimension of discrimination in particular, the General Assembly adopted the Declaration on the Elimination of Discrimination Against Women in 1967, which led to the approval of the Convention on the Elimination of All Forms of Discrimination Against Women (CEDAW) in 1979 and its entry into force in 1981. Moving beyond formal legal and political equality, the CEDAW also differentiates aspects of social, public and private equality to emphasize the importance of access for women to education, healthcare and economic means. Resulting from the Fourth World Conference on Women held in Beijing in 1995,[3] the Beijing Platform for Action for Equality, Development and Peace spells out twelve areas for action, detailing especially gender-specific needs with respect to health, education, poverty and access to

[2] On the evolution of human rights instruments at the UN, see Quataert 2009. Reilly 2009 discusses the development of women's human rights and feminist critiques.

[3] The conference in Beijing was preceded by the UN Declaration on the Elimination of Violence Against Women (1993) and the World Conference on Human Rights (1994), which also attended to the connection between gender issues and children's and indigenous peoples' rights.

economic resources, but also adding sections on the environment, on women and peace, on women and the media and on the young girl in order to analyze and redress the dimensions of gender inequalities in a more comprehensive and fine-grained manner. The Platform also emphasizes the importance of developing institutional mechanisms and forms of cooperation between governmental and non-governmental organizations to reduce gender inequalities systematically. During the conference and in the dissenting comments on the Platform, the governmental representatives of many Islamic and Catholic countries, along with the United States and the Holy See, mounted a very vocal opposition to the Platform's endorsement of women's reproductive freedom. As a result of this very public disagreement, discussions around the Beijing conference – and, by implication, issues of gender equality – have often been perceived as crucially focused on women's health and especially women's reproductive health, even though the Platform documents a much more comprehensive approach.

Security Council Resolution 1325, approved in 2000, marks a further shift, as it focuses on the role of women in politics, outlining the importance of involving women in conflict resolution and in security and peace measures. Resolution 1325 emphasizes the inclusion of a gender perspective in assessing the implications of armed conflicts and lays out programs on gender, peace and security to promote equal training and professional involvement of women and men in peace-building missions and to counter one-dimensional gender perspectives that view women solely as victims of male violence in conflicts. Taking up the focus on women's involvement and empowerment, the Millennium Development Goals (MDGs) address the continued gender differential in education, poverty reduction, care-giving to the young, sick, and elderly, and access to paid formal employment and to top-level positions in the private and political sectors. Moreover, the MDGs take a strong stance on the link between legal and regulatory measures and the need for cultural change by emphasizing the cultural success of quotas, where they have been implemented, and the importance of special measures to transform cultural perceptions of leadership and women's roles as leaders.

Over the course of the more than forty years since the Declaration on the Elimination of Discrimination against Women was adopted, the UN discourse on gender inequalities has expanded from the early efforts to institute legal international instruments to assert the equal rights of women to a focus on implementing practices of empowerment. From the late 1990s on and especially in the 2000s, the UN women's divisions' emphasis has moved to ensuring the collection of gender-disaggregated data, the allocation of funds for gender mainstreaming, and the implementation of mechanisms for accountability. Equally, while violence – often extreme violence – against women and girls remains an urgent issue (not so much of gender inequality, but of gender discrimination), it is clear that discussions and programs have moved from considering women in the first place as needing special protection to considering women as partners in the process of their empowerment.

Among the continued challenges in greater progress towards women's empowerment remains the current emphasis on micro-economics (for example, micro-loans) at the expense of macro-economic policies that take a gender perspective into account (UN General Assembly 2009). To boost efforts, current UN documents identify as further priorities strengthening governments' cooperation with civil society and increasing data collection, especially data more thoroughly disaggregated according to sex, age, race, ethnicity, socio-economics and ability. Finally, most recent reports begin to emphasize the need for men's greater involvement in efforts towards women's empowerment and participation in the reworking of the cultural understanding of masculinity and men's roles.

Gendered dignity and its discontents: theoretical reflections

Canvassing the development of the discourse on gender inequalities and the means of redress within the UN context reveals rather strikingly that human dignity as a key concept is mostly absent from these discussions. In ethical and political discussions of gender issues, human dignity tends to appear frequently in discussion on biomedical ethics and on extreme violence against women.[4] In debates on gender inequalities as part of the broader set of problems being addressed in feminist and queer political theory, human dignity plays no significant conceptual role. However, the sparseness of references to dignity within this debate is instructive, insofar as it signals the difficulties inherent in appealing to human dignity as a philosophical resource in the context of overcoming gender inequalities. This section will address two problematics, namely (1) invoking dignity as inadvertently abetting traditional gender regimes and privileges and (2) reducing gender inequalities to a women's issue, and will conclude by suggesting what a gender perspective adds to considerations on human dignity.

Invoking dignity as inadvertently abetting traditional gender regimes

UN debates and documents on gender equality invoke human dignity in two ways. The few times when the term 'dignity' appears in the main texts of the documents, the concept is cited in order to establish the equal rights of women and men and to give texture to practices of equality that enact reciprocal respect and self-respect to strengthen mutual, equal partnerships between the genders. That said, in the UN documentation on women's rights and empowerment, the dignity of women tends to be more often explicitly invoked by states to reaffirm rather than to tackle existing gender norms. In reports on their own

[4] Further exceptions are discussions of *Menschenwürde* (human dignity) especially with respect to German constitutional law; see Baer 2009: 417–68.

progress towards establishing women's rights, some states comment on their commitment to protecting women's dignity, by, for instance, focusing on banning images of women that could be construed as pornographic. At the same time, these states tend to ignore the broader platform that calls for women to assume positions of public leadership, also in the media, and for representations of women in a variety of roles and responsibilities to highlight their contribution at all levels in all sectors of society.[5] In this context, the references to dignity ground a position that ends up thwarting rather than furthering women's equality with men because the substantive interpretation of women's dignity reasserts a lopsided understanding of dignity as primarily concerned with protecting women and their bodies from exploitation, a focus that in turn upholds traditional gender norms.

These conservative invocations of dignity pertaining specifically to women signal that references to dignity as a fundamental value do not necessarily aid projects of overcoming gender inequalities. The problem is that in the context of attending to gender matters the understanding of dignity, especially with regard to women, is already culturally over-determined as especially a matter of their bodies, their (proper) sexuality and their needing protection. If dignity is invoked as a value and norm to protect and further the integrity of bodies and ways of living, then the context of gender inequalities reveals how the substantive interpretations of a person's dignity as gendered remain delimited by the implied assumptions about dignified femininity and masculinity. In turn, being perceived as undignified in one's behaviour exposes one differentially more to violence and inequalities or to the indifference of others in the face of violence or discrimination that one might suffer.

In a global perspective, the gesture of protecting women's dignity also runs a broader risk of inadvertently reiterating the stereotyped colonialist narrative of the 'poor, brown woman' who must be rescued by the 'strong, white man'.[6] Frequently, gender discrimination against non-white, lower-class and disabled women tends to be more readily viewed in terms of physical violations of their human dignity, while discrimination against white, able-bodied, middle- and upper-class women in the northern hemisphere tends to be viewed as an issue of infringements of their equal rights. Countering the often well-intentioned but inadvertent repetition of structural discrimination requires considering as crucial elements the intersectionality of gender and race, class, ability, age and other markers in order to diagnose structural gender inequalities and build coalitions across these differentials to abolish these inequalities.[7]

[5] See, for instance, the section on 'Media and Women' in the 2010 Ugandan government's report on progress in women's empowerment in light of the fifteenth anniversary of the Beijing conference.

[6] On the problem of this stereotypical colonialist narrative, see Spivak 1988.

[7] On the introduction of intersectionality into feminist criticism, see Crenshaw 1991; Alcoff and Mendieta 2003.

Reducing gender inequalities to a women's issue

Not only does women's human dignity as a trope call for careful conceptual and discursive analyses, the undergirding understanding of 'gender' equally requires critical scrutiny insofar as it tends to lend itself to equivocating between 'gender inequalities' and 'discrimination against women'. On UN websites and in its current publications, gender has been defined as socially constructed and as requiring broader analysis with respect to its intersections with other categories, among which disability and sexuality tend often not to make the more standard list of class, race and age. However, the UN definition still presents the socially and historically diverse system of gender norms and roles as mapping onto biologically discreet identities of two sexes, namely, women and men:[8] 'Gender' 'refers to the social attributes and opportunities associated with being male and female and the relationships between women and men and girls and boys, as well as the relations between women and those between men' (UN Office of the Special Adviser on Gender Issues and Advancement of Women, undated). Within this framework, gender-sensitive considerations to overcome inequalities tend to focus almost entirely on discrimination against women and girls. This conceptual narrowing obfuscates how substantive gender equality also requires transforming the roles of men and expectations of masculinity. In addition, this – often implicit – understanding of 'gender issues' as primarily 'women's issues' also renders invisible other inequalities on the basis of gender identity (discrimination of transgender, transsexual and intersex individuals) and on the basis of sexual orientation (discrimination based on one's own sex/gender in relation to one's partners' sex/gender).

At the UN, gender identity and sexual orientation have most recently emerged as the next frontier in discussions of gender equality (cf. Organization of American States 2009). Similar to the early stages in the women's human rights movement, these efforts have so far focused on decriminalizing and protecting sexual minorities and transgender, intersex and genderqueer individuals from physical and psychological violence.[9] However, bringing genderqueer lives into greater focus also opens up a context for a critical affirmation of gendered human dignity. Laying claim to the human dignity of sexual and gender minorities can be potentially powerful and less ambiguous than it is in the context of women's dignity alone, because genderqueer behaviour is so often stereotyped as 'undignified'. By extending genderqueer rights beyond establishing private

[8] This definition constitutes an advance in light of the difficulties that arose from the use of 'gender' in the context of the Beijing conference, where the Vatican suspected 'gender' to be code for homosexuality.

[9] In the gender equality debates at the UN, sexual orientation and genderqueer identities have been largely avoided, because gender variation and non-heterosexual sexuality have often been denounced as 'Western' and 'Neo-colonial' impositions by a number of African and Islamic governments.

individual freedoms and ensuring tolerance, the claim for the recognition of the human dignity of genderqueer people seeks to make possible a dignified life supported by self-respect and respect by others, especially where this respect is not predicated on conforming to heterosexual and heteronormative norms.

Just as gender injustices and inequalities are not reducible to experiences of violence against women, an enhanced understanding of lived dignity for all humans opens the way to establishing material equality for all by ensuring access to resources and decision-making for those who are differentially more exposed than others to discrimination and violence based on the expressions of their gender and sexuality. Against invoking dignity too uncritically, an encompassing critical gender perspective alerts us to how long histories of power complicate well-intentioned normative invocations of dignity as value and ideal.

References

Alcoff, L., and Mendieta, E. (eds.). 2003. *Identities: Race, Class, Gender, and Nationality.* Malden, MA: Blackwell

Baer, S. 2009. 'Dignity, Liberty, Equality: A Fundamental Rights Triangle of Constitutionalism', *University of Toronto Law Journal* 59(4): 417–68

Cornell, D. 2002. *Between Women and Generations: Legacies of Dignity.* New York: Palgrave

Crenshaw, K. 1991. 'Mapping the Margins: Intersectionality, Identity Politics, and Violence Against Women of Color', *Stanford Law Review* 43(6): 1241–99

Krook, M. L., and Childs, S. (eds.). 2010. *Women, Gender, and Politics: A Reader.* Oxford University Press

Lorber, J. (ed.). 2010. *Gender Inequality: Feminist Theories and Politics.* Oxford University Press

Organization of American States. 2009. 'Statement on Human Rights, Sexual Orientation and Gender Identity', 4 June 2009. www.unhcr.org/refworld/docid/49997ae312.html

Quataert, J. H. 2009. *Advocating Dignity: Human Rights Mobilizations in Global Politics.* Philadelphia, PA: University of Pennsylvania Press

Reilly, N. 2009. *Women's Human Rights: Seeking Gender Justice in a Globalizing Age.* Cambridge: Polity

Spivak, G. C. 1988. 'Can the Subaltern Speak?', in L. Grossberg and C. Nelson (eds.), *Marxism and the Interpretation of Culture.* Urbana, IL: University of Illinois Press, 271–303

UN Office of the Special Adviser on Gender Issues and Advancement of Women. Undated. 'Concepts and Definitions', www.un.org/womenwatch/osagi/conceptsandefinitions.htm

56

The rise and fall of freedom of online expression

MATHIAS KLANG

At first glance, the connection between human dignity and technology is a tenuous one. We strive to see ourselves as autonomous subjects, uncontrolled by the everyday technology around us. Often technology is promoted as being the very basis for increased freedom. Access to the Internet is increasingly seen as the basis for democratic participation, mobile telephone technology is marketed as increasing our freedom and mobility, and social media are presented as a cornerstone for access to knowledge and the antidote to the authoritarian state. Therefore, personal technology, or access to the Internet, has come to symbolize a democratic cornerstone: a realm wherein the individual may engage in public discourse and access information vital to personal development and necessary for true democratic participation. This is particularly true for most of the digital technology that has come to dominate much of the public discourse: for example, the mobile phone, the Internet and social networks.

In recognition of its role in freedom of expression, individual autonomy and development and recognizing its value in social participation and democratic participation, a discussion has arisen as to whether access to the Internet should be made into a right: whether states have the responsibility to guarantee that Internet access is broadly available. Several countries have enacted measures to protect individuals' access to the Internet (Lucchi 2011).

This freedom is, however, under attack by a wide range of factors (marketing, peer pressure, the digitalization of everyday services and the choice to remain outside the digital realm) which create the risk that our autonomy is infringed upon rather than supported by technology.

As convenience encourages the adoption of technology, it increasingly pervades our daily lives and creates fresh concerns about the ways in which many of our core values are affected. Mobile phones allow us to communicate in a way that is not limited by location, but they also raise surveillance concerns; the Internet is the greatest tool for accessing human knowledge but also the source of an unfathomable amount of offensive material; social networks free us from the shackles of time and space in developing human relationships, but also change the very nature of concepts such as friendship, stalking and privacy.

Freedom of expression is recognized as a key component in a democratic society. Without the ability to spread information, others would not be able to participate freely in these ideas and arguments thus hampering personal development and the dignity of individuals and creating an adverse effect on democratic growth.

Our ability to practise the right to freedom of expression depends upon our access to communications technology. Without the technological ability to spread information, the fundamental right to free expression is moot. Therefore, in order to ensure human dignity, and the human rights which safeguard it, it is vital (1) to understand the technology we rely on, (2) to recognize the legal, economic, social and technological controls placed in technology, and (3) to ultimately ensure that technology, for the most part, serves to promote human dignity. This chapter focuses on the ways in which individuals' freedom of speech is impacted by the economic and social goals of those who provide us with our technology.

Every modern democracy maintains rules ensuring citizens' rights to communicate. These rights are often philosophically grounded, and include not only the right to disseminate but also the right to seek out information. The right to freedom of communication can be understood as grounded in three motivations (Schauer 1982): freedom of communication is necessary for arriving at the truth, it is fundamental for democracy and it is fundamental for self-fulfilment.

For the main part of our history, efficient information transfer has been hampered by space and time. The advent of writing worked to overcome these barriers to an extent, but the ability to spread information was still limited by the speed at which information could be transmitted. Innovations such as the printing press and the telegraph revolutionized the communications infrastructure by enabling messages to be sent at a fraction of the time and cost – and the development of radio, telephone and television of the past century now enable real time communication. Each of these innovations has created a need for a reappraisal of the values protected by our human rights conventions to ensure human rights are not weakened through technological development.

However, these earlier communications networks were controlled at the point of access. The right to communicate has always been hampered by the practical ability to do so. In a sense, individuals' abilities to veritably communicate with mass audiences have made the right of communication largely into a moot point. Recent decades have, once again, seen radical advances in communications technology. The dissemination of Internet access in general and the World Wide Web in particular have enabled the potential for individual mass communication.

Viewed from the perspective of freedom of expression, this latter innovation creates an interesting tension. How should states react when well-established, but inoperable rights suddenly become actionable? When the physical limitations to communication are alleviated, are we still prepared to accept the freedom to access and spread information as a fundamental human right?

The Internet revolution

Today, we tend to accept the Internet, and the World Wide Web, as an 'invention'. However, in reality, this is a convenient fiction as it is the cumulative result of a series of technical, social and economic developments which have led us to the point where we think nothing of calling across an ocean to talk, to use our telephones to browse the Internet or to post information on a social network.

The revolutionary factor is found in the level of access to global communications that we have today. This access is not limited to the ability to consume information produced and presented by others but the, relatively novel, ability to produce and disseminate our own material. This shift in personal technology has revolutionized personal habits, business models and therefore naturally affects politics and our understanding of freedom of expression.

The 1990s was the early period of popular Internet access and it was during this phase that discussions about the ability and desirability of regulating the Internet began. The early discussions were split between those who felt that the technology needed to be regulated and those who thought it could – and should – not be regulated. John Perry Barlow (1996) published A Declaration of the Independence of Cyberspace, arguing that governments had no legitimacy to govern the Internet, David Johnson and David Post (1996) argued that territorially based law-making and enforcement was inadequate for a global communications medium, and Lawrence Lessig (1999) explained that in a world made up of computer code it was the programmer, not the legislator that held the power.

Limiting speech rights in democratic states

To be clear, countries' attitudes towards the Internet are not uniformly positive. Although this chapter focuses on the question of limiting freedom of expression in liberal democracies, it is important to note that several countries claim the right and ability to censor online information. The organization Reporters Without Borders publishes an annual 'Enemies of the Internet' report, in which they list countries and levels of Internet suppression. In their latest 2012 report, the 'enemies list' included Bahrain, Belarus, Burma, China, Cuba, Iran, North Korea, Saudi Arabia, Syria, Turkmenistan, Uzbekistan and Vietnam. These states combine content filtering with access restrictions and maintain tight control over the Internet as a whole.

States have also been involved in monitoring and limiting access to social networking sites. In preparation for the 20th anniversary of the 1989 Tiananmen Square protests, China blocked access to several sites. Blocking access to social media is not uncommon. The largest social network (Facebook) has sparked concern and has been blocked in a wide range of states for longer or shorter periods. This list includes a range of countries as diverse as Syria (Oweis 2007), to the United Kingdom (Booth, Laville and Malik 2011). For the most part, the blocking of social media is part of a larger strategy to control online information.

An additional point of conflict is that even in democratic states the attitude towards freedom of expression is not uniform. The Anglo-American legal systems have a marked preference for the 'marketplace of ideas'[1] metaphor, which encourages almost all communication with the understanding that the stronger ideas will triumph over the weaker. Civil law systems prefer a moderated version of the marketplace where a range of expressions are not protected by free speech. Naturally, in a global communications infrastructure, these differences create tensions as illustrated by the *LICRA* v. *Yahoo!* case. In this case,[2] the Internet service provider Yahoo! maintained online auction sites which could be accessed globally. Among the items on auction were Nazi memorabilia. Article R645-1 of the French Criminal Code prohibits the public wearing or exhibiting of uniforms, insignias and emblems which 'recall those used' by organizations declared illegal in application of Article 9 of the Nuremberg Statute, or by a person found guilty of crimes against humanity. The case illustrates national variations in freedom of expression and the tensions brought about by a global communications infrastructure. This case brought into focus the question of the locus of activities on servers accessible via the Internet and the competency of national courts to enforce national legislation on online actions.

The rise of walled gardens

At the turn of the millennium, the technology discussion began to focus on the concepts of user-generated media, web2.0 and social media. The appearance of these showed that a change was occurring among Internet users: they not only consumed information created by organizations, but also began to create material themselves. The primary motor for this discussion was the increased popularity of blogs and blogging as a communications tool.

The twenty-first century saw the launch of projects such as the encyclopaedia Wikipedia (2001), social networks such as LinkedIn (2003) and Facebook (2004), video sharing sites such as YouTube (2005) and micro blogging applications such as Twitter (2006). That year also saw the launch of the iPhone and the increased dominance of iTunes as a marketplace. Taken together, this was heralded as a revolution in communications, and in 2006 *Time* chose the social media user as its Person of the Year.[3] Naturally, the barriers of time and space had been removed much earlier but this communication came about in the

[1] This has its origins in John Stuart Mill and in Justice Oliver Wendell Holmes' dissent in *Abrams* v. *United States*, 250 US 616, 624 (1919).

[2] *Ligue contre le racisme et l'antisémitisme et Union des étudiants juifs de France* v. *Yahoo! Inc. and Société Yahoo! France.* Tribunal de grande instance Paris, 22 May 2000.

[3] Time Magazine Person of the Year 2006, www.time.com/time/magazine/article/0,9171,1570810,00.html (accessed 28 April 2013).

ability of ordinary people to access the network and to participate in mass communication, not as consumers but as senders of information. In other words, information dissemination was no longer exclusive.

The phenomenal growth and dissemination of the early World Wide Web was due not only to its technological makeup but also to its fundamental principle of openness. When Tim Berners-Lee created the necessary protocols, he laid the foundations for its openness both in not limiting it through technological measures, but also in the way he announced it in 1991 without implementing licensing schemes or securing legal property rights. However, this openness also enabled the creation of so-called 'walled gardens' within the open Internet. The walled garden is a metaphor describing systems where service providers create closed online environments where they maintain control over applications, content and media. Access to these walled gardens is regulated through licensing where the service provider is able to limit the users rights. Tim Berners-Lee's openness has enabled the implementation of Walled gardens and he has regularly voiced his concern over the ways in which data is collected and presented in ways that are detrimental to the users (Katz 2012).

Personalization and bubbles

One of the biggest assets of walled gardens is their ability to collect and analyze huge amounts of user data, which is primarily used to create better marketing systems and through this generate revenue for the service providers. The fundamental principle is based on the idea that service providers such as Google and Facebook are able to learn a great deal about individual users through the information that is required (login data, email addresses), offered freely (online searches, links users click on) and analysis of large quantities of data. This data collection serves two main purposes: first, to tailor the online experience to the individuals' preferences, and, second, to sell this information to third parties.

Personalization began as a positive goal where each user would have the ability to tailor flows of information to suit his or her individual tastes. Nicholas Negroponte (1996) referred to this as the creation of the 'daily me'. However critics soon pointed to the detrimental effects of this kind of personalization. Cass Sunstein (2001) pointed out that, by choosing only information we agree with, we limit the questioning of established ideas and stifle the public debate. David Weinberger (2004) warned that such systems would create echo chambers: 'Internet spaces where like-minded people listen only to those people who already agree with them'.

This echo chamber effect is multiplied when service providers actively implement personalization strategies, as they tend to prioritize the information they deem fitting for the user's profile. Commenting on the personalization trend, Eric Schmidt, the former CEO of Google, has said 'It will be very hard for people to watch or consume something that has not in some sense been tailored for them' (quoted in Jenkins 2012). And Mark Zuckerberg, Chairman and CEO of Facebook, stated: 'A *squirrel* dying in front of your house may be more relevant to your interests right now than people dying in Africa' (quoted in Pariser 2011). While these positions may be technically correct, taken from a freedom-of-expression and access point of view they are highly problematic – in particular when these are the views of the information providers.

The drive towards personalization is problematic since the Internet service providers such as Google and Facebook are not providing their users with unbiased information. Google attempts to provide the user with the most interesting search results for that particular person; Facebook prioritizes status updates from a selection of the user's friends. In either case, the service provider has made a choice as to which information the individual user needs to see and what information she does not need to see. This lack of unbiased information is compounded by the user's beliefs that technology is inherently neutral and has no political goals of its own (Winner 1985).

Searching for the term 'information' on Google returns 11,070,000,000 hits in 0.24 seconds. The choice of which results to show is based on algorithms weighted by what Google thinks the user is looking for. This is not a neutral ranking. Nor is the flow of information produced by a user's Facebook friends displayed neutrally; it is a selection decided upon by Facebook, based on their understanding of what that user is looking for. In effect, Facebook picks the most suitable individuals from your friends and effectively filters out information from the friends it deems to be unsuitable. There are several other companies treating user data in this way; the ones described above are rather the rule than the exception. Both Google and Facebook have argued that what they are doing is necessary in order to provide a better service, and that it would be impossible or useless to present all information equally. Also should any real criticism arise from users the companies are quick to point out that they are not a public service, users freely choose to use their services at no cost, and users are free to leave at any time. While the first two arguments are true, services such as these are rapidly becoming fundamental to modern communications and in many cases opting out is not a veritable option – opting out is equal to choosing not to communicate.

Memory: the dark side of data

Our technological ability to collect, analyze, store and access data has the potential to enable increased participation in civil society and therefore could become a major element in the democratic debate. However, as discussed above, the privatization of the web provides a false sense of participation in open public debate. Advanced web technology's ability to collect, store and retrieve information has also created new types of problems, found for instance in the discussion on the 'right to forget' or the 'right to be forgotten' (Mayer-Schonberger 2009; Bernal 2011). In essence, the argument is that individuals' past mistakes should be left in the past, in particular when facts may be presented in a misleading or unduly harsh fashion. Take, for example, the problem of the Spanish doctor.

In 1991, one of Spain's leading newspapers, *El Pais*, published an article about a plastic surgeon, Dr Guidotti Russo, accused of malpractice.[4] The charges were eventually dropped and everything could have been forgotten had it not been for the web. With the digitalization of newspaper articles and the effectiveness of search engines, Dr Russo is once again harmed by the past. When searching for information about Dr Russo on Google, the *El Pais* article about being accused of malpractice appears prominently, while news of his innocence is not to be found. In 2011, Dr Guidotti Russo asked the Spanish courts to compel Google to remove the offending article from their search results. He is not asking for the removal of the article from the *El Pais* database. The difference is interesting as each of the removals may be construed as varying levels of censorship. By removing the article from the newspaper, it becomes totally unavailable; by removing it from Google it becomes relatively non-discoverable.

Recently, these types of cases have been surfacing, and a discussion concerning the right to be forgotten has arisen, and proposals have been made to include such a right in legislation. While it is easy to see the damage arising from technology, attempts to amend online information may be more agreeable to civil law than to the Anglo-American tradition.

Smartphones and apps

The public debate is not being stifled, as it was in the past, by imprimatur and censorship, but rather by the limitations applied to our ability to choose whom we communicate with and the constant surveillance being applied to our digital communications.

Even though the tension between the increased potential to access and participate in an open and free public debate and the limitations of walled gardens has been recognized, there are further problems to be faced in the future of web-based communications. Once again, the chokehold is applied to the root of our communications infrastructure. Since the launch of the iPhone in 2007, the demand for and the use of smartphones has rapidly increased. Since then, these devices have been developed further to include tablet computers, and, seen collectively, they are rapidly changing the ways in which the user accesses information.

From the perspective of freedom of expression, the problem with smartphones and tablets is that access to Internet-based information is more focused on applications ('apps') on the devices. These apps are designed to carry out specific tasks, often connected to a specific source of information, and bring with them two specific information problems. First, the apps are often used

[4] 'El riesgo de querer ser esbelta', www.elpais.com/articulo/sociedad/riesgo/querer/ser/esbelta/elpepisoc/19911028elpepisoc_3/Tes (accessed 28 April 2013).

to collect data about the users much in the same way as the walled gardens discussed above. Second, the app market is a more or less controlled environment. The apps not only control the flows of information but also often have limitations placed on them by the device controller. The result is that we are moving further away from the open web and back into a system of controlled environments.

Therefore, the technological infrastructure of modern communication carries with it an inherent paradox: we are more than ever able to communicate with others while, at the same time, the communications of ordinary individuals have never been subjected to the levels of control, monitoring and analysis as we face today. Through this increased control and manipulation of technology the potential beneficial effects on human dignity are subverted and there is a growing need to view the regulation of technology from a human rights perspective.

Conclusion

The advanced technological communications infrastructure available to many in developed countries has the potential to enable individuals to record and transmit ideas at a lower cost and to a wider audience than ever before in history. As such, the Internet, social media and our mobile devices could be seen as vital tools in ensuring human development and as an important element in the protection of human rights and dignity. However, in order to fulfil this potential, these technologies must be prevented from being turned into advanced infrastructures of surveillance and control. This chapter has pointed to the ways in which technology with freedom-enhancing potential can be used to serve the interests of small groups rather than the protection and development of human rights – unless legal safeguards are enacted to ensure the rights to technology include rights to use them without excessive corporate surveillance and control.

References

Barlow, J. P. 1996. 'A Declaration of the Independence of Cyberspace'. (8 February 1996), https://projects.eff.org/~barlow/Declaration-Final.html, accessed 28 April 2013

Bernal, P. 2011. 'A Right to Delete?', *European Journal of Law and Technology* 2(2)

Booth, R., Laville, S., and Malik, S. 2011. 'Royal Wedding: Police Criticized for Pre-Emptive Strikes Against Protesters'. *Guardian*. (29 April), www.guardian.co.uk/uk/2011/apr/29/royal-wedding-police-criticized-protesters (accessed 28 April 2013)

Jenkins, H. W. 2012. 'Google and the Search for the Future', *Wall Street Journal*, http://online.wsj.com/article/SB10001424052748704901104575423294099527212.html (accessed 28 April 2013)

Johnson, D. R., and Post, D. G. 1996. 'Law and Borders: The Rise of Law in Cyberspace', *Stanford Law Review* 48: 1367

Katz, I. 2012. 'Tim Berners-Lee: Demand Your Data from Google and Facebook', *Guardian* (18 April), www.guardian.co.uk/technology/2012/apr/18/tim-berners-lee-google-facebook (accessed 28 April 2013)

Lessig, L. 1999. *Code and Other Laws of Cyberspace.* New York: Basic Books

Lucchi, N. 2011. 'Access to Network Services and Protection of Constitutional Rights: Recognizing the Essential Role of Internet Access for the Freedom of Expression', *Cardozo Journal of International and Comparative Law* 19(3): 2, www.cjicl.com/uploads/2/9/5/9/2959791/cjicl_19.3_lucchi_article.pdf (accessed 28 April 2013)

Negroponte, N. 1996. *Being Digital.* New York: Vintage Books

Mayer-Schonberger, V. 2009. *Delete: The Virtue of Forgetting in the Digital Age.* Princeton University Press

Oweis, K. Y. 2007. 'Syria Blocks Facebook in Internet Crackdown'. Reuters Online (23 November), www.reuters.com/article/2007/11/23/us-syria-facebook-idUSOWE37285020071123 (accessed 28 April 2013)

Pariser, E. 2011. *The Filter Bubble: What the Internet Is Hiding from You.* London: Penguin

Schauer, F. 1982. *Free Speech: A Philosophical Enquiry.* Cambridge University Press

Sunstein, C. 2001. *Republic.com.* Princeton University Press

Weinberger, D. 2004. 'Is There an Echo in Here?' Salon.com (February), www.salon.com/2004/02/21/echo_chamber/ (accessed 28 April 2013)

Winner, L. 1985. 'Do Artefacts Have Politics?', in D. Mackenzie and J. Wajcman (eds.), *The Social Shaping of Technology.* Buckingham: Open University Press

Part VII

Biology and bioethics

57

The threefold challenge of Darwinism to an ethics of human dignity

CHRISTIAN ILLIES*

Many (such as Frances P. Cobbe) regard Darwin's *Origin of Species* as the final nail in the coffin of theism, and his *Descent of Man* as sounding the '[death] knell of the virtue of mankind'.[1] Yet Darwin insisted that an evolutionary explanation of our moral sense in no way harms ethics; but, rather, gives it a surer foundation. The question of whether Darwin's insights can provide this foundation, or whether they are in fact harmful to ethics, is still discussed today. In what follows, I will look at a particular aspect of this debate, namely, the importance of Darwinism for a Kantian style of dignity ethics.

By 'Darwinism' I mean an evolutionary theory where natural selection is the central explanatory concept for the development of natural phenomena (including human beings and their behaviour). I will look at this as a *scientific theory*, not at evolutionary theory as an overall worldview. Some authors, such as Daniel Dennett, have tried to push evolutionary theory in this direction (as a worldview), and argued on its basis for a naturalistic metaphysics which would obviously not be compatible with dignity ethics (Dennett 1996). I will concentrate on the implications of the scientific theory alone.

I understand 'human dignity' in the Kantian tradition as a special normative status, based upon the claim that *all* human beings are rational and free (or at least have the potential to be free), where this actual or potential autonomy is the basis of universal human dignity. Kantian dignity ethics is a type of moral cognitivism; it is based upon the assumption that it is a rational claim to attribute dignity universally to all humans.

As I will argue, there are three versions of the evolution-theory challenge to a Kantian kind of dignity ethics, but dignity ethics can withstand them all. However, it might have to be substantially modified in light of evolutionary theory.

* I am grateful to Gabriele De Anna, Sebastian Krebs and Graeme Napier for helpful critiques and clarifying suggestions.

[1] Darwin quotes a critique by Frances Power Cobbe in a footnote of the second edition of the book in 1874. See Darwin 1817: 99 n. 6.

Animals can be like humans

A typical member of the species *homo sapiens* has some characteristics that make him excel amongst all other animals, namely, reason and autonomy. In most versions of dignity ethics, these abilities justify the claim that human beings, and human beings alone, have a special status. 'Morality, and humanity as capable of it, is that which alone has dignity', Kant writes (1889: 53).

A typical transcendental justification for this claim goes as follows. Moral norms or values only become real if there are rational, autonomous beings to realize them in actions. Hence morality depends on autonomous agents as its *raison d'être.* Without autonomous agents, there cannot be any morality. Therefore, the first transcendentally derived moral demand is to defend the freedom and rationality of free rational agents because a moral scheme which does *not* do so would undermine its own basis and thus be self-contradictory. It follows that, if dignity is based on autonomy and reason (or at least the potential for it), then only free rational beings have dignity. Because animals lack these cognitive abilities, it is argued, they do not belong to this privileged class. As Kant says in his *Lecture on Ethics*: 'So far as animals are concerned, we have no direct duties. Animals . . . are there merely as means to an end. That end is man' (Kant 1963: 239).

The evolutionary perspective undermines the notion of any such privileged status for human beings because it presents an evolutionary continuum between human and non-human animals (see for example Bugynar, Stöwe and Bernd 2004; Sommer 2011). The mental skills of humans might be not entirely different from the skills of non-human animals. Does it follow that dignity ethics collapses because 'any adequate defence of human dignity would require some conception of human beings as radically different from other animals' (Rachels 1990: 171–2)? No, there is no cogent reason why this should be. Dignity is accorded to agents who are rational and free – that is why Kant talks not so much about 'human beings' but about the respect we owe to *all rational beings.* If some animals are freer and more rational than we have hitherto thought, then they also have dignity. Yet all criteria for human dignity – rationality, freedom, autonomy etc. – are still in place.[2] Dignity ethics claims that human beings have a *unique status*, but it does not have to claim that humans are *unique in having such a status.*

Humans can be like animals

Let us look at things the other way round. Perhaps human beings are *not* free agents who can act morally, but are rather much more like animals and thus do not deserve to be treated differently to all other animals.

[2] To be sure, there is the problem of how to justify the attribution of dignity in the case of marginal human agents who seem to lack full autonomy and freedom – but this problem is independent from the status of animals.

Determined by our genes?

Are we determined by our biological nature? Although often accused of determinism by critics, evolutionary theory in fact rarely makes deterministic claims.[3] Scientists even talk about 'freedom' when it comes to human actions and decisions (Dawkins 1976) and deny that any biologist believes in 'genetic determinism' (Wilson 1998: 205). Evolutionary biology does not identify precise instincts or strict patterns of human behaviour, but rather probabilities or statistical laws describing behaviour.

Why Darwinism cannot say much more about human behaviour becomes obvious when we look at the structure of its explanations of moral behaviour. According to evolutionary theory, human beings are born with certain genetic dispositions to feel, judge or act in certain ways which are morally relevant. These dispositions can be called 'primary phenotypic adaptations'. But human beings also seem to have innate dispositions which allow them to regulate themselves by responses (for example, blame) and to set up entire ethical systems. We can call these systems 'secondary phenotypic behaviour', because they are a level over and above the primary (Rauscher 1997). On this second (cultural) level, the behavioural dispositions are coordinated and stabilized by mechanisms of social affirmation – religious commands, for example, or civil laws (Wilson 1978: 167). Secondary phenotypic behaviour seems to have its own (cultural) history and its own mechanisms of development (cultural inheritance is probably Lamarckian rather than Darwinian), but it is not entirely independent of primary phenotypic behaviour. Normative principles make normative assessments of the interactive behavioural dispositions with which our genes provide us (for example, jealousy, cooperation, mating preferences, even attitudes towards infanticide).

Consequently, what an actual agent does will always be shaped on both primary and secondary phenotypic levels, and it is the secondary one that explains why an evolutionary account of human behaviour is on the whole probabilistic rather than deterministic: genes are just one among many different types of causes that must be considered; and it is by no means clear whether we will ever be able to identify a sufficient set of causes (genetic and cultural) which fully determines human behaviour. Of course, *cultural determinism* remains a possibility, but it is certainly not a thesis for which evolutionary theory is likely to provide strong arguments or evidence.

Are human beings driven by selfishness?

Evolutionary Theory explains human behaviour in a way that might invite yet another objection. Are we programmed to be psychological egoists (and thus

[3] Some biologists do argue deterministically, for example William Provine, and most prominently Charles Darwin who wrote in 1838: '[O]ne doubts existence of free will every action determined by hereditary constitution, example of others or teaching of others' (Darwin 1838).

not worth being respected as moral agents)? After all, natural selection favours winners, who care primarily about their own genes and their proliferation. As products of a long evolutionary history, we should have been selected as egoists whose 'ultimate goal' (Steven Pinker's term) is evolutionary success.[4] According to this account, we are never truly moral, at least not if morality is about acting out of some genuine (self-less) concern for others, or about doing the right thing *for its own sake*.

What exactly does it mean to say that natural selection favours selfishness? First, the theory claims that genes are the unit of selection (as sociobiology has powerfully argued). The prevalent genes in a population (including the gene-pool of *Homo sapiens*) should be those that have the phenotypic effects most favourable to their own replication. Second, evolutionary theory argues that natural selection works on behaviour. Evolutionary psychology gives details to this by claiming that our brain consists of specialized (often unconsciously operating) neural circuits ('modules') which have been selected to solve problems our hunter-gatherer ancestors faced. If we combine the two claims we have an account of the human being as a creature guided by its genes to act in ways which are in its evolutionary interest.

There is, however, no direct path from successful ('selfish') genes to selfish behaviour. Moreover, to act selfishly (i.e. with egoistic motives) is often not the best way to promote one's evolutionary success. And that is why our genes give us rather different motives, like hunger, curiosity, cooperative interests, and rivalry. Darwin distinguishes between the 'standard' and the 'motive' of conduct, the former being related to the outcome of the action or the good that it promotes (such as reproductive success), the latter to the subjective motives of the agent (Darwin 1817: 120).[5] Thus, even if the genes direct our behaviour in the interest of our genes, they have not programmed us as psychological egoists on the phenotypic level.

But then, if genes affect us in such a way that we are not conscious of their effect (or 'standard'), do they then make us have *hidden* selfish motives? Richard Alexander, for example, argues that natural selection has shaped us to be unaware of our impulses, because this self-ignorance allows us to deceive others more efficiently (Alexander 1975: 96). This is implausible for two reasons. On the one hand, it is not clear what this unconscious motive might be. There seems to be nothing suppressed or waiting to be discovered here. No psychoanalyst will ever help us discover that we only *thought* that we were hungry, but that, in fact, this was really an unconscious selfish desire to proliferate. Such a 'hidden selfish motive' cannot be discovered in any obvious way; neither can its existence

[4] Cf. www.flyfishingdevon.co.uk/salmon/year3/psy339evaluation-evolutionary-psychology/evaluation-evolutionary-psychology.htm#pc-ep.

[5] In his critique of Sidgwick's Utilitarianism, he writes: 'With respect to the latter theory, the standard and the motive of conduct have no doubt often been confused, but they are really in some degree blended.'

be proved or disproved. If it is in the interest of our genes to behave in some situations altruistically (to feel love and sympathy towards our siblings, for example), then our genes have probably programmed us to have these motives or feelings. But what point would there be in postulating a second, *deeper*, selfish motive behind it? The idea of an unconscious psychological egoism is based upon confusion, as Stephen Pinker suspects: 'The confusion comes from thinking of people's genes as their *true self*, and the motives of their *genes* as their deepest, truest, unconscious, motives. From there it is easy to draw the cynical and incorrect moral that all love is hypocritical' (Pinker 1999: 401).

Debunking practical reason

A third challenge of evolutionary theory is to be found on the meta-ethical level. Richard Joyce and others argue that evolutionary explanations for moral beliefs debunk the meta-ethical tenet that morality is something real and that human beings have moral knowledge (Singer 1982, Joyce 2006). Following Erik Wielenberg, we can formulate the 'Evolutionary Debunking Thesis' (EDT):[6]

> If S's moral belief D can be given an evolutionary explanation, then S's moral belief D is not knowledge. (Wielenberg 2010)

Exponents of the EDT do not deny that we *regard* some of our moral beliefs as universally valid. But it is exactly this objectivist viewpoint which, they argue, is an *illusion* with respect to the nature of moral judgments, an illusion our genes provide for us, in order that we might be successful cooperators (Ruse and Wilson 1985). Dignity ethics should take EDT seriously; after all, dignity ethics claims to provide some moral knowledge.

Let us look at an example of an *evolutionary* explanation of the belief that all human beings have dignity (or at least some special normative status). It is argued first that every human being believes that *he or she* has this status. The belief has been positively selected because it enhances genetic fitness: if S sees herself as more than merely a thing amongst other things (more than an entity that others may use *ad lib*), then S is motivated to prevent others from doing harm to her. Such behaviour will increase her chances of survival and reproduction (Joyce 2006: 111) and that would explain S's belief D *of S* (everyone thinks *he* or *she* has a special normative status).

Why should D be expanded to others? Here, Wielenberg suggests a 'Likeness Principle' at work: 'Consider the principle that things that are alike with respect to their known properties are alike with respect to their unknown properties (call this *Likeness Principle*). Recognizing this principle, or being disposed to reason in accordance with it, provides many advantages' (Wielenberg 2010: 445). Wielenberg argues that it is in general an advantage to treat like cases alike. We

[6] I have changed P into D in Wielenberg's formulation because I am investigating the belief that humans have dignity.

must therefore think that special normative status should be given to *anyone like us*: S's belief D becomes a general belief about everyone having D.[7]

If an evolutionary explanation on these lines is correct, would it debunk any belief in human dignity? The immediate answer seems to be 'no': it is certainly possible that S's moral belief D finds an evolutionary explanation *and* that the belief D is also correct. The functionality of our moral beliefs and their correctness could coincide, and EDT would be wrong. This is, after all, the situation with some theoretical beliefs. Evolution has shaped us so that we tend to believe some facts about the world; for example, that events are causally connected ('belief C') and that the world really is ordered in terms of cause and effect (C is in fact true). It is plausible to assume C because it is functionally advantageous (fitness-enhancing) to have veridical representations of the world, i.e. to believe that the world is ordered in the way in which it actually is.[8]

We cannot rebut EDT so easily, however. Even if the truth of D is logically compatible with an evolutionary explanation of our belief D, we find D much 'harder to buy' once we know the 'biological machinery behind this illusion' (Wright 1994: 339). Here is a difference between theoretical and practical beliefs. In the case of theoretical beliefs, we have a situation wherein C (the way the world really is) is a *part of the explanation* for the selective advantage of the belief C. Someone who tends to look for causes will understand better how things work and will deal more successfully with the world. But in the case of moral beliefs there is no such explanatory connection: erroneous beliefs about moral facts (if there are any moral facts) do not seem to decrease our fitness in an obvious way. Someone who does not believe in the dignity of others is not 'punished' by the realities of our world like the man who ignores causality.

Consider this interesting thought-experiment by Darwin. In his response to the objection by Frances Cobbe, quoted above, he writes that our moral beliefs have been selected *only* because they increased our fitness, *not* because they are true:

> If, for instance, to take an extreme case, men were reared under precisely the same conditions as hive-bees, there can hardly be a doubt that our unmarried females would, like the worker-bees, think it a sacred duty to kill their brothers, and mothers would strive to kill their fertile daughters; and no one would think of interfering. (Darwin 1817: 99)

7 Wielenberg leaves it open whether it increases directly our fitness to think that everyone has *d*. It might merely be an indirect effect of an otherwise advantageous principle that we generally apply.

8 Evolutionary theory does not have to hold that it is different with theoretical beliefs; they could also be false. R. Trivers argues in this sense that 'the conventional view that natural selection favours nervous systems which produce ever more accurate images of the world must be a very naive view of natural selection' (Dawkins 1976: vi). A similar doubt about the trustworthiness of our beliefs has already been raised by Charles Darwin in a letter to William Graham dated 3 July 1881 (Darwin 1887: 315–16).

We seem, then, to have no reason to assume that our moral beliefs are in accordance with moral facts.[9] If they were, it would be a 'striking coincidence between the independent normative truths posited by the realist and the normative views that evolutionary forces pushed us toward', as Sharon Street writes (Street 2008).

The first observation is that the coincidence is not as striking as Street suggests. After all, we have many innate beliefs and many of them do *not* coincide with the truths posited by the realist. If evolutionary theory is right, then we have innate xenophobic beliefs, or beliefs that stepchildren have less importance than biological children. There are a lot of predispositions which incline us to believe A, B, C, D, etc. and only very few of these beliefs coincide with the alleged moral truths promoted by dignity ethics. We are, after all, an ambivalent mixture of good and bad impulses pulling us in different directions, as we all know only too well. (But worse: some moral demands find no easy resonance in us; these are examples of moral truths which do not coincide with innate beliefs.) Thus, the coincidence is much smaller than Street thinks: it is merely that D is amongst the *various* beliefs (good and bad) that we might hold 'naturally'.

Second, it is not so 'striking' to find a 'coincidence' between some moral truths and some innate beliefs. After all, morality is about human well-being - and so is much of what is functional in evolutionary terms. In most cases, human well-being is a necessary condition for reproductive success. Moral truths and innate beliefs do not, however, coincide completely. Whereas morality demands support of the universal well-being of the species (or wider), the focus of evolutionary-functional beliefs is the individual and its siblings or offspring. A certain coincidence is therefore to be expected rather than to be found surprising.

Finally, the moral fact D and my belief D might not be entirely disconnected. The human belief D is (just as much as our other moral beliefs) both the starting point and part of the explanation and justification of D: that we have moral beliefs at all, that we can reason about them (dismiss some and uphold others), and that we can distinguish between truth and illusion – these are all capacities essential to human reason and autonomy. And they are the basis for attributing dignity to human beings in the first place. In other words, while the fact C explains (via natural selection) our belief C, in the moral case it is our belief D, and our reflection upon it, that explains (via justification) the moral fact D.

[9] We might not have good reasons to attribute dignity to the bee-like humans in Darwin's story in any case: they seem to be determined to make certain (functional) judgements. Thus, they lack the autonomy that is the prerequisite for a being having dignity.

Conclusion

This threefold evolutionary challenge cannot, in the end, undermine the idea of inviolable human dignity. That is the conclusion of the analysis above: Kantian dignity ethics remain compatible with Darwinism as a scientific theory.

If taken seriously, however, an evolutionary understanding of the human being requires dignity ethics to think critically about some of its basic concepts and ideas – and probably to modify many of its claims. We have seen that the line between human beings and animals cannot be drawn as sharply as many have thought; and this might require us to attribute dignity to some non-human animals. We seem not to be unique: just at one end of a spectrum. A second insight arising from this has importance for any ethical system focusing on autonomy as its core value. If human beings have dignity *because* they are free and rational beings that can act morally, then it is important to understand that human freedom is a very complex phenomenon. Human beings are influenced and motivated much more by innate impulses than traditional analyses of freedom would suggest. This understanding will have practical consequences. It helps us to see more clearly, for example, how human beings can be manipulated, and, therefore, see how they may be protected from any such attack on their freedom.

If dignity ethics can learn these lessons from evolutionary theory, then Darwinism is certainly not ringing the '[death] knell of the virtue of mankind' but might, rather, cause dignity ethics to find more secure philosophical footings.

References

Alexander, R. 1975. 'The Search for a General Theory of Behavior', *Behavioral Sciences* 20: 77–100

Bugynar, T., Stöwe, M., and Bernd, H. 2004. 'Ravens, Corvus Corax, Follow Gaze Direction of Humans Around Obstacles', *The Royal Society* 271: 1331–6

Darwin, C. 1817. *The Descent of Man, and Selection in Relation to Sex*. London: John Murray

1838. Notebook quoted after http://darwin-online.org.uk/content/frameset?itemID=F1582%26;viewtype=text%26;pageseq=1 (accessed 26 March 2012)

Darwin, F. (ed.). 1887. *The Life and Letters of Charles Darwin Including an Autobiographical Chapter*. London: John Murray

Dawkins, R. 1976. *The Selfish Gene*. Oxford University Press

Dennett, D. 1996. *Darwin's Dangerous Idea: Evolution and the Meanings of Life*. New York: Touchstone

Joyce, R. 2006. *The Evolution of Morality*. Cambridge, MA: MIT Press

Kant, I. 1889. 'Fundamental Principles of the Metaphysic of Morals', in *Critique of Practical Reason And other Works on the Theory of Ethics*, trans. T. Kingsmill Abbott. London, New York, Toronto: Longmans, Greens and Co.

1963. *Lectures on Ethics*, trans. L. Infield. New York: Harper & Row

Pinker, S. 1999. *How the Mind Works*. London: Penguin

Rachels, J. 1990. *Created from Animals: The Moral Implications of Darwinism*. Oxford University Press

Rauscher, F. 1997. 'How a Kantian Can Accept Evolutionary Metaethics', *Biology and Philosophy* 12: 303–26

Ruse, M., and Wilson, E. O. 1985. 'The Evolution of Morality', *New Scientist* 1478: 108–28

Singer, P. 1982. 'Ethics and Sociobiology', *Philosophy and Public Affairs* 11(1): 40–64

Sommer, V. 2011. 'Kulturnatur, Naturkultur: Argumente für einen Monismus', *Zeitschrift für Kulturphilosophie* 2011(1): 335–65

Street, S. 2008. 'Reply to Copp: Naturalism, Normativity, and the Varieties of Realism Worth Worrying About', *Philosophical Issues* 18: 207–28

Wielenberg, E. 2010. 'On the Evolutionary Debunking of Morality', *Ethics* 120: 441–64

Wilson, E. O. 1978. *On Human Nature*. Cambridge, MA: Harvard University Press

1998. *Consilience: The Unity of Knowledge*. New York: Random

Wright, R. 1994. *The Moral Animal: Why We Are, the Way We Are: The New Science of Evolutionary Psychology*. London: Little, Brown & Company

58

On the border of life and death: human dignity and bioethics

MARCUS DÜWELL

A greater number of explicit references to human dignity can be found in bioethical debates than in virtually any other context. This may have its ground in the subject-matter of bioethical debates, namely, questions of life and death, which undoubtedly concern the dignity of a person. It may, however, also be a consequence of the strong influence that various religions and ideologies have on these debates. It seems that, in bioethics, the term 'human dignity' is quite often used in a way that seems to distinguish different ideological camps, which gave rise to the idea that the term would be connected to a conservative-communitarian network with strong links in various religious circles.

The underlying problem in discussing the role of human dignity in bioethics is that most approaches in bioethics are not appropriate for developing an adequate understanding of human dignity as a foundational concept from which the human rights are derived.[1] I briefly discuss two examples: Jonsen and Toulmin (1988) claimed that bioethical debates should centre on *cases*, rather than principles (Düwell 2012: 51–8). They argued that the appropriate way to deal with bioethical cases would be to compare between those cases where we agree in our moral judgments and those cases of medical practice where we are uncertain about what we ought to do. By a critical discussion and comparison of cases it would be much more likely that we would come to an agreement than if we focus on abstract principles and their contested philosophical background theories. Such case-oriented, sometimes even anti-theoretical approaches are quite dominant in bioethics. If human dignity is to be interpreted as a principle from which human rights can be derived,[2] it would be difficult to relate this principle to a case-oriented approach in the first place.

But even those approaches in bioethics that explicitly deal with principles have conceptual problems in relating to human dignity. The dominant approach is the so-called 'principlism' of Beauchamp and Childress (2008). This approach assumes that there are four principles (autonomy, beneficence, non-maleficence and justice) that would be the normative reference-point in

[1] For a critical discussion, see Düwell 2012: 64–108.

[2] Concerning the possible interpretation of human dignity in general, see the philosophical introduction in Chapter 2 of this volume.

all bioethical debates. The task of ethical discourses is to specify these four principles with regard to concrete bioethical questions, and to determine their relative weight in a concrete judgment. The approach was often criticized; it was argued that it is unclear which criteria ought to guide the weighing-process, and also that these four principles are simply an articulation of common intuitions lacking any further justification of their validity (Düwell 2012: 96–102). The more important point in this context is, however, that with principlism there is only place for a specific kind of a 'principle'. Human dignity as foundational principle from which the human rights are derived, is obviously another kind of principle than the four that according to Beauchamp and Childress have to be balanced against each other.

These two examples show that the question of how the dominant bioethical approaches relate to the human rights framework and the possible philosophical conceptualizations of this framework in general will need to be discussed. This discussion is all the more necessary as the important international regulatory documents in biolaw are part of the human rights framework.

References to human dignity have developed since the end of the Second World War. Andorno and Düwell (2013) have argued that three phases of the relevant debates in bioethics may be distinguished.

(1) Directly after the Second World War (and as a direct response to the crimes of physicians in Nazi concentration camps), the focus lay especially on the protection of human beings in human experiments. The Nuremberg Code is the most prominent articulation of this concern.
(2) Between the 1970s and 1990s we see an expansion of areas that are regulated with explicit reference to human dignity (for example, abortion, genetic diagnosis, euthanasia), where these references mainly concern the dignity of the *individual* person.
(3) Since the end of the 1990s we increasingly find references to the dignity of the *human species*, for example in an appeal to enhance the characteristics of the human species or in a concern regarding interventions in the human genome that may alter central features of the human being in a way that violates its dignity.

This chapter aims to systematically and critically reconstruct the role of 'human dignity' in bioethical debates under the headings: (1) Who has dignity? (2) What are the normative consequences of having dignity? (3) The dignity of the human species.

Who has dignity?

In bioethics, there have been many debates concerning the question who is the *object of moral concern*: who is to be ascribed so-called 'moral status' (cf. Düwell 2012: 109–24) and thus should morally be taken into account. Different ethical theories would connect different normative implications with the ascription of moral status, and only in some approaches would moral status refer to the much more specific status of a 'bearer of dignity' that is entitled to the entire set of (human) rights. In bioethics, the terminology is not always clear. When, for example, the concept of 'dignity of the creature' was introduced in a debate concerning the constitution of Switzerland, it was clearly not the intention to ascribe the same dignity to animals and plants that we ascribe to human beings. This claim was generally interpreted in the sense that animals should be an object of moral concern, although the precise nature of this moral status remains somewhat vague.[3]

Bioethics is particularly concerned with questions regarding the *beginning and the end of human life*. Cases of 'brain death' have been heavily disputed since as early as the end of the 1950s. With the introduction of the heart-lung machine it became possible to continue the basic bodily functions of patients whose brain functions had been irreversibly destroyed. At the same time, the use of organs for transplantation purposes became a realistic option. This raised the question: what is the moral status of brain-dead patients? Sometimes this question was phrased in terms of a problem concerning the end of human life, or as the question whether or not a brain-dead patient is still a human being. Such a conceptualization would interpret the moral question as a question of philosophical anthropology: it asks what the human being is from the perspective of the debate concerning persons with reduced brain functions. One can, however, also ask: is the brain-dead patient a person with dignity, and how ought we to deal with him? Since human dignity is seen as the basis of human rights,[4] this would raise the conceptual question whether human beings in all phases of their life are rights-bearers in the strict sense, and when the status of a 'being with dignity' begins and ends. And this, in turn, gives rise to the following question: on the basis of what features do we ascribe human dignity? Is it simply membership of the human species, or do we ascribe dignity on the basis of characteristics such as rational capacities? In the latter case: what if those capacities are irreversibly destroyed (as in cases of brain death), would we still have reason to assume that the being in question holds dignity? Similar questions were raised with regard to coma patients. The difference is, however, that there exists a large variation between cases that are diagnosed as coma, and also the diagnosis involves much more uncertainty than in cases of brain death. The uncertainty of the diagnosis gives rise to important precautionary reasons to treat those patients as beings with dignity.

A similar debate took place at the 'other end' of human life, particularly with regard to the status of human embryos and foetuses. Here, it was questioned to what extent we have to ascribe human dignity to an embryo in the first

[3] See Chapter 60 by Heeger and Chapter 61 by Schaber in this volume.

[4] Concerning the general conceptual question about the relationship between human dignity and human rights see the philosophical introduction in Chapter 2 of this volume.

stages of its development. Some scholars argue that we have to ascribe human dignity to human beings from conception onwards on the basis of a concept of personhood that does *not* involve rational capacities. At the other end of the spectrum we find the position that ascribes human dignity depending on the existence of *developed* rational capacities. The latter position, however, is not sincerely advocated. Nearly everybody would see newborn human babies as possessing dignity, and ascribe the right to life to them. Some have asked whether we have obligations to prolong the life of a baby with such a severe handicap that it would lead an extremely painful life.[5] Here, the main question is not whether such a baby has human dignity, but what kind of moral obligations would follow from having dignity: does it imply a prohibition of killing *in all cases*?

Authors who link human dignity to the capacity of rationality offer various arguments why we should ascribe dignity to human beings in a stage of development in which no rational capacities are detected. A first set of arguments refers to precaution: since we do not know precisely in which stage rational capacities are developed, we should play it safe and ascribe the dignity status before we phenomenologically or empirically perceive such a development. With regard to embryos and foetuses this argument is, however, of limited importance, since we can be quite certain that embryos and newborns have *not* developed rational capacities. This can, however, at least explain why we ascribe rights to babies before they actually show signs of reflective capacities.

A second set of arguments involves a plea for the extension of the scope of moral protection before the actual development of personal or rational capacities. The *potential* to develop rational capacities is argued to be sufficient for moral status. There are various versions of these arguments. Some would, for instance, say that the continuity of the development between the embryo and the rational person does not allow for sharp distinctions. Others would argue that the potentiality argument does not apply to the fertilized egg, but only to the embryo after the early phases of differentiation, because only after the end of those differentiations is there an ontological identity between the embryo and the future person (Steigleder 1998). It is important to note that such an ontological concept of potentiality significantly differs from a much more unspecific concept where it would be unclear why it could not be applied to sperm cells or unfertilized eggs as well.

A *third* set of arguments does not refer to the moral status of the embryo and newborn but to a possibility that certain uses of such beings could undermine respect for human dignity as such. If we would offer the possibility to exclude

[5] Many scholars, such as Peter Singer and Helga Kuhse (Kuhse and Singer 1985), argue in this context for positions that are probably incompatible with human dignity. This incompatibility is, however, not based on the particular case of disabled babies; it is rather that the ethical tradition they adhere to has no conceptual room for human dignity and inalienable rights in the first place.

human beings from the strict protection of human dignity, this could engender abuse or form a slippery slope because it makes disputable who is a human being and who is not – parallels to Nazi practices when Jews were denied the status of a human being are omnipresent in this debate. This argument does, however, not suffice to explain why we should opt for an ascription of the dignity status from conception onwards; it would for example be possible to see birth as the beginning of the dignity status to avoid such abuse.

Different scholars will ascribe a different role to these kinds of arguments: some will propose to use them (particularly the potentiality argument) to extend the full status of a being of human dignity to all early stages of the development of a human being, while others would opt for a gradualistic concept. The latter would require either that we regard the ascription of human dignity not as an all-or-nothing decision, but that we allow for different grades of dignity (which seems to threaten the idea that all human beings are equal in human dignity), or that potential human persons do not have human dignity, but rather a lower moral status. This latter position would necessitate an explanation of under which conditions such a lower status could overrule the rights and liberties of agents.

In any case, it is not at all evident at what point in the development of a being we have to see him or her as a being with dignity. The need for justification lies not only with the side of those who defend arguments from potentiality or precaution but with all positions.

But a more fundamental problem underlies these considerations: the basis on which we ascribe human dignity to beings must necessarily be connected to particular capacities of human beings, otherwise it would not be intelligible why we ascribe this status in the first place. But it is not obvious that those capacities are necessarily correlated to biological features that we can empirically test or phenomenologically experience. Besides this there is a great number of practical problems: it may for example be impossible to protect the dignity of each individual if we expect specific institutions to judge whether or not rational capacities are present. This too may be a reason to support a broader scope of protection of human dignity.

The normative consequences of having dignity[6]

Since the Nuremberg Code, the central point of reference in bioethical debates has been the idea that human beings – as a consequence of having dignity – have to give informed consent if they are involved in human experiments. In the decades since Nuremberg, the justification, scope, role and rules of application for this requirement were matters of bioethical debate (cf. Manson and O'Neill 2007; Beyleveld and Brownsword 2007). Informed consent was regarded as

[6] For an extensive analysis of the questions in this context, cf. Beyleveld and Brownsword 2001, especially 145–266.

mandatory not only in the case of experiments on human beings, but for medical treatment in general. With this extension, the question whether informed consent is a realistic and desirable requirement became more pressing. This requirement sets standards for physicians' communication skills and patients' involvement and comprehension that are impossible to be met. It also seems to engender bureaucracy. In addition, the focus on informed consent led to the question to what extent physicians have to fulfil wishes of patients that go beyond the traditional task of medicine (for example, plastic surgery, extension of life span). Does the requirement of informed consent demand that physicians fulfil all the preferences of their patients, or does informed consent merely protect the patient against unwanted treatment? If we see informed consent as grounded in respect for human dignity, the justification would entail that the person has to give authorization if something is to be done to him or her. This requirement for authorization, however, does not justify all claims regarding fulfilment of preferences since the human rights regime is not about fulfilment of preferences but about rights; the question is therefore what we have a right to.

With specific interpretations of human dignity it is not clear to what extent the normative consequences only result in the protection of individuals against direct violations of their *negative liberty* (their right not to be harmed), or whether respect for human dignity also requires duties that correlate with *positive rights* of patients (rights to be supported). This is particularly relevant in healthcare ethics, since the accessibility of medical treatment determines to a great extent the scope of opportunities and choices agents have. Would respect for the dignity of persons imply the obligation of states to provide effective access to a healthcare system? Questions arise here as to how to determine the threshold of medical treatment that should be financially supported, how much solidarity can be expected from society and the state, and so on.

While most seem to agree that patients' authorization is required for making actions of physicians morally acceptable, it is contested whether there are limits to what the patient may ask, limits that are related to our understanding of human dignity. In the debate about *euthanasia* and *assisted suicide* it was discussed whether physicians could be required to end the life of patients or support their attempts to commit suicide. Some arguments would refer to the intrinsic therapeutic aim of medicine and the question whether euthanasia would be compatible with this. There are, however, other arguments, which are much more focused on human dignity. Some see human dignity as demanding a fundamental restriction of the acts of other human beings, perhaps even forming a kind of taboo (in the line of Durkheim 1897). Often in the debate, respect for human dignity is linked to the doctrine of 'sanctity of life' that considers killing people as crossing the Rubicon. The idea of sanctity of life has, however, quite different roots than the human rights concept (for a critical discussion, cf. Bayertz 1996; Düwell 2012: 128–34). Others would claim that human beings have a right to 'die with dignity' and that this would not only make it *permissible* to help them if they are in extremely desperate and/or painful situations, but would even *oblige* us to provide help. This latter concept would, however, presuppose that people would lose their dignity if they die in an 'undignified' manner. This way of referring to 'dignity' is conceptually different from human dignity understood as the foundation of human rights. In the latter sense, one would not lose one's dignity by dying in a miserable and perhaps humiliating way. The argument would run rather the other way around: precisely because the patient *has* human dignity, others are categorically obliged to respect the dying person and should help him or her. If we understand human dignity as respect for the authority human beings should have over themselves, this would imply that euthanasia or assisted suicide can only be justified if it is compatible with or even called for by this respect. Such a justification would, however, give clear limitations concerning the legitimate appeal to human dignity. It would strictly exclude that anyone other than the disabled and ill person judges the value of his or her life, and whether this life is dignified.

The dignity of the human species

A variety of debates do not solely concern the dignity of individual persons, but also touch upon more collective[7] dimensions in the use of modern biotechnology. Some of these debates are discussed under the heading 'post-human' or 'transhuman' dignity,[8] which would entail an obligation of humans to develop technology further, so that the biological limitations of the species may be transcended. So far no elaborate argument has been given for the claim that such an obligation follows from the concept of human dignity. The scope of relevant debates, though, by far extends the specific discussion about posthumanism.

In the Kantian tradition (but not only there) human dignity would imply that human beings have worth beyond all price. Thus, the individual human being cannot be substituted, and is excluded from exchange of goods. But to what extent does this worth exclude ownership of parts of the human body, or patents on inventions of genetic material that may be developed into a human being (see Beyleveld and Brownsword 2001: 171–218)? These questions are part of debates about intellectual property and patent law. One could consider questions such as whether the dignity of the human person is in principle incompatible with ownership and commodification of those inventions or material.[9] For commodification or ownership, the consent or authorization of the agents involved would be required, and it is questionable whether such authorization is at all possible regarding these kinds of technologies. It is furthermore disputed whether the probable or possible consequences of the application of those technologies are such that it is likely that the societal order is changed in a way that

[7] See Chapter 35 by Werner in this volume.

[8] Bostrom 2005; see also Sandel 2007 and Chapter 33 by Weiss in this volume.

[9] See Chapter 59 by Campbell in this volume.

would affect human dignity. Habermas (2003), for example, voices the concern that cloning, gene therapy and pre-natal genetic diagnosis may result in a dependency between generations. If the parent generation were allowed to determine central genetic characteristics of their offspring, this would affect the changes of the younger generation to develop themselves as independent and free persons. This would arguably risk infringing upon human dignity because a legal and political order based on human dignity would demand a relation of equality between generations – which is precisely what is thought to be undermined by the use of certain technologies. One may have doubts regarding the validity of Habermas' specific position, but the general line of his argumentation is certainly relevant: whether the new technologies are compatible with human dignity depends on the question whether or not those technologies may have consequences that fundamentally undermine equality within the social order or undermine the possibility of a human being to understand him- or herself as free and autonomous being.

Human dignity is not only a concept aimed to protect human beings against atrocities like those in the Nazi concentration camps, but is a concept that should provide normative orientation with regard to a broad spectrum of possible technological developments. How that can be operationalized requires much more discussion, that would need in particular to reflect critically on the methods, theories and principles that are used in bioethics, and whether these are appropriate in understanding the human rights framework in general.

References

Andorno, R., and Düwell, M. 2013. 'Menschenwürdebegriff in der Bioethik', in J. C. Joerden, E. Hilgendorf and F. Thiele (eds.). *Menschenwürde und Medizin: Ein interdisziplinäres Handbuch.* Berlin: Duncker & Humblot, 465–81

Bayertz, K. (ed.). 1996. *Sanctity of Life and Human Dignity.* Dordrecht: Springer

Beauchamp, T. L., and Childress, J. F. 2008. *Principles of Biomedical Ethics.* Oxford University Press

Beyleveld, D., and Brownsword, R. 2001. *Human Dignity in Bioethics and Biolaw.* Oxford University Press

2007. *Consent in the Law.* Oxford: Hart Publishing

Bostrom, N. 2005. 'In Defense of Posthuman Dignity', *Bioethics* 19(3): 202–14

Durkheim, E. 1897. *Le suicide: Etude de sociologie.* Paris: Alcan (trans. J. A. Spaulding and G. Simpson, Suicide: A Study in Sociology. Glencoe, IL: The Free Press, 1951)

Düwell, M. 2012. *Bioethics – Methods, Theories, Domains.* London, New York: Routledge

Habermas, J. 2003. *The Future of Human Nature,* trans.W. Beister. Rehg: Polity Press

Jonsen, A., and Toulmin, S. 1988. *The Abuse of Casuistry: A History of Moral Reasoning.* Berkeley, CA: University of California Press

Kuhse, H., and Singer, P. 1985. *Should the Baby Live? The Problem of Handicapped Infants.* Oxford University Press

Manson, N. C., and O'Neill. O. 2007. *Rethinking Informed Consent in Bioethics.* Cambridge University Press

Sandel, M. 2007. *The Case Against Perfection: Ethics in the Age of Genetic Engineering.* Cambridge, MA: Harvard University Press

Steigleder, K. 1998. 'The Moral Status of Potential Persons', in E. Hildt and D. Mieth (eds.). *In Vitro Fertilization in the 1990s: Towards a Medical, Social and Ethical Evaluation.* Aldershot: Ashgate

59

Human dignity and commodification in bioethics

ALASTAIR V. CAMPBELL*

The meaning of human dignity

This chapter is concerned with how the concept of human dignity relates to the current debates in biomedical ethics about the commodification of the human body and its parts. Before considering the specific topics dealt with in this discussion, I shall clarify how I am using the term 'human dignity'. In accordance with the approach of this volume as a whole, my use depends on the way in which the concept functions in the Universal Declaration of Human Rights (UDHR) of 1948. It appears in the very first sentence of the Preamble to the Declaration:

> Whereas recognition of the inherent dignity and of the equal and inalienable rights of all members of the human family is the foundation of freedom, justice and peace in the world...

As this wording makes clear, dignity is closely aligned to human rights, but also to the *human family* – not merely to the rights of individual members. This emphasis on human solidarity will be very important for my exposition of the issues in the current move towards the commodification of human bodily materials through what has been called the 'tissue economy' (Waldby and Mitchell 2006). In the decades since the UDHR was adopted, biomedical ethics developed dramatically in the United States and other Western nations; however, the debate rapidly seemed to place the sole focus on a notion of autonomy, narrowly understood as the individual's capacity of free choice. Such a narrow focus cannot be justified if we look at the detailed requirements of the UDHR, based on the core concepts of inherent dignity and *equal* and inalienable rights. Just a few of the specific requirements of the UDHR illustrate this:

- Article 1: All human beings are born free and equal in dignity and rights. They are endowed with reason and conscience and should act towards one another in a spirit of brotherhood.

* Much of the material in this chapter is derived from my book, *The Body in Bioethics* (Routledge-Cavendish, 2009), in which the issues are discussed in greater detail.

- Article 25: Everyone has the right to a standard of living adequate for the health and well-being of himself and of his family, including food, clothing, housing and medical care and necessary social services, and the right to security in the event of unemployment, sickness, disability, widowhood, old age or other lack of livelihood in circumstances beyond his control.
- Article 29: Everyone has duties to the community in which alone the free and full development of his personality is possible.

As these clauses make plain, human dignity depends on freedom certainly, but that is just one of the elements which make up the moral requirements of a humane society. These include brotherhood (modern sensibility would use a gender-neutral term like 'solidarity'), welfare rights, rights to health and well-being and (notably) the acceptance of *duties to the community*, not merely private, individual rights claims on that community. It is from the perspective of this rich understanding of human dignity that I shall be arguing against the currently popular notion that there is no problem regarding the commodification of the human body and its parts. To treat one's body as merely a commodity, a possession which one can trade to personal advantage, I shall argue, undercuts the values of human welfare, human interdependence and one's responsibilities to the human community upon which human dignity depends.

Biomedicine and the commodification of the human body

I shall discuss two interrelated areas in this section: first, the trade in human tissue, consequent upon the increasing interest of biomedical researchers in both cell lines and potential therapies using stem cells; and, second, the trade in 'high value' body parts and tissue – notably blood and organs.

The tissue economy

The demand for human tissue from the medical and scientific community and from the biotechnology and pharmaceutical industries is now massive. Andrews and Nelkin sum up the situation in their study of the US market in human tissue, *Body Bazaar*:

> The business of human bodies is a growing part of the $17 billion biotechnology industry comprising more than thirteen hundred biotechnology firms. Those companies extract, analyze, and transform tissue into products with enormous potential for future economic gain. Their demands for skin, blood, placenta, gametes, biopsied tissue, and sources of genetic material are expanding. The blood we all provide routinely for diagnostic purposes is now useful for the study of biological processes and the genetic basis of disease. Infant foreskin can be used to create new tissue for artificial skin. Umbilical cords are valued as a source of stem cells . . . Cell lines derived from the kidneys of deceased babies are used to manufacture a common clot-busting drug . . . And human DNA can even be used to run computers, since the four chemicals – represented by the letters CATG – provide more permutations than the binary code. (Andrews and Nelkin 2001: 2f)

This treasure trove of human materials has spawned a new type of criminal – the bio-pirate. Michael Mastromarino, a former dentist who owned a New Jersey-based firm called Biomedical Tissue Services (BTS), was convicted in 2008 in a New York court for conspiring with funeral directors in several states to strip the body parts of corpses, awaiting burial or cremation, including arm and leg bones, skin and (possibly) heart valves and veins. The products were then sold on to companies providing materials for dental implants, bone implants, skin grafts and many other medical procedures. It emerged that more than one thousand corpses had been 'harvested' in this way. (Bones were replaced with PVC piping or broomsticks to conceal what had been done from the relatives.) More than 10,000 people received these tissues, some of them from persons infected with AIDS or other infectious diseases. Mastromarino was convicted and sentenced 18 to 54 years in prison. However, it is clear that he is not the first – and probably not the last – 'bio-pirate'. Andrews and Nelkin report several other earlier cases, including the sale of organs and brain parts from an infant by a morgue assistant, the sale of spines by the director of a medical school anatomy mortuary, and the routine sale of body parts, without the knowledge or consent of families, by mortuaries and crematoria in California (Andrews and Nelkin 2001: 160).

Clearly, such practices are utterly unethical, as well as probably illegal (although the laws under which people can be convicted are somewhat fuzzy and outmoded in many jurisdictions). But even if we discount these macabre fringes of the tissue market, what are we to make of the use of the huge amounts of quite legally obtained human tissue, held in numerous medical facilities and tissue banks throughout the world? (Estimates of the total amount are very hard to compute, but a calculation of tissue held only in the United States, published in 1999, suggested a total of at least 307 million specimens with an ongoing accumulation rate of more than 20 million samples per year. See Weir and Olick 2004: Chapter 2.) Does it matter that tissue donated freely and willingly for the purpose of improving medical research can now become a source of major profit for most parties involved, *except* the original donor? If there was consent (at least of some kind), and if no harm is caused to the original donors, why should we be concerned about it?

I shall return to this central question at the end of this chapter. First, however, we turn to even more obvious examples of the commodification of the human body: trade in blood and in transplantable organs.

High-value body parts

Blood and organs like hearts and kidneys are literally life-saving resources in medicine, yet both are in very short supply internationally. So far as blood is concerned, it is widely accepted that only a voluntary donation system can ensure a safe blood supply. However, less than 45 per cent of donated blood worldwide is collected in developing and transitional countries, yet these make up 80 per cent of the world's population (World Health Organization 2008).

The goal of 100 per cent voluntary unpaid blood donations, set by World Health Organization in 1997, had been achieved by only 49 of the 124 countries surveyed in 2006. Many of these countries still rely heavily on family/replacement donors and paid donors, both known to be less safe sources than regular donations from unpaid donors. Moreover, in these poorer countries, the facilities for screening donors and blood may either be inadequate or absent altogether. Even when we look at a highly developed country like the United States, we find that, while *whole* blood donations are now entirely from unpaid sources, blood plasma donors are still paid. Thus, the question of the safety of these products becomes crucial, especially since they are widely exported to meet the needs of other countries.

The situation with transplantable organs is even worse. Since its development as a life-saving measure in the second half of the last century, organ transplantation has expanded exponentially in terms of survival rates, the number of people on the waiting list for the procedure, and the range of transplantable organs. Advances in immuno-suppression and in prevention of infection have led to improvement in both the survival of the recipients and of the transplanted organs. At the same time, there has been an increase in repeat transplantations (following failure of the graft) and in multiple organ transplants. The range of conditions for which transplantation is offered has widened, and transplantable organs now include kidney, liver (or sections of liver), pancreas, heart and lung. Brain-dead donors can provide all of these organs, while kidney and sections of the liver and pancreas can also be obtained from living donors. Survival outcomes are better from living (related or unrelated) donors than from cadaveric donors, and, in the case of kidney failure, better from transplantation than from dialysis.

A consequence of this dramatic expansion in life-saving potentiality has been a worldwide demand for organs from either living or cadaveric sources, far exceeding their current availability. In light of this, many bioethics authors have argued that we need to introduce a 'regulated market' in kidneys from living donors. In other words, they believe that these body parts should be regarded as commodities, to be traded (albeit with regulations to protect donors and recipients) on a worldwide market. (We do not find the same kinds of arguments in favour of a market in blood, presumably because the hazards to the recipients of a trade in blood are very evident.)

Are there plausible objections to the view that a regulated market makes organ trade morally acceptable, assuming for now that such regulation can prevent the exploitation evident in the current illegal market (a somewhat bold assumption!)? The basic argument against the sale of one's organs is that, although they are alienable (I can have them removed from my body and transferred to another), they ought not to be regarded as fungible or commensurable. That is: organs ought not to be dealt with as though they were commodities whose value can be determined in a market of demand and supply. To do so, it is argued, is to reduce one's body to a mere object amongst other objects, to fail to respect its special place as a part of my identity – my embodied self. Thus, in donating part of my body to help another, I make a personal investment in the other's welfare and survival; I give of myself to the other. But in treating my body merely as a means to income, I demean myself by using my body (parts) in an instrumental way.

However, some authors have argued that equating organ sales with lack of respect for personal identity is a conceptual confusion. For example, Wilkinson (2003) argues that (a) there is no necessary connection between commodification of bodies and commodification of persons (consider X who buys an organ from a friend Y who needs some money; X may commodify the organ but not the friend Y); and (b) empirically there is little reason to regard organ sale as worse than widely accepted practices such as the buying and selling of labour (consider manual labour workers in some countries paid at the lowest possible rates by companies outsourcing the manufacture of their brand name products). So if we are to prohibit organ sale, then we have to prohibit (at least some) of these widely accepted practices.

However, in response to this type of argument one may point out that examples of exploitation in some areas of social life do not provide a justification for the spread of such exploitation to other social interactions. Moreover, defenders of the marketability of organs do not provide any principles for preventing what we might call 'market creep' in the sale of body parts. On what basis do we draw a line in the authorization of the dismantling of the bodies of the poor to meet medical needs? Gill and Sade (2002) refer to this argument in relation to the possibility of heart transplants and point out (rightly) that the law could not authorize the killing of a person to provide a heart to another. There are simpler examples. There are many body parts without which a person can still function adequately, which are also transplantable and useful for those with medical or surgical needs. Examples would be people who seek replacement of a severed hand, an operation which has been carried out using a hand from a cadaver, but which would be more effective using the hand of a living person. So why should someone not offer their hand for sale? We need to ask why such sales should be prevented *in principle*. Where should we draw the line between acceptable and unacceptable trading in one's bodily resources?

Conclusion: preserving our shared human dignity

I return to the core concepts of the UDHR: freedom *and* equality; a common life where adequate social security and healthcare give everyone the chance of a life of dignity and self-development; rights, yes, but also duties; membership of the human family in which solidarity is a guiding principle. Relating such normative concepts to the question of the commodification of the body leads us naturally to the notion of the 'bio-commons'. The metaphor of a commons which must be protected from commercial interests has its ground in the history of 'enclosures'. When, in eighteenth-century Britain, common land, free to all for grazing, was taken over by powerful landowners, this resulted in massive suffering for the rural poor. So the metaphor of a 'bio-commons' promotes the idea that human materials and the information derived from them should be openly accessible so that they can be used for the benefit of all humankind, rather than for the benefit of the powerful (see Dickenson 2007: Chapter 8 and Waldby and Mitchell 2006: Chapter 5). By such a sharing for mutual benefit, the human origins of tissues, organs and blood would be properly recognized and the dignity of our common heritage respected and preserved.

I conclude that the notions of human dignity and solidarity, enshrined in the Universal Declaration of Human Rights – and in many other subsequent international declarations – require that the human body and its parts be treated, not as tradable assets, but as essential aspects of our shared, embodied humanity. Of course, every individual has a fundamental right to bodily integrity. Nothing in this account implies that the community in some sense 'owns' the bodies of its individual members (whether before or after death) or that it has claims on the use of such parts, against the will of the individual. Rather, our nature as embodied selves provides us for opportunities for altruism, the giving to 'unknown strangers' described in Titmuss' classic study, *The Gift Relationship* (Titmuss 1970). It is for these reasons that a full understanding of human dignity must lead us to oppose the idea of a market in body parts, condemn the involvement of some members of the medical profession in such activities, and require international commitment to effective ways of giving all persons access to the bio-commons.

References

Andrews, L. B., and Nelkin, D. 2001. *Body Bazaar: The Market for Human Tissue in the Biotechnology Age.* New York: Crown Publishers

Dickenson, D. 2007. *Property in the Body: Feminist Perspectives.* Cambridge University Press

Gill, M. B., and Sade, R. M. 2002. 'Paying for Kidneys: The Case Against Prohibition', *Kennedy Institute of Ethics Journal* 12: 17–45

Titmuss, R. M. 1970. *The Gift Relationship: From Human Blood to Social Policy.* London: George Allen & Unwin

Waldby, C., and Mitchell, R. 2006. *Tissue Economies: Blood, Organs, and Cell Lines in Late Capitalism.* Durham, NC: Duke University Press

Weir, R. F., and Olick, R. S. 2004. *The Stored Tissue Issue: Biomedical Research, Ethics, and Law in the Era of Genomic Medicine.* Oxford University Press

Wilkinson, S. 2003. *Bodies for Sale: Ethics and Exploitation in the Human Body Trade.* London: Routledge

World Health Organization. 2008. 'Blood Safety and Donation', www.who.int/mediacentre/factsheets/fs279/en/index.html (accessed October 2010)

60

Dignity only for humans? A controversy

ROBERT HEEGER

A critical comment on the ascription of dignity to non-human living beings

Should dignity be ascribed only to humans or also to non-human living beings? We are faced with this problem if we take note of a recent bioethical discussion about the 'dignity of creatures'. This discussion was prompted by an amendment to the Swiss Federal Constitution. A plebiscite of May 1992 had voted into the Constitution that the federal government in its regulations of gene technologies shall take into account the dignity of non-human creatures, that is: of animals, plants and other organisms. The vote for the demand that the dignity of these creatures be taken into account indicates that wide sections of the Swiss population worried about moral problems caused by genetic engineering – in short: whether human beings have a moral obligation to set limits to their interference with the life of animals, plants and other organisms, and, if so, which limits should be set. Hitherto used moral criteria, such as the avoidance of pain and suffering in animals, were thought insufficient for tackling these problems. A more far-reaching criterion was deemed necessary in order to include moral concerns beyond animal pain and suffering. But the fierce debate following the plebiscite showed that it is far from clear what moral content the concept of dignity of non-human creatures should be taken to have. The Swiss authorities commissioned two teams to clarify the concept and to explore its implications for the genetic engineering of non-human creatures. The reports of the teams give expression to two interpretations of the concept that were prevailing in the discussion (Schmidt 2008: 196). The first report (Praetorius and Saladin 1996) tries to determine a concept of dignity of non-human creatures by analogy with a Kantian concept of human dignity. The second report (Balzer, Rippe and Schaber 1998) suggests that the concept should be seen as corresponding with the concept of inherent value of non-human beings. I will describe both interpretations and criticize them for what I take to be their problematic features. Finally, I will raise the question of whether we should ascribe dignity to all living beings or only to human persons, bearing in mind the role of the concept of dignity as a ground for human rights.

Dignity of creatures as an extension of human dignity

According to the first report, the concept of dignity of creatures is akin to the concept of human dignity. Its meaning should be clarified by starting out from the concept of human dignity. To respect human dignity means to assume that every human being has intrinsic value and must be taken into account regardless of the cost, and to have dignity means to be in the world for the sake of oneself and not for the purposes of others (Praetorius and Saladin 1996: 20, 29). In this interpretation, the Kantian idea of the human being as an end in itself and a bearer of absolute intrinsic value is discernible. However, in contrast to Kant, the report widens the application of the concept of dignity. Dignity extends to non-human creatures. This gives rise to the question what content the concept of dignity has if it is said to be applicable to both human beings and non-human creatures. The answer of the report is this: first, the concept of dignity of creatures cannot have exactly the same meaning as the concept of human dignity, due to the significant role *reason* plays in the conceptualization of human dignity. But, second, both concepts have a core meaning in common. This core meaning is the specific intrinsic value of a being, its 'integrity' (Praetorius and Saladin 1996: 86). Human beings and non-human creatures have this feature in common, because both are organic wholes that can make their needs or wishes understood by human beings (Praetorius and Saladin 1996: 36). Since both concepts share this core meaning, the concept of dignity of non-human creatures should get an interpretation that leans on the concept of human dignity. It should be taken to mean the specific intrinsic value of non-human creatures to which we owe respect (Praetorius and Saladin 1996: 87).

The report also deals with the question what implications the concept of dignity has for the genetic engineering of non-human creatures. The demand that the dignity of non-human creatures be taken into account should lead to a new perception of other living beings – with far-reaching practical consequences regarding, for instance, the treatment of animals. To treat animals solely as means to achieve human ends is to grossly disregard their intrinsic value. To subject them to genetic engineering for human purposes is to make them serve better as objects for human use (Praetorius and Saladin 1996: 93). Such serious interferences with their lives are in principle morally inadmissible. They can only be justified if human life would otherwise be threatened (Praetorius and Saladin 1996: 44).

This interpretation of the concept of dignity of non-human creatures is problematic. It starts out from a Kantian concept of human dignity and tries to extend it to non-human creatures. It implies that there is an analogy between human dignity and the dignity of non-human creatures. The dignity it ascribes to these creatures is supposed to give them inviolability similar to human inviolability. However, the report fails to justify the stated analogy. It omits the important question whether non-human creatures meet the prerequisite conditions of the ascription of dignity. According to a Kantian concept, persons have dignity in virtue of their autonomy, that is, in virtue of their ability to exert self-determination, to be moral agents. This self-determination requires minimally that persons can transcend immediate urges and everyday needs and can reflectively evaluate their own and others' wishes, needs and interests. But as far as we know, non-human creatures cannot acquire this capacity. Therefore, a Kantian concept of dignity cannot be extended to non-human creatures.

Dignity of creatures as inherent value

The second report argues that the concept of dignity of non-human creatures should not be seen as an extension of the concept of human dignity. One important reason it gives is that the constitutional article demands to take into account the dignity of non-human creatures regardless of whether they have or lack the cognitive capacities that are prerequisites for human dignity (Balzer, Rippe and Schaber 1998: 42). The report proposes an interpretation that is independent of the concept of human dignity. It says, instead, that the concept of dignity in the constitutional article corresponds with the concept of inherent value (Balzer, Rippe and Schaber 1998: 42–8). What its concept of inherent value comprises can be explained by considering two questions. First, why should inherent value be ascribed to non-human creatures? Second, what moral content does the ascription of inherent value have?

In answer to the first question, the report states that inherent value should be ascribed to non-human creatures because they can be said to have three characteristics. First, they have a good of their own. Second, they pursue individual goals, they have their own ends, strive to survive, adapt to their environment and reproduce. Third, they are organic entities; they exist as individuals (Balzer, Rippe and Schaber 1998: 43–4). Most important is that they possess a good of their own. The report puts in more concrete terms what this good consists in with regard to genetic engineering. It is neither an original purpose of the species nor the integrity of the genome, but the uninhibited development of those functions and abilities that members of the respective species, as a rule, can develop (Balzer, Rippe and Schaber 1998: 52–7). So, whether or not the own good of non-human creatures is impaired by genetic engineering should be determined in view of (expected or empirically demonstrated) phenotypes of the transgenic animals or plants, for example, the transgenic animals' ability to grow, procreate or move. The report also provides an answer to the question regarding the moral content of the ascription of inherent value: that a non-human creature has inherent value implies that human beings must take it into account for its own sake, show it moral respect for its own good. From the ascription of inherent value the report draws the moral conclusion that it is *prima facie* wrong to impair those functions and abilities of a non-human creature that members of its species can normally develop. This conclusion is in turn decisive for the report's moral assessment of genetic engineering: if genetic interventions impair the normal functions and abilities, then they are *prima facie* wrong, that is to say, they are morally inadmissible, unless they can be justified by other morally relevant reasons (Balzer, Rippe and Schaber 1998: 15, 57–8).

There is reason to challenge this answer. It is doubtful whether the concept of inherent value does have the stated moral content, for the report's term 'inherent value' is ambiguous. It seems to stand for two different concepts of inherent value. One concept has a directly obligating character. To state that a living being has inherent value is to raise a moral claim. The report says, for instance: all living beings have inherent value and that means that we should not see them only as means, but recognize them as beings with their own good (Balzer, Rippe and Schaber 1998: 48, 50). This concept of inherent value is egalitarian and resembles the concept of inherent worth set forth, for example, in Taylor's theory of environmental ethics (Taylor 1986: 75–80, 156–8). However, in several important passages the report does not hold to this concept, but gives preference to a different one: an inherent value is a value that admits of degrees and can be weighed against the value of other goods. Living beings can have a higher or lower inherent value and their value is proportionate to their complexity and abilities (Balzer, Rippe and Schaber 1998: 49–50). This implies that living beings can differ in value as judged against a standard of value. Certain properties inherently related to them, such as their abilities, are the objects of this valuation. That a being has 'inherent value', then, means that it is valuable as far as these properties are concerned. This concept of inherent value is a non-moral concept. It does not yet have the moral implication that we must take non-human creatures into account for their own sake. In order for such a moral obligation to follow, a non-moral concept of inherent value must first gain moral significance.

It may be argued that this concept too already has moral significance, since the report develops the concept of dignity of non-human creatures 'within a bio-centric framework', which is to say, by starting out from the bio-centric thesis that all living beings have to be taken into account morally (Balzer, Rippe and Schaber 1998: 38, 42, 48). However, the report does not set out how this bio-centric thesis is connected with the report's concept of a value of non-human creatures that allows of degrees and can be weighed against the value of other goods. It does not show why the bio-centric thesis supports the view that a standard of value be introduced in order to determine how valuable living beings are in comparison with other living beings or other goods. The report needs an argument that explains how its concept of inherent value inherits moral significance from the bio-centric thesis. On the condition that such an argument can be provided and that the bio-centric thesis is tenable, the ascription of inherent value can be said to imply that non-human creatures should be taken into account for their own sake.

Should we ascribe dignity to non-human living beings?

We have looked into two interpretations of the concept of dignity of non-human creatures. Do they give us good reason for applying the concept of dignity to non-human living beings? The first interpretation fails in this respect. It tries to ascribe dignity to non-human living beings by extending a Kantian concept of human dignity to them. But a Kantian concept of dignity cannot be extended to non-human living beings because it is tied to prerequisite conditions which, as far as we know, non-human beings cannot meet. The second interpretation does not get into these difficulties. It suggests that the ascription of dignity to non-human living beings corresponds to the ascription of inherent value, which entails the moral claim that these beings be taken into account for their own sake. However, this interpretation leaves us with a problem. It equates the ascription of inherent value with the ascription of dignity. But we may reasonably agree with the moral claim that non-human living beings be taken into account for their own sake, even though we would refuse to ascribe dignity to them. We can justify this by pointing out that there is a difference between the obligation to show consideration for a being and the obligation to respect the dignity of a being. To which beings do we have the latter obligation? That depends on the concept of dignity we have reason to advocate. The strongest candidate is the concept of the dignity of the human person. This concept plays a fundamental role in the Universal Declaration of Human Rights. It is the dignity of the human person that is to be protected by human rights. Philosophers have tried to adumbrate the concept in its close connection to human rights. The concept has been determined as the specific value and inviolability of the human person in virtue of its normative agency. One important component of this agency is the autonomy to choose and pursue one's own conception of a worthwhile life (Griffin 2008: 33, 45, 156). This concept of dignity does not rule out moral obligations to non-human living beings, for human dignity and human rights do not cover the whole of morality. Still, the concept implies a special position of the human person and is not applicable to non-human living beings. If we stick to it, then we should not ascribe dignity to non-human living beings.

References

Balzer, P., Rippe, K. P., and Schaber, P. 1998. *Menschenwürde vs Würde der Kreatur: Begriffsbestimmung, Gentechnik, Ethikkommissionen.* Freiburg im Breisgau, Munich: Alber Verlag

Griffin, J. 2008. *On Human Rights.* Oxford University Press

Praetorius, I., and Saladin, P. 1996. *Die Würde der Kreatur (Art. 24novies Abs. 3 BV).* Bern: BUWAL

Schmidt, K. 2008. *Tierethische Probleme der Gentechnik: Zur moralischen Bewertung der Reduktion wesentlicher tierlicher Eigenschaften.* Paderborn: Mentis Verlag

Taylor, P. W. 1986. *Respect for Nature: A Theory of Environmental Ethics.* Princeton University Press

61

Dignity only for humans? On the dignity and inherent value of non-human beings

PETER SCHABER

In 1992, an article was incorporated by referendum in the Swiss Constitution mandating that the federal government regulations on the use of genetic material should take into account the dignity of non-human beings. Paragraph 1 of the article states:

> The federal government shall issue regulations on the use of the genetic material of animals, plants, and other organisms. It thereby shall take into account, the dignity of non-human beings ['*die Würde der Kreatur*'] as well as the safety of human beings, animals, and the environment, and shall protect the genetic diversity of animal and plant species.

According to the legal interpretation, the dignity of non-human beings pertains to all individual organisms, animals, plants and micro-organisms. What is meant by the dignity of non-human beings? How does it relate to human dignity? And why should we ascribe it to all non-human beings? If animals had dignity, their moral status might be the same or at least close to the one humans have. They might have, provided that dignity is the basis of human rights, the same rights humans have. On the other hand, if they do not have dignity, the rights humans have might trump the claims that could be made on behalf of animals.

Non-human and human dignity

One might argue that the dignity of non-human beings is just an extension of the concept of human dignity. What we ascribe to humans when we talk of their dignity is also something that should be ascribed to non-humans. Of course, the meaning of the concept of human dignity is contested. But, one could argue, whatever turns out to be the proper understanding of human dignity, it should also be ascribed to non-humans. But why should we do this? Advocates of the view that we should extend dignity to all living organisms give two reasons: first, humans would not have the properties due to which they have dignity if there were no other living organisms. Dignity pertains also to the necessary conditions of the properties which convey dignity to humans. Second, Living organisms have their own teleonomic structure, they are beings that pursue their own ends.

The first argument provides us with a reason to extend dignity not just to all living organisms, but rather to all natural entities on which the dignity-conveying properties of humans depend. This does not correspond to what the official understanding of Article 120 of the Swiss Constitution demands, yet one could think that this is what should be done. Taking the argument seriously, one would have to draw an even more radical conclusion and argue that all natural preconditions for human dignity in the world have dignity themselves.

The argument presupposes an idea of conditionality that says: X is a necessary condition for Y; Y has dignity, so has dignity as well. In other words, dignity has to be ascribed to X because it is a condition without which beings would not have dignity.

But it is not clear why this should follow. The normative properties we ascribe to something do not necessarily correspond to the normative properties we ascribe to their necessary conditions. There would be no valuable things if there were no atoms. But this in itself is not seen as a reason to ascribe value to atoms. And, in addition: the conditionality argument might, in the dignity case, prove too much: if the conditions that are necessary for beings to have dignity therefore have dignity as well, then not just living beings, but most non-living entities such as molecules and electrons, would have dignity. It is not clear whether this extension of human dignity can sensibly be defended.

Inherent value

Some authors argue that the dignity of non-human beings should not be taken as an extension of human dignity, but should be understood in a different way. Ascribing dignity to non-human beings, according to this view, is just saying that they have inherent value, that is: a value they have independently of the value they have for other beings. Their inherent value can be understood as moral status: they count for their own sake. Our behaviour towards them should be restricted, not by reasons that are based on our interests and needs, but by reasons that result from the affirmation that they possess value. In other words, that non-human beings have inherent value means that we should behave morally towards them, irrespective of the value they have for human beings as well as for other living beings.

Why should inherent value be ascribed to non-human beings? Many hold the view that non-human beings have inherent value due to the fact that they have an individual good. Things can happen and be done to them which are good or bad for them. What it means for something to be good or bad for a non-human being can be understood (a) in a subjectivist way and (b) in a objectivist way. According to the subjectivist view, things are good or bad for non-human beings when they experience them as good or bad, respectively. And, according to the objectivist view, things are good and bad for non-human beings without being experienced by them as such. Supporters of the subjectivist position hence limit inherent value to sentient beings, while supporters of the objectivist position take all living beings to have inherent value.

The subjectivist position cannot account for the intuition that it would be wrong to use drugs or breeding techniques to make sure that, for instance, pigs could tolerate extremely restrictive living conditions without experiencing it as bad. The subjectivist view could not object to such a practice, because it is not bad for the pig according to this view, given that it does not experience it as bad. This can be seen as a reason to reject the subjectivist position. It leaves us with the objectivist position and requires us to extend inherent value to all living beings whose lives can sensibly be judged in terms of quality. But what exactly does it mean to have a good of one's own? An answer is needed to determine what it means to take the inherent value of a being into account either by respecting or by promoting it. Three answers have been given.

According to the first proposal, the inherent value of a living being is preserved when this being is capable of developing into a typical representative of the species it belongs to. The individual's own good refers to certain species-specific features that distinguish the individual as a member of its species. On this view, it is the purpose of living beings to develop their species-specific features. This is, for instance, not the case with Tracy, the transgenic sheep, who produces the pharmaceutical product Alpha-1-Antitryspin (AAT) in her milk. Tracy's situation fails to live up to this aim, given that producing pharmaceutical products is not what sheep normally do. Tracy does not possess the species-specific features of a sheep, even though the transgenic change does not infringe upon her functioning. To respect the dignity of living beings is to respect their species-specific features.

According to the second proposal, the inherent value of a living being is respected when its genetic make-up is preserved. In other words, a living being lives a good life when its individual genetic make-up develops to maturity. Given that breeding does not change the individual genetic make-up, this position allows animal husbandry, but it does prohibit the production of transgenic animals. Breeders do not change the individual genetic make-up. Genetic engineering does change the genetic make-up, and is thus, on this view, incompatible with the inherent value of the beings concerned. It must be stressed that this is held to be wrong not because it violates the species' limits, but rather because it allows for the possibility to infringe upon the individual value of the living being itself.

According to the third proposal, the individual good of a living being is related to those functions and operations that a member of the species can normally perform. Any reduction or limitation of an individual's capabilities infringes on the good of a being and disrespects its inherent value. This is the case regardless of whether the concerned individual is able to realize it or not. On this view, the individual good of a living being does not consist in this individual being able to develop all species-specific features. It rather consists in its being able to perform those functions a member of its species can normally perform (for example, growth, reproduction, motion or social functioning). An infringement of such functions would interfere with the good of the living being and thus be a way of disrespecting its inherent value. The dignity of living beings is violated if the individual being's own good is infringed upon. And this is the case if the living being is prevented from performing those functions that members of the species can normally perform.

To illustrate the three positions: the dignity of Tracy, the transgenic sheep, is infringed upon according to the first position because the change in its genes prevents it from living the life of a normal sheep, producing a pharmaceutical product sheep normally do not produce. Given that its genetic make-up has not been preserved, its dignity is also violated if we follow the second proposal. However, it need not be violated according to the third proposal, provided Tracy is able to live out her normal functioning (for example, be able to move, grow, reproduce and live together with other sheep).

An equivocation?

Finally, one has to ask whether the talk of dignity of living beings is just an equivocation. Is what is meant by the inherent value of beings completely different from human dignity? Does the inherent value of beings share certain essential features with human dignity? The answer depends, of course, on what we mean by human dignity. Authors in a Kantian tradition think that dignity does not allow for any trade-offs. Human dignity should not be weighed against other values. Thus, violations of dignity cannot be justified by the advantages such violations would bring about. The dignity of humans trumps any advantage in terms of any kind of value, no matter how great.

Could it be true that we would never be justified in impairing functions a cow would normally perform, however big the benefits were we could expect from doing so? It is unlikely that this form of trumping could sensibly be linked to the inherent value of non-human beings. And this is also probably not what was aimed for in the Swiss Constitution.

It can also be questioned whether the inherent value of non-living beings has anything to do with human dignity if the latter is understood as what is paradigmatically violated by acts of humiliation and degradation. It is hard to imagine that non-human beings can be the objects of such kinds of treatment. If human dignity is taken in such a sense, the inherent value of non-human beings must be understood in a different way.

There is the further question whether the concept of inherent value has moral significance (see Chapter 60 of this volume). The answer to this question depends on the meaning of the concept of inherent value. It might be understood as referring to reasons for action: 'X has inherent value' then means: 'The properties due to which X has an inherent value are reasons to treat and not treat it in certain ways.' The latter need not be objects of moral duties we have. It might in a much weaker sense be something we should do.

If living beings have inherent value, then certain treatments are appropriate, others are not. To destroy or to fail to promote the good on which the inherent value of a being is based must then be regarded as inappropriate, if not, depending on the concept of inherent value, as morally wrong. The inherent value of a being should be respected, preserved or promoted. This is not because this would serve the purposes human beings pursue. Living beings must rather be treated in these ways because of what they are. More precisely, they must be treated this way because of the properties that give them inherent value. What this amounts to might differ from what we owe to the inherent dignity of humans. But it might be what is actually meant by the talk of the dignity of creatures.

References

Attfield, R. 1995. 'Genetic Engineering: Can Unnatural Kinds be Wronged?', in P. Wheale and R. McNally (eds.), *Animal Genetic Engineering: Of Pigs, Oncomice, and Men.* London: Pluto Press, 201–10

Balzer, P., Rippe, K. P., and Schaber, P. 1998. *Menschenwürde vs Würde der Kreatur: Begriffsbestimmung, Gentechnik, Ethikkommissionen.* Freiburg im Breisgau, Munich: Alber

2000. 'Two Concepts of Dignity for Humans and Non-Human Organisms in the Context of Genetic Engineering', *Journal of Agricultural and Environmental Ethics* 13: 7–27

Fox, M. 1990. 'Transgenic Animals: Ethical and Animal Welfare Concerns', in P. Wheale and R. McNally (eds.), *The Bio Revolution, Cornucopia or Pandora's Box.* London: Pluto Press, 31–45

Heeger, R. 2000. 'Genetic Engineering and the Dignity of Creatures', *Journal of Agricultural and Environmental Ethics* 13: 43–51

Praetorius, I., and Saladin, P. 1996. *Die Würde der Kreatur*, Schriftenreihe Umwelt No. 260, Bern

Rolston, H. 1988. *Environmental Ethics: Duties to and Values in The Natural World*, Philadelphia, PA: Temple University Press

Saladin, P., and Schweizer, R. 1995. *Kommentar zu Art. 24novies*, in J. Aubert *et al.* (eds.), *Kommentar zur Bundesverfassung der Schweizerischen Eidgenossenschaft.* Basel, Zürich, Bern: Helbing und Lichtenhahn/Schulthess, Stämpfli, 58–73

Singer, P. 1993. *Practical Ethics.* Cambridge University Press

Sitter-Liver, B. 1995. 'Würde der Kreatur: Grundlegung, Bedeutung, Funktion eines neuen Verfassungsprinzips', in J. Nida-Rümelin and D. V. d. Pfordten (eds.), *Ökologische Ethik und Rechtstheorie.* Baden-Baden: Nomos, 355–64

Taylor, P. 1986. *Respect for Nature: A Theory of Environmental Ethics.* Princeton University Press

62

Human dignity and future generations

MARCUS DÜWELL*

The questions of whether we have obligations towards future generations, why we have such obligations and what these obligations entail, are important topics of discussion in contemporary moral and political philosophy. While there seems to be political consensus on the view that we are obligated to adopt a policy of sustainability, the reasons why we should endorse such an obligation are highly contested. The dominant argument can be found in the so-called 'Brundtland definition' of 'sustainable development': 'sustainable development is development that meets the needs of the present without compromising the ability of future generations to meet their own needs' (United Nations 1987: 37). In this line of thought, the obligation towards future generations is a normative reason for a sustainable politics. Of course, we also have reasons to act sustainably because of the rights of current (particularly the younger) generations, but various aspects of a sustainable politics are only necessary if we take future generations into account. Such an obligation to a long-term sustainable policy would assume that there is something about future generations that gives us obligations towards them. But if we attribute rights to future generations, we would assume that human rights should be attributed to beings that do not and may never exist. This problem is quite extensively discussed in terms of 'rights of future generations' or 'intergenerational justice' (for example, Grosseries and Meyer 2009; Hiskes 2009) but the concept of human dignity is hardly ever referred to. In the following I will briefly explain (1) the obstacles we are facing if we talk about human dignity in the context of future generations; (2) what such a conceptualization could look like; and (3) what further philosophical and practical issues arise from this.

Why should we talk about human dignity in the context of future generations?

In providing a normative framework for obligations towards future generations we have basically two options.

* The work reported on in this chapter has benefited from participation in the 'Rights to a Green Future' network, financed by the European Science Foundation. I thank Rutger Claassen and Klaus Steigleder for helpful comments.

We can start with the *obligations that we have towards existing human beings* and assume that we have the same or similar obligations towards future generations. In international law our obligations towards others are conceptualized in terms of human rights and this framework is binding also for the domestic level insofar states obliged themselves to form their legal order in accordance with the provisions of the human rights framework. On the view of this framework, it is assumed that human beings have human rights on the basis of their human dignity. The obligations that follow from this normative status are thought to override other practical considerations.[1] If we would attempt to base an obligation regarding future generations on this framework, we would have to show that we have to act in a sustainable way to fulfil our duties towards future generations and that those obligations are a consequence of the duties we have towards the dignity of human beings.

An alternative route would assume that we have a responsibility towards nature for nature's sake, or an obligation towards God not to destroy his property, the cosmos (for example, Taylor 1986; Rolston 1988). The problem with this approach is that it would assume that there are normatively more important considerations than respect for the dignity of the human being, and hence the basic assumption of the human rights regime – that human dignity may not be overruled by other action-guiding considerations – would be rejected. Respect for human dignity would be subordinated to the obligations that we have towards nature, god or the cosmos. Such an eco- or bio-centric position is quite popular because it seems to articulate the broadly shared conviction that it is morally wrong to destroy large parts of the globe for human interests and that the exercise of our liberty should thus be limited. Often the anthropocentrism of modern morality is held responsible for this development. However, the proposed bio- or eco-centric alternatives are by no means uncontroversial, and – more importantly for our purposes here – incompatible with an ethics of human dignity, since they would force us to revise the overriding priority of the human rights framework. It is therefore worthwhile to investigate how a concept of responsibility for future generations on the basis of an ethics of human dignity would look and which philosophical presuppositions are necessary for its justification. The question would thus be whether the human rights framework itself could provide a basis for obligations for a sustainable politics.

Can we apply the concept of human dignity to future generations?

In talking about future generations, we are confronted with a variety of conceptual and normative problems under which the most famous one would be the so-called *non-existence* and *non-identity-problem*, which questions whether and under which conditions we can harm future generations at all (Parfit 1984;

[1] These conceptual presuppositions are explained in the philosophical introduction in Chapter 2 of this volume.

Roberts and Wassermann 2009). Focused on our context, the problem would be the following: if we think that we are obligated to respect the dignity of other people, we usually presuppose their existence. Future generations, however, are generations of beings that are not yet born. Whether or not they will exist depends on our decisions; we can simply decide not to bring them into existence. If we were to do so, we would perhaps miss important life opportunities for ourselves and it might be particularly sad for those who would be the last people on Earth, but it would not be a rights violation of future generations because they simply do not exist and never will. To say that they have a right to be brought into existence would assume that there are already individuals that have pre-existing rights, which is conceptually impossible. Some people assume that we have an obligation to ensure that humankind continues to exist, but it would be the question whether these obligations could be based on the principle of human dignity. It would be another concept of dignity if we were to speak about the *dignity of the human species as such or a collective dignity*, bypassing the rights and dignity of the individual and assuming that the species would be a kind of collective agent. We should therefore investigate whether we could justify a categorical obligation to continue the life of the human beings on the basis of the same concept of human dignity that forms the basis of the human rights framework. An option would be to ask whether we could decide to end human existence by stopping reproduction in general and still be committed to the conviction that we have to respect the absolute worth of human beings. If the conviction that human beings have unconditional moral worth is morally so fundamental important that it forms the basis of the human rights framework, it could be inconsistent with this assumption to finish the existence of humankind. But even if we assume that we have an obligation to bring human beings into existence because of general obligations to preserve the existence of humanity, it is not plausible to assume that this obligation would be a duty corresponding to the rights of specific future beings to be brought into existence.[2]

But we can leave this question open here and wonder whether we have other duties towards future generations. The world population is growing more rapidly than ever before. We therefore have strong reasons to assume that there will continue to be human beings in the future, human beings that are not yet born. But does this mean we have moral obligations towards those future generations? Should the rights that are grounded in their purported dignity status be implemented in global and national regulatory orders? This would depend on how we conceptualize human dignity. If we understand human dignity as a normative status that prohibits using those who possess it as objects or 'a mere means', it is not obvious how this relates to future generations: since they do not exist, it seems rather impossible for us to treat them as objects. Even if we destroy the Earth for our purposes, we may be said to ignore

[2] I am grateful to Klaus Steigleder for clarifying comments on this point.

future generations, but we cannot be said to treat them as a mere means.[3] An approach that understands the obligations human dignity gives rise to in terms of the prohibition of humiliating treatment (Margalit 1996) runs into a similar problem: to humiliate someone (as in torture or rape) presupposes a form of contact between human beings, from which we can doubt that this is applicable to our relationship to future generations. However, if we understand human dignity as the basis of the whole human rights regime, then it seems possible that our behaviour today may violate the dignity of future generations.

If human dignity is the basis from which human rights are derived, the whole spectrum of actions that these rights prohibit or prescribe is based on the concept of human dignity. Now, human rights basically exclude those actions that disrespect human beings and protect their rights to exercise freedoms; they prescribe that governments must be accessible for and controlled by citizens and that they must have economic and cultural opportunities. In short, to respect human dignity means to treat human beings in such a way that they are able to live their own life (in this line, cf. Gewirth 1992).

Regarding future generations, however, many of these rights seem to fall outside the scope of our influence. We don't know how they will live and which interests and values they will have: whether or not future generations will live in families; how they will organize their social life; whether they will build opera houses; whether they will have democratic societies; whether they will live in states that are similar to ours and whether they will drink single malt whisky. We don't know those things and it seems unclear whether we influence their life in respects that are important for them. We could therefore conclude that it is not clear to what extent we may violate their rights.

But in another respect our actions today do influence basic conditions of their life. The emissions we produce have influence on the global climate, the level of the oceans, the temperature on the globe etc.; we are using natural resources that will probably be extremely valuable for them, and our reproductive behaviour is responsible for an extreme growth of the world population. In all these respects we have a large influence on the basic conditions of their life. It is evident that all these influences affect aspects of their life that are as important to them as they are to us, since future generations will share some of our basic biological features. Whatever aims they may have, whatever goals they may wish to achieve in life, they will always need some quality of the environment and access to some basic goods in order to realize the goals that they want to achieve. That means that, even if we don't know what future generations will value and how they

[3] The prohibition on treating human beings as a 'means only' is prominently formulated in Kant's 'formula of humanity'. But I assume that this prohibition is a consequence of the more broadly formulated obligation in Kant to treat human beings as an 'end in itself'. In this sense, I assume that Kant's concept of human dignity has a much broader scope than the prohibition of instrumentalization of human beings.

will live, we have all reason to assume that we influence the basic conditions of their life. *If human rights form a protection against standard threats to human existence and aim to ensure equal access to those goods that are required for human beings in order to be able to live a life of their own, then it seems inevitable that we have the possibility to violate the rights of future generations.*

Perhaps such an approach to human rights is surprising because discussions on human rights often just focus on individual liberties. In order to protect individual liberties, however, the human rights regime needs to safeguard certain goods that function as the *condition* for effectuating these liberties. If the freedom of speech, access to public offices or freedom of religion is to be protected by the human rights regime, then those goods that are in a basic sense necessary to enjoy those rights have to be protected in the first place. If we have a right to be governed by a democratically elected government, it is impossible to respect this right without giving access to political information and educating people to the extent that they have the skills required for understanding this information. Relevant for the human rights regime are hence not only the interests and goals of *individual* people, but also specific goods, which are important for human agents *in general.*

In this context, Gewirth speaks of 'generic rights' (Gewirth 1978: 64, see also Gewirth 2001), 'rights to the necessary conditions of agency'. These conditions are in part different for various agents, depending on various cultural, historical and individual circumstances of actions. Furthermore, it is possible that human beings evolve in various respects in the future. But we have reasons to assume that humans in the future will share some basic biological aspects with us and that they will have at least some fundamental interests[4] equivalent to ours. Wherever and whenever human beings exist, they have the right to water to drink and air to breathe, are in need of social recognition and other physical, psychological and social conditions that form *generic conditions for agency.* To determine these rights in detail is more complex because those generic conditions are not just the conditions for mere survival but those goods that are necessary for a meaningful way of realizing goals of action. In any case, it is obvious that the destruction of basic generic goods would violate the human rights of future generations.

It is in this context important to notice that with regard to the generic rights there is a significant difference to cases that are often discussed in the context of future generations. Parfit (1984) starts his discussion about the so-called 'non-identity problem' with reference to cases of children with severe disabilities. The example of an abortion of such a child is used as an example that shows it is

[4] To talk here about 'goods' and 'needs' in the explication of human rights does not imply any commitment to an 'interest theory of rights' (rights that are based in interests of agents). In a 'will theory of rights' (the rights are based in the will of agents), generic rights must be presupposed because they are necessary for enabling agents to form goals and realize them, independently of the aims they want to achieve.

impossible to harm future generations, because such an abortion would avoid the existence of just such a child, and therefore nobody would be harmed. In the case of environmental rights, all future right-holders are affected, independently of their specific features. Of course, it will be difficult in light of the non-identity problem to formulate comparative judgments that will compare whether some generations are better off in comparison to others if different strategies with regard to environmental policies had been taken. But this difficulty does not exclude that in principle we can violate their generic rights.

If we assume that there will be future generations, then we have to assume that they have some generic (particularly environmental) rights that are fundamentally important because the goods that are protected by those rights are fundamental life conditions. Those rights are so fundamental that they directly affect their dignity as human beings, that is, the dignity of beings that should be enabled to live a life of their own. Whether or not we can violate their dignity depends not on the existence of the right-holders but on the influence we have on the goods to which they have a right. With regard to some environmental rights, it is obvious that we violate their rights in respect of these goods.

With a commitment to the dignity of all human beings we are obliged to give normative priority to ensure and create those conditions that are necessary for enabling human beings to live an autonomous life, independently of the time in which they live. Since the consequences of our actions have become more far-reaching for the future during the last decades, the scope of our responsibility has become broader – which makes it necessary to rethink the human rights regime in an intergenerational perspective. This would imply reformulating the human rights regime in a very fundamental way. We would not just add another right to the existing human rights lists; we would have to rethink the whole human rights regime in an intergenerational perspective. This would be a fundamental shift for the entire regulatory regime. In the context of such a fundamental shift, it is necessary to ask whether this change is consistent with the normative basis of the human rights, that is, whether it is consistent with the general interpretation of the concept of human dignity. Because of the far-reaching nature of these changes, the case of future generations is a particularly appropriate one in which to reflect on the role of human dignity as the foundation of the human rights regime. If my argument so far is correct, it is not only consistent with the concept of human dignity to take future generations into account, it is even normatively required.

Questions for the dignity of future generations

In the previous section, it was argued that we are able to violate the dignity and rights of future generations. But there are various questions which need to be answered in order to develop this position in detail. I will briefly mention five questions:

(1) We would need criteria to determine under which conditions changes of the environment are so far-reaching that the impact on the life of future generations would constitute a serious violation of their rights. This implies that we would have to be able to determine some *thresholds* for unacceptable environmental consequences of our actions.
(2) In order to respect the dignity of future generations, we would have to be able to *compare the relative importance of their basic rights with the rights of contemporaries*. The question will be how much weight potential rights violations of future generations will hold *vis-à-vis* the exercise of liberties by current generations. That is all the more important as it is likely that effective protection of the environmental rights of future generations implies that current generations have to reduce their travel, their use of energy, their reproductive behaviour etc. To justify those far-reaching consequences, it would be necessary to set priorities in the comparison of environmental rights of future generations with the rights of current generations.
(3) We don't know *how many future generations* there will be, nor *how many people there will be in each generation*. With regard to the use and distribution of natural resources and also with regard to climate change, it would nonetheless make a difference whether we have to think about five or five hundred generations. It is, however, impossible to predict this. It would, for example, be difficult to make comparative judgments about how policies today would affect future generations and comparative judgments about the respective rights violations. A concept of intergenerational human dignity would be needed to deal with this problem.
(4) It is impossible to predict how various actions will influence the environmental conditions of future generations. We are confronted with many *risks* and *uncertainties* with regard to the consequences of our actions. In order to determine our obligations towards future generations, we would have to be able to distinguish between morally acceptable and unacceptable risks and uncertainties. This problem is not really new: with regard to nuclear energy we are accustomed to discussing the question whether the risk of nuclear waste is acceptable with regard to the rights of future generations. However, if we broaden the scope of this problem to all environmental conditions of the life of future generations, this becomes very complex; it is often impossible to make a calculation of the risks. Under such circumstances of uncertainty, scholars refer to the 'precautionary principle'. This entails that we – because of the importance of the goods that are at stake – should refrain from some actions for precautionary reasons, even if we cannot predict a real risk. But even though the precautionary principle plays a significant role in legal regulations and in the scholarly literature, there are as yet no convincing criteria for the application of this principle. We should at the very least be able to explain when the respect for the dignity of future generations makes it obligatory for us to act in a precautionary manner.

(5) It is not evident whether a sustainable politics that respects the basic rights of future generations can be implemented in the context of the democratic state. Current generations tend to use elections to vote for political parties that support their interests, while future generations have no vote. This question is clearly related to the concept of democracy and the relationship between human dignity and democracy. If our democratic rights are based on human dignity (we have a right to decide about our government because we have human dignity) then there could be a conflict between our democratic rights and the environmental rights of future generations. The question is to what extent the respect for the dignity of future generations may justify restrictions in the exercise of our democratic rights or whether this respect should be a reason to think about a structural representation of future generations within the existing democratic institutions.

References

Gewirth, A. 1978. *Reason and Morality.* Chicago University Press

1992. 'Human Dignity as the Basis of Rights', in M. J. Meyer and W. A. Parent (eds.). *The Constitution of Rights: Human Dignity and American Values.* Ithaca, NY: Cornell University Press, 10–28

2001. 'Human Rights and Future Generations', in M. Boylan (ed.), *Environmental Ethics.* Upper Saddle River, NJ: Prentice-Hall, 207–12

Grosseries, A., and Meyer, L. (eds.). 2009. *Intergenerational Justice.* Oxford University Press

Hiskes, R. P. 2009. *The Human Right to a Green Future: Environmental Rights and Intergenerational Justice.* Cambridge University Press

Margalit, A. 1996. *The Decent Society.* Cambridge, MA: Harvard University Press

Parfit, D. 1984. *Reasons and Persons.* Oxford University Press

Roberts, M. A., and Wassermann, D. T. (eds.). 2009. *Harming Future Persons: Ethics, Genetics and the Nonidentity Problem.* Dordrecht: Springer

Rolston, H. 1988. *Environmental Ethics: Duties to and Values in The Natural World.* Philadelphia, PA: Temple University Press

Taylor, P. W. 1986. *Respect for Nature: A Theory of Environmental Ethics.* Princeton University Press

United Nations. 1987. *Report of the World Commission on Environment and Development: Our Common Future*

Appendix 1

Further reading

Arendt, H. 1951. *The Origins of Totalitarianism.* New York: Harcourt Brace Jovanovich

Balzer, P., Rippe, K., and Schaber, P. 2000. 'Two Concepts of Dignity for Humans and Non-Human Organisms in the Context of Genetic Engineering', *Journal of Agricultural and Environmental Ethics* 13: 7–27

Baranzke, H. 2002. *Würde der Kreatur? Die Idee der Würde im Kontext der Bioethik.* Würzburg: Königshausen und Neumann

Barilan, Y. M. 2012. *Human Dignity, Human Rights, and Responsibility: The New Language of Global Bioethics and Biolaw.* Cambridge, MA, London: MIT Press

Bayertz, K. (ed.). 1996. *Sanctity of Life and Human Dignity.* Dordrecht: Springer

Beitz, C. 2009. *The Idea of Human Rights.* Oxford University Press

Benhabib, S. 2011. *Dignity in Adversity: Human Rights in Troubled Times.* Cambridge: Polity Press

Beyleveld, D., and Brownsword, R. 2001. *Human Dignity in Bioethics and Biolaw.* Oxford University Press

Bostrom, N. 2005. 'In Defense of Posthuman Dignity', *Bioethics* 19(3): 202–14

Cantor, N. L. 1993. *Advance Directives and the Pursuit of Death with Dignity.* Bloomington, IN: Indiana University Press

Capps, P. 2009. *Human Dignity and the Foundations of International Law.* Oxford, Portland, OR: Hart Publishing

Cicero, M. Tullius. 1913. *De officiis*, ed. and trans. W. Miller. Cambridge, MA: Harvard University Press

Collste, G. 2002. *Is Human Life Special? Religious and Philosophical Perspectives on the Principle of Human Dignity.* Bern: Peter Lang Verlag

Dean, R. 2006. *The Value of Humanity in Kant's Moral Theory.* Oxford University Press

Denis, L. 2007. 'Kant's Formula of the End in Itself: Some Recent Debates', *Philosophy Compass* 2:(2): 255–7

Dillon, R. S. (ed.). 1995. *Dignity, Character, and Self-Respect.* New York, London: Routledge

Donnelly, J. 1987. 'Human Rights and Human Dignity: An Analytic Critique of Non-Western Conceptions of Human Rights', in E. F. Snyder and S. Sathirathai (eds.), *Third World Attitudes Toward International Law.* Dordrecht: Springer, 341–57

2002. *Universal Human Rights in Theory and Practice.* Ithaca, NY: Cornell University Press

Düwell, M. 2010. 'Human Dignity and Human Rights', in P. Kaufmann, H. Kuch, C. Neuhäuser and E. Webster (eds.). *Humiliation, Degradation, Dehumanization: Human Dignity Violated*. Dordrecht: Springer, 215–30

Dworkin, R. 1977. *Taking Rights Seriously*. Cambridge, MA: Harvard University Press

Egonnson, D. 1998. *Dimensions of Dignity: The Moral Importance of Being Human*. Dordrecht: Springer

Forst, R. 2012. *The Right to Justification*. New York: Columbia University Press

Gaita, R. 2000. *A Common Humanity: Thinking about Love and Truth and Justice*. London, New York: Routledge

Geddert-Steinacher, T. 1990. *Menschenwürde als Verfassungsbegriff: Aspekte der Rechtsprechung des Bundsverfassungsgerichts zu Art. 1 Abs. 1 Grundgesetz*. Berlin: Duncker & Humblot

Gewirth, A. 1978. *Reason and Morality*. Chicago University Press

1992. 'Human Dignity as the Basis of Rights', in M. J. Meyer and W. A. Parent (eds.), *The Constitution of Rights: Human Dignity and American Values*. Ithaca, NY: Cornell University Press, 10–28

1992. *Community of Rights*. Chicago University Press

Girad, C., and Hennette-Vauchez, S. (eds.). 2005. *La dignité de la personne humaine: Recherche sur un processus de juridicisation*. Paris: Droit et Justice

Griffin, J. 2008. *On Human Rights*. Oxford University Press

Gröschner, R., Kirste, S., and Lembcke, O. 2008. *Die Menschenwürde – entdeckt und erfunden im Humanismus der italienischen Renaissance*. Tübingen: Mohr Siebeck

Grotius, *De jure belli ac pacis libri tres*, trans. F. W. Kelsey. New York: Oceana

Haakonssen, K. 1996. *Natural Law and Moral Philosophy: From Grotius to the Scottish Enlightenment*. Cambridge University Press

Habermas, J. 2003. *The Future of Human Nature*, trans. H. Beister and W. Rehg. Cambridge: Polity Press

2010. 'The Concept of Human Dignity and the Realistic Utopia of Human Rights', *Metaphilosophy* 41(4): 464–80

Harris, G. W. 1997. *Dignity and Vulnerability: Strength and Quality of Character*. Berkeley, CA: University of California Press

Hart, H. L. A. 2001. 'Are There Any Natural Rights?', in P. Hayden (ed.), *The Philosophy of Human Rights*. St Paul, MN: Paragon House, 151–62

Heeger, R. 2000. 'Genetic Engineering and the Dignity of Creatures', *Journal of Agricultural and Environmental Ethics* 13: 43–51

Hill, Thomas E., Jr. 1992. *Dignity and Practical Reason in Kant's Ethical Theory*. Ithaca, NY: Cornell University Press

Ignatieff, M. 2001. *Human Rights as Politics and Idolatry*, ed. A. Gutman. Princeton University Press

Jellinek, G. 1982. *The Declaration of the Rights of Man and of Citizens: A Contribution to Modern Constitutional History*, trans. M. Farrand. New York: H. Holt

Joas, H. 2011. *Die Sakralität der Person: Eine neue Genealogie der Menschenrechte*. Frankfurt am Main: Suhrkamp

Joerden, J. C., Hilgendorf, E., and Thiele, F. (eds.). 2013. *Menschenwürde und Medizin: Ein interdisziplinäres Handbuch*. Berlin: Duncker & Humblot

Kamali, M. H. 2002. *The Dignity of Man: An Islamic Perspective*. Cambridge: Islamic Texts Society

Kant, I. 1998. *Groundwork of the Metaphysics of Morals*, trans. M. J. Gregor. Cambridge University Press

Kass, L. R. 2002. *Life, Liberty and the Defense of Dignity: The Challenge for Bioethics*. San Francisco: Encounter Books

Kateb, G. 2011. *Human Dignity*. Cambridge, MA, London: Belknap Press of Harvard University Press

Kemp, P., Rendtorff, J., and Johansen, N. M. (eds.). 2000. *Bioethics and Biolaw*, vol. II, *Four Ethical Principles*. Copenhagen: Rhodos International Science and Art Publishers and Centre for Ethics and Law

Kerstein, S. J. 2002. *Kant's Search for the Supreme Principle of Morality*. Cambridge University Press

Korsgaard, C. M. 1996. *Creating the Kingdom of Ends*. Cambridge University Press

Kraynak, R. P., and Tinder, G. (eds.). 2003. *In Defense of Human Dignity: Essays for Our Time*. Notre Dame, IN: University of Notre Dame Press

Löhrer, G. 1995. *Menschliche Würde: Wissenschaftliche Geltung und metaphorische Grenze der praktischen Philosophie Kants*. Freiburg im Breisgau, Munich: Alber

Luban, D. 2007. *Legal Ethics and Human Dignity*. Cambridge University Press

Macklin, R. 2003. 'Dignity as a Useless Concept', *British Medical Journal* 327: 1419–20

Malpas, J., and Lickiss, N. (eds.). 2007. *Perspectives on Human Dignity: A Conversation*. Dordrecht: Springer

Margalit, A. 1996. *The Decent Society*. Cambridge, MA: Harvard University Press

Maritain, J. 1966. *Man and the State*. University of Chicago Press

McCrudden, C. 2008. 'Human Dignity and Judicial Interpretation of Human Rights', *European Journal of International Law* 19(4): 655–724

Menke, C., and Pollmann, A. 2007. *Philosophie der Menschenrechte zur Einführung*. Hamburg: Junius Verlag

Meyer, M. J. 1989. 'Dignity, Rights, and Self-Control', *Ethics* 99: 520–34

Morsink, J. 1999. *The Universal Declaration of Human Rights: Origins, Drafting and Intent*. University of Philadelphia Press

Mutua, M. 2002. *Human Rights: A Political and Cultural Critique*. Philadelphia, PA: University of Pennsylvania Press

Nussbaum, M. 2002. 'The Worth of Human Dignity: Two Tensions in Stoic Cosmopolitanism', in G. Clark and T. Rajak (eds.), *Philosophy and Power in the Graeco-Roman World: Essays in Honour of Miriam Griffin*. Oxford University Press, 31–49

2006. *Frontiers of Justice: Disability, Nationality, Species Membership*. Cambridge, MA: Belknap Press of Harvard University Press

Pico della Mirandola, G. 1965. *Oration on the Dignity of Man*, trans. C. G. Wallis. Indianapolis, IN: Bobbs-Merrill Company

President's Council on Bioethics. 2002. *Human Cloning and Human Dignity: An Ethical Inquiry*. Washington, DC

2003. *Being Human: Readings from the President's Council on Bioethics*, Washington, DC

2008. *Human Dignity and Bioethics*. Washington, DC

Pufendorf, S. 1991. *On the Duty of Man and Citizen*, ed. J. Tully. Cambridge University Press

Quataert, J. H. 2009. *Advocating Dignity: Human Rights Mobilizations in Global Politics*. Philadelphia, PA: University of Pennsylvania Press

Rosen, M. 2012. *Dignity: Its History and Meaning*. Cambridge, MA: Harvard University Press

Sensen, O. 2011. *Kant on Human Dignity*. Kantstudien Ergänzungshefte 166, Berlin, Boston: Walter de Gruyter

Shue, H. 1980. *Basic Rights: Subsistence, Affluence, and US Foreign Policy*. Princeton University Press

Skinner, B. F. 1971. *Beyond Freedom and Dignity*. Indianapolis, IN, Cambridge: Hackett Publishing Company

Soulen, R. K., and Woodhead, L. (eds.). 2006. *God and Human Dignity*. Grand Rapids, MI, Cambridge: William B. Eerdmans Publishing Company

Stetson, B. 1998. *Human Dignity and Contemporary Liberalism*. Westport, CT: Praeger Publisher

Thomson, J. J. 1990. *The Realm of Rights*. Cambridge, MA: Harvard University Press

Tierney, B. 1997. *The Idea of Natural Rights*. Grand Rapids, MI, Cambridge: William B. Eerdmans Publishing Company

Trinkaus, C. 1970. *In Our Image and Likeness: Humanity and Divinity in Italian Humanist Thought*. Chicago University Press

Tuck, R. 1979. *Natural Rights Theories: Their Origin and Development*. Cambridge University Press

Vögele, W. 2000. *Menschenwürde zwischen Recht und Theologie*. Gütersloh: Gütersloher Verlagshaus

Waldron, J. 2012. *Dignity, Rank and Rights*, ed. M. Dan-Cohen. Oxford University Press

Wellman, C. 1999. *The Proliferation of Rights: Moral Progress or Empty Rhetoric?*. Boulder, CO: Westview Press

Whitman, J. Q. 2004. 'The Two Western Cultures of Privacy: Dignity Versus Liberty', *Yale Law Journal* 113(6): 1151–1221

Appendix 2

Universal Declaration of Human Rights

Preamble

Whereas recognition of the inherent dignity and of the equal and inalienable rights of all members of the human family is the foundation of freedom, justice and peace in the world,

Whereas disregard and contempt for human rights have resulted in barbarous acts which have outraged the conscience of mankind, and the advent of a world in which human beings shall enjoy freedom of speech and belief and freedom from fear and want has been proclaimed as the highest aspiration of the common people,

Whereas it is essential, if man is not to be compelled to have recourse, as a last resort, to rebellion against tyranny and oppression, that human rights should be protected by the rule of law,

Whereas it is essential to promote the development of friendly relations between nations,

Whereas the peoples of the United Nations have in the Charter reaffirmed their faith in fundamental human rights, in the dignity and worth of the human person and in the equal rights of men and women and have determined to promote social progress and better standards of life in larger freedom,

Whereas Member States have pledged themselves to achieve, in cooperation with the United Nations, the promotion of universal respect for and observance of human rights and fundamental freedoms,

Whereas a common understanding of these rights and freedoms is of the greatest importance for the full realization of this pledge,

Now, Therefore, The General Assembly proclaims THIS UNIVERSAL DECLARATION OF HUMAN RIGHTS as a common standard of achievement for all peoples and all nations, to the end that every individual and every organ of society, keeping this Declaration constantly in mind, shall strive by teaching and education to promote respect for these rights and freedoms and by progressive measures, national and international, to secure their universal and effective recognition and observance, both among the peoples of Member States themselves and among the peoples of territories under their jurisdiction.

Article 1

All human beings are born free and equal in dignity and rights. They are endowed with reason and conscience and should act towards one another in a spirit of brotherhood.

Article 2

Everyone is entitled to all the rights and freedoms set forth in this Declaration, without distinction of any kind, such as race, colour, sex, language, religion, political or other opinion, national or social origin, property, birth or other status. Furthermore, no distinction shall be made on the basis of the political, jurisdictional or international status of the country or territory to which a person belongs, whether it be independent, trust, non-self-governing or under any other limitation of sovereignty.

Article 3

Everyone has the right to life, liberty and security of person.

Article 4

No one shall be held in slavery or servitude; slavery and the slave trade shall be prohibited in all their forms.

Article 5

No one shall be subjected to torture or to cruel, inhuman or degrading treatment or punishment.

Article 6

Everyone has the right to recognition everywhere as a person before the law.

Article 7

All are equal before the law and are entitled without any discrimination to equal protection of the law. All are entitled to equal protection against any discrimination in violation of this Declaration and against any incitement to such discrimination.

Article 8

Everyone has the right to an effective remedy by the competent national tribunals for acts violating the fundamental rights granted him by the constitution or by law.

Article 9

No one shall be subjected to arbitrary arrest, detention or exile.

Article 10

Everyone is entitled in full equality to a fair and public hearing by an independent and impartial tribunal, in the determination of his rights and obligations and of any criminal charge against him.

Article 11

(1) Everyone charged with a penal offence has the right to be presumed innocent until proved guilty according to law in a public trial at which he has had all the guarantees necessary for his defence.
(2) No one shall be held guilty of any penal offence on account of any act or omission which did not constitute a penal offence, under national or international law, at the time when it was committed. Nor shall a heavier penalty be imposed than the one that was applicable at the time the penal offence was committed.

Article 12

No one shall be subjected to arbitrary interference with his privacy, family, home or correspondence, nor to attacks upon his honour and reputation. Everyone has the right to the protection of the law against such interference or attacks.

Article 13

(1) Everyone has the right to freedom of movement and residence within the borders of each state.
(2) Everyone has the right to leave any country, including his own, and to return to his country.

Article 14

(1) Everyone has the right to seek and to enjoy in other countries asylum from persecution.

(2) This right may not be invoked in the case of prosecutions genuinely arising from non-political crimes or from acts contrary to the purposes and principles of the United Nations.

Article 15

(1) Everyone has the right to a nationality.
(2) No one shall be arbitrarily deprived of his nationality nor denied the right to change his nationality.

Article 16

(1) Men and women of full age, without any limitation due to race, nationality or religion, have the right to marry and to found a family. They are entitled to equal rights as to marriage, during marriage and at its dissolution.
(2) Marriage shall be entered into only with the free and full consent of the intending spouses.
(3) The family is the natural and fundamental group unit of society and is entitled to protection by society and the State.

Article 17

(1) Everyone has the right to own property alone as well as in association with others.
(2) No one shall be arbitrarily deprived of his property.

Article 18

Everyone has the right to freedom of thought, conscience and religion; this right includes freedom to change his religion or belief, and freedom, either alone or in community with others and in public or private, to manifest his religion or belief in teaching, practice, worship and observance.

Article 19

Everyone has the right to freedom of opinion and expression; this right includes freedom to hold opinions without interference and to seek, receive and impart information and ideas through any media and regardless of frontiers.

Article 20

(1) Everyone has the right to freedom of peaceful assembly and association.
(2) No one may be compelled to belong to an association.

Article 21

(1) Everyone has the right to take part in the government of his country, directly or through freely chosen representatives.
(2) Everyone has the right of equal access to public service in his country.
(3) The will of the people shall be the basis of the authority of government; this will shall be expressed in periodic and genuine elections which shall be by universal and equal suffrage and shall be held by secret vote or by equivalent free voting procedures.

Article 22

Everyone, as a member of society, has the right to social security and is entitled to realization, through national effort and international cooperation and in accordance with the organization and resources of each State, of the economic, social and cultural rights indispensable for his dignity and the free development of his personality.

Article 23

(1) Everyone has the right to work, to free choice of employment, to just and favourable conditions of work and to protection against unemployment.
(2) Everyone, without any discrimination, has the right to equal pay for equal work.
(3) Everyone who works has the right to just and favourable remuneration ensuring for himself and his family an existence worthy of human dignity, and supplemented, if necessary, by other means of social protection.
(4) Everyone has the right to form and to join trade unions for the protection of his interests.

Article 24

Everyone has the right to rest and leisure, including reasonable limitation of working hours and periodic holidays with pay.

Article 25

(1) Everyone has the right to a standard of living adequate for the health and well-being of himself and of his family, including food, clothing, housing and medical care and necessary social services, and the right to security in the event of unemployment, sickness, disability, widowhood, old age or other lack of livelihood in circumstances beyond his control.

(2) Motherhood and childhood are entitled to special care and assistance. All children, whether born in or out of wedlock, shall enjoy the same social protection.

Article 26

(1) Everyone has the right to education. Education shall be free, at least in the elementary and fundamental stages. Elementary education shall be compulsory. Technical and professional education shall be made generally available and higher education shall be equally accessible to all on the basis of merit.
(2) Education shall be directed to the full development of the human personality and to the strengthening of respect for human rights and fundamental freedoms. It shall promote understanding, tolerance and friendship among all nations, racial or religious groups, and shall further the activities of the United Nations for the maintenance of peace.
(3) Parents have a prior right to choose the kind of education that shall be given to their children.

Article 27

(1) Everyone has the right freely to participate in the cultural life of the community, to enjoy the arts and to share in scientific advancement and its benefits.
(2) Everyone has the right to the protection of the moral and material interests resulting from any scientific, literary or artistic production of which he is the author.

Article 28

Everyone is entitled to a social and international order in which the rights and freedoms set forth in this Declaration can be fully realized.

Article 29

(1) Everyone has duties to the community in which alone the free and full development of his personality is possible.
(2) In the exercise of his rights and freedoms, everyone shall be subject only to such limitations as are determined by law solely for the purpose of securing due recognition and respect for the rights and freedoms of others and of meeting the just requirements of morality, public order and the general welfare in a democratic society.
(3) These rights and freedoms may in no case be exercised contrary to the purposes and principles of the United Nations.

Article 30

Nothing in this Declaration may be interpreted as implying for any State, group or person any right to engage in any activity or to perform any act aimed at the destruction of any of the rights and freedoms set forth herein.

Index

Lightning Source UK Ltd.
Milton Keynes UK
UKHW051309220919
350230UK00020B/270/P

9 780521 195782